WHO WAS WHO
IN THE
NAPOLEONIC
WARS

WHO WAS WHO
IN THE
NAPOLEONIC WARS

PHILIP J. HAYTHORNTHWAITE

ARMS AND
ARMOUR

Arms & Armour
An Imprint of the Cassell Group
Wellington House, 125 Strand, London WC2R 0BB

Copyright © Philip J. Haythornthwaite, 1998

First published 1998

British Library Cataloguing-in-Publication Data:
a catalogue record for this book is available from the
British Library

ISBN 1-85409-391-6

Distributed in the USA by Sterling Publishing Co. Inc.,
387 Park Avenue South, New York, NY 10016-8810.

Designed and edited by DAG Publications Ltd.
Designed by David Gibbons; layout by Anthony A. Evans;
edited by Michael Boxall.

Printed and bound in United States.

ACKNOWLEDGEMENTS
The author extends especial thanks to
Dr. John A. Hall and to Thomas E. DeVoe.

CONTENTS

Introduction, 7
Footnote References, 12

A to Z of Personalities, 13

INTRODUCTION

Thomas Carlyle asserted that: 'History is the essence of innumerable biographies',[1] and 'The history of the world is but the biography of great men.'[2] This compilation of biographical notices of personalities of the Napoleonic Wars includes not only the 'great men' but many individuals of lesser fame, but arguably no less importance; for, especially in the military field, the 'great men' could not have achieved their successes without the efforts of their countless followers. Some of these became famous to a lesser extent, but for most the lament of Jonathan Leach was prophetic: 'Ere many years elapse, if the names of Vimeira, Talavera, Salamanca, Vittoria, &c., &c., should be partially remembered, the actors in those scenes (with a few exceptions) will be entirely forgotten'.[3] Alexander Pope may have stated that 'The proper study of mankind is man',[4] but in such a work of finite length, in whatever subject, only a limited section of mankind can be included, and it is likely that no two opinions would arrive at the same selection. Despite Sir Charles James Napier's remark that 'Few men read observations and notes ... for the small merit they contain is like a bad gold mine, and will not ... repay the trouble of working',[5] some introductory comments are necessary to this register of personalities of the Napoleonic era.

For this purpose, the term 'Napoleonic Wars' has been taken to include the French Revolutionary period, which brought about the rise of Napoleon and the wars which bear his name; and to include the Anglo–American War of 1812, significant causes of which arose from the existing Napoleonic conflict. Personalities involved exclusively in warfare in India during this period, however, have not been included, even though this has resulted in the omission of such interesting and colourful characters as Tipu Sultan of Mysore, the Peshwa Baji Rao II, Doulut Rao Sindhia of Gwalior, the bandit supreme Doondia Wao, and Sir George Barlow, the Governor of Madras who was described as a repulsive despot who brought about what amounted to a mutiny of the officers of the Madras Army.

The length of any entry is not intended as a direct reflection upon the importance of the subject, and for reasons of space in most cases there is opportunity only to recount brief biographical facts, in some cases concentrating only upon the incidents which brought a personality to prominence. For those who achieved most of their fame in subsequent years, the text concentrates upon their actions in the Napoleonic Wars rather than upon their more famous later careers. Anecdotes and contemporary comments are included in some cases, though the use of such material has been limited by constrictions of space. Although many political figures are included, emphasis has been placed upon military personalities, though high rank alone has not necessarily been taken as a criterion for inclusion; there were, for example, no less than 647 general officers in the British *Army List* of July 1815, of whom only 148 were employed, and only 25 of these served in the Waterloo campaign. It could be argued that, for example, Karl Theodore Körner, the latter-day Tyrtaeus, had more influence upon his time by the effect of his patriotic poetry than did many general officers of no especial distinction, and that the latter individuals made less mark upon the history of the period than memorialists like Jean Roch Coignet or Benjamin Harris, who spent their military careers at the bottom of the ladder of promotion.

In addition, some personalities prominent in other fields have been included, in cases where the events of the Napoleonic Wars exerted some bearing upon their careers. The extent to which the military and political events of the period affected the lives of those not primarily concerned in either of those fields was considerable, as may be demonstrated by a few examples in addition to those, like Körner, who appear in the main body of this work. In Germany, notably Prussia, probably a higher proportion of what might have been termed the 'educated classes' served in the military during the 'War of Liberation' than did the equivalent population of other nationalities, as a consequence of the surge of patriotic feeling which called to the colours many who would not otherwise have entered military service; for example, the poet Joseph, Freiherr von Eichendorff (1788–1857) and the philosopher and educational reformer Friedrich Froebel

(1782–1852) were among those who served in Lützow's corps in 1813–14.

Other examples of how the war and its personalities entangled the lives of those known more from other fields of endeavour than as military or political figures might include a number of characters from the sciences and arts. The astronomer Johann Encke (1791–1865) served in the Hanseatic Legion and became a lieutenant in the Prussian artillery; the physicist Henry Kater (1777–1835) served as an officer in the British Army until 1814; Sir Roderick Murchison (1792–1871), the geologist who originated the term 'Silurian System' in his book of that title in 1839, carried the Colours of the 36th Foot at Vimeiro. The astronomer Sir Edward Sabine (1788–1883, also noted for his work on terrestrial magnetism) entered the Royal Artillery in 1803, served at the siege of Fort Erie and rose to the rank of major-general in 1856; Jean Victor Poncelet (1788–1867), the mathematician and engineer, one of the developers of modern geometry, was an engineer officer in the French Army who began his researches on projective geometry while a prisoner of war, having been captured during the Russian campaign of 1812.

The dramatist Charles Etienne (1778–1845) was secretary to Maret and accompanied Napoleon on his perambulations: the author and poet Alphonse Lamartine (1790–1869) served briefly in the *Garde du Corps* at the Bourbon Restoration. Other literary figures of note involved in some way with the Napoleonic Wars included Friedrich Klinger (1752–1831, originator of the term *Sturm und Drang*), a general in Russian service; Richard Cumberland (1732–1811) was lieutenant-colonel commandant of the Tunbridge Wells Volunteers; Jacob Grimm (1785–1863) was Jérôme Bonaparte's library superintendent and later secretary to the Hessian minister at the Allied headquarters in 1813; Walter Savage Landor (1775–1864) served briefly as a volunteer in Spain in 1808. The Irish poet Thomas Moore (1779–1852), author of such immortal verses as *The Minstrel Boy*, *Oft in the Stilly Night* and the song to which the 28th Foot marched out of Brussels en route for Waterloo, *The Young May Moon*, was for a time registrar of the Admiralty prize-court in Bermuda, and was friendly with the rebel Robert Emmet. The violin virtuoso Nicolo Paganini (1784–1840) was musical director at the court of Napoleon's sister Elisa; Henry 'Orator' Hunt

(1773–1835), the radical politician and speaker 'Peterloo', was a member of the Wiltshire Yeoman (and challenged his commanding officer to a du when he was expelled from the unit!); Sir Mos Montefiore (1784–1885), the London banker an Stock Exchange broker, best known for his efforts improve the welfare of the Jewish people and in th future of Palestine, attained the rank of captain the Surrey Militia. The German philosopher Johan Gottlieb Fichte (1762–1814) took no active part in th war (though was depicted as a member of the *Lan sturm*),[6] but lectured in support of the 'War of Libe ation'. His wife helped nurse the wounded an caught a hospital fever; she survived but Fich himself succumbed and died on 27 January 1814.

Many names may be found with more than on spelling, both in contemporary and later source Indeed, some individuals changed their name the spelling of their name, during their lifetim (perhaps the commonest reason for a change name being the inheritance of property from a rela tive of a different name). The most obvious exan ples of those who amended the spellings of the name include Napoleon himself and his Britis adversary, who began his military career as Arth Wesley but like the rest of his family subsequent adopted the spelling 'Wellesley'. Napoleon surname, Buonaparte, was changed to the (now more familiar 'Bonaparte', though the origina version was used in some English-language pub cations throughout his life, and even the revise spelling of his name attracted criticism from thos who on principle found fault with everything he did (Even his address was cause for facetious commer by the hostile British press: 'The Address of the *Fir Consul* is a curious one. "To *Bonaparte*, Malmaison." That a man of *good parts* should take *bad house* is somewhat singular. If he had state that the *tenure* of his mansion was *precarious*, th world would be inclined to give him full credit fo the admission!'[7] In fairness, such puns were muc in vogue; Napoleon himself made his famous crac about the heroic Mouton, to the effect that 'm sheep is a lion', and it was said that Victor receive his title duc de Bellune as a deliberate pun upon h nickname of '*beau soleil*', transforming 'handsom sun' into *belle-lune*, beautiful moon.

Many personalities were referred to by a nam different from their own after being awarded, o heriting, a title of nobility. In general, in this work individuals are referred to and listed according to the name which is most familiar or by their ultimate title; but the alternatives are also listed , with details of where the appropriate text can be found; so that, or example, the entry for duc d'Elchingen directs the reader to the entry for Ney, and so on.

Confusion between persons of similar name occurs in some later works, as it must have occurred at the time. Occasionally individuals might become known by an additional name to differentiate one from another – for example Merlin of Thionville and Merlin of Douai – and a practical solution adopted in the Prussian service was to identify those of the same name by the addition of a number, perhaps most famously 'Pirch I' and 'Pirch II'. (Such a system was used in the British Army, but only within regiments as a way of distinguishing members of the rank and file who had the same name, sometimes a very necessary distinction: for example, in the Strathspey Fencibles in 1793 there were seventeen privates and three NCOs named John Grant, sixteen John McDonalds (plus one NCO), not to mention twelve John McDonells. Such numbering was not adopted for officers, however, even in the case of the above regiment which during its brief existence had thirteen commissioned John Grants, and some difficulties might arise as a result).

Subtle differences in title might avoid confusion between, say, Lord James Hay and James, Lord Hay (both officers of the 1st Foot Guards at Waterloo), but in other cases a similarity of names could lead to embarrassing consequences. When two James Stuarts were issued commissions on the same day, and had their intended regiments mixed up, the one who should have been appointed to the 67th but joined the 25th instead was surprised when his namesake marched into the 25th's mess and 'in a stentorian voice, and in broad Scotch, roared out: "Whaur is the domned scoundrel that has ta'en my name?"'[8] The two subsequently joined their correct regiments, the 'impostor' being known thereafter as 'Jamie Stuart, the Pretender'!

Alternative spellings may be encountered of even the most familiar names, and no great pains appear to have been taken in many early sources to ensure an accurate or consistent rendition; indeed, the matter seems at times to have been virtually ignored. A review of Siborne's *History of the War in France and Belgium* lamented that 'very few readers have a memory capable of retaining so many names; nor can their wish be very great to remember numerous names of men whom they never heard of before – names, too (many of them), of excessive length, and so rugged as to defy pronunciation by English lips ... our heads turn dizzy with endeavouring to remember them. Some pages ... completely bristle with them ... We hope that Captain Siborne is preparing an abridgement [in which] nine out of ten of these hard names will, no doubt, be omitted ...'[9] Variations in spelling are particularly evident in cases where the name was originally not rendered in the Roman alphabet, notably Russian names which had to be spelled phonetically; for example, the name usually spelled 'Arakcheev' appears in Clausewitz's work on the 1812 campaign as 'Aractschejef', and similar variations abound. It was presumably the complexity of the spelling or pronunciation of the name 'Chichagov' (this spelling being the least complicated of a number of versions) which so perplexed Napoleon that he always referred to that individual not by name but by his rank, 'the Admiral'. At the extreme, some names appear to have been so difficult to manage that they appear in some sources changed almost unrecognisably; such was the fate of the gallant Major Ernst von Burgwedel, who led the 3rd Hussars of the King's German Legion at Benavente, who appears as 'Bagwell' in more than one British account.

Even in what might be termed 'official' contemporary sources, variation in spelling may occur; Miles Nightingall, for example, corrected the spelling of his own name in his copy of the 1801 *Army List* (when he was but a lieutenant-colonel), yet as late as 1815, when he had risen to the eminence of Lieutenant-General Sir Miles Nightingall, KCB, the *Army List* spelled his name correctly twice (in the list of generals and as colonel of the 6th West India Regiment), but still managed to mis-spell it when listing him as CinC Bengal.

A common practice in English-language works is the Anglicisation of some first names; hence 'Napoleon' instead of 'Napoléon', 'Emperor Francis' instead of 'Kaiser Franz', 'Queen Louise' instead of 'Königin Luise', 'Archduke Charles' instead of 'Erzherzog Karl (Carl)', and so on. In this work a somewhat arbitrary system has been used, in that personalities are referred to by the name which is most familiar in English-language sources, even though this is not strictly the most accurate rendition. Similarly, titles of nobility are given in the terms which are, perhaps, the most familiar; hence the use of 'prince' instead of the German 'Fürst', if the individual concerned might be more familiarly styled by the former translation. The British titles 'Honourable' (for the son of a peer) and 'Right Honourable' have not been included in the titles of those who held them; but the post-nominal 'Bt.' (baronet) has been retained.

The military ranks which are given in the title to each entry are those ultimately attained by the individual (though not all grades of general are necessarily differentiated for this purpose), rather than the rank they held during or at the conclusion of the Napoleonic conflict.

Orders and decorations held by individuals have not been listed, if for no other reason than to economise on space, as those held by even middle-ranking officers could be extensive. As an example, Wilhelm von Dörnberg, most familiar for his participation in the Waterloo campaign, although not a personality of crucial significance, numbered among his honours the Grand Cross of the Guelphic Order (Hanover), Knight Commander of the Order of the Bath (Great Britain), the Order of Alexander Nevsky, the Order of St. Anne, the Order of St. George (all of Russia), the Order of Military Merit (Prussia), the Military Order of William (Netherlands) and the Order of the Golden Lion and Order of the Iron Helmet (both Hesse).

SOURCES

The most obvious source of biographical material are published studies of individuals; for some of the personalities listed in this work, brief details of such works (and of their own writings) are quoted, although such lists are by no means comprehensive, and are intended merely as a suggestion for further reference. Preference has been given to English-language editions, and in most cases where details of English translations are given, the original foreign-language publication is not quoted. The biographies listed exist mostly in book form; only in a few cases are entries in periodicals cited. For a general bibliography on all aspects of the Napoleonic Wars, including the listing of many biographies, and important critical essays on many topics, *Napoleonic Military History: A Bibliography* (ed. D. D. Howard, London, 1986) is invaluable. An excellent modern bibliographical essay on the Napoleonic Wars in general appears in C. Esdaile's *The Wars of Napoleon*, London, 1995.

Biographical essays or shorter notices are to be found in many works that do not concentrate specifically upon the Napoleonic Wars or personalities. These range from 'general' works such as *Encyclopedia Britannica* (the 11th edition of 1910–11 is still useful though of course 'dated'), to those that concern the personalities of a particular nation or biography in general, for example the British *Dictionary of National Biography*, the *Biographie Universelle* and *Nouvelle Biographie Générale*. Biographical notices appear in some more general works concerned with the Napoleonic period, notably *Dictionary of the Napoleonic Wars*, D. G. Chandler, London, 1979, an important reference to all aspects of the period.

More specific biographical material can be found in a number of works of major significance, dedicated to certain armies or services of the Napoleonic era, some of which were published relatively shortly after the event. For the French Army and Navy, reference should be made to *Dictionnaire Biographique des Généraux et Amiraux Français de la Révolution et de l'Empire*, G. Six, Paris, 1934, and to the same author's *Les Généraux de la Révolution et de l'Empire*, Paris 1947. A more modern work is *Les Etoiles de Napoléon: Maréchaux, Amiraux, Généraux 1792–1815*, A. Pigeard, 1996. An English-language work which covers civil as well as military personalities is *In Flight with the Eagle: A Guide to Napoleon's Elite*, R. Horricks, Tunbridge Wells, 1988. Although no comparable work exists that deals exclusively with British personalities of the Napoleonic Wars, earlier works (though not comprehensive) include, for example, *The Royal Military Calendar*, ed. Sir John Philippart, London, 1820 (covering officers of field rank still serving at that date); *A Naval Biographical Dictionary*, W. R. O'Byrne, London, 1849 (concerning officers serving or retired in 1845; a revised edition, not completed, was published in 1861); *Royal Naval Biography, or Memoirs of the Services of all Flag Officers ...* , J. Marshall, London, 1823; and *The Naval Biography of Great Britain ... during the Reign of His Majesty George III*, J. Ralfe, London, 1828.

Other sources cover, in varying detail, personalities associated with a particular campaign, for example *Memoirs of the British Generals Distinguished during the Peninsular War*, J. W. Cole, London 1856. More specific are works which concern a single battle, notably *Napoleon's Generals: The Waterloo Campaign*, T. Linck, the first parts published in Kidderminster and Castletown, I.o.M., 1990–1, and subsequently in one volume, Chicago, n.d. (extensive biographical texts on French general officers who served in the Waterloo campaign); and *The Waterloo Roll Call*, C. Dalton, London 1904 (2nd enlarged edn., originally published 1890; lists all British officers present at the battle, but excludes the King's German Legion, and in many cases biographical details are very brief).

While all the above are recommended as being of great value, some caution is advisable when using earlier works, and the extensive obituaries and encomiums published at the time or shortly after the event, which are not necessarily the most balanced view of any individual. Samuel Johnson remarked that every man's life is best written by himself, but those autobiographical works of Napoleonic characters which do exist, while generally of great value, are necessarily based upon one viewpoint. Evaluations of the career and merits of an individual may be found to conflict; even at the time there were often divergent opinions, not to mention the (sometimes repeated) re-evaluations of subsequent years. Objectivity was in short supply in some works, which appear almost hagiography rather than biography; conversely others were so contentious as to be the subject of acrimonious exchanges (for example those between Beresford and William Napier). Blood was shed in a duel between Gourgaud and Ségur over their conflicting perceptions of Napoleon and the 1812 campaign (Marbot thought them both wrong in their various extremes!), but contemporary criticism was generally more reserved, if not always founded upon the highest principles of accuracy. (When reviewing Captain Basil Hall's *Patchwork*, the *United Service Journal* remarked on 'an unaccountable backsliding from orthodox John Bullism

in extolling Buonaparte as a "lion who, when alive, with a single playful pat of his majestic paw, would have crushed a hundred thousand Cockneys, had they dared to cross his path!". Hear not this, ye dwellers within the sound of Bow bells, or woe be to the Captain! ...'[10]) Even within the opinions and experiences of a single individual, comments regarding a person known to them might vary very considerably, between official statements intended for public consumption and opinions expressed in private correspondence.

Finally, some contemporary reports in relation to individuals are wholly unreliable, especially those published in the popular press; for example, readers of *The News* (London) for 25 June 1815 would have seen a report that at Waterloo Jérôme Bonaparte had personally killed Murat, 'whether by accident, or intentionally, is not mentioned, and that Bonaparte himself was wounded', as inaccurate a story as any to arise out of the entire period. Even obituaries and similar texts are not necessarily accurate in relation to facts; dates of births and deaths may be found to vary (and in some cases such dates are even now unknown), and even memorial inscriptions may not be entirely accurate (see, for example, the entry for Sir Henry Shrapnel).

1. 'On History'.
2. 'Heroes and Hero-Worship'.
3. Leach, Lieutenant-Colonel J. *Rough Sketches of the Life of an Old Soldier*. London, 1831, p. 405.
4. 'Essay on Man'.
5. Napier, Sir Charles James. *Lights and Shades of Military Life*. London, 1850, p. viii. 6. A somewhat humorous portrait is reproduced in *Die Grosse Zeit*, T. Rehtwisch, Leipzig 1913, for example.
7. *Morning Herald*, 26 Aug 1800.
8. Stuart, Colonel W. K. *Reminiscences of a Soldier*. London, 1874, vol. I, p. 10.
9. Anon. 'On Some Recent Writers of Military History', in *Colburn's United Service Magazine*, 1845, vol. III, pp. 17–18.
10. *United Service Journal*, 1841, vol. I, pp. 406–7.

FOOTNOTE REFERENCES

The following list gives full details of those works identified only by authors' names in the footnotes that record sources of quotations.

Anon. *The Court and Camp of Bonaparte*. London, 1831

Beamish, N. L. *History of the King's German Legion*. 1832–7

Bunbury, Sir Henry. *Memoirs and Literary Remains of Lieutenant-General Sir Henry Edward Bunbury, Bt.*, ed. Sir Charles Bunbury. London 1868

– *Narratives of Some Passages in the Great War with France 1799–1810*. London, 1854; repr. with intr. by Sir John Fortescue. London, 1927

Clausewitz, General C. von. *The Campaign of 1812 in Russia*. London, 1843

Costello, E. *Adventures of a Soldier*, London, 1852, 1967 edn. ed. A. Brett-James.

Cust, Sir Edward. *Annals of the Wars of the Eighteenth Century, Annals of the Wars of the Nineteenth Century*. London, 1862

D'Urban, Sir Benjamin. *The Peninsular Journal of Major-General Sir Benjamin D'Urban 1808–17*, ed. I. J. Rousseau, London, 1930; repr. as *The Peninsular Journal 1808–17*. London, 1988

Ellesmere, Earl of. *Personal Reminiscences of the Duke of Wellington*. London, 1904

Fortescue, Hon. Sir John. *History of the British Army*. London, 1899–1920

Fraser, Sir William, Bt. *Words on Wellington*. London, 1899

Griffiths, A. J. *The Wellington Memorial*. London, 1897

Harris, B. *The Recollections of Rifleman Harris*, ed. H. Curling, London, 1848, r/p ed. C. Hibbert, London, 1970

Kincaid, Sir John. *Random Shots from a Rifleman*. London, 1835; Maclaren's combined edn. (with *Adventures in the Rifle Brigade*. London, 1830) London, 1908

La Rochejaquelein, marquise de. *Memoirs of the Marchioness de Larochejaquelein* (sic). Edinburgh, 1816

Las Cases, marquis de. *Memoirs of the Life, Exile and Conversations of the Emperor Napoleon*. London, 1834

Leach, Lieutenant-Colonel J. *Rough Sketches of the Life of an Old Soldier*. London, 1831

Lejeune, baron. *Memoirs of Baron Lejeune*, trans. Mrs A. Bell. London, 1897

Macdonald, Marshal. *Recollections of Marshal Macdonald, Duke of Tarentum*, ed. C. Rousset, trans. S. L. Simeon. London, 1892

Marbot, baron. *Memoirs of Baron de Marbot*, trans. A. J. Butler. London, 1913

Maxwell, Sir Herbert. *The Life of Wellington*. London, 1899

Moore Smith, G. C. *The Life of John Colborne, Field Marshal Lord Seaton*. London, 1903

Napier, Sir George. *Passages in the Early Military Life of General Sir George T. Napier*, ed. General W. C. E. Napier. London, 1884

Napier, W. F. P. *History of the War in the Peninsula*. London, 1828–40

Napoleon. *Confidential Correspondence of Napoleon Bonaparte with his Brother Joseph*, London, 1855

Oman, Sir Charles. *History of the Peninsular War*. Oxford, 1902–30

Palmer, A. *Russia in War and Peace*. London, 1972

Russell, J. *Nelson and the Hamiltons*. London, 1969

Ségur, P. de. *History of the Expedition to Russia*. London, 1825

Simmons, G. *A British Rifle Man*, ed. W. Verner. London, 1899

Smith, Sir Harry. *The Autobiography of Sir Harry Smith*, ed. G. C. Moore Smith. London, 1910

Stanhope, Earl. *Notes on Conversations with the Duke of Wellington*. London, 1888

Tomkinson, W. *The Diary of a Cavalry Officer in the Peninsular War and Waterloo Campaign*, ed. J. Tomkinson. London, 1895

Warre, Sir William. *Letters from the Peninsula 1808–12*, ed. Revd. E. Warre. London, 1909

Wellington, Duke of. *Dispatches of Field Marshal the Duke of Wellington*, ed. J. Gurwood. London, 1834–8

Wilson, Sir Robert. *Narrative of Events during the Invasion of Russia*, ed. Revd. H. Randolph. London, 1860

– *Private Diaries of Travels ...*, ed. Revd. H. Randolph. London, 1861

Colburn's United Service Magazine: in footnotes as *CUSM*

Edinburgh Evening Courant: in footnotes as *Edinburgh*

Gentleman's Magazine: in footnotes as *Gent's Mag.*

London Gazette: in footnotes as *Gazette*

United Service Journal: in footnotes as *USJ*

ABBOT, Charles, Baron Colchester (1757–1829)

A significant personality in the British parliament, Charles Abbot was Speaker of the House of Commons throughout the Napoleonic Wars (1802–17), and was ennobled as Baron Colchester upon his retirement. Like many members of society, he was involved in military affairs in a peripheral way, commanding a cavalry troop of the North Pevensey Legion, raised in 1803. He should not be confused with his namesake, **Charles Abbott, 1st Baron Tenterden of Hendon (1762–1832)**, a distinguished lawyer and eventually Lord Chief Justice of England.

Colchester, Lord. *Diary and Correspondence of Charles Abbot, Lord Colchester*, ed. 2nd Lord Colchester. London, 1861; *Speeches of the Rt. Hon. Charles Abbot ... in communicating thanks of the House of Commons to Military Commanders 1807–1816*. London, 1829 (includes biography)

ABERCROMBY, Lieutenant-General Sir Ralph (1734–1801)

Great Britain's most distinguished and capable general of the Revolutionary Wars, Ralph Abercromby was a worthy man, beloved by the army. Son of George Abercromby of Tullibody, Clackmannanshire, he was destined for the Scottish bar but preferred a military career. Commissioned in 1756, he served in the Seven Years War but declined to serve in the War of American Independence out of sympathy with the colonists, and retired as colonel in 1783. He served as MP for Clackmannanshire until he surrendered the seat to his brother, and resumed his military career upon the commencement of the Revolutionary Wars, serving in The Netherlands, most effectively as CinC West Indies (capturing St. Lucia, St. Vincent and Trinidad), and was appointed CinC Ireland in 1797. His humanitarian instincts caused him to eschew military oppression, and having met with opposition he resigned shortly before the 1798 rebellion. One of the few to emerge with credit from the expedition to The Netherlands in 1799, he conducted the expedition to Egypt with skill and devotion to duty despite the handicaps of age, extreme short sight and difficulties posed by his own government. Struck in the leg by a ball towards the end of his decisive victory at Alexandria, he died aboard ship a week later, and was buried at Malta. His concern, as he was carried from the field in a soldier's blanket, was typical: that he should be given the name of the soldier lest the man lose his blanket. The Duke of York's tribute, in a general order, was apt: 'His steady observance of discipline, his ever-watchful attention to the health and wants of his troops, the persevering and unconquerable spirit which marked his military career, the splendour of his actions in the field and the heroism of his death, are worthy the imitation of all who desire, like him, a life of heroism and a death of glory.' Characteristically he had declined a peerage and grant of land in the West Indies for merely doing what he considered his duty, but in

belated recognition his wife (Mary Anne Menzies) was created Baroness Abercromby of Aboukir and Tullibody. His second and fourth sons, **Lieutenant-General Sir John (1772–1817)**, and **Colonel Alexander (1784–1853)**, enjoyed distinguished military careers during the Napoleonic Wars, the latter commanding a brigade in the Peninsula and serving as assistant quartermaster-general at Waterloo. The family name is sometimes rendered as 'Abercrombie'.

Dunfermline, J. *Lieutenant-General Sir Ralph Abercromby, KB*, a memoir written in 1861 by his son James, later Lord Dunfermline

SIR JOHN ABERCROMBY
(ENGRAVING BY NICHOLLS)

ABERDEEN, George Hamilton Gordon, 4th Earl of (1784–1860)

A significant statesman of the mid 19th century, and British Prime

SIR RALPH ABERCROMBY
(PRINT BY JOHN KAY)

THE EARL OF ABERDEEN

Minister at the commencement of the Crimean War, having succeeded his grandfather as Earl of Aberdeen in 1801, George Gordon was appointed British Minister at Vienna, and signed the Treaty of Töplitz between Great Britain and Austria in October 1813. Accompanying the Emperor, he was present at the Battle of Leipzig, attended the Congress of Châtillon and was involved in the negotiations of the Treaty of Paris. He was a personable young man, but inexperienced; Metternich called him a 'dear simpleton of diplomacy'. During tours of Europe in his youth he had met Napoleon.

Balfour, Lady S. *Life of George, Fourth Earl of Aberdeen*. London, 1922; Chamberlain, M. E. *Lord Aberdeen: A Political Biography*. London, 1983; Iremonger, L. *Lord Aberdeen*. London, 1978; Stanmore, Lord. *The Earl of Aberdeen*. London, 1893

ABISPAL, Count of, see **O'DONNELL, Henry**

ABRANTES, duc d', see **JUNOT**

ACTON, Sir John Francis Edward (1736–1811)
Born at Besançon of English family, John Acton served in the Tuscan navy with such distinction that in 1779 Queen Maria Carolina of Naples persuaded her brother, Grand Duke Leopold of Tuscany, to allow him to re-organise the Neapolitan navy. Acton became a 'favourite' of the Queen, and was an industrious CinC of the army and navy, and Prime Minister. His principal policy, with the assistance of the British Ambassador Sir William Hamilton, was to substitute the influence of Austria and Great Britain for that of Spain, thus arousing French hostility (Hamilton noted that 'I can perceive him to be an Englishman still').[1] Acton fled Naples with the royal family in 1798, returned with them, was briefly deprived of his authority in 1804 by French pressure, but was restored and accompanied the royal family to Sicily in 1806. In November 1791 he had succeeded his cousin as 6th Baronet Acton of Aldenham, and in 1799, by papal dispensation, at the age of 63 married the daughter of his brother Joseph, who was not yet 14 years of age. A curious circumstance affected Sir John's funeral in Palermo: furious rainstorm forced the mourners to take shelter, leaving the body unprotected in the streets for almost a whole day. He is often referred to as 'General Acton', but should not be confused with his brother **Joseph Edward Acton, (1737–1830)** who was also a general in Neapolitan service, and whose son Henry served at Waterloo as a lieutenant in the British 13th Light Dragoons.
1. Russell, p. 6.

ADAM, Albrecht (1786–1862)
Famous for his vivid, eye-witness illustrations of the 1812 Russian campaign, Adam was a Bavarian painter, engraver and lithographer. He served in the campaign as an officer in the Topographical Bureau of the Italian Army; his illustrations were published in his most significant military work, *Voyage de Willenberg en Prusse jusqu'à Moscou en 1812*. Munich, 1828.

ALBRECHT ADAM: A SELF-PORTRAIT SHOWING HIM AT WORK DURING THE RUSSIAN CAMPAIGN OF 1812.
(PRINT AFTER ALBRECHT ADAM)

ADAM, General Sir Frederick (1781–1853)

Grandson of the 10th Lord Elphinstone, he was educated at the Military Academy at Woolwich and commissioned in the army in 1795. He served in The Netherlands in 1799, in Egypt and the Mediterranean, having attained the command of the 21st Foot in 1805. In 1813 he commanded a brigade in Catalonia, and had his left arm and hand injured severely at Ordal (12 September 1813). Appointed major-general on 4 June 1814, he commanded the 3rd British Brigade of the 2nd Division in the Waterloo campaign, and was wounded during the battle. From 1824 to 1831 he was Lord High Commissioner for the Ionian Islands, and from 1832 to 1837 Governor of Madras. He received a knighthood of the Bath in June 1815, and rose to the rank of general (1846).

Reumont, A. von. *Sir Frederick Adam: A Sketch of Modern Times.* Privately printed, 1855

ADDINGTON, Henry, 1st Viscount Sidmouth (1757–1844)

Entering British politics as MP for Devizes in 1784 as a consequence of his friendship with William Pitt, his conscientious career secured

HENRY ADDINGTON, 1ST VISCOUNT SIDMOUTH (PRINT AFTER COPLEY)

him the position of Speaker in 1789, and he remained a supporter of Pitt until the latter's resignation over Catholic Emancipation. Enjoying the confidence of the king, Addington became Prime Minister (First Lord of the Treasury and Chancellor of the Exchequer) in March 1801, and negotiated the Peace of Amiens. Pitt withdrew his support over Addington's unwillingness to prepare for a renewal of the war, and after it recommenced he resigned (April 1804). A brief reconciliation with Pitt saw Addington elevated to the peerage as Viscount Sidmouth (January 1805) and a re-admission to government, but further disagreements led him to resign in July. He served in the Grenville/Fox administration but left in 1807 over proposals to permit Roman Catholics to hold military commissions; Lord President of the Council under Perceval, he became Home Secretary under Liverpool until 1821, and was blamed for the severity of the suppression of unrest during his term of office. He left government in 1824 but spoke against both Catholic Emancipation (1829) and the Reform Bill (1832). An honest and industrious man who remained true to his principles, he had no very outstanding talents and was perceived as dull and pedestrian; he was nicknamed 'the doctor' from the profession of his father.

Pellew, Hon. G. (ed.). *Life and Correspondence of the Rt. Hon. Henry Addington, 1st Viscount Sidmouth.* London, 1847; Ziegler, P. *Addington.* London, 1965

ALAVA, General Miguel Ricardo (1770–1843)

Distinguished by being present at both Trafalgar and Waterloo, albeit on different sides, Miguel Ricardo Maria Juan de la Mata Domingo Vincente Ferrer Alava de

MIGUEL RICARDO ALAVA (PRINT AFTER G. DAWE)

Esquivel (he used only his first two names) was born in Vitoria of noble family, entered the Spanish Navy and served at Trafalgar aboard *Principe de Asturias*; his uncle, Vice-Admiral don Ignacio Maria Alava, was 2i/c of the Spanish fleet at the battle. Having transferred to the army, Miguel joined the independence party after the beginning of the Peninsular War and was appointed Spanish attaché to Wellington's headquarters. He became a close friend of Wellington and accompanied him throughout the Peninsular War, recalling with amusement how he would inquire each day of the hour at which they would set out on the morrow, and what they might expect for dinner; the answer was always the same, so that Alava came to regard with horror the words 'daylight' and 'cold meat'! Appointed lieutenant-general in 1814 and ambassador to The Netherlands, he was re-assigned to Wellington's HQ for the Waterloo campaign. The subsequent internal unrest in Spain led to periods of exile in England and France (when he received much help from his friend Wellington), interspersed with ambassadorial appointments in both countries, until his retirement as ambassador in London in 1841, after which he lived in France.

A succinct modern biography in English by J. Vidal-Abarca appears in *La Batalla de Vitoria 175 Años Despues*. Vitoria, 1988

ALBEMARLE, General George Thomas Keppel, 6th Earl of (1799–1891)

GEORGE THOMAS KEPPEL,
6TH EARL OF ALBEMARLE

A member of a family which had produced a number of distinguished officers (most notably Admiral Augustus, Viscount Keppel, 1725–86), George Keppel owes his 'Napoleonic' fame to longevity, being one of the last British survivors of Waterloo: as an ensign in the 3rd Bn, 14th Foot, he celebrated his 16th birthday three days before the Battle of Quatre Bras. Despite the title of his earldom, which he inherited from his brother in 1851, he was not related to the famous Duke of Albemarle, General George Monck (1608–69), whose title became extinct in 1688 and was re-created for Arnold van Keppel in 1697.

Albemarle, 6th Earl. *Fifty Years of My Life*. London, 1876

ALBUFERA, duc d', see SUCHET

ALEXANDER I, Tsar of Russia (1777–1825)

TSAR ALEXANDER I
(ENGRAVING BY T. W. HARLAND AFTER F. BOLK)

The son of Tsar Paul I and Maria Fedorovna, daughter of Frederick Eugene of Württemberg, Alexander succeeded as Tsar after the murder of his father in March 1801. To his contemporaries he remained an intriguing contradiction, ruler of the most autocratic state in Europe, yet possessed of such liberal ideas that he declared in 1807 that he would abolish serfdom if only it were possible within Russian society. Napoleon styled him 'the Talma of the North', a reference to the great French actor François-Joseph Talma (1763–1826), implying that Alexander was equally ready to play any part which circumstances demanded; but in the final analysis Alexander retained his absolute powers. In foreign policy he extended the borders of his state more than his two most illustrious predecessors, Peter and Catherine the Great, had done, and confirmed Russia's status as a leading European power. Alexander's initial admiration for Napoleon faded with his youthful idealism, and Russia opposed France until forced to accede to the Treaty of Tilsit; the resulting alliance soured over economic

affairs, Napoleon's creation of the Duchy of Warsaw and his seizure of the lands of the Duke of Oldenburg who was married to the Tsar's sister. The breakdown of Russo-French relations culminated in Napoleon's invasion of Russia, during which the Tsar remained steadfastly unwilling to negotiate, and the influence of Alexander and Russia was of crucial importance in the subsequent campaigns. Alexander played an important role at the Congress of Vienna, and was instrumental in the creation of the Holy Alliance. Expressing himself oppressed by the burdens of state, he died at Taganrog in 1825. A legend that he had relinquished his position to become a religious hermit, not unlikely considering his character, was certainly untrue. A pleasant and affable man, the melancholy of his later life was increased by an unhappy, arranged marriage at the age of 16 with Princess Maria Louisa of Baden; the death of his only legitimate child in 1808; and later that of a much-loved illegitimate daughter. For all his liberal inclinations, he left Russia in its state of absolutism and serfdom.

Almedigen, E. M. *Emperor Alexander I*. London, 1964; Hartley, J. M. *Alexander I*. London, 1994; Palmer, A. *Alexander I, Tsar of War and Peace*. London, 1974; Troyat, H. *Alexander of Russia, Napoleon's Conqueror*. London, 1984

ALI PASHA (known as Arslan (the Lion), Pasha of Iannina (1741–1822)

Born at Tepeleni, Albania, of the family which had held the position of Bey, he progressed from brigandage to a repossession and enhancement of his family's hereditary office, by defeating rivals under the guise of supporting the Ottoman Empire. Established as the Pasha of Iannina, he became virtual sovergn of Albania, defeated the ɪristian Suliots and concluded ɪs own diplomatic alliances. He ᵣst favoured France, then formed ᵤ alliance with Russia and Great ʳitain, and by 1803 was master of ʟbania, Epirus and Thessaly, with ɪs sons Pashas of the Morea and ᵉpanto. To possess the port of ᵤrga, Ali concluded an alliance ɪth Napoleon in 1807, but turned ᵣ the Allies when French troops ᵉre not withdrawn. In March ʃ14 the Pargiots seized their town ᵣom the French and handed it to ʈe British, to save it falling to Ali; ᵤt amid protests from the oppoᵗtion in Britain, Parga was ceded ᵣ the Ottoman Empire (1817) and ᵉnce to Ali. To curb the power of ɪeir virtually independent provinᵗal pashas, the Ottoman Empire ᵤoved against Ali in 1820; after a ᵉge of Iannina he sued for ᵉace, met with the Ottoman ᵤmmander Khurshid Pasha and ᵗter a friendly meeting was ᵤbbed in the back as he left ʃ822). Although he could be ᵤrtrayed merely as a ferocious ᵤnqueror, Ali was a remarkable ʰaracter who maintained Iannᵤa as a centre of culture, and has ᵉen styled 'the Mohammedan ᵤnaparte'.

Baggally, J. W. *Ali Pasha and ᵣeat Britain*. Oxford, 1938

ʟTEN, Field Marshal ᵣr Charles (Karl), Count ʃ764–1840)

ᵤn of Baron Alten and a member ᵣf an old Hanoverian family, he ᵤntered the Hanoverian Army in ʃ781, served in The Netherlands in ʃ793–5 and entered British service ᵥith the King's German Legion. ʟfter serving in the Hanoverian ʃ805), Copenhagen and Walcherᵤn expeditions, he was employed ᵤ the Peninsula, ultimately ᵤmmanding the Light Division as ᵤajor-general from July 1810 and ᵤolonel of the 1st Light Bn, KGL. ʈe led the British 3rd Division in

the Waterloo campaign (severely wounded), commanded the Hanoverians in the occupation of France, and in 1818 returned to Hanover where he became Minister of War and Foreign Affairs, and a field marshal, while retaining his major-generalcy in the British Army; he was ennobled as Count von Alten. Jonathan Leach, who served under him in the Peninsula, described his inspiring style of command: 'He was always with the most advanced party, whether it happened to be cavalry or infantry; and in his quiet, cool manner, did the business to admiration.'[1] He should not be confused with **Victor, Baron Alten**, majorgeneral in the British Army and colonel of the 2nd KGL Hussars, who died in 1820 as a lieutenantgeneral in the Hanoverian Army and colonel of the 2nd Hussars.

1. Leach, p. 324.

ALVINTZI (or ALVINZI, or ALVINCZY de BERBEREK), Field Marshal Baron Josef (1735–1810)

A Transylvanian, he served in the Austrian Army during the Seven Years War (especially distinguished at Torgau) and against the Turks. Appointed *Feldmarschall-Leutnant* in 1790, he relinquished command in The Netherlands after being injured falling from a horse, but took the field in the early Revolutionary Wars and enjoyed his greatest success at Neerwinden and in raising the siege of Charleroi, where he was wounded by a shell. He had no such triumphs in Italy, being defeated by Napoleon at Arcola and Rivoli. As *Feldzeugmeister* he led a commission on the reform of the Austrian Army in 1798, and subsequently became *Feldmarschall* and served as Governor of Hungary. He died of apoplexy and at his own request was buried in a soldiers' cemetery, that he might

lie with the men who had shared his campaigning.

A brief memoir in English appears in Cust, Sir Edward. *Annals of the Wars of the Eighteenth Century*. London, 1862, vol. V, pp. 281–2

AMHERST, General Jeffrey, Baron (1717–97)

Best known for his successes in command of British troops in North America during the Seven Years War, and a full general from 1778, Jeffrey Amherst spent the later part of his life as acting or actual Commander-in-Chief of the British Army, until his supplanting in 1795 removed a somewhat dead hand from the control of the military establishment. Despite his early valuable services, Henry Dundas was surely right in describing him as a worthy and respectable old man whose period of influence and supreme command had produced nothing but mischief. His son, William Pitt Amherst, 1st Earl Amherst (1773–1857), best known as Governor-General of Bengal 1823–8, was commander of the St. James's Volunteers from their formation in 1797. He was unrelated to the other Jeffrey Amherst (d. 1815) who also served in America and became a majorgeneral in 1798, but whose principal service in the Napoleonic era was as commandant of the Evesham Volunteers.

ANDERSON, Lieutenant-General Paul (1767–1851)

He is best remembered as the closest friend and confidant of Sir John Moore, into whose regiment (51st) he was commissioned in 1788. He served as Moore's ADC from The Netherlands expedition of 1799, and at Alexandria was wounded so severely as to virtually lose the use of his right arm. After a period of regimental service he served as Acting Adjutant-General under Moore, and it was in Anderson's arms that Moore died. He remained a lifelong friend of the Moore family and of Lady Hester Stanhope, who was believed to have been Moore's fiancée; she named Anderson as her executor. He served at Walcheren, then at Malta, became major-general in 1819 and attained the rank of full general five weeks before his death. In his retirement at Bath he assembled relics of Moore, and commissioned George Jones to produce a painting of Moore's burial. Anderson's younger brother Robert was killed at Alexandria while serving with the 42nd.

ANDREOSSY, General Antoine-François, comte (1761–1828)

An eminent French soldier of Italian noble descent, Andréossy joined the French artillery in 1781 after a brilliant career at the school of artillery. He served as an engineer in Italy in 1796–7 and with Napoleon in Egypt, assisted in the coup of Brumaire, and was promoted to *général de division* in January 1800. Although employed as inspector-general of artillery and with Napoleon's headquarters in the 1805 campaign, most of his appointments were diplomatic: as ambassador to London during the Peace of Amiens, to Vienna 1808–9 (and as military governor of the city during the French occupation), and to Constantinople (1812–14). Reconciled with the Bourbons, he was elected as Deputy for the *département* of the Aude in 1827. Elected to the Académie des Sciences in 1826, his numerous publications included treatises on artillery (notably its use in sieges), military history (including a study of the pontoneers in Italy), an account of the Languedoc Canal (credit for which he accorded his ancestor François Andréossy,

1633–88), and scientific works such as observations on Egyptian lakes and the Black Sea, based on his experiences in those regions.

ANGLESEY, 1st Marquess of, see UXBRIDGE

ANGOULEME, Louis de Bourbon, duc d' (1775–1844)

Son of comte d'Artois (later Charles X), he arrived in southern France, under the alias of comte de Pradel, at the end of the Peninsular War with the intention of leading a royalist movement. He made a triumphal entry into Bordeaux on 12 March 1814 and announced that he was taking over the city in the name of the king, using the presence of Allied forces to impose restitution of royal authority over a population more anti-Bonaparte than pro-Bourbon. This brought a stinging rebuke from Wellington, to the effect that Angoulême might do as he wished but should not expect help from the Allied army to impose Bourbon rule, and that as he was performing military duties allocated him by the British and Allied governments, 'I will not give the assistance of the troops under my command to support any system of taxation or of civil government which your Royal Highness may attempt to establish'[1] without a popular declaration of support for the Bourbons. Judge-Advocate-General Larpent summarised Angoulême's character as affable and good-tempered without displaying any obvious talents; and Angoulême also gave some offence to the French ex-imperial troops he reviewed at Toulouse by wearing British-style uniform and having his aides dressed in British hussar costume.

1. Wellington, 29 Mar 1814, vol. XI, p. 611.

Guichen, E. de. *Le duc d'Angoulême*. Paris, 1909

ANTOMMARCHI, Francesco (1789–1838)

Born in Corsica, he studied medicine at Pisa and Florence. He was chosen by Cardinal Fesch to serve as Napoleon's physician at St Helena where he arrived September 1819, and remained there for the rest of Napoleon's life. He performed the post mortem on Napoleon, and wrote an account of his experiences.

Antommarchi, F. *The Last Days of the Emperor Napoleon*. 1825

ARAKCHEEV, General Alexei Andreevich, Count (1769–1834)

His chief military fame lies with his re-organisation of the Russian artillery, begun during the reign of Tsar Paul I but mainly after 1801 during the reign of Alexander I whose friend and confidant he became. The artillery reforms, including the introduction of the 'System of 1805', were of great benefit, and in January 1808 Arakcheev was appointed Inspector-General and War Minister, and played an important part in the direction of the Swedish War of 1809. Although succeeded as War Minister by Barclay de Tolly, he remained the Tsar's close adviser, and undertook the establishment of military colonies after the end of the Napoleonic Wars, in an attempt to establish a different form of land tenure. In this, as in his artillery reforms, he became highly unpopular for what some perceived as brutal enforcement of regulations; following the Tsar's death, Arakcheev retired in 1826 and the military colony system was modified completely by Alexander's successor. Clausewitz described Arakcheev as 'A Russian in every sense of the word, of great energy and cunning ... the Emperor had great confidence in him; however, the conduct of war being a thing quite strange to him, he mixed himself up in [very] little.'[1]

1. Clausewitz, p. 9.

Jenkins, M. *Arakcheev, Grand Vizier of the Russian Empire.* London, 1969

ARMSTRONG, Brigadier-General John, jun. (1758–1843)

Son of Brigadier-General John Armstrong, sen. (*d*.1795), who served with Pennsylvanian troops in the Seven Years War and with the Continental Army during the War of American Independence, John Armstrong, jun. also served in the latter war (ADC to Mercer and Gates), and then pursued a political career which included US ambassadorship to France (1804–10). Appointed brigadier-general in 1812, in January 1813 he became Madison's Secretary of War; blamed for the failure of the expedition against Montreal, and for the British capture of Washington, he was forced to resign in 1814 and undertook no further public duties.

ARNDT, Ernst Moritz (1769–1860)

ERNST MORITZ ARNDT
(LITHOGRAPH AFTER C. ENGLEBACH)

This German poet and historian was known during the Napoleonic era for violently anti-French publications, for example *Geist der Zeit*, the tone of which was such that he had to seek refuge in Sweden. He returned to Germany in late 1809 with a false identity, had close contact with important members of the anti-French party, and in 1812 went to St. Petersburg to help the war against Napoleon. He produced not only many pamphlets which inspired the 'War of Liberation' but also popular songs like 'Was ist das deutsche Vaterland?' Despite involvement in reform movements after the Napoleonic Wars, not all his work was political, but it was for his patriotic sentiments that he is perhaps best remembered.

ARTOIS, Charles-Philippe, comte d' (Charles X of France) (1757–1836)

The fourth child of the dauphin (son of Louis XV) and thus brother of Louis XVI, he was not especially concerned with politics before the French Revolution, being known rather for an extravagant lifestyle which aroused some unpopularity. At the Revolution he became a leader of the *émigrés*, canvassing support throughout Europe. His

CHARLES-PHILIPPE, COMTE D'ARTOIS (CHARLES X OF FRANCE); SHOWN AT RIGHT WITH LORD ADAM GORDON AT LEFT.
(PRINT AFTER JOHN KAY)

only military adventure was in the expedition to the Ile d'Yeu in 1795, in support of the Vendéen rising; but instead of boosting morale by leading the royalists in person, he declined to cross to the mainland, sending a sword of honour to Charette instead, which as the latter predicted was as good as a death-warrant. Artois returned to Great Britain where he remained until the Bourbon restoration, living part of the time at Holyrood. During his brother's reign as Louis XVIII, Artois led the ultra-royalist faction, succeeded to the throne as Charles X in 1824, and remained so autocratic that his fall, in the 1830 revolution, was inevitable. He again sought refuge in Britain (Holyrood was again put at his disposal) and he remained in exile for the remainder of his life. His unyielding belief in the supremacy of autocratic monarchy exemplifies the well-known saying that the Bourbons had neither learned nor forgotten anything during the Napoleonic interregnum.

ASTURIAS, Prince Ferdinand of the, see FERDINAND IV, King of Spain

AUCHMUTY, Lieutenant-General Sir Samuel (1756–1822)

Born in New York of Scots origin, he served as a Loyalist in the War of American Independence and was granted a British regular commission. Possessing neither money nor influence, he went to India to further his career in the British Army, and prospered; he was adjutant-general to Sir David Baird's force in Egypt, emerged from the South American expedition with an enhanced reputation (having captured Montevideo in February 1807), was promoted to major-general, served as CinC Madras 1810–13 and commanded the expedition which captured

Java, winning the decisive victory at Cornelis (28 August 1811). On his return home he was promoted to lieutenant-general and was CinC Ireland in 1821; he was found dead after falling from his horse in Phoenix Park in August 1822. He held the colonelcy of the 78th Highlanders from January 1812 until his death. He should not be confused with **General Sir Samuel Benjamin Auchmuty**, who served in the Peninsula with the 7th Foot and in a number of staff appointments, including ADC to Lowry Cole, became a general officer in 1841 and held the colonelcies of the 7th and 65th.

AUERSTADT, duc d', see DAVOUT

AUGEREAU, Marshal Pierre-François-Charles, duc de Castiglione (1757–1816)

PIERRE AUGEREAU
(ENGRAVING BY T. JOHNSON AFTER R. LEFEVRE)

One of Napoleon's most famous Marshals, he was a Parisian of humble parentage who remained unpolished all his life. His early career in the French army ended when he deserted after killing an officer, and from 1777 to 1784 he claimed to have served in the Russian and Prussian armies, evidently deserting from both; rejoining the French Army in 1784, he may have been seconded to Neapolitan service, or may just have wandered there, plying his trade as a dancing- and fencing-master. He prospered when joining the French Revolutionary forces from 1790, becoming a general in December 1793. He was nicknamed 'le grand Prussien' from his instance on drill and discipline and for his personal appearance ('he was always dressed irreproachably ... hair curled and powdered, long queue, his long riding-boots highly polished, and withal a most martial bearing'[1] according to Marbot), which contrasted markedly with the shabby appearance of most of the French troops. He served against Spain but won most distinction with the Army of Italy under Napoleon, notably at Castiglione, from where in 1808 he took his ducal title. His relations with Napoleon became somewhat strained – having played an important role in the coup of 18 Fructidor (4 September 1797) he prevaricated during the coup of Brumaire – but was reconciled and was created a Marshal in 1804. He commanded a corps in 1805, at Jena, and most famously at Eylau, where he performed his duty though so ill that he had to be held in the saddle by his aides, and was wounded in the arm by a grapeshot and bruised by his falling horse. After commanding the Army of Catalonia in 1809, Augereau was transferred to Germany, held Prussia during the 1812 campaign, served at Leipzig, commanded the Army of the Rhône in 1814 but abandoned Lyons and in due course declared his support for Louis XVIII. The king confirmed his rank and titles, but upon Napoleon's return in 1815 Augereau attempted to change sides again; having been disowned by Napoleon for treason in 1814, he was also dismissed by the king after Waterloo, and died at his estate at La Houssaye on 12 June 1816. A capable tactician, he was not especially skilled in handling larger formations; Napoleon remarked that he 'seemed to be tired and disheartened by victory, of which he always had enough. His person, manners, and his language, gave him the air of a bravo. This ... he was far from being, when he once found himself sated with honours and riches, which he had bestowed upon himself on every occasion that offered, and by every means in his power.'[2] He suffered considerably from ill-health and his military performance declined in consequence. Although described as an uncouth braggart and an unmitigated looter, he was also brave and generous to his friends, popular with those who knew him well, and devoted to both his wives; his first wife, Gabrielle, having died in 1806.

1. Marbot, vol. I, p. 10. 2. Las Cases, vol. I, p. 189.

Elting, Colonel J. R. 'The Proud Bandit: Augereau', in D. G. Chandler (ed.). *Napoleon's Marshals*. London, 1987

BABEUF, François-Emile (alias Gracchus) (1760–97)
Styling himself Gracchus Babeuf after the name of a distinguished plebeian family of ancient Rome, he was an agitator and journalist noted for his violent and extreme views during the French Revolution and after. In 1794 he published his journal *Le Tribun du peuple* (originally *Journal de la liberté de la presse*) and continued, despite being arrested several times, to expound extreme opinions in violent opposition to the Directory. Prompted by the threat of insurrection by socialists and Jacobins, the Directory arrested him in May 1796, ignored a somewhat vain and deluded letter which he sent to them (in which he claimed to be of equal power to the government), and put him on trial in April 1797 as the leader of the conspiracy, even though more important individuals were implicated. Condemned to death, Babeuf stabbed himself but was taken to the scaffold and beheaded. He had claimed that he was certain of immortality, but is now perhaps best known as an early proponent of socialism.
Advielle, A. *Histoire de Gracchus Babeuf*. Paris, 1884.

BACLER D'ALBE, General Louis-Albert-Ghislain, baron (1761–1824)
One of Napoleon's most valuable staff officers, he was an artist who joined the French Army in 1793, employing his talents as a geographical and cartographic expert, serving in Italy 1794–6. From September 1804 he took control of the topographical department of Napoleon's personal headquarters and became one of his most trusted assistants, working with the Emperor whenever maps were consulted and plans drawn up. Baron Fain described how, during their daily planning, both

Napoleon and Bacler d'Albe would climb upon the map-table to study dispositions in greater detail, sometimes banging their heads together as they crawled over the maps. Promoted to *général de brigade* in 1813, and created a baron from 1809, he became director of the *Dépot de la Guerre* in 1814, and continued to serve the Bourbons until his retirement in 1820. His eldest son, Joseph-Albert, served as ADC to Philippe de Ségur in the 1812 campaign.

BAGGOVOUT (or BAGAVUT), General Karl Federovich (1761–1812)
A Russian general of Estonian extraction, he served with distinction against the Turks in the annexation of the Crimea (1783–4), against the French in 1805 and against the Swedes in 1808. During Napoleon's invasion of Russia in 1812 he commanded the Russian II Corps, holding the right wing, later left wing, at Borodino. He was killed by a cannon-shot at Tarutino later in the campaign.

BAGRATION, General Peter (1765–1812)
Descended from the Georgian noble family of Bagratides, he entered the Russian army in 1782. Service in the Caucasus and Poland brought him to the attention of Suvarov, whom he accompanied in the campaigning in Italy and Switzerland, and was distinguished by the capture of Brescia. He won further accolades in 1805, notably at Hollabrunn, and served at Austerlitz, Eylau, Heilsberg and Friedland; in 1808 he captured the Åland Islands, and in 1809 commanded at Rassowa and Tataritza against the Turks. In the 1812 campaign he commanded the Second West Army, when his relations with Barclay de Tolly were distinctly strained; but he retained his command under Kutuzov and led the Russian left

wing at Borodino, where he was shot in the leg. Only with reluctance did he allow himself to be carried away; infection set in and he died on 24 September, declaring that he could die happy when assured that negotiations with Napoleon would not take place while an armed Frenchman was still in Russia. Although he may have lacked the ultimate spark of military genius, Bagration was regarded highly by society and his own men (who made a pun on his name to produce the term 'God of The Army'),[1] and, despite a taciturn demeanour and a fierce temper, Robert Ker Porter called him 'an honour to human nature'. Wilson described him as 'of short stature, with strong dark features, and eyes flashing with Asiatic fire. Gentle, gracious, generous, chivalrously brave, he was beloved by every one, and admired by all who witnessed his exploits. No officer ever excelled him in the direction of an advance or rear guard'.[2] Ségur thought him the antithesis of the cold, scientific Barclay de Tolly, representing instead the 'martial, bold and vehement instinct' of Suvarov, 'terrible in battle, but acquainted with no other book than nature, no other instructor than memory, no other counsels than his own inspirations,' an 'old Russian' (in terms of tradition, not age) who at the beginning of the 1812 campaign 'trembled with shame at the idea of retreating without fighting'.[3] His death was a severe loss to the Russian Army.

1. Palmer, p. 122. 2. Wilson, *Narrative*, p. 156. 3. Ségur, vol. I, p. 226

BAINBRIDGE, Commodore William (1774–1833)

WILLIAM BAINBRIDGE

A native of Princeton, New Jersey, he went to sea as a merchant sailor, and was commissioned in the US Navy in 1798. After service against the Barbary pirate states, in the War of 1812 he succeeded Isaac Hull in command of USS *Constitution*, his most celebrated action being the capture of HMS *Java* on 29 December 1812, off Brazil. His rewards included a gold medal from the US Congress, and the freedom of New York and Albany.

BAIRD, General Sir David, Bt. (1757–1829)

Born at Newbyth in Aberdeenshire, he was commissioned in the British Army in 1772 and went to India in 1779. Wounded and captured by Hyder Ali of Mysore at Parambakum (10 September 1780), he was imprisoned in appalling conditions at Seringapatam by Hyder and the son who succeeded him in 1782, Tipu Sultan. He was released in 1784 and, after service at the Cape, gained condign revenge when,

commanding a brigade as major-general in the Fourth Mysore War, he led the storming of Seringapatam where Tipu was killed. Believing himself unjustly treated when Arthur Wellesley was made governor of the captured city, Baird declined an East India Company pension. After commanding the force sent from India to Egypt in 1801, on his return to India he again thought himself ill-used in comparison with Wellesley and resigned his command. Captured by a French privateer on his way home, he was exchanged, knighted in 1804 and promoted to lieutenant-general. He led the expedition to the Cape with success, but was recalled after permitting Home Popham to undertake the unauthorised foray

SIR DAVID BAIRD
(ENGRAVING AFTER A. J. OLIVER).

to South America. Nevertheless, he was given command of the 2nd Division in the expedition to Copenhagen in 1807, where he was wounded in the left hand, and was appointed 2i/c to Moore in the Peninsula. At Corunna he should have succeeded to command of the army upon Moore's fatal injury, but at almost the same time was himself hit by grapeshot, which necessitated amputation of his left arm. Although actual command devolved upon Sir John

Hope, as nominal senior officer Baird wrote the covering letter which accompanied Hope's dispatch. It was his last active duty; in his view, at least, he was overlooked for further employment as a result of personal and political enmities, although he received a baronetcy (1809) and the rank of full general (1814), and served as CinC Ireland 1820–2. His baronetcy devolved upon his nephew, also David Baird, who was wounded severely while defending Hougoumont as an ensign in the 3rd Foot Guards.

Haley, A. *Our Davey: General Sir David Baird*. Liverpool, 1989; Hook, T. E. *The Life of General Rt. Hon. Sir David Baird, Bart.* London, 1832; Wilkin, W. H. *The Life of Sir David Baird*. London, 1912

BALL, Rear-Admiral Sir Alexander John, Bt. (1759–1809)

A protégé of Admiral Rodney, he was commissioned in the Royal Navy in 1778 and rose to the rank of captain in 1783. Originally Nelson had no opinion of him (supposedly because of Ball's use of epaulettes on his uniform, a French style disliked by traditionalists!), but after Ball, as commander of HMS *Alexander*, helped save the flagship in a

SIR ALEXANDER BALL

storm, Nelson became a devoted friend. After serving in *Alexander* at Aboukir Bay, Ball was ordered to the blockade of Malta, and in 1801 was appointed Governor of the island, which post he held until his death; he was created a baronet in 1801 and attained flag rank in 1805. His rule in Malta was popular and benevolent, but a memorialist noted that although he was 'devoted to the Maltese interest ... They, however, are an ungrateful set of wretches; their bigotry would not permit that the bells should be rung at his funeral; even his leniency seemed to make them disrespect him ... We are all in mourning here for a month, and all public amusements are suspended for eight days after the funeral. He was most exemplary for virtue, honour, and friendship; and died embalmed in our tears, and wafted to heaven in our sighs.'[1]
1. *Gents Mag.*, suppl. 1809, p. 1234

BALLESTEROS, General Francisco

Captain-General of Andalusia, he was one of the most active, if not especially talented or successful, Spanish leaders of the Peninsular War. He achieved a number of minor victories, served at Albuera and sustained resistance in Andalusia; but his political ambitions led to his downfall. He endeavoured to attach his troops to him personally, financed by means of extortion, and was resentful of obeying orders (his inactivity was ascribed as one reason for the failure of Wellington's siege of Burgos); and Wellington's nomination as generalissimo of the Allied forces in the Peninsula prompted him to denounce the proposal as dishonourable to Spain, and to attempt a *coup d'état*. The Cortes ordered his arrest (in the event his army displayed no loyalty to him personally), and he was imprisoned in the fortress of Ceuta in North Africa, and later at Frenegal in Estremadura.

BARAGUEY D'HILLIERS, General Louis, comte (1764–1813)

Perhaps best remembered as a dragoon commander, he was commissioned in the French Army in 1787; *général de brigade* by 1793, after a period under political arrest he joined the Army of Italy and after serving at Rivoli was promoted to *général de division*. Given a divisional command for the expedition to Egypt, he was left behind at Malta (his division being taken over by Menou) and sent home for reasons of ill health, only for his ship (the frigate *La Sensible*) to be captured by HMS *Seahorse* (27 June 1798). The crew and passengers were released in Sardinia, but Baraguey and his ADCs were retained as prisoners of war. After exchange he became Chief of Staff to the Army of the Rhine, and his association with dragoons from 1804–5 included command of a division and the experiment in which dismounted dragoons served as infantry. After serving at Elchingen, he was employed in Italy 1806–9, and in Catalonia until 1812; he was ennobled as comte in 1808. In the 1812 Russian campaign, Baraguey served as Governor of Smolensk, and was then given a division under Victor; after the surrender of one of his brigades he was removed from command pending an inquiry, but died at Berlin in January 1813. Marbot, at least, had no opinion of him; he described Baraguey as 'one of Napoleon's mistakes', after whose command the dragoon arm 'felt the disorder into which Baraguey had thrown it', though his opinion was evidently soured by the belief that in Russia he had surrendered his command on the understanding that he would not be taken prisoner – a singular concept! – and added that Baraguey had anticipated the judgment of the court-martial by dying of grief![1]
1. Marbot, vol. II, pp. 555–6.

BARBAROUX, Charles-Jean-Marie (1767–94)

A Marseilles lawyer, he took up the revolutionary cause with enthusiasm, and was deputed to go from there to the Legislative Assembly to denounce the departement's directorate as royalist conspirators. He instigated the dispatch from Marseilles of the volunteer battalion which participated in the insurrection of 10 August 1792 in Paris. A member of the Girondin party in the Convention, he opposed Robespierre and Marat, and voted for the execution of the king, but eventually had to flee to the Bordeaux region; apprehended, he tried to shoot himself but was only wounded, and was guillotined at Bordeaux. He was so extraordinarily handsome that he was known as 'the Antinoüs' (after the Emperor Hadrian's 'favourite' who drowned himself in the Nile in AD 130).

BARBE-MARBOIS, François, marquis de (1745–1837)

He held diplomatic and political office under monarchy, republic, empire and monarchy again, serving each master with servility. Son of the master of the mint at Metz, he was a diplomat under the *ancien régime*, became a member of the *Conseil des Anciens* in 1795, was transported to French Guiana in 1797 but was released by Napoleon; appointed a Councillor of State and Minister of Finance 1802–5, he negotiated the sale of Louisiana to the USA. Politically influential and from 1808 president of the *cour des comptes* – an office he relinquished finally in 1834 – he turned against Napoleon in 1814, was granted a peerage by Louis XVIII was confirmed in his office, and served as Minister of Justice 1815–16. Caulaincourt recorded Napoleon as remarking that he had been deceived by Barbé-Marbois' resemblance of honesty, but found him unprincipled, envious and untalented, but in the court of accounts could do no damage! He published several works, including an account of his deportation to Guiana, a history of the ceding of Louisiana and an essay on San Domingo, where he held his first government post.

BARCLAY, Captain Robert Heriott (1786–1837)

Born in Fife, the son of a clergyman, he joined the Royal Navy as a midshipman in 1798 and rose to lieutenant in 1805. He served in HMS *Swiftsure* at Trafalgar, and lost his left arm in an attempted cutting-out at Noirmoutier Roads in April 1808. In December 1809 he went to North America; promoted commander in March 1813, he led the British flotilla on Lake Erie and was commander of the British force defeated by Perry. Severely wounded in the action (his right arm was almost crippled), he was exonerated by the court-martial following the defeat, but received little further employment, retiring shortly after becoming captain in October 1824.

BARCLAY DE TOLLY, Field Marshal Mikhail Andreas, Prince (1761–1818)

One of the most outstanding figures in the Russian military hierarchy, he was most skilled as an administrator and reformer, but had a considerable battlefield career. Born in Livonia of Scots ancestry, he was the son of a pastor and served for fourteen years as an 'other rank' in the Russian Army before he was commissioned. After service against Swedes, Poles and Turks he became major-general in 1799

MIKHAIL BARCLAY DE TOLLY
(PRINT AFTER SAINT-AUBIN)

and lieutenant-general in 1806; he performed sterling service against Napoleon, notably at Pultusk and Eylau (where he was wounded). Appointed Minister of War in 1810, he instituted reforms of major benefit to the Russian military and, being a favourite of the Tsar, was appointed to command the First West Army for the 1812 campaign, despite opposition from traditionalists who resented 'foreign' commanders. In particular, his relations with Bagration were very poor, and could have had severe consequences had not Kutuzov been recalled to supreme command. Sir Robert Wilson believed that the appointment of a new commander at this juncture was essential, describing Barclay as 'a brave soldier and a good officer, but not a captain with a master mind equal to the need'.[1] As a general he was cautious, as demonstrated by his withdrawal in the face of Napoleon's advance, for which he was criticised; Ségur contrasted the fiery Bagration with the 'cool valour, the scientific, methodical and tenacious genius of Barclay, whose mind, German like his birth, was for calculating everything, even the chances of the hazard, bent on owing all to his tactics, and nothing to fortune'.[2] After commanding the

right wing at Borodino, the union of the First and Second West Armies led Barclay to retire on grounds of ill-health, but he remained War Minister until 1813. In that year he again took the field and was appointed Russian CinC after Bautzen; he led the Russians in France in 1814, was promoted to field marshal, in 1815 again led the army which invaded France, and was made a prince. If his greatest contribution was in the fields of reform and administration, where he demonstrated his greatest skill, he was not a bad general despite the criticism he received at the time, and his policy of declining a major battle at the outset of the 1812 campaign prevented the Russian forces from being enveloped and destroyed piecemeal.

1. Wilson, *Narrative*, p. 130. 2. Ségur, vol. I, p. 226.

Josselson, M., and Josselson, D. *The Commander: A Life of Barclay de Tolly*. Oxford, 1980

BARHAM, Admiral Charles Middleton, Baron (1726–1813)

Born at Leith and great-grand-nephew of the Civil War general John Middleton, 1st Earl (*c*.1619–74), he served as Comptroller of the Navy 1778–90 and was awarded a baronetcy in

CHARLES MIDDLETON, BARON BARHAM
(ENGRAVING AFTER J. DOWNMAN)

October 1781. In his 79th year he was brought out of retirement by his friend William Pitt to be First Lord of the Admiralty, and thus held that office, which he executed with industry and experience, at the time of Trafalgar; he was ennobled as Baron Barham of Barton Court and Teston, Kent, in May 1805. Upon his death it was stated that his life had been 'eminently distinguished by every active, public, and private virtue',[1] but not everyone was so impressed: St. Vincent said he had made more money from the sale of offices at the Navy Board than any of his predecessors, that he lacked experience of active service, was only capable of minor administrative tasks and of advocating a system of morality for his seamen, Middleton being a noted Methodist!

1. *Gent's Mag.*, June 1813, p. 597.

Laughton, Sir John (ed.). *Letters and Papers of Charles, Lord Barham*. London, 1907–11

BARLOW, Joel (1754–1812)

This American poet, politician and diplomat was living in France during the beginning of the Revolutionary period, and sympathised with its ideals (some of his writings were banned in Great Britain); after serving as US consul in Algiers (1795–7) he was appointed American plenipotentiary to France. Travelling to meet Napoleon to negotiate a commercial treaty, he became involved in the retreat from Moscow and died from exposure in Poland on Christmas Eve 1812.

BARNARD, General Sir Andrew Francis (1773–1855)

One of the British Army's best and most popular regimental commanders, he was born in County Donegal. He saw extensive service in the West Indies, The Netherlands, Mediterranean and Canada before being gazetted to the 95th Rifles as lieutenant-colonel in March 1810. He served in this regiment with the greatest distinction; severely wounded in command of the 3/95th at Barrosa, he commanded a brigade of the Light Division from August 1811, led the division after Craufurd's death at Ciudad Rodrigo until after Badajoz, and was desperately wounded by a bullet through the body at Nivelle. When assured that death was not imminent, he declared that 'If any man can recover, I know I shall';[1] and when he rejoined his brigade exactly one month later he was greeted by prolonged and spontaneous cheering. Barnard was wounded again while commanding the 1/95th at Waterloo, and was appointed by Wellington to lead the British division during the occupation of Paris. From 1821 he held important posts in the royal household, and rose to the rank of full general (1851). Not only a skilled soldier, Barnard was universally popular with those under his command: 'If a thorough knowledge of their profession, calm, cool courage, great presence of mind in action, frank and gentlemanly manners, and the total absence of what may be termed teazing (*sic*) those under their command, I do say ... that both Baron Alten and Colonel Barnard merited the high estimation in which they were held.'[2] Apparently the most for which Barnard was criticised was the dense smoke produced by the cigars he smoked in the Peninsula!

1. Simmons, p. 322. 2. Leach, p. 262.

Powell, A. *The Barnard Letters*. 1928

BARNAVE, Antoine-Pierre-Joseph-Marie (1761–93)

A lawyer from Grenoble, he was acknowledged as one of the greatest orators of the French Revolution. Although a supporter of the principles of the revolution and until 1791 a leading Jacobin, he later spoke in favour of the retention of the monarchy, and made a good impression upon the king and queen when entrusted with escorting them back to Paris from Varennes; they probably made a similar impression upon him. He retired to Grenoble in 1792, but was denounced for his support for the monarchy, and after a period of imprisonment was executed in November 1793. Unusually, he was a Protestant.

BARNES, General Sir Edward (1776–1838)

Entering the British Army in 1792, after service in the West Indies, he was on Wellington's staff in the Peninsula, and as a major-general commanded a brigade of the 7th Division (December 1812–December 1813) and then a brigade of the 2nd Division until the end of the war. For the 1815 campaign he served as adjutant-general, but such duties must not have been to the taste of a man who had been described in 1813 as falling upon the enemy like a bulldog, and hence he was described as 'our fire-eating adjutant-general'. This was exemplified at Quatre Bras when he could not resist the temptation to lead the 92nd (which had been under his command in the Peninsula) in the charge during which Cameron of Fassiefern was killed; Barnes was himself wounded at Waterloo. He became a popular Governor of Ceylon (1824–31) and then until 1833 was CinC India with the local rank of general; he held the colonelcies of the 31st, 78th and 2/Rifle Brigade, and was MP for Sudbury 1837–8.

BARRAS, Paul-François-Jean-Nicolas (1755–1829)

Known as one of the most immoral and avaricious leaders of the French revolutionary era, he was descended from a noble Provençal family, entered the

PAUL BARRAS
(ENGRAVING AFTER RAFFET)

French Army at the age of 16 and served in the East Indies 1776–8 and 1782–3; he was captured at the surrender of Pondicherry in 1778. Espousing the revolution, he became one of the administrators of the *département* of the Var and (perhaps because of his military background) served as political commissioner with the French Army in the south-east, where he encountered Napoleon Bonaparte during the siege of Toulon. Having supported the overthrow of Robespierre, he was charged with the defence of the Convention during the attempted coup of 13 Vendémiaire (1795) and sought Napoleon's assistance, greatly increasing the latter's prestige. Barras became one of the Directors, whose conduct was such that the unpopularity of the government made Napoleon's coup of Brumaire (1799) relatively easy. Barras' political career ended with the fall of the Directory – perhaps not unwillingly as he may have had some complicity in the coup – and he retired to enjoy his vast, dubiously accumulated wealth; his notorious immorality, both public and private, did much to bring about the downfall of the Directory and was one cause of the low esteem in which it was held. A tall, handsome man, he was described as somewhat sinister in appearance, and his vulgar manners showed no evidence of his genteel background. Although his relations with Napoleon were always good – the Empress Josephine was one of Barras' ex-mistresses – Napoleon recognised his failings, remarking that he had no talent for oratory, no idea of business, no knowledge of military affairs (having left the army as a captain) and as a Director 'he did not possess the qualifications requisite to fill that situation'. Of his fortune, Napoleon thought that 'the manner in which it had been acquired, by favouring the contractors, impaired the public morals'. Barras, he said, 'spoke sometimes in moments of agitation, and his voice filled the house. His intellectual capacity did not allow him to go beyond a few sentences, but the animation with which he spoke would have produced the impression that he was a man of resolution; this however he was not; and he had no opinion of his own upon any part of the administration of public affairs.'[1]

1. Las Cases, vol. II, p. 257.

Barras, P. F. N. *Memoirs of Barras, Member of the Directorate*, ed. G. Duruy, trans. C. E. Roche. London, 1895–6

BARRERE (or BARERE) de VIEUZAC, Bertrand (1755–1841)

A provincial lawyer, Barrère became a member of the French National Assembly, and later the Convention, and appears to have given his allegiance to whichever party was in the ascendant – at first attacking Robespierre, then joining him, and finally denouncing him. Although described as a mild and amiable man, he is perhaps best remembered for his declaration that 'The tree of liberty cannot flourish if it is not watered by the blood of a king.' Despite attempts to stay on the winning side, he was sentenced to transportation in 1795, and after his escape lived in obscurity. He was employed as a minor agent by Napoleon and declared himself a royalist after Napoleon's fall, but in 1815 was banished as a regicide and lived in Brussels until permitted to return, and was even given a small pension by Louis-Philippe. He appears in David's painting *Oath in the Tennis Court*, writing up the proceedings for his paper *Point du Jour*, and was the last surviving member of the Committee of Public Safety to which he had been appointed in April 1793. It was said that he originated the phrase 'nation of shopkeepers' which as often been attributed to Napoleon: Barrère referred to the British as a *nation boutiquière* in a speech concerning the battle of the Glorious First of June, on 16 July 1794.

BASSANO, duc de, see MARET

BATHURST, Henry, 3rd Earl (1762–1834)

One of the foremost British politicians of the era, he was MP for Cirencester from 1783 until he succeeded his father as 3rd Earl in 1794. He served in a number of government posts under his friend William Pitt, was President of the Board of Trade and Master of the Mint under Portland and Perceval, was briefly Foreign Secretary (1809) and from June 1812 until 1827 was Secretary for War and the Colonies under Lord Liverpool. In this position he contributed much towards sustaining Wellington in the Peninsula, and many of Wellington's important dispatches were addressed to him. Bathurst served as Lord President of the Council during Wellington's ministry of 1828–30. He was supposedly the last man to wear his hair in a queue, cutting it off only in 1828.

BEAUHARNAIS, General Alexandre, vicomte de (1760–94)

Born in Martinique of an old French noble family, he served in the French Army during the War of American Independence, and at the commencement of the Revolution was a member of the National Assembly, of which he became president. Although in his military career he had risen only to the rank of major, in 1793 he was appointed general of the Army of the Rhine; a brave but not enterprising man, he failed in tasks assigned to him, most notably preventing the fall of Metz, and retired. Accused of treason and complicity in the fall of Metz, he was guillotined on 23 June 1794. He is best remembered as the first husband of the Empress Josephine (from whom he had separated in 1782) and as father of Eugène de Beauharnais. His brother François, marquis de la Ferté-Beauharnais (1756–1847) was a confirmed royalist who served in the *Armée de Condé*, but later returned from emigration and served Napoleon in diplomatic posts.

BEAUHARNAIS, Eugène de, Viceroy of Italy (1781–1824)

The son of Alexandre de Beauharnais, he first encountered Napoleon when, as a boy, he asked for the return of the sword of his guillotined father. Eugène at first resented Napoleon's marriage to his mother, the widow of the father he revered, but he became one of the most loyal and capable subordinates of his step-father, and displayed considerable military skill in the service of the Empire. He accompanied Napoleon to Italy in 1796–7 and to Egypt – wounded at Acre –

EUGÈNE DE BEAUHARNAIS
(PRINT AFTER ALBRECHT ADAM)

and was promoted to general in 1804. In the following year he was appointed Viceroy of Italy, where his rule (albeit depending upon Napoleon's instructions) was beneficial; in 1809 he commanded the Army of Italy (with Macdonald as his assistant), was checked at Sacile but won a victory at Raab, and served with distinction at Wagram. He led the Army of Italy in the 1812 campaign, performing well at Borodino and, especially, at Maloyaroslavets, played an important role at Lützen and defended Italy with some skill in 1814, displaying unswerving loyalty to his step-father. The marriage between Eugène and Princess Auguste-Amélie of Bavaria had been arranged by Napoleon, but became a true love-match, and having promised his father-in-law not to become involved any further in Napoleon's schemes, he did not rejoin the Emperor in 1815. Eugène retired to Munich with the titles of Duke of Leuchtenberg and Prince of Eichstädt, spending his time helping the old soldiers and comrades of Napoleon, until his tragically early death from cerebral haemorrhages. A genuinely good man, whose motto 'Honour and Fidelity' fitted him perfectly, his character was

assessed accurately by Bourrienne: 'an excellent heart, a fine courage, strict honour, great generosity and frankness, with an obliging and amiable temper'.[1]

1. Anon., p. 257.

Beauharnais, E. de. *Mémoires et Correspondance politiques et militaires du prince Eugène*, ed. Baron A. Ducasse. Paris, 1858–60; Epstein, R. *Prince Eugène at War 1809: A Study of the Role of Prince Eugène de Beauharnais in the Franco–Austrian War of 1809*. Arlington, Texas, 1984; Montagu, V. M. *Eugène de Beauharnais: the Adopted Son of Napoleon*. London, 1913; Oman, C. *Napoleon's Viceroy: Eugène de Beauharnais*. London, 1966; Vaudoncourt, F. F. G. *Histoire politique et militaire du Prince Eugène Napoléon, vice-roi d'Italie*. Paris, 1828

BEAUHARNAIS, Hortense de, Queen of Holland (1783–1837)

The daughter of Alexandre de Beauharnais, and sister of Eugène, she became Napoleon's step-daughter upon the re-marriage of her mother, the Empress Josephine. At Napoleon's instigation she entered into an unhappy marriage with Louis Bonaparte, becoming in turn Queen of Holland and Duchesse de Saint-

HORTENSE DE BEAUHARNAIS, QUEEN OF HOLLAND (ENGRAVING BY F. FRENCH AFTER GÉRARD)

Leu. One of her sons became the Emperor Napoleon III; another, by her lover General Auguste Flahaut, was Charles-Auguste-Louis-Joseph (1811–65), who was created duc de Morny by his half-brother Napoleon III. Hortense was the author of the very popular marching-song *Partant pour la Syrie*, sung by generations of French soldiers.

Beauharnais, H. *The Memoirs of Queen Hortense*, ed. J. Hanoteau. New York, 1927; Taylor, I. *Queen Hortense and her Friends*. 1907; Wright, C. *Daughter to Napoleon*. New York, 1961

Beauharnais, Josephine de, see **JOSEPHINE, Empress**

BEAULIEU, General Johann Peter, Baron (1725–1819)
A native of Brabant who joined the Austrian Army at the age of 18 and served on the staff of Marshal Daun during the Seven Years War, he had the distinction of being one of the very first to engage the French at the commencement of the Revolutionary Wars, when he defeated General Biron's column near Valenciennes on 29 April 1792. He commanded the left wing at Jemappes and later in 1794 was Chief of Staff in The Netherlands, but when sent to command in Italy was defeated by Napoleon, notably at Montenotte and Lodi, whereupon he retired to his estate near Linz. Interested in art and architecture (he had been employed to decorate the imperial palaces), he collected works of art and in 1789 during the Flemish insurrection, which as Governor of Malines he helped suppress, his house and its treasures were attacked by rebels, and his only (adopted) son shot in its defence. Thereupon Beaulieu displayed the 'singularly calm and stoical disposition' which characterised his military service, remarking to his followers, 'My friends, this is not a

time for tears; we must conquer.'[1] Three of his brothers were killed in Austrian service, at Breslau, Hochkirch and in the War of the Bavarian Succession.
1. A brief memoir in English is in Cust, vol. V, pp. 279–80

BECKWITH, Lieutenant-General Sir Thomas Sidney (1772–1831)
Among the best of the 'outpost' commanders in the British Army, he was the son of Major-General John Beckwith, who had led the 20th in their celebrated charge at Minden. Commissioned in 1791, Sidney's fame arose from his association with the 95th Rifles, which he joined (as the Experimental Corps of Riflemen) in 1800. Lieutenant-colonel from 1803, he assisted Moore in the development of light infantry training at Shorncliffe, served in Denmark in 1807 and in the Peninsula from its commencement until he returned home ill in 1811, having commanded a brigade of the Light Division with great success. In 1812 he went to Canada as assistant quartermaster-general and served in the War of 1812; major-general in 1814, he was appointed CinC Bombay in 1829 and lieutenant-general in 1830; he died in India. He was praised universally as a man more concerned with the efficiency of troops in the field than with parade-ground precision. 'always averse to tease and torment the old soldier with more than a certain *quantum* of drill'[1] but instead gaining their confidence by kindness, 'the surest way to make the soldiers follow him cheerfully through fire and water, when the day of trial came; for they well knew that he was the last man on earth who would give them unnecessary trouble, or, on the other hand, would spare neither man nor officer, when the good of the service demanded

their utmost exertions'.[2] Kincaid remarked that he had 'a tall commanding figure and noble countenance, with a soul equal to his appearance – he was, as Napier says, "a man equal to rally an army in flight"... the life and soul of the fray ... and his calm, clear, commanding voice was distinctly heard amid the roar of battle, and cheerfully obeyed ... nothing more than a familiar sort of conversation with the soldier ... "Now, my lads, we'll just go back a little if you please ... we'll just walk quietly back, and you can give them a shot as you go ..."'[3] Sidney Beckwith should not be confused with his brother, **General Sir George Beckwith (1753–1823)**, who performed much valuable service in the West Indies, was knighted for the capture of Martinique in 1809 and became full general in 1814; nor with their nephew, **Major-General John Charles Beckwith (1789–1862)**, of the 95th, who served as a brigade-major in the Light Division during the Peninsular War and, as a major, serving as assistant quartermaster-general, lost a leg at Waterloo.
1. Leach, p. 112. 2. Ibid., p. 121. 3. Kincaid, pp. 237–8.

BEDOYERE, Charles de la, see **LA BEDOYERE**

BEECHEY, Sir William (1753–1839)
A notable British portrait-painter, his subjects included a number of military personalities; he was knighted and elected to the Royal Academy after exhibiting a huge canvas of George III and the Prince of Wales reviewing troops in 1798, which was bought by the king himself.

BEETHOVEN, Ludwig van (1770–1827)
Born in Germany and latterly resident in Vienna, the great

composer deserves inclusion here not only for his pre-eminence in the music of the time, but for some connections with the events of the period. He derived inspiration from the period of the French Revolution, and his Third Symphony, op. 55, the 'Eroica', was written in 1804 in honour of Napoleon; but upon learning that Napoleon had made himself emperor, Beethoven almost destroyed the score. Another composition, performed at the Congress of Vienna, was entitled *Wellingtons Sieg oder die Schlacht bei Vittoria'*, known in English as *Wellington's Victory'* or the *Battle' Symphony.*

BELLANGE, Joseph-Louis-Hippolyte (1800–66)

Bearing the same name as the perhaps better-known early 17th-century French artist Jacques, Hippolyte Bellangé (as he is known) was a pupil of Gros and made his reputation as a painter of Napoleonic battle-scenes. His most famous publication was *Uniformes de l'Armée française depuis 1815* (*c.*1831). Although not working contemporaneously with the Napoleonic period, his work is generally accurate, and impressive if sometimes theatrically composed, for example his well-known print of the last stand of the Old Guard at Waterloo.

BELLEGARDE, Field Marshal Heinrich Joseph Johannes, Count (1756–1845)

Born in Dresden and beginning his career in the Saxon Army, he transferred to Austrian service in 1771 and won distinction against the Turks (1788–9) and as a general officer in The Netherlands 1793–4). As *Feldmarschall–Leutnant* he was Archduke Charles' deputy in command of the Army of the Lower Rhine (1796), accompanied him to Italy in the following year, and in 1799 led a corps in

Switzerland and Italy. He served in the Marengo campaign and in 1805 was temporarily appointed president of the war council, then commanded the right wing at the second battle of Caldiero. In 1809 he played an important role in the battles of Aspern–Essling and Wagram, where he commanded I Corps. As *Feldmarschall* Bellegarde served as Governor of Galicia (1810–13) and led the Austrian forces in Italy 1813–15. Described as a very gallant officer, he was a capable subordinate and a useful administrator, if not an independent commander of the highest ability. Involved in measures intended to reform the Austrian forces, in 1798 he had the foresight to propose the implementation of a *corps d'armée* system, which would have been of considerable benefit, only for it to be rejected by the more reactionary element of the military establishment.

BELLIARD, General Augustin-Daniel, comte (1769–1832)

He began his military career in the French National Guard, but later served in a number of staff appointments, including at Valmy, and after Arcola became *général de brigade*. In the Egyptian campaign, as Governor of Cairo, he surrendered the city to the British without opposition; of undoubted personal bravery, this decision (which angered some French opinion) was based upon his humanity and a commendable reluctance to sacrifice lives uselessly. In 1805 he served as Murat's chief of staff, then Joseph Bonaparte's, again with Murat in 1812, and as a cavalry commander in 1814 had the dubious distinction of carrying to Napoleon the news of the surrender of Paris. Belliard accepted the Bourbon restoration but joined Napoleon again in 1815, being sent as envoy to

Murat; and later again accepted the Bourbons. He became interested in archaeology during the Egyptian campaign, was of great help to the scholars who accompanied the arm, and wrote a ten-volume history of the expedition.

Belliard, General A. D. comte. *Histoire scientifique et militaire de l'expédition française en Egypte.* Paris, 1830–6; *Mémoires du Comte Belliard.* Paris, 1842

BELLUNE, duc de, see VICTOR

BENEVENTE, duc de, see TALLEYRAND

BENNIGSEN, General Levin August Theophil, Count (1745–1826)

LEVIN BENNIGSEN

Born in Brunswick of Hanoverian family, he was a page at court and began his military career in the Hanoverian Foot Guards, but retired in 1764 and entered Russian service in 1773. He was distinguished in wars against the Turks, in the Polish War (1793–4) and against the Persians (1796); and took an active part in the conspiracy which led to the assassination of Tsar Paul I. It appears that his subsequent career was not helped by Alexander I's knowledge of his implication in the plot, and (among others) was resented as a 'foreigner' by elements within the Russian military hierarchy. Nevertheless, in 1801 he was appointed Governor-General of Lithuania, general in 1802, and commanded the Russian army which fought at Pultusk and Eylau, but temporarily retired from command following his crushing defeat at Friedland. In 1812 he served as Kutuzov's chief of staff and defeated Murat at Vinkovo, but had no opinion of Kutuzov and retired after disagreements with him. After Kutuzov's death he returned as commander of the Army of Reserve, and was ennobled as a count on the evening of the last day of the Battle of Leipzig in recognition of his crucial role in the action. Thereafter he commanded the forces operating in north Germany, and retired in 1818 to settle on his estate in Hanover. His son, Count Alexander (1809–93) was distinguished as a Hanoverian statesman.

Bennigsen, Count L. *Mémoires du Général Bennigsen*, ed. G. Cazalas, Paris, 1907–8

BENTINCK (or CAVENDISH-BENTINCK), General Lord William Henry (1774–1839)

Second son of the 3rd Duke of Portland, he served as Governor of Madras from 1803 until his recall following the sepoy mutiny at Vellore in 1807; military representative to the Spanish government in 1808, he commanded a brigade of the 1st Division in the Corunna campaign, and was later British commander in the Mediterranean. In June 1813 he replaced Murray in command of the forces in eastern Spain, and in spring 1814 invaded north Italy, occupying Tuscany and Genoa; something of an idealist, he had plans for liberal constitutions in these areas but they were repudiated by the Austrians and unsupported by the British government. He

LORD WILLIAM HENRY BENTINCK (ENGRAVING BY G. STODART AFTER LAWRENCE)

WILLIAM BERESFORD (ENGRAVING AFTER SIR WILLIAM BEECHEY)

returned to India as Governor-General in 1827, which office he held until 1835. A Member of Parliament at various times between 1796 and his death, representing four seats, he held the colonelcies of the 11th and 20th Light Dragoons. His brother, **Major-General Lord Frederick Bentinck (1781–1828)**, commanded the advance-guard of Murray's expedition to Tarragona.

Rosselli, J. *Lord William Bentinck and the British Occupation of Sicily 1811–1814*. Cambridge, 1956; *Lord William Bentinck: the Making of a Liberal Imperialist 1774–1839*. London, 1974

BERESFORD, Marshal William Carr, Viscount (1768–1854)

A natural son of the 1st Marquess of Waterford, he entered the British Army in 1785 and lost an eye in a shooting accident in Nova Scotia in the following year. He served with the 69th at Toulon, became lieutenant-colonel of the 88th in 1795 and served with them in India, and commanded a brigade in Baird's force in Egypt. Present at the Cape in 1806, he went from there on the disastrous South American expedition and was captured at Buenos Aires. At the end of 1807 he went to

Madeira as Governor and CinC in the name of the Portuguese monarchy, and after serving in the Peninsula under Moore and Wellington was appointed Marshal of the Portuguese Army on 2 March 1809. His task of re-organising it, by overhauling the entire military system and introducing a small number of British officers was accomplished with great distinction and produced a vital component of Wellington's Peninsula army. Awarded a knighthood of the Bath and a Portuguese peerage after Busaco, Beresford proved to be a first-rate administrator, but his limitations as a field commander were revealed when he commanded at Albuera, after which he became briefly despondent. However, he remained a most important figure in the Allied command, served subsequently with distinction and was wounded severely at Salamanca; at the end of the war he was created Baron Beresford of Albuera and Cappoquin, up-graded to a viscountcy in 1823. He left Portuguese service in 1819 upon the dismissal of British officers after the revolution; thereafter he supported Wellington in politics and was Master-General of the Ordnance 1828–30. In his later years he became involved in a famous war of words with William

pier who was critical of his abil-
es, and wrote of Albuera: 'No
neral ever gained a great battle
th so little increase of military
putation as marshal Beresford.
s personal intrepidity and
ength, qualities so attractive for
e multitude, were conspicuously
splayed, yet the breath of his
vn army withered his laurels ...
e person of the general-in-chief
is indeed seen every where, a
llant soldier! but the mind of the
eat commander was seen no
here.'[1] Napier's strictures were
obably too harsh, and indeed
ellington nominated Beresford
replace himself should he be
led: 'the ablest man I have yet
en with the army, and the one
ving the largest views, is Beres-
rd. They tell me that when I am
t present he wants decision ...
it I am quite certain he is the
ly person capable of conducting
arge concern ... if it was a ques-
m of handling troops, some of
u fellows might do as well, nay,
tter than he; but what we want
w is some one to feed our
ops, and I know of no one fitter
r the purpose than Beresford.'[2]
Napier, W., vol. II, pp. 547, 554. 2.
iffiths, p. 308.

RG, Grand Duke of, see
URAT

RNADOTTE, Marshal Jean-
ptiste-Jules (later Charles-
an), later Charles XIV of
veden) (1763–1844)

guably the most successful of
poleon's subordinates, Jean-
ptiste (he later added the name
les) entered the French Army in
80, served in the East Indies and
se to the rank of sergeant-
ajor. A vehement republican
ho had 'Death to Tyrants'
ttooed on his arm!), he pros-
ered during the French Revolu-
m and had risen to *général de
vision* by October 1794. He
rved under Napoleon in Italy

JEAN-BAPTISTE BERNADOTTE
(CHARLES XIV OF SWEDEN)
(ENGRAVING BY T. BLOOD AFTER SHEPPERSON)

and became associated with the
Bonaparte family by marriage, in
August 1798, to Désirée Clary,
Joseph's sister-in-law. Although
he declined to assist Napoleon's
coup d'état, he was among the
first creation of marshals in 1804,
and handled his corps with credit
in the Ulm–Austerlitz campaign,
receiving the title of Prince
of Ponte Corvo. Thereafter his
fortunes declined; he was severely
criticised by Napoleon for his
delay in supporting Davout at
Auerstädt, and after mishandling
his corps at Wagram he was
dismissed from the army. He was
re-employed in command of the
force to oppose the Walcheren
landing, but in September 1809
Napoleon deprived him of all
appointments. His future lay to
the north: having shown great
kindness to Swedish prisoners in
the late war with Denmark, he
was approached by the Swedish
government as a successor to
King Charles XIII, who had no
heir. Napoleon thought the idea
absurd, but on 21 August 1810
Bernadotte was elected as Crown
Prince, changing his name to
Charles-Jean and his religion to
Lutheran. Napoleon's seizure of
Swedish Pomerania in 1812
forced Bernadotte towards the

Tsar and those who opposed the
French; thus he took Sweden into
the Sixth Coalition and in 1813–14
led her troops as commander of
the Army of the North, winning
the actions of Grossbeeren and
Dennewitz and playing an important role at Leipzig. He was
accused of deliberate delaying in
the Leipzig campaign and in
France, the latter perhaps out of
consideration for his native
country, for he may have entertained hopes of succeeding
Napoleon, but this was never realistic as most Frenchmen regarded
him as a traitor. Napoleon
certainly did: 'in his intoxication,
he sacrificed both his new and his
mother country, his own glory,
his true power, the cause of the
people, and the welfare of Europe
... He is now the only upstart
sovereign in Europe.'[1] Nevertheless, it is perhaps ironic that
the once die-hard republican
achieved something which even
Napoleon did not: the foundation
of a royal dynasty which still
endures. In February 1818
Bernadotte became King Charles
XIV of Sweden (Carl XIV Johan)
and proved a moderate and good
ruler, unifying Norway and
Sweden, although his inherent
conservatism led some in the
Swedish parliament to call for his
abdication in 1840 in favour of his
son Oscar (1799–1859), who actually succeeded as Oscar I upon his
father's death. Oscar married
Josephine Beauharnais, Eugène's
daughter and thus grand-
daughter of the Empress Josephine.

1. Las Cases, vol. IV, p. 110.

Barton, Sir Dunbar P. *Bernadotte, the First Phase 1763–99*.
London, 1914; *Bernadotte and
Napoleon 1799–1810*. London,
1921; *Bernadotte, Prince and King
1810–44*. London, 1925; Dewes, S.
Sergeant Belle-Jambe. London,
1943 (the title is from Bernadotte's
early nickname, 'Sergeant Pretty-

Legs', from his handsome appearance); Heathcote, T. A. 'Sergeant Belle-Jambe', in *Napoleon's Marshals*. ed. D. G. Chandler. London, 1987 (includes a fuller bibliography); Palmer, A. *Bernadotte*. London, 1990; Lord Russell of Liverpool. *Bernadotte, Marshal of France and King of Sweden*. London, 1981

BERNARD, General Simon (1779–1839)

This French officer of engineers served as Napoleon's aide 1805–12 and in the Waterloo campaign, and was especially distinguished during the defence of Torgau (which fell in January 1814 after a three–month siege). After the Napoleonic Wars he emigrated to the USA where he became a general of engineers and worked on a number of engineering projects, including forts and the Chesapeake and Ohio Canal. He returned to France after the 1830 revolution, was appointed lieutenant–general of engineers by Louis-Philippe, and served as Minister of War in 1836.

BERNSTORFF, Christian Gunther, Count von (1769–1835)

A member of an important family of Danish diplomats (notably his father, Andreas Peter 1735–97, and great-uncle, Johann Hartwig 1712–72), he held a number of important diplomatic posts until he succeeded his father as Foreign Minister in 1797. In 1800 he became Prime Minister and supervised foreign policy during the period including hostilities against Great Britain in 1801 and 1807. His authority was the greater because of the insanity of the Danish king, Christian VII. Following his retirement in 1810, Bernstorff held diplomatic posts, represented Denmark at the Congress of Vienna and from 1818 transferred his services to Prussia,

becoming head of the foreign ministry.

BERRY, Charles-Ferdinand, duc de (1778–1820)

The last French prince to hold the title of duc de Berry (or Berri, derived from the province of that name), he was the younger son of comte d'Artois (later Charles X) and brother of duc d'Angoulême. At the revolution he emigrated with his father, served in the *Armée de Condé* and with the Russians, before settling in Britain in 1801. In 1814 he returned to France, and was appointed CinC of the army by Louis XVIII upon Napoleon's return, but having few loyal troops retired to Ghent until after Napoleon's defeat. His marriage to an Englishwoman, Anna Brown (by whom he had two daughters) was dissolved in 1814 for political reasons, and he married instead Princess Caroline of Naples (1798–1870). In February 1820 he was assassinated when leaving the opera in Paris.

BERRY, Rear-Admiral Sir Edward, Bt. (1768–1831)

SIR EDWARD BERRY
(PRINT PROBABLY AFTER W. GRIMALDI)

One of Nelson's closest and bravest companions, he was the son of a London merchant of Norfolk origin, and entered the

Royal Navy by the influence [of] Lord Mulgrave, once a pupil [of] Berry's uncle. He served in t[he] War of American Independen[ce] and at the First of June, w[ith] Nelson's First Lieutenant in HM[S] *Agamemnon*, was present at [St] Vincent as a 'passenger' in HM[S] *Captain* and was the first to boa[rd] the *San Nicolas*, and as Nelso[n's] flag captain commanded HM[S] *Vanguard* at Aboukir B[ay]. Exchanged after his capture [in] HMS *Leander* when carryi[ng] home the dispatch of the victo[ry] his place was taken by Thom[as] Hardy, who was evidently mo[re] capable, but Berry command[ed] HMS *Agamemnon* at Trafalgar a[nd] in Duckworth's victory at S[an] Domingo. He became a baronet [in] 1806 and rear-admiral in J[uly] 1821, but never held an admira[l's] command because of ill-heal[th]. Probably the greatest complime[nt] paid to this outstandingly bra[ve] seaman was when, accompanyi[ng] Nelson to St. James's, he heard t[he] king lament the loss of Nelso[n's] right arm; whereupon the admi[ral] replied that he still had his rig[ht] hand, presenting Berry to t[he] king.

BERTHIER, Marshal Louis-Alexandre, prince de Neuchât[el] (1753–1815)

Arguably the most important of [all] Napoleon's subordinates, he w[as] unimpressive in independe[nt] command but invaluable as Chi[ef] of Staff. Born at Versailles, [he] followed his father into milita[ry] engineering, and served [in] America under Rochambeau; [at] the Revolution he served in t[he] Versailles National Guard a[nd] aided the escape of Louis XV['s] aunts. Although periodica[lly] unemployed, being thought to [be] a royalist, his administrati[ve] ability led to posts as chief of sta[ff] and when sent to Italy as a gener[al] his talents made him an ide[al] assistant for Napoleon. He serv[ed]

LOUIS BERTHIER
(ENGRAVING BY H. DAVIDSON AFTER GROS)

s Chief of Staff and Minister of
Var (1800–7), became a Marshal
ı the first creation and Prince of
ʃeuchâtel (1806) and of Wagram
ı809). He had been in nominal
ommand of the Army of Reserve
ı the Marengo campaign (as First
'onsul Napoleon was officially
ıenied military rank), but his
ıilings as a general were
xposed at the beginning of the
ı809 campaign. Thereafter he
ontinued as Chief of Staff, and
ıthough Napoleon regarded him
s a friend he may never have
ıppreciated his true worth, once
ıescribing Berthier as merely a
ʃhief clerk' and at least once
ıattering his head against a wall
ı an outburst of rage. Berthier
ıecame progressively more
ıorose, especially after Napoleon
ırranged his marriage to a
ʃerman noblewoman instead of
ı his beloved mistress, Madame
ʃisconti, whose husband died
ıhortly after the marriage;
ıerthier declared 'To what a
ıiserable condition I am
ıeduced! With a little more
ʃonstancy, Madame Visconti
ıight have been my wife!'[1] His
ıisery increased as he claimed to
ʃe overworked to the point of
ıeath and, weary of incessant
ıampaigning and having support-
ıd the Bourbons at the time of

Napoleon's first abdication, he
remained loyal to them in 1815.
On 1 June 1815 he fell to his death
from a window at Bamberg,
perhaps murdered, perhaps an
accident, or perhaps suicide
prompted by the fact that Russian
troops were marching past *en
route* for France, to oppose the
old master he had abandoned.
His talents as Chief of Staff were
prodigious, involving incessant
hard work and great attention to
detail; as Napoleon remarked,
'Nature has evidently designed
many for a subordinate situation;
and among these is Berthier. As a
chief of staff he had no superior;
but he was not fit to command five
hundred men.'[2]

1. Anon., p. 241. 2. Ibid., p. 242.

Derrécagaix, General V. B. *Le
Maréchal Berthier, Prince de
Wagram et de Neuchâtel*. Paris,
1904–5; Raeuber, C. 'Duty and
Discipline; Berthier', in *Nap-
oleon's Marshals*, ed. D. G. Chan-
dler. London, 1987; Watson, S. J.
*By Command of the Emperor: A
Life of Marshal Berthier*. London,
1957

BERTHOLLET, Claude-Louis, comte (1748–1822)

Born in Savoy, he practised as a
physician before he made his
name as a chemist; originally an
opponent of Lavoisier's work
against the phlogistic theory, from
1785 he declared himself
convinced by it. His work was
varied; during the early Revolutionary period, with the assistance
of Monge, he worked on improvements in iron manufacture, developed a process for the production
of saltpetre for gunpowder,
published a notable work on
dyeing, and his *Essai de statique
chimique* of 1803 was the foundation of chemical physics. He went
with Monge to Italy to select works
of art for the French national
collection, and was the chief
organiser of the scientists who

formed the Egyptian Institute
which accompanied Napoleon's
expedition. Involved in the action
between French and Mameluke
flotillas at Shubra Khit, he
weighted his pockets with the
intention of drowning himself
rather than be killed by the
Mamelukes, but changed his mind
and fought on until the day was
won. He accompanied Napoleon
back to France, became a senator
and was ennobled as comte, and
was appointed a peer of France by
the Bourbons.

BERTRAND, General Henri-Gratien, comte (1773–1844)

HENRI BERTRAND

Probably the most loyal of all
Napoleon's followers, he was an
engineer officer who served in the
French Army from the beginning
of the Revolutionary Wars;
promoted to colonel in Egypt, he
became *général de brigade* in
1800, and in 1804 inspector-
general of engineers and an aide
to Napoleon. He accompanied the
emperor in the great campaigns,
always serving with fidelity,
became *général de division* in May
1807, comte in 1808, and supervised the construction of the
Danube bridges in the 1809
campaign. Governor of Illyria
1811–12, he commanded IV Corps

in 1813, was distinguished at Leipzig, and in November of that year was appointed Grand Marshal of the Palace. He accompanied Napoleon to Elba, in the Hundred Days and to St. Helena; the latter must have tested Bertrand's loyalty severely, for his

FANNY BERTRAND

half-English wife Fanny, who had already lost a child on Elba, after unsuccessfully pleading with Napoleon not to allow her husband to accompany him into exile, rushed from his cabin (aboard HMS *Bellerophon*) and attempted to throw herself overboard ('Is she not mad?' was Napoleon's comment!). Nevertheless, Madame Bertrand dutifully followed her husband to St. Helena, the general remaining there until Napoleon's death. He was allowed to keep his rank by Louis XVIII, became a Deputy in 1830, and it was entirely appropriate that so devoted a subject was selected to accompany Napoleon's remains on the homecoming to France in 1840.

Bertrand, H. G. *Napoleon at St. Helena: Memoirs of General Bertrand*. London, 1953 (from *Cahiers de Sainte-Hélène*, ed. P. F. de Langle. Paris, 1949–59); Girard de Vasson, J. *Bertrand, le Grand-Maréchal de Sainte-Hélène*. Paris, 1935

BESSIERES, Marshal Jean-Baptiste, duc d'Istrie (1768–1813)

One of Napoleon's most loyal and popular subordinates, he was born in Preissac and was intended for his father's medical profession; instead, he turned to soldiering at the beginning of the French Revolution, though he was no radical: a devout Roman Catholic, his conservatism was demonstrated by the fact that he powdered his hair throughout his military career, long after the fashion was outdated. He served as a member of Louis XVI's Constitutional Guard in the defence of the Tuileries, then enlisted as a cavalry trooper and after service in the Army of the Pyrenees rose to the rank of captain. With the assistance of his childhood friend Joachim Murat, he was appointed commander of Napoleon's Guides and after service in Italy and Egypt, assisting Napoleon in the coup of Brumaire, and leading the Guard cavalry at Marengo, he was included in the first creation of the marshalate in 1804. Given command of the cavalry of the Guard, he led a vital charge at Austerlitz and performed well at Eylau, but his abilities in independent command were not outstanding, seeming to suffer from over-caution; although when commanding a corps in Spain he did win the Battle of Medina del Rio Seco. Reverting to subordinate cavalry commands, he impressed all who saw him for his calm demeanour when commanding the rearguard at Aspern–Essling; created Duke of Istria in May 1809, he succeeded Bernadotte in command of the forces opposing the Walcheren expedition, fell briefly out of favour for opposing Napoleon's divorce upon religious grounds, then returned to Spain (receiving some unfair criticism for supposed inaction at Fuentes de Oñoro). After commanding the

JEAN-BAPTISTE BESSIÈRES (ENGRAVING BY C. STATE AFTER RIESENER)

Guard cavalry in the Russian campaign of 1812, at Rippach near Weissenfels on 1 May 1813 he was struck by a ricocheting ball and killed instantly; 'thus, after living like Bayard, be died like Turenne'. It was a grievous blow to the army and he was mourned universally especially by the Guard who adored him; 'always kind, humane, and generous, of antique loyalty and integrity, and, whether considered as a citizen or as a soldier, an honest, worthy man. He often made use of the high favour in which he stood to do extraordinary services and acts of kindness ...'[2] If not quite the Bayard as he was sometimes described – not everyone liked him: he had a longstanding feud with Lannes which almost developed into violence on the night of Aspern–Essling after Bessières objected to the manner in which Lannes (his superior) had given him orders, and it transpired that he had been unfaithful to his wife with a chorus-girl from the Paris opera – and despite his somewhat limited military talents, his 'rare union of valour, prudence and humanity'[3] made him one of the most loyal and valuable of Napoleon's subordinates. His brother **Bertrand, Baron Bessières (1773–1855)** was a divisional general in the French rmy who retired upon the restoration of the Bourbons; his last public act was an attempted defence of Ney.

Las Cases, vol. I, p. 341. 2. Ibid. 3. Anon., p. 244.

Bessières, A. de. *Le Maréchal Bessières, duc d'Istrie*. Paris, 1941; Esdaile, C. 'The Misnamed Bayard: Bessières', in *Napoleon's Marshals*, ed. D. G. Chandler. London, 1987; Rabel, A. *Le Maréchal Bessières*. Paris 1903

BEURNONVILLE, Marshal Pierre Riel (or Ryel), marquis de (1752–1821)

Originally destined for the church, instead he made the army his career, became a lieutenant-general and served at Valmy and Jemappes. French Minister of War in February 1793, he was ousted, but when sent as subordinate to Dumouriez (who called him his Ajax) he was one of those appointed to arrest his commander. Handed over to the Austrians in April 1793, he was exchanged in April 1795, replaced Moreau in command of French forces in Holland, and in 1798 became inspector-general of infantry. In 1800 he went to Berlin as ambassador, and in 1802 to Madrid; in 1805 he was made a senator and in 1814 served in the provisional government following Napoleon's abdication. He followed Louis XVIII to Ghent in 1815, and after the second restoration was created a marquis and Marshal of France. Although not involved in the great Napoleonic campaigns, it was said that he was present at no less than 172 engagements in 1791–93.

BEXLEY, Baron, see VANSITTART

BEYLE, Henri (known as Stendhal) (1783–1842)

This great French author served in the Napoleonic Wars largely by virtue of his family connections with Daru. Having served as a lieutenant in the 6th Dragoons 1800–2, as ADC to General Michaud in Italy, and having resigned in July 1802 after having to rejoin his regiment for tedious garrison duty, in 1806, by the influence of his cousin Pierre Daru, Beyle obtained a post in the commissariat. He served until 1814, participating in the Russian campaign of 1812 and witnessing Bautzen. His literary career prospered after the Napoleonic Wars, and although he had not been an unqualified admirer of Napoleon, he was fascinated by him and wrote a *Vie de Napoléon* as an answer to criticisms by Madame de Staël, though it was not published in his lifetime; and evidence of the Napoleonic experience can be found in some of his work.

Stendhal: *Correspondance de Stendhal 1800–1842*, intro. M. Barrès. Paris, 1908; *Journal de Stendhal 1801–1814*. Paris, 1888; Wood, M. *Stendhal*. London, 1971

BIANCHI, General Vicenz Friedrich, Baron, Duke of Casalanza (1768–1855)

This Austrian engineer officer, commissioned in 1787, attained the rank of general officer in 1807 after service against the Turks; he was among the Allied commanders defeated at Dresden, but as *Feldmarschall-Leutnant* he achieved his greatest success in 1815, defeating Murat at Tolentino, for which service he received his Neapolitan dukedom.

Bianchi, F. von. *Freiherr von Bianchi, duca de Casalanza*. Vienna, 1857

BILLAUD-VARENNE, Jacques-Nicolas (1756–1819)

Destined for the Church but adopting a legal career instead, he was one of the most extreme of the French Jacobin politicians. A vehement republican, he agitated for the execution of the king and queen, was one of the directors of the September Massacres, and had an awesome reputation during his service as a *représentant en mission* in the *départements* of the Nord and Pas-de-Calais. A member of the Committee of Public Safety, he attacked Robespierre for being too moderate; but was himself arrested and a commission was appointed to investigate his cruelty. In 1795 the Convention ordered his banishment to Guiana; during his exile his principal occupation was breeding parrots, and he spent the last years of his life in Haiti. Napoleon remarked that of all the sanguinary monsters of the Revolutionary period, he was the worst.

BLAKE, General Joachim (1759–1827)

Born at Malaga of Irish descent, he was one of the best Spanish commanders of the Peninsular War, if one of the least fortunate. A colonel in 1808, he was appointed Captain-General of Galicia, but was defeated at Medina del Rio Seco, Zornoza and Espinosa, whereupon he was replaced by La Romana. In 1809 he was given command of the forces of Aragon, and later Catalonia, won an action against Suchet at Alaniz (23 May 1809) but was later defeated at Maria and Belchite, and resigned the Catalonian command after failing to relieve Gerona. In April 1810 he was appointed to lead the 'Army of the Centre' at Cadiz, but was defeated at Baza by Milhaud and performed with lack of distinction (at least in British eyes) at Albuera. In July 1811 he was appointed Captain-General not only of his own Murcian forces but of Valencia and Aragon, but was defeated by Suchet, besieged in Valencia and surrendered in January 1812; he was kept in close confinement at Vincennes for the remainder of the war. In his later life he attained the reputation of a political liberal. Although his military skill was probably limited, he was possessed of genuine courage and organisational ability, without the over-confidence or unrealistic expectations which brought disaster to other Spanish commanders, and some of his defeats were exacerbated by ill-luck and circumstances beyond his control.

BLANE, Sir Gilbert, Bt. (1749–1834)

Having been Lord Rodney's private physician, this Scottish medical practitioner did much to improve the health of seamen; it was largely through his efforts that the consumption of lime juice became compulsory in the Royal Navy as a preventive against scurvy. His publications included *Observations on the Diseases of Seamen* (1795), and in 1812 his baronetcy was a reward for his work on the maladies suffered during the Walcheren expedition. His son, Hugh Seymour Blane, served as an ensign in the 3rd Foot Guards at Waterloo; the baronetcy became extinct after the 4th Baronet was killed at Jutland.

BLIGH, Vice-Admiral William (1754–1817)

Although best known as the victim of the mutiny aboard HMS *Bounty* in 1789, Bligh (who had accompanied James Cook on his second expedition in HMS *Resolution*) also served in the Napoleonic Wars. His ship HMS *Director* was the first of the North Sea Fleet to be affected by the 'Great Mutiny' of 1797, but fought at Camperdown shortly after; and at Copenhagen he commanded HMS *Glatton* which, experimentally, was armed entirely with carronades. In 1805 Bligh went to New South Wales as Governor and suffered his third

mutiny in 1808, of the New South Wales Corps (alias the 'Rum Puncheon Corps'!). Returning to England in 1811, he was promoted to rear-admiral, and to vice-admiral in 1814; despite his record of suffering mutinies, perhaps (as in New South Wales) exacerbated by a harsh manner of exercising authority, he was a brave and determined officer. He should not be confused with Richard Rodney Bligh, the vice-admiral who was 2i/c to Hyde Parker at Jamaica, whom the latter rather unjustly sent home.

Hawkey, A. *Bligh's other Mutiny*. London, 1975; Kennedy, G. *Captain Bligh: the Man and his Mutinies*. London, 1989; Mackaness, G. *The Life of Vice-Admiral William Bligh*. Sydney, 1931

BLUCHER, Field Marshal Gebhard Leberecht von, Prince of Wahlstadt (1742–1819)

GEBHARD VON BLÜCHER (ENGRAVING BY T. W. HARLAND AFTER F. C. GRÖGER)

Probably the most famous Prussian soldier of the Napoleonic Wars and one of Napoleon's most implacable opponents, he was born near Rostock in Mecklenburg, the son of a retired officer, entered the Swedish cavalry at the age of 14 but transferred to Frederick the Great's service after being

captured by the Prussian Despite much experience as hussar officer, when h complained about lack of promo tion Frederick reputedly said tha he could go the devil; so from 1773 to 1786 he became a farme Reinstated, Blücher rose command a hussar regiment, wa greatly distinguished against th French in 1793–4 and by 1801 wa a lieutenant-general. He was leading member of the 'wa party' irredeemably hostile to th French, and in 1806 fought as cavalry commander, continuin the struggle after the disaster o Jena–Auerstädt until compelle to surrender from want o supplies, at Ratkau on November 1806. Totally oppose to any collaboration wit Napoleon, he spent the nex several years in virtual wilder ness, doing what he could reform the Prussian Army bu even being relieved of his post a Governor of Pomerania in 1812 a a result of French pressure. I the 'War of Liberation', howeve he was immediately given hig command (of the Army of Silesia with Gneisenau as chief of staf This was an ideal collaboratio blending Gneisenau's clear calcu lation with Blücher's fire t produce an excellent partner ship; never a great tactician, th nickname bestowed upo Blücher by his troops, wh adored him, was descriptive o his basic military philosophy 'Marschall Vorwärts' ('Marsha Forward'). His tenacity an refusal to accept defeat was a vita asset in 1813–14, overcomin reverses and maintaining morale the Army of Silesia playing crucial role in Napoleon's defea On the day of his victory ove Marmont at Mockern (16 Octobe 1813) he was promoted to *Gener alfeldmarschall*, and in June 181 he was created Prince o Wahlstadt (in Silesia, on th tlefield of the Katzbach where had defeated Macdonald on 26 tober 1813). The old Marshal's domitable spirit was crucial in e Hundred Days campaign en in command of the ussian forces in The Nether- ds; having given his word to pport Wellington, he was deter- ned to follow that course of tion even though Gneisenau nted to retire to re-organise er Ligny, and the continuing ussian collaboration with ellington was the reason for poleon's defeat at Waterloo. (It significant in assessing the rtnership that Blücher had to gue with Gneisenau on this int: it was more a genuine llaboration rather than the one ing subservient to a superior). tiring because of ill-health and d age, Blücher died at his Sile- n estate on 12 September 1819.

the end of his life he retained e fiery temperament appro- iate to an old hussar, and ellington, after remarking that e last time he met Blücher the d man seemed to be mentally stable, imagining himself to be egnant with an elephant, added at 'He was a very fine fellow, and henever there was any question fighting, always ready and eager if anything too eager.'[1] With his ssionate hatred of the French d his loyalty to his cause and ies, despite his limitations, he rsonified the finest type of ghting general', personally and orally brave, fêted by his allies d adored by his troops.

Stanhope, p. 120.

Gneisenau, A. W. A. *The Life and mpaigns of Field-Marshal Prince ücher, of Wahlstatt* (sic), trans. J. Marston. London, 1815; Park- son, R. *The Hussar General: The fe of Blücher, Man of Waterloo.* ndon, 1975 (the most important ography in English, including a etailed bibliography of other ographical works)

BOCK, Major-General Eber- hardt Otto Georg von (*d.* 1814)

This distinguished Hanoverian officer was colonel of the 1st Dragoons of the King's German Legion, major-general in the British Army from 25 July 1810, and commander of the KGL heavy cavalry brigade which won the notable action at Garcia Hernandez (23 July 1812) during the pursuit after Salamanca. The combat involved the rare event of infantry in square being broken by cavalry, although the decision to charge in the manner which occurred seems to have been made by the squadron- comman- ders of the KGL Dragoons involved. Bock himself – described by Kincaid as small, slender and with a hump on one shoulder – was so short-sighted that he had to ask Assistant Adjutant-General Lieutenant-Colonel John May, 'will you be so good as to show us the enemy?';[1] May pointed him in the general direction of the French and accompanied him as he led his forward elements in the charge, leaving the following squadrons to charge on their own initiative and to overthrow the squares. Returning to England in January 1814 after valuable service in the Peninsula, Bock was drowned when the transport *Bellona* was wrecked on the coast of France; lost with him was his son, Captain Lewis von Bock of the KGL 2nd Hussars.

1. Beamish, vol. II, p. 82.

BOGUE, Captain Richard (1782–1813)

The son of a Hampshire doctor, he was commissioned in the Royal Artillery in 1798, was posted to the Royal Horse Artillery in 1803 and became a captain in 1806. He served in the Corunna campaign, but is remembered for com- manding the rocket troop at Leipzig, attached to Bernadotte's army, where he was killed by a

RICHARD BOGUE
(PRINT AFTER J. SLATER)

shot through the head. Sir Charles Stewart described him as a 'gallant and deserving officer ... alike an ornament to his profession and a loss to his friends';[1] his skill with rockets was much complimented, and he was described as 'most distinguished ... no less from professional accomplishments than from the private virtues of the heart'.[2] Bernadotte awarded him a posthumous knighthood of the Order of the Sword, and gave his widow 10,000 dollars. Only a month before Bogue's death, she had lost her brother, Captain William Hanson of the 20th Light Dragoons, in the Peninsula; and her husband's half-brother, Captain Joseph Bradby Bogue, had died in July 1806 while com- manding HMS *Terpsichore* in the East Indies.

1. *Gazette*, 3 Nov 1813. 2. *Gent's Mag.*, 1813, vol. II, p. 507

Bogue's diary of the Corunna campaign was published in Leslie, J. H. *The Services of the Royal Regiment Of Artillery in the Penin- sular War*. London, 1908, vol. II, pp. 37–69

BON, General Louis-André (1758–99)

Having served in the French Army as an ordinary soldier 1776–84, he was elected lieutenant-colonel at the time of the Revolution (1792) and rose to *général de brigade* in 1795. He served in Italy (wounded at Arcola), commanded a division in 1797, and served with distinction in the Egyptian campaign, again with a divisional command, notably at the Battle of the Pyramids. He was mortally wounded in the storming of the breach at Acre on 10 May 1799, in the final and unavailing attack.

BONAPARTE, Carlo (Charles-Marie Buonaparte) (1746–85)

CARLO BONAPARTE

A lawyer descended from a family of minor nobility, of Italian extraction which settled in Corsica in 1529, Carlo Buonaparte (as the surname was spelled originally) was a somewhat foppish and unreliable character little distinguished except as the father of three kings and, most notably, an emperor (his second son, Napoleon). Carlo favoured the French link with Corsica rather than the nationalist position, which brought him some favours, but his most profound contribution in creating the Bonaparte dynasty was his marriage in 1764 to Letizia Ramolino, who was a much greater influence on the family than was Carlo, who died of stomach cancer at Montpellier in 1785. It is perhaps a comment

on his standing in the Napoleonic pantheon that it was not until 1951 that his body was taken back to Ajaccio to be laid beside Letizia in the chapel built by Napoleon III.

General histories of the Bonaparte family include Markham, F. *The Bonapartes*. London, 1975; Stacton, D. *The Bonapartes*. London, 1967; Masson, F. *Napoléon et sa Famille*. Paris, 1897–1900; Seward, D. *Napoleon's Family*. London, 1986

BONAPARTE, Caroline (Maria-Annunciata Caroline), Queen of Naples (1782–1839)

Born at Ajaccio on 25 March 1782, Napoleon's youngest sister had several suitors, but married Murat in January 1800, conse-

CAROLINE BONAPARTE (FROM AN ENGRAVING BY A. E. ANDERSON AFTER GÉRARD).

quently becoming in succession Grand Duchess of Berg and, in August 1808, Queen of Naples. She proved to be a great assistance to her husband, taking on the reins of government during his absence, though was not notably faithful; she pursued a somewhat notorious affair with Junot, for example. She was popular with the Neapolitans but her energies were always directed to her own and Murat's advancement; consequently her cordial relations with

Napoleon became strained a culminated in alliances betwe Naples and Napoleon's enem in an attempt to retain the thro Napoleon blamed Caroline m than Murat for this unavail 'treachery', and after Mura death she sought refuge first Austria and later Florence. intelligent but calculating wom she was described by Napoleon having 'solid sense, strength character, and boundless am tion',[1] and by Talleyrand as hav 'Cromwell's head on the sho ders of a pretty woman'.[2]
1. Las Cases, vol. I, p. 192. 2. Anc p. 107.

Bear, J. *Caroline Murat, A Bi raphy*. London, 1972; Cole, H. *T Betrayers: Joachim and Carol Murat*. London, 1972; Gagnière, *La Reine Marie-Caroline Naples*. Paris, l886; Weiner, M. *T Parvenu Princesses: Elisa, Paul and Caroline Bonaparte*. Lond 1964.

BONAPARTE, Elisa (Marie-Anne Elise), Grand Duchess Tuscany (1777–1820)

ELISA BONAPARTE (ENGRAVING BY R. G. TIET AFTER PRUD'HON)

Napoleon's eldest sister was bo in Ajaccio on 3 January 1777, a married Félix Bacciochi, a we connected Corsican, in May 17 (his baptismal name was Pasqua it he changed it to Félix after the improvement in his fortunes). He remained in his wife's shadow, for Elisa was determined upon a royal career; in 1805 Napoleon gave them the principality of Piombino and the republic of Lucca, of which Elisa took control, even conducting her own foreign policy. Her competence led Napoleon to allocate her a wider territory, as Grand Duchess of Tuscany, in 1808. Relations became strained over suspicions that she favoured Murat's case over that of her brother, and upon the collapse of the empire she and her family fled to Genoa, then to Bologna. After detention by the Austrians they were allowed to settle near Trieste, where Elisa died, having adopted the title of Countess of Compignano. Her husband, from whom she was estranged for some time, was described as having a 'peaceable disposition [which] formed a striking contrast with the active, bustling spirit of his wife. He seems to have been considered a good sort of man, who did not care to apply himself to business, and only sought to indulge in the comforts and advantages of the situation.'[1]

1. Anon., p. 93.

Fleuriot de Langle, P. *Elisa, soeur de Napoléon.* Paris, 1947; Marmothan, P. *Elisa Bonaparte.* Paris, 1898; Rodocanachi, E. *Elisa Bonaparte en Italie.* Paris, 1900; Weiner, M. *The Parvenu Princesses: Elisa, Pauline and Caroline Bonaparte.* London, 1964

BONAPARTE, Jérôme, King of Westphalia (1784–1860)

The youngest, least serious and perhaps least talented of Napoleon's brothers was born in Ajaccio on 15 November 1784, and followed his brother's fortunes with little real success. Leaving the Consular Guard after being wounded in a duel with Davout's

JÉRÔME BONAPARTE, KING OF WESTPHALIA
(ENGRAVING BY M. HAIDER AFTER GROS)

brother, he transferred to the navy, where his career was undistinguished despite attaining the rank of admiral. He left his ship in America and married Elizabeth Patterson of Baltimore, but Napoleon refused her admission to his territory and she had to settle at Camberwell, where she gave birth to a son. Napoleon had the marriage annulled, and married Jérôme to Princess Frederica Catherina of Württemberg. Jérôme commanded a Bavarian division in 1806 and was appointed King of Westphalia by Napoleon, which was of little benefit to that state: Jérôme's extravagant lifestyle compounded an already parlous economy, there was an abortive revolt by army officers in 1809, and the participation of Westphalian troops in Spain and the 1812 Russian campaign almost reduced the country to bankruptcy. In 1809 Jérôme commanded X Corps and in 1812 VIII Corps, but went home early from the latter campaign after a row with Napoleon concerning his lethargic conduct. Westphalia rose against him in 1813 and he fled to Switzerland, later Trieste, but returned to command a division during the Waterloo campaign, in which he was most noted for uselessly expending resources in vain

attempts to capture Hougoumont. After the collapse, he threw himself upon the mercy of his father-in-law, who kept him under semi-arrest; given the title Count of Montfort in 1816, Jérôme was allowed to leave after two years and lived in Trieste, Italy and Switzerland until he returned to France in 1847. His career resurrected, he became Marshal of France and President of the Senate. His children included Napoleon Joseph Charles Paul (1822–91), known as 'Plon-Plon', who became heir to the Napoleonic succession; and Jérôme Napoleon (1805–70), Elizabeth Patterson's child, who resided in Baltimore, whose elder son served with the French Army in the Crimea and the younger son as Roosevelt's Navy Secretary 1905–6 and later US Attorney General. Good-natured but indolent, Jérôme was not devoid of talent but preferred the privileges of royal status to its duties; Napoleon remarked that he 'was an absolute prodigal. He plunged into boundless extravagance, and the most odious libertinism. His excuse perhaps may be his youth, and the temptations by which he was surrounded.'[1] He was less generous when in 1813 he was alleged to have told Jérôme to go away: 'You are hateful to me. Your conduct disgusts me. I know no one so base, so stupid, so cowardly; you are destitute of virtue, talents and resources ...'[2]

1. Las Cases, vol. II, p. 193. 2. Anon., pp. 76–7.

Du Casse, Baron A. (ed.). *Mémoires et Correspondance du roi Jérôme et de la reine Cathérine.* Paris, 1861–6; Kircheisen, F. M. *Jovial King: Napoleon's Youngest Brother.* London, 1932; Martinet, A. *Jérôme Napoléon, Roi de Westphalie.* Paris, 1902; Mitchell, S. *A Family Lawsuit: the Story of Elizabeth Patterson and Jerome Bonaparte.* New York, 1958

BONAPARTE, Joseph, King of Naples and Spain (1768–1844)

JOSEPH BONAPARTE, KING OF SPAIN
(ENGRAVING BY L. RADOS AFTER J. B. BOSIO)

Although the eldest of the Bonaparte brothers, he spent his career in Napoleon's shadow. Born at Corte in Corsica on 7 January 1768, he was trained in law and served as a diplomat: Minister to Parma and Rome, Member for Corsica in the Council of Five Hundred, negotiator of the Convention of Montfontaine (his country house) with the USA, and the Treaties of Lunéville and Amiens. In 1805 Joseph acted as head of government while Napoleon was campaigning, and in 1806 was sent to Naples with a French army, accepting the crown himself (31 March 1806) after the expulsion of the Bourbons. Genuinely concerned with improving the lot of his subjects, he made such beneficial reforms in Naples as his treasury would allow, and only with reluctance did he surrender the crown to Murat to take up that of a new kingdom, Spain. Never accepted by the majority of the Spanish population, his imposition as king by Napoleon was a primary cause of the Peninsular War, in which he attempted to do his best although possessed of few military talents and completely under the domi-

nation not only of Napoleon but even to some extent of the generals appointed to assist him. His complaints brought little result, and he offered to resign the crown, writing to Napoleon that 'I have not your entire confidence, and yet without it my position is not tenable ... even at Madrid I am every day counteracted ... if I must be insulted in my own capital ... denied the right of naming the governors and the commanders who are always before me, and make me contemptible to the Spaniards and powerless to do good ... I ought not to be king of Spain, and my happiness requires me to cease to be so ...'[1] Only after Joseph's flight from Spain following the defeat of Vittoria did Napoleon accede to his wishes, blaming him unfairly for many of the ills of the Peninsular War. In 1814, as Napoleon's deputy, Joseph gave Marmont authority to negotiate a truce, leading to the surrender of Paris, causing Napoleon further dissatisfaction. After the Hundred Days, Joseph lived in America as the Comte de Survilliers, also visiting England, Genoa and Florence, retiring to the latter after leaving the USA in 1839, and dying there on 28 July 1844. A kind man of liberal inclination if lacking energy, his tastes were not for kingship and conquest (fond of literature, he published a romance entitled *Moina* in 1799), and he would have been happier had he been allowed to live quietly with his wife, Julie Clary, whom he married in Marseilles in 1794 and similarly had no taste for regality. Napoleon's comment on Joseph is probably accurate: 'Joseph rendered me no assistance; but he is a very good man. His wife ...

is the most amiable creature that ever existed. Joseph and I were always attached to each other, and kept on very good terms. He loves me sincerely, and

I doubt not that he would d every thing in the world to serv me. But his qualities are on suited to private life. He is of gentle and kind dispositio possesses talent and informatio and is altogether a very amiab man. In the discharge of the hig duties which I confided to hin he did the best he could. H intentions were good; and there fore the principal fault rested n so much with him as with m who raised him above his prop sphere.'[2]

1. Napoleon, vol. II, pp. 46–7. 2. L Cases, vol. II, p. 192.

Abbott, J. S. C. *History of Josep Bonaparte*. New York, 186 Connelly, O. *The Gentle Bonapart* London, 1968; Du Casse, Baron / (ed.). *Mémoires et Correspon dance politiques et militaires d Roi Joseph*, Paris 1854–7 (a sectio in translation being *The Confiden tial Correspondence of Napoleo Bonaparte with his Brother Josepl* London, 1855); Glover, M. *Th Legacy of Glory: the Bonapart Kingdom of Spain*. New York, 197 Ross, M. *The Reluctant King Joseph Bonaparte, King of the Tw Sicilies and Spain*. London, 1976

BONAPARTE, Letizia (Maria-Letizia), 'Madame Mère' (1750–1836)

LETIZIA BONAPARTE
(ENGRAVING BY T. JOHNSON)

apoleon's mother exerted upon
m an influence immeasurably
eater than that of his father.
etizia Ramolino (actually Maria-
etizia) was born in 1750 (or
ossibly 1749) into a family resi-
ent in Corsica from the mid 15th
entury, married Carlo Bonaparte
: the age of 14 and produced thir-
en children, eight of whom
irvived infancy. She followed her
usband's changing fortunes with
onstancy, and after his death
icceeded in her hard struggle to
iise her children. Simple and
raightforward, she continued
ie frugal lifestyle developed
uring her early privations, and
ever wanted the outward show
nd opulence which Napoleon
'ished to shower upon her.
ideed, he complained that she
:arried her parsimony to a most
idiculous extreme. I offered to
irnish her with a very consider-
ible monthly income, on condi-
on that she would spend it, [but
he] was very willing to receive the
noney provided she were
ermitted to hoard it up ... all her
ear was that she might one day be
educed to beggary. She had
nown the horrors of want, and
ney now constantly haunted her
nagination ...[yet she] would will-
ngly have given me her all, on my
eturn from the island of Elba; and
fter the battle of Waterloo, she
vould have surrendered to me all
he possessed in the world, to
.ssist me in re-establishing my
ffairs. This she offered to do; and
vould, with but a murmur, have
loomed herself to live on brown
)read.'[1] Although living in virtual
etirement, graced by the title
Madame Mère', she maintained
:great interest in the welfare of her
:hildren and was renowned for
ier common sense (Napoleon
·emarked that: 'She had the head
)f a man on the shoulders of a
voman.')[2] She joined Napoleon at
Elba and was privy to the plans for
nis return; and after the Hundred

Days retired to Rome, only
becoming involved in wider affairs
than her own when she made an
unanswered plea for Napoleon's
release in 1818. Respected by all
who knew her, she remained the
firmest foundation of the Bonaparte family, and as Napoleon
stated: 'She is indeed a kind
mother.'[3] She is sometimes named
as 'Laetitia', but herself always
used the spelling 'Letizia'.

1. Las Cases, vol. II, p. 191. 2. Anon.
p. 8. 3. Las Cases, vol. II, p. 191.

Bonaparte-Wyse, O. *The Spur-
ious Brood: Letitia Bonaparte and
her Children*. London, 1969;
Decaux, A. *Napoleon's Mother*.
London, 1962; Stirling, M. *A Pride
of Lions: a Portrait of Napoleon's
Mother*. London, 1961 (New York
edition entitled *Madame Letizia*);
Tschudi, C. *Napoleon's Mother*.
London, 1910

BONAPARTE, Louis, King of Holland (1778–1846)

LOUIS BONAPARTE, KING OF HOLLAND
(ENGRAVING BY W. MILLER)

Born at Ajaccio on 2 September
1778 and educated under
Napoleon's supervision, after
training as a gunner Napoleon's
brother Louis accompanied him
as an aide in Italy and Egypt; in
1804 he was promoted to general.
In 1802 Napoleon arranged for
him a most unfortunate marriage

to Josephine's daughter Hortense,
and in June 1806 pushed Louis
into the position of King of
Holland, despite protests that his
health was not up to the task.
Nevertheless, Louis proved too
good a king for Napoleon's taste,
refusing the kingdom of Spain
(which went instead to Joseph),
behaving with kindness towards
his Dutch subjects, and relations
between the two deteriorated
greatly when Louis refused
to implement the Continental
System. Finally Napoleon annexed
Holland (9 July 1810), Louis abdicated and went abroad, first to
Bohemia, but finally settled in
Italy, using the title of comte de
Saint-Leu, producing a number of
unremarkable literary works and
free from the unwanted responsibilities of state and a wretched
marriage. His third son, Charles
Louis Napoleon (1808–73) became
the Emperor Napoleon III.
Napoleon's comment on Louis
was that he 'had been spoiled by
reading the works of Rousseau'![1]

1. Las Cases, vol. II, p. 189.

Bonaparte, L. *Documents
historiques et Réflexions sur le
gouvernement de la Hollande*.
Paris, 1829 (Louis' own account of
his reign in Holland); Duboscq, A.
Louis Bonaparte en Hollande.
Paris, 1911

BONAPARTE, Lucien, Prince of Canino (1775–1840)

Born at Ajaccio on 21 May 1775 and
debarred from a military career by
defective eyesight, Napoleon's
brother Lucien, was active in politics, supporting the Jacobins and
entering the Council of Five
Hundred in 1798. As president of
that body he was of great assistance to Napoleon at the *coup* of
Brumaire; but thereafter dissen-
sions with Napoleon led to a
decline in his influence. In 1800 he
was appointed Minister at Madrid
and further displeased his brother
by signing the preliminaries of

peace in June 1801 (and, it was said, laid the foundations of his vast fortune on the financial deal involved). Lucien finally broke with Napoleon over his re-marriage (his first wife having died), Napoleon wishing a dynastic alliance but Lucien insisting on marrying his mistress, Marie Jouberthou. He retired to an estate at Canino, near Rome; but declining all royal favours offered by Napoleon if he gave up his wife, in 1810 took his family and servants aboard ship, bound for the USA. The vessel was captured by the British, and for the rest of the war Lucien lived on parole on an estate he bought at Thorngrove, near Ludlow. He

LUCIEN BONAPARTE
(ENGRAVING BY T. JOHNSON)

returned to Italy in 1814 and received the papal title of Prince of Canino, but briefly returned to France to support Napoleon during the Hundred Days. At its conclusion he returned to Italy where he died on 29 June 1840. He directed much of his energy in later life towards literature, including his epic poem *Charlemagne, ou l'église délivrée* (1814), of which Napoleon remarked, 'How much labour, ingenuity and time has been thrown away upon this book! What a wreck of judgement and taste!.'[1] Conversely, one of Lucien's reported remarks was

an accurate prediction: during one of many violent disagreements during Lucien's brief tenure as Minister of the Interior during the Consulate, he flung his watch at Napoleon's feet and said: 'You will one day be smashed to pieces as I have smashed that watch; and a time will come when your family and friends will not have a resting-place for their heads.'[2] Despite such disagreements, however, Las Cases commented of Lucien in 1815 that 'it would have been difficult for any man to have been more upright and steady in his political views, or to have evinced greater attachment and good-will towards his brother.'[3]

1. Las Cases, vol. III, p. 288. 2. Anon., pp. 40–1. 3. Las Cases, vol. I, p. 70.

Bonaparte, Lucien. *Memoirs.* London, 1836; Jung, T. *Lucien Bonaparte et ses Mémoires.* Paris, 1882–3

BONAPARTE, Napoleon, see Napoleon I

BONAPARTE, Napoleon François-Joseph-Charles, see Napoleon II

BONAPARTE, Pauline (Marie-Paulette), Princess Borghese (1780–1825)

Born at Ajaccio on 20 October 1780, the second, most beautiful, carefree and flirtatious of Napoleon's sisters, Pauline, married General Victor-Emmanuel Leclerc in 1797. The union was not especially felicitous, and after his death at San Domingo in 1802 she returned home, and in August 1803 married Prince Camillo Borghese. She lived with him in Rome for a time but tired of such a life and returned to Paris, where her lifestyle caused much scandal. Although she remained loyal to Napoleon, her treatment of Marie-Louise led to her removal from court, yet in 1814 she accompa-

nied her mother to Elba. Afte Napoleon's final defeat sh returned to Italy, living in gre style in the Borghese palace and i her own house in Rome, the Vil Paolina; reconciled with he husband, she died in Florence o 9 June 1825. Pauline's extrava gances were as well known as he beauty; Napoleon remarked tha 'She might have been immense rich, considering all that I gav her; but she gave all away in he turn.'[1] No amount of lectures o the virtues of thrift by *Madam Mère* changed her habits; when Nice, for example, she arrange for a post-wagon to bring her th latest Paris fashions daily. She wa

PAULINE BONAPARTE
(ENGRAVING BY M. HAIDER AFTER R. LEFEVRE)

described as more fascinating than classically beautiful, with 'eyes of a gentle blue, and generally suffused with a sort o coquettish sleepishness which .. wooed and won the imagination more effectually than the brightest sparkle from the haughtiest eye'. She is perhaps best remembered by Canova's great sculpture which depicted her as the naked Venus; when she was asked how she could possibly have exposed herself thus, she remarked typically that there was a fire in the room where Canova was working!

Las Cases, vol. II, p. 191. 2.
on., pp. 100–1.
Dixon, P. *Pauline: Napoleon's*
orite Sister. New York, 1961;
tzen, L. *Imperial Venus: the*
ry of Pauline Bonaparte-
rghese. London,1974; Weiner,
The Parvenu Princesses: Elisa,
uline and Caroline Bonaparte.
ndon, 1974

ONCHAMPS (or BONCHAMP), aarles-Melchior-Artus, arquis de (c.1760–93)

ais gallant officer had served in
e royal forces before the French
evolution, and in 1793 was
osen to lead the royalist insur-
nts in the Vendée. The Marquise
e la Rochejaquelein described
m as: 'thirty-two years of age,
ad had served with distinction in
dia, under M. de Suffren. His
lour and talents were unques-
oned; he was considered as one
the most able of the chiefs; and
s troops as the best disciplined.
e had no ambition, no preten-
ons, was gentle, of an easy
mper, much loved by the army,
ad possessing its confidence. But
e had the misfortune of being
ounded in most of the engage-
ents, and the army often
eprived of his presence'[1]
onchamps was mortally wound-
d at the Battle of Cholet (17
ctober 1793) by grapeshot in the
.omach; his last act was to order
ne release of some 6,000 repub-
can prisoners who had been
armarked for execution by the
oyalists, an act of magnanimity
/hich cost them dear, as the
x-prisoners were freed to take up
rms again. The marble statue
/hich surmounts Bonchamps'
omb in the church of Saint-
lorent was the work of Pierre
ean David, known as David
'Angers, whose father was
mong the prisoners spared by
3onchamps' typical act of
.umanity.
. La Rochejaquelein, pp. 110–11.

BONET (or BONNET), General Jean-Pierre-François, comte (1768–1857)

Having joined the French Army in
1786 and twice deserting, Bonet
prospered during the Revolutionary Wars, fighting at Hohenlinden and from 1808 in the
Peninsula. He is probably best
remembered for succeeding to
command of the French Army at
Salamanca following the wounding of Marmont, having previously
been operating independently,
Napoleon ordering him (over
Marmont's head) to re-occupy the
Asturias. Joining the main army
before the battle of Salamanca and
commanding the 8th Division,
Bonet was the senior of
Marmont's subordinates and was
within a few yards of the Marshal
when he was wounded, so took
command immediately; but
within an hour he was himself
seriously wounded, and the
command passed to Clausel. He
served in the 1813 campaign,
including Lützen, Bautzen and
Dresden, was captured in
November 1813, and during the
Hundred Days commanded part
of the Paris garrison. He remained
in the service after the Bourbon
restoration, retired in 1848 and in
1852 became a senator.

BORGHESE, Camillo Filippo Ludovico, Prince (1775–1832)

A member of an ancient Italian
noble dynasty, he joined
Napoleon's family in 1803 when he
became the second husband of
Pauline Bonaparte. In 1806 he was
created Duke of Guastalla and in
1809 appointed Governor-General
of the *départements au delà des*
Alpes, based at Turin, despite his
estrangement from Pauline. This
was largely an honorific appointment; it had been remarked of
him earlier, when serving in the
national guard of Rome, 'he was
remembered for the more than
Roman indolence of his disposi-

tion, and the perfect stoicism with
which he performed the duties of
his military toilette, amidst the
crash of empires, and the dissolution of the entire frame of European society. He was then called
"the citizen Borghese", but was so
far removed from the character,
that it was pasquinaded of him,
that he displayed, like the Egyptian
sultan, a new habit every day, and
sent his linen to Paris to be
washed'; and that within a few
months of his marriage, he
'reverted to the frivolous and dissipated habits of his youth'.[1] Eventually, despite many scandalous
dalliances in the interim, Pauline
and Camillo were reconciled. He

CAMILLO BORGHESE
(ENGRAVING BY T. JOHNSON AFTER GÉRARD)

died at Florence, where he had
made his home, in 1832.
1. Anon., pp. 95–6.

BOUCHOTTE, Jean-Baptiste-Noël (1754–1840)

A cavalry captain at the outbreak
of the French Revolution, he was
given command of the French
forces at Cambrai, where he
distinguished himself sufficiently
to be appointed Minister of War
after the defection of Dumouriez.
He performed the job competently
until the end of March 1794; after
a trial during the revolutionary
upheavals, at which he was

acquitted, he returned to his native Metz, and after holding minor public office 1799–1805 passed the remainder of his life in retirement.

BOUILLE, General François-Claude-Amour, marquis de (1739–1800)

A relative of Lafayette, he had a distinguished career in the French Army, especially in the West Indies during the War of American Independence. Hostile to the Revolution, he suppressed the risings of the garrisons of Metz and Nancy, and attempted to aid the escape of the royal family. He then fled abroad to continue the fight against the republicans, issuing a famous declaration from Luxembourg to the effect that 'if they touched one hair of his Majesty's head, he would come to Paris, and not leave one stone upon another'.[1] After seeking support in several countries, Bouillé settled in England; the cavalry regiment which he formed, Bouillé's or the Uhlans Britanniques, which existed 1793–6, was remarkable as being the only British unit of the period armed with lances. He was described as a man of courage and integrity, 'justly celebrated for his military talents, the rectitude of his character, and the honourable conduct'[2] which he pursued against Great Britain during the American War, his loyalty to his king, and for being 'an officer of great merit, but somewhat passionate'.[3] He published a memoir of the events of the Revolution (1795), and died in London on 14 December 1800.
1. *Gent's Mag.*, Dec, 1800, p. 1215.
2. Ibid. 3. Ibid.

BOURMONT, Marshal Louis-Auguste-Victor, comte de Ghaisne (1773–1846)

Originally a member of the *Gardes Françaises*, he was a royalist all his life, yet attained high rank in Napoleon's army. After service with the *Armée de Condé* he attempted further subversion, but, having made submission, was allowed to live in Paris until continuing royalism led to his arrest. A prisoner for more than three years, he fled to Portugal in 1804, and offered his services to Junot upon the French invasion of that country. Employed on the staff, he was arrested on his return to France after Cintra, but with Junot's support was given an imperial commission. He served in Italy, with Eugène's staff in Russia, was captured and escaped, and was promoted to *général de division* after his defence of Nogent (February 1814). After serving the Bourbons during the first restoration, he was given a divisional command in Gérard's corps in 1815, but deserted to the Allies on the first day of the Waterloo campaign. His treachery was not especially appreciated: Blücher was contemptuous of him, remarking that the white cockade in Bourmont's hat meant nothing: a cur (*Hundsfott*) remained a cur! His defection also produced a memorable piece of by-play between Napoleon and Gérard, who said he trusted Bourmont and would answer with his head. Napoleon tapped Gérard's cheek and said, 'This head's mine, isn't it? But I need it too much!'[1] Bourmont prospered under the Bourbons, was Minister of War in 1829 and was promoted to Marshal following successes in Algeria in 1830; but the 1830 revolution ended his French career, and after serving Dom Miguel in the Portuguese civil war (1833–4) he retired to Rome, returning to France only after the amnesty of 1840.
1. Maxwell, vol. II, pp. 7–8.

BOURRIENNE, Louis-Antoine Fauvelet de (1769–1834)

A school friend of Napoleon, he used their acquaintance to secure the position of assistant Napoleon in Italy, his knowled of legal and diplomatic matte being useful in the drafting of t Treaty of Campo Formio. He we to Egypt as Napoleon's secreta and assisted in the coup Brumaire, but lost his position a consequence of financial irreg larities. Appointed French env to Hamburg in 1805, he amassed fortune from bribes to evade t Continental System and w recalled in disgrace in 1810. 1814 he joined the Bourbons a in 1815 accompanied the king Ghent; he was a Deputy 1815– but failed to be re-elected after t fall of his patron, Villèle, and fl to Belgium to escape his credito His fame rests with his *Memoirs Napoleon Bonaparte*, an inte esting if unreliable work. Na oleon supposedly remarked him that he, Bourrienne, would immortal, because he w Napoleon's secretary; whereupe Bourrienne defeated the arg ment by asking Napoleon to nan Alexander's secretary! After tw years of mental instability, he di at Caen in 1834.

Bourrienne, L. A. F. d *Mémoires*, Paris 1829; Englis translations from 1830, includir an abridged edition of 1836; subs quently reprinted, including th edited by R. W. Phipps, Londo 1893

BOUVET, de Précourt Amiral François-Joseph baron (1753–1832)

An officer who had served wit Suffren, he rose rapidly in the na after the revolution had cause the emigration of many of th senior and most experienced off cers. Promoted to rear-admiral i 1793, he was 2i/c of the Frenc fleet at the Battle of the Gloriou First of June, flying his flag in L Terrible; but after the failure of th expedition to Bantry Bay, in whic he commanded the van of th leet, he was dismissed and had to support himself by running a school. Napoleon restored him to duty, but he saw no further service after commanding the squadron that was sent to occupy Guadeloupe during the Peace of Amiens. His name is perhaps most familiar by being borne by the French battleship of 1896 which was sunk by a mine off the Dardanelles in 1915.

BOYD, Brigadier General John Parke (1764–1830)

Born in Massachusetts of a Scottish father, he served as an officer in the US Army 1786–9 but then went to India, obtaining employment as an officer in the service of the Nizam of Hyderabad. Returning home, he was appointed colonel of the 4th US Infantry in October 1808, served at Tippecanoe (1811) and on 26 August 1812 was promoted to brigadier general. He held that rank throughout the War of 1812, commanded at the defeat of Chrysler's Farm, and was honourably discharged in 1815. In the following year he went to England to claim compensation for a cargo of saltpetre seized by a British ship *en route* from the East Indies.

BRENTON, Vice-Admiral Sir Jahleel, Bt. (1770–1844)

This distinguished British naval officer was born of an American loyalist family in Rhode Island, the son of Admiral Jahleel Brenton (1729–1802). Early in his career he served in the Swedish Navy while awaiting employment in the Royal Navy, was present at St. Vincent and Algeciras, and made his name as a frigate commander. Wrecked off the French coast in 1803, he resumed his career after exchange, and his most famous action occurred on 3 May 1810 in the Bay of Naples, when in command of HMS *Spartan* he beat off a flotilla of twelve Neapolitan vessels, despite being so short-handed that a Royal Engineer surveyor and the purser had to direct the ship's gunnery. Brenton was even praised by Murat (at that time king of Naples), but received wounds which precluded further active service, although subsequently he served ashore and became vice-admiral in 1830. Two brothers also served in the Royal Navy: Lieutenant James Wallace Brenton, killed near Barcelona in 1799 when serving with HMS *Petrel*, and Captain Edward Pelham Brenton, best known for his history of the Royal Navy and biography of St. Vincent, and whose own career was recorded by Jahleel.

Brenton, Sir Jahleel. *Memoir of Captain Edward Pelham Brenton.* London, 1842; Raikes, Revd. H. *Memoir of the Life and Services of Vice-Admiral Sir Jahleel Brenton, Bt.*, London, 1846

BRIDPORT, Admiral Alexander Hood, Viscount (1727–1814)

Brother of Samuel, Lord Hood, he entered the Royal Navy in 1741 and became a captain fifteen years later; he served in the Seven Years War, at Quiberon (1759) and Ushant (1778), was promoted to rear-admiral in 1780 and participated in the relief of Gibraltar. Vice-admiral in 1787, he was Howe's 2i/c at the Battle of the Glorious First of June (flying his flag in HMS *Royal George*), for which he was ennobled as Baron Bridport of Cricket St. Thomas. In the following year he succeeded Howe as commander of the Channel Fleet and fought the inconclusive action off Belle Ile (23 June 1795); then served ashore helping to direct the war, and was involved in attempts to suppress the 'great mutiny' of 1797 (in which he was not particularly successful: the intervention of old Howe was required before the men returned to their duty). Back

ALEXANDER HOOD, VISCOUNT BRIDPORT (ENGRAVING BY FREEMAN AFTER LEMUEL ABBOTT)

at sea in 1798, he supervised the blockade of France, failing to stop the French expedition to Ireland, and the escape of Bruix's Atlantic fleet in 1799, which attracted criticism, until in 1800 he retired after 59 years' service, his peerage being advanced to a viscountcy in reward for a lifetime of exertion.

A brief account of the Hood family is in Cust, Sir Edward. *Annals of the Wars of the Eighteenth Century.* London, 1862, vol. V, pp. 287–9; Hood, D. *The Admirals Hood.* London, 1942

BRISCALL, Revd. Samuel (1788–1848)

Probably the most famous military clergyman of the era, he was the son of a Stockport surgeon who became a Chaplain to the Forces in 1808. After serving in the Corunna campaign, he returned to the Peninsula in June 1809 and was appointed to headquarters in September 1810, in effect becoming senior chaplain to the army. After a break on account of ill-health, he returned in 1813 and, enjoying Wellington's particular favour (who found him an assiduous and sincere man), was appointed his chaplain in Paris in 1814, was present in the Waterloo campaign and as senior chaplain to the army of occupation. He was awarded the curacy of Stratfield Saye, in Wellington's gift, where he remained until 1836, as well as a living in Lincolnshire, also at the Duke's behest.

Glover, M. 'An Excellent Young Man: the Rev. Samuel Briscall', in *History Today*, August, 1968

BRISSOT (called Brissot de Warville), Jacques-Pierre (1754–93)

The son of an innkeeper and cook near Chartres (leading to the quip that he inherited all the heat from his father's stove), he assumed the name de Warville. He trained as a lawyer, but became a pamphleteer which earned him a sojourn in the Bastille and exile in England, until upon the French Revolution he became prominent as leader of the Girondins (also sometimes styled Brissotins). For a period he practically directed French foreign policy, the declarations of war upon the Emperor and Great Britain being much to his account, and he helped give the war its revolutionary-propagandist aspect. Though an intelligent and capable man, he was unable to prevail over internal upheavals and was guillotined with other Girondins on 31 October 1793. He had edited the *Patriote français* 1789–93, and was such an admirer of America (which he visited in 1788) that he dressed in a style resembling that of a Quaker.

BROCK, Major-General Sir Isaac (1769–1812)

A native of Guernsey and nephew of Admiral Sir James Saumarez, he was commissioned in the British Army at the age of 15, was a lieutenant-colonel by 1797, commanded the 49th in North Holland in 1799 and served aboard the fleet at Copenhagen, but won his fame in North America. He served with his regiment in Canada

1802–5, returned in 1806 to command the garrison at Quebec, became a major-general in June 1811 and three months later took over the civil administration of Upper Canada as well as the military, as 'President and Administrator' of the province. In this role, despite meagre resources, he successfully opposed the American invasion in 1812, compelling the surrender of General William Hull by bluff on 16 August, and on 13 October commanded the Anglo–Canadian forces in the victory at Queenston. Brock led one of the earlier attacks to stabilise his position, which allowed reinforcements to win the day; but while cheering on the York Militia he was shot through the body and died almost immediately. A tall, commanding man who had been a great boxer and swimmer in his youth, he had an affable, courteous manner and was universally liked, admired and respected, characteristics which must have been of use in maintaining the morale of the outnumbered Anglo–Canadians at the commencement of the War of 1812. In 1824 his body was removed from Fort George and returned to Queenston Heights, where he had fallen, and a monument was erected there; in 1840 it was blown up by an Irish American. It was replaced by a larger monument in tribute to the man who had saved the Niagara frontier from American invasion; and Brockville, Ontario, was named after him.

Oman, Sir Charles. 'How General Isaac Brock Saved Canada', in *Studies in the Napoleonic Wars*. London, 1929; Tupper, F. B. *Life and Correspondence of Major-General Sir Isaac Brock*. London, 1847 (written by his nephew)

BROGLIE, Marshal Victor-François, duc de (1718–1804)

An outstanding member of a

distinguished French noble and military family, he followed his father as a leading commander in the French Army. Appointed Marshal of France after successes in the early Seven Years War, he was somewhat disgraced by his defeat at Vellinghausen in 1761 and was not again employed until 1778. Vehemently opposing the Revolution, he commanded *émigré* forces in 1792, and died at Münster in 1804. His most notable military contribution was the devising of a divisional system, adumbrating Napoleon's *corps d'armées*, by which various arms were combined into a single, flexible structure. Despite his opposition to the Revolution, his son, **Victor-Claude, prince de Broglie (1757–94)**, was an equally ardent adherent to revolutionary principles, was a member of the Jacobin Club and sat in the Constituent Assembly. A professional soldier like his father, he served as chief of staff to the French army on the Rhine, but despite his beliefs fell victim to the Terror and was executed at Paris in June 1794.

BROKE, Rear-Admiral Sir Philip Bowes Vere, Bt. (1776–1841)

A member of an old Suffolk family, he entered the Royal Navy in 1792, served at St. Vincent and after some years of unemployment following promotion to captain in 1801, in 1806 he was appointed to command the frigate HMS *Shannon*. A most capable officer, he trained his crew to the peak of efficiency, which was demonstrated when on 1 June 1813 he encountered the USS *Chesapeake* off Boston, the result of a courteous challenge he had issued to the commander of the American frigate, James Lawrence. In one of the most famous and fiercely contested frigate actions of the period, *Chesapeake* was captured

SIR PHILIP BOWES VERE BROKE

after Broke led a boarding-party; coming after reverses against the US Navy, it made Broke a national hero and he was rewarded with a baronetcy. During the action he was so severely wounded by a cutlass blow to the head that he was unable to serve again, and he never fully recovered from the injury. His younger brother Charles served in the Peninsula, was assistant quartermaster-general at Waterloo, and, having adopted an additional surname, died as Major-General Sir Charles Broke-Vere in 1843.

Brighton, Revd. J. G. *Admiral Sir P. B. V. Broke, Bart.: A Memoir*. London, 1866; Padfield, P. *Broke and the Shannon*. London, 1968

BRONTE, Duke of, see **NELSON**

BROWN, General Jacob Jennings (1775–1828)

One of the best American commanders of the War of 1812, he was born in Pennsylvania but settled in New York. In 1798 Brown was military secretary to Alexander Hamilton, then Inspector General of the US Army, and by 1810 had attained the rank of brigadier general in the state militia. He commanded part of the state frontier at the beginning of the War of 1812 and, after

repelling the British attack at Sackett's Harbor, became brigadier general in the regular army (July 1813). In January 1814 he was promoted to major general and succeeded Wilkinson in command of the forces at Niagara; he commanded at Chippewa and was severely wounded at Lundy's Lane. In recognition of his services he received the freedom of New York, and as General of the Army commanded the US Army from March 1821 until his death. A deeply religious man of impressive bearing and calm demeanour, he was styled 'The Fighting Quaker'.

BRUEYS D'AIGALLIERS, Vice-Admiral François-Paul (1753–98)

FRANÇOIS BRUEYS D'AIGALLIERS

A native of Languedoc, he entered the French Navy in 1766, served in the War of American Independence, became captain in 1792, was temporarily suspended during the political upheavals of the early Revolutionary Wars, but was reinstated and as *contre-amiral* captured the Ionian Islands in 1796. *Vice-amiral* in 1798, he commanded the naval forces in the Egyptian expedition, and in his flagship *L'Orient* led the fleet at the Battle of Aboukir Bay. Dreadfully wounded early in the action, with

both legs shattered, he refused to be taken below, remarking that a French admiral should die on his quarterdeck; and was killed by a roundshot from HMS *Swiftsure* before *L'Orient* blew up. Napoleon wrote a most sensitive letter of condolence to his widow.

BRUIX, Vice-Admiral Eustache (1759–1805)

EUSTACHE BRUIX
(ENGRAVING AFTER A. MAURIN)

He joined the French Navy in 1778 and served in the West Indies; like many others, he was suspended during the political turmoil of the early Revolutionary Wars, but was reinstated in 1794 and participated in the abortive expedition to Ireland in 1796. *Contre-amiral* from 1797, he served as Minister of Marine 1798–9, and led the unsuccessful attempt to relieve the French expedition to Egypt. In 1803 he commanded at Boulogne, but from the following year was occupied in staff appointments until his death.

BRUNE, Marshal Guillaume-Marie-Anne (1763–1815)

The son of a lawyer, he abandoned his own legal studies when in debt from gambling to work as a printer and would-be author. An ardent supporter of the Revolution

GUILLAUME BRUNE
(ENGRAVING BY E. HEINEMANN AFTER BENOIST)

and friend of Danton, he was appointed to high command with only the experience as a captain of the National Guard, though he was a tall, impressive man of martial bearing. He served alongside Napoleon at the 13th Vendémiaire as *général de brigade*, and in 1796 was *général de division* in the Army of Italy; in 1798 he commanded the French forces which occupied Switzerland, succeeded to command of the Army of Italy at the time of the Egyptian expedition, and in 1799 commanded the French forces which opposed the Anglo–Russian expedition to North Holland. His service in Italy in 1800, and as ambassador to Constantinople from 1802 to 1804 was unimpressive, however, though he was appointed a Marshal at the first creation. Governor-General of the Hanseatic towns in 1807, he was dismissed because of his continuing republican expressions, and was not reconciled with Napoleon until the Hundred Days, when he was appointed to command the Army of the Var. After Napoleon's fall he was *en route* for Paris when he was murdered by a royalist mob in Avignon on 2 August 1815.

Shepperd, A. 'The Patagonian: Brune', in *Napoleon's Marshals*, ed. D. G. Chandler. London, 1987

(the title of this biography refers to a nickname given to Brune by Danton, relating to his tall build and manner)

BRUNSWICK, Friedrich Wilhelm, Duke of (1771–1815)

FRIEDRICH WILHELM, DUKE OF BRUNSWICK
(PRINT PUBLISHED BY ACKERMANN)

Son of Duke Karl Wilhelm Ferdinand and his wife, the daughter of Frederick, Prince of Wales, Friedrich Wilhelm, 'the Black Duke', was one of Napoleon's most intractable opponents. He succeeded to the dukedom after his father's death; his lands were seized by the French and Napoleon reputedly said '*Je veux l'écraser, lui et toute sa famille.*'[1] In 1809 the Duke formed his 'Black Legion' for Austrian service, which, following Austria's defeat, marched across Germany to be evacuated by British ships, and transferred to British service to continue the fight. Restored to his duchy in 1813–14, the Duke formed a new national army and led it in the Waterloo campaign, only to be shot dead at Quatre Bras while rallying his young soldiers. His hatred of the French was exemplified by the black uniforms and death's head insignia with which he equipped his troops, and in the anti-French camp he was regarded as the model of a patriot:

'He is the only German Prince who has shown a determined mind, and a readiness to sacrifice his property; had every one acted as he had done with firmness and disinterestedness, the German nation would not have been reduced to the wretched state in which she is at present.'[2] The close ties with England were demonstrated by the fact that Friedrich Wilhelm's son, Duke Karl II, who succeeded him as a minor, ruled until he came of age under the regency of the British Prince Regent, later George IV.

1. Anon. *Account of the Operations of the Corps under the Duke of Brunswick.* London, 1810, p. 5. 2. Ibid., p. 38.

BRUNSWICK, Karl Wilhelm Ferdinand, Duke of (1735–1806)

KARL WILHELM FERDINAND, DUKE OF BRUNSWICK
(ENGRAVING BY R. HOUSTON AFTER I. G. QJESENIS)

Succeeding his father, Karl, as Duke of Brunswick in 1780, he proved to be a model 'enlightened' sovereign, but his main reputation was as a soldier. His military experience began in 1757 under the Duke of Cumberland and continued under his uncle, Ferdinand of Brunswick. Married to the daughter of Frederick, Prince of Wales, he served his uncle, Frederick the Great, as a Prussian field marshal, and was appointed to lead the Allied forces for the invasion of France in 1792; but his liberal sentiments were so well known that he had also been offered command of the French army in the same year. His command was complicated by the presence of the King of Prussia, and after the defeat of Valmy, restricted by the king's presence and unable to collaborate with his allies, he resigned and returned to his duchy. In 1803 he undertook a successful diplomatic mission to Russia, and in 1806 at the request of Queen Louisa was prevailed upon to take command of the Prussian Army once more, but again found his freedom of action complicated by the king and his advisers. He was mortally wounded at Auerstädt and died near Hamburg on 10 November 1806. His son and heir, Duke Friedrich Wilhelm, carried on the fight against the French until his death at Quatre Bras.

Fitzmaurice, Lord. *Charles William Ferdinand, Duke of Brunswick*. London, 1901

BUBNA und LITIC (or LITTITZ), Field Marshal Ferdinand, Count (1768–1826)

This Austrian general first saw active service against the Turks in 1788, and during the Napoleonic Wars exerted considerable influence, notably as adjutant-general. Promoted to *Feldmarschall-Leutnant* after Wagram, he performed some diplomatic missions to France in 1813, and in the same year commanded a light division of the Army of Bohemia's advance guard. He served at Dresden and Leipzig, and after the war in Italy was appointed Governor of Lombardy in 1818.

BUGEAUD DE LA PICONNERIE, Marshal Thomas-Robert, duc d'Isly (1784–1849)

Best known for his achievements in Algeria 1836–46 against Abd-el-Kader, which won him promotion to Marshal of France in 1843 and the dukedom which took its title from his victory of Isly (14 August 1844), he began his military career during the Napoleonic Wars. From a noble family, in 1804 he entered the *vélites* of the Imperial Guard, served in the Austerlitz campaign, was commissioned in 1806 and served in the 1806–07 campaigns. In the Peninsula from 1808, he was especially distinguished during the second siege of Saragossa, was colonel by the time of the first restoration, rejoined Napoleon during the Hundred Days and served in the Army of the Alps. His military career was resurrected after the 1830 revolution. In addition to his martial skills, his great interest and expertise was in agriculture. To the student of the Napoleonic Wars he is familiar for his classic account of the sensations experienced when attacking a British line, which for example appears in translation by Oman, Sir Charles. *Wellington's Army*. London, 1912, pp. 91–2, and in Chandler, D. G. *The Campaigns of Napoleon*. London, 1967, p. 348.

Bugeaud, T. R. *Aperçus sur quelques détails de la guerre*. Paris, 1846; Ideville, comte H. d'. *Memoirs of Marshal Bugeaud*, trans. and ed. C. M. Yonge. London, 1884

BULOW, Dietrich Heinrich, Freiherr von (1757–1807)

Dietrich von Bülow followed his elder brother, Friedrich Wilhelm, into the Prussian Army in 1773, but after sixteen years' service became tired of routine, left to travel in Europe and America and followed a number of occupations as diverse as theatre management and glass exporting, none with financial success. Reduced to making a living from minor literary work, he published *Geist der Neueren Kriegssystems* (Hamburg 1799), the most influential of a number of works on military history and theory. This attempted to reduce strategy to a predictable science, without much success, but he was more innovative in tactical theory which recognised the importance of skirmish tactics and light infantry. His criticisms of established Prussian practice aroused the enmity of the establishment, which regarded them as almost treasonable; he was arrested as a madman but when proven sane was incarcerated in Colberg, from where he passed into Russian custody, and died in prison at Riga, probably from neglect, in 1807.

BULOW, General Friedrich Wilhelm, Freiherr von, Graf von Dennewitz (1755–1816)

Highly educated and of distinguished ancestry, he entered the Prussian Army in 1768 and was commissioned in 1772, but it was his musical abilities which first brought him to notice (he was greatly interested in all arts and sciences). In 1792 he was

FRIEDRICH WILHELM BÜLOW VON DENNEWITZ
(ENGRAVING BY T. JOHNSON)

appointed military tutor to Prince Louis Ferdinand, served in the campaigns of 1793–4 (receiving the *Pour le Mérite* for the siege of Mainz), but the tribulations of his brother Dietrich caused him both anguish and financial loss (investing in the unsuccessful attempt to export glass to the USA), and the death of his wife and two children were even more dreadful blows. He served with distinction under Lestocq in 1806–7, and thereafter devoted himself to the reformation of the Prussian Army. *Generalleutnant* from March 1813, he made a great contribution to success in the 'War of Liberation', winning the actions of Gross-beeren and Dennewitz, taking his title from the latter, which raised his popularity almost to that of Blücher. His corps played an important part in the Leipzig campaign, after which he was sent into The Netherlands, and joined Blücher for the victory of Laon. Appointed full general, he was briefly CinC in Prussia before commanding IV Corps in the Hundred Days campaign, in which he was especially distinguished as leader of the Prussian units which arrived on Napoleon's right flank at Waterloo, the importance of which was crucial. As Wellington reported, 'The operation of General Bülow upon the enemy's flank was a most decisive one; and, even if I had not found myself in a situation to make the attack which produced the final result, it would have forced the enemy to retire if his attacks should have failed, and would have prevented him from taking advantage of them if they should unfortunately have succeeded.'[1] Von Bülow died shortly after returning to his command in Prussia following the conclusion of the war.

1. Wellington, vol. XII, p. 484.

Ense, V. von. *Leben des General Grafen Bülow von Dennewitz*. Berlin, 1854

BUNBURY, Lieutenant-General Sir Henry Edward, Bt. (1778–1860)

Son of the caricaturist Henry William Bunbury (1750–1811), he was commissioned in the Cold-stream Guards in 1795; ADC to the Duke of York, he served in the 1799 campaign in North Holland, in the Mediterranean in 1805 and at Maida. Under-Secretary of State for War 1809–16, and major-general from June 1814, he went on a mission to Wellington's head-quarters in that year and was sent to inform Napoleon of the decision to exile him to St. Helena. Later MP for Suffolk, he was married to Louisa Emilia, daughter of General Edward Fox and niece of Charles James Fox, in 1830 he married Emily Louisa, daughter of Sir George Napier, a family related to his first wife (who had died in 1828), and succeeded his uncle, Sir Thomas Charles (1740–1821) as 7th Baronet. Bunbury is perhaps best known for his *Narratives of Some Passages in the Great War with France 1799–1810*, London, 1854, which Sir John Fortescue described as the best military history in English (1927 edn., p. xiii). Sir Henry should not be confused with another memorialist, Thomas Bunbury, who served with the 20th Portuguese Line and 3rd *Caçadores* in the Peninsula, commanded the 80th Foot in the Sutlej campaign, and wrote *Reminiscences of a Veteran: Personal and Military Adventures in the Peninsula*, 1861.

Bunbury, Sir Charles. *Memoir and Literary Remains of Lieutenant-General Sir Henry Edward Bunbury, Bart*. London, 1868

BUONAPARTE

The original spelling of Napoleon's family name; from about 1796 he adopted the French spelling 'Bonaparte', q.v.

BURDETT, Sir Francis, Bt. (1770–1844)

Succeeding his grandfather Sir Robert (1716–97) as 5th Baronet, he was a noted radical and parlia-mentary and social reformer, and MP for Boroughbridge, Westminster and North Wiltshire. He was a stern critic of the British government, making vehement attacks upon subjects as diverse as the building of barracks (to 'use the troops paid by the people to subdue the people',[1] flogging (where his agitation was said to have helped amend the regulations), and the conduct of the war; for example, his was the only dissenting voice against the motion to reward Wellington in 1812 (in which debate he complained about progress in the Peninsula while admitting that he knew nothing of military affairs!). In April 1810 he was arrested for breaching parliamentary privilege (by writing an article for Cobbett's newspaper); mobs assembled to support him, three people were killed when the Life Guards opened fire, and the arrest was only made when parliamentary officers forced the kitchen window of his house, from where he was taken to the Tower.

1. *Edinburgh* , 7 May 1812.

Patterson, M. W. *Sir Francis Burdett and His Times*. London, 1931

BURGHERSH, Lord, see WESTMORLAND, Earl of

BURGOYNE, Field Marshal Sir John Fox, Bt. (1782–1871)

Best known as the principal British engineer at the com-mencement of the Crimean expe-dition, he served with some distinction in the Napoleonic Wars, in Egypt in 1807, in the Corunna campaign and with Wellington from 1809, becoming commanding engineer on his staff after Vittoria. He received brevets as major and lieutenant-colonel for Ciudad Rodrigo and Badajoz, and served at New Orleans, but only attained the rank of major-general in 1838; he became field

JOHN FOX BURGOYNE
(ENGRAVING BY W. J. EDWARDS)

marshal in January 1868. He was a natural son of General John Burgoyne (1722–92), best known for his surrender at Saratoga in 1777, and the opera singer Susan Caulfield. His son, Captain Hugh Talbot Burgoyne, RN (1833–70), won the Victoria Cross in the Crimea and died when HMS *Captain* sank in the Bay of Biscay.

Head, Sir Francis. *Sketch of the Life and Death of Field Marshal Sir John Burgoyne*. London, 1872; Wrottesley, Hon. G. *Life and Correspondence of Field Marshal Sir John Fox Burgoyne*. London, 1872

BURKE, Edmund (1729–97)

In the context of the Revolutionary and Napoleonic Wars, this great British politician and writer is remembered chiefly for his great work *Reflections on the Revolution in France*, published in 1790. Entering parliament as MP for Wendover (though of Irish birth), he held office only briefly but was extremely influential as an independent of radical leanings, criticising the king and supporting the American colonists before the War of Independence. Upon the outbreak of the French Revolution he was still allied with Fox and the Whigs and subsequently supported Pitt, his *Reflections* winning wide acclaim (it went through eleven editions in little over a year) but completing his estrangement from those with whom he had been associated for most of his political career. Although his great work received some criticism for exaggeration, he predicted the extremism which took hold of the Revolution; Scott remarked that no political prophet ever viewed the future with a surer ken. Perhaps the best known of its memorable expressions is: '... the age of chivalry is gone. That of sophisters, economists, and calculators, has succeeded; and the glory of Europe is extinguished for ever'; and it confirmed Burke's enduring reputation as a political writer and philosopher.

Ayling, S. *Edmund Burke: His Life and Opinions*. London, 1989; Prior, Sir James. *Memoir of the Life and Character of Edmund Burke*. 1824

EDMUND BURKE (ENGRAVING BY W. H. EGLETON AFTER REYNOLDS)

BURNEY, (later d'ARBLAY) Frances ('Fanny') (1752–1840)

The British novelist Fanny Burney had established her literary reputation before the Napoleonic era, but its events had a great effect upon her life: in 1793 she married the French *émigré* artillery officer, Alexandre d'Arblay, who had been an aide to Lafayette. They lived in France from 1801, but she returned to England in 1812 so that their 18-year-old son would not be conscripted. During the Hundred Days she was in Brussels and left an account of the confusion there at the time of Waterloo, but when General d'Arblay (as he had become) was given permission to live in England, they settled there; he died at Bath in 1818. Fanny's diaries are an interesting source for an account of contemporary society.

d'Arblay, Frances. *The Diaries of Madame d'Arblay*, ed. C. F. Barrett (her niece). London, 1854.

BURNS, Robert (1759–96)

ROBERT BURNS

The great Scottish poet produced a few significant works of relevance to military matters. Himself a member of the Dumfries Volunteers (and receiving a large military funeral), probably his best-known military work is the poem *The Dumfries Volunteers*, also known by its first line, 'Does Haughty Gaul Invasion Threat?' Other Burns poems were thought worthy of publication in 'patriotic' works at the time; for example, *The Anti-Gallican* (1804) published *Bruce's Address* and *Song of Death. Epistle to Colonel de Peyster* (ex-8th Foot) was addressed to Burns' commander in the Dumfries Volunteers, and *The Soldier's Return* is another memorable poem with a military theme, with the famous first line, 'When wild war's deadly blast was blawn ...'

BURRARD, Lieutenant-General Sir Harry, Bt. (1755–1813)

Forever associated with the shameful Convention of Cintra, he was commissioned in the Coldstream Guards in 1772, served in the War of American Independence and in The Netherlands 1793–5, in 1798 was promoted to major-general and was 2i/c of the Ostend expedition. Commanding the 1st Division as Cathcart's 2i/c in Denmark in 1807, he was rewarded by a baronetcy, of Lymington, which he represented in parliament 1780–1806. In 1808 he was sent to the Peninsula as Dalrymple's deputy, where he forbade Arthur Wellesley from pursuing the French after his victory at Vimeiro. After 'Dowager' Dalrymple and 'Betty' Burrard – with Wellesley an unwilling additional signatory – had concluded the Convention of Cintra, which allowed the French to escape with the plunder of Portugal, all three were recalled to face an inquiry, in which only Wellesley was exonerated; Burrard held no active command thereafter, forever tarnished by Byron's condemnation, 'For chiefs like ours in vain may laurels bloom.' His eldest son, Paul, was mortally wounded at Corunna where he served as Moore's ADC; his second son, a midshipman in the Royal Navy, was drowned in October of the same year by the upsetting of a boat from the royal yacht *Royal Sovereign* in Weymouth harbour, and his fourth son, Ensign William Burrard of the 1st Foot Guards, was mortally wounded at San Sebastian. Burrard himself died in October 1813.

BUTLER, Lady Elizabeth (1846–1933)

Although later than the period, the artist Elizabeth Southernden Thompson, who married General Sir William Butler in 1877, painted some of the most frequently reproduced pictures of Napoleonic scenes. Her work is characterised by realistic and sympathetic treatment of the hardships endured by the common soldiers, executed with great care and attempts to achieve accuracy. Although only a minority of her work features Napoleonic events, it includes two of the best-known battle-paintings: 'Scotland For Ever', showing the charge of the 2nd Dragoons at Waterloo, and 'Quatre Bras', which Ruskin heralded as the first pre-Raphaelite battle-painting. These illustrate both her great talent and the hazards of reliance upon non- contemporary images: she depicts the 28th Foot wearing the 'Belgic' shako, when they almost certainly retained the previous 'stovepipe' cap, and shows the 2nd Dragoons with a guidon, which was not carried on campaign. Nevertheless she occupies a position in the first rank of battle-painters alongside the like of Détaille.

Spencer-Smith, J., and Underwood, P. *Lady Butler, Battle Artist.* 1987

BUXHOWDEN, Field Marshal Friedrich Wilhelm, Count (1750–1811)

An Estonian German who had married an illegitimate daughter of Catherine the Great, he came to prominence in the Russian Army under Suvarov in Poland (1793–4), but it is as a lieutenant-general in command of the first three columns of the Allied army at Austerlitz that he was best known. He did not give the impression of any great education or capability; he was encumbered with an enor-

mous train of servants, baggage and hunting-dogs, and his subordinate Langeron remarked that as the battle went against them, he seemed scarcely in possession of his wits. Despite his lack of success at Austerlitz, he commanded the Russian 2nd Army in the 1806–7 campaign, being sent west to reinforce Bennigsen; there was rivalry between the two, and Buxhöwden was blamed unfairly for not arriving at Pultusk. He was senior to Bennigsen, briefly commanded the Russian forces at the beginning of 1807, but was recalled and Bennigsen given the command. He was appointed to organise the administration of Finland following its ceding to Russia by Sweden by the Treaty of Fredrikshavn (17 September 1809).

BUZOT, François-Nicolas-Léonard (1760–94)

A lawyer from Evreux, he was a Deputy of the Girondin group in the Convention, who voted for the death of the king but solicited a reprieve. He warned of the danger of the Parisian mob, which made him unpopular; known as an honest man unprepared to compromise his beliefs, he was proscribed with the Girondins in June 1793, escaped from Paris, and in Normandy attempted to raise an insurrection against the Convention. When this failed he was outlawed, fled to the Bordeaux region and committed suicide in June 1794.

BYNG, Field Marshal Sir John, Earl of Strafford (1772–1860)

Commissioned in the British Army in 1793, he served in The Netherlands 1793–4, in Ireland during the 1798 rebellion, at Copenhagen and Walcheren, and from September 1811 led a brigade of the 2nd Division in the Peninsula. Major-General from June 1813, in the Waterloo campaign he commanded the 2nd British (Foot Guards) Brigade of the 1st Division. Promoted to lieutenant-general in May 1825, general in November 1841 and field marshal in October 1855, he commanded in Ireland 1828–31 and in May 1835 was ennobled as Baron Strafford, upgraded to Viscount Enfield and Earl of Strafford in September 1847, resurrecting the title of a distant and less fortunate kinsman, Thomas Wentworth, Earl of Strafford (1593–1641). Admiral John Byng (shot in 1757, *pour encourager les autres* according to Voltaire) was another kinsman, and Sir John's grandson was the greatly distinguished Field Marshal Julian, Viscount Byng of Vimy (1862–1935).

BYRON, George Gordon, Baron (1788–1824)

The great poet's significance in the context of the Napoleonic Wars is limited to some of his verses, notably in *Childe Harold's Pilgrimage* ('There was a sound of revelry by night', as the Duchess of Richmond's ball is memorably described), but he is also an example of how the wars touched the lives of many outside the spheres of military or political life. Byron inherited his title from his great-uncle William, 5th Baron (1722–98) only because his direct heir, his grandson Lieutenant William Byron of the 18th Foot, had been killed on 31 July 1794 during the siege of Calvi.

LORD BYRON
(ENGRAVING AFTER THOMAS PHILLIPS)

CABARRUS, François, count (1752–1810)

A French-born soap manufacturer in Spain, he became prominent in financial and mercantile circles via his San Carlos bank and company which traded with the Philippines. As adviser to the government of King Charles III, he instituted many financial reforms, but fell out of favour with the more reactionary Charles IV and was even imprisoned (1790–2) before being re-employed and ennobled. Upon the deposition of the king by Napoleon, he was appointed Minister of Finance to Joseph Bonaparte, but died in 1810 probably from a combination of work and alcohol. His daughter Thérèse, a legendary beauty, was originally married to comte de Fontenay, then became the wife of the revolutionary Jean Tallien and caused him to moderate his views, saving many lives by her entreaties. They were divorced in 1805 and she married comte de Caraman, later prince de Chimay.

CADORE, duc de, see CHAMPAGNY

CADOUDAL, Georges (1771–1804)

The son of a miller, Cadoudal (sometimes called just 'Georges') was a leader of the Chouans and a committed royalist. He fought against the French republicans in the Vendée and Quiberon, and continued his struggle until his supporters were defeated in the field. Thereafter he worked conspiratorially, and despite an interview with Napoleon in Paris, who tried to convince him of the futility of his actions, refused to compromise. At various times he took refuge in England; it was said that he was implicated in the plot to blow up Napoleon in the rue St. Nicaise in December 1800, for which two royalists, Carbon and St. Régent, were executed (though

Cadoudal denied that he originated the plan). Plotting with Pichegru and Moreau, Cadoudal returned to Normandy in August 1803, to execute a plot to seize Napoleon; he evaded capture for some six months but finally was arrested and, declining to beg for pardon, was executed in Paris in June 1804. Bourrienne, who witnessed his interview with Napoleon, said that he had the bearing and manners of a rude soldier, but the soul of a hero; Napoleon was slightly less generous, saying that he had courage and nothing more, and that he refused to believe that no matter what exertions he made for the royalists, they would still regard him as nothing more than a miller's son.

CAFFARELLI du FALGA, General Louis-Marie-Joseph Maximilien de (1756–99)

Commissioned as an engineer in 1775, he became one of Napoleon's closest friends during the Egyptian campaign. Although he was suspended and imprisoned during the revolutionary period, he remained a convinced republican of extreme views; during the voyage to Egypt he argued that property was a form of theft and that after twenty years' work tenants should become landowners. He lost his left leg campaigning on the Rhine, was promoted to *général de brigade* in 1795, and commanded the engineers and supervised the Scientific Commission in Egypt. He was hit in the arm during the siege of Acre; Larrey amputated it, but he fell victim to fever and died two weeks later, on 27 April 1799. It was said that during the delirium of fever he roused to coherence whenever Napoleon visited him, proof of the 'sort of reverential respect' he had for his chief,[1] and according the Bourrienne one of his last requests was that he be

read Voltaire's preface to Montesquieu's *L'Esprit des Lois*. His brother, **General Marie-François Auguste comte (1766–1849)**, entered the French Army in 1792 from Sardinian service, fought at Marengo with the Consular Guard, became *général de division* in 1805 and served Napoleon as an aide and in diplomatic missions. In October 1810 he commanded the 'Division of Reserve of the Army of Spain' and ultimately the Army of the North, but was accused of lacking energy in failing to suppress guerrilla activity in the Biscay region (though the problem was probably too great for his resources), and he was recalled in January 1813 and replaced by Clausel. In 1814 he escorted the Empress and the King of Rome to Vienna, and, having rallied to Napoleon in 1815, found no favour under the Bourbons, until ennobled as a peer of France in 1831.

1. Las Cases, vol. I, p. 141.

CALDER, Admiral Sir Robert, Bt. (1745–1818)

Second son of the old Scottish family Calder of Muirton, he entered the Royal Navy in 1759, became captain in 1782, served at St. Vincent and was knighted after bearing the victory dispatch to England, became a baronet in the following year, rear-admiral in 1799 and vice-admiral in 1804. In 1805 his fleet blockaded Ferrol and Corunna where Napoleon's invasion preparations were in hand; on 22 July he intercepted Villeneuve's fleet on passage to Brest, and with his outnumbered force fought an indecisive action, capturing two Spanish vessels. Calder discontinued the fight and Villeneuve refused to engage again, taking refuge in Ferrol; stung by criticisms of timidity despite having frustrated the French plans, Calder demanded a court-martial, which was held in December 1805. Although exonerated of cowardice he was reprimanded severely, a verdict which dismayed him; he 'appeared deeply affected – he turned round, and retired without a word ... scarcely lifted up his head, which was apparently bowed down by the weight of the sentence pronounced upon him'.[1] His reputation was later restored, he became an admiral in 1810 and in 1815 was appointed to command at Portsmouth.

1. *Gent's Mag.*, Jan 1806, p. 81.

CALVERT, General Sir Harry, Bt. (*d.*1826)

SIR HARRY CALVERT
(ENGRAVING BY GOLDINGS)

One of the most distinguished staff officers of the period, he served in The Netherlands campaign 1793–4, but is best known as the British Army's Adjutant-General 1799–1820, a position he held with distinction. He was colonel of the 14th Foot from 1806 until his death, the regiment being nicknamed 'Calvert's Entire' from the fact that his family were brewers. He was awarded a baronetcy in 1818; the son who succeeded him assumed the surname of Verney on inheriting the estates of that family, which included among its members Sir Edmund Verney, Charles I's standard-bearer who was killed at Edgehill.

Calvert, Sir Harry. *Journals and Correspondence of Sir Harry Calvert, Bart ... the Campaigns in Flanders and Holland 1793–94*, ed. Sir Harry Verney. London, 1853

CAMBACERES, Jean-Jacques Régis de, duc de Parme (1753–1824)

JEAN JACQUES CAMBACÉRÈS
(ENGRAVING BY H. WOLF AFTER H. F. SCHONIN)

A lawyer, born in Montpellier, he espoused the French Revolution, but by concentrating upon legal and legislative matters managed to avoid becoming tainted with its worst excesses. His attitude to the trial of Louis XVI was typical: while voting for the king's guilt, he cast doubt upon the legality of proceedings and recommended that the penalty be postponed, thus absolving himself of culpability as a regicide. He served as President of the Committee of Public Safety and was instrumental in concluding peace with Spain; and although his moderation was so unappealing to the Directors that temporarily he retired from public duty, in July 1799 he became Minister of Justice by Sieyès' influence. He supported the coup of Brumaire and in December 1799 was appointed Second Consul, thereafter playing an important role in Napoleon's career. He became Arch-Chancellor of the Empire and President of the Senate, and contributed greatly to the formation of what became the *Code Napoléon*; created Duke of Parma in 1808, he remained an important statesman whose opinions Napoleon always took into consideration. He joined Napoleon in 1815 and until 1818 was exiled, living in Brussels; and upon his return took no further part in public life. In return for his loyalty and advice, Napoleon seems to have excused aspects of his character which he might otherwise have criticised, not least Cambacérès' reputation as a gourmet whose long dinners even interrupted matters of state. The duchesse d'Abrantès described his appearance as rather fantastic, with old-fashioned ruffles, queue, gold-buckled shoes polished with English blacking, and tricorn hat.

Aubriet, A. *Vie de Cambacérès.* Paris, 1825; Papillard, F. *Cambacérès.* Paris, 1961; Vialles, P. *L'Archichancelier Cambacérès.* Paris, 1908

CAMBON, Pierre-Joseph (1756–1820)

One of the most able financiers of the French Revolution, Cambon, a Protestant, forsook his family cotton business for politics, helping to form the Jacobin Club in his native Montpellier. He was the last President of the Legislative Assembly, voted for the death of the king, and worked on the Committee of Public Safety, but is probably best known for his efforts in creating the *Great Book* to finance the public debt, that being the name for the register of fund-holders. He resisted Robespierre and was forced to flee, but returned to France in 1795, living in retirement on his estate near Montpellier, until exiled as a regicide in 1816. He died near Brussels.

CAMBRIDGE, Adolphus Frederick, Duke of (1774–1850)

ADOLPHUS FREDERICK, DUKE OF CAMBRIDGE (ENGRAVING BY W. SKELTON AFTER BEECHEY)

The seventh son of King George III, he was created Earl of Tipperary and Duke of Cambridge in 1801; he was appointed a field marshal in the British Army on 26 November 1813, but that, like his colonelcies of the Coldstream Guards (from September 1805) and the 60th (from 1827) was largely honorific. He was married to Augusta, daughter of Landgrave Frederick of Hesse–Cassel; his son, George William Frederick Charles, also Duke of Cambridge (1819–1904) had a much more active military career, serving in the Crimea, becoming field marshal in 1862 and serving as Commander-in-Chief 1856–95.

CAMBRONNE, General Pierre-Jacques-Etienne, vicomte (1770–1842)

His fame is probably founded upon something he never said, a somewhat unusual notoriety. Entering the French Army in 1792, he had a distinguished record even before he entered the 1st *Tirailleurs-Chasseurs* of the Imperial Guard as a major in 1809. He served in Russia and Spain, commanded the 3rd *Voltigeurs* at Dresden, took command of the 2nd *Chasseurs*, was wounded at Hanau and four times at Craonne, and had attained the rank of *général de brigade* in 1813. He commanded the 'Elba Battalion' in exile, and the 1st *Chasseurs* in 1815, his moment of immortality coming at Waterloo, when his Guardsmen made their last stand. Called upon to surrender, his reply – according to tradition – was '*La Garde meurt mais ne se rend pas!*' (The Guard dies but does not surrender), but actually was probably '*Merde!*', the imprecation which became known as '*le mot de Cambronne*'. Wounded, he was taken prisoner when his aiguillette

CAMBRONNE AT WATERLOO (PRINT AFTER GEORGES SCOTT)

was seized by Hew Halkett, commander of the 3rd Hanoverian Brigade. Pardoned by the Bourbons, Cambronne resumed his military career, being ennobled as vicomte in 1822, before retiring in the following year.

Braunschvigg, L. *Cambronne: Sa Vie civile, politique et militaire ...* Nantes, 1894.

CAMDEN, John Jeffreys Pratt, 2nd Earl and 1st Marquess (1759–1840)

Son of the 1st Earl Camden, whom he succeeded in 1794, the 2nd Earl entered British politics at an early age, and held a number of appointments before being appointed Lord-Lieutenant of Ireland in 1795. He was greatly concerned to maintain tranquillity, but was pessimistic and not especially well-served by his subordinates. He was replaced by Cornwallis before the 1798 rebellion was over, but subsequently was Secretary for War and the Colonies (1804) and Lord President of the Council (1805, 1807–12); he became 1st Marquess in 1812. He commanded the Sevenoaks Troop, and later West Kent Regiment, of Yeomanry, and from 1809 the Weald of Kent Local Militia. In 1814 as Lord- Lieutenant of the county, with some yeomanry he escorted Louis XVIII to Dover to sail for France.

CAMELFORD, Thomas Pitt, 2nd Baron (1775–1804)

A cousin of William Pitt (his father, the 1st Baron, 1737–93, was a nephew of the Earl of Chatham), Thomas the 2nd Baron had a colourful career in the Royal Navy, surviving the wreck of the *Guardian* (see entry for Riou), physically attacking his erstwhile commanding officer, Captain George Vancouver, and killing a brother officer, ostensibly for mutiny, in Antigua. He left the service and was arrested in

France under suspicion of planning to assassinate Napoleon with a repeating pistol, but was freed on Napoleon's order. Known for a wild lifestyle, he was killed in a duel with Captain Thomas Best, at a time when he may have been involved with Cadoudal, and other attempts on Napoleon's life; 'his imperfections and his follies were often brought before the publick; but the counter-balancing virtues were but seldom heard of '.[1]

1. *Gent's Mag.*, Mar, 1804, p. 285.

Tolstoy, N. *The Half-Mad Lord: Thomas Pitt, 2nd Baron Camelford.* London 1978

CAMERON, Colonel John, of Fassiefern (1771–1815)

JOHN CAMERON OF FASSIEFERN.

One of the best-known regimental officers of the British Army, he was a member of an ancient Highland family. In 1793 he was commissioned in the British Army and in 1794 joined the 100th, later 92nd Foot, the Gordon Highlanders, with whom he was to spend his career. He served in Corsica, Ireland, North Holland in 1799, Egypt, Walcheren and the Peninsula and was especially distinguished at Maya. Lieutenant -colonel from June 1808, colonel from June 1814, he was shot dead at Quatre Bras and was buried on

the following day by his foster-brother Ewen McMillan, who had accompanied him as a private in the 92nd throughout the campaigns. 'Fassiefern' was revered by his men in the manner of an old clan chief, but though a splendid soldier he was the sternest of disciplinarians, 'the very devil' in the punishment of dirty or drunken soldiers according to one of his men.[1] His father was awarded a baronetcy and an augmentation to the family arms as a tribute to his service.

1. Gardyne, C. G. *The Life of a Regiment.* London, 1929, vol. I, p. 359.

Clerk, Revd. A. *Memoir of Colonel John Cameron, Fassiefern,* Glasgow, 1858.

CAMPBELL, Lieutenant-General Sir Colin (1776–1847)

One of Wellington's best staff officers, he ran away to sea before becoming an officer in the Breadalbane Fencibles in 1795. He served with the 78th in India, distinguished at Ahmednuggur and wounded severely at Assaye, and most valuably as a staff officer in the Peninsula. As a colonel in the Coldstream Guards, he was HQ commandant at Waterloo; despite the importance of this position he remained a poor linguist and would order his dinner as if it were soldiers to be commanded ('*Bif-tek, venez ici*').[1] He became lieutenant-general and was Governor of Nova Scotia (1833) and Ceylon (1840–7). He should not be confused with his namesakes: one, later Lord Clyde; the other, Lieutenant-Colonel Colin Campbell, who commanded the 3/1st in the Peninsula and Waterloo campaigns, and was wounded seriously at Quatre Bras; nor with the Peninsular divisional commanders Alexander Campbell (later lieutenant-general and baronet, 6th Division 1810–11), and Henry Frederick Campbell (later general, 1st Division 1812).

1, Stanhope, p. 299.

CAMPBELL, Field Marshal Sir Colin, Baron Clyde (1792–1863)

SIR COLIN CAMPBELL,
BARON CLYDE

Renowned for his leadership of the Highland Brigade in the Crimea, and for commanding the forces which suppressed the Indian Mutiny (for which he became field marshal and 1st Baron Clyde), he was born in Glasgow, the son of a carpenter named Macliver, and adopted the surname Campbell in tribute to a maternal uncle who financed his education and obtained for him a commission in the 9th Foot. With them he served at Vimeiro, Corunna, Walcheren and in the Peninsula from 1811, being wounded leading the forlorn hope at San Sebastian and at the Bidassoa; as a captain in the 60th from November 1813 he served in America from August 1814.

Burne, Sir Owen. *Clyde and Strathnairn*. London, 1895; Forbes, A. *Colin Campbell, Lord Clyde*. London, 1895; Shadwell, Lieutenant-General L. *The Life of Colin Campbell, Lord Clyde*. Edinburgh, 1881

CAMPBELL, Thomas (1777–1844)

This Scottish poet, an important literary figure of his time, wrote a number of poems with a military theme, influenced by contemporary events, most notably perhaps *The Battle of the Baltic* (Copenhagen, 1801) and *Hohenlinden*. The latter, and *The Soldier's Dream*, were composed on a tour of Germany begun in 1800; when Ratisbon was taken by the French shortly after his arrival, he took refuge in a Scottish monastery, and returned home from northern Germany on the outbreak of hostilities between Great Britain and Denmark.

Beattie, W. *Life and Letters of Thomas Campbell*. 1849

CAMUS, Armand Gaston (1740–1804)

A lawyer before the French Revolution, the principles of which he embraced, he served in the States-General and National Convention, helped improve the commissariat, and was one of the commissioners appointed to arrest Dumouriez, only to be turned over by that general to the Austrians. Exchanged in 1795, he returned to his duties as official archivist, and true to his convictions – he had voted for the king's death – took no part in the Napoleonic regime.

CANINO, Prince of, see BONAPARTE, Lucien

CANNING, George (1770–1827)

One of the most influential European statesmen of the 1820s, and a friend of William Pitt, he entered British politics as an MP in 1793. He served as Under-Secretary at the Foreign Office 1796–9 and joint Paymaster of the forces 1800–1, and as Treasurer of the Navy in Pitt's second ministry. Foreign Secretary under Portland (1807–9), in manoeuvring to be the latter's successor he attempted to have Castlereagh dismissed; disappointed, he resigned in September 1809 and shortly after was challenged to a duel by Castlereagh and shot in the thigh. This affair prompted his absence from public office for some time, though he undertook a mission to Lisbon in 1812 and re-entered the cabinet (having become reconciled with Lord Castlereagh) in 1816. Canning's real mark on European affairs dates from his appointment as Foreign Secretary in 1822, from which office he succeeded Liverpool as Prime Minister in 1827. His ministry was not expected to last, having had to rely upon Whig support as some Tories were unwilling to serve under a man whom they disliked; Wellington, for example, resigned as Commander-in-Chief, claiming that Canning had treated him like a dog and even considered calling him out. Canning was Prime Minister for only a few months; worn out with the effort of constructing a government, he never fully recovered from a cold caught at the Duke of York's funeral, and died in August 1827. He had a great reputation as a wit and orator, perhaps his most famous quotation being that concerning his recognition of the independence of the ex-Spanish colonies in South America: 'I called the New World into existence to redress the balance of the old.'

GEORGE CANNING (ENGRAVING BY T. BLOOD
AFTER NOLLEKENS)

Bagot, J. (ed.). *George Canning and his Friends*. London, 1909; Dixon, P. *Canning, Politician and Statesman*. London, 1976; Hinde, W. *Canning*, London, 1973; Stapleton, A. G. *The Political Life of George Canning*. London, 1831; Rolo, P. J. V. *George Canning: Three Biographical Studies*. London, 1965; Temperley, H. W. V. *George Canning*. London, 1905

CANOVA, Antonio (1757–1822)

In 1802 the Italian Canova, the most famous neo-classical sculptor, accepted Napoleon's invitation to Paris where he became an admirer. He produced a number of studies of Napoleon, notably two enormous statues, one in bronze in Milan and another, in marble, which was presented to Wellington and placed in Apsley House. Probably his most celebrated work is the nude statue of Pauline Bonaparte as Venus, executed in 1808. In 1815 he was commissioned by the Pope to retrieve works of art which had been taken to France during the Napoleonic Wars; such was his success that he was ennobled by the Pope as Marquis of Ischia, and granted a pension.

CAPODISTRIAS, Joannes, Count (1776–1831)

Best known as the first President of Greece, after which appointment he signed himself Joannes or Ioannes Capodistrias, Giovanni Antonio Capo d'Istria was a member of an ancient and distinguished Corfiote family ennobled as counts by the Duke of Savoy in 1689. From 1800 he was involved in the governance of the Ionian Islands, where he supported Russian influence; but upon the transfer to France by Tilsit he declined to assist the French and instead entered the Russian foreign ministry. In 1811 he assisted the embassy at Vienna and in 1812 was diplomatic chief

to Chichagov's mission on the Balkan frontier. Appointed councillor of state, he was attached to Barclay de Tolly's command in 1813 and was present at Lützen, Bautzen, Dresden and Leipzig, then went to Switzerland as Allied envoy and was very influential at the Congress of Vienna. Enjoying the trust of the Tsar, in 1815 he became a secretary of state, but after sharing the foreign ministry with Nesselrode his influence declined as a more reactionary mood took over imperial policy, and in 1822 he resigned. In 1827 he was elected President of Greece, the culmination of a lifetime's concern for that nation; but his presidency was beset by internal strife, he was felt to be too Russian, and in October 1831 he was assassinated.

Woodhouse, C. M. *Capodistria, the Founder of Greek Independence*. Oxford, 1973

CARACCIOLO, Commodore Francesco, Prince (1732–99)

A member of a noble Neapolitan family, he had served in the British Navy during the War of American Independence, and at Toulon. As a senior officer in the Neapolitan Navy he escorted Ferdinand IV to Sicily upon the approach of the French, but then returned to Naples to secure his own property, the interests of which perhaps causing him to accept the principles of the French Revolution. He took command of the navy of the new Parthenopean Republic, and on the collapse of that state and the withdrawal of the French, he attempted to escape but was captured by royalists and taken in fetters to Nelson's flagship, HMS *Foudroyant*. Although this was British territory, perhaps in the knowledge that the Queen of Naples wanted him hanged, Nelson permitted a court-martial to be held with Neapolitan officers sitting in judgement; they

convicted Caracciolo and he was hanged immediately from the yardarm of the Neapolitan frigate *Minerva*. His body was thrown into the sea from where it emerged later, enabling a Christian burial to take place. Although he was strictly guilty of treason, Nelson was much criticised for allowing Great Britain to become involved in Neapolitan internal affairs.

CARNOT, General Lazare-Nicolas-Marguerite (1753–1823)

LAZARE CARNOT
(ENGRAVING BY J. MASSARD)

Meriting the contemporary description of him as being 'the organiser of victory', he was the most influential French military figure of the Revolutionary era. From a middle-class Burgundian family, he was commissioned as an engineer in 1773; he supported the Revolution, voted for the execution of Louis XVI, and though prominent in politics was best known for his military skills. Although only a captain, virtually all military administration was his responsibility, including the *levée en masse* and *amalgame*, and as a member of the Committee of Public Safety from August 1793 his role was actually that of Minister of War and Chief of Staff. His influence was immense; the army which

Napoleon inherited probably owed more to him than to any other source, and indeed the infant French republic might not have survived without his efforts. In 1795 he was appointed a Director, was forced to flee abroad in 1797 but returned after the coup of Brumaire; from early 1800 he served as Minister of War and participated in campaigning on the Rhine. His republicanism led him into conflict with Napoleon, however, and from early 1801 he largely retired from public life, remaining a senator and devoting his time to writing and science. His greatest work, commissioned by Napoleon as a textbook for the Metz engineering school, was *De la Défense des Places Fortes* (1810), which was translated for the use of almost every European army. The crisis of 1814 led to his return to active duty, and as *général de division* and Governor of Antwerp he conducted a brilliant defence. In 1815 he rallied to Napoleon and became Minister of the Interior, but was proscribed at the second restoration and spent the remainder of his life in exile, mainly at Magdeburg. His influence on the French military was immense, and his theory of 'active defence' was highly influential in the science of fortification. Napoleon commented upon his honesty and patriotism: 'Carnot was laborious, sincere on every occasion, but unaccustomed to intrigue and easily deceived ... he displayed on every occasion great moral courage ... he spoke and voted against the establishment of the empire; but his conduct, open and manly, gave no uneasiness ... faithful, laborious, full of probity, and always sincere.'[1] Carnot's sons also contributed greatly to their country: the eldest, Sadi (1796–1832), also an engineer officer, was a prominent scientist ('Carnot's Principle' is fundamental in the theory of thermody-

namics); the second, Lazare (1801-88), was a leading politician whose son Marie became fourth president of the Third Republic and was assassinated by an Italian anarchist in 1894; and another son was a distinguished mining engineer and a leading analytical chemist.

1. Las Cases, vol. II, pp. 260–1.

Carnot, H. *Mémoires sur Carnot*. Paris, 1863; Picaud, A. *Carnot, l'organisateur de la victoire*. Paris, 1885–7; Reinhard, M. R. *Le Grand Carnot 1753–1823*. Paris, 1950–2; Tissot, P. F. *Mémoires historiques et militaires sur Carnot*. Paris, 1824; Watson, S. *Carnot 1753–1823*. 1954.

CARRA SAINT-CYR, General Claude, comte (1760–1834)

Commissioned into the French Army in 1774, he served in the War of American Independence and by 1795 had risen to *général de brigade*. He accompanied General Aubert-Dubayet to the Ottoman Empire in a diplomatic capacity (and married his widow in 1799), served as Consul-General in Wallachia and returned to France in 1798. After serving in Italy in 1799 he commanded a brigade of Monnier's division at Marengo (two battalions of the 19th *Demi-Brigade Légère*), and when Monnier fell from favour with Napoleon was credited with commanding the right flank. In 1803 he became *général de division*, in 1806 Governor of Magdeburg and in 1808 a baron; in 1809 he led the 2nd Division of IV Corps at Aspern–Essling with distinction, and at Wagram. As Governor of Hamburg he fell from favour in 1813 when he lost the city, and later permitted some 2,000 men to be killed or captured as they advanced on Lüneburg, by not supporting them; but did return to service under Vandamme and retired only in 1832, having served as Governor of French Guiana 1814–19.

Bayet, comte F. du. *Les Généraux Albert Du Bayer, Carra St. Cyr, et Charpentier*. Paris, 1902

CARRIER, Jean-Baptiste (1756–94)

A lawyer before the French Revolution, he was a Jacobin Deputy to the Convention who voted for the death of the king and was prominent in the overthrow of the Girondins. In October 1793 he was sent to Nantes to extinguish revolt, and there gained a fearful reputation; finding that shooting and guillotining was not the most efficient method of slaughter, he had boatloads of enemies sunk in the Loire, perhaps as many as 4–5,000 unfortunate victims being slain, including women and children, though estimates range up to 15,000; Scott commented that not even the demons of Hell could have matched his conduct. He was recalled in February 1794 and in October put on trial, having attacked Robespierre; he claimed that his excesses in Nantes had been necessary to suppress revolt, but he was convicted and guillotined.

CARTEAUX, General Jean-François (1751–1813)

One of the generals who rose to high rank during the French Revolution without having the necessary skills to justify promotion, he became a painter after some military service under the *ancien régime*. An aide to Lafayette in 1789, after suppressing unrest in Marseilles (where he committed no excesses) he became *général de division* in 1793. As commander at Toulon he encountered Napoleon, who was his chief of artillery; here Carteaux revealed his ignorance (Bourrienne remarked that there was nothing martial about him) and argued against Napoleon's plans, but even Madame Carteaux took Napoleon's part against him ('Let the young man alone, he knows more about it than you do, for he never asks your advice'![1] Carteaux was then transferred to the Army of Italy, then the Alps, was disgraced and imprisoned but later held a number of commands, including administrator of Piombino (1803–5) before retiring in 1810.

1. Las Cases, vol. I, p. 92.

CASABIANCA, Commodore Louis de (1762–98)

Best known as the subject of a poem, he was a Corsican who served in the French Navy during the War of American Independence, became a captain in 1792 and represented Corsica at the Convention. He achieved immortality as captain of the 120-gun *L'Orient*, Brueys' flagship, at Aboukir Bay. Conflicting accounts exist of exactly what happened, but supposedly his 10-year-old son Giacomo would not leave his wounded father, or vice versa, when the ship began to burn; other accounts suggest that they did leave but drowned before they could be rescued. The devotion of the son was the subject of Felicia Hemans' poem *Casabianca*, which is perhaps better known by its first line, 'The boy stood on the burning deck'. Louis' uncle, **General comte Raphael de Casabianca (1738–1825)**, was appointed commander in Corsica by the French revolutionary government in place of Paoli, and became *général de division* after his defence of Calvi against the British. He served in Italy 1794–6, entered the senate and became comte in 1806. He supported Napoleon in 1815 but was reconciled with the monarchy thereafter.

CASTANOS, General Francisco Xavier, Duke of Bailen (1756–1852)

One of the foremost Spanish commanders of the era, he was trained in Germany and as commander of the Army of Andalusia on 21 July 1808 compelled the French general Dupont to surrender at Bailen. This, the high point of Castaños' career, albeit at the very beginning of his period of command, caused a sensation and provided the title of his dukedom. Thereafter he was not so successful, relinquishing command of the Army of the Centre after his defeat at the Tudela (23 November 1808). In January 1810 he saved the members of the Central Junta from a mob, and was appointed a member of the Regency until his deposition in September 1810. In February 1811 he succeeded La Romana as Captain-General of Estremadura, and collaborated with Beresford at Albuera. Described by Lejeune as 'a very intelligent man, with prepossessing and dignified manners',[1] he enjoyed Wellington's confidence, who could rely upon him while possessing no illusions about his military limitations. In spring 1812 the Galician, Estremaduran and Castilian commands were unified under Castaños (as Wellington had recommended), but in June 1813 he was replaced for political reasons; Wellington lamented the fact, writing to War Minister Juan O'Donoju that Castaños 'has served his country in close concert with me for the last three years, and who in the whole course of that time has never differed in opinion from me on any subject of importance,'[2] and called it a 'harsh and unjust' decision.[3] Castaños continued to serve his country in the years after the Peninsular War, as a member of the Council of State (from 1825), President of the Council of Castile (1843) and as tutor to Queen Isabella II.

1. Lejeune, vol. II, p. 105. 2. Wellington, 2 July 1813, vol. X, p. 492. 3.

Ibid., 24 June 1813, to Henry Wellesley, p. 564.

Priego y Llovera, P. *El Grande de España: Capitan-General Castaño.... Madrid, 1958.

CASTIGLIONE, duc de, see AUGEREAU

CASTLEREAGH, Robert Stewart, Viscount, 2nd Marquess of Londonderry (1769–1822)

ROBERT, VISCOUNT CASTLEREAGH (ENGRAVING BY T. W. HARLAND AFTER LAWRENCE)

One of the leading British statesmen of the age, he adopted the courtesy title of Viscount Castlereagh when his father became Earl of Londonderry in August 1796. His early career was concerned with his native Ireland, commanding the Londonderry Militia and entering the Irish House of Commons when barely 21 years of age. He acted as Chief Secretary for Ireland and was much concerned with the suppression of the 1798 rebellion, then entered the Westminster parliament as MP for Down. An inveterate opponent of the French, he was Secretary for War and the Colonies from 1805 until the fall of the ministry after Pitt's death, and occupied the same post under Portland in 1807. He was a major supporter of the Peninsula expedi on – Wellington remarked that a brother could not have done more but his reputation was damaged by Walcheren and the duel with Canning, and he resigned. In March 1812 he returned as Foreign Secretary – an office held until his death – and led the House of Commons after Perceval's murder. As the leading influence in the foreign policy of Liverpool's ministry, he played a crucial role in European politics, devoted to the elimination of France as a military threat and being instrumental in the maintenance of a united front against Napoleon. The Treaty of Chaumont, negotiated when he visited Allied headquarters, he regarded as his own, and as the senior British representative at the Congress of Vienna helped maintain union against Napoleon in 1815 despite the revelation of the secret treaty of January 1815 between Great Britain, Austria and France against the territorial aspirations of Russia and Prussia. He succeeded as 2nd Marquess of Londonderry (a title granted in January 1816) in April 1821, and continued in office until August 1822 when, exhausted and perhaps suffering from mental illness, he cut his throat with a penknife, a sad end to a career of crucial importance in the outcome of the Napoleonic Wars. His half-brother was Charles Stewart, Wellington's adjutant-general.

Alison, A. *Lives of Lord Castlereagh and Sir Charles Stewart, the Second and Third Marquesses of Londonderry*. Edinburgh, 1861; Bartlett, C. J. *Castlereagh*. London, 1966; Castlereagh, Viscount. *Correspondence, Despatches and Other Papers of Viscount Castlereagh*, ed. 3rd Marquess. London, 1848–53 (first four vols. entitled *Memoirs and Correspondence of Viscount Castlereagh*); Derry, J. W. *Castlereagh*. London, 1976; Hinde, W. *Castlereagh*. London 1981; Hyde, H. M. *The Strange Death of Lord Castlereagh*. London, 1959; Webster, C. K. *The Foreign Policy of Castlereagh 1812–1815*. London, 1931

CATHCART, General William Schaw, 1st Earl (1755–1843)

WILLIAM, 1ST EARL CATHCART

Succeeding his father, General Charles, 9th Baron Cathcart, in 1776, he served in the British Army during the War of American Independence, in The Netherlands 1793–5 (promoted to major-general), and in the Hanoverian expedition. Lieutenant-general from 1801, he commanded in Ireland 1803–5 and in Scotland 1807–12, the latter duty interrupted when he was chosen to lead the expedition to Denmark. Rewarded with a viscountcy and promoted to general, in 1812 he was sent to Russia as Ambassador (which post he held until 1820), accompanying the Allied HQ throughout the campaigns of 1813–14 and exercising diplomacy towards the maintenance of a united front against the French. He was elevated to an earldom in July 1814. His eldest son, William (1782–1804), a captain in the Royal Navy, died of yellow fever in Jamaica. The second son,

General Charles Murray Cathcart (1783–1859), who succeeded as 2nd Earl, joined the 2nd Life Guards in 1800, served in the Mediterranean, Walcheren, the Peninsula and as assistant quartermaster-general at Waterloo, and was CinC Canada 1846–9. From 1807 he was known as Lord Greenock, from which title the mineral Greenockite (cadmium sulphide) was named, he being an amateur scientist who detected such crystals in 1840. The fourth son, **Lieutenant-General Sir George Cathcart (1794–1854)**, served as ADC to his father 1813–14 and to Wellington at Waterloo; Governor and CinC at the Cape in 1852, he wrote *Commentaries on the War in Russia and Germany in 1812 and 1813* (London, 1850), and was killed at Inkerman while commanding the 4th Division.

CATHELINEAU, Jacques (1759–93)

An itinerant salesman, he felt impelled to leave his wife and five children to join what he appears to have regarded as a royalist crusade at the time of the Vendéen rebellion. Although militarily uneducated he was evidently a powerful presence: 'Never was there a more gentle, modest or virtuous man, perfectly unassuming, and commanding the more respect on that account. He possessed a very superior understanding, a powerful eloquence, and natural talents for war. The peasants adored him, and felt towards him the most profound respect. His reputation for piety was such, that the soldiers called him "The Saint of Anjou", and placed themselves, when they could, near him in battle, imagining that they could not be wounded at the side of so holy a man.'[1] After some notable successes, he was appointed generalissimo of the royalist

forces, but was shot leading the attack on Nantes (29 June 1793) and died some two weeks later.
1. La Rochejaquelein, p. 113.

CAULAINCOURT, General Armand-Augustin-Louis, marquis de, duc de Vicence

ARMAND DE CAULAINCOURT (ENGRAVING BY G. KRUELL AFTER GÉRARD)

(1773–1827)

The son of General Gabriel-Louis de Caulaincourt, who embraced the French Revolution but retired in 1792, he entered the French Army at the age of 14, was deprived of his commission and arrested as an aristocrat, but enlisted in the ranks and rose again under the protection of Hoche. After undertaking a diplomatic mission to Russia, he was appointed aide to Napoleon upon his return (August 1802), and was unjustly blamed for his very peripheral role in the kidnapping of the duc d'Enghien. Napoleon's Master of Horse 1804–13, he was *général de division* in 1808 and became Duke of Vicenza in 1808; Ambassador to Russia 1807–11, he served as one of Napoleon's closest aides in the 1812 campaign. In 1813–14 he represented Napoleon at all the important diplomatic negotiations with the Allies, replaced Duroc as Grand Marshal of the Palace in

1813, and was Foreign Minister from November 1813 until the abdication, and again during the Hundred Days. Proscribed after the second restoration, he was allowed to return to France after the intervention of the Tsar; he wrote a notable account of the 1812–14 period in his memoirs. Although known as Napoleon's chief diplomatic aide, he was also a very experienced soldier, and by the age of 29 had served in thirteen campaigns and been twice wounded. At Napoleon's side throughout the 1812 campaign, he showed remarkable fortitude when informed of his brother's death at Borodino, sitting completely impassive in his saddle but for tears streaming down his cheeks; concerned at his distress Napoleon asked if he wanted to retire, to which Caulaincourt made no reply, merely half-raised his hat in a gesture of thanks, and loyally remained at his post.

Caulaincourt, General A. A. L. *Memoirs of General de Caulaincourt, Duke of Vicenza*, ed. J. Hanoteau, trans. H. Miles and G. Libaire. London, 1935–8 (memoirs originally published as *Souvenirs du duc de Vicence*, 1837–40); abridged version is *With Napoleon in Russia*, ed. G. Libaire. New York, 1935

CAULAINCOURT, General Auguste-Jean-Gabriel, comte de (1777–1812)

Brother of Armand de Caulaincourt, he served in the French cavalry from 1792, was wounded at Marengo, and from 1804 served Louis Bonaparte, becoming his Master of Horse in Holland. *Général de brigade* in 1808, *de division* in 1809, he served in the Peninsula and was ennobled as comte in 1810. In the 1812 campaign he superintended Napoleon's HQ until sent to replace Montbrun at Borodino; he found Montbrun's aides in tears at

the death of their general. 'Follow me,' he told them; 'weep not fo him, but come and avenge hi death!' Murat ordered him to lea his heavy cavalry against the Grea Redoubt; he replied: 'You shall se me there presently, dead or alive.' Leading the charge, he was sho dead as he entered the redoubt.
1. Ségur, p. 348.

CAVENDISH-BENTINCK, General Lord William, see BENTINCK

CHAMBARLHAC de LAUBE-SPIN, General Jacques-Antoine, baron de (1754–1826)

Having served in the royal army he was distinguished by service in the French Army during the revolutionary wars, notably in Italy and was promoted to *général d* *brigade* on the field of Arcola. Hi best-known service was probably as a divisional commander unde Victor at Marengo, though Coignet of the 96th *Demi-brigade* from his perspective as an ordinary 'ranker', was unimpressed by his performance at this battle claiming that after his orderly was killed, Chambarlhac disappeared and was only seen again after the fighting was over, whereupon the 96th fired a volley in hi direction. Nevertheless, he wa promoted to *général de division* in 1803 and served in a number o staff appointments, receiving a barony in 1811. He was unemployed after the Bourbon restoration.

CHAMPAGNY, Jean-Baptiste de Nompère de, duc de Cadore (1756–1834)

After service in the French Navy during the War of American Independence, and some politica activity during the revolutionary period, he served as French Ambassador to Vienna 1801–4, and from August of the latter year was Napoleon's Minister of the Inte-

r. He proved so capable that in
gust 1807 he succeeded Tal-
rand as Foreign Minister, until
placed in 1811, and was made
c de Cadore. He attracted some
rdly unbiased criticism for
ecuting Napoleon's foreign
licy: 'Falsehood, perfidy, injus-
e, spoliation in the worst accep-
ion of the terms, distinguished
s official career ... he unblush-
gly laid down the principle, that
at which policy rendered
cessary, justice must, of course,
thorize"... which the very thief
his career to the gallows does
ot avow to himself.'[1] He
pported the Bourbons at the
st restoration but rejoined
apoleon for the Hundred Days,
r which he was deprived of his
sition as a peer of France until
19. Talleyrand once remarked
at Champagny did in twenty
urs what Napoleon had told
m to do in twenty-four, whereas
(Talleyrand) would have taken
ree weeks.[2]

Anon., pp. 147–8. 2. Palmer, A.
etternich. London, 1972, p. 62.

**HAMPIONNET, General Jean-
tienne (1762–1800).**

orn in Valencia, after service in the
ench royal army he was elected
command a battalion during the
rly Revolutionary Wars, and rose
prominence after service on the
hine. In command of the Army of
ome, he was so successful that he
ptured Naples, leading to the
tablishment of the Parthenopean
epublic (23 January 1798), where-
oon his command was re-desig-
ated as the independent Army of
aples. Perhaps too assiduous in
s duties for his own good, he fell
ctim to political manoeuvring,
as recalled and sent for trial, but
e new Directory of June 1799
stored him to duty as
ommander of the Army of the
ps; worn out by exertion and the
nequal struggle with which he
ad been charged, he died in

January 1800 at Antibes. The
duchesse d'Abrantès remarked of
the unfairness of the Directory in
sacrificing the glory of one of the
nation's loyal servants for resisting
the schemes of avaricious politicians.

**CHANDLER, Brigadier General
John (1760–1841)**
Born in Massachusetts, he was an
itinerant blacksmith who
attained considerable affluence,
served in Congress 1805–8,
became a major general of militia
and in November 1812 a regular
brigadier general. A politician
rather than a soldier, he was criticised for possessing little or no
military talent, and on 5 June
1813 at Stony Creek, having been
unhorsed, he was captured when
he wandered into British lines.
He was discharged from the US
Army in June 1815, and represented Maine in the Senate
1820–9.

CHAPPE, Claude (1763–1805)
A member of a French family
which produced a number of
engineers and scientists, Chappé
is remembered as the inventor of
the telegraph, which had important military use. In 1792 he introduced the first mechanical
semaphore, consisting of three
movable arms upon an upright
post, the positions of which each
represented a word or letter; the
22 stations he constructed
between Lille and Paris were so
efficient that news of the capture
of Condé in 1793 took only twenty
minutes to arrive at the capital.
Chappé originally called his invention the Tachygraphe, and was
appointed to superintend the
system; but rival inventors so
questioned the origin of the
scheme that he became depressed
and committed suicide. From
then until 1830 the post of administrator of telegraphs was held in
turn by his four brothers.

**CHARETTE DE LA CONTRIE,
François-Athanase de
(1763–96)**

FRANÇOIS CHARETTE DE LA CONTRIE
(ENGRAVING BY W. GREATBATCH)

A member of an ancient French
family, he served as a naval officer
from 1779 until he left to marry a
wealthy widow in 1790. An ardent
royalist, he emigrated but
returned to France to take part in
the defence of the Tuileries, and
was sought out to help lead the
royalist rebellion in the Vendée.
One of their best leaders, he
commanded the Army of Bas-
Poitou or Army of the Marais, and
even after the general defeat
continued the fight. In the spring
of 1795 he made peace on behalf
of his followers – giving rise to criticism that he had split the royalist
cause – but took the field again
when informed of the projected
expedition to Quiberon. Dismayed
when the comte d'Artois refused
to cross from the Ile d'Yeu to the
mainland, where his presence
would have provided a huge boost
to morale, sending Charette an
ornamental sword instead, the
general remarked that it was actually his death warrant, as the
revolt could not succeed without
the royal presence. Nevertheless,
he bravely continued the struggle,
declining safe passage to England
for himself and his family, until his

small band was ambushed on 23 March 1796. Wounded and captured, he was sentenced to death and shot at Nantes on 30 March. He was reported to have expressed bitterness against the princes who failed to aid him, but his last words before he gave the order to fire were 'Vive le Roi!' His reputation, however, remained undimmed; the marquise de La Rochejaquelein admitted that Charette and Stofflet damaged the cause by their rivalry, but that he: 'acquired immortal glory. The boldness of his measures, his fertility in resources, and constancy, never subdued in the most desperate situations, mark him a great man. Wounded, pursued from place to place, with scarcely twelve companions left, this general was still such an object of fear to the republicans, as to induce them to offer him a million of livres, and a free passage to England; which he refused, choosing to persevere in the unequal struggle.'[1] Napoleon thought Charette 'the only great character, the true hero' of the wars in the Vendée, and when Las Cases remarked that in the navy he had been 'a common-place sort of man, destitute of information, ill-tempered and extremely indolent', Napoleon replied that it demonstrated that 'true decision of character always develops itself in critical circumstances'.[2]

1. La Rochejaquelein, pp. 482–3. 2. Las Cases, vol. IV, pp. 89–90.

Charette, G. *Charette: Roi de la Vendée*. Paris, 1951.

CHARLES IV, King of Spain (1748–1819)

The second son of Charles III of Spain, he succeeded because of the mental incapacity of his elder brother, Don Philip, in 1788. Unfortunately he was not a great deal better; Sir Charles Oman's description of a 'benevolent imbecile' embraces the common

CHARLES IV, KING OF SPAIN
(MEDALLIC PORTRAIT)

perception of his mental capacity and good nature.[1] During his reign he was controlled by his unscrupulous wife, Queen Maria Luisa of Parma (his first cousin), and the chief minister, her 'favourite' Godoy; he seemed conscious only of anything which appeared to attack the dignity of monarchy, preventing liberalisation. By allowing the Queen and Godoy to rule, he abdicated responsibility long before his actual abdication of the throne in favour of his son (18 March 1808); he then withdrew his decision, abdicating again in May in favour of Napoleon, which allowed Joseph Bonaparte to ascend the throne. Charles was kept a virtual prisoner at Valençay in France, accepted a pension from Napoleon and, with his son now heading the family, died in Rome in January 1819.

1. Oman, vol. I, p. 13.

CHARLES X, King of France, see ARTOIS

CHARLES XIII, King of Sweden (1748–1818)

Brother of King Gustavus III and nephew of Frederick the Great, Charles, Duke of Sudermania, commanded the Swedish Navy during the 1788 war with Russia, and acted as regent between the assassination of Gustavus III (1792)

CHARLES XIII, KING OF SWEDEN
(MEDALLIC PORTRAIT)

and the coming of age of his so Gustavus IV (1796), during whi time real power resided with t Minister Gustaf Adolf Reuterhol After the deposition of Gustavus on the grounds of insanity (March 1809), the Duke of Sude mania was again appoint temporary regent by t conspiracy of army officers whi had dethroned the king; and on June was elected as King Charl XIII. By this time he was ailing a childless, and relinquished t reins of government as soon Bernadotte was elected as Crow Prince. By the Treaty of Kiel (January 1814) Norway w acquired by Sweden, so th Charles became the first king the united state; but he w monarch only in name, and di in February 1818.

CHARLES (Karl Ludwig), Fiel Marshal, Archduke of Austria, Duke of Teschen (1771–1847)

The most outstanding Austri commander of the era, he w born in Florence, the third son Emperor Leopold II and broth of Francis II; adopted by the Du of Saxe–Teschen (to whose duc he succeeded in 1822), he w trained as a soldier from yout Charles commanded a brigade Jemappes and, as Governor of th Austrian Netherlands, was disti guished at Neerwinden, b feated at Wattignies and ·urus. Field·marshal from 1796, led the Army of the Rhine, nning the actions of Rastadt, ·berg and Würzburg, then mmanded in Italy without ccess before returning to the ine theatre and more victories. · retired temporarily from mmand following difficulties of llaboration with his Russian ·ies, served as Governor of hemia and Minister of War, but 1805 commanded in Italy. llowing the defeat of that year led the re-organisation and construction of the Austrian ·ces, probably his most impor- ·t contribution, and was in ·erall command in 1809. He ·hieved the rare success of ·licting a defeat on Napoleon, at ·pern–Essling (which had an ·ctric effect throughout Europe), ·t was overwhelmed at Wagram. ·ereupon he retired from field mmand, but his defeat should ·t obscure his talents as a ·neral, and especially as a ·former, when he had to contend ·th reactionary elements within ·e establishment. His military ·itings were influential, though ·s theories, like his strategy ·lowing Aspern–Essling, might · criticised for being over

cautious; Clausewitz claimed that he attached more importance to the possession of ground than to the destruction of the enemy (the opposite of Napoleon's strategy), which may have had a malign influence in the war of 1866. This, however, contrasted with his courage in battle, the most cele- brated example being his rallying of Regt. No. 15 (Zach) at Aspern– Essling, by grasping their colours, although he always made light of the story, saying that a man of his small stature could hardly have carried so heavy a flag! In 1815 he married Princess Henrietta of Nassau–Weilburg, and their eldest son, Archduke Albert (Friedrich Rudolf Albrecht, 1817–95), victor of Custozza (1866), was one of the leading military figures of his generation.

Angeli, M. von. *Erzherzog Carl also Feldherr und Heeresorgan- isator.* Vienna, 1896–7; Criste, O. *Erzherzog Carl von Oesterreich.* Vienna and Leipzig, 1912; Charles, Archduke. *Principes de la Stratégie ...*, trans. Jomini and Koch. Paris, 1818; *Ausgewählte Schriften weiland Sr. K. Honheit Erzh. Carl v. Oesterreich*, ed. Archdukes Albert and William. Vienna, 1862 (compi- lation of the Archduke's writings); Rothenberg, G. E. *Napoleon's Great Adversaries: The Archduke Charles and the Austrian Army 1792–1814.* London, 1982 (not a biography *per se* but the leading study of the subject in English)

CHARLES AUGUSTUS (Karl August), Duke of Saxe-Weimar-Eisenach (1757–1828)

One of the most influential princes of the smaller German states, he succeeded his father in infancy. A man of many talents and liberal disposition, he was a patron of Goethe and Schiller and employed Johann Herder to reform his state's education, and was equally influential in politics, as a leader of the 'league of princes' (*Fürsten-*

bund), formed in 1785 under Fred- erick the Great, in opposition to the Holy Roman Empire. As a Prussian general officer he was present at Valmy and Kaiser- slautern, and in the Jena campaign. To avoid losing his land he was forced to join the Confed- eration of the Rhine (it was said that only the pleading of his duchess, Louise of Hesse–Darm- stadt, prevented Napoleon from deposing him), but abandoned the French alliance in 1813 and commanded an Allied corps in The Netherlands in 1814. The Congress of Vienna elevated his state to a grand-duchy, he became the first German prince to grant a liberal constitution (5 May 1816), and at his death was mourned as a great humanitarian. His son, **'Bernhard of Saxe–Weimar' (1792–1862)**, was distinguished as a soldier, notably when commanding a brigade of the 2nd Netherlands Division in the Waterloo campaign, particularly at Quatre Bras; he rose to command the forces in the Dutch East Indies. His son, William Augustus Edward (1823–1902), served in the British Army in the Crimea and attained the rank of field marshal in 1897.

CHARLES JOHN, Crown Prince of Sweden, see BERNADOTTE

CHARLET, Nicolas-Toussaint (1792–1845)

This well-known painter, engraver and lithographer was the son of a French cavalryman whose early death in the service left his family in poor circumstances. Military subjects formed a great part of his work; a die-hard Bonapartist who had served in the National Guard and fought at the Clichy Gate in 1814, he studied under Gros and became best known for his mili- tary prints, including such works as *Costumes Militaires* (1817), *La Vielle Armée Française, Costumes*

ARCHDUKE CHARLES
(ENGRAVING BY T. W. HARLAND AFTER KELLERHOVEN)

de l'ex-Garde, Costumes Militaires Françaises (1818), etc. Although his work tends to glorify Napoleon and especially the Imperial Guard, it is most distinctive, often 'atmospheric' and of high artistic quality.

CHARTRES, duc de, see LOUIS-PHILIPPE

CHASSE, General David-Henri, baron de (1765–1849)

Originally in the Dutch Army, Chassé served in the French Army in the last decade of the 18th century before returning to Dutch service, in which he became major-general in 1806. In the Peninsula he attained the French rank of *général de brigade* and received a barony, and was distinguished at Maya. He was wounded at Arcis-sur-Aube, but is best known as one of those who by a quirk of politics in 1815 fought against the forces alongside which he had served most of his career. As a lieutenant-general he commanded the 3rd Netherlands Division with distinction during the Hundred Days; his advance in the later stages of the Battle of Waterloo helped repel the final assault of the Imperial Guard. He defended the citadel of Antwerp during the Belgian rebellion, holding out from October 1830 until forced to surrender in December 1832.

CHASSELOUP-LAUBAT, General François, marquis de (1754–1833)

One of the most noted military engineers of his generation, he entered the French engineers in 1774 and despite his noble background retained his commission during the Revolution. Distinguished in the early campaigns, he commanded the engineers at the siege of Mainz (1796) and became chief engineer of the Army of Italy, and *général de division* in 1799. After the 1800 campaign he spent much time in Italy, on fortification work, but served with Napoleon in 1806–7 (at the sieges of Colberg, Danzig and Stralsund) and in Russia in 1812. He accepted the Bourbon restoration and remained loyal to them in 1815; ennobled as comte by Napoleon, Louis XVIII honoured him with a marquisate, but despite taking no part in the last campaigns he did vote against the condemnation of Ney. His thoughts on artillery and fortification were first published as *Correspondance d'un Général Français* in Paris in 1801, and reprinted thereafter; his style of fortification was centred upon the use of strong bastions and outworks.

CHATEAUBRIAND, François-René, vicomte de (1768–1848)

The most celebrated French literary figure of his age, he was one of those who reacted against the excesses of the French Revolution, though not opposed to it in its early stages. An aristocrat, commissioned into the French Army in 1788, he left for America in 1791 but returned to oppose the Revolution, being wounded at Thionville as an officer of emigrants. His brother died on the scaffold, his family were imprisoned, and Chateaubriand sought refuge in England until his return to France in 1800. His literary works attracting notice – he became a leading figure in the French Romantic movement – he was appointed attaché to the French embassy in Rome in 1803, and subsequently envoy to the Valais, but he resigned in protest at the execution of the duc d'Enghien (Napoleon accused Chateaubriand of 'malevolence and want of integrity' during his period in Rome.)[1] Later writings caused offence to Napoleon, notably a comparison with Nero in 1807 and an address on Chénier in 1811 which was so anti-Bona-partist that Napoleon forbade publication. Chateaubriand w[elcomed the Bourbon restoratior[Louis XVIII claimed that [his supportive pamphlet he wrote w[as worth 100,000 men – but [he temporarily fell from favour ov[er criticism of royalist excess[es. Thereafter he served as Amba[ssador to Berlin, London a[nd Rome, briefly as Foreign Minist[er and as French representative [at the Congress of Verona.

1. Las Cases, vol. II, p. 232.

Chateaubriand, F. R. *Mém-oires.* 1849–50, English trans. Teixeira de Mattos, 1902; Paint[er, G. D. *Chateaubriand: a Biograph[y,* London, 1977

CHATHAM, General John Pitt, 2nd Earl of (1756–1835)

Eldest son of William Pitt, who[m he succeeded as 2nd Earl in 177[8; he pursued both a political a[nd military career (rising to the ra[nk of general in January 1812). In t[he administration of his broth[er William he was First Lord of t[he Admiralty (1788–94), Lord Pri[vy Seal (to 1796) and Lord Preside[nt of the Council (to 1801). In 1799 [he commanded a brigade in t[he expedition to North Holland, w[as Master-General of the Ordnan[ce 1801–6 and 1807–10, was appa[r-ently suggested for command [of the Peninsula expedition, and [in 1809 was appointed to lead t[he military element of the Walcher[en expedition. (It was suggested th[at Canning secured this appoi[nt-ment, expecting that its succe[ss would enable Chatham to becom[e prime minister, in which ca[se Canning himself would have exe[r-cised the actual power.)[1] Althoug[h Chatham had been a valuab[le member of the Cabinet and a goo[d Master-General, he was extreme[ly indolent, was said never to trav[el without a mistress and was [so unpunctual that he was known [as 'the late Lord Chatham'; but wh[at-ever his abilities, the project w[as

mplicated by factors outside his
ntrol and the expedition was a
saster. Subsequently he served
Governor of Gibraltar 1820–35.
For an example of this rumour
e Stanhope, p. 289; Wellington
ems to have believed it: see
lesmere, p. 130.

HAUMETTE, Pierre-Gaspard
763–94)

njoying a varied career –
cluding the study of medicine
d the law before he came to
rominence during the French
evolution – his abilities gave him
nsiderable influence in Paris,
here he was elected President of
e Commune. An excellent
rator, who spoke in favour of
ood morals, industry and patrio-
sm, and a social reformer, he is
erhaps best known for his
tempts to replace Roman
atholicism with the worship of
eason, though he acceded to the
rinciple of freedom of private
orship. A leader of the attacks on
e Girondins, he was himself
ttacked by Robespierre and
gether with the Hébertists, was
ndemned and executed on 13
pril 1794.

HAUNCEY, Commodore Isaac
772–1840)

orn in Connecticut, he went to
a in the merchant service before
e was commissioned in the US
avy in 1798. He served with
istinction in the Mediterranean
nd was head of the Brooklyn navy
ard when appointed to command
e naval forces on the Lakes in
e War of 1812. He took
ommand at Sackett's Harbor in
october 1812, created a flotilla and
was able to oppose the British
otilla of Sir James Yeo with
uccess, eventually blockading the
ritish at Kingston. After the war
e again served in the Mediter-
anean and from 1833 was a
ember of the board of naval
ommissioners, of which he was

president at his death in January
1840.

CHENIER, André (1762–94)

The famous French poet, whose
literary reputation grew after his
death, served briefly in the army,
and at the outbreak of the French
Revolution was secretary to the
ambassador in London. He
returned to France in 1790 and
was antagonistic towards the
direction of political change,
believing that the early stages of
the Revolution had achieved the
necessary reforms. In March 1794
he was arrested, tried upon a false
charge of conspiracy and guillotined on 25 July; during his
imprisonment he wrote some of
his best works, including the
poem *La Jeune Captive*, which
became famous after his death.
His brother, **Marie-Joseph-
Blaise Chénier (1764–1811)**, had
a lesser literary reputation, and
also had a brief military career. He
supported the Revolution and
displayed his republican sympathies in his play *Charles IX*, was a
member of the Convention and
Council of Five Hundred, voted for
the death of Louis XVI and in 1795
composed a report advocating
strictures upon *émigrés* and
clergy. His political career declined over suspicions of moderation, and in 1802 over opposition
to Napoleon, but he was later
reconciled with the Emperor for a
time and was appointed inspector-
general of public education. His
work included national songs,
most notably the 'Chant du
Départ'.

CHICHAGOV, Admiral Pavel
(1767–1849)

A great Anglophile, this Russian
commander had been raised in
England, married a Miss Proby in
Paddington and later became a
naturalised British subject. He was
in command of the Russian
squadron which co-operated with

the British in The Netherlands
expedition of 1799 and had been
Russia's Navy Minister 1808–12,
but his significance results from
his role in the opposition to
Napoleon's invasion of Russia. In
1812 he was appointed to
command the Army of the Danube
(or Moldavia) which was freed for
operations against Napoleon by
the Peace of Bucharest which
ended hostilities with the Ottoman
Empire. He was perhaps not the
ideal choice: his subordinate
Langeron stated that he had only
limited knowledge of military
affairs, was prone to conceiving
impracticable plans, harsh and
autocratic and too obstinate to
take advice; but was so completely
honest that he tended to despise
his own nation for the corruption
he believed was rife. In 1812 he
marched north, pushed back
Schwarzenberg's corps on the
right flank of the *Grande Armée*
and attempted to block Napoleon's escape-route at the
crossing of the Berezina. He
allowed himself to be surprised
at Borisov, having unwisely
bivouacked in a too forward position, and was deceived about the
French dispositions, so that
despite his efforts the *Grande
Armée* was able to fight its way
through. His name – which may
be found with a number of
different spellings, for example
'Tchitchagoff' or 'Tchitchagov' –
so perplexed Napoleon that he
was unable to pronounce it,
always referring instead to 'the
Admiral'.

Tchitchagoff (*sic*), P. *Mémoires
de l'Amiral Tchitchagoff*. Leipzig,
1862

CHLOPICKI, General Jozef
Gregorz (1771–1854)

His first military service was in the
army of his native Poland in the
1792–4 war, after which, like many
Polish *émigrés*, he joined the
Polish Legion in Italy. He won

considerable distinction before attaining command of the 1st Regt. of the Vistula Legion, which he led in the Peninsula, notably at Saragossa: tasked with repelling a relief-force, he defeated Palafox at Epila (23–4 June 1808), for which and for the storming of the city (1809) he was awarded a French barony and the rank of *général de brigade*. He played an important role in Suchet's victory at Saguntum, and in 1812 commanded a brigade of the Vistula Legion attached to the Imperial Guard, being wounded at Smolensk. In 1814 he entered Russian service as a general officer, but was involved in the Polish rebellion of 1830, briefly as its head, and was severely wounded at Grochow; after which he retired, resentful of subordinates whom he considered to have let him down. His name is sometimes rendered as 'Chlopiski'

CHRISTIAN VII, King of Denmark (1749–1808)

CHRISTIAN VII, KING OF DENMARK
(MEDALLIC PORTRAIT)

Son of Frederick V, whom he succeeded in 1766, at the time of the Napoleonic Wars he was insane following a life of debauchery and drunkenness; he had divorced his wife, Caroline Matilda (1751–75), sister of George III of Great Britain, after she had been imprisoned for some time.

As he was incapable of ruling, power rested with ministers such as Bernstorff and the Crown Prince Frederick, who succeeded to the throne as Frederick VI on Christian's death in 1808.

CHRISTIAN VIII, King of Denmark (1786–1848)

The son of Frederick VI, in 1813 he was sent to Norway as Governor to cement the allegiance of that territory with Denmark, in the face of a movement which favoured union with Sweden. Instead, he favoured liberalism and those seeking independence, and was elected King of Norway (May 1814); but was unable to resist Sweden which, by the Treaty of Kiel (14 January 1814) had been granted Norway as a 'punishment' for Denmark's support of Napoleon. After barely two weeks' hostilities, negotiations ensured that Norway passed to the Swedish crown, albeit with the maintenance of their own constitution; Christian resigned his crown and lived virtually in retirement until he succeeded Frederick VI as King Christian VIII of Denmark in 1839.

CHURCH, General Sir Richard (1784–1873)

Although probably most famous as 'the liberator of Greece', his first contact with that nation came when he was an officer in the British Army. Born of a Quaker family in Cork, he ran away to the army and his father purchased him a commission in the 13th Foot. He served in Egypt, became a captain in the Royal Corsican Rangers (with whom he fought at Maida), and in 1807 was assistant QMG to the expedition which took the Ionian Islands. He conceived a plan for a corps of Greeks in British service; the Duke of York's Greek Light Infantry was formed in March 1810, with Church in command, and he led it (and was severely wounded in the arm) at

the storming of Santa Maura. Th[e] unit was taken officially on to th[e] British establishment in Februar[y] 1811, with Church as 2i/c, and [in] 1813 he formed a 2nd Regt. The[ir] disbandment (October 181[5–] January 1816) left him unem[-] ployed, and subsequently h[e] served in the Neapolitan Army as [a] general and in 1827 accepte[d] command of the Greek forces [in] the War of Independence. H[e] passed the remainder of his life [in] Greece, and died in Athens. He [is] probably the subject of a paintin[g] by Denis Dighton showing th[e] most exotic military costume [of] the entire Napoleonic er[a,] presumably worn as a field office[r] of the Greek Light Infantr[y,] including a version of Gree[k] national dress, classical helme[t,] cuirass and greaves (see Haswe[ll] Miller, A. E., and Dawnay, N. [P.] *Military Drawings and Paintings [in] the Royal Collection*, vol. [I,] London, 1966).

Church, E. M. *Chapters in a[n] Adventurous Life*. Edinburg[h] 1895; Poole, S. L. *Sir Richar[d] Church*. London, 1890

CLAIRFAIT, Field Marshal François, see CLERFAYT

CLARENCE, Duke of, see WILLIAM IV

CLARK, George Rogers (1752–1818)

This American frontier militar[y] leader, who played a considerab[le] part in the War of American Inde[-] pendence, was involved briefly i[n] the Revolutionary Wars when i[n] 1793 he was appointed a genera[l] in the French Army with the inten[-] tion of raising a force to attac[k] Spanish possessions west of th[e] Mississippi; but the US govern[-] ment demanded that he sur[-] render his commission, an[d] nothing came of the plan. He wa[s] the brother of William Clar[k] (1770–1838) the explorer and join[t] eader of the Lewis and Clark expedition.

CLARKE, Field Marshal Sir Alured (1745?–1832)

Little is known of his background. He was commissioned in the British Army in 1759 and served in the War of American Independence. As a major-general in 1795, he was sent with a force to India, with orders to reinforce the Cape if necessary, and his arrival in support of Craig secured the capture of that territory. He then proceeded to India, commanding in Bengal in 1797 and as lieutenant-general was CinC India 1797–1801 before returning home. He was full general from April 1802 and became field marshal in July 1830.

CLARKE, Marshal Henri-Jacques-Guillaume, duc de Feltre (1765–1818)

HENRI CLARKE (ENGRAVING BY C. STATE AFTER G. D. J. DESCAMPS)

Descended from an English baronet, he was born in Landrecies, the son of an ex-officer of the French Army, and was himself commissioned at an early age. He served with the Army of the Rhine under Custine, temporarily fell from favour but was appointed to the Topographical Bureau and became *général*

de division in December 1795. In November 1796 he was sent to Italy by the Directory to report on General Bonaparte, but became instead a loyal supporter, and upon Napoleon's assumption of power was appointed a councillor of state and ambassador to Etruria. After serving as Governor of Vienna and Berlin 1805–6, he succeeded Berthier as War Minister in 1807, holding that position with some distinction until 1814, though proving somewhat ineffective without Napoleon's guiding hand at the time of the Malet conspiracy. He joined the Bourbons in 1814 and was appointed their War Minister in 1815, accompanying Louis XVIII to Ghent. He retained the post until 1817, becoming a Marshal in 1816, and somewhat unpopular for his treatment of old officers. Much more of a bureaucrat than a soldier, he was said to be rather pompous (Napoleon made fun of his boast of descent from the Plantagenets); and, remembering his harsh governance of Berlin, it was reported that King Frederick William III told him in 1814 that 'If I have any advice to give you, it is that you never again shew your face in Prussia.'[1]

1. Anon., p. 153.

CLARKE, Mary Anne (c.1776–1852)

Née Thompson, she was the wife of a bankrupt stonemason, 'a very pretty, sprightly, gaily-disposed girl, very fond of shewing herself, and attracting attention',[1] when she became the mistress of Frederick, Duke of York. He paid her £1,000 per annum from 1802, but such was her extravagant lifestyle that she began to swindle tradesmen and finally to take bribes against a promise to use her influence on the Duke to gain military, civil and ecclesiastical preferments. On becoming aware of this the Duke broke off the rela-

MARY ANNE CLARKE

tionship and promised her a pension of £400 p.a., but, besieged by creditors, she attempted to blackmail him. When this failed, her latest friend, Colonel Gwylym Lloyd Wardle, Radical MP for Okehampton, raised the matter in parliament; a committee of inquiry established that bribes had been paid but that there was no evidence of the Duke being influenced; but he had to resign as CinC, albeit temporarily. Mrs. Clarke continued her career and in February 1814 was sentenced to nine months in Marshalsea prison for blackmailing the Chancellor of the Exchequer for Ireland. She died at Boulogne on 21 June 1852.

1. *Gent's Mag.*, Feb 1809, p. 164.

CLARY, Désirée, Queen of Sweden (1777–1860)

She was a daughter of a Marseilles banker whose family had been befriended by Joseph Bonaparte. Désirée was at first betrothed to him, but Napoleon persuaded Joseph to marry her elder, plainer, sister Julie, who had a larger dowry. Napoleon himself then became betrothed to Désirée, and her subsequent suitors included Junot and Marmont. In August 1798, however, she married Bernadotte instead, and thus in due course became Queen of Sweden. It was said that Napoleon

DÉSIRÉE CLARY (ENGRAVING BY R. G. TIETZE AFTER GÉRARD)

was more lenient with Bernadotte than he would otherwise have been because of his old affection for her. For much of her married life she lived in Paris, but lived in Sweden after Bernadotte's death; their son became King Oscar I of Sweden. She later used a Latin version of her name, Desideria.

Bearne, C. M. *A Queen of Napoleon's Court: The Life Story of Désirée Bernadotte*. London, 1905

CLAUSEL, Marshal Bertrand, comte (1772–1842)

First distinguished in the early Revolutionary Wars, notably in the Pyrenees, he served in Italy (1798–9) and San Domingo, and as a *général de division* from December 1802 in Naples (1806) and Dalmatia (1808–9), but he is best known for his Peninsula service. He commanded the 1st Division of VIII Corps (1810–11), later the 2nd Division of the Army of Portugal, to command of which he succeeded at Salamanca after the wounding of Marmont and Bonet. Replaced by Souham in September 1812, after a period of sick leave he replaced Caffarelli in command of the Army of the North (January 1813); later in the year he was appointed commander of the left wing of Soult's army and served with

distinction in the battles of the Pyrenees. He rallied to Napoleon in 1815 and was appointed to command on the Pyrenean frontier. After Waterloo he fled to America with a royalist sentence of death over him, but was permitted to return in 1820 and entered politics as a Liberal. In 1830 he was given a brief command in Algeria, became Marshal in the following year, and in 1835 was CinC Algeria, but was recalled after his repulse at Constantine in the following year.

CLAUSEWITZ, General Karl Maria von (1780–1831)

KARL MARIA VON CLAUSEWITZ

One of the most famous of all military theorists and philosophers, his work has influenced generations, and arose from his own service in the Napoleonic wars. Born near Magdeburg, he entered the Prussian Army in 1792, served on the Rhine 1793–4 and then, with Scharnhorst's training and recommendation, began a career on the general staff. He was aide to Prince August in 1806, from 1809 helped Scharnhorst in his reforms and was esteemed so highly that he was appointed military tutor to the Crown Prince. In 1812 he entered Russian service rather than serve in the enforced collab-

oration with Napoleon, and served on the Russian staff with Wittgenstein; he helped negotiate the defection of Yorck's Prussians by the Treaty of Tauroggen and as Wallmoden's chief of staff conducted the action at Göhrde. Rejoining the Prussians in 1814, he served as Thielmann's chief of staff in the Hundred Days, became major-general in 1818 and was director of the Berlin staff college until 1830. In 1831 he was Gneisenau's chief of staff on the Polish frontier, but like his chief fell victim to cholera and died at Breslau on 18 November 1831. The influence of his writing – most published posthumously – was immense, notably his masterpiece *Vom Kriege* (*On War*), which contained his belief that 'War is nothing more than a continuation of politics by other means', and that (as Napoleon demonstrated) the object should be the destruction of the enemy's field army by a decisive battle. Clausewitz's historical works – the final seven of the ten volumes published as *Hinterlassene Werke über Krieg und Kriegsführung* (Berlin 1832–7) are less well known, but his account of the 1812 campaign – the translation is entitled *The Campaign of 1812 in Russia* – which was published in 1843, has been reprinted as recently as 1992. It is upon his writings on the theory and philosophy of war, however, that his reputation endures, despite later criticism, and perhaps no other figure from his era made so great an impression upon the conduct of war in the succeeding century and a half. His name was commemorated in the German Army by the title of Field Artillery Regt. No. 21 (1st Upper Silesian).

Clausewitz, C. (*sic*) von. *On War* (translations include London 1873, and by M. Howard and P. Paret, New York, 1976); *The Campaign of 1812 in Russia*

London, 1843 (repr. with intro. by
. F. Nafziger. London, 1992);
loward, M. *Clausewitz*. Oxford,
983; Paret, P. *Clausewitz and the
tate*. Oxford, 1976; Parkinson, R.
lausewitz: a Biography. London,
971

LAY, Henry (1777–1852)

This leading American statesman
and orator played a not inconsiderable part in the War of 1812.
Appointed Speaker of the House of
Representatives in 1811, he was a
powerful advocate of opposition to
Great Britain, declaring that in the
cause of honour and independence, weak though the country
might be, it should be prepared to
oppose both the British and
French if necessary, and that resolution and spirit were the only
security. One of those who
impelled Madison towards conflict, he later served as a peace
commissioner who negotiated an
end to hostilities by the Treaty of
Ghent.

CLERFAYT, General François-Sébastien-Charles-Joseph de Croix, Count of (1733–98)

A Walloon, Clerfayt (or 'Clairfait')
entered the Austrian Army in 1753
and served with distinction during
the Seven Years War, remaining
loyal during the 1787 Netherlands
revolt and, as *Feldmarschall-Leutnant*, won further distinction in
the Turkish War. In 1792 he
commanded the Austrians in
Brunswick's army, enjoyed some
success in The Netherlands,
notably at Neerwinden, but was
checked at Wattignies and then
had little good fortune as
successor to Saxe–Coburg in
overall command. On the Rhine in
1795 he successfully relieved
Mainz, but his conclusion of an
armistice was not approved and
he resigned. Cust commented that
although Clerfayt was a cautious
commander, he was brave and
skilful, 'immensely beloved and

valued by his soldiers and by his
country',[1] and deserved a better
end to his military career.
1. Cust, vol. IV, pp. 299–300.

CLERK, John (d.1812)

Although not a seaman, John
Clerk of Edlin was apparently a
major influence in the development of naval tactics, by his theory
of 'breaking the line' as a way of
bringing about a close action
against an enemy unwilling to
engage. He published his *Essay on
Naval Tactics* for private circula-
tion in 1782, a copy being lent by
General Debbeig to Sir John
Jervis, who asked where he might
buy one for himself. 'It is not to be
bought,' answered the general. 'I
had this copy from the author,
who is a particular friend of mine;
he had but a few copies printed,
all of which he has given away
among his friends.' 'Since that is
the case', said Jervis, 'you shall not
have this copy back again; it is too
good a thing for you, who are a
landsman. I will keep it to myself.'[1]
The work seems to have made a
profound impression, the tactic of
'breaking the line' being put into
effect as early as the Battle of the
Saints (1782), and Duncan, who
apparently advised Clerk to
reprint his work because naval
officers were circulating hand-
written copies among themselves,
adopted the scheme at Camperdown. The system achieved its
most famous success under
Nelson, who attacked at Trafalgar
in two columns.
1. *Morning Chronicle*, 3 November
1798, which contains a lengthy
analysis.
    Clerk, J. *An Essay on Naval
Tactics, Systematical and Historical*. 1782, 2nd edn. 1790, 3rd and
fullest edn., Edinburgh, 1804

CLINTON, Lieutenant-General Sir Henry (1771–1829)

Younger son of General Sir Henry
Clinton (1738?–95), British CinC

during part of the War of American Independence, and brother
of William, he was commissioned
in 1787, served with the Prussians
in The Netherlands in 1789, was
on the Duke of York's staff 1793–4,
ADC to Cornwallis in Ireland in
1798, and in 1799 was a liaison
officer with the Russian forces in
northern Italy. He served in India
(including Laswaree), was attached to the Russian HQ in the
Austerlitz campaign, commanded
a Guards flank battalion in Sicily
1807–8 and was Moore's adjutant-
general in the Corunna campaign.
Major-general in July 1810, lieutenant-general June 1814, from
February 1812 he commanded the
6th Division of the Peninsular
army (less much of 1813), received
the KB for his conduct at Vittoria
and led the 2nd Division at
Waterloo. A brave and able divisional commander, he was
perhaps unsuited for higher
command, which is probably why
Wellington declined to give him
more responsibility when the
opportunity arose. He was MP for
Boroughbridge 1808–18.

CLINTON, General Sir William Henry (1769–1846)

Elder brother of Sir Henry
Clinton, he entered the British
Army in 1784, served in The

SIR HENRY CLINTON
(ENGRAVING BY J. JENKINS)

Netherlands 1793–4 and 1799 (in the latter campaign as the Duke of York's ADC), went on military missions to the Russians in Italy and to Sweden in 1808, and was Governor of Madeira (1802). Major-general from 1808, lieutenant-general from 1813, he briefly commanded British forces at Alicante (October–November 1812), was present at Castalla, and was angered by Murray's handling of the Tarragona episode. From September 1813 he succeeded Bentinck in command of the forces in Catalonia, even though the latter had reported him so diffident and fearful of responsibility that the anxiety of command might ruin his constitution, though Bentinck stated that a more honourable man could not exist. Clinton requested that Wellington send someone more senior to replace him, but retained his command as no one could be spared. He returned to the Peninsula to command British troops in Portugal 1826–8 and became a full general in 1830; he was an MP 1794–6 and 1806–29.

CLOOTS (or Clootz), Jean-Baptiste du Val de Grâce, Baron von (1755–94)

One of the most eccentric personalities of the French Revolution, Cloots was a Prussian nobleman of great wealth (much of which he dissipated) who supported revolutionary ideals and established himself in Paris as 'orator of the human race'. In 1792, after contributing 12,000 *livres* to French war funds, he was given French citizenship and elected to the Convention, where he voted for the death of Louis XVI; he declared that his heart was French and his soul *sans-culotte*. He published a work entitled *La République Universelle* (1792), abandoned his title and changed his name to Anarchsis Cloots (Anarchsis being the name of a

young Scythian philosopher in Jean-Jacques Barthélemy's *Voyage du jeune Anarchsis en Grèce)* (1787), and as a violent, antimonarchist atheist, urged the destruction of religion. Excluded from the Jacobin Club by Robespierre, he was unfairly implicated in the trial of the Hébertists and, his background and vast fortune being sufficient for condemnation, was guillotined on 24 March 1794.

CLYDE, Field Marshal Baron, see CAMPBELL, Sir Colin

COBBETT, William (1763–1835)

WILLIAM COBBETT
(ENGRAVING AFTER J. R. SMITH)

This famous British author, politician and journalist was a vociferous critic of the government during the Napoleonic Wars, his *Weekly Political Register*, begun in 1802, presenting the Radical viewpoint. His literary output was enormous (and costly because frequently provoking legal action), though in military affairs it exhibited some naïvety, for example his assertion that French dispatches were more reliable that British, as with Soult's Albuera account which he claimed must be true else Soult 'would not dare, Duke as he is, to say so';[1] and declared that the Peninsular War was a hopeless enterprise, 'nothing but a

drain on this country, without the smallest chance of any ultimate benefit'.[2] He was not without military experience, having served 1784–91 and become sergeant major in the 54th Foot; which presumably caused him to play a leading part in the agitation to outlaw flogging, which was the cause of his most severe penalty: he was imprisoned in Newgate for two years and fined £1,000 for libel following criticisms of the flogging of members of the Cambridgeshire Local Militia at Ely in 1809. He continued to edit his *Register* from gaol!

1. *Weekly Political Register*, 22 June 1811, column 1546 (unpaginated but columns numbered). 2. Ibid., 9 Nov 1811, column 581.

Briggs, A. *William Cobbett.* Oxford, 1967; Cobbett, W. *The Autobiography of William Cobbett,* ed. W. Reitzel. London, 1947; Chesterton, G. K. *William Cobbett.* London, 1926; Cole, G. D. H. *The Life of William Cobbett.* London, 1927; Green, D. *Great Cobbett: The Noblest Agitator.* Oxford, 1985; Spater, G. *William Cobbett: the Poor Man's Friend.* Cambridge, 1982

COCHRANE, Admiral Lord Thomas, Earl of Dundonald (1775–1860)

THOMAS COCHRANE,
EARL OF DUNDONALD

on of the 9th Earl of Dundonald, whom he succeeded as 10th Earl in 1831, Thomas, Lord Cochrane, was one of the most audacious naval officers of the era. Originally commissioned in the 104th Foot, he transferred to the Royal Navy and as a lieutenant in command of the brig HMS *Speedy* wrought such havoc upon French and Spanish shipping in the Mediterranean that he earned the nickname '*Le Loup de Mer*' ('Sea Wolf'). His fame was assured by his capture by boarding of the Spanish frigate *El Gamo* (6 May 1801) despite a huge disparity in size (319 men to Cochrane's 54); and after exchange following capture (when *Speedy* took on three ships of the line) he was promoted to captain and continued raiding and coastal forays in the frigates *Pallas* and *Impérieuse*. Despite such success, he aroused the wrath of the naval and political establishment, as a critic of government policy in his role as MP (Honiton 1806, Westminster from 1807), and although he performed his duties successfully in the attack on Basque Roads in April 1809, to which he had been assigned as the acknowledged expert on raids and cutting-out, he was associated with the failure of his superior, Gambier, and received no further employment. In 1814 his enemies seized their chance when he was implicated – via his criminal uncle, Colonel Andrew Cochrane-Johnstone – in the great Stock Exchange Fraud; though entirely innocent he was gaoled for a year and cashiered. Thereafter he used his skills to good effect in the navies of Chile, Brazil and Greece in those nations' struggle for independence, and in 1832 his name was cleared; re-appointed to the Royal Navy, he served as admiral commanding the North American and West Indian station 1848–51, and became Admiral of the Fleet.

His own comment that 'my life has been one of unmerited suffering'[1] is a melancholy reflection on the career of one of the greatest seamen of the age.

1. *Autobiography*, vol. II, p. 399.

Cochrane, A. *The Fighting Cochranes*. London, 1983; Dundonald, 10th Earl of. *The Autobiography of a Seaman*. London, 1860; Dundonald, 11th Earl of, and Foxbourne, H. R. *The Life of Thomas, Lord Cochrane, 10th Earl of Dundonald*. London, 1869; Thomas, D. *Cochrane: Britain's Last Sea-King*. London, 1978

COCKBURN, Admiral Sir George, Bt. (1772–1853)

Having joined the Royal Navy as a boy, he came to notice when in command of the frigate HMS *Minerve*, which captured the Spanish frigate *Santa Sabina* off Cartagena on 20 December 1796 (and lost it upon the arrival of reinforcements; Nelson was aboard *Minerve* and was thus officially in command, and curiously the Spanish captain was Don Jacobo Stuart, great-grandson of King James II). Cockburn served at St. Vincent, commanded the naval forces at the capture of Martinique (1809), and as rear-admiral from 1812 attracted some opprobrium in the USA when, as 2i/c to Warren, he was implicated in the burning of Washington. In 1815 he conveyed Napoleon to St. Helena and remained in charge of him until the arrival of Sir Hudson Lowe; towards the ex-emperor he behaved correctly but (understandably) without much sympathy, although he drank Napoleon's health on his birthday. Napoleon complained when Cockburn restricted his movements and read his correspondence, and objected when Cockburn remarked that 'he knew no person by the title of 'Emperor' at St. Helena'.[1] Las Cases remarked that 'we cannot pardon the affected

familiarity with which he treated us ... We can never forgive the haughty and self-complacent air with which he addressed Napoleon by the title of *General*'.[2] Subsequently Cockburn served as a Lord of the Admiralty and MP for Portsmouth; vice-admiral in 1819, admiral in 1837 and admiral of the fleet in 1851, he inherited the baronetcy from his brother in 1852.

1. Las Cases, vol. II, p. 14. 2. Ibid., p. 77.

CODRINGTON, Admiral Sir Edward (1770–1851)

SIR EDWARD CODRINGTON

Best known as the commander of the Allied fleet at Navarino, he served as signal-lieutenant in HMS *Queen Charlotte* at the Glorious First of June, commanded HMS *Orion* at Trafalgar, was present at Walcheren and in operations along the east coast of Spain, and was captain of the fleet under Sir Alexander Cochrane in the later stages of the War of 1812. Rear-admiral in 1814, he attained the rank of admiral in 1837; MP for Devonport 1832–9. His eldest son Edward (1803–19) was lost while on service as a midshipman; his second son, Sir William Codrington (1804–84) succeeded Raglan as commander in the Crimea, and his third, Sir Henry

William (1808–77) rose to the rank of admiral of the fleet.

Bourchier, Lady J. *Memoir of the Life of Admiral Sir Edward Codrington*. London, 1873 (written by his daughter)

COIGNET, Captain Jean-Roch (1776–1850)

By virtue of his memoirs he is one of the best-known 'ordinary' soldiers of Napoleon's army. Enlisting in 1797, he served in Italy with the 96th *Demi-brigade*, which enabled him to write a most graphic account of Marengo; his later campaigns were spent in the Imperial Guard, in which he was promoted to sergeant, and in 1812 was commissioned as a staff officer during the Russian campaign. His list of engagements resembles a roll-call of the battles of the *Grande Armée*, culminating with Waterloo, and he retired on half-pay in 1816. For an uneducated man who only learned to write at the age of 33, his memoirs are a deserved classic.

Coignet, J.-R. *The Note-Books of Captain Coignet*, intro. Hon. Sir John Fortescue. London, 1928.

COLBERT, General Auguste-François-Marie de (1777–1809)

One of three brothers who made a notable mark in the Napoleonic army (Edouard, born 1774, Alphonse, born 1776), he was the son of *maréchal-de-camp* comte de Colbert-Chabanais, who died in 1790. His rise was rapid; enrolling at the age of 16, he progressed to become ADC to Grouchy and Murat, served in Italy and Egypt and, despite his youth, after Marengo was given command of the 10th *Chasseurs à Cheval*. He served under Ney in the 1805 campaign, became *général de brigade* in December 1805, and commanded Ney's advance-guard with great courage and distinction at Jena (Ney remarked that he always slept peacefully when

Colbert was in command of his outposts). Continuing his career as a dashing leader of light cavalry in the Peninsula, when leading the cavalry of Ney's VI Corps he somewhat unwisely attempted to capture the bridge at Cacabellos in the face of determined resistance (3 January 1809), and was shot through the head and killed. (He had been singled out by Rifleman Thomas Plunket of the British 95th, a noted rascal and marksman, it was said in response to an offer of a reward by Sir Edward Paget to any man who hit the daring Frenchman on the grey horse). Lejeune wrote of the army's regret at the loss of 'a very interesting man, one of the flower of the army on account of his fine figure, his courteous bearing, and his chivalrous courage.'[1] Colbert's father-in-law was comte de Canclaux, a distinguished general of engineers.

1. Lejeune, vol. I, p. 115.

Colbert-Chabanais, A. N. J. *Traditions et Souvenirs, ou Mémoires touchant le Temps et la Vie du Général Auguste Colbert*. Paris, 1863–73; Ojala, J. A. *Auguste de Colbert*. Salt Lake City, 1979

COLBERT, General Edouard de, comte de Colbert-Chabanais (1774–1853)

Elder brother of Auguste-François-Marie, and also a cavalryman, he came to notice in the Egyptian campaign, and in 1802 was given charge of the administration of the Mamelukes of the Consular Guard. After serving as ADC to Junot and Berthier and commanding the 7th Hussars, he was appointed a baron of the empire and in March 1809 became *général de brigade*, commanding the light cavalry of II Corps in the campaign of that year, being wounded and distinguished at Wagram. In 1811 he was given command of the 2nd (ex-Dutch or 'Red') Lancers of the Imperial

Guard, led the Guard light hors[e] in Russia and in 1813–14, retaine[d] command of the re-titled 'Cheva[u]x Légers de France' at the fir[st] restoration, but rallied [to] Napoleon in 1815. Wounded in th[e] left arm on 16 June, he led h[is] lancers at Waterloo with his ar[m] in a sling, a famous example of th[e] bravery and devotion of Nap[oleon's followers. He was impris[on]ed briefly at the secon[d] restoration, spent some months i[n] exile and was unemployed for [a] decade, but when restored t[o] favour became a peer of Franc[e] (1832) and Inspector-General [of] Cavalry. He was injured by th[e] device which killed Mortier, bu[t] survived until his death at Paris i[n] December 1853.

COLBORNE, Field Marshal Sir John, Baron Seaton (1778–1863)

SIR JOHN COLBORNE

One of the best battalio[n] commanders of the British Army[,] he was commissioned in 1794[,] served in North Holland, Egyp[t] and at Maida, and at Corunna a[s] Moore's military secretary. He returned to the Peninsula in late[r] 1809 as attaché to the Spanish Army, witnessing the defeat a[t] Oçana, and was then appointed t[o] command the 2/66th as lieutenant-colonel. He led them a[t] usaco and commanded the rigade at Albuera that was annihilated by French cavalry, 'a most unfortunate affair for me, though I had nothing to do with the arrangement, but merely obeyed the orders of General Stewart',[1] as he wrote. In July 1811 he took command of the 2nd Light Infantry, one of the finest regiments in the army, and with them achieved great fame. He was severely wounded at Ciudad Rodrigo, as George Napier recalled: 'in such horrid pain [that] his spirits were quite sunk ... his arm was broken close up to the joint of the shoulder, which, and the scapula itself, were split ... [there was] no suffering in human life which he would not endure, if necessary, either for his country or his friends. Few men are like him; indeed except the Duke of Wellington, I know no officer in the British army his equal. His expansive mind is capable of grasping anything ... his genius for war so powerful that it overcomes all obstacles ... He has, with the most intrepid bravery, a coolness of head ... nothing can take him by surprise or flurry him'.[2] Colborne recovered to resume command of his regiment in July 1813, and led it for the remainder of the war. His fame was assured at Waterloo when he employed the above-mentioned attributes to wheel his 2nd to assail the flank of a column of Imperial Guard, which greatly helped to repel Napoleon's last attack. Subsequently he served as CinC and Governor-General of Canada at the time of the 1837–8 rebellions, was justly ennobled as Baron Seaton in 1839, and became field marshal in 1860.

1. Moore Smith, p. 161. 2. Napier, G., pp. 220–1.

Moore Smith, G. C.: *The Life of John Colborne, Field Marshal Lord Seaton.* London, 1903

COLE, General Sir Galbraith Lowry (1772–1842)

SIR GALBRAITH LOWRY COLE
(PRINT AFTER LAWRENCE)

One of Wellington's most reliable divisional commanders, he was the second son of the 1st Earl of Enniskillen. Commissioned in 1787, he served in a number of staff appointments, including ADC to the CinC Ireland (wounded at Vinegar Hill), military secretary to Hutchinson in Egypt, and commander of the left at Maida. Major-general from 1808, he commanded the 4th Division in the Peninsula from October 1809, save for an absence from late 1811 to July 1812, and a further three months' leave to recover from a wound received at Salamanca. Capable and extremely brave, he was less impressive when entrusted with a larger command, as at Roncesvalles; and at Orthes John Colborne recalled him as being in somewhat of a lather: 'He was much excited and said, "Well, Colborne, what's to be done? Here we are, all coming back as fast as we can." I was rather provoked and said, "Have patience, and we shall see what's to be done."'[1] Probably his most famous action was in mounting the counter-attack at Albuera, without Beresford's order; claims were made that Henry Hardinge initiated the

manoeuvre, but as Cole told him, 'I fully admit that the merit of originating the movement rests with you, but the credit for having incurred the responsibility is mine.'[2] Known for giving the best dinners in the Peninsula army (for which he kept a travelling kitchen and herds of sheep and goats as part of his HQ), Cole was justly popular; as George Napier recalled: 'He would never permit officer or *private soldier* to want anything that he had, or that it was in his power to procure for him; and though a hot-tempered man, he is as kind and generous as he is brave, and a more truly gallant, enterprising soldier never breathed.'[3] Cole was promoted to lieutenant-general in June 1813, general in 1830, and after the Napoleonic Wars served as Governor of Mauritius and Cape Colony. He had once been a suitor for the hand of Kitty Pakenham, but she married Wellington instead.

1. Moore Smith, p. 201. 2. *USJ,* 1840, vol. III, p. 248. 3. Napier, G., p. 152.

Cole, M. Lowry, and Gwynn, S. *Memoirs of Sir Lowry Cole.* London, 1934

COLLINGWOOD, Vice-Admiral Cuthbert, Baron (1750–1810)

CUTHBERT COLLINGWOOD (ENGRAVING BY W. HULL AFTER H. HOWARD)

Nelson's great friend and deputy, he went to sea at the age of 11, was a midshipman for almost fifteen years, served in the War of American Independence (including Bunker Hill), was captain of HMS *Barfleur* at the Glorious First of June, served at St. Vincent in HMS *Excellent*, and became vice-admiral in 1799. At Trafalgar he commanded one of the columns of attack in HMS *Royal Sovereign*, and succeeded to command of the fleet after Nelson's death. Ennobled and appointed to command in the Mediterranean, he remained on that service until his death aboard HMS *Ville de Paris* on 7 March 1810, off Port Mahon, despite requests that he return home on grounds of ill-health; but on being told that he was needed he 'said that he never in his life had declined a call'.[1] A very skilled seaman, he was universally liked and admired for his abilities and kindness, and was greatly entertaining by constant punning and good humour. 'One prejudice he had ... he deemed it to be the bounden duty of every Englishman, to hate a Frenchman as his natural foe; and no man ever hated the national character, and the nation, more cordially than he.'[2] Although lamenting the long separations from his family, he always put duty first; and when at home would walk around his native Northumberland with pocketsful of acorns, which he planted at every suitable place, to ensure a supply of oak for the next-but-several generations of warships.

1. *Gent's Mag.*, May, 1810, p. 486. 2. Ibid.

Hughes, E. (ed.). *The Private Correspondence of Admiral Lord Collingwood*. London, 1957; Murray, G. *The Life of Admiral Collingwood*. London, 1936; Newnham Collingwood, G. L. (ed.). *A Selection from the Public and Private Correspondence of Vice-Admiral Lord Collingwood*. London, 1828 (compiled by his son-in-law); Warner, O. *The Life and Letters of Vice-Admiral Lord Collingwood*, Oxford, 1968

COLLOT D'HERBOIS, Jean-Marie (1750–96)

An actor by profession, he was a figure of some influence in the French Revolution. His popular pamphlet *L'Almanach du Père Gérard* advocated a constitutional monarchy, but he became increasingly radical, and as a Paris Deputy to the Convention was the first to advocate the abolition of the monarchy, and voted for the death of the king. A member of the Committee of Public Safety from September 1793, he suppressed the revolt of Lyons with great brutality, using cannon loaded with grapeshot to slaughter prisoners *en masse* (it was said that he had a grudge against the city, having once been booed off the stage there). In May 1794 he was the victim of an attempted assassination by one Henri Ladmiral, who had determined to shoot either him or Robespierre for the good of the country, but his pistol at first misfired, and then he missed; but Collot fell victim to the Thermidorian reaction at the end of Robespierre's rule, was denounced and in March 1795 was transported to Guiana, where he died of fever in the following year.

COLVILLE, General Sir Charles (1770–1843)

Third son of John, 8th Lord Colville of Culross (1724/5–1811), a veteran of Fontenoy and Culloden), Charles was commissioned in the British Army in 1787; he served in the West Indies, in Ireland during the rebellion, commanded the 13th Foot in Egypt and in Bermuda in 1808, and was temporary Governor and CinC Grenada. Major-gener⊥ from 1810, in October of that ye⊥ he took over a brigade of the 3⊥ Division in the Peninsula, w⊥ distinguished at El Bodon and ⊥ December 1811 commanded t⊥ 4th Division, being shot throug⊥ the thigh and losing a finger ⊥ Badajoz. On his return aft⊥ recovery in 1813 he reverted to ⊥ brigade command in the 3rd Di⊥ sion, until appointed to lead t⊥ 5th Division in December 181⊥ succeeding to command t⊥ investing force at Bayonne aft⊥ Hope's injury. With local rank ⊥ lieutenant-general, he led the 4⊥ Division in the Waterloo cam⊥ paign, but missed the battle ⊥ commanding the reserve at H⊥ Subsequently he was Cin⊥ Bombay (1819–25) and Govern⊥ of Mauritius (1828–33); he died ⊥ 27 March 1843. His wife Jan⊥ survived him by only two month⊥ dying in consequence of a misha⊥ when a candle set her dress aligh⊥ Colville's elder brother wa⊥ Admiral John Colville (1768–184⊥ who succeeded as 9th Baron, an⊥ who was himself succeeded b⊥ Charles' elder son Charles Joh⊥ (1818–1903), 1st Viscount Colvill⊥ the younger son, Sir Willia⊥ James (1827–1903), had a disti⊥ guished military career, notably i⊥ the Crimea.

Colville, J. *The Portrait of ⊥ General*. Salisbury, 1980

COMBERMERE, Field Marshal Viscount, see COTTON

COMPANS, General Jean-Dominique, comte (1769–1845⊥

Destined for the priesthood, bu⊥ entering military service in 179⊥ he served with the French Army a⊥ Toulon and in Italy (commandin⊥ a brigade in 1799), was Lanne⊥ chief of staff in 1805 (wounded a⊥ Austerlitz), became *général d⊥ brigade* in 1806 and comte in 180⊥ but is perhaps best known for hi⊥ service in the Russian campaign ⊥

12. Commanding the 5th Division of I Corps, he won great distinction by his skilful co-ordination of infantry and artillery in capturing and holding the Shevardino Redoubt two days before Borodino. In the battle proper he was shot in the shoulder when leading the advance of I Corps, which frustrated his plan to outflank the position. He served in the 1813 campaign and was twice wounded at Mockern. Having accepted the Bourbon restoration, he rallied to Napoleon in 1815 but declined a command in the Army of the North.

Compans, J. D. *Le Général Compans 1769–1845, d'après ses notes de Campagne et sa Correspondance*, ed. M. Ternaux-Compans. Paris, 1912

CONDE, Louis-Joseph, prince de (1736–1818)

The title 'Prince of Condé' was borne by a branch of the house of Bourbon, including among its holders Louis II, 'the Great Condé' (1621–86), the victor of Rocroi and a general of high repute. Prince Louis-Joseph, son of Louis Henri, duc de Bourbon (Minister of Louis XV), was a distinguished commander in the Seven Years War, and on the advent of the French Revolution became a leader of the royalist *émigrés*, going first to Brussels in 1793. Together with the duc de Bohan he raised the royalist standard at Coblenz and gave his name to the *Armée de Condé*, which served with the Allied forces from 1793, paid originally by Austria, from 1795 by Great Britain, entering Russian service in 1797 and after that country's exit from the war, by Great Britain again. In 1800 Condé went to England where he lived for a time, returning to France only in 1814, and during the Hundred Days accompanied Louis XVIII to

Ghent. His son, Louis-Henri-Joseph, duc de Bourbon (1756–1830) was the last to hold the title *Prince de Condé*; he served with the *Armée de Condé* and during the Hundred Days attempted to raise a royalist revolt in the Vendée.

CONDORCET, Marie-Jean-Antoine-Nicolas Caritat, marquis de (1743–94)

This French philosopher and mathematician became involved in politics at the time of the Revolution; it was said that he concealed violent passion under a calm exterior, which was compared to a snow-covered volcano. A member of the Legislative Assembly and Convention, he was a republican but did not support the execution of the king, and was condemned for supporting the Girondins. For eight months he was hidden by the widow of the sculptor Vernet, during which time he wrote his best-known work, *Esquisse d'un Tableau historique des progrès de l'esprit humain*; but leaving his shelter so as not to risk the safety of his hostess, he was arrested and flung into gaol. On the following morning he was found dead, either from natural causes or perhaps self-administered poison. His widow Sophie (1764–1822) was the elder sister of Marshal Grouchy; she shared her husband's ideals and thus her salon attracted those opposed to the concepts of empire and monarchy.

Cahan, L. *Condorcet et la Révolution Française*. Paris, 1904; Guillois, A. *La Marquise de Condorcet*. Paris, 1897; Schapiro, J. S. *Condorcet and the Rise of Liberalism*. New York, 1934. A collected edition of Condorcet's work was published by his widow 1801–4, and his *Oeuvres*, ed. A. C. O'Connor and M. F. Arago, Paris, 1847–9

CONEGLIANO, duc de, see MONCEY

CONGREVE, Sir William, Bt. (1772–1828)

Best known for the invention of the military rocket which bears his name, he was the son of a general but never held a British commission. His father being Comptroller of the Royal Laboratory at Woolwich, young Congreve had opportunity and encouragement to develop his rocket, which he demonstrated in 1805. He was present when it was used in action at Boulogne (1806), Copenhagen, Basque Roads and Walcheren, and it was employed by the 'rocket brigade' of the Royal Artillery in the later Peninsular War, at Leipzig and at Waterloo, with mixed effect. Wellington was no great admirer of so inaccurate a weapon, but its effect on enemy morale could be profound, as Wittgenstein remarked. 'They look as if they were made in hell, and surely are the devil's own artillery'.[1] In 1814 Congreve succeeded his father as baronet and Comptroller of the Royal Laboratory, but his only military rank was a lieutenant-colonelcy in the Hanoverian artillery (1811), promoted to major-general in 1818. A great favourite of the Prince Regent, he was an MP from 1812 and had a wide scope of scientific interests, including such diverse projects as artillery, printing, clocks, steam-engines, canals and even a perpetual motion machine. He is sometimes confused with his father, **Lieutenant-General Sir William, Bt. (1741?–1814)**, who entered the Royal Artillery in 1755, served in America during the Seven Years War and War of Independence, was a great favourite of the Prince of Wales and Duke of York and commanded the latter's artillery in The Netherlands 1793–4. A great expert on artillery, he was Comptroller of the Royal Laboratory from 1783 until his death, and invented the block-trail artillery carriage. Major-general in 1802 and lieutenant-general and baronet from 1808, in April 1814 'after a long life devoted to his country',[2] he appears to have taken his own life.

1, *Edinburgh*, 11 April 1814. 2. *Gent's Mag.*, May, 1814, p. 519.

Congreve, W. *Details of the Rocket System*. London, 1814; Carman, W. Y. 'Sir William Congreve 1741–1814', in *Journal of the Society for Army Historical Research*, vol. LI, 1973

CONSALVI, Cardinal Ercole (1757–1824)

Born in Rome and a leading statesman representing the papal authority, he believed in the divine right of kings and thus opposed the tenets of the French Revolution, as might have been expected from a protégé of Henry, Cardinal Duke of York. His views led him to be imprisoned in 1798 by the Roman Republic, but he escaped and was instrumental in the appointment of Pius VII as Pope, whose Prime Minister he became. He was a leading figure in the negotiations which led to the Concordat, arriving in Paris in June 1801 where Napoleon found him a hard bargainer but a realist and personally charming. Conflict between Napoleon and Rome led to his resignation in 1807, and despite Napoleon's apologies he refused to attend the marriage with Marie-Louise, and was confined at Rheims for three years. After Napoleon's abdication Consalvi was papal representative to the Allied sovereigns and at the Congress of Vienna, and helped re-organise the papal states until his retirement in the year before his death.

Consalvi, Cardinal E. *Mémoires*, ed. J. Crétineau-Joly. Paris, 1864

CONSTANT de REBECQUE, Henri-Benjamin (known as CONSTANT, Benjamin) (1767–1830)

BENJAMIN CONSTANT (ENGRAVING BY T. JOHNSON AFTER L. VALLIER)

Born in Lausanne, the son of a general in Dutch service, he became involved in French politics from about 1796 when he published two pamphlets in defence of the Directory; his views were moderate, having been influenced by Whig beliefs during his education in England. In December 1799 he became a member of the Tribunate, but his independence angered Napoleon and resulted in his dismissal in 1802. A great favourite of Madame de Staël, he followed her into exile in 1803 and their association did not end completely even after Constant's second marriage in 1808. In 1813 he published a work attacking Napoleon, which was well received by the Allies, and he supported the Bourbon restoration; but having left Paris upon Napoleon's return in 1815, he returned, probably because of his infatuation with Madame Récamier. Meeting Napoleon at the Tuileries, he decided to support him and was appointed a councillor of state, consequently being forced into exile (at Brussels) upon the second restoration.

He was permitted to return [to] France in 1816 and was active [in] liberal politics thereafter. H[is] most important writings inclu[de] his semi-autobiographical nov[el] *Adolphe* (published London, 181[5]) *De la religion considérée dans s[a] Source, ses formes, et s[es] développements* (Paris, 1825–31) and his *Journaux intimes*. H[e] should not be confused wit[h] general Jean Victor Constant [de] Rebecque (1773–1850), who serve[d] with the Prince of Orange in th[e] Peninsula and was his mo[st] capable and energetic chief of sta[ff] in the Waterloo campaign.

Nicolson, H. *Benjamin Constan[t]* London, 1949

'CONSTANT' (WAIRY, Louis-Constant), 1778–1845)

Known almost universally as ju[st] 'Constant', he was Napoleon['s] senior valet for almost the who[le] of the Empire period. Born in th[e] Jemappes region of Belgium, th[e] son of an hotelier, he went int[o] service with Eugène de Beauha[r]nais, having been recommende[d] to Josephine, transferred to he[r] service and became Napoleon['s] closest and most faithful attenda[nt] from 1800 to 1814. His memoir[s] were largely the product of othe[r] hands, but provide an interestin[g] if not altogether reliable view o[f] Napoleon as seen by a clos[e] servant.

Wairy, L. C. *Memoirs o[f] Constant, the Emperor Napoleon['s] Head Valet*, trans. P. Pinkerto[n] London, 1896 (orig. pubd. Paris 1830–1)

CONSTANTINE, Grand Duke (1779–1831)

Younger brother of Tsar Alexande[r] I, he was raised by Catherine I[I] who, it was said, chose his nam[e] to emphasise Russia's intention o[f] capturing Constantinople. H[e] entered military service at an earl[y] age, but though personally brav[e] showed little aptitude for com[mand]

mand; but after distinguishing himself at Novi the Tsar accorded him the title of *Tsarevich*, which officially belonged only to the direct heir. He continued to serve in the army after his brother's accession to the throne, commanding the Guard Corps at Austerlitz – having a near escape by shooting the horse of a Mameluke who had vowed to take his head as a trophy – and although an advocate of the French alliance led V Corps in 1812, and served in 1813–14. He was appointed CinC Poland, in effect ruling that territory from the creation of the 'Congress Kingdom', and resigned his position as heir to the throne in order to marry a Polish lady, Johanna Grudzinska; he remained unwilling to become involved in the Decembrist revolt of 1825 which sought to put him on the throne in place of his younger brother Nicholas. He was taken by surprise by the Polish revolt of 1830 and proved incapable of quelling it. He died of cholera at Vitebsk in June 1831.

CONTE, Nicolas-Jacques (1755–1805)

A mechanical engineer and inventor of the first rank, Conté was of humble origin but came to notice by his artistic talent. Redirecting his energies to science, he became a leading figure in ballooning, led the aviation establishment at Meudon and became head of military ballooning in 1796. In 1795 he lost the use of his left eye by a hydrogen explosion in his experiments, and worked on many other projects, notably the artificial plumbago made from graphite and clay for use in pencils, which still bears his name, the genuine article having been denied to France by British hostilities. With the rank of *chef de brigade*, he led the balloon corps in Egypt, where his ability to invent and manufacture virtually anything the army required was a vital asset. On his return to France he was appointed to supervise the preparation of the publication on the expedition, but died before its completion.

COOKE, Lieutenant-General Sir George (1768–1837)

Brother to the Duke of York's private secretary, 'Kangaroo' Cooke, he was commissioned in the 1st Foot Guards in 1784, and served in The Netherlands in 1794 and 1799 (severely wounded); major-general from June 1811, he took command of the British troops at Cadiz after Graham's criticism of the Spanish at Barrosa precluded him from remaining in that command. Cooke is best known as commander of the 1st Division (of Foot Guards) at Waterloo, where he lost his right arm. He received the KCB in October 1815 and became lieutenant-general in 1821; his sister Penelope having married the 6th Earl Cardigan in 1794, Sir George was uncle to the 7th Earl, of Crimea fame.

CORBINEAU, General Jean-Baptiste-Juvenal, comte (1776–1848)

Commissioned into the French Army in 1792, he saw extensive service during the Revolutionary Wars, in Poland (1807) and in the Peninsula (1808–11), being ennobled as a baron in 1808 and promoted to *général de brigade* in 1811; but his real fame dates from the Russian campaign of 1812, when he was responsible to a considerable degree for saving the *Grande Armée*. He commanded a cavalry brigade of II Corps, which was 'borrowed' by Wrede and removed to his VI Corps, operating to the north of the main advance. At least according to Marbot, this had been done without authorisation and much to Corbineau's dissatisfaction. Eventually he challenged Wrede to produce the authorisation for the appropriation of his brigade, and when this was not forthcoming, Corbineau marched off in the direction of Oudinot's II Corps, a manoeuvre of some hazard but helped by the presence in the brigade of the 8th *Chevau-Légers-Lanciers*, originally the lancers of the Vistula Legion, whose Polish composition allowed them to understand the local civilians. Finding his intended route blocked, Corbineau was directed by some peasants to a ford over the Berezina near Studianka, of which the French had no prior knowledge; and after he rejoined Oudinot the information provided the route of escape from the converging Russian forces which had intended to maroon what remained of the retreating *Grande Armée* on the far bank of the Berezina. Corbineau was promoted to *général de division*, became an imperial ADC in 1813, and helped save Napoleon from Cossacks at Brienne.

CORDAY D'ARMONT, Marie-Anne-Charlotte (1768–93)

CHARLOTTE CORDAY
(ENGRAVING BY W. GREATBATCH AFTER MARKE)

She made her mark on the French Revolution by a single act on 13 July 1793. An attractive, intelligent and well-read young woman from

Normandy and descended from an impoverished noble family (an ancestor was the dramatist Corneille), she determined to assassinate Marat following his persecution of the Girondins, with whose political views she was in sympathy; and, it was said, she held him responsible for the execution of an army officer of whom she was enamoured. She went to Paris, bought a knife, and gained an audience with Marat (who was in his bath) on the pretext of bringing him information about traitors in Caen. She stabbed him through the heart and he died almost immediately; she was apprehended and guillotined on 17 July.

CORNWALLIS, General Charles, 1st Marquess (1738–1805)

CHARLES, 1ST MARQUESS CORNWALLIS
(ENGRAVING BY W. HOLL AFTER COPLEY)

Marquess Cornwallis (to which title he was elevated in 1793) is best known as the British commander who surrendered at Yorktown, but he was also involved in the Napoleonic era. Governor-General and CinC India from 1786, upon his return he served as Master-General of the Ordnance (1795–1801) and in June 1798 became Lord-Lieutenant and CinC Ireland, effectively ending the rebellion by his defeat of

Humbert at Ballinamuck. His conduct made him very popular with his troops; when marching with a force to Athlone, 'the attention and kindness extended ... to the troops under his command, completely won their hearts; like a true soldier, he sought no comfort or refreshment for himself while one of his men remained unsupplied, and even then shewed himself content with the coarsest fare and meanest accommodation'.[1] In 1802 he helped negotiate the Treaty of Amiens, when he made a lasting impression on Napoleon, being the first Englishman 'who gave me, in good earnest, a favourable opinion of his nation ... in every sense of the word, a worthy, good, and honest man ... I have preserved an agreeable recollection of him in every respect, and it is certain that a request from him would have had more weight with me, perhaps, than one from a crowned head.'[2] In 1805 Cornwallis returned to India as Governor-General, but his health collapsed and he died in that October at Ghazipur. His brother, **Admiral Sir William Cornwallis (1744–1819)**, who entered the Royal Navy in 1755, saw much service in the West and East Indies (assisting in the reduction of

SIR WILLIAM CORNWALLIS
(ENGRAVING BY BARTOLOZZI)

Pondicherry), became rear-admiral in February 1793 and vice-admiral in July 1794. Serving in the Channel in June 1795, he won some fame when, retiring before a greatly superior French force, he turned to assist two slow-sailing ships, a gesture of defiance which persuaded the French to abandon the pursuit, believing that British reinforcements must be at hand. In 1796 he survived a court-martial for disobeying an order to go to the West Indies (insisting his health was not sufficiently strong), became an admiral in 1799 and commanded in the Channel 1801 and 1803–6. He was very popular with his men, who gave him the affectionate nicknames of 'Billy Blue' and 'Billy-go-tight', the latter from his stout build.

1. *Morning Chronicle*, 6 Sept 1798.
2. Las Cases, vol. II, pp. 273–5.

Cornwallis, 1st Marquess. *Correspondence of Charles, 1st Marquis Cornwallis*, ed. C. Ross. London, 1859

CORVISART DES MARETS, Jean-Nicolas, baron (1755–1821)

An outstanding figure in French medicine of the period, he met Napoleon in 1801 and was appointed his 'First Physician'. He exercised some influence, especially over the appointment of those who might be his rivals (Larrey suffered in this way), but later lost favour by not approving of Napoleon's second marriage. He was not Napoleon's personal surgeon, however; from 1796 until 1814 that position was occupied by Alexandre-Urbain Yvan (1765–1839).

COTTEREAU, Jean (1767–94)

A smuggler and dealer in contraband salt, he was the original leader of the Chouans who rose in rebellion against the French republicans; many, but not all, were Bretons, and most were basically brigands. The name 'Chouan', applied both to Cottereau and his followers, was a local term for the *chouette* or screech-owl, whose call was imitated by the Breton rebels. From August 1792 Cottereau conducted a guerrilla war and collaborated with the Vendéen royalist forces, but was mortally wounded in an ambush and died in February 1794; the Chouans continued their guerrilla activities for some time, their most famous leader being Georges Cadoudal.

COTTON, Admiral Sir Charles, Bt. (1753–1812)

Going to sea in 1772, he became a captain and commanded HMS *Majestic* at the Glorious First of June, and HMS *Mars* in 1795, one of the ships involved in Sir William Corwallis' retreat and stand in the face of heavy odds. Rear-admiral in February 1797, vice-admiral in April 1802 and admiral in April 1808, Cotton is best remembered for commanding the naval forces at the beginning of the Peninsular War, notably for his support for the Portuguese and vehement opposition to the Convention of Cintra. He was later CinC Mediterranean and in 1811 was given command of the Channel Fleet, but died suddenly near Plymouth on 23 February 1812, 'an excellent commander, a good man, and inviolably attached to his King and Country'.[1]

1. *Gent's Mag.*, Mar, 1812, p. 299.

COTTON, Field Marshal Sir Stapleton, Bt., Viscount Combermere (1773–1865)

Probably Wellington's best cavalry general, he was commissioned in the British Army in 1790, served in The Netherlands (1793–4), the Cape (1796) and in the Fourth Mysore War. Major-general from 1805, in 1808 he went to the Peninsula as deputy to William Payne,

STAPLETON COTTON, VISCOUNT COMBERMERE

and replaced him as cavalry commander in June 1810; he succeeded to the family baronetcy in 1809. On the night of Salamanca he was shot accidentally by a sentry whose challenge he had failed to answer, which led to his being invalided home in December 1812. He rejoined in June 1813, the delay partly caused by dissatisfaction at not receiving a peerage for his service at Salamanca and partly because he was unwilling to serve under Beresford, his junior in the British Army; but in May 1814 he became Baron Combermere of Combermere (Cheshire). Wellington was denied his services at Waterloo when Uxbridge was given the cavalry command, but Combermere replaced him in the army of occupation. Wellington admitted that he was not the best man to command an army, but still entertained a high opinion of his abilities, and recommended him for chief command in India, where he was spectacularly successful by his capture of Bhurtpore (Bharatpur) in January 1826, for which he received a viscountcy. It was his last active service. He held a number of important posts subsequently, becoming field marshal in October 1865; he was MP for Newark 1806–14.

Combermere, Viscount. *Memoirs and Correspondence of Field-Marshal Viscount Combermere, from his Family Papers*, ed. Mary, Viscountess Combermere and W. W. Knollys. London, 1866; Smyth, Lieutenant-Colonel N. M. 'Stapleton Cotton, Viscount Combermere, Field-Marshal', in *Cavalry Journal*, 1912, vol. VII, pp. 271–82.

COUTARD (or COUTHARD), General Louis-François, comte (1769–1852)

Having joined the French Army in 1791 and become distinguished for his part in the defence of Genoa, he was ennobled as baron in 1808, but his most famous service was at Ratisbon in April 1809. As commander of the 65th Line, he was ordered by Davout (whose cousin he had married) to hold his position as long as possible. On 19 April he hung on, repelling Austrian attacks, but lost heavily and reported himself short of ammunition; but the promised re-supply never arrived, and outnumbered ten to one and without the material to destroy the Ratisbon bridge as ordered, he surrendered. In reality it was his only option to avoid further losses in a hopeless cause, but it was a severe tactical blow to Napoleon; yet although reprimanded, Coutard was excused when the facts became fully known. Subsequently he served in Spain, became *général de brigade*, commanded a brigade of Merle's 9th Division in II Corps in the Russian campaign of 1812, and was wounded near Vilna. He became comte in 1816 and enjoyed a brief political career, but retired in 1831 after declining to serve under Louis-Philippe.

COUTELLE, Jean-Marie-Joseph (1748–1835)

One of the earliest exponents of military aviation, he was appointed, with Conté, to supervise the establishment of the French Army's balloon service. Appointed captain in April 1794, and commander of the 1st *Aërostier* company, he took his balloon *L'Entreprenant* on active service; aerial observation was used to good effect at Fleurus and subsequently, but the section taken to Egypt (with Coutelle, as *chef de brigade*) was not used effectively and the corps was disbanded in 1799. Thereafter Coutelle was employed in a minor staff position as *sous-inspecteur aux revues*, and retired in 1816. He was apparently the first man to experience anti-aircraft fire, when an Austrian roundshot grazed the basket of *l'Entreprenant* while observing near Maubeuge.

COUTHON, Georges (1755–94)

A lawyer at the beginning of the French Revolution, he was initially a supporter of constitutional monarchy, but became a close associate of Robespierre, in the Convention voted for the death of the king and was the first to demand the arrest of the Girondins. As a member of the Committee of Public Safety, in August 1793 he accompanied the army sent against Lyons, accepted the city's surrender in October and established the commission to seek out the rebels, but the worst reprisals occurred after he was replaced by Collot d'Herbois. He aided the persecution of the Hébertists and devised the law which denied the right of a defence to those tried by Revolutionary Tribunal. He was arrested and executed with Robespierre, after an abortive attempt to stab himself and then feign death; as he suffered from paralysis of the legs, which were contracted, he had to be laid sideways on the guillotine.

COVINGTON, Brigadier General Leonard (1768–1813)

One of the most senior American officers killed in the War of 1812,

he was born in Maryland and served as an officer in the US Army 1792–5, including the actions at Fort Recovery (30 June 1794) and Fallen Timbers. He served in Congress 1805–7, was commissioned as colonel of light dragoons in 1809 and was breveted as brigadier general in August 1813. Mortally wounded at Chrysler's Farm, he died two days later.

COWLEY, Baron, see WELLESLEY, Henry

CRADOCK (later 'CARADOC'), General Sir John Francis, 1st Baron Howden (1762–1839)

SIR JOHN CRADOCK, BARON HOWDEN
(PRINT AFTER LAWRENCE)

Son of the Archbishop of Dublin, he was commissioned in the British Army in 1777, served in the West Indies and as brevet major-general was wounded at Ballinamuck. He commanded a brigade in Egypt, and in India from 1803 as CinC Madras he was held partially responsible for the mutiny at Vellore (from his lack of understanding of Indian cultural and religious traditions), and was recalled. In 1808 he was appointed to command British forces in Portugal but proved unenterprising and pessimistic, and much to his dismay in April 1809 was replaced by Arthur Wellesley; 'to

the day of his death this supercession would at times recur painfully to his recollection'.[1] He then served briefly as Governor and CinC Gibraltar, and in the same capacities at the Cape (1811–14). He received an Irish peerage in 1819 and the English barony of Howden in 1831; 'considered one of the handsomest men of his day, his Lordship was also an accomplished scholar, and possessed a grace and dignity of manner peculiarly attractive. His nature was truly kind and affectionate, his benevolence unbounded, and his charity unostentatious.'[2]

1. *USJ*, 1839, vol. III, p. 97. 2. Ibid. p. 98

CRAIG, General Sir James Henry (1748–1812)

Son of Hew Craig, judge at Gibraltar, he entered the British Army at the age of 15, served with distinction in the War of American Independence and as a tactical expert corresponded with Dundas about the Prussian system. He served as the Duke of York's chief of staff in The Netherlands, becoming major-general in October 1794; in 1795 he commanded the expedition to the Cape and after the capture of the territory remained as Governor until 1797. After serving in Bengal he was promoted to lieutenant-general (January 1801) and in 1802 returned to England to command the Eastern District. In March 1805 he was appointed CinC Mediterranean (where it was hoped the climate would be beneficial to his poor health), but he found co-operation with the Russians and Neapolitans difficult; yet he made Sicily secure before his health broke down and he resigned, sailing for home in April 1806. From August 1807 to October 1811 he was Governor of Lower Canada, and was promoted to full general on 1 January 1812;

but died on 12 January, 'of a lingering and painful disease, borne like a man and a soldier'.[1] Bunbury described him as a short, broad man, so muscular as to be a 'pocket Hercules', intelligent and skilled, and despite hot temper and some pomposity was beloved by those under his command, to whom he exhibited great kindness.

1. *Gent's Mag.*, January 1812, p. 92.

CRAUFURD, Major-General Robert (1764–1812)

ROBERT CRAUFURD.

'Black Bob' Craufurd (a name appropriate both to his complexion and stern demeanour) was one of the British Army's toughest fighters and most unyielding disciplinarians. From a family of old Scottish gentry, he was commissioned in 1779 and became devoted to his profession, perhaps as a result of meeting Frederick the Great at the Prussian annual manoeuvres. After service in the Third Mysore War, he accompanied his elder brother on his mission to Austrian headquarters, served subsequently in a variety of significant staff positions, and was one of few commanders to emerge with credit from the South American expedition. MP for East Retford 1801–5, he was a friend of William

Windham and thus became an unofficial military adviser to the Ministry; but it was as head of the Light Brigade, later Division, in the Peninsula that he won his real fame. His command of this élite formation was marked by harsh discipline, necessary to keep his command functioning even under such trials as the retreat to Vigo; total concern with the welfare of his troops; and unwavering determination coupled with personal bravery which sometimes caused difficulties, as at the Coa when his reluctance to withdraw put his troops in jeopardy. Near Guinaldo he remained on the enemy side of a river almost a day after he had been ordered to retire; on his return, Wellington remarked that he was glad to see him safe. 'Oh, I was in no danger, I assure you,' replied Craufurd. 'But I was, from your conduct,' said Wellington.[1] Craufurd was wounded by a shot through the lungs which lodged in the spine, while directing the Light Division's stormers at Ciudad Rodrigo, and died four days later, an irretrievable loss to the army. Unusually for so unyielding a disciplinarian, he was worshipped by many of his men, as articulated by Benjamin Harris, who thought him 'the very picture of a warrior. I shall never forget Craufurd if I live to a hundred years. He was in everything a soldier ... No man but one formed of stuff like General Craufurd could have saved the brigade from perishing altogether [on the retreat to Vigo]; and, if he flogged two, he saved hundreds from death ... he seemed an iron man; nothing daunted him – nothing turned him from his purpose. War was his very element, and toil and danger seemed to call forth only an increasing determination to surmount them.'[2]

His brother, **Lieutenant-General Sir Charles Gregan**

Craufurd (1761–1821), was commissioned in 1778, was ADC to his friend the Duke of York, and in 1793–4 served as British representative to the Austrian HQ in The Netherlands: he performed the same service in 1796 until a severe wound at Amberg prevented him from undertaking any further active service. He became lieutenant-general in 1810 and succeeded Robert as MP for East Retford (until 1812). The Craufurd brothers' uncle was Quentin Craufurd, a friend of the French royal family; his carriage was used by Louis XVI on the flight to Varennes; another kinsman was Captain Thomas Craufurd of the 3rd Foot Guards, killed at Hougoumont, and they were also related to Sir William Fraser, Bt., author of the well-known *Words on Wellington* (London, 1889), his mother, the Craufurd brothers' niece, having married Sir James Fraser, Bt., Uxbridge's ADC at Waterloo.

1. Craufurd, as below, p. 185. 2. Harris, pp. 102, 92–3.

Craufurd, Revd. A. H. *General Craufurd and his Light Division.* London. n.d. (written by Craufurd's grandson)

CREEVEY, Thomas (1768–1838)

This Whig MP held only minor political office, but is remembered for his journals and correspondence which illuminate the political and social life of the era. Although hostile to the Wellesley family (in 1810 he organised a petition against a pension for Wellington), when in Brussels in 1815 he found Wellington not at all resentful, and it was to Creevey that the Duke made his famous remark about the outcome of the 1815 campaign depending upon 'that article', the British infantryman.

Creevey, T. *The Creevey Papers*, ed. Sir Herbert Maxwell. London, 1904; *Creevey's Life and Times: A*

Further Selection from the Correspondence of Thomas Creevey, ed. J. Gore. London, 1934

CROKER, John Wilson (1780–1857)

This politician and author, born in Galway, is remembered best by the posthumous publication of his memoirs, journals and correspondence. He came to notice in 1809 after making a speech in defence of the Duke of York relative to the Clarke affair, and was appointed Secretary to the Admiralty, a position he held with distinction for more than twenty years. Despite a disagreement over the tactics involved in the siege of San Sebastian, he was a loyal friend and supporter of Wellington. A great opponent of the Reform Bill, he quit parliament in 1832 because he refused to sit in a 'reformed' house; his literary work was also extensive and included a poem on Talavera. Rees Gronow remarked on his sneering countenance and bitter remarks about all people and subjects when he dined with him in 1815!

Brightfield, M. J. *John Wilson Croker*. 1951; Croker, J. W. *The Correspondence and Diaries of John Wilson Croker*, ed. L. J. Jennings. London, 1884; *The Croker Papers*, ed. B. Pool. London, 1967

CUESTA, General Don Gregorio Garcia de la (1740–1812)

Few generals can have been as reviled by their allies as was the unfortunate Cuesta, one of Spain's best-known commanders of the period. A Castilian, who had first fought the French in 1793, he was appointed Captain-General of Estremadura in 1808. Defeated at Medina del Rio Seco and Medellin, he commanded the Spanish army which collaborated with Arthur Wellesley in the Talavera campaign, but was unwilling or unable to fulfil his obligations, so that the British had to fight virtually unsupported; Cuesta refused to supply his allies and even abandoned their wounded to the French. Infirm and immobile, he travelled in a lumbering coach and when mounted had to be held in the saddle by servants. British opinion was universally condemnatory; Benjamin D'Urban, who noted that at Medellin Cuesta 'behaved with the fire of five-and-twenty' until ridden down by his own bolting cavalry, wrote of Talavera that, 'With such Allies it is impossible to act – Treachery or Panic?'[1] John Colborne called him 'a perverse, stupid old blockhead';[2] Edward Costello, 'that deformed-looking lump of pride, ignorance and treachery ... the most murderous-looking old man I ever saw';[3] William Warre, an 'obstinate surly old ignorant fellow ... quite superannuated, and so violent and obstinate that everybody feared him but his enemies'.[4] Such opinions being typical, Cuesta's retirement in August 1809, following a stroke, was greeted with great relief. He died in Majorca in 1812.

1. D'Urban, pp. 48, 68–9. 2. Moore Smith, p. 130; 3. Costello, p. 21; 4. Warre, p. 74.

CUMBERLAND, Field Marshal Ernest Augustus, Duke of, later King of Hanover (1771–1851)

The fifth son of King George III, created Duke of Cumberland and Teviotdale in 1799, Ernest attracted much rumour and innuendo. As a cavalry general in the Hanoverian Army he lost the sight of an eye at Tournai in May 1794, and after Hanover withdrew from the war he returned to England, rising to field marshal in the British Army in November 1813, and commanding the Hanoverian Army in 1813–14. In British politics he was an extreme reactionary, opposing all reform

ERNEST AUGUSTUS, DUKE OF CUMBERLAND (ENGRAVING BY W. SKELTON AFTER W. OWEN).

and especially Catholic Emancipation. His stern demeanour and dislike of publicity gave him a sinister reputation, the wilder rumours including that he had fathered a son on his sister Sophia, of having attacked the wife of the Lord Chancellor and of having been the cause of the suicide of a wronged husband; but the most famous proven case involved a murderous attack made upon him by his valet Sallis, who was found with his throat cut. No motive for the attempted assassination or suicide was discovered, but they led to rumours that Cumberland had murdered him. Even his marriage (May 1815) was controversial, to his cousin Princess Frederica of Mecklenburg–Strelitz, who had jilted his brother, the Duke of Cambridge, and was said to have murdered her two previous husbands. The marriage caused a rift in the royal family and Cumberland went abroad, returning to oppose parliamentary reform, and upon the death of William IV he became King of Hanover, being popular with the majority of his subjects despite his reactionary attitudes.

Willis, G. M. *Ernest Augustus, Duke of Cumberland and King of Hanover*. London, 1954

CURELY, General Jean-Nicolas (1774–1827)

According to his friend General De Brack, author of the celebrated work on light cavalry tactics (*Light Cavalry Outposts*, London, 1876), he was one of the best exponents of this specialised service, and the personification of every military virtue. Born of peasant stock, he enlisted in the French 8th Hussars in 1793 and saw much service in the Revolutionary Wars, coming to special notice when at Afflenz on 12 November 1805, with a handful of men, he routed an enemy regiment. Subsequently commissioned in the 7th Hussars, he served under Lasalle in 1806–7 and won great distinction in 1809. After recovering from a shot in the left knee at Wagram, he served in Catalonia, and with the 20th *Chasseurs à Cheval* in 1812 helped Corbineau find the vital ford over the Berezina. He commanded the 10th Hussars 1813–14, was appointed *général de brigade* after making a charge at Montmirail, and was given another brigade in 1815 but only reached the army after the rout had begun. Curély received no further active employment and was retired officially in 1825; though poorly rewarded for service in twenty campaigns, 38 battles and almost fifty lesser engagements, and six wounds, his reputation as a tactician and leader was established by De Brack's assessment (his own self-effacing memoir was never intended for publication). Had he been given the opportunity, he might have become the most famous cavalry general of all.

Sheppard, Captain E. W. 'Napoleon's Best Light Cavalrymen', in *Cavalry Journal*, 1930, vol. XX, pp. 72–86; Thoumas, General. *Le Général Curély: itinéraire d'un Cavalier Léger de la Grande Armée 1793–1815*. Paris, 1887

CUSTINE, General Adam-Philippe, comte de (1740–93)

Born in Metz, the unfortunate Custine served in the army as a captain during the Seven Years War and as a colonel in the War of American Independence. Elected to the States-General in 1789 as representative of the nobility of Metz, he embarked on active service again in 1791, commanding the Army of the Vosges and in 1793 replacing Dampierre as commander of the Army of the North. After some success he fell victim to prevarication and inactivity, which may have been failings in military ability but were not treasonable; yet he was accused of absurd charges tantamount to having deliberately helped the enemy, and a ridiculous accusation that he never entertained republicans at his table. Still protesting his innocence, he was condemned and executed, one of those French generals of the Revolutionary era who fell victim to his own side rather than by the hand of the enemy.

CZARTORYSKI, Adam George, Prince (1770–1861)

A Polish nobleman, son of Prince Adam Casimir Czartoryski (1734–1823) and a British mother, Isabella Fleming, he was compelled to enter the Russian Army after the Third Partition of Poland and the confiscation of the family estates. He and his younger brother Constantine so impressed the Empress Catherine that she appointed them gentlemen-in-waiting, and Tsar Paul made him ADC to the Tsarevich Alexander. Upon the latter's accession he assumed great importance, foreign affairs being almost entirely in his hands from 1804 until he lost favour in 1807; but he remained on the best of terms with Alexander and was influential at the Congress of Vienna, drafting most of the memoranda on Polish affairs without reference to the principal Russian representative, Nesselrode. He never trusted Napoleon in relation to Polish affairs and opposed the creation of the Duchy of Warsaw, but participated in the government of the 'Congress Kingdom'; for a time he headed the administration during the 1830 revolution, and at its end went into exile in France for the remainder of his life.

Kukiel, M. *Czartoryski and European Unity 1770–1861*. New York, 1955; Zawadski, W. H. *A Man of Honour: Adam Czartorysky*. Oxford, 1993

DABROWSKI, General Jean Henri, see **DOMBROWSKI**

DALHOUSIE, General Sir George Ramsay, 9th Earl of (1770–1838)

Succeeding his father as Earl of Dalhousie in 1787, Ramsay commanded the 2nd Foot in the West Indies, Netherlands and Egypt, but is best remembered as a divisional commander under Wellington, becoming major-general in April 1808 and lieutenant-general in June 1813. He commanded the 7th Division in the Peninsula from October 1812 until the end of the war, apart from a three-month break in the winter of 1813–14, and was generally quite competent, though at times committed errors, notably in disobeying orders about the road to be taken on the retreat from Burgos, and arriving late for his allotted task at Vittoria. He served as Lieutenant-Governor of Nova Scotia (1816), Governor of Canada (1819–28) and CinC India (1830–38). His younger brother was Lieutenant-General John Ramsay (1775–1842) who served as Dalhousie's military secretary in Canada and India.

DALLAS, Alexander James (1759–1817)

Born in Jamaica of a Scottish family, and educated in Great Britain, he settled in Philadelphia in 1783 and embarked upon a legal and political career. In October 1814 he was appointed Secretary to the US Treasury, and did much towards solving the financial crisis caused by the War of 1812 and which had frustrated his predecessors. In addition to his valuable work on US finances, he served as Secretary at War from March 1815, and resigned in 1816.

DALLEMAGNE, General Claude, baron (1754–1813)

Serving in the army as an 'other rank' from 1773, including the War of American Independence, he was commissioned in 1791 and performed much useful service in Italy, notably when commanding an élite corps of grenadiers assembled from the whole army. Becoming *général de division* in 1796, he retired from active service in 1799 but returned in 1807 and participated in the resistance to the Walcheren expedition, before retiring again with the reward of a barony shortly before his death.

DALMATIA, Duke of, see **SOULT**

DALRYMPLE, General Sir Hew Whiteford, Bt. (1750–1830)

Byron's lines, 'Here folly dash'd to earth the victor's plume/For chiefs like ours in vain may laurels bloom', were written largely in condemnation of the unfortunate Dalrymple. After long service he was appointed Governor of Gibraltar in 1806; intelligent if cautious, he served well there and in 1808 was appointed to command the British expedition to the Peninsula, not only for his knowledge of Spain but because he was politically more acceptable

SIR HEW DALRYMPLE
(PRINT AFTER J. JACKSON)

than Moore or Wellesley. Arriving only after the latter's victory at Vimeiro, he concurred with his deputy Burrard's decision not to follow up the success, but instead negotiated the shameful Convention of Cintra. All three generals were called before an inquiry, from which only Wellesley was exonerated; the latter was scathing about his commander, declaring him stupid, incapable and without an idea of what to do, and the army's opinion may be gauged from the nickname 'Dowager Dalrymple'. Following the censure of the Cintra inquiry he received no further active command, but became a general in 1812, and in 1814 he petitioned for some reward in recompense for his hurt at being criticised; perhaps surprisingly, he received a baronetcy.

Dalrymple, Sir Hew. *Memoir written by General Sir Hew Dalrymple Bart. of his Proceedings as connected with the Affairs of Spain*, ed. A. J. Dalrymple. London, 1830; Fanshawe, Admiral Sir E. G. *Hew Dalrymple at Gibraltar and Portugal in 1808*. London, n.d.

DAMPIERRE, Auguste-Henri-Marie-Picot, marquis de (1756–93)

Having left the army after service in America under Rochambeau, he returned to serve in the Revolutionary Wars, initially as commander of the 5th Dragoons. Distinguished by his bravery and loyalty, notably in leading an attack at Jemappes witnessed by Du-mouriez (despite being described as having a gloomy disposition), he was appointed to command the Army of the North after the latter's defection. His period of command was short: encouraged by the political commissioners to advance in early May 1793 in an attempt to relieve Condé, when leading a counter-attack on the village of Raismes he was mortally wounded when a cannon-ball struck off his leg.

DANTON, Georges-Jacques (1759–94)

GEORGES DANTON (ENGRAVING BY T. W. HARLAND)

A leading personality of the Revolution, he was a lawyer of impressive appearance, athletic build, a loud voice and opinions which, Saint-Just remarked, made even Freedom tremble. In 1790 he was chosen to command the National Guard of his own district in Paris, where he was president of the Cordeliers' Club, and because of his popular following and influence was appointed Minister of Justice in August 1792. He was blamed by some for complicity in the September Massacres, and resigning his ministerial post became the leader of the most vehemently revolutionary members of the Convention. An original

member of the Committee of Public Safety, he led the exhortations to resist the enemy in the early Revolutionary Wars, devised the means to harness republican fervour to galvanise the army, made a number of trips to enthuse the forces and has been styled the man who saved the French from defeat. He played a role in the proscription of the Girondins and Hébertists, but himself fell victim to internal conflicts and to his rival Robespierre; despite a position of great power, Danton was condemned for having conspired with foreigners and royalists. He defended himself with vigour, but was executed on 5 April 1794.

Barthou, R. *Danton*. 1932; Beesly, A. H. *Life of Danton*. 1899; Hampson, N. *Danton*, London, 1978. Warwick, C. F. *Danton and the French Revolution*. 1909

D'ARBLAY, Madame, see BURNEY, Frances

DARU, Pierre-Antoine-Noël-Bruno, comte (1767–1829)

One of Napoleon's most loyal and dedicated subordinates, he served in the French artillery before beginning his career as a commissary in 1793, utilising his skills of administration, industry and honesty. In 1799 he was head of Massena's commissariat in Switzerland, and held the same post under Napoleon in 1800 and in the campaigns of 1805, 1806–7 and 1809. He was much more than merely an organiser, procurer of supplies and accountant: he was a signatory of the armistice which ended hostilities in northern Italy in 1800, and as *Intendant–Général* of the imperial household became a trusted adviser to Napoleon. Universally admired, he became Secretary of State in 1811; Napoleon remarked that 'he was a man distinguished for probity and for indefatigable application to business. At the retreat from

Moscow [his] firmness and presence of mind were remarkable and ... he laboured like an ox while displaying the courage of a lion.'[1] On one occasion, while taking Napoleon's dictation in the middle of the night, Daru fell asleep in mid-sentence and awoke to find Napoleon doing the writing himself. He apologised, explaining that he had been working without sleep for several days and nights. 'Why did you not inform me?' said Napoleon, kindly. 'I do not want to kill you. Go to bed. Good night, M Daru.'[2] In addition to his ability and willingness to handle excellently all tasks thrown upon him, Daru was an enthusiast for literature and published works as diverse as a poetic translation of Horace and histories of Venice and Brittany. He rallied to Napoleon in 1815, and after the second restoration became a member of the Chamber of Peers and spoke against ultra-royalist policies.

1. Las Cases, vol. III, p. 206. 2. Ibid. p. 207

Nanteuil, H. de la Barre de. *Le Comte Daru ou l'Administration militaire sous la Révolution et l'Empire*. Paris, 1966

DAVID, Jacques-Louis (1748–1825)

The most influential French painter of his generation, and the leading neo-classicist, David was distantly related to Boucher but instead of the latter's rococo adopted a more austere style. Although Louis XVI had been his chief patron, David embraced the Revolution, was elected to the Convention and became its president, and voted for the execution of the king. His pictures were enormously popular, exemplifying republican virtues, perhaps most notably *The Oath of the Horatii* (1785), as well as those with more immediate political connection such as *Marat*. Briefly imprisoned after the fall of Robespierre, he became an enthusiastic admirer of Napoleon and as painter to the Emperor completed a number of almost propagandist works such as *Napoleon crossing the Alps* and the *Coronation*. Forced into exile as a regicide at the Bourbon restoration, he settled in Brussels where he remained for the remainder of his life. From the earlier, stern neo-classical style, his later work shows the beginnings of the influence of Romanticism; and his portraits in particular are wonderfully executed. He should not be confused with the sculptor Pierre-Jean David (1789–1856), known from his place of birth as David d'Angers, whose best work was executed in the post-Napoleonic period.

DAVOUT, Marshal Louis-Nicolas, duc d'Auerstädt, prince d'Eckmühl (1770–1823)

LOUIS NICOLAS DAVOUT (ENGRAVING BY R. A. MULLER AFTER C. GAUTHEROT)

Probably the most capable of Napoleon's Marshals, Davout (whose name may be found rendered as Davoût or Davoust) was commissioned in his father's regiment in 1788; dismissed because of over-zealous support for the Revolution, he was elected lieutenant-colonel of the 3rd Battalion of Yonne Volunteers. He

came to prominence for service at Neerwinden and in an unsuccessful attempt to intercept Dumouriez's defection, and became *général de brigade*; but had to resign as a *ci-devant* aristocrat until his rank was restored after the fall of Robespierre. He served on the Rhine and in Egypt under Desaix, was promoted to *général de division* in 1800, and, having impressed Napoleon, was the youngest of the first creation of Marshals of the Empire in 1804. His connection to Napoleon was made closer by his appointment as colonel-general of the Imperial Guard Grenadiers, and his marriage to the sister of Leclerc, Pauline Bonaparte's husband. In 1805 he led III Corps in a notable forced march to Austerlitz, where he commanded Napoleon's right, and won more fame by his victory at Auerstädt in 1806, which name he took for the dukedom he was awarded in March 1808. He led the decisive flank-attack at Eylau, and in 1809 was distinguished at Eckmühl (for which he was awarded the title of prince in that August) and Wagram; and in 1812 commanded I Corps, which his stern discipline made the best in the army. In 1813–14 he held Hamburg with great resolution, and in 1815 was Napoleon's War Minister and Governor of Paris, probably a waste of his battlefield talents. After two years of disfavour and internal exile he was reinstated by the Bourbons, and in 1819 became a member of the Chamber of Peers. Although not especially military in appearance (bald, and wearing powerful spectacles), his talents were considerable. A stern, dour disciplinarian, he had few gracious attributes (hence the nickname 'the Iron Marshal') and his reputation suffered from his governorships of the Duchy of Warsaw (from 1807) and Hamburg, where he was known as 'the terrible Davout' or 'the Hamburg Robe-

spierre'; the Abbé de Pradt remarked that 'no despotism could exceed that of this old soldier of liberty: he filled all Poland with dread, and brought much disgrace on the French name'.[1] In fairness one must say that he was given the most difficult tasks and carried them out with minute care and, if never especially liked, was the epitome of the dedicated, brave and determined professional; and though he assembled a large fortune, he was never a blatant plunderer like other Marshals. His considerable ability was not always best employed nor was his advice always heeded; for example, he advocated a wide flank-march at Borodino, which might have avoided the butchery of a frontal attack, only for Napoleon to rebuff him: 'Ah! you are always for turning the enemy; it is too dangerous a manoeuvre!'[2]

1. Anon., p. 335. 2. Ségur, vol. I, p. 321.

Blocqueville, marquise de. *Le Maréchal Davout raconté par les siens et lui-même.* Paris, 1878–80 (compiled by Davout's daughter); Chandler, D. G. 'The Iron Marshal: Davout', in *Napoleon's Marshals*, ed. Chandler. London, 1987 (includes a bibliography); Davout, L. N. *Correspondance du Maréchal Davout, prince d'Eckmühl*, ed. C. de Mazade. Paris, 1885; *Operations de 3e Corps 1806–07*, ed. L. Davout. Paris, 1896; Gallagher, J. G.: *The Iron Marshal: A Biography of Louis N. Davout.* Champaign, Illinois, 1976; Hourtoulle, H. F. G. L. *Davout Le Terrible.* Paris, 1975; Vigier, J. *Davout, Maréchal de l'Empire.* Paris, 1898 (written by Davout's grandson)

DAVY DE LA PAILLETERIE, General Thomas, see DUMAS

DEARBORN, Major General Henry (1751–1829)

Originally a New Hampshire medical practitioner, he was a

lieutenant colonel who had served in the War of American Independence and as Jefferson's Secretary at War; already a major general of Massachusetts Militia, in January 1812 he was appointed senior major general with responsibility for the northern frontier. Despite his earlier military record, he proved unfitted for higher command, and his inept strategy was a contributory factor in Hull's surrender at Detroit. Known to the army as 'Granny', he was relieved of command in July 1813 when his ineptitude became obvious (Secretary at War Armstrong stated that the burden was too heavy for him to carry with advantage to the nation or credit to himself), yet he was nominated as Secretary at War in March 1815, only for the offer to be withdrawn after protests and rejection by the Senate. He served as US Ambassador to Portugal 1822–4.

DECAEN, General Charles-Mathieu-Isidore, comte (1769–1832)

After serving with distinction at Hohenlinden, and becoming *général de division* in 1799, in 1802 he was appointed commander of the French possessions in the East Indies. Finding Pondicherry indefensible, he made his base at Ile de France (Mauritius) from August 1803, re-organised the military forces and did what he could to damage British commerce with India. Despite sturdy resistance, Mauritius was captured by the British in 1810; Decaen was wounded but permitted to return to France, from 1811 commanding the French army in Catalonia, in 1814 the forces in the Bordeaux region, and during the Hundred Days he commanded in the eastern Pyrenees.

Decaen, C. M. I. *Mémoires et journaux du Général Decaen*, ed. E. Picard and P. Pallier. Paris, 1911;

Gautier, M. L. E. *Biographie du Général Decaen*. Caen, 1850

DECATUR, Commodore Stephen (1779–1820)

Having joined the US Navy in 1798, he came to prominence in the operations against Tripoli in 1804: as a lieutenant commanding the gunboat *Number Four*, he captured an enemy vessel by an audacious boarding action in which he killed the enemy captain in single combat. In the War of 1812 he won greater fame when, as captain of USS *United States*, he captured the frigate HMS *Macedonian* off Madeira in a violent action. In 1813 he was appointed commodore of a squadron at New York, but in January 1815 was forced to surrender in his flagship USS *President* to a British squadron. Subsequently he served against the Mediterranean corsairs again, and was killed in a duel with another naval officer, James Barron. He is perhaps best remembered for his declaration when proposing a toast in 1816: 'May she always be in the right; but our country, right or wrong.'

Mackenzie, A. S. *Life of Decatur*. Boston, 1846

DECRES, Admiral Denis, duc de St. Germain (1761–1820)

Best known as Napoleon's Minister of Marine, Decrès, comte and later duc de St. Germain, also had a distinguished career at sea. Having entered the navy of the *ancien régime*, he rose to the rank of rear-admiral (1797) and came to prominence during operations in the Mediterranean. For the Egyptian expedition he commanded the convoy of transports, but his greatest exploit was in attempting to carry a message from Vaubois, the Governor of Malta, that the island could not hold out much longer. Decrès sailed in the 74-gun *Guillaume Tell*, but encountered HMSs *Pene-*

lope, *Lion* and *Foudroyant*, and surrendered only after 'a most obstinate Defence of Three Hours and a Half'[1] in which his ship was so shot to pieces as to be quite unmanageable, which earned him great praise. As *vice-amiral* and Minister of Marine he exerted influence over Napoleon's maritime policy, and was also concerned with the affairs of the Seamen of the Imperial Guard as well as with the naval battalions deployed in land campaigns. He accepted the Bourbon restoration and was killed in 1820 by a charge of gunpowder under his bed, apparently laid by his valet.

1. Dispatch of Captain Manley Dixon, HMS *Lion*, in *Gazette*, 3 June 1800.

DEJEAN, General Pierre-François, comte (1780–1845)

He gained his first military experience as ADC to his father, the French engineer general Jean-François-Aimé Dejean; then transferred to the cavalry, served in the 1805–6 campaigns and attained command of the 11th Dragoons in 1807. After service in the Peninsula he became *général de brigade* (August 1811), in 1812 led a brigade of the 5th Heavy Cavalry Division of I Cavalry Corps, became an imperial ADC (February 1813) and *général de division* (March 1814). In 1815 he became involved in the controversy over the fatal counter-marching of d'Erlon's corps in the Waterloo campaign: Napoleon thought that he was involved in a reconnaissance of d'Erlon's position and the confusion which occurred, but Dejean declared that his mission on the French left was totally unconnected with d'Erlon, whose troops he did not see, and thus was blamed unfairly. At the second restoration he lived in exile until 1818, but became a peer upon his father's death and was returned to duty in 1830.

DELABORDE, General Henri-François, comte (1764–1833)

In British annals he is remembered as the first French commander to be defeated by Wellington. The son of a Dijon baker, he enlisted as a private in 1783, advanced rapidly after the Revolution, becoming *général de division* in 1793. Chief of staff at Toulon, he served in the Pyrenees and in Germany with Moreau, and in 1807 commanded Junot's 1st Division in the Peninsula. He commanded against, and was defeated by, Arthur Wellesley at Rolica, and in 1809 led the 3rd Division of Soult's II Corps. Ennobled in 1808, he led the 1st Division of the Imperial Guard in the 1812 Russian campaign, was still with the Guard when wounded at Pirna in August 1813, and having rejoined Napoleon in 1815 received no further employment after the Bourbon restoration.

DE LOUTHERBOURG, Philippe-Jacques (1740–1812)

This Strasbourg-born artist was elected to the French Academy in 1767, but lived in England from 1771 and became a naturalised subject (hence he is sometimes styled Philip James). Hired by David Garrick as a scenery painter at Drury Lane Theatre, where he was a great success, he was elected to the Royal Academy in 1781. He painted a number of important military canvases, including naval subjects for Greenwich Hospital such as *Lord Howe's Victory off Ushant*, as well as *The Siege of Valenciennes* and *The Landing in Egypt*; sketches for such works demonstrate his meticulous attention to detail of uniforms, equipment and portraits. He later became interested in more arcane matters, including faith-healing, and was involved with the alchemist and fraudster Count Alessandro Cagliostro (1743–95).

DE LANCEY, Colonel Sir William Howe (c.1781–1815)

SIR WILLIAM DE LANCEY

Born in New York of an eminent Loyalist family (his father, Stephen, who died as Governor of Tobago, was the son of General Oliver De Lancey), he appears to have been commissioned in the British Army at a remarkably early age (though his date of birth is uncertain). He served with distinction as a staff officer in the Peninsula (he received the Gold Cross with five clasps), but is best remembered as deputy quartermaster-general in the Waterloo campaign, the Duke of Wellington having insisted that he be given this appointment in preference to Sir Hudson Lowe. At Waterloo, De Lancey was hit in the back by a roundshot, and despite the ministrations of the young wife whom he had married only on 4 April 1815, he died a week later, universally lamented both for his abilities and his personality. His wife Magdalene, sister of Captain Basil Hall, RN, wrote a moving account of her experiences, published as *A Week at Waterloo in 1815*, ed. Major B. R. Ward. London, 1906.

DELORT, General Jacques-Antoine-Adrien, baron (1773–1846)

Commissioned after less than a year's service (1792), he served on Sérurier's staff in Italy before joining the French cavalry; he served with the 9th Dragoons at Austerlitz, in Italy 1806–7 and in the Peninsula, mostly under Suchet, becoming a baron in October 1810 and *général de brigade* in July 1811. He won fame for his victory over O'Donnell's Spanish army at Castalla (21 July 1812), served in France in 1814, becoming *général de division* in February, and succeeded Pajol in command of the 2nd Division of II Cavalry Corps. Although not an ardent Bonapartist, which raised doubts about employing him in 1815, he led the 14th Cavalry Division of IV Cavalry Corps in the Waterloo campaign, receiving two wounds to add to those sustained in earlier campaigns. Unemployed until the advent of Louis-Philippe, from 1830 he held a number of significant military posts, and served as a Deputy; he was made a peer of France in 1837 and retired in 1841.

DELZONS, General Alexis-Joseph, baron (1775–1812)

Although probably best remembered as one of the generals of the *Grande Armée* who perished in Russia, he had had a long experience of earlier service. Volunteering during the Revolutionary Wars, he served in Italy (including Dego, where he was wounded, Lodi and Rivoli), Egypt, and at Wagram and Znaim (again wounded). *Général de brigade* on his return from Egypt, *de division* in 1811, he led the 13th Division of Eugène's IV Corps in 1812. He survived Borodino but was killed at Maloyaroslavets while urging on his division which, after absorbing much heavy fire, was beginning to waver in its attack. Delzons was hit in the head by a ball and killed on the spot; his brother, Major Jean-Baptiste Delzons (1787–1812) attempted to carry him away but was himself mortally wounded while so doing.

DENON, Dominique-Vivant, baron de (1747–1825)

After a career as a minor French diplomat and a popular member of royal society as a literary and antiquarian expert, from 1787 he devoted himself to artistic and antiquarian pursuits, living abroad for part of the Revolutionary period. He became a friend of Napoleon after they had met at Josephine Beauharnais' salon, so with his artistic skills and knowledge of ancient artefacts it was natural that he should accompany the Egyptian expedition as part of the scientific commission. He followed Desaix in the campaign in Upper Egypt, which involved some hazard, such as an occasion when Menou and a part-civilian party were ambushed; Denon and others defended themselves successfully but the artist Joly became so hysterical that he could not even flee, and was killed. On his return to France, Denon published *Voyage dans la Basse et la Haute Egypte pendant les campagnes de Bonaparte en 1798 et 1799* (Paris, 1802; London, 1807), which confirmed his reputation as an artist and archaeologist; his work was the first to popularise the art and antiquities of ancient Egypt. He became the first director of the Louvre and later accompanied Napoleon on his campaigns as artistic adviser, his work including the evaluation of captured works of art.

Châtelain, J. *Dominique-Vivant Denon et le Louvre de Napoléon.* Paris, 1973

DENUELLE, Charles-Léon, comte (1806–81)

Known as 'comte Léon', he was an illegitimate son of Napoleon, by Eléonore Denuelle de la Plaigne, to whom Napoleon had been introduced by his sister Caroline. Although their liaison was of short duration, Napoleon acknowledged its product and made a bequest to him in the seventh codicil of his will. The child was ennobled as comte in 1815 and granted a pension, which was abolished by the Bourbons. Eléonore married three times, finally becoming countess of Laxburg when she married the Minister of State of the Grand Duchy of Baden. A spendthrift and a gambler, Léon appealed for help to Napoleon III who paid his debts and granted him a pension.

Dodds, D. W. *Napoleon's Love Child: A Biography of Count Léon.* 1974.

D'ERLON, Marshal Jean-Baptiste Drouet, comte (1765–1844)

Perhaps the most celebrated example of confused or mistaken orders during the entire period are those which led to comte d'Erlon's corps taking no part in the battles of Ligny or Quatre Bras, where its presence at either could have been decisive. A native of Rheims, he joined the army in 1782 but only gained a commission during the Revolutionary Wars, rising to *général de brigade* (1799) and *de division* (August 1803), after service at Hohenlinden. He was ennobled as comte d'Erlon after the campaigns of Austerlitz and Friedland (where he was wounded while serving as Lannes' chief of staff). In the Peninsula he proved to be one of the most capable subordinate commanders: he led IX Corps at Fuentes de Oñoro, the 5th Division under Soult in 1812, and was successively commander of the Armies of the Centre, then Portugal, the 'lieutenancy' of the Centre in 1813 and the left wing of the army at Nivelle and Nive. Although employed by the Bourbons after the first restoration, he rejoined Napoleon in 1815 and was given command of I Corps; and the unfortunate events of 16 June have tended to overshadow his otherwise capable service. Napoleon, however, seems not to have blamed him, and he commanded the right at Waterloo, where his tactics showed little evidence of lessons learned from Peninsula experience. Sentenced to death *in absentia* by the Bourbons, he ran an inn at Bayreuth until an amnesty in 1825 permitted his return to France where he resumed duty under Louis-Philippe (in whose interests he had been involved in a number of conspiracies), and although his period as Governor-General of Algeria (1834–5) was undistinguished, he became a Marshal of France in 1843. He should not be confused with **Jean-Baptiste Drouet (1763–1824)**, a minor political figure of the Revolution, chiefly known for recognising the royal family on their flight to Varennes, which led to their arrest. An extreme member of the Convention, as commissioner to the army he was captured at Maubeuge (breaking his leg while trying to escape by jumping from a window!); he had to flee for a time after helping Babeuf's Jacobin conspiracy, and again (as a regicide) at the restoration, but returned to live under an alias.

DESAIX (correctly Desaix de Veygoux), General Louis-Charles-Antoine (1768–1800)

One of the most celebrated of Napoleon's early companions, he was born of a noble but impoverished family. He was commissioned in 1783 but embraced the principles of the Revolution. His abilities were soon recognised and he became *général de brigade* in September 1793 and *de division* in the following year. Greatly distinguished in command of Jourdan's right wing in 1795 and under Moreau in 1796, notably in the

LOUIS CHARLES DESAIX
(ENGRAVING BY TIETZE AFTER GUÉRIN)

defence of Kehl, his popularity equalled that of Moreau and Bonaparte, but he became a devoted follower of the latter. Entrusted with an important command in the Egyptian expedition, he conquered Upper Egypt while Napoleon was away in Syria, and was not only skilled militarily but behaved with such humanity towards the local populace that he was nicknamed 'the Just Sultan'. He signed the Convention of El Arish but was detained by Keith for some time, returning home only just in time for the climax of the Marengo campaign. Detached from the army on the day of the battle, he hurried back towards the sound of gunfire and arrived to find the Austrians poised for victory; Desaix remarked that the battle was lost, but, 'There is yet time to win another.' While leading the attack which turned the battle in Napoleon's favour he was shot through the heart, conceivably by accident by his own side; stories that he exclaimed 'Dead!', or 'Tell the First Consul that I die with regret because I feel that I have not done enough to be remembered by posterity'[1] are probably apocryphal, because the surgeons who embalmed his body found the heart so shattered that they doubted that he could have spoken

a single word. He was admired and lamented universally; even in England, the country of his nation's bitterest enemies, he was described as 'esteemed by the French soldiers, honoured by the Austrians, and loved by all who knew him'.[2] Napoleon remarked that Desaix 'lived only for noble ambition and true glory; his character was formed on the ancient model', as such would never have been a rival, and that his death was 'the greatest loss he could possibly have sustained';[3] he might have thought differently had Desaix lived, knowing that he had saved Napoleon from defeat and that the laurels of Marengo were at least in part Desaix's.

1. 'Other Interesting Particulars respecting the Battle of Marengo' by 'C. J.', in *British Military Library or Journal*. London, 1801, vol. II, p. 422. 2. *Monthly Review*. London, 1804, Appendix p. 541. 3. Las Cases, vol. I, p. 148.

Martha-Beker, F. *Le Général L. C. A. Desaix*. Paris, 1852; Sauzet, A. *Desaix, le 'Sultan juste'*. Paris, 1954

DESGENETTES, René-Nicolas Dufiche, baron (1762–1837)

One of the most celebrated medical practitioners of the era, and actually baron des Genettes (he amended his name as a tribute to republican sympathies), he served in Italy and with the Egyptian expedition as Physician-in-Chief. He represented Medicine in the Institute of Egypt, and it was said that to calm fears of contagion he inoculated himself with pus from plague victims (which he later denied, and Larrey said he only pretended to do it);[1] and he also opposed Napoleon's order to poison plague victims at Jaffa, though this probably did not occur in the way that it was often told. Ennobled as a baron by Napoleon, he was appointed Inspector-General of Medical Services and in the 1812 campaign

was Physician-in-chief to the *Grande Armée*. Captured by the Russians, he was set free by the Tsar because of his reputation as a humanitarian and after Larrey's intercession, though he showed little gratitude to the latter. He was captured again at Leipzig and again released, served in the Waterloo campaign, and at the end of the wars retained a revered position in the French medical establishment, including the appointment in 1832 as Physician-in-Chief to the Invalides.

1. See, e.g., Richardson, R. G. *Larrey: Surgeon to Napoleon's Imperial Guard*. London, 1974, p. 165.

Desgenettes, R. N. D. *Histoire médicale de l'Armée d'Orient*. Paris, 1802

DESMOULINS, Lucie-Simplice-Camille-Benoist (1760–94)

A lawyer at the beginning of the

CAMILLE DESMOULINS
(ENGRAVING BY W. GREATBATCH)

Revolution, and despite an unprepossessing appearance, violent manner and stammer, he made a political mark by haranguing the populace from the table of a cafe, pistol in hand, urging the uprising which led to the fall of the Bastille. He achieved fame as a pamphleteer, was one of the first to call for a republic, and became Danton's secretary, a member of the Convention and an associate of Robespierre. His publication *Vieux Cordelier* was critical of the Hébertists and approved of by Robespierre, but it also exposed the horrors of the Revolution, and his association with Danton caused Robespierre to denounce Desmoulins as a moderate. He was tried with Danton and his faction, Desmoulins raging at the court and calling them murderers until he was dragged away, and resisted violently on the day of his execution, 5 April 1794. His wife Lucile, whom he had married in 1790, was also condemned on a false charge and executed eight days later; she impressed all with her dignified bearing, so different from the rage of her husband on the scaffold.

Methley V. M. *Camille Desmoulins: A Biography*, London 1914

DESPARD, Colonel Edward Marcus (1751–1803)

Born in Queen's County, one of five out of six brothers who served in the British Army or Navy, he was commissioned in 1766 and served with distinction in the West Indies. When he was unable to gain redress for his dismissal on unfair charges from his post as Governor of the Mosquito Coast and Honduras, after a period in custody, he formed an insane scheme to assassinate the king and seize the Tower and Bank of England, with a few other conspirators who were members of a revolutionary society known as 'Free and Easy'. Despard was arrested and with six others was tried for high treason; they were the last people in Great Britain to be sentenced to be hanged, drawn and quartered. They were executed on 21 February 1803 (in the event the punishment involved only hanging and decapitation after death); Despard died proclaiming his innocence. His

dreadful fate seems not to have impaired the career of his brother, **General John Despard (1745–1829)**, who attained the rank of general in June 1814 and held the colonelcy of the 5th West India Regiment from 1809.

Bannatine, J. *Memoirs of Edward Marcus Despard*. London, 1899.

DESSAIX, General Joseph-Marie, comte (1764–1834)

Not to be confused with the more celebrated Desaix, he was born in Savoy and qualified in medicine before joining the Paris National Guard in 1789. In 1792 he formed the Légion des Allobroges, served at Toulon, in the Pyrenees and in Italy, and was captured at Rivoli. Elected to the Council of Five Hundred in 1798, he opposed the coup of Brumaire, but in 1803 became *général de brigade*. He distinguished himself in 1809, notably in holding a bridgehead over the Piave with an advance-guard of *voltigeurs*, was promoted to *général de division* and ennobled as comte. In Russia in 1812 he led the 4th Division of I Corps, and at Borodino twice took command when successive commanders were wounded (Compans and Rapp); exposed to heavy fire throughout, he had a brandy bottle broken by a bullet which hit his saddle-holster, and finally was incapacitated by a shot in the left arm. He took service under the Bourbons but in 1816 was imprisoned briefly by them for rejoining Napoleon during the Hundred Days, and saw no further service.

Dessaix, J. *Le Général Dessaix*. Paris, 1879; Girod de l'Ain, General Baron. *Dix Ans de mes Souvenirs militaires*. Paris, 1873 (written by Dessaix's ADC)

DESSALINES, Jean-Jacques, Emperor Alexandre I of Haiti (1758–1806)

One of Toussaint l'Ouverture's

generals, he renewed the fight against the French in Haiti following Toussaint's arrest, in a war conducted with great barbarity. Following the French evacuation he assumed total power, first as Governor for life and from October 1804 as self-proclaimed Emperor Alexandre I. His rule was marked by continued bloodshed (he began with a massacre of whites), until he was assassinated in a revolt against his tyranny in 1806, which introduced a period of civil war between the rivals for his succession, Henri Christophe (1767–1820) and Alexandre Sebas Pétion (1770–1818), which lasted until the latter's death.

DESSOLLES, General Jean-Joseph-Paul, marquis de (1767–1828)

Despite noble birth, he rose to the rank of *général de brigade* (1797) and *de division* (1799) in the French Army during the Revolutionary Wars, served in Italy and under Moreau at Hohenlinden. After a period of voluntary retirement (out of loyalty to Moreau) he was sent to the Peninsula, where he led the largest divisional command in Spain, the Reserve Division some 8,500 strong at the beginning of 1809. Recalled in 1811, he was invalided home from the Russian campaign and in 1814 joined the Bourbons, to whom he remained loyal in 1815. In 1817 he was ennobled as a marquis and in the following year held the portfolio of Foreign Minister and President of the Council of Ministers.

DETAILLE, Jean-Baptiste-Edouard (1848–1912)

Although not a personality of the Napoleonic era, he deserves a mention as one of the great battle-painters of history, renowned chiefly for scenes of the Franco–Prussian War (in which he

EDOUARD DETAILLE

rved in the *Gardes–Mobiles*), but qually adept at pictures of the apoleonic age, which were accu- tely rendered and evocative of e Napoleonic legend, for ample his *Vive l'Empereur!* (a large of French hussars), and *aut les têtes! La mitraille n'est pas e la merde!* (Lepic and the renadiers à Cheval of the Impe- al Guard at Eylau).

Humbert, J. *Edouard Detaille: Héroïsme d'un Siècle*. Paris, 1979; e is also featured in Goetschy, G. *es Jeunes Peintres Militaires*. aris, n.d.

E WINTER, Admiral Jan illem (1750–1812)

native of Holland, he entered the avy of that state in 1761 but as a eutenant was forced to emigrate ter the 1787 rebellion, which as 1 ardent republican he had upported. He entered the French rmy, served in the campaigns of 792–3 and became *général de rigade*; when Holland was verrun in 1795 he returned home nd was given command of the eet of the new Batavian Republic s rear-admiral, rising to vice- dmiral in 1796. He improved the eet but led it to heroic defeat by uncan at Camperdown, being aptured when his flagship rijheid was forced to strike. uncan found him an agreeable

companion who spoke excellent English (and presumably an enter- taining guest, because de Winter was an excellent flute-player) and was impressed by his gallantry (he was the only man left alive on his quarterdeck when he surren- dered). Exchanged in 1797, he served as Batavian Ambassador to France 1798–1802 before resuming command of the fleet, making a cruise to the Barbary states and negotiating a peace with Tripoli. Louis Bonaparte appointed him a Marshal and Count of Huessen, and as commander of both army and navy he served against the Walcheren expedition. Upon the incorporation of the Kingdom of Holland into the French empire, Napoleon made de Winter inspector-general of the northern coasts and commander of the fleet at the Texel.

DIAVOLO, Fra (Michele Pezza) (l771–1806)

'Fra Diavolo' – the latter appropri- ately signifying 'devil' – was the name adopted by the notorious Italian bandit Michele Pezza who in 1799 was enlisted into Cardinal Ruffo's 'Army of the Holy Faith' as the leader of a band of brigands intent on reconquering the Parthenopean Republic on behalf of the Bourbons of Naples. Diavolo was more military than some and wrought considerable havoc among the French and their allies – he was created Duke of Cassano for his successes – but perpetrated excesses which horrified even his own side; Joseph Bonaparte put a price on his head. Having attacked the French in Calabria, he did the same from Sicily and returned to the mainland where he was even- tually arrested, tried and shot. Despite his cruelty, his audacity and courage won a degree of popularity, and he was the subject of the 1830 opera *Fra Diavolo* by Daniel Auber (1782–1871).

DIBDIN, Charles (1745–1814)

This British musician, author, actor and song-writer occupies a minor niche in the chronicles of the Napoleonic Wars by virtue of his sea-songs, their morale- boosting aspect meriting a govern- ment pension of £200 p.a. from 1803 (but withdrawn during the Grenville administration); the best-known is probably the moving *Tom Bowling*. Such was the popularity of his verses that it was said that he brought in more recruits to the navy than did the press-gangs, and earned him the sobriquet of 'the Tyrtaeus of the British Navy', after the Spartan poet of the 7th century BC whose marching-songs and martial odes were popular with the Spartan troops at about the time of the second Messenian War.

DICKSON, Major-General Sir Alexander (1777–1840)

The son of Admiral William Dickson, he was commissioned in the Royal Artillery in 1794 and served in Malta and South America, but is best known as Wellington's chief gunner in the Peninsula. Initially Wellington had difficulty in finding a competent artillery chief, but found the ideal man in Dickson; though he had to invoke Dickson's commission as lieutenant-colonel in the Portuguese artillery to enable him to be placed over his seniors in the Royal Artillery, Dickson wearing his Portuguese uniform to avoid giving them offence. At Vittoria and subsequently he commanded the entire Allied artillery with skill and resolution. In 1815 Dickson returned from America (where he had served at New Orleans) only to find that an artillery chief (Sir George Wood) had been appointed to Wellington's army, so during the Hundred Days he commanded the battering train. He was always referred to by his brevet rank of lieutenant-colonel, but as promotion in the Ordnance services was by seniority, even with his vast experience and competence, his regimental rank was that of captain throughout the period. He eventually became major-general. His diaries and letters form an important source for the history of the Peninsular War.

Dickson, Sir Alexander. *The Dickson Manuscripts*, ed. Major J. H. Leslie. Woolwich, 1905, repr. Cambridge, from 1987; 'Artillery Services in North America in 1814 and 1815', ed. Leslie, in *Journal of the Society for Army Historical Research*, vol. VIII, 1929

DIEBITSCH (later DIEBITSCH-ZABALKANSKY), Field Marshal Hans Karl Friedrich Anton, Count von (1785–1831)

HANS VON DIEBITSCH
(PRINT AFTER STEINMETZ)

Born in Silesia, the son of an ADC of Frederick the Great, he was one of a number of Prussian officers who entered Russian service, though in his case earlier than most. Wounded at Austerlitz, he served at Eylau and Friedland, became major-general in 1812 and, commanding Wittgenstein's advance-guard, helped negotiate the Convention of Tauroggen which brought York's Prussians to the Allied side. He was further distinguished at Dresden and

Leipzig, and gave useful advice in 1814 (advocating the drive on Paris). He had considerable influence upon Tsars Alexander and Nicholas (ennobled by the latter), attended the Congress of Vienna, became chief of the Russian general staff and won great renown in the Russo–Turkish War (1828–9); for his success in the Adrianople campaign he was promoted to field marshal and given the honorary name 'Zabalkansky' to commemorate his crossing of the Balkans. He was given command of the forces engaged in suppressing the Polish insurrection, but died (of cholera or suicide) on 10 June 1831.

DIGHTON, Denis (1792–1827)

Military Painter to the Prince Regent, he is well known for his depictions of contemporary troops, including scenes from the Peninsular War. A fine draughtsman, his pictures are full of character and generally quite authentic, though less trustworthy in the treatment of foreign uniforms than those which depict British troops (he held a commission in the 90th Foot 1811–12). Some of his battle-scenes are especially effective, his skill in handling water-colour compensating for any slight errors in proportion. He made drawings at Waterloo in 1815 and accompanied George IV on his tour to Scotland, but loss of royal favour seems to have affected his mind; he retired to Saint-Servan in Brittany and died there. His father, Robert Dighton (1752–1814), exhibited as a professional artist at the age of 17, and was also an actor. Although not primarily a 'military' artist, he made many caricatures-cum-character studies at Brighton and London 1801–4, and some more finished, spectacular water-colour portraits (like that of his son Robert in the uniform of the Prince of Wales's

Volunteers) which are meticulo[us] records of regimental uniform[s]. His reputation was somewh[at] damaged by his unauthoris[ed] removal of prints from the Briti[sh] Museum. Robert Dighton, ju[nior] (1786–1865) produced milita[ry] caricatures and some superb finished portraits, but was more serving officer than an art[ist] (commissioned April 1809, lie[u]tenant 1812, served in the Peni[n]sula 1810–12 and was wound[ed] with the 1/38th at Bayonne, ha[lf] pay November 1834). A third so[n] Richard (1795–1880) was also a[n] artist, and also produced caric[a]tures (including some under th[e] pseudonym 'Simon Pure').

Haswell Miller, A. E., an[d] Dawnay, N. P. *Military Drawin[gs] and Paintings in the Royal Colle[c]tion*. London, 1966–70 (contain[s] many reproductions of th[e] Dightons' work); Rose, D. *Li[fe,] Times and Recorded Works [of] Robert Dighton*. London 1981

DJEZZAR PASHA, Ahmed (c.1735?–1804)

Governor of Acre and command[er] of Ottoman forces in Syria, he w[as] one of the most unusual and ter[ri]fying opponents encountered [by] Napoleon. Ahmed had fled h[is] native Bosnia, possibly after [a] murder, and entered Ottom[an] service, ultimately as a Mamelu[ke] in the service of Ali Bey of Cair[o.] Nicknamed 'the Butcher', he eli[m]inated Ali Bey's opponents [by] assassination. Of violent temper[a]ment, he quarrelled with Ali B[ey,] took service under Emir Yusuf [of] the Druses, quarrelled with hi[m] and finally acquired the appoin[t]ment as Pasha of Acre. He w[as] accused of great atrocities, esp[e]cially against Christians, and it w[as] said that all the inhabitants [of] Syria hated his oppression. He w[as] politically astute and defend[ed] Acre – with the help of Sidn[ey] Smith and Louis-Edmond [de] Phélipeaux – stalwartly, if not in hion entirely in accord with the ꞁets of European warfare: after ꞁ first French attack Djezzar had ꞁveral hundred Christian pris- ꞁers (including Napoleon's dip- ꞁnat messenger, Mailly de ꞁâteaurenard) strangled and ꞁeir bodies flung into the sea to ꞁ found by the French. Ever of an ꞁdependent mind, Djezzar re- ꞁsed to co-operate with the ꞁand Vizier and his army which ꞁer advanced through Syria, as if ꞁsentful of all invaders, whether ꞁench or 'friendly' Turks.

ꞁKHTUROV, General Dmitri ꞁrgeivich (1756–1816)

ꞁobably best known for an action ꞁring the 1812 campaign, this ꞁssian general was widely expe- ꞁnced in important commands: ꞁ Austerlitz he commanded the ꞁ Column of the Allied army and ꞁved bravely in conducting a ꞁhting retreat, led the reserve at ꞁlau, and VI Corps at Borodino. ꞁthough described as something ꞁ a courtier – on one occasion ꞁring the 1812 campaign Barclay ꞁ Tolly had to call him to his duty ꞁhile Dokhturov was serving ꞁttuzov with his lunch! – he was ꞁcognised as a worthy man, and ꞁ was he who headed off the ꞁench line of retreat and engaged ꞁem at Maloyaroslavets, and held ꞁs ground until reinforcements ꞁrived and the *Grande Armée* ꞁtired. His name is sometimes ꞁndered as 'Doctorov'.

ꞁOLGORUKI, General Prince ꞁeter Petrovich (1776–1806)

ꞁ member of an influential ꞁssian noble family, he was a ꞁusted aide and favourite of the ꞁar and a rival of Czartoryski. ꞁe most militant of Alexander's ꞁdes, he served as his 'general- ꞁljutant' in the Austerlitz ꞁmpaign, being employed as a ꞁenipotentiary in negotiations ꞁth the French, most notably at ꞁ interview with Napoleon before

the battle. Dolgoruki exhibited such arrogance and intransigence that Napoleon told him in no uncertain terms to be off and tell his master that he (Napoleon) would not stand for such insults. From this meeting and Dolgo- ruki's reconnaissance the Allies were led into fatally under-esti- mating Napoleon's strength and circumstances.

DOMBROWSKI (sometimes 'DABROWSKI'), General Jan Henryk (otherwise styled **Jean Henri**), (1755–1818)

Born near Cracow, after service in the army of Saxony, where he was raised, he entered the service of his native Poland in 1791, serving with Kosciusko before emigrating. In January 1797 he formed a Polish Legion for the Cisalpine Republic, which served in the Italian campaigns, and rose to the rank of *général de brigade*. In 1806 he raised a Polish division for Napoleon, served with it at Fried- land, and in 1812 commanded the 17th Division of Poniatowski's Polish V Corps of the *Grande Armée*. Stationed to the south and east of Minsk, Dombrowski was ordered to hold the bridge over the Berezina at Borisov, to enable the retreating army to escape; he arrived there on the night of 20/21 November to find imperfect preparations for the defence of the position, and when heavily attacked at dawn had to withdraw before reinforcements could arrive, losing the river-crossing which could have been cata- strophic for Napoleon. He was wounded in the subsequent fighting around the Berezina; in 1813 he succeeded to Ponia- towski's command after that Marshal's death at Leipzig, and in 1814 returned to Poland. In 1815 he was appointed a general by the Tsar and given the task of re- organising the Polish Army, but retired in 1816.

DOMMARTIN, General Elzéar-Auguste Cousin de (1766–99)

Probably best remembered as the commander of Napoleon's artil- lery in Egypt, he was commis- sioned in 1785, served at Toulon and in Italy, and was appointed commander of the artillery of the Rhine in 1797. Unwittingly, he played a part in Napoleon's rise to fame: as a captain he had commanded the artillery at Toulon until seriously wounded; and it was by chance that Napoleon was in the area at the time and had the influence to be appointed in Dommartin's stead. In the East, Dommartin con- ducted the sieges of El Arish and Acre, but died from blood poison- ing after being wounded in a skir- mish.

DOMON, General Jean-Simon, baron (1774–1830)

One of the lesser rank of French cavalry generals, he was elected an officer on his first day of service in 1792, transferred to the cavalry in 1799, served with the 3rd Hussars at Elchingen (wounded) and Jena, and with the 7th Hussars at Eylau, Friedland and Wagram. Baron from October 1810, he commanded the 8th Hussars in the Russian campaign of 1812, becoming *général de brigade* and taking command of Piré's brigade of the 1st Light Cavalry Division after its commander was wounded. During the campaign Murat had him transferred to Neapolitan service as lieutenant-general, with which he served in 1813. He accepted employment under the Bourbons at the first restoration but rallied to Napoleon and led the 3rd Cavalry Division (corps cavalry for III Corps) at Ligny, and was wounded at Waterloo. He was recalled to duty by the Bourbons as Inspector-General of Cavalry, and led a cavalry division in Spain in 1823.

DONKIN, General Sir Rufane Shaw (1773–1841)

Son of a British Army officer who became a general in 1809, he received his first commission at the age of five, and actually joined the army when he was 14. After service in the West Indies, at Ostend and in Denmark, he commanded a brigade of the 3rd Division in the Peninsula from June to October 1809, including Talavera. Major-general from 4 June 1811, he served as quarter-master-general in the Mediterranean and eastern Spain (1810–13), commanded a division in the Third Maratha (or Maratha and Pindari) War, and administered the Cape of Good Hope 1820–1; Port Elizabeth he named in memory of his late wife. Lieutenant-general in 1821, general in 1838, he was MP for Berwick 1832–7, Sandwich 1839, and in 1835 became Surveyor-General of the Ordnance. A member of the Royal Society and the author of a work on the course of the Niger (1829), he took his own life in 1841.

DONOUGHMORE, Earl of, see HUTCHINSON

DONZELOT, General François-Xavier, comte (1764–1843)

Probably best remembered as the commander of the 2nd Division of d'Erlon's I Corps in the Waterloo campaign, where his tactical skills were shown to be not of the highest order, he had spent much of his career in staff appointments. He enlisted in 1783, was commissioned in 1792, served as Desaix's chief of staff in Egypt and towards the end of the campaign was leading a brigade. Augereau's chief of staff in 1805, from 1807 he was Deputy Governor, and from March 1808 Governor, of the Ionian Islands, territory which British conquest reduced to Corfu, which he held until 1814. *Général de brigade* from Egypt, *de division*

from 1807, he was ennobled as baron in 1808 and by the Bourbons as comte in 1819; he served as Governor of Martinique 1818–26 where he exercised his talent for organisation and administration to good effect.

Rossignol, A. *Le Général comte Donzelot*. Besançon, 1903

DORNBERG, Lieutenant-General Sir Wilhelm Kaspar Ferdinand von (styled 'Sir William de Dörnberg' in British sources) (1768–1850)

WILHELM VON DÖRNBERG
(PRINT AFTER GRIMM)

One of the last Prussians to surrender in 1806, he joined the Westphalian army of Jérôme Bonaparte with the intention of raising insurrection; but when that failed he became commandant of the Hussars of the Duke of Brunswick's 'Black Legion' in September 1809, in British service. Promoted to major-general in the British Army on 1 January 1812, and appointed colonel-commandant of the 1st Light Dragoons of the King's German Legion in June 1815, he served in north Germany and The Netherlands in 1813–14 and commanded Wellington's 3rd Cavalry Brigade in the Waterloo campaign. In this position he was involved in the delay in transmitting intelligence from Wellington's

'observing officer', Colquhou Grant, at the outset of th campaign; stationed at Mo Dörnberg received a report from French agent relating to th presumed intended direction Napoleon's advance, and tran mitted only an emasculat version to the Duke, then riding him in person when he realis the error; but the criticism he h received from some sources somewhat unjust. Wounded Waterloo, he later became a lie tenant-general in Hanoveri service and was ambassador to Petersburg.

Dörnberg-Hausen, H. vo *Wilhelm von Dörnberg*. Marbur 1936

DOULCET, Louis Le, see PONTECOULANT

DROUET, Jean-Baptiste, see D'ERLON

DROUOT, General Antoine, comte (1774–1847)

ANTOINE DROUOT
(LITHOGRAPH AFTER MAURIN)

One of the most respect commanders of Napoleon's Imp rial Guard, he had the distinctio of being present at the most dec sive naval battle of the Napoleo Wars and at the climax: Trafalg and Waterloo. Commissioned e artillery in 1793, he served in he Netherlands and Germany including Fleurus and Hohen-den) and as a gunnery expert as attached to the fleet, serving at afalgar aboard *Indomptable*. appointed head of the Guard tillery in 1808, he led it in Spain nd at Wagram, where a hit on the ght foot left him with a limp; nnobled as a baron in 1810, he d the Guard artillery in Russia, otably at Borodino, and was appointed *général de brigade* anuary 1813) and an imperial de. Further distinguished in 13 (including Lützen, Bautzen, resden and Leipzig) he became *néral de division* in September d comte in October; he fought rough the 1814 campaign and evotedly followed Napoleon to ba, of which he became overnor. He commanded the uard in the Waterloo campaign d was tried for treason by the ourbons, a case in which the killed Napoleon took great terest; he was acquitted but eclined to serve under the Bour-ons and retired to his native ancy. Universally admired, he as described by Macdonald as he most upright and modest man have ever known – well lucated, brave, devoted, simple manners. His character was fty and of rare probity.'[1] He ways carried a Bible and eclaimed from it; and for reason superstition on days of battle ways wore his old artillery niform, in which he had never een wounded.

Macdonald, vol. II, p. 351.

Nollet-Fabert, J. *Biographie du énéral Drouot*. Nancy, 1850

UBOIS DE CRANCE, General dmond-Louis-Alexis 747–1814)

though probably more a politi-ian than a soldier, he was sponsible for some of the most portant reforms in the French Army. Originally a member of the *Maison du Roi*, he supported the Revolution, was elected to the States-General and as Secretary of the Constituent Assembly was much concerned with military reforms, being among the first to advocate a conscription involving all members of society. As a member of the Convention he voted for the execution of the king, and was instrumental in the introduction of vital military reforms: the rapid promotion of worthy junior officers, the intro-duction of multi-arm divisions and the integration of new and experienced troops in the *amal-game*. In August 1793 he was appointed a *représentant-en-mission* to the army tasked with suppressing the revolt at Lyons, but was recalled for not exhibiting sufficient energy, though it was said that the city had refused to surrender while he commanded the besiegers, so inveterate an opponent was he. Charges were brought against him, including that he had made himself absolute commander of the army, which he had brought to a state of discipline, that he usually wore military uniform rather than the dress of a *représentant*, of having the superciliousness of a tactician, and of preferring a regular siege to costly attacks; all of which were surely reasons for praise rather than for criticism, and he easily justified his conduct. Excluded from the Jacobin Club at Robe-spierre's instigation, he supported the move against the latter, and became a member of the Committee of Public Safety and, under the Directory, of the Council of Five Hundred. In 1799 he was appointed Minister of War, but being opposed to the coup of Brumaire he retired from public office.

Jung, H. F. T. *Dubois de Crancé, l'Armée et la Révolution 1789–1794*. Paris, 1884

DUBRETON, General Jean-Louis, baron (1773–1855)
'One of the most resourceful and enterprising officers whom the British army ever encountered,'[1] was Sir Charles Oman's descrip-tion of him, and it is surely accu-rate. Commissioned in 1790, he went to the West Indies in 1802 and was captured by the British; and it was after his release that he played the most important role in his career. Promoted to *général de brigade* in 1811, he was appointed Governor of Burgos with orders to delay Wellington's victorious progress as long as possible. Despite the comparatively weak state of the defences, Dubreton not only delayed Wellington but defied all attempts to take the city; after thirty-five days of siege (September–October 1812) it was relieved and Wellington's army commenced a retreat second only to that to Corunna. Despite the insufficient resources deployed by the besiegers, Dubreton's resource-ful defence was a crucial factor, and thus he was one of few French commanders who could legiti-mately claim a success over one of the greatest commanders of the age. He became *général de division* in December 1812, served in Germany in 1813 (including Hanau) but did not rejoin Napoleon in 1815; consequently his barony was awarded by Louis XVIII and he remained in the royal army until his retirement in 1831.
1. Oman, vol. V, p. 23.

DUCKWORTH, Vice-Admiral Sir John Thomas, Bt. (1748–1817)
Entering the Royal Navy in 1759 and commissioned in 1770, he commanded HMS *Orion* at the Glorious First of June, served in the Mediterranean and at the capture of Minorca, and became rear-admiral (1799) and vice-admiral (1804). He achieved his greatest triumph on 6 February 1806 off San Domingo, when with

his flagship HMS *Superb* and six other ships of the line he defeated Admiral Leissegues' French squadron of five ships of the line, three being taken and two wrecked when driven ashore, which as he said 'will fairly add another sprig of laurel to our naval history'.[1] He was less successful in the following year when attempting to force the Dardanelles. From 1810 he commanded off Newfoundland, and in 1815 at Plymouth, which command he held until his death. His son, Lieutenant-Colonel George Duckworth, commanded the 1/48th at Albuera; he was hit in the left breast by a musket-ball, but 'the same noble blood which runs in the veins of the father flowing equally warm in those of the son, he could not be induced to quit the field';[2] he was then mortally struck by a ball in the throat. By a dreadful coincidence, news of his death reached his home on the day before the funeral of his only son, a child of four.

1. Dispatch, 7 February 1806 in *Gazette*, 23 March 1806. 2. *Gent's Mag.*, 1811, vol. I, p. 679.

DUCOS, Pierre-Roger, comte (1754–1816)

Despite a lack of outstanding political talent, he achieved high office in the wake of the Revolution. A lawyer, he was elected to the Convention and voted for the death of Louis XVI, and was President of the Council of Five Hundred at the time of the coup of 18 Fructidor. At the end of his term of office he became a judge, and became a member of the Directory by the influence of his friend Barras, who could thus count upon his support. Ducos assisted in the coup of Brumaire, and served briefly as Third Consul; Napoleon honoured him (he was ennobled as comte and served as Vice-President of the

Senate), but in 1814 he sided with the Bourbons, who made him a peer of France; yet he was exiled as a regicide in 1816 and died in March of that year as the result of a coach accident at Ulm.

DUGOMMIER, General Jacques-Coquille (1738–94)

The owner of extensive estates in Martinique, he supported the Revolution and returned to France in 1791 to resume the military career which had begun in the Seven Years War and which he had given up in 1782. *Général de division* from November 1793, he replaced the incompetent François Doppet as commander of the forces besieging Toulon, and concluded the operation successfully (the political representatives with the army wanted to replace him for his perceived slowness; Dugommier's artillery commander, Napoleon Bonaparte, esteemed his chief and helped him organise the victory). Dugommier then transferred to the Pyrenean front but was killed by a mortar bomb on 17 November 1794.

DUGUA, General Charles-François-Joseph (1744–1802)

Commissioned in 1760, he retired in 1777 but returned from service in the *gendarmerie* in the Revolutionary Wars, becoming *général de division* while a staff officer in the army that was besieging Toulon. He served in the Pyrenees, commanded the cavalry reserve of the Army of Italy and was a member of the Council of Five Hundred, but his main fame rests with his divisional command during the Egyptian campaign, in which he was appointed Commandant of Cairo from February 1799. He has been described as a benign individual, but some of his suggestions in this office were fairly extreme: to curb rampant prostitution and

the diseases it caused, he sa[id] that the only solution was [to] drown the prostitutes in the Ni[le] and that as Napoleon w[as] ordering so many executions [he] proposed employing a headsma[n] to economise on ammunitio[n]. After repatriation following t[he] surrender of French forces [in] Egypt, Dugua went to S[a]Domingo as chief of staff [to] Leclerc, and died there of yello[w] fever.

DUHESME, General Philibert-Guillaume, comte (1766–1815)

Of humble background, he w[as] elected an officer in the Fren[ch] National Guard in 1789, served [in] the army in The Netherlands an[d] became *général de brigade* (179[4]) and *de division* in Novemb[er] 1794. Service under Moreau ga[ve] rise to unfounded charges [of] cowardice, and in Italy from 179[?] he was acquitted of plunderi[ng] (which charges were probab[ly] not unfounded). He commande[d] part of the Army of Reserve in t[he] Marengo campaign (though n[ot] present at the battle), but h[is] intransigent republicanism an[d] difficult manner led to his bei[ng] consigned to relatively unimpo[r]tant duties in Italy, until posted [to] Spain in 1808. There he failed [to] take Gerona, and as Governor [of] Barcelona behaved in so cru[el] and rapacious a manner th[at] Augereau dismissed him (the[re] was ill-feeling between the tw[o] which may have influence[d] this decision), and Duhes[me] returned to France in disgrac[e.] Napoleon declined to have hi[m] prosecuted on the grounds that [it] would give too much satisfactio[n] to the Catalans! In late 181[3] Duhesme was recalled to du[ty,] served in 1814 as a division[al] commander under Victor an[d] was ennobled as comte for h[is] services. He accepted th[e] Bourbon restoration and thoug[h] joining Napoleon comparative[ly]

PHILIBERT DUHESME AT DIRSHEIM, 20 AUGUST 1797
(PRINT AFTER PERRIGEON)

ate in 1815 was given command of the Young Guard, which he led with distinction at Waterloo, attempting to hold Napoleon's right flank; near Plancenoit he was mortally wounded by a musket-ball in the head. These actions late in his career con-firmed his resolution and abili-ties as a divisional commander which might otherwise have been overshadowed by his earlier reputation for rapacious brutality.

Duhesme, P. G. *Mémoires de Duhesme*. Paris, 1823

DUMAS, General Mathieu, comte (1753–1837)

Born in Montpellier of noble family, he entered the army in 1773, served as ADC to Rocham-beau in America, and after some years exploring the eastern Mediterranean was present at the siege of Antwerp in 1787. A liberal during the Revolution, he escorted Louis XVI back from Varennes and in 1792 was elected President of the Legislative Assembly; but his politics proving insufficiently extreme, he deemed it prudent to go abroad on three occasions, until returning finally after the coup of Brumaire. In 1800 he organised the Army of Reserve at Dijon, became *général de division* in 1805, and as Napoleon's quar-termaster served in the Austerlitz campaign. Minister of War for Joseph Bonaparte in Naples, he went to Spain and in November 1808 became assistant QMG to the French forces there; assistant chief of staff in the Danube campaign in 1809, and ennobled as comte in 1810, he served as *Intendant-Général* to the *Grande Armée* in the 1812 Russian campaign, but fell ill and was replaced by Daru. Taken prisoner in 1813, he took service under the Bourbons after the restoration, but was persuaded by Joseph Bonaparte to support Napoleon in 1815, when he was tasked with organising the National Guard. Retired at the second restoration, he was reinstated and served on the Council of State 1818–22, and again after the 1830 revolution in which he was involved; he became a peer of France in 1831. He worked on a noted military history of 1798–1807 (*Précis des Evéne-ments militaires*, Paris, 1818–26), which he had begun in 1800 and which ran to nineteen volumes; and translated Napier's *History of the War in the Peninsula*.

Dumas, M. *Souvenirs de Lieu-tenant-Général comte Mathieu*

Dumas de 1770 à 1836. Paris, 1839 (English title *Memoirs of his own Time*), published posthumously by his son

DUMAS, General Thomas-Alexandre (also known as DAVY DE LA PAILLETERIE) (1762–1806)

Born in San Domingo, he was the natural son of Antoine Alexandre Davy, marquis de la Pailleterie, and a Negro woman, Marie Dumas. He accompanied his father to France in 1780, enlisted in the army and rose from the ranks; *général de division* in 1793, he commanded in the Western Pyrenees and served in the Alps, but is probably best remembered for commanding the cavalry in the Egyptian expedition. He was a formidable man: known as 'the Black Devil' during his service in the Tyrol, amazing stories were recounted of his Herculean strength, and his bravery and resolution were said to equal it. He was no diplomat, however, and voiced the concerns of other generals over Napoleon's conduct of the Egyptian campaign; so that when he asked for leave to return to France to escape the Egyptian climate, Napoleon readily let him go, which ended his military career. His son was the author Alexandre Dumas (1802–70) and his grandson, Alexandre Dumas '*fils*' (1824–95), both gaining reputations which overshadowed that of their brave sire.

Hautrive, E. d'. *Un Soldat de la Révolution: le Général Alexandre Dumas.* Paris, 1897

DUMERBION, General Pierre-Jadart (1737–97)

After long service in the army dating from the Seven Years War, he became *général de division* in May 1793, and in the following January was given command of the Army of Italy. Steady rather than inspirational, he took care to consult the army's political representatives to avoid falling foul of political intrigue, and was sufficiently generous to recognise that the successes he achieved in Italy were the result of the abilities of his chief of artillery, Napoleon Bonaparte. He relinquished his command in favour of Schérer in November 1794 and retired in the following May.

DUMOURIEZ, General Charles-François (1739–1823)

CHARLES FRANÇOIS DUMOURIEZ
(ENGRAVING BY W. GREATBATCH)

The son of a commissary, he began his military service as a volunteer in the French Army in 1757 during the Rossbach campaign; commissioned later in the Seven Years War, he was employed in Corsica in 1768 and subsequently on secret missions, notably to Poland. At the Revolution, perhaps seeing an opportunity for advancement, he joined the Jacobin Club, and later the Girondins. In March 1792 he became Foreign Minister and was largely responsible for the declaration of war on Austria, and later in the year took command of the Army of the Centre. He won the victory of Jemappes and shared that of Valmy with Kellermann, but was defeated at Neerwinden in January 1793, which provoked h[is] famous 'treason'. He had n[o] sympathy with the extremis[m] which had seized the Revolutio[n] and doubtless feared for his li[fe] from his own government; so h[e] began to plot with the Austrian[s] and turned over to them the poli[t]ical commissars sent by th[e] French government to investiga[te] his conduct. He called on h[is] troops to march on Paris an[d] overturn the government; whe[n] this failed he fled with his frien[d] the duc de Chartres (later Kin[g] Louis-Philippe) to the Austrian[s]. Thereafter he was involved i[n] royalist intrigues until in 1804 h[e] settled in England, where h[e] became a military adviser to th[e] government and was given [a] pension; he never returned t[o] France, and died at Henley-on[-] Thames. Although his politica[l] ambitions may have caused him t[o] betray his country, his own senti[ti]ments were quite different fro[m] those of his masters, and th[e] conflict was highlighted b[y] Lafayette, who noted that althoug[h] in his memoirs Dumouriez ha[d] praised the stormers of th[e] Bastille, at the time he ha[d] submitted a report on how t[o] prevent the Bastille from falling t[o] an insurrection. Some politica[l] leaders he treated with disdai[n] notably snubbing Marat wh[o] inquired why he had discipline[d] some troops who had kille[d] emigrant deserters. Whether hi[s] defection was caused by persona[l] reasons or for the perceived goo[d] of his country, as Thier[s] remarked, it should not b[e] forgotten that in the early part o[f] the Revolutionary Wars he was to [a] considerable extent the saviour o[f] that country.

Dumouriez, C. F. *La Vie et le[s] Mémoires du Général Dumourie[z].* Paris, 1823 (an English editio[n] *Memoirs ... written by himsel[f]* trans. J. Fenwick, was published i[n] Dublin in 1794); Rose, J. H., an[d]

roadbent, A. M. *Dumouriez and ~~th~~e Defence of England*. London, ~~1~~908

~~D~~UNCAN, Admiral Adam, ~~V~~iscount (1731–1804)

ADAM DUNCAN
(PRINT AFTER HOPPNER)

~~I~~n his youth said to be the most ~~h~~andsome man in the Royal Navy, ~~h~~e was born in Dundee of an ~~a~~ncient Scottish family and ~~e~~ntered the navy at an early age. ~~C~~aptain by 1761, his promotion ~~w~~as slow, perhaps influenced by ~~t~~he fever he contracted at the ~~c~~apture of Havana which ~~p~~recluded him from serving again ~~i~~n warm climates. He became a ~~r~~ear-admiral in 1787 (vice-admiral ~~1~~793, admiral 1795), it being said ~~t~~hat even this promotion had ~~m~~uch to do with his marriage in ~~1~~777 to the niece of Henry Dundas, ~~w~~hose influence was crucial in ~~D~~uncan's advancement. Having ~~d~~eclined command in the Mediter-~~r~~anean on medical grounds, not ~~u~~ntil 1795 was he appointed to lead ~~t~~he North Sea Fleet, and it was ~~f~~ortunate that he was there at the ~~t~~ime of the 'great mutiny'. An inspi-~~r~~ational leader, by force of person-~~a~~lity he ensured that two ships ~~t~~ook no part; to the crew of his ~~f~~lagship HMS *Venerable* he made a ~~m~~oving speech which reduced ~~e~~very man to tears,[1] and a similar speech to the crew of HMS *Adamant* produced only one seaman who challenged his authority. At six feet three and of athletic build, Duncan possessed great strength; so with one hand he held the man by his collar over the side of the ship and asked the crew to look at the wretch who would deprive him of his command! With these two loyal ships he blockaded the Dutch fleet in the Texel, sailing to and fro and signalling to an imaginary fleet beyond the horizon, until the mutiny was suppressed and the remainder of the fleet returned to duty. This was followed by his crowning victory over de Winter at Camperdown (11 October 1797), for which he was rewarded with the viscountcy of Duncan of Camperdown and the barony of Duncan of Lundie (the family lord-ship in Perthshire). Duncan was known not only as a brave and capable seaman, but had 'a coun-tenance that indicated great intelli-gence and benevolence. His private character was that of a most affectionate relative, and a steady friend; and, what crowns the whole with a lustre superior to all other qualities or distinctions, a man of great and unaffected piety.'[2] He died aged 73 'of the gout in his stomach'[3] and was suc-ceeded by his son Robert, a captain in the Ayrshire Militia.

1. Obit. in *Gent's Mag.*, Sept, 1804, p. 878; an abbreviated version is in Lloyd, C. *St. Vincent and Camper-down*. London, 1963, pp. 111–12. 2. *Gent's Mag.*, Sept, 1804, p. 879. 3. Ibid., Aug, 1804, p. 790.

Camperdown, Earl of. *Admiral Duncan*. London, 1898

DUNDAS, General Sir David, Bt. (1735–1820)
Known as 'Old Pivot' from the style of manoeuvres he favoured, he was one of the most influential figures in the British Army. The son of an Edinburgh merchant, he

SIR DAVID DUNDAS
(PRINT AFTER R. OWEN)

served in the Seven Years War, became major-general in 1790, commanded a brigade in The Netherlands in 1794, succeeded to command of the expedition to Toulon and then to Corsica, and as lieutenant-general (1797) served in the campaign in North Holland (1799). His greatest contribution was the production of the first universally accepted manual for drill and manoeuvres, published in 1788 as *Principles of Military Movements*, and re-issued with official sanction in 1792 as *Rules and Regulations for the Move-ments of His Majesty's Infantry*, and often styled 'the Eighteen Manoeuvres'. It was somewhat Prussian in style and had failings (light infantry tactics were almost ignored), but in ensuring that the British Army operated in a uniform manner it was a work of great significance. (Moore once remarked that it would have been even better but for 'those damned eighteen manoeuvres'. '"Why-ay," says Sir David, slowly, "ay, people don't understand what was meant. Blockheads don't under-stand!"')[1] The reaction of some towards the drill-book may be gauged from the remark made to him by 'an old crony and coun-tryman' who saw Dundas' own brigade in sad disorder in The

Netherlands: 'I say, David, whar's your peevots noo?'[2] Dundas served as Quartermaster-General 1796–1803 and as commander of Southern District 1803–5 at the height of the invasion alarm (he was largely responsible for the construction of the Martello Towers along the south coast), and having retired on grounds of ill-health, as a full general (from April 1802) he was recalled as Commander-in-Chief during the Duke of York's forced absence after the Clarke scandal. In this role Dundas was not a success; George Napier claimed that he 'had the greatest antipathy to giving any man promotion who was not as old as himself ... the crusty old fellow could not bear the idea of promotion; and, except his money, he would sooner part with anything else ... thank God, the old boy is gone, and the Lord defend us from ever seeing such another at the head of the army'.[3] Despite such opinions, and despite in later days a thin, austere and aged-looking appearance, Dundas was a worthy and significant figure in the British establishment.

1. Bunbury, *Narratives*, p. 30. 2. *CUSM*, 1843, vol. II, p. 292. 3. Napier, G., p. 84.

DUNDAS, Henry, 1st Viscount Melville (1742–1811)

Born and educated in Edinburgh, he followed his family's legal profession and was considerably distinguished even before entering parliament in 1774. A talented speaker (with a strong and probably attractive Scots accent), he became a firm friend of William Pitt and served as Home Secretary 1791–4 and Secretary at War 1794-1801. In the latter office he was very influential, even when advocating schemes not favoured by Pitt, with varying degrees of success. His own military knowledge was limited to a

commission in the Royal Edinburgh Volunteers, and Sir John Fortescue remarked that he was the worst man for the job, 'so profoundly ignorant was Dundas of war that he was not even conscious of his ignorance',[1] which was probably somewhat harsh; yet his instructions were sometimes confusing or contradictory and sometimes made without benefit of professional military advice. He left office in 1801 but returned with Pitt in 1804 as First Lord of the Admiralty, having been ennobled as Viscount Melville in 1802. In 1806 he was impeached for misappropriation of public funds (when Treasurer of the Navy 1783–1801), and though acquitted of everything but negligence, he never again held office. He died in Edinburgh in May 1811, of 'ossification of the heart'. 'A man so long in possession of uncommon power, must necessarily have excited much envy and malice; and few have had more of it than Lord Melville. They who disapprove the politicks of Mr. Pitt, of course execrate his coadjutor; but ... a large number of comprehensive minds will consider him a powerful and efficient statesman, who ... was sometimes excessive in his profusion, and too careless in his means and instruments ...'[2]

1. Fortescue, vol. IV, p. 72. 2. *Gent's Mag.*, 1811, vol. I, p. 677.

Furber, H. *Henry Dundas, First Viscount Melville.* Oxford, 1931; Matheson, C. *The Life of Henry Dundas, First Viscount Melville.* London, 1933

DUNDONALD, Admiral Earl of, see COCHRANE

DUPONT DE L'ETANG, General Pierre-Antoine, comte (1765–1840)

The name of Dupont will forever be associated with one of the French Army's worst reverses of

the period. Originally in Dutc service, he joined the Frenc Army in 1791 and became *géné. de brigade* after capturing a Austrian regiment at Menin, an *de division* in 1797. He supporte the coup of Brumaire, wa Berthier's chief of staff in th Marengo campaign, and signe the Convention of Alessandria; h was distinguished at Haslach as divisional commander under Ne in 1805 and won further laurels i 1806–7, notably at Friedlanc Ennobled as comte, he wa appointed to lead the 2nd Corps c Observation of the Gironde; bu after some early success, whe sent to subdue Andalusia he wa cut off and forced to capitulat with his entire force at Baile (19–23 July 1808). The total los was about 17,600 surrendered an 2,000 casualties, though in fairnes much was against him from th beginning, notably the fact tha most of his troops were inexperi enced; but Napoleon greeted th news with fury: 'Dupont ha dishonoured our flag. What inca pacity, what cowardice!'[1] and ha Dupont and his subordinate arrested on their return to France but on reading the report of ar investigative commission he founc that Dupont had a legitimate defence against all charges excep ineptitude, so after nine months imprisonment he was released. Ir February 1812, however, he wa re-arrested and tried without a chance to prepare a defence or be legally represented; the judicia commission deemed it not in the wider interest to hold a public trial, but recommended that he be deprived of rank and dismissed Instead, Napoleon imprisonec him, and he was only released upon the fall of the empire. Re-employed by the Bourbons, he was Minister of War 1814–15, fled on Napoleon's return, and became a minister of state at the second restoration. He served as a

PIERRE DUPONT SURRENDERS AT BAILEN (PRINT AFTER MAURICE ORANGE)

were handled severely. D'Urban became a colonel in British service, major-general in Portuguese, received a KCB in 1815 and remained with the Portuguese until 1816, when he returned to a sequence of British staff appointments: Governor of Antigua, Demerara and British Guiana; Governor and CinC at the Cape 1834–8 (where the city of Durban was named after him. He was removed because of his attempts to extend British territory by the proclamation of Queen Adelaide's Province, which was repudiated by the government in London), and became CinC Canada from 1847 until his death at Montreal; he had been promoted to major-general in the British Army in 1819, and lieutenant-general in 1837.

D'Urban, Sir Benjamin. *The Peninsular Journal of Major-General Sir Benjamin D'Urban, 1808–17*, ed. I. J. Rousseau, 1930; reprinted as *The Peninsular Journal, 1808-17*. London, 1988

DUROC, General Géraud-Christophe-Michel, duc de Frioul (1772–1813)

'The Emperor told me that Duroc was the only man who possessed his intimacy and entire confidence: "He was a pure and virtuous man, utterly disinterested, and extremely generous"[1]; such was the remarkable testimony given by Napoleon about his most loyal subordinate. The son of a French officer, Duroc began military training in 1789 but emigrated at the Revolution; commissioned in the artillery on his return (1793), he met Napoleon at Toulon, served in Italy, became Napoleon's aide and was seriously wounded in Egypt. In 1798 he became Napoleon's senior ADC, *général de brigade* in 1801, *de division* in 1803, and Grand Marshal of the Palace in 1805. He undertook diplomatic missions and negotia-

Deputy 1815–30 and retired in 1832; he wrote some military treatises and poetry, including a verse translation of Horace.

1. Napoleon, 3 Aug 1808, vol. I, p. 333.

Dupont, P. A. *Mémoires du Général Dupont: Relation de la Campagne d'Andalousie*. Paris, 1824

D'URBAN, Lieutenant-General Sir Benjamin (1777–1849)

The son of a naval, later civilian, medical practitioner, he was commissioned in the British Army in 1793, served in The Netherlands and West Indies, and after a number of staff appointments was selected by Beresford as QMG of the Portuguese Army. He served throughout the Peninsular War without taking leave, in nine major actions from Busaco to Toulouse, as well as at Medellin (where he rescued Cuesta) and as a cavalry brigadier at Majalahonda (11 August 1812), where with little blame to himself save perhaps excessive daring, his Portuguese

tions, including the Treaty of Schönbrunn, the armistices with the Tsar in 1807 and of Znaim, and the negotiations for the abdication of Charles IV of Spain; and commanded Oudinot's grenadiers at Austerlitz. As director of the imperial household he was a skilled organiser, and his advice to Napoleon, upon whom he was generally in attendance, was invaluable. At Bautzen he was mortally wounded by the cannonball which also killed the engineer general Kirchner, but lived long enough for an emotional last meeting with Napoleon. The latter was greatly moved, saying that: 'Duroc was the only person who had possessed his unreserved confidence, and to whom he could freely unburden his mind ... Duroc loved the Emperor for himself ... What a servant! What a friend'! What a treasure! How many storms he has soothed! How many rash orders, given in the moment of irritation, has he omitted to execute, knowing that his master would thank him the next day ... Duroc had more influence over the Emperor's resolutions than is imagined. His death was probably, in this respect, a national calamity.'[2]

1. Las Cases, vol. I, pp. 99, 338. 2. Ibid., pp. 339–40.

La Tour, J. J. *Duroc, duc de Frioul* ..., Paris, 1913.

DURUTTE, General Pierre-François-Joseph, comte (1767–1827)

A native of Douai, he joined the French Army in 1792, served at Jemappes and became a staff officer under Moreau in 1795. He became *général de division* in 1803, but his long association with Moreau and lack of enthusiasm for Napoleon led to his being given garrison duties until 1809. In that year he served as a division commander under Eugène and became a baron in August (comte August 1813); in 1812 he led the 32nd Division of Augereau's Corps in the Russian campaign, served in 1813 and held Metz as Governor, January–March 1814. He was employed by the Bourbons, but reverted to Napoleon in 1815, and is probably best known for commanding the 4th Division of d'Erlon's I Corps in the Hundred Days campaign. He fought valiantly at Waterloo, his division occupying the extreme right of Napoleon's line, and towards the end of the battle lost his right eye and arm to sabre cuts. Thus disabled, he was retired in October 1815 and lived in Belgium for the remainder of his life.

DU TEIL, Jean-Pierre, and Du Teil, the Chevalier, see TEIL

BLE, General Jean-Baptiste, aron (1758–1812)

o a considerable extent the aviour of Napoleon and the rande Armée in 1812, he was the n of a gunner NCO. He joined he artillery in 1773, was commisioned in 1775 and became énéral de brigade in September 793 and de division in the llowing month. He commanded he artillery of the Army of the orth from 1794 and of the Rhine 1800, was a popular Governor f Magdeburg 1806–8 and in 808–9 was Jérôme Bonaparte's Minister of War in Westphalia. nnobled as baron in 1808, in 810–11 he led Massena's artillery n the Peninsula, notably at iudad Rodrigo and Almeida, and or the Russian campaign was iven command of the Grande rmée's pontoon-train. During he retreat from Russia, and gainst Eblé's protests, Napoleon, elieving that they would not be eeded, ordered the destruction f the pontoons at Orsha, and the orses to be used to transport rtillery; but on his own initiative blé distributed tools and metal ittings among his pontoniers, and nanaged to keep two field forges nd other equipment. Only ecause of this foresight, was he ble to construct the bridges over he Berezina, and to maintain hem, which permitted the Grande Armée to escape the trap et for them by the Russians' lestruction of the bridge at Borisov. The exertions of Eblé and his pontoniers were truly heroic, and were duly recognised. On the llness (later death) of Lariboisière, the army's artillery commander, Eblé took over, and n January 1813 Napoleon appointed him inspector-general of artillery, unaware that the gallant Eblé had died on 30 December 1812, of the exertions involved in the retreat from Moscow. Too late for his elevation to comte to be

made official, as a gesture of esteem to this worthy man, Napoleon made his widow a comtesse in April 1813.

Chuquet, A. *Human Voices from the Russian Campaign of 1812*, trans. H. M. Capes. London, 1913 (trans. of Chuquet's *Etudes d'Histoire*, vol. V; contains a brief biography of Eblé)

ECKMUHL, Prince of, see **DAVOUT**

ELBEE, Joseph-Louis-Maurice Gigost d' (1753–94)
Born in Dresden of French parents, d'Elbée had retired from the French Army at the age of thirty, had emigrated in 1791 but returned in the following year to save his estate from confiscation. In 1793, with some reluctance, he was persuaded by the royalists of his own locality to lead them in rebellion against the revolutionary government which he opposed. After the death of Cathelineau he was elected to lead the Vendéen army, as being a minor noble with some military training. Madame La Rochjaquelein described him as 'of a small stature, extremely devout, enthusiastic, and possessed an extraordinary calm courage. His vanity, however, was easily wounded, which made him irritable, although ceremoniously polite. He had some ambition, but narrow, as well as all his views. His tactics consisted of rushing on with these words, "My friends, Providence will give us the victory." His piety was very sincere, but as he saw it was a means of attaching and animating the peasants, he carried it to a degree of affectation and charlatanry, often ridiculous. He had about his person images of saints, read sermons and exhortations to the soldiers, and, above all, spoke incessantly of *Providence*, and to such a degree, that the peasants, much as they loved him, and

respected every thing connected with religion, called him, without meaning a joke, "*General Providence*". In spite of these little foibles M. d'Elbée was in reality so estimable and virtuous a man, that he inspired every one with respect and attachment.'[1] Although some derided his military abilities, his enemies respected his skill in concentrating his forces to fight and in adopting the tactics which suited them best, hence his successes. Severely wounded at Cholet (17 October 1793), he took refuge on the Island of Noirmoutier, and was too ill to resist when the republicans arrived in the following January. Unable to stand, he was placed in a chair and shot, exhibiting great bravery; his wife, who had refused to escape when she could have saved herself, was executed next day.

1. La Rochejaquelein, pp. 111–12.

ELCHINGEN, duc de, see **NEY**

ELIZABETH, Madame (Elizabeth-Philippine-Marie-Hélène) (1764–94)
Generally known as 'Madame Elizabeth', this French princess was the daughter of Louis, Dauphin of France, and Marie Josephine of Saxony, and was sister to Louis XVI to whom she was entirely devoted. She accompanied him on the flight to Varennes and, condemned for assisting him, supplying funds for *émigrés* and

'MADAME ELIZABETH'
(ENGRAVING BY W. GREATBATCH)

SIR JOHN ELLEY

GILBERT ELLIOT, EARL OF MINTO (ENGRAVIN
BY W. J. EDWARDS AFTER G. CHINNERY)

encouraging the royal troops, was guillotined on 10 May 1794, actually for no other reason than that she was the king's sister. She met her end with great fortitude and under the duress of imprisonment was described as 'an angel of goodness'.

ELLEY, Lieutenant-General Sir John (1766–1839)

Unusually for an officer of the British Army, he rose to high rank from relatively humble origins; the son of a Holborn eating-house keeper, and apprenticed to a Leeds tanner, he enlisted as a private in the Royal Horse Guards in 1789. He was hardly a typical 'other rank', however, coming from a relatively prosperous background and blessed with superior abilities; distinguished in The Netherlands 1793–5, he was commissioned in 1794 and became a major in 1804. In the Peninsula he served as assistant adjutant-general to Paget and Cotton, receiving much praise from the latter, and was wounded at Salamanca; he was also acknowledged as a most accomplished swordsman. At Waterloo he served as deputy adjutant-general, and returned home in 1818; he became a knight of the Bath in January 1815, major-

general in 1819 and lieutenant-general in 1839, was Peelite MP for Windsor in 1835 and was buried in St. George's Chapel, Windsor. Amusingly, he featured in the libellous poem *The Blueviad* written by Edward Goulburn in 1805, as 'Lothario': 'Wife, Maid or Virgin, are to him the same/And each at his desire, must yield their fame'!

MacKenzie, Colonel R. H. 'Lieutenant-General Sir John Elley, KCB, KCH', in *Cavalry Journal*, 1913, vol. VIII, pp. 215–20

ELLIOT, Gilbert (Elliot-Murray-Kynynmound), Earl of Minto (1751–1814)

Best remembered as a successful Governor-General of India (1806–13), Gilbert Elliot (who changed his name to Elliot-Murray-Kynynmound in October 1797) came from a distinguished Scottish family, entered parliament in 1776 and was British envoy to Vienna 1799–1801. His part in the history of the Napoleonic era was most marked during the period he administered Corsica (1794–6) when it was controlled by Great Britain, at which time it was considered expedient that Paoli be absent. In October 1797 he was ennobled as Baron Minto (of Minto, in

Roxburghshire) and elevated February 1813 to Earl of Minto. H aunt Jane (1737–1805) wrote tl memorable ballad *Flowers of tl Forest*.

Minto, Countess of. *Life ar Letters of Sir Gilbert Elliot, Fir Earl of Minto, from 1751 to 180* London, 1874

ELPHINSTONE, Admiral George, see KEITH, Viscount

ELPHINSTONE, Major-Genera William George Keith (1782–1842)

Grandson of Charles, 10th Baro Elphinstone, he commanded th 33rd Foot at Waterloo, but is be known as the general who led th disastrous retreat from Kabul i 1842, during which he died o fatigue, having been taken pris oner. After the Kabul débâcle cri icisms of his conduct at Waterlo were made, though in his defenc Colin Halkett said that 'his behav iour was in every respect that of gallant officer', and Captai Joseph Harty stated that he 'neve saw a soldier more cool an possessed of more courage' Elphinstone's brother Charles, o the Royal Navy, was lost whe HMS *Blenheim* was wrecked in th Indian Ocean in 1807; a sad coin cidence, because their uncl

harles had been lost when HMS
rince George was accidentally
urned in 1758.
, *USM*, 1842, vol, II, pp. 404–5.

MMET, Robert (1778–1803)

lthough not actively involved in
1e 1798 Irish rebellion, this son
f a notable Irish physician
upported its aims and in 1800–2
avelled in Europe, meeting
xiled leaders of the United
rishmen and in October 1802
apoleon. He returned to Ireland
o plan a renewed rising, which
niscarried totally when put into
ffect on 23 July 1803; he was
pprehended on 25 August,
onvicted of treason, and hanged
n 20 September 1803. Some
omance attached to the story by
irtue of his love affair with Sarah
urran (daughter of the noted
awyer and politician John
hilpot Curran (1750–1817), who
lefended Lord Edward Fitzgerald
nd Wolfe Tone), but she later
narried Major Robert Sturgeon,
i distinguished officer of the
Royal Staff Corps in the Penin-
ular War. Robert Emmet's
rother Thomas Addis Emmet
1764–1827) was a distinguished
awyer and one of the more
autious leaders of the United
rishmen, who was imprisoned
1798–1802. Subsequently he went
o Paris and was involved in
oreparations for a renewed
nsurrection with French assis-
ance, but after the failure of
Robert's rising he emigrated to
he USA, where he became a
uccessful lawyer.

ENGHIEN, Louis-Antoine-Henri
de Bourbon-Condé, duc d'
(1772–1804)

The subject of one of the 'crimes'
of Napoleon which had a
profound effect upon opposition
to him in Europe, he was the son
of the prince de Condé. He left
France at the outbreak of the
Revolution and joined the *Armée*

LOUIS ANTOINE, DUC D'ENGHIEN
(ENGRAVING BY O. GROSCH AFTER C. RAUSCH)

de Condé; upon its disbandment
after the Peace of Lunéville, he
married Princess Charlotte, niece
of Cardinal de Rohan, and settled
at Etterheim in Baden. In 1804
Napoleon heard that he was implicated in royalist plots, notably with
Cadoudal and Pichegru (which in
fact he was not); but Napoleon
ordered that he be seized by a raid
in March 1804 which brought him
to France, a violation of neutral
territory. When Napoleon learned
the truth the indictment was
changed, Enghien was accused of
bearing arms against France and
of supporting a new coalition
against that country, was condemned and shot in the moat of
Vincennes castle, where he was
buried, despite a plea from
Josephine that he be spared. The
act sullied Napoleon's reputation
and encouraged opposition to
him, but he remained unrepen-
tant, even remarking in his will
that 'in like circumstances I would
do as much again'.[1]

1. *Napoleon's Last Will and Testament*, ed. J. P. Babelon and S.
d'Huart, trans. A. de Jonge. London, 1977, p. 38.
 Welschinger, H. *Le Duc
d'Enghien*. Paris, 1888

ERSKINE, General James, see
ROSSLYN, 2nd Earl of

ERSKINE, Thomas, 1st Baron
(1750–1823)

The career of Lord Erskine exemplifies how the military events of
the period touched the lives of
those occupied in quite different
fields. He won distinction as a
lawyer (and some criticism for
defending Thomas Paine), and
was Lord Chancellor during the
Grenville administration; and
having in early life been an officer
in the Royal Navy and 1st Royals,
commanded the Law Association
Volunteers, to which he was
gazetted as lieutenant-colonel in
July 1803. He was not especially
successful as a soldier: he used his
legal skills to ensure that volunteers could resign at will, against
the intentions of the government,
and it was said that he was unable
to give orders to his unit without
the aid of a crib-card, so that in
1804 the general who inspected
his corps 'had the condescension
to try and instruct them in some
manoeuvres!'[1] Erskine also coined
the term 'brutal and insolent
soldiery'.
1. *Morning Chronicle*, 29 Oct 1804.

ERSKINE, Major-General Sir
William, Bt. (1777–1813)

The son of Lieutenant-General Sir
William Erskine, Bt., Sir William,
jun. (who inherited the baronetcy
in 1795) was a somewhat unusual
general in that he was generally
believed to be insane. Commissioned in 1786 and MP for Fife
1796–1805, he became major-
general in April 1808 and was sent
to the Peninsula, Sir David Dundas
having a high opinion of him.
Wellington queried the appointment, saying that he believed
Erskine was mad; Torrens replied:
'No doubt he is sometimes a little
mad, but in his lucid intervals he
is an uncommonly clever fellow;
and I trust he may have no fit
during the campaign, though he
looked a little wild before he
embarked'.[1] From February to

May 1811 Erskine commanded the 5th Division (less a period in command of the Light Division and cavalry), and from May to July, and again in 1812, he led the 2nd Cavalry Division. He had very bad sight and his reputation as a rash and incompetent commander was demonstrated by his mishandling of the action at Sabugal (retrieved by his subordinates), and by allowing the Almeida garrison to escape. His mental health seems to have broken down completely and he was killed at Lisbon in February 1813 'in consequence of throwing himself out of a window in a fit of delirium, which caused instant death',[2] although Judge-Advocate-General Larpent believed that he lived long enough to claim that he had not intended to commit suicide.

1. Fortescue, vol. VII, p. 419. 2. *Gent's Mag.*, June 1813, p. 595.

Fry, M. I., and Davies, G. 'Wellington's Officers in the D.N.B.', in *Journal of the Society for Army Historical Research*, vol. XXXIII, 1955, notes some corrections to the accepted version of Erskine's career, including his date of birth which is usually given as 1769.

ESPAGNE, General-Jean-Louis-Brigitte, comte (1769–1809)

Born in Auch, he is remembered as a fine leader of cuirassiers. He served as a trooper in the cavalry during the *ancien régime*, as an officer in the Revolutionary Wars, commanded the 8th Cavalry (originally the sole regiment equipped with cuirasses), and became *général de brigade* in 1799, *de division* in 1805. After service in Italy under Jourdan and as Massena's chief of staff, he was distinguished with his cuirassier division at Heilsberg, where he received seven lance-wounds, and in March 1808 was ennobled as comte. In 1809 he led the 3rd Heavy (cuirassier) Divi-

sion, which at Aspern–Essling was required to make repeated charges to stabilise the centre of the French position. Espagne led from the front, and when the corner of his cocked hat was shot through he merely turned the undamaged part to the front; but in a renewed charge against an Austrian battery he was hit by cannon-fire and killed. Buried on Lobau Island, his was a grievous loss of a brave and skilled cavalry general.

ESPANA, General Carlos José d'Espignac (1775–1839)

Born at Foix in south-western France, this emigrant officer entered Spanish service in 1792, but is best remembered as a divisional commander during the Peninsular War. He escaped from the defeat of the Battle of the Gebora, commanded Castaños' infantry at Albuera, and led a division at Salamanca; and in the latter campaign his most famous (or notorious) service occurred, when he withdrew the garrison of Alba de Tormes castle which had been posted to deny the French use of the bridge at that place, which enabled the defeated French to escape. Appointed Governor of Madrid, he continued to serve in conjunction with Wellington, commanding a division of the Spanish 4th Army. He was in charge of the blockade of Pamplona and was wounded in a French sally, typical of the reckless bravery he displayed on many occasions, and accepted the city's surrender after having threatened to give no quarter otherwise. He served with Wellington to the end of the war, but as a diehard absolutist fled upon the triumph of the Liberals in 1820, returning with the French to restore the rights of Ferdinand VII. He gained a dreadful reputation by mass executions in Catalonia, underwent a period in exile after Ferdi-

nand's death but was allowed t[o] return home; but his conduc[t] must not have been forgotte[n] because he died when mutinou[s] soldiers threw him into the Rive[r] Segre with a millstone tied aroun[d] his neck.

ESPOZ Y MINA, General Francisco, see MINA

ESSLING, prince d', see MASSENA

ESTAING, Admiral Charles-Hector, comte d' (1729–94)

Best known for his service in th[e] French Navy in India during th[e] Seven Years War, and in the War o[f] American Independence, after th[e] peace of 1783 he turned to politic[s] as a reformer but loyal supporte[r] of the monarchy. He supporte[d] Marie-Antoinette during her tria[l] for which he was himself trie[d] and executed in April 1794.

EVANS, General Sir George De Lacy (1787–1870)

SIR GEORGE DE LACY EVANS
(ENGRAVING BY W. J. EDWARDS AFTER CLAUDET[)]

Famous for leading the British Legion in the Carlist War and the 2nd Division in the Crimea, he saw much service during the Napoleonic Wars. Joining the army as a volunteer in 1806, he was commissioned in 1807, served in India, with the 3rd Dragoons in the Peninsula (Vittoria, Pyrenees, Toulouse), in America (Bladensburg, New Orleans) and at Waterloo as ADC to Sir William Ponsonby. He rose to the rank of general (1861) while holding a Spanish lieutenant-generalcy.

Spiers, E. M. *Radical General: Sir George De Lacy Evans 1787–1870*. Manchester, 1983

EXELMANS, Marshal Remy-Joseph-Isidore, comte (1775–1852)

REMY JOSEPH EXELMANS

A native of Bar-le-Duc, he entered the army in 1791 and was commissioned in 1796. After good service in Italy he became ADC to Murat, was distinguished in the Austerlitz campaign, and after serving as a regimental cavalry commander in 1806 became Murat's senior ADC in 1807 as *général de brigade*. Ennobled as baron in March 1808, he was captured in Spain in the same year but broke his parole and escaped from England, where he had been sent, in 1811. Murat appointed him master of the palace, but he preferred a military career, joined the Imperial Guard cavalry and in 1812 was promoted to *général de division* after

Borodino, succeeding to the command of Pajol's division after the latter had been wounded. Commanding a division of II Cavalry Corps in 1813, he was handled severely at the Katzbach, partly as a consequence of his own dispositions and insufficient caution; but he became comte in September 1813 and commanded part of the Guard cavalry in 1814. He took service under the Bourbons at the first restoration (surviving a trial for conducting correspondence with Murat), but rejoined Napoleon in 1815, leading II Cavalry Corps in the Waterloo campaign. At the second restoration he had to live abroad until 1819 after denouncing the execution of Ney as an assassination; active in the 1830 revolution, he was rewarded by Louis-Philippe (including reinstatement as a peer of France), and as a supporter of Louis Napoleon, in 1851 was appointed a Marshal of France, a reward which would have been unlikely during the First Empire because of his lack of tactical aptitude. His death resulted from a fall from his horse.

Thoumas, C. A. *Le Maréchal Exelmans*. Paris, 1891

EXMOUTH, Admiral Sir Edward Pellew, 1st Viscount (1757–1833)

Best known for commanding the British fleet which bombarded Algiers in 1816, he also had a distinguished career during the Napoleonic Wars. Born at Dover of a Cornish family, he joined the Royal Navy in 1770 and became known for bravery and daring; he served in the War of American Independence (he carried news of Burgoyne's surrender to England), was knighted in 1793 when as captain of the frigate HMS *Nymphe* he captured the French frigate *Cléopâtre* (the first major British naval success of the

SIR EDWARD PELLEW, VISCOUNT EXMOUTH (ENGRAVING BY J. ROGERS AFTER W. OWEN)

war), and made another notable capture in 1794 (the French frigate *Pomone*). In 1796 he received a baronetcy for saving the passengers and crew of the transport *Dutton*, which he boarded from shore after it had grounded at Plymouth; elected MP for Dunstable in 1802 (a supporter of Pitt) he became rear-admiral in 1804, CinC East Indies (to 1809), CinC North Sea 1811, and Mediterranean 1814. Ennobled as Baron Exmouth in 1814, in 1815 he again commanded in the Mediterranean, during which time he landed an expedition at Marseilles to support the royalists, and led them in person to occupy Toulon. He was advanced to a viscountcy after his service at Algiers, and retired after serving as Port Admiral at Plymouth (1817–21). His brother was Admiral Sir Israel Pellew, who as captain of HMS *Conqueror* at Trafalgar sent his captain of marines, James Atcherley, to accept Villeneuve's surrender. On being told that Atcherley represented Captain Pellew, Villeneuve remarked that he was pleased to have surrendered to an officer as distinguished as Sir Edward; when Atcherley said that it was Edward's brother, Israel, Villeneuve exclaimed 'What, are there two of them? Alas!' Exmouth's eldest sons followed him into the Royal Navy: Captain Pownoll Bastard (1786–1833, later 2nd Viscount) and Admiral Sir Fleetwood Broughton Reynolds (1798–1861); Israel's son Edward was a captain in the 1st Life Guards (commissioned November 1813) and was killed by a brother officer in a duel at Paris in 1819.

Ostler, E *The Life of Admiral Viscount Exmouth.* London, 1835; Parkinson, C. Northcote. *Edward Pellew, Viscount Exmouth.* London, 1934. An account of Exmouth's Algiers service is in Perkins, R., and Douglas-Morris, Captain K. J. *Gunfire in Barbary.* Havant, 1982

FABER DU FAUR, General Christian G. von (1780–1857)

As a subaltern in the Württemberg artillery, this notable military artist survived the retreat from Moscow and published impressive scenes of the campaign in a series of lithographs (Stuttgart 1831–43); an excellent draughtsman, his work is a major source for the campaign and includes some of the most famous images of the period. He attained the rank of general in the Württemberg army.

Faber du Faur, C. G. von, and Kaussler, F. von. *La Campagne de Russie (1812) d'après le journal illustré d'un témoin oculaire*. Paris n.d. [1895]

FABRE D'EGLANTINE, Philippe-François-Nazaire (1750–94)

The dramatist Philippe Fabre (who added the 'd'Eglantine' later) was a native of Carcassonne, and is perhaps better known for his political activities. An ardent supporter of the Revolution, he was a member of the Jacobin Club, was Danton's secretary, and in the Convention voted for the execution of Louis XVI. He was a bitter opponent of the Girondins and was concerned in the creation and nomenclature of the republican calendar. Condemned on a charge of corruption, he was guillotined in April 1794.

FAIN, Agathon-Jean-François, baron (1778–1837)

A civil servant under the Directory, the Paris-born Fain entered the office of the secretary of state as an archivist during the Consulate; in 1806 he was appointed to Napoleon's personal staff and became his confidential secretary in succession to Méneval, and accompanied him throughout the later campaigns. Ennobled in 1809, Fain retired at the second restoration (until recalled as cabinet secretary by Louis-Philippe in 1830) and devoted much time to writing histories of 1812–14 and 1794–5; of the first, Las Cases remarked that 'Baron Fain has presented us with a record of national glory, and he is justly entitled to the gratitude of his countrymen' in recording the prodigies performed by Napoleon and his forces, 'an episode of miracles'.[1] Fain's memoirs, published in 1908, are a valuable source for the period during which he was one of Napoleon's closest associates.

1. Las Cases, vol. IV, p. 116.

Fain, A. J. F. *Mémoires du Baron Fain, Premier Secrétaire du Cabinet de l'Empereur*. Paris, 1908. *Memoirs of the Invasion of France by the Allied Armies and of the last Six Months of the Reign of Napoleon*. London, 1834 (published in French a decade earlier)

FANE, General John, see WESTMORLAND

FAVRAS, Thomas de Mahy, marquis de (1744–90)

After service in the French Army during the Seven Years War, he raised a legion in support of the insurrection in The Netherlands in 1787. With the outbreak of the Revolution he became involved in schemes in support of the monarchy, involving his old associate, the comte de Provence (later Louis XVIII), but was betrayed and arrested. Despite evidence which was stated to be insufficient, he was condemned and executed in February 1790, without implicating any of the other conspirators (though it was reported that he had offered to reveal a name in exchange for a pardon). The Count of Provence more than once denied complicity, and it was said that Favras was condemned to placate the mob.

FELTRE, duc de, see CLARKE

FERDINAND III, Grand Duke of Tuscany, Archduke of Austria, Grand Duke of Würzburg (1769–1824)

One of the most enlightened and benevolent of rulers, he was the second son of Emperor Leopold II, succeeding his father as Grand Duke of Tuscany when Leopold became emperor in 1790. Ferdinand attempted to remain neutral in the wars but had to flee when the French entered Tuscany in 1799, and although Florence was recovered with Austrian assistance and by a popular rising in his name, by the Treaty of Lunéville Tuscany was converted to the kingdom of Etruria, and Ferdinand returned to Austria. In return for losing Tuscany, in 1802 he received the electorship of Salzburg, which he exchanged in 1805 for Würzburg, and as Grand Duke of

FERDINAND III, GRAND DUKE OF TUSCANY
(MEDALLIC PORTRAIT)

that state in September 1806 entered the Confederation of the

Rhine, which he left in November 1813. The Congress of Vienna returned Würzburg to its previous Bavarian possession, and in September 1814 Ferdinand was welcomed back to Tuscany by almost all the population. He left briefly in 1815, but after Napoleon's final defeat ruled there benevolently until his death, maintaining much of the French legislation introduced during his absence, so that the transition from French rule to the old regime was accomplished without the excesses which occurred in some other states.

FERDINAND IV, King of Naples (1751–1825)

FERDINAND IV, KING OF NAPLES
(MEDALLIC PORTRAIT)

When Charles of Bourbon succeeded as King Charles III of Spain in 1759, he relinquished the throne of Naples and Sicily and was succeeded by his 8-year-old son Ferdinand (IV of Naples, III of Sicily, I of the Two Sicilies). Somewhat ignorant and boorish, Ferdinand was among the least appealing heads of state of the period, and was nicknamed *il rè lazzarone* (the *lazzaroni* being the lowest form of peasant), or, from his nose, *il rè nasone*; but he retained the devotion of the *lazzaroni*. In 1768 he married Maria Carolina, daughter of Empress Maria-Theresa and sister of Marie-Antoinette, an ambitious and dominating woman who

came to control both king and kingdom, and under whose influence Naples became involved in the war with France. After briefly occupying Rome in 1798, Ferdinand fled before the advancing French, abandoning Naples for the safety of the British fleet. On the return of the royalists, who overturned the brief Parthenopean Republic, no mercy was shown to the republicans. In January 1806 Ferdinand again fled to Sicily before the French, Napoleon installing Joseph Bonaparte, then Murat, as king in his stead. Ferdinand remained in Sicily under British protection, his repressive regime tempered by the adoption of a liberal constitution under pressure from the British Minister, Lord William Bentinck. Ferdinand virtually abdicated responsibility, appointing his son as regent, and Maria Carolina was sent to Austria, where she died in 1814. Restored to his land in 1815, Ferdinand proclaimed himself King of the Two Sicilies and abolished the Sicilian constitution, which heralded a period of repression, rebellion, cruelty, violence and Austrian military intervention, a sad situation not improved by the accession of the corrupt Francis I on Ferdinand's death in January 1825.

Acton, H. *The Bourbons of Naples*. London, 1956

FERDINAND VII, King of Spain (Prince of the Asturias) (1784–1833)

Posterity has dealt severely with his reputation; Sir Charles Oman, for example, described him as a 'coward and a cur'.[1] Prince of the Asturias and son of King Charles IV and Queen Maria Louisa, he was deliberately excluded from affairs of state, at odds with his parents and violently opposed to their favourite, Godoy. Involved in 1807 in a plot against the latter, by which he intended to seek Napoleon's protection, when discovered he

FERDINAND VII, KING OF SPAIN
(MEDALLIC PORTRAIT)

was accused by Godoy of plotting against his father, and to save himself betrayed his accomplices. Under pressure from the population Charles IV abdicated in March 1808 and Ferdinand succeeded to the throne, whereupon Charles withdrew his abdication; but by the Conference of Bayonne (April–May 1808) both Charles and Ferdinand were forced to surrender the crown to Napoleon who ultimately installed Joseph Bonaparte as king. While the overwhelming majority of the Spanish population was fighting the Peninsular War in Ferdinand's cause, he was living in semi-imprisonment at Valençay, amusing himself in such harmless pastimes as embroidery and cutting out paper patterns. Napoleon himself remarked on the unusual nature of his detention: 'The fact is, he was scarcely guarded at Valençay, and that he did not wish to escape. If any plots were contrived to favour his evasion, he was the first to make them known ... His applications to me for a wife at my hands were incessant. He spontaneously wrote me letters of congratulation upon every event that occurred in my favour.'[2] When restored to his throne in 1814, Ferdinand revoked the (somewhat impracticable) constitution of 1812 which had been passed by the *cortes* without his consent, and began to rule autocratically; this provoked the liberal rising of 1820 which forced him to accede to the constitution, until restored to his former status by French invasion. Thereafter there were brutal reprisals, and even in deciding his succession Ferdinand managed to precipitate another round of bloodshed, by consenting to the right of succession of his daughter in preference to his brother, Don Carlos, thereby initiating the Carlist Wars.

1. Oman, vol. I, p. 16. 2. Las Cases, vol. II, p. 293.

FERDINAND D'ESTE, Archduke (1781–1835)

One of the oldest princely houses of Italy, the family of Este produced a number of important military figures. The third wife of the Emperor Francis II (later I) was Maria Ludovica Beatrix of Este, whom he married in 1808; her brother was the Archduke Ferdinand, who as *Feldmarschall- Leutnant* was a capable commander of the Austrian Army. Despite his youth, in 1805 he was appointed nominal commander in Germany and wisely advocated caution, though as *de facto* commander, Mack's view prevailed. Ferdinand refused to be confined at Ulm with the rest of Mack's force and broke out with some cavalry, 1,800 of whom succeeded in reaching safety. In 1809 he commanded VII Corps, detached on the northern frontier; marching into Poland he defeated Poniatowski at Raszyn (19 April) but the diversion was not as great as had been intended: with Russia declaring war on Austria on 5 May, and with a threat to his rear, he had to retreat, deprived of reinforcements by the Wagram campaign.

FERSEN, Hans Axel, Count von (1755–1810)

This Swedish statesman entered the French Army in 1779, served as an aide to Rochambeau in the War of American Independence, and became a great favourite at the French court, especially with Marie-Antoinette. Having returned to Sweden in 1788, he was sent back to Paris by King Gustavus III to assist the French royal family; he was involved in the abortive flight to Varennes, and in February 1792 audaciously stole in to see the royal family during their confinement, but his efforts to render assistance were in vain. He served Gustavus IV and was a known supporter of his son to succeed him after the 1809 coup, in place of the king's uncle, who became Charles XIII, and an unfounded rumour spread that Fersen had been implicated in poisoning the latter's elected successor, the Prince of Augustenburg. As Earl Marshal, Fersen received the Prince's body when it was conveyed to Stockholm on 20 June 1810, and he was beaten to death by a mob which accused him of being the prince's murderer; the inaction of troops nearby led to suspicions that it might have been a convenient way to remove one who was not a supporter of the then king.

Fersen, H. A. von. *Rescue the Queen: A Diary of the French Revolution*. London, 1971

FESCH, Cardinal Joseph (1762–1839)

Half-brother of Letizia Bonaparte, as Napoleon's uncle he was an influential figure in the youth of the Bonaparte children. Archdeacon of Ajaccio, and revered in the district, during the revolutionary period he took secular employment after leaving Corsica with Letizia and her family, and laid the foundation of a considerable fortune serving as a commissary with Napoleon's Army of Italy. After Napoleon became First Consul, Fesch resumed his ecclesiastical career and featured in the negotiations leading to the Concordat, for which he was

CARDINAL JOSEPH FESCH
(ENGRAVING BY M. HAIDER AFTER J. MAGLIOLI)

rewarded with the archbishopric of Lyons (1802) and the appointment as cardinal in the following year. From 1804 Napoleon made him ambassador to Rome, and through him made his demands upon the Pope; but Fesch's relations with his nephew became progressively strained, especially after the annexation of the papal states and virtual detention of the Pope, and Fesch refused Napoleon's offer of the archbishopric of Paris. At the restoration he retired to Rome (although he resumed his duties at Lyons during the Hundred Days and was named a senator), and spent the remainder of his life in retirement in Rome, surrounded by a vast art collection, and caring for Letizia for the remainder of her life. When Napoleon needed a priest to be sent to St. Helena, it was to Fesch that the request was made.

Lyonnet, J. B. *Le Cardinal Fesch*. Lyons, 1841

FEZENSAC, duc de, see MONTESQUIOU-FEZENSAC

FITZGERALD, Lord Edward (1763–98)

The fifth son of James, 1st Duke of Leinster, he was commissioned in the army in 1779, served in the 19th Foot and was severely wounded at Eutaw Springs (8 September 1781) during the War of American Independence; he later served as a major in the 54th where Cobbett, at that time their sergeant-major, described him as the only truly sober, honest, humane and conscientious officer he had ever encountered. A member of parliament from an early age, Fitzgerald's Whig sympathies (Charles James Fox was his cousin) may have influenced his support for the French Revolution, which was reinforced by a trip to France in which he lodged with Paine and married a girl of dubious parentage named Pamela (c.1776–1831), who was believed to be a natural daughter of Philippe 'Egalité', duc d'Orléans. They created a stir when they returned to Dublin – the idealistic and handsome Fitzgerald had his hair cropped in 'revolutionary' style – and such was his denunciation of the government that he was called to the bar of the Irish Parliament to apologise. In 1796 he joined the United Irishmen and visited Hamburg to negotiate French assistance; though a vehement advocate of early rebellion, due to his high birth it seems that the government was unwilling to act against him until forced. When his refuge in Dublin was disclosed a party was sent to arrest him (19 May 1798); he resisted violently, stabbed the police chief who tried to make the arrest and killed a yeomanry officer (Captain Ryan) by fourteen thrusts with a dagger, and was only caught when the Dublin town-major, Henry Sirr, shot him in the shoulder. Fitzgerald had powerful friends (his mother, daughter of the 2nd Duke of Richmond, canvassed the support of the Prince of Wales and Duke of York, and the Duke of Richmond spoke to the king), who aimed to postpone the trial until the Irish rebellion had ended, in

hope of securing a more favourable climate; but the wound in his shoulder became infected, and he died on 4 June 1798. Despite the sincerity of his beliefs and a most engaging personality, he was probably too impulsive and inexperienced to make an ideal leader of the movement, to which leadership his position in society had propelled him.

Moore, T. *Life and Death of Lord Edward Fitzgerald*. London, 1831, revised as *The Memoirs of Lord Edward Fitzgerald*, ed. M. MacDermott. London, 1897; Tillyard, S. *Citizen Lord: Edward Fitzgerald*. London, 1997

FLAHAUT DE LA BILLARDERIE, General Auguste-Charles-Joseph, comte de (1785–1870)

Perhaps best remembered as the lover of Hortense de Beauharnais, wife of Louis Bonaparte and Queen of Holland, he was ostensibly the son of the comte de Flahaut (guillotined in 1793), but was believed to be a natural son of Talleyrand; his mother, the comtesse, is probably better known as Madame de Souza, wife of the Portuguese Ambassador to France, who became Auguste's adopted father. In exile until 1798, Flahaut entered the army in 1800, became ADC to Murat, served in the campaigns of 1805–7 and in Spain in 1808, and despite long liaisons with Countess Potocka and Caroline Bonaparte (Murat's wife), became the lover of Hortense. Their son, Charles Auguste Louis Joseph Demorny, later duc de Morny, was born in 1811. These affairs seem not to have inhibited Flahaut's career: he served as Eugène's aide in Russia, became *général de brigade* in 1812, *de division* in October 1813, and ADC to Napoleon. After service in the Hundred Days (as Napoleon's aide) he was saved from exile by

Talleyrand's influence, but later went abroad; while in England he married Margaret Elphinstone, daughter of Viscount Keith. Flahaut returned to France in 1827, where he became a peer and lieutenant-general under Louis-Philippe, and served as ambassador to Vienna 1841–8 and to Great Britain 1860–2. He had a most distinguished grandson: his daughter Emily married the 4th Marquess of Lansdowne and their son Henry, the 5th Marquess, held among other posts those of Viceroy of India (1888–94) and the Secretaryships of State for War (1895–1900) and Foreign Affairs (1900–5) in the British government.

FLETCHER, Lieutenant-Colonel Sir Richard, Bt. (1768–1813)

One of the most expert military engineers of the period, he saw service in the West Indies, with the Ottoman forces 1799–1800 (he helped fortify E1 Arish and Jaffa), and in the Danish expedition (1807), but made his name as Wellington's chief engineer in the Peninsula, where he served from 1809. He is perhaps best known as a principal designer of the Lines of Torres Vedras, but also supervised the great sieges of Ciudad Rodrigo, Badajoz and San Sebastian. At Badajoz he was wounded in a singular manner, when a ball struck his purse and drove a dollar into his thigh, but though convalescent for two weeks, he continued to supervise the work carried out by his subordinates. Rewarded with a baronetcy, Fletcher was killed at San Sebastian: 'the fatal shot entered the spine of the back, and occasioned his instant death'; and having been Wellington's chief engineer so long, and giving 'constant proof of superior skill and abilities',[1] his loss was greatly lamented.

1. *Gent's Mag.*, Nov, 1813, p. 499.

FLORIDABLANCA, José Monino y Redondo, Count of (1728–1808)

The distinguished chief minister of King Charles III of Spain, he at first retained his office upon the accession of Charles IV and encouraged the formation of the first coalition against republican France; but the Queen persuaded Charles to dismiss him, and he was imprisoned in the castle of Pamplona (being saved from starvation only by the intervention of his brother). Upon his release he was allowed to return to his estates, but in 1808 used his influence to advocate the establishment of a central *junta* to rule Spain in the absence of Ferdinand VII, in preference to the existing, unco-ordinated provincial *juntas*. In September 1808 Floridablanca was elected head of the resulting 'Supreme *Junta*' but his health was not sufficiently sound for the task and he died on 20 November.

FOLEY, Admiral Sir Thomas (1757–1833)

One of Nelson's most trusted subordinates, Thomas Foley was a member of an ancient family of South Wales gentry, entered the Royal Navy in 1770 and saw much active service under Keppel and Rodney. At the beginning of the French Revolutionary Wars he was sent to the Mediterranean as flag-captain to Admiral John Gell, and later to Sir Hyde Parker. He served at Toulon as flag-captain to Admiral Sir Charles Thompson, and in command of HMS *Goliath* played a most significant role at Aboukir Bay, upon his own initiative sailing between the French line and the shore to attack them from an unexpected side, which had a profound effect upon the course of the action. At Copenhagen Foley commanded Nelson's flagship, HMS *Elephant*, but ill-health compelled him to decline the appointment as Nelson's

SIR THOMAS FOLEY

captain of the fleet in the operations which led to Trafalgar. From 1808 until the end of the war he commanded in the Downs, rose to the rank of admiral and died when commanding at Portsmouth in 1833; his coffin was constructed of planks from *Elephant*'s quarter-deck. Regarded as one of the most able officers of the period, he had a commanding presence (tall, with a bluff manner and very loud voice), and a reputation for kindness to those under his command.

Herbert, J. B. *Life and Services of Admiral Sir Thomas Foley*. Cardiff, 1884

FOUCHE, Joseph, duc d'Otrante (1763–1820)

'A furious partiality for clandestine operations'[1] was Las Cases' comment on Fouché, one of the most sinister figures of the period. Born near Nantes and intended for a maritime career like his father, his talents and constitution directed him to the teaching profession, via the Oratorian Order which had educated him. At the Revolution, known for the vehemence of his ideals, he was elected to the Convention where he gravitated towards the Jacobins, voted for the execution of the king and assisted Collot d'Herbois in the brutal suppression of revolt at Lyons. Ever prepared to sacri-

fice principle for personal gain or survival, he turned against the Jacobins at the time of the coup of 9 Thermidor, but was expelled from the Convention as 'a thief and a terrorist, whose crimes would cast eternal disgrace on any assembly of which he was a member'.[2] Ingratiating himself with the Directory, he was appointed ambassador to the Cisalpine Republic, and in mid 1799 became Minister of Police, in which office he attained great power, and after supporting the coup of Brumaire was retained by Napoleon. He was effective in suppressing opposition to Napoleon, but was temporarily deprived of office (1802–4) when Napoleon became worried about his increasing power; but his network of agents was so effective at the time of the Cadoudal conspiracy that he was reinstated. With good reason Napoleon remained suspicious of his loyalty, and despite having ennobled him as duc d'Otrante, dismissed him in June 1810 when clandestine foreign negotiations (including those with Great Britain) came to light. Napoleon sent him to Rome as Governor, but discovered that Fouché had not surrendered important documents from his old job; to escape the Emperor's

JOSEPH FOUCHÉ
(ENGRAVING BY L. WOLF AFTER J. GIRARDET)

anger Fouché intended to go to America, but Elisa Bonaparte pleaded on his behalf and he was allowed to settle in France. Later he was appointed Governor of Illyria, and at the restoration ingratiated himself with the Bourbons, while maintaining contact with Napoleon; at the time of the Hundred Days Fouché declined the ministry of police when it was offered by the king, but accepted it from Napoleon and resumed his old duties, while keeping contact with Metternich and the royalists in order to secure his position irrespective of the outcome. Consequently he abandoned Napoleon upon his defeat, was elected president of the commission which governed France provisionally after the abdication and was taken into Louis XVIII's government until old resentments on the part of the royalists caused him to resign in September 1815. He acted as ambassador at Dresden until the proscription of regicides caused his dismissal in 1816, and he retired to Trieste to enjoy the immense fortune which he had accumulated during his years of power. Bourrienne summarised Fouché as belonging to no party, serving those whom he knew would triumph, and at the same time intriguing for their overthrow so as to secure his own position; in this he was undoubtedly skilled, and his formidable intelligence network made him a valuable servant. Napoleon had no illusions about him, remarking that 'Intrigue was to Fouché a necessary of life. He intrigued at all times, in all places, in all ways, and with all persons ... He made it his sole business to look out for something that he might be meddling with';[3] it was often said that Fouché's ugly foot was sure to be thrust in everybody's shoes, and Caulaincourt recorded Napoleon as stating that Fouché would steal anything upon which

he could lay his hands. For all that, Napoleon found him a valuable tool, and like Talleyrand he was above all a survivor. There is some point to Scott's remark that it was a wonder how such an arch-plotter managed to die in bed.

1. Las Cases, vol. I, p. 12. 2. Anon., p. 162. 3. Las Cases, vol. II, p. 66.

Cole, H. *Fouché, the Unprincipled Patriot*. London, 1971; Cubberly, R. E. *The Role of Fouché during the Hundred Days*. Madison, 1969; Fouché, J. *The Memoirs of Joseph Fouché, Duke of Otranto*, London 1825 (orig. pubd. Paris, 1818); Madelin, L. *Fouché*, Paris, 1901

FOUQUIER-TINVILLE, Antoine-Quentin (1746–95)

Notorious as the public prosecutor of the Paris Revolutionary Tribunal from March 1793 to July 1794, he gained a fearsome reputation as a ruthless instrument of the faction in power, giving legality to purges and executions. He fell with Robespierre, and after a long trial in which his defence was that he was obeying the orders of the Committee of Public Safety, he was convicted and guillotined in May 1795.

FOURES, Pauline (1781–1869)

The illegitimate daughter of an unknown father and a cook named Bellisle, which name she adopted, she married a *chasseur* lieutenant named Fourès and accompanied him to Egypt, where her beauty was noticed by General Napoleon Bonaparte. He sent her husband out of the way to Malta, only for him to be captured by the British and paroled; on his return to Egypt he found his wife installed as Napoleon's mistress and known by the nickname 'Cléopâtre'. Pauline divorced her outraged husband and set her sights higher, but to Napoleon it was a passing affair and she had to make her own way back to France in 1800. Napoleon gave

minor diplomatic employment to her second husband, Henri de Ranchoup, and claimed that in 1811 he met Pauline at a masked ball and gave her 60,000 francs. In 1816 she left her husband and went to Brazil with an ex-Imperial Guard officer, Jean Auguste Bellard, operating a lucrative trade in rare wood until in 1837 she settled in Paris with a collection of monkeys and parrots. Having written a novel and taken up painting during her earlier residence in Paris, she wrote a second and lived comfortably to a great age.

Régis, R. *Pauline Fourès ... maîtresse de Bonaparte en Egypte*. Paris, 1946

FOURNIER-SARLOVEZE, General François, comte (1773–1827)

In many ways the archetypal, dashing light cavalry officer, he was born in Sarlat, and was commissioned in the French Army in 1792. Known for a somewhat haughty, arrogant manner which caused a number of duels, he was cashiered for fraud and absence without leave in 1794 but reinstated, served in 1797 as aide to Augereau, in Germany and Italy, and was arrested briefly in 1802 for suspected complicity in a plot against Napoleon; there seems to have been mutual dislike between them. Nevertheless, his fighting qualities were appreciated and he served as Lasalle's chief of staff in 1807, becoming *général de brigade* in June of that year, and a baron in 1808. He fought in the Peninsula as cavalry commander of IX Corps, including Fuentes de Oñoro, and in Russia in 1812 commanded the cavalry of IX Corps, a force drawn from Berg, Baden, Hesse–Darmstadt and Saxony, which made the vital charges at Studianka during the crossing of the Berezina. Promoted to *général de division*, Fournier served in the 1813 campaign, including Leipzig, but received no further employment after renewed criticism of Napoleon. He was reinstated by the Bourbons, advanced to comte (and permitted to add 'Sarlovèze' to his name, from his place of birth) and became Inspector-General of Cavalry (1819), but was retired after falling from favour.

FOX, Charles James (1749–1806)

CHARLES JAMES FOX (ENGRAVING BY W. H. EGLETON AFTER REYNOLDS)

One of the great figures in British political history, Fox was the third son of the 1st Lord Holland and his wife Caroline, daughter of the 2nd Duke of Richmond. Highly intelligent, with a love of literature, classics and languages, he entered parliament in 1768 and became a Lord of the Admiralty in 1772, but the gambling which plagued his career, and his reputation as a rake, found no favour with George III, and he was dismissed. Associated with the Rockingham Whigs, he spoke forcibly in opposition to the War of American Independence, served as Foreign Secretary under Rockingham (1782–3) and in coalition with Lord North under Portland, but then went into opposition for almost the whole of his subsequent career. He became a stern opponent of William Pitt and a close associate of the Prince of Wales, and his unwillingness to

condemn the progressive excesses of the French Revolution brought him great unpopularity; even his old associate Burke publicly renounced their friendship in the House of Commons in 1791, and Fox almost withdrew from parliament entirely. In May 1798 he was even dismissed from the privy council for publicly proclaiming the sovereignty of the people. The fall of Pitt and peace with France brought him back into public life, however, and Napoleon (who met him during Fox's trip to Paris in 1802) had hopes of a more permanent peace should Fox take over the reins of government. Pitt's death left Fox as the country's leading statesman, and as such he could no longer be excluded from office; as Grenville's Foreign Secretary he was able to warn Talleyrand of a plot to assassinate Napoleon, which gave an opportunity for the opening of tentative negotiations for peace, but Fox was suspicious and not inclined to accede to French demands. His health had begun to fail when he took office, and dropsy became apparent in the summer of 1806; he died on 13 September. Napoleon found he 'possessed a noble character, a good heart, liberal, generous, and enlightened views. I considered him an ornament to mankind, and was very much attached to him'; yet found Fox ready to defend his own country no matter how much he disagreed with its government. With men like Fox and Cornwallis, Napoleon said, 'I should always have agreed ... we should have done great things together'.[1] Fox's younger brother, **General Henry Edward Fox**, had served in the War of American Independence and was ADC to the king; he was appointed to command British forces in the Mediterranean and to represent Great Britain at the Neapolitan court at the time when Charles James was Foreign Secretary. A kindly, affable man with no

taste for ostentation, he was unsuited for the job on grounds of both health and ability, and Sir John Moore was sent as his 2i/c with the implicit purpose of taking active command of the troops.

1. Las Cases, vol. II, pp. 274–5.

Butterfield, H. *Charles James Fox and Napoleon*. London, 1962; Derry, J. *Charles James Fox*. London, 1972; Fox, C. J. *Memorials and Correspondence of Charles James Fox*, ed. Lord John Russell. London, 1853–7; Lascelles, E. *The Life of Charles James Fox*. Oxford, 1936; Reid, L. *Charles James Fox*. London, 1969; Russell, Lord John. *Life and Times of Charles James Fox*. London, 1859–66

FOY, General Maximilien-Sébastien, comte (1775–1825)

MAXIMILIEN FOY

One of Napoleon's most able divisional commanders, Foy was the son of a French soldier who had fought at Fontenoy, and an English mother. Commissioned in the artillery in 1792, he was imprisoned in 1794 for criticising the extremes of the government; he served under Moreau in 1796–7, in Switzerland under Massena and in Italy in 1800. His rise in rank was inhibited by his republican principles and opposition to Napoleon's elevation to emperor, but in 1807 he accompanied

Sébastiani to Constantinople and made his name in the Peninsula. He commanded the artillery reserve at Vimeiro and a brigade of Delaborde's division at Corunna; taken prisoner by the Portuguese at Oporto in March 1809, he was almost murdered in mistaken revenge, saving himself by holding up two hands to show that he was not the one-armed and much hated Loison. Wounded commanding a brigade of Heudelet's division at Busaco, he was sent by Massena to explain to Napoleon the position in front of the lines of Torres Vedras. (Wellington discovered that Foy was regularly sending into the British lines for English newspapers, their only way of receiving news as they were cut off from France; on investigation Foy claimed he was only checking his investments in British government stock!). Ennobled as baron in September 1810 and promoted to *général de division*, Foy led the 1st Division of the Army of Portugal with distinction at Salamanca, but it was badly mauled at Garcia Hernandez next day; distinguished in the Pyrenees, he was wounded at Orthez by a shrapnel-ball in the shoulder. He accepted the Bourbon restoration but rallied to Napoleon in 1815, was elevated to comte and led the 9th Division at Waterloo, becoming bogged down in the fighting around Hougoumont and suffering a bad bruise on the shoulder from a musket-ball. Reconciled with the Bourbons, he took up a staff appointment in 1819 but made a greater mark in politics as a liberal Deputy with a justified reputation for honesty and sincerity; he made a notable protest about French intervention in Spain. His political career, and his task of writing the history of the Peninsular War, were curtailed by his early death in November 1825, and such was his reputation and popularity that some 100,000 mourners attended his funeral.

Foy, M. S. *Histoire de la Guerre de la Péninsule sous Napoléon.* Paris, 1827 (English edn. *History of the War in the Peninsula.* London, 1829); Girod de l'Ain, M. *Vie Militaire du Général Foy.* Paris, 1900 (includes the journals of this able and gallant officer)

FRANCIS I, King of the Two Sicilies (1777–1830)

Son of Ferdinand IV of Naples (later Ferdinand I of the Two Sicilies), Francis was heir to the throne and came to some prominence in 1812, when under the influence of the British Minister, Lord William Bentinck, Sicily was granted a constitution and Francis was appointed regent. After the end of the war Ferdinand reasserted his authority, and when Francis succeeded as king in 1825 he proved as reactionary as his father, being characterised as a corrupt libertine.

FRANCIS II, Holy Roman Emperor (Emperor Francis I of Austria) (1768–1835)

EMPEROR FRANCIS II (FRANCIS I OF AUSTRIA)
(ENGRAVING BY BLOOD AFTER SHEPPERSON)

The last Holy Roman Emperor, Francis II was the son of Leopold II and Maria Louisa, daughter of Charles III of Spain, and succeeded his father on 1 March 1792. He relinquished the title of

Holy Roman Emperor in 1806 following Napoleon's domination of Germany after the Austrian defeat of 1805, and was henceforth Francis I of Austria (not to be confused with the Holy Roman Emperor Francis I, husband of Maria Theresa, 1708–65). The first half of his reign was dominated by the wars against France, in which Austria played a leading role, and although Francis retained a hand in the military decisions as supreme ruler of his dominions, he put much faith in civilian and military advisers, for example his brother the Archduke Charles and Chancellors such as Colloredo; from 1809 foreign affairs were entrusted to Metternich. The relationship between civilian and military functionaries caused some conflict, complicated by Francis' establishment of a military section within the *Staatsrat* (government) which overlapped the duties of the *Hofkriegsrat* (military council); but Francis' patience and determination ensured that Austria retained an influential position, though successive defeats precluded its forces from remaining in the field throughout. Following the defeat of 1809, Austria was forced into an alliance with France, cemented by Napoleon's marriage to Francis' daughter Marie-Louise in 1810, and it resulted in Austria's provision of a corps to cover Napoleon's right flank during the invasion of Russia in 1812; and Austria's abandonment of the alliance in 1813 proved to be a vital factor in the defeat of Napoleon. Francis himself sometimes accompanied the army on campaign; it was to protect him from a perceived French threat that the action of Villers-en-Cauchies was fought in 1794, and he was present at Austerlitz, Dresden and Leipzig. After the end of the war he followed a path of conservatism and opposition to liberal policies, which caused some criticism, but he remained popular with the mass of his subjects. He was married four times: in 1788 to Elizabeth of Württemberg, who died in childbirth in 1790; later that year to his cousin Maria Theresa, daughter of Ferdinand IV of Naples; after her death in 1807 to Maria Ludovica Beatrix d'Este; and after her death to Carolina Augusta of Bavaria (1816).

Meynert, H. *Kaiser Franz I.* Vienna, 1872

FRASER, Lieutenant-General Alexander Mackenzie (1756–1809)

Alexander Mackenzie, who adopted the name Mackenzie Fraser in 1803, was commissioned in 1778 and served as ADC to Sir Augustus Eliott at the siege of Gibraltar, in India, in The Netherlands (1794–5) and at the Cape. Major-general from 1802, in 1807 he led the expedition to Egypt, commanded the 3rd Division in the Corunna campaign and the 4th Division at Walcheren. He contracted fever there and died at the house of his brother-in-law (the Attorney-General, Sir Vickery Gibbs) in Hayes, Middlesex, in September 1809. Colonel of the 78th from 1796, he was described as 'mild as a Lamb, and as a Lion strong; he was rather above 5 feet 11 inches high, and well put together; and he had so benevolent a look when speaking, you were assured his heart went with the words'.[1] He should not be confused with Major-General John Randoll Mackenzie, who was killed while in command of a brigade at Talavera, a member of an ancient family from the Black Isle, Ross-shire, who transferred to the army from the marines in 1794, served with Mackenzie Fraser in the 78th and was 'a zealous, steady, cool soldier; a mild and most friendly man' who was 'adored' by the 78th.[2]

1. *Gent's Mag.*, Oct, 1809, p. 902. 2. Ibid., Aug, 1809, p. 780

FRAZER, Colonel Sir Augustus Simon (1776–1835)

SIR AUGUSTUS FRAZER
(PRINT AFTER HEAPHY)

Born at Dunkirk, the son of Colonel Andrew Frazer of the Royal Engineers, he was commissioned in the Royal Artillery in 1793, served in The Netherlands 1794–5 and 1799, at Buenos Aires, and from November 1812 in the Peninsula, being appointed to command the army's horse artillery five months later. Brevet lieutenant-colonel for Vittoria (where he risked his life to drag the mortally wounded French General Sarrut from under the hooves of his own horse artillery), he commanded the horse artillery in the Waterloo campaign where it was said that it was largely at his instigation that the more effective 9pdrs were issued to replace 6pdrs. Knighted in 1814 and colonel from 1825, he was Director of the Royal Laboratory, Woolwich, from 1828 until his death. His letters from the Peninsula and Netherlands were published in 1859 and mark him as 'a thorough soldier, a perfect gentleman, a delightful companion, and a modest and unassuming man'.[1]

1. Mackenzie, as below, and in Dalton, C. *The Waterloo Roll Call.* London, 1904, p. 210.

Frazer, Sir Augustus. *Letters of Colonel Sir Augustus Simon Frazer*, ed. Major-General E. Sabine. London, 1859; Mackenzie, Colonel R. H. 'Colonel Sir Augustus Frazer', in *Cavalry Journal*, vol. V, 1910, pp. 131–7 (repr. from RUSI *Journal*)

FREDERICK I, King of Württemberg (1754–1816)

Friedrich Karl Wilhelm II (Frederick), Duke of Württemberg, succeeded his father Frederick Eugene in 1797. Frederick II continued his father's opposition to France (which had already resulted in French invasion), and the state was again invaded; compelled to make peace, in March 1802 he ceded his possessions on the left bank of the Rhine (receiving territory styled 'New Württemberg' in compensation), and was granted the title of Elector by Napoleon. In 1805 he joined France in a military alliance, receiving territory by the Peace of Pressburg, and on 1 January 1806 took the title of King of Württemberg (the designation Frederick I should not be confused with the previous duke Frederick I, 1557–1608). He joined the Confederation of the Rhine in 1806, supported Napoleon against

FREDERICK I, KING OF WÜRTTEMBERG
(MEDALLIC PORTRAIT)

Prussia and Austria and was rewarded with more territory; in the Russian campaign of 1812 the 14,000 of his troops who served in III Corps were all but annihilated, and in November 1813 he changed sides by concluding the Treaty of Fulda with Austria, which secured his royal title and territory, and after which his troops served with the Allies. Despite being exceptionally corpulent, Frederick was an energetic ruler (he commanded his forces in person in the 1809 campaign, for example), ambitious and autocratic. By his second wife, Charlotte Augusta Matilda, Princess Royal of Great Britain (1766–1828), whom he married in 1797, he became son-in-law to George III. Surrounded by dissent over the constitution he proposed for Württemberg, Frederick died on 30 October 1816, and was succeeded by his son William I (1781–1864); he had quarrelled with his father over support for Napoleon, and in 1814 commanded a corps of the Allied forces with some distinction.

FREDERICK AUGUSTUS I, King of Saxony (1750–1827)

FREDERICK AUGUSTUS I, KING OF SAXONY
(ENGRAVING BY STEINLA AFTER VOGEL)

Succeeding his father Frederick Christian as Elector of Saxony in 1763, he assumed power on coming of age in 1768. A modest, unassuming and conscientious man, he was too loyal even to dismiss the inefficient and was prone to manipulation by his ministers and generals; Napoleon declared him the most honest man who ever held a sceptre. In foreign policy he tried to avoid dangerous connections, declining the throne of Poland in 1791, involved Saxony as little as possible in the Revolutionary Wars and in 1796 concluded a treaty of neutrality with France. In 1806, however, he supported Prussia, but after the defeat joined the Confederation of the Rhine and had his title upgraded to the status of king. Thereafter he supported Napoleon loyally, and in 1807 became nominal Grand Duke of Warsaw, and even in 1813 refused to violate his allegiance to the French Emperor. He was present at the battle of Dresden, and after the Saxon army changed sides during the Battle of Leipzig he was taken prisoner by the Allies. Only Austria's desire for a buffer between themselves and Prussia prevented the annexation of his entire state; after much wrangling at the Congress of Vienna he was left with less than half his original territory, Prussia appropriating the rest. He never lost popularity with his subjects, however, and spent the remainder of his reign attempting to repair the damage wrought upon Saxony by the war, and amply deserved his sobriquet 'the Just'.

Bonnefons, A. *Un Allié de Napoléon, Frédéric Augustus, Premier Roi de Saxe, 1763–1827*. Paris, 1902.

FREDERICK WILLIAM II, King of Prussia (1744–97)

He succeeded his uncle Frederick II 'the Great' in 1786; his father was Augustus William, second son of Frederick William I. He was a pale shade of his namesake grandfather and his uncle; lacking energy and determination, he neither attempted to resolve internal discontent by liberal reforms, nor pursued the previous vigorous foreign policy, and was much influenced by the mystics Johann Wöllner and Johann von Bischoffswerder, the former virtually assuming the role of prime minister. Frederick William had little interest in the army, which had been the bedrock of the Prussian state, and neglected it; his military intervention in The Netherlands in 1787 was of no benefit to Prussia, and

FREDERICK WILLIAM II, KING OF PRUSSIA
(MEDALLIC PORTRAIT)

after the early campaigns of the Revolutionary Wars made a separate peace with France (by the Treaty of Basle, April 1795), which was regarded by his allies as an act of betrayal. Prussia's reputation was thereby somewhat discredited, and its finances exhausted, upon his death in 1797. He was legitimately married twice, contracted two polygamous marriages and had an acknowledged mistress.

FREDERICK WILLIAM III, King of Prussia (1770–1840)

Son of Frederick William II and his second wife, Frederika Louise of Hesse–Darmstadt, he succeeded to the throne on his father's death in 1797, having served in the

FREDERICK WILLIAM III OF PRUSSIA
(ENGRAVING BY BLOOD AFTER BOLK)

1792–4 campaigns, and having married Princess Louise of Mecklenburg–Strelitz in 1793. Although somewhat lacking in decisiveness, he tried to remedy the worst aspects of his father's reign by lifting some of the more repressive laws and improving finances. Encouraged by Queen Louise, he opposed Napoleon in 1806 and was defeated massively, losing much of his territory and being forced into the role of client-state; but this led to a movement for national regeneration and patriotism, led by Frederick's ministers Stein and Hardenberg, and in military affairs by Scharnhorst and Gneisenau, though the Queen's support ended with her early death in 1810. Prussian forces supported Napoleon in the Russian campaign of 1812, but the defection of Yorck's troops propelled the King into the Allied camp. Having been forced to adopt a policy in accordance with popular sentiment, Frederick William committed Prussia fully to the 'War of Liberation', thereby playing a major role in the events leading to Napoleon's downfall; he was present at a number of actions, including Bautzen, Dresden and Leipzig. After the war he played a subsidiary role to that of the Tsar and Metternich,

and despite his opposition to liberalism retained the affection of his people. Although Prussia did not regain all her lost territory, she became the leading German state and laid the foundation of the German Empire. Frederick William wrote two accounts of his military services in the campaigns of 1792 and 1793.

FREIRE (or FREYRE), General Manuel (1765–1834)

He came to prominence as a cavalry commander during the Peninsular War, commanded the Spanish 3rd or Army of Murcia (1810–11) until replaced by Nicolas Mahy, but is best known for his command of the Army of Galicia which won the action at San Marcial (31 August 1813) which Wellington refused to support so that none of the credit would be deflected from the Spaniards. Freire was unable to prevent his troops from looting, however, and this prompted Wellington to send them back to Spain for fear that they would antagonise the French populace, writing to Freire: 'I am not entering France to pillage; I have not had thousands of officers and soldiers killed and wounded so that the rest can plunder the French';[1] but Freire's troops were recalled for the blockade of Bayonne, and fought with determination (if without notable success) at Toulouse.

1. Wellington, 14 Nov 1813, vol. XI, p. 287 (originally written in French)

FREIRE DE ANDRADE, General Bernardino (1764–1809)

Perhaps best remembered for the nature of his demise, he was the general given command of the Portuguese forces organised in 1808 to resist French occupation; he had previously fought against the French in the Roussillon campaign of 1793. He came into

conflict with Arthur Wellesley and in March 1809 displayed great timidity when his army gathered at Braga. As the French advanced, Freire, in the teeth of open mutiny among his troops who wished to fight, attempted to flee but was seized by some of his own men, and command of the army was given to his deputy, Baron Eben. When the latter left Braga a mob of militiamen dragged Freire from the gaol into which he had been thrown and piked him to death in the street. The subsequent rout of the Portuguese at Braga perhaps vindicates Freire's opinion of the capabilities of his army.

FREIRE DE ANDRADE, General Gomes (1752–1817)

Born in Vienna, the son of the Portuguese envoy, he served against the French in the Roussillon campaign (1793) but after the French invasion of 1807–8 entered French service. He commanded the 2nd Division at the first siege of Saragossa (in which one of his two brigades was composed of Portuguese troops in French service), and after serving in the Russian campaign, he was appointed Governor of Dresden (August 1813). Captured when that city fell to the Allies in November, he was released from captivity in the following year and returned to Portugal, where in 1817 he was executed for being a leader of the military revolt in Lisbon, which was crushed by Beresford.

FRERE, John Hookham (1769–1846)

A boyhood friend of Canning and a member of a family of Suffolk gentry, he was MP for West Looe 1796–1802 and a great supporter of Pitt. Appointed Under-Secretary of State in 1799, he served as envoy to Lisbon (1800) and to Madrid (1802–4), and in 1808 was appointed Plenipotentiary to the

Spanish Central *junta*. This role brought him into conflict with Moore, Frere wishing to pursue the most aggressive course, not even contemplating the retreat which was forced upon him; he even tried to undermine Moore's authority and accused him of doing as much mischief as he could short of actually attacking the Spanish. This was taken as proof of his unfitness for a diplomatic post, and although not censured he was perceived as having endangered the British Army by intemperate advice; he was recalled and held no other government appointment, though he did decline a diplomatic mission to Russia. He spent the remainder of his life in literary pursuits (notably his verse translations of Aristophanes) and from 1820 lived in Malta. His nephew, Sir Bartle Frere, also entered public service and has been blamed for precipitating the Zulu War of 1879.

Festing , G. *John Hookham Frere and his Friends.* London, 1799; Frere, J. H. *The Works of John Hookham Frere.* London, 1872 (includes biography by W. E. and Sir Bartle Frere)

FRERON, Louis-Marie-Stanislas (1754–1802)

Son of the journalist Elie Fréron (known for his attacks on Voltaire), he was an ardent supporter of the Revolution and editor of the extreme publication *L'Orateur du Peuple.* Sent with Barras to establish the authority of the Convention at Marseilles and Toulon in 1793, he gained a reputation for cruelty and mass execution (even by cannon-fire). At first a close collaborator with Robespierre, he later became an opponent and helped bring about his ruin. Initially disapproved of by Napoleon – he had fallen in love with Pauline Bonaparte – he was nevertheless appointed Prefect of

San Domingo at the time of the French expedition, and died there.

FRIANT, General Louis, comte (1758–1829)

Perhaps best remembered as the Colonel of the Grenadiers of the Imperial Guard, he served in the *Garde Française* 1781–7, entered the Paris National Guard in 1789 and was elected to field rank in 1792. *Général de brigade* from June 1795, after service in Italy he became *général de division* during the Egyptian campaign; in 1805 he commanded the 2nd Division of Davout's III Corps, was distinguished at Austerlitz and Auerstädt, was wounded at Eylau and (still with Davout) at Wagram, and became comte in 1808. In 1812 he led the 2nd Division of Davout's I Corps, and in August was rewarded with the Colonelcy-in-Chief of the *Grenadiers à Pied*, but within a month was wounded twice at Borodino. In 1813–14 he led the Old Guard with distinction and after the restoration commanded the re-named *Grenadiers de France*, but rejoined Napoleon in 1815 and led the Grenadiers of the Old Guard at Waterloo, where he was wounded in the hand. He retired into private life in September 1815. One of Napoleon's best divisional commanders (who doubtless profited from being Davout's brother-in-law), Friant was both a brave and able soldier and a capable administrator.

Friant, J. F. *Vie Militaire du Lieutenant-Général Comte Friant.* Paris, 1857 (written by his son)

FRIMONT, General Johann Maria Philipp, Count of Palota, Prince of Antrodocco (1759–1831)

Having entered the Austrian cavalry in 1776 and been commissioned during the War of Bavarian Succession, he made his reputation as a cavalry leader in the

French Revolutionary Wars, most notably at Marengo, and became major-general in the following year. He served in Italy in 1805 and 1809, becoming *Feldmarschall-Leutnant*; in 1812 he led the cavalry of Schwarzenberg's Austrian Auxiliary Corps in the Russian campaign and in early 1813 took command of that formation when Schwarzenberg, having signed a convention of neutrality, was recalled to Vienna. Frimont served in the campaigns of 1813 and in France in 1814, and in 1815 commanded Austrian forces in Italy. In the occupation of France until 1818, he commanded at Venice the following year and in 1821 led the Austrian forces against rebels in Naples, for which he received promotion to *General der Cavallerie* and from Ferdinand IV the title of Prince of Antrodocco. He later suppressed a number of revolts in northern Italy.

FRIOUL, duc de, see DUROC

FULTON, Robert (1765–1815)

Born in Pennsylvania of Irish parents, he went to England to study painting, and then became an engineer. Contacts with the Duke of Bridgewater and James Watt led him to study canal construction, but it was in France that he demonstrated a steam-powered boat, and a submarine warship. The latter was demonstrated at Brest in 1801, but Napoleon did not pursue the project, and despite further work on submarine explosives, neither the British nor the US governments took up the idea. Instead, Fulton made progress on steam navigation, had a steam-vessel running on the Hudson in 1807, and in 1814–15 he built for the US government the first steam-powered warship, the paddle-wheeler *Fulton*.

GAETA, duc de, see **GAUDIN**

GAINES, Major General Edmund Pendleton (1777–1849)

He was born in Virginia, and as a lieutenant in the US Army, he was the officer who arrested the ex-Vice President Aaron Burr near Fort Stoddart (19 February 1807) on charges of treason. Rising to the rank of brigadier general in the War of 1812, Gaines commanded at the successful defence of Fort Erie, for which he was promoted to major general and received a gold medal from Congress; shortly afterwards he was wounded by a shell and relinquished command. He later served in the Seminole War. Although described as somewhat irascible and vain, he was remarkably brave under fire; when shot in the mouth by a Seminole, he merely remarked that it was mean of them to knock out his teeth when he had so few left![1]

1. Fredriksen, J. C. *Officers of the War of 1812.* Lewiston, 1989, p. 30.

Silver, J. W. *Edmund Pendleton Gaines: Frontier General.* Baton Rouge, 1949

GALLATIN, Albert (1761–1849)

Born and educated in Geneva, he emigrated to America in 1780 and after military service became a leading politician. Jefferson appointed him Secretary of the Treasury in 1801 and he continued in office under Madison, and so was responsible for financing the early stages of the War of 1812. In May 1813 he went to St. Petersburg as an envoy, to take advantage of Russia's offer to mediate between Great Britain and the USA, and in February 1814 resigned from the Treasury (Secretary of the Navy William Jones having acted as his locum). Gallatin was one of the delegation which negotiated the Treaty of Ghent and he remained in Europe until 1828, serving as US

Ambassador to the French court 1816–23.

GAMBIER, Admiral James, Baron (1756–1833)

JAMES, BARON GAMBIER
(ENGRAVING BY HOLL AFTER BEECHEY)

Despite rising to high rank he was not one of the Royal Navy's brightest ornaments. Born in the Bahamas (where his father was Governor), he was commissioned in 1767 and rose by family influence; he commanded HMS *Defence* at the Glorious First of June, became rear-admiral in the following year and a Lord of the Admiralty, in which role he was not especially distinguished. Vice-admiral in 1801 and admiral in 1805, he received a barony after commanding the fleet in the Danish expedition, and in 1808 took command of the Channel Fleet, in which post he completely mishandled the attack on Basque Roads in April 1809 when he failed, despite the urgings of Lord Cochrane, to destroy a French fleet that was entirely at his mercy. He was court-martialled, but it was hardly likely that such a well-connected supporter of the government would be convicted; consequently it was adjudged that his conduct was 'marked by zeal, judgement, ability, and an anxious attention to the welfare of His

Majesty's Service', and that the court 'do adjudge him to be Most Honourably Acquitted'.[1] He commanded the Channel Fleet until 1811, and in 1814 was the commissioner who negotiated the Treaty of Ghent; he became Admiral of the Fleet in 1830. Gambier was a deeply religious man, hence his nickname 'Dismal Jimmy', and his habit of distributing tracts among the seamen was thought by some, including Cochrane, to be highly detrimental to discipline. One of his subordinates at the time of Basque Roads, Rear-Admiral Harvey, went further; a gallant Trafalgar officer who compared Gambier unfavourably with Nelson, he declared to Gambier's face that 'he never saw a man so unfit for the command of the fleet'[2] and that he himself 'was no canting Methodist, no hypocrite, nor no psalm-singer';[3] but whatever the truth of the assertion, Harvey was dismissed the service for speaking disrespectfully to a superior.

1. *Gent's Mag.*, Aug, 1809, p. 775. 2. Dundonald, Earl of. *The Autobiography of a Seaman.* London, 1861, vol. I, p. 357. 3. *Gent's Mag.*, May, 1809, p. 472.

Minutes of a Court Martial holden on board HMS Gladiator *... on ... James Lord Gambier.* London, 1809

GANTEAUME, Amiral Honoré-Joseph-Antoine, comte (1755–1818)

Originally a merchant seaman, he served in the French Navy during the War of American Independence, commanded the 74-gunner *Trente-et-un Mai* with distinction at the Glorious First of June, and was thrice wounded. As rear-admiral he was Brueys' chief of staff for the Egyptian campaign, survived the destruction of *L'Orient* at Aboukir Bay, and then served in the land campaign until he sailed home with Napoleon in the frigate *Le Muiron*. From 1800 he commanded the Brest fleet, making two abortive attempts to rescue the Egyptian expedition and leading **a** successful mission to resupply the French in the West Indies (1802). Vice-admiral in 1804 and comte in 1810, he served briefly as Minister of Marine and was rewarded with the colonelcy of the Seamen of the Imperial Guard; but accepted the restoration and remained loyal to the Bourbons during the Hundred Days, becoming a peer of France at the second restoration.

GARDANE (or GARDANNE), General Claude-Matthieu, comte (1766–1818)

Perhaps better known as a diplomat, he was commissioned during the Revolutionary Wars, became *général de brigade* in 1799 after service under Moreau, and despite losing favour with Napoleon became an imperial ADC in 1805. In 1807, perhaps because his family was known in the near east, he was appointed envoy to Persia, in the hope of cementing an alliance in preparation for an attack on British India, Persia hoping to receive French help in their war against Russia. Tilsit rendered the latter impossible, and though Gardane temporarily eliminated British influence in Persia, he realised that there was no chance of Persian co-operation in an attack on India, so returned to France in 1809. Although Napoleon was not entirely satisfied with this, Gardane was ennobled as comte and sent to

Massena's army in the Peninsula, where he fell into great disfavour. Ordered to reinforce Massena with a convoy of munitions, he indulged in a fruitless and costly march and counter-march, lacking the resolution to push on and deliver his cargo, before retiring to where he had begun. So strange was this manoeuvre that Wellington commented that they 'retired with great precipitation ... this march, if it was ordered by superior authority, and is connected with any other arrangement, had every appearance, and was attended by all the consequences of a precipitate and forced retreat'.[1]

1. Wellington, to Liverpool, 8 Dec 1810, vol. VII, p. 31.

GARDANNE, General Gaspard-Amédée (1758–1807)

Having served in the army until 1784, he was elected as a field officer in 1792, served at Toulon and in Italy, and was confirmed as *général de brigade* in March 1797. Governor of Alessandria instead of going to Egypt, he was captured upon the capitulation, but exchanged, and *général de division* from January 1800, is perhaps best remembered for leading a division of Victor's corps at Marengo, where he served with great distinction. In 1805 he held a divisional command under Massena in Italy, served with the Army of Naples (including the siege of Gaeta) and in 1807, notably at the siege of Danzig where his division and that of Schramm helped repel the Russian attempt at relief (15 May 1807). Gardanne survived only a further three months, dying of fever in August.

GASSENDI, General Jean-Jacques-Basilien, comte (1748–1828)

An artillery officer as early as 1769, he was Napoleon's superior officer in 1788; he commanded the siege train at Toulon, but his

most memorable service was probably as commander of the artillery park of the Army of Reserve in 1800, when he helped devise the methods of transporting ordnance over the Alps using 'sledges' made of hollowed tree trunks to drag gun-barrels and sledges on rollers to transport other equipment. After service at Marengo his subsequent duties were administrative commandant of the Auxonne artillery school (1802–3), then Inspector-General of Artillery and *général de division* in 1805, and comte in 1809. Councillor of State and senator (1813), he voted for Napoleon's abdication and was appointed a peer of France by the Bourbons, but supported Napoleon in 1815 and was only reinstated as a peer in 1819.

GAUDIN, Martin-Michel-Charles, duc de Gaeta (1756–1841)

One of Napoleon's most valuable civil subordinates, he had served under the *ancien régime* and at the Treasury under revolutionary governments. On Lebrun's recommendation, Napoleon appointed him Minister of Finance in 1799, and he proved so capable that he remained in office until 1814, and again during the Hundred Days. He reformed the national finances, notably in taxation and rating, founded the Bank of France (of which he became Governor in 1820), and was rewarded in 1809 with the dukedom of Gaeta. In 1815 he was appointed a peer of France and was elected as a Deputy.

GAZAN, General Honoré-Théodore-Maxime, comte de la Peyrière (1765–1845)

Probably best known for his Peninsula service, his military career began under the *ancien régime* and continued with success in the Revolutionary Wars, in Germany

d Italy. *Général de brigade* in
99, he was promoted to *de divi-
n* on the day of the 3rd Battle of
rich (25 September 1799), and in
00 was besieged in Genoa.
lding a divisional command in
05–7, his most notable action
s at Durrenstein (11 November
05), when his division, under
ortier's direction, fought a
sperate battle against over-
elming numbers and suffered
severely that it took no further
rt in the campaign. After serving
der Lannes at Pultusk, Gazan
s transferred to Spain in 1808,
mmanding the 2nd Division of V
rps at the second siege of
ragossa, was wounded at
dajoz and again when leading
s division in the great attack upon
e heights' at Albuera. Early in
13 he succeeded Soult as
mmander of the Army of the
uth, and attracted some criti-
m from Jourdan for retiring at
ttoria, apparently without orders.
1 the re-organisation of French
rces in the Peninsula (July 1813)
ult chose him as chief of staff, in
ich capacity he signed the
mistice at the end of the war.
zan's wife was captured at
ttoria; Wellington sent her back
her husband in her own
rriage. Gazan retired from active
ty in 1815, but subsequently held
number of staff appointments
fore his final retirement in 1832,
which year he was appointed a
er of France.

ENTZ, Friedrich von
764–1832)

n of a Prussian civil servant and
mself employed as such, he
me to prominence through his
lent opposition to the French
volution and to Napoleon.
ginning with his translation of
rke's *Reflections on the Revolu-
n in France* (1794), Gentz's
thorship was prodigious and
pular, his invective against
ance and in favour of Austria

and Great Britain bringing financial rewards from both those
countries. This, and his support
for liberal reforms, made his position in Prussia untenable, so in
1802 he went to Austria where he
was appointed an imperial councillor (and after meeting Pitt on a
trip to London was granted a
British pension). Continuing his
anti-French stance, in 1806 he
drafted the King of Prussia's letter
and proclamation to Napoleon,
and in 1809 the Austrian proclamation announcing war against
France. From 1812 he was a friend
of and adviser to Metternich, on
whom his influence was considerable; his knowledge of the participants and events lent great
authority to his position as Secretary to the Congress of Vienna and
all others up to Verona (1822). He
has been described as a literary
mercenary (as Napoleon considered him), who sold his skill with
the pen instead of being the
leading political commentator of
the generation, which had seemed
his destiny; certainly he was a
spendthrift who squandered funds
on gambling and women, but his
political acumen was considerable
and his intellectual talents were
always in demand. Wellington
characterised him as 'a very able
man, but very venal; he took
money from all quarters',
including even the Duke himself.[1]
1. Stanhope, p. 225.

Buckland, C. S. B. *Friedrich von
Gentz's Relations with the British
Government 1809–12.* London,
1933; Mann, G. *Secretary of
Europe: the Life of Friedrich von
Gentz, Enemy of Napoleon.* New
Haven, Connecticut, 1946; Sweet, P.
R. *Friedrich von Gentz: Defender of
the Old Order.* Madison, 1941

GEORGE III, King of Great
Britain (1738–1820)

Son of Frederick, Prince of Wales,
he succeeded his grandfather
George II in 1760 and enjoyed one

GEORGE III (ENGRAVING BY SKELTON AFTER
SIR WILLIAM BEECHEY)

of the longest reigns of any British
monarch. Although he never lost
popularity with the majority of his
subjects – the nickname 'Farmer
George' exemplified the perception of a homely, decent and practical individual – his reign was not
the most happy. At his accession,
Great Britain was involved in the
Seven Years War, which the king
helped to end by the removal of the
elder Pitt as chief minister, but the
loss of the American colonies and
the fall of his favoured minister,
Lord North, was a severe blow to
national prestige. George accepted
the installation of the younger Pitt
and maintained an active role in
politics, but from 1788 was
afflicted with apparent insanity
(which may have had a physiolog-
ical origin). He supported entirely
the struggle against France, but
was never completely happy with
Pitt and remained vehemently
opposed to any attempt to grant
concessions to Roman Catholics,
as being contrary to his coronation
oath. This precipitated Pitt's resignation and another bout of the
king's illness, but he accepted Pitt's
return after the renewal of the war,
and at this critical period George
became the popular figurehead
representing the national will to
resist Napoleon. After Pitt's death
he accepted the 'ministry of all the

talents' despite its inclusion of Fox, who represented everything the king disliked (a Whig and one who had a bad influence on the Prince of Wales), but its replacement was the last political act of great significance in which the king took part, for in 1811 his mental health collapsed irrevocably and the Prince of Wales became regent. George spent his last, tragic years in insanity and blindness. His marriage to Charlotte Sophia of Mecklenburg–Strelitz was happy and produced fifteen children: George, Prince of Wales; Frederick, Duke of York; William, Duke of Clarence (later William IV); Edward, Duke of Kent; Ernest, Duke of Cumberland (later King of Hanover); Augustus, Duke of Sussex; Adolphus, Duke of Cambridge; and Princes Octavius and Alfred, who died in infancy; and six Princesses: Charlotte, Augusta, Elizabeth, Mary, Sophia and Amelia. It was the death of the latter, George's favourite child, which helped precipitate his final breakdown.

Aspinall, A. (ed.). *The Later Correspondence of George III*. Cambridge, 1962–70; Brooke, J. *King George III*. London, 1972; Long. J. C. *George III*. 1962

GEORGE, Prince of Wales (Prince Regent, later King George IV) (1762–1830)

Eldest son of King George III, he was in many ways the opposite of the perception of his father as the epitome of decency and prudence. A devotee of gambling and profligacy from an early age, he established a rival 'court' at Carlton House which attracted the opponents of his father's ministers, notably Charles James Fox and other leading Whigs, which served only to increase the conflict between the king and his son. In 1785 the prince secretly married Maria Fitzherbert (1756–1837), a union officially illegal (she was a

GEORGE, PRINCE OF WALES (LATER KING GEORGE IV)(ENGRAVING BY W. SKELTON AFTER THOMAS PHILLIPS)

Roman Catholic and the king's permission had not been granted) but which brought the prince more happiness than his wretched official marriage to Princess Caroline of Brunswick in 1795. This union produced one child, Princess Charlotte, who died in 1817; the royal couple formally separated, but Caroline's presence blighted his life, especially after George's accession as king. Institution of divorce proceedings on the grounds of Caroline's outrageous conduct and adultery served to make George even more unpopular than his notorious lifestyle, popular opinion supporting the queen against a husband known for his own adulterous affairs. George III's incapacity from 1811 led to the prince becoming regent, when he took over all his father's duties; his own reign as King George IV from 29 January 1820 saw a diminution in the powers of the crown, notably in the appointment of ministers, and eventually he relented in his opposition to Catholic Emancipation as proposed by his last Prime Minister, the Duke of Wellington. Having by his spendthrift ways considerably reduced the popularity and standing of the monarchy, George IV died on 26 June 1830 and was succeeded by

his brother the Duke of Claren[ce] as King William IV. Geor[ge] supported the war against Fran[ce] and from 1796 held the colone[lcy] of the 10th Hussars; and in la[ter] life, apparently after copio[us] alcohol at dinner, would ma[ke] claims about his own milita[ry] prowess. Gronow recounted h[ow] he claimed to have led the Hous[e]hold Cavalry at Waterloo, to whi[ch] Wellington replied diplomatica[lly] that he had heard his Royal Hig[h]ness say so before; and on anoth[er] occasion George claimed that [he] had personally ordered [an] augmentation to the Peninsu[lar] army, and called on Wellington [to] confirm the truth of the fanta[sy] 'Sir, I was in Spain at the time,' w[as] the reply![1] On being informed [of] Napoleon's death with the wor[ds] 'your greatest enemy is dea[d]' George replied 'Is she, by —', [a] telling comment on his relatio[n]ship with his wife.[2]

1. Ellesmere, p. 127. 2. Fraser, 228.

Aspinall, A. (ed.). *The Cor[re]spondence of George, Prince [of] Wales 1770–1812*. London, 196[2–]71; *The Letters of King Geor[ge] IV 1812–30*. Cambridge, 19[3x]; Hibbert, C. *George IV, Prince [of] Wales 1762–1811*. London, 19[7x]; Hibbert, C. *George IV: Regent a[nd] King 1811–30*. London, 197[x]; Priestley, J. B. *The Prince of Ple[a]sure and his Regency, 1811–[2x]*. London, 1969

GEORGES, Mademoiselle, see WEIMER

GERARD, François-Paschal-Simon, baron (1770–1837)

One of the leading French painte[rs] of the period, he was born in Ro[me] (where his father worked for t[he] French ambassador) and studi[ed] under David, through whose infl[u]ence he obtained a revolutiona[ry] tribunal post (thus avoiding mi[li]tary service), but from the dread[ful] duties of which he absent[ed] mself on grounds of ill-health. rom about 1800 he was recognised as one of the foremost ortraitists (he exhibited no less an fourteen portraits at the 1810 lon, so vast was his output), but e also executed narrative works, ch as *Bataille d'Austerlitz* (1810).

was Gérard who suggested to avid that in the great painting of apoleon's coronation, the empor should be shown crowning sephine instead of himself; but er the rivalry between them (and ith Gros) turned to animosity. espite having been a great vourite with Napoleon, he tained his position as court inter after the restoration, and as ennobled by Louis XVIII in 19. His popularity declined with e rise of romanticism, but his ortraits remain as a brilliant illuination of the period.

ERARD, Marshal Etienne- aurice, comte (1773–1852)

mong the most able of Napoleon's nerals, he entered the army in 91 and was commissioned in the llowing year; his long association ith Bernadotte began in 1795 hen he was appointed to his staff, d continued until Austerlitz where Gérard, as senior ADC, was ounded in the leg). *Général de igade* from November 1806, he d a brigade of Augereau's corps at lau, then became Bernadotte's ief of staff and served in enmark and at Wagram, and was nobled as baron in May 1809. ter serving in IX Corps in Spain cluding Fuentes de Oñoro), he turned to France, ill; in 1812 he cceeded to command the 3rd vision of Davout's I Corps after udin was mortally wounded, coming *général de division* in ptember 1812. In 1813 he held a visional command under Macnald (including at Lützen and utzen) before being appointed to ad XI Corps, but almost immediely was wounded at the

Katzbach, and on returning to duty was again assigned a division under Macdonald, being wounded again at Leipzig. In 1814 he was appointed to lead II Corps, and having accepted the Bourbon restoration was sent to replace Davout as head of XIII Corps at Hamburg. Although not enthusiastic about Napoleon's return, he commanded IV Corps in the Waterloo campaign, which began inauspiciously for him when Bourmont, whom he had recommended, defected to the Allies. After service at Ligny, Gérard was wounded at Wavre, his advice to Grouchy to march towards the sounds of battle having been ignored. He left France at the second restoration but returned in 1817 and became involved in politics as a liberal Deputy; he was influential in the 1830 revolution, and was appointed a Marshal and Minister of War. He commanded the French Army in Belgium in 1831–2 and captured Antwerp, and again held the portfolio as war minister briefly in 1834. A close associate of Louis-Philippe, he held a number of posts until he resigned with the abdication of that monarch, and was a senator for a short time before his death in April 1852.

GERICAULT, Jean-Louis- Alexandre-Théodore (1791–1824)

Born in Rouen, he studied painting under Carle Vernet and Gros, and became a leading member of what might be termed the French 'realistic' school. Perhaps most famous for his portrayal of horses, he attracted great attention in 1812 with the exhibition of his portrait of Lieutenant Dieudonné of the Imperial Guard (titled *Officier des Chasseurs à Cheval*), and two years later with *Cuirassier blessé*. During the Hundred Days he joined the royal *Mousquetaires* and accompanied the king to The Nether-

lands, but later favoured more liberal politics, perhaps exemplified by his great and controversial picture *Le Radeau de la Méduse* (the Raft of the Medusa) exhibited in 1819; the hostility it aroused was a reason for his subsequent residence in London. Short though his career was – he was killed in a riding accident – he was a considerable influence upon the Romantic movement, and notably upon Delacroix.

GILLRAY, James (1757–1815)

Born in Chelsea, the son of a Scottish soldier who had lost an arm at Fontenoy, he became the greatest British caricaturist. An apprentice engraver who had been a strolling player, in 1778 he entered the Royal Academy school as a student of Bartolozzi; despite accompanying de Loutherbourg to The Netherlands campaign, sketching figures for the latter's 'Siege of Valenciennes', Gillray found no success as a conventional artist, but as a caricaturist and political satirist he was without peer. He lived with his publisher and print seller, Miss (or Mrs) Hannah Humphrey, whose shop-window became one of the great attractions of London for its display of Gillray creations; and despite the often venomous satire, his work was genuinely witty and appreciated even by most of those they satirised, until it became a mark of political standing to be the subject of a Gillray. Despite many satires on George III, the events of the French Revolution and subsequent wars revealed Gillray's patriotic side, and his caricatures of Napoleon were among the most savage, depicting a ridiculous, dwarf-like figure of bombast and ridicule, while Gillray glorified his 'John Bull' as the epitome of British resistance to Napoleon. After producing a large number of memorable caricatures on the subject of the Napoleonic conflict,

Gillray's mental health broke down (he had been known as a heavy drinker) and from 1811 he produced no further work.

Hill, D. *Mr. Gillray the Caricaturist*. London, 1965

GIRARD, General Jean-Baptiste, baron (1775–1815)

Perhaps best remembered as the defeated French commander at Arroyo dos Molinos (which somewhat unfairly overshadows his successes), he entered the army in 1793 and served in an unofficial staff appointment even before being commissioned in 1796. He served as aide to Monnier in Italy (including the defence of Ancona and Marengo), on Murat's staff in the Austerlitz and Jena campaigns, and from November 1806 was *général de brigade*. In 1807 he commanded a brigade under Suchet in Lannes' V Corps, and led it in Spain under Mortier, winning renown at Arzobispo (8 August 1809), and later in the year took command of the division, the appropriate promotion being confirmed in December when he was recovering from a wound sustained at Ocaña. In August 1810 he defeated La Romana at Villagarcia, but his command was badly mauled attacking 'the heights' at Albuera, and after his surprise and rout at Arroyo dos Molinos (27 October 1811) he was recalled in some disgrace. In 1812 he was given a relatively minor command, 28th Division of IX Corps, but it performed a vital service at the Berezina in helping to keep open Napoleon's route of escape, during which Girard was wounded. Commanding a Polish–Saxon division in 1813, he was severely wounded at Lützen, and was then besieged in Magdeburg, capitulating only after receiving news of Napoleon's abdication. In 1815 he rallied to Napoleon and led the 7th Division of II Corps at Ligny, where he was hit several

times, once in the lung; Napoleon visited him on the evening of the battle and conferred upon him the title duc de Ligny, but he died in Paris on 27 June.

GIRON, General Pedro Agostin, duque de Ahumada (1788–1842)

Nephew of Castaños, he was an important Spanish commander during the Peninsular War, leading the 4th Army (of Galicia) which collaborated with Wellington from 1813, arriving too late to participate in the victory of Vittoria, and serving at Tolosa. Shortly afterwards, Giron was removed from his command by the Regency, like Castaños, much to Wellington's dismay; he complained that not only had Giron been given the command by his (Wellington's) desire, but that he 'had conducted himself entirely to my satisfaction'.[1] In the event, though replaced by Freire at the head of the Galician army, Giron himself replaced Henry O'Donnell as commander of the Andalusian army, which he led for the remainder of the campaign.

1. Wellington, vol. X, p. 493.

GNEISENAU, Field Marshal August Wilhelm Anton, Graf Neithardt von (1760–1831)

Best known as Blücher's assistant, which does not fully recognise his own talents, he was the son of a Saxon officer named Neithardt, and was raised in poverty. After two years at Erfurt University he entered Austrian service (1779) and in 1782 that of the Margrave of Anspach–Bayreuth, when he took the name Gneisenau from some lost family estates in Austria. After service in British pay during the War of American Independence, he was granted a Prussian commission in 1786, garrison duty enabling him to study his profession in detail; he served as a staff officer at Jena, but it was his defence of

AUGUST WILHELM VON GNEISENAU (ENGRAVI[NG] BY VON SCHALL AFTER F. KRÜGER)

Colberg in 1807 which broug[ht] him to prominence. As chief engineers he aided Scharnhorst reconstructing the Prussian Arm[y] but the fall of Stein from Fren[ch] pressure led to his tempora[ry] retirement. After travels to Russi[a] Sweden and England he return[ed] to Berlin and played a leading r[ole] in the 'patriotic' movemer[nt] becoming Blücher's chief of sta[ff] with the renewal of hostiliti[es] against France. They formed one [of] the greatest command partne[r]ships in history, Gneisenau's calc[u]lating intelligence combining wi[th] Blücher's fire and determinatio[n] the advance on Paris was large[ly] Gneisenau's work, and their re[la]tionship may be gauged fro[m] Blücher's remark to Henry Har[d]inge after Ligny, that 'Gneisena[u] has given way', hardly norm[al] comment from a general regardi[ng] a subordinate. Wellington state[d] that Gneisenau was 'very deep [in] strategy ... in tactics ... not so mu[ch] skilled. But Blücher was just th[e] reverse – he knew nothing of pla[ns] of campaign, but well understood [the] field of battle.'[1] Gneisenau wa[s] ennobled as count (*Graf*) in 181[4] and with senior officers passe[d] over so that his association wi[th] Blücher could continue, in 1815 h[e] succeeded to command of th[e] Prussian forces when Blücher wa[s] mporarily disabled at Ligny. He arboured mistrust of Wellington's motives (and so his conduct has tracted some criticism from ritish authors), and his inclination as to withdraw to re-organise; but rtunately for the Allied cause, lücher recovered in time to onvince Gneisenau that they must onour their commitment to upport Wellington, and the defeat f Napoleon resulted. Gneisenau onducted the pursuit after 'aterloo, but soon retired on both ealth and political grounds. He eturned to service in 1818 as overnor of Berlin, was field marshal from 1825 and in 1831 was ppointed to command the Army f Observation on the Polish fronter, only to die from cholera on 24 ugust of that year, a sad end for ne of the greatest of Prussian enerals.

Stanhope, pp. 118–19.

Pertz, G. H., and Delbrück, G. es Leben des Feldmarschalls rafen Neithardt von Gneisenau. erlin, 1864–80 (first three volmes by Pertz, final two by elbrück); Delbrück, H. Das Leben es G. F. M. Grafen von Gneisenau. erlin, 1894.

OBEL, Jean-Baptiste-Joseph 1727–94)
ne of the most significant ecclesistics of the Revolutionary period, e was suffragan bishop of Basle hose political career began with is election to the States-General. rofessing support for the Revolution and a member of the Jacobin lub, he was elected constitutional ishop of Paris and in November 793 appeared before the Convention wearing a red 'bonnet of berty' and laid down his symbols f ecclesiastical office, declaring at he did so out of respect to the eople. He was one of the first to elebrate the 'goddess of reason' nd while never professing theism, was regarded as an theist by Robespierre, and by the

Hébertists as one of themselves; consequently he was included in their purge and guillotined on 12 April 1794.

GODOY, Alvarez de Faria, Rois Sanchez y Zaragoza, Manuel de, Duke of Alcudia, 'Prince of the Peace' (1767–1851)
Offspring of an ancient but impoverished Spanish noble family, he joined the royal *garde du corps* in 1784, where his handsome appearance and pleasant character attracted the attention of Princess Maria Luisa, who became queen upon the accession of her husband as Charles IV in 1788. She dominated her husband, so with

her support Godoy was promoted to positions for which he was quite unfitted: a minister in 1791, ennobled as Duke of Alcudia, he was prime minister 1792–8 until French opposition caused his removal. During this period he at first endeavoured to remain uncommitted in the Revolutionary Wars, only for Spain to be virtually bankrupted in the war against France (1793–5); but for his role in negotiating the Peace of Basle (1795) he was awarded the title 'Prince of the Peace' (sometimes rendered as 'Prince of Peace' though strictly the definitive article should be included: *Principe de la Paz*). Never having lost the confi-

THE ARREST OF GODOY (PRINT AFTER MAURICE ORANGE)

dence of the king and queen, he returned to office in 1801, and together with the court pursued a disastrous policy: an alliance with France which, with Napoleon's intrigue and conflict between the king and his heir, culminated in the fall of the royal family and the genesis of the Peninsular War. Before that happened, a popular revolt had driven Godoy from office; the rising at Aranjuez on 17 March 1808 forced him into hiding under a pile of mats in an attic, but he was recognised when hunger drove him out and he was arrested upon the instigation of Prince Ferdinand. Thinking to use his influence with the king, Napoleon had him released, and he accompanied Charles IV into exile until the king's death in Rome in 1819. Having been extremely rich (by virtue of gifts from the king and queen and from speculation and frauds), Godoy was reduced to poverty; an attempt in 1833 to redeem his estates confiscated in 1808 was unsuccessful, and he lived his last years on a small pension granted by Louis-Philippe; he died in Paris. Alava remarked that his circumstances were so reduced that when the Spanish Prince Don Francisco visited Paris in 1838, Godoy had to take a public omnibus to visit him; yet the prince was Godoy's own son, 'and so like that anybody may see it is so'.[1] (At the king's behest Godoy had married the king's cousin, the Infanta Teresa de Borbón, even though he continued to live with the mistress who was the mother of his two children, and his relationship with the queen is well-known). Godoy's career is remarkable for the fact that he was so highly regarded by the king and queen that they put him before their own son and heir, and equally for the ruinous state to which Spanish finances were reduced during his stewardship. Although his life was profligate and

his ambitions great (including the wish to become a sovereign prince), some of his intentions were not necessarily unfortunate: he did try to keep in check the Inquisition and the most reactionary forces, and even tried to suppress bullfighting.

1. Stanhope, p. 121.

Chastenet, J. *Godoy, Master of Spain*, trans. J. F. Huntington. London, 1953; D'Auvergne, E. B. *Godoy, The Queen's Favourite*. Boston, 1913; Godoy, M. *Memoirs of Don Manuel Godoy*, London 1836

GOETHE, Johann Wolfgang von (1749–1832)

JOHANN VON GOETHE
(PRINT BY S. BENDIXEN AFTER C. VOGEL)

The work of the great German poet, dramatist and philosopher was not profoundly affected by the events of the wars of the era, though he was involved in some of them. With his friend and patron, Charles Augustus of Saxe–Weimar–Eisenach, he was present at Valmy and the siege of Mainz, and published his accounts of these events in *Campagne in Frankreich* and *Belagerung von Mainz*. Goethe was an admirer of Napoleon, whom he met at Weimar in 1808, and his admiration was reciprocated; Napoleon had read Goethe's *Die Leiden des jungen Werthers* ('The Sorrows of

Young Werther') as a young ma[...] and his remark about Goethe[...] '*Voilà un homme!*' – is well know[...] In October 1808 Goethe w[...] awarded the *Légion d'honneur*. [...] had no great sympathy for th[...] movement which arose aroun[...] the 'War of Liberation', so th[...] national enthusiasm whic[...] inspired the writings of others ha[...] no great effect upon his wor[...] Among the other characters of th[...] Napoleonic age whom Goeth[...] encountered, he left an ear[...] account of Emma Hamilton's 'att[...]tudes', which impressed him [...] much as they did others who sa[...] her impressions of figures fro[...] classical antiquity.

GOHIER, Louis-Jérôme (1746–1830)

A lawyer until he became involve[...] in politics (originally he repr[...]sented Rennes in the State[...] General), he was a man of abili[...] and ambition. Minister of Justic[...] March 1793–April 1794, in Jun[...] 1799 he became a member of th[...] Directory; he was its last presiden[...] and despite professing admiratio[...] for Napoleon, and a great frien[...]ship between Gohier's wife an[...] Josephine, Napoleon had n[...] success in winning him over. A[...] ardent republican, after the coup [...] Brumaire Gohier refused to resig[...] his post, so effectively was depose[...] From 1802 until the annexation [...] Holland he served as Frenc[...] consul-general at Amsterdam, an[...] declined a similar post in the US[...] on grounds of ill-health.

GOLDSMITH, Lewis (*c.*1767–1846)

As a political writer, he had th[...] unusual distinction of writing f[...] both sides during the Napoleoni[...] Wars. Born in England of Por[...]uguese extraction, in 1801 h[...] published an attack on Britis[...] policy and in 1802 moved [...] France, establishing an English[...] language newspaper with th[...]

encouragement of Talleyrand and Napoleon, to view British affairs from a French perspective. He was employed in some secret service work for Napoleon, but his republican sympathies declined and in 1809 he returned to England, where in 1811 he founded a violently anti-French newspaper, *The Anti-Gallican Monitor* (later *The British Monitor*). He also wrote a number of works critical of Napoleon, and claimed that the latter had tried to bribe him to stop. He returned to Paris in 1825.

GOMM, Field Marshal Sir William Maynard (1784–1875)

SIR WILLIAM GOMM

A significant figure in the British Army in the earlier Victorian period, notably as CinC India (1850-5) and field marshal from 1868, he saw most of his hardest active service during the Napoleonic Wars. Commissioned as ensign at the age of ten (in recognition of the gallantry of his father, Lieutenant-Colonel William Gomm, killed at Guadeloupe in 1794), he carried the Colours of the 9th Foot in The Netherlands in 1799, served at Ferrol, Hanover (1805), Copenhagen, in the early Peninsular War and at Walcheren, before returning to the Peninsula for the remainder of the war, for the most part as Assistant Quarter-

master-General. He held the same post (as captain and lieutenant-colonel in the 2nd Foot Guards from July 1814) at Waterloo; his horse George was one of the longest-serving equine veterans of the battle, living until 1841.

Gomm, W. M. *Letters and Journals of Field Marshal Sir William Maynard Gomm ... from 1799 to Waterloo*, ed. F. C. Carr-Gomm. London, 1881

GORCHAKOV, General Andrey Ivanovich, Prince (1768–1855)

The Russian noble family of Gorchakov (alternative spellings include Gortchakov) provided a number of significant military personalities during the Napoleonic Wars. Prince Andrey served at Friedland and held an important command in 1812–14 (at Borodino he controlled Raevsky's VII, Borozdin's VIII and Sievers' IV Cavalry Corps, virtually the whole of the Second West Army). **General Alexander Ivanovich Gorchakov (1769–1825)** served under his kinsman Suvarov against the Turks, and against the French in Italy and Switzerland (1799) and Poland (1806–7). **General Prince Mikhail Dimitrievich Gorchakov (1795–1861)** began his military career in 1807, serving against France 1812–14, but won greatest renown in Poland in 1831 and especially by his assumption of command of Russian forces in the Crimea in 1855, including the defence of Sebastopol. His brother, **General Petr Dimitrievich Gorchakov (1770–1868)**, also served against France in 1812–14, but was most distinguished in operations against the Turks 1828–9, and came out of retirement for the Crimean War, leading VI Corps at Alma and Inkerman. The cousin of the last two, **Prince Alexander Mikhailovich Gorchakov (1798–1883)**, was a Russian foreign minister of great renown, being appointed chancellor of the empire in 1863

and only relinquishing the foreign ministry in 1882.

GORDON, Alexander, 4th Duke of (1743–1827)

He was associated with the raising of four regiments: the 89th Highlanders, in which he was a captain (1759), two regiments of Gordon Fencibles (1778 and 1793), and the 100th, later 92nd, in 1794, which as the Gordon Highlanders became one of the British Army's most famous units. Better known, however, is the story of how the Duke's wife, Jane Maxwell, assisted in the formation of the 100th (having in 1775 helped raise a company of the 71st for her brother). A remarkable beauty (known as 'Bonnie Jean'), she dressed in uniform and with her daughters helped encourage recruits; the most famous story concerns how she would put the bounty-coin between her lips, so that each recruit claimed not only the coin but a kiss as well, surely the most remarkable method of recruiting adopted during the period. Doubts have been raised about the accuracy of the story (one authority noted that 'the legend of the Duchess of Gordon's kiss ... will ultimately take rank with other pretty fairy tales',[1] but it

GEORGE, MARQUESS OF HUNTLY, LATER 5TH DUKE OF GORDON (ENGRAVING BY W. HALL AFTER A. ROBERTSON)

remains a most attractive story. The Duke's eldest son George (1770–1838), who succeeded as 5th Duke, is better known as the Marquess of Huntly; having served with the 42nd and the 3rd Foot Guards, in The Netherlands and including Valenciennes, he became lieutenant-colonel commandant of the 100th, served as brigadier-general during the Irish rebellion, was wounded at Egmont-op-Zee (1799) and rose to the rank of general.

1. Bulloch, J. M. 'The Duchess of Gordon as a Recruiter', in *Scotland for Ever*. London, n.d. (*c.* 1915); the same title was used for a pamphlet published by Bulloch in 1908

GORDON, Lieutenant-Colonel Sir Alexander (1786–1815)

One of Wellington's most trusted ADCs, he was the third son of George, Lord Haddo and Charlotte, *née* Baird, and was thus Sir David Baird's nephew, and brother of the 4th Earl of Aberdeen, the Prime Minister. He served as Baird's ADC at the Cape (1806), at Copenhagen and in South America before his Peninsula service, received a knighthood of the Bath in January 1815, and as lieutenant-colonel in the 3rd Foot Guards was mortally wounded at Waterloo as Wellington's ADC, not surviving the amputation of a leg. Wellington had Gordon laid in his own bed, himself sleeping in his cloak, but Gordon died during the night of the battle; Wellington was greatly affected by the loss and wrote in the Waterloo dispatch that he 'was a most promising officer, and a serious loss to His Majesty's service'.[1] He should not be confused with three Peninsula officers of similar name: Captain Alexander Gordon of the 15th Hussars, the author of a notable account of the Corunna campaign; Lieutenant-Colonel Alexander Gordon of the 83rd, killed at Talavera; and Lieutenant-General William

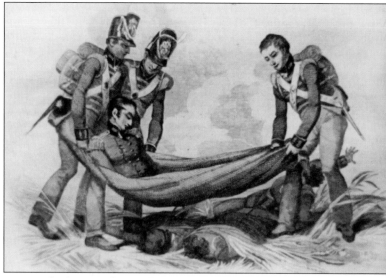

SIR ALEXANDER GORDON IS CARRIED WOUNDED FROM THE FIELD OF WATERLOO

Alexander Gordon, who as a captain in the 50th was wounded at Vittoria. Nor should he be confused with **General Sir James Willoughby Gordon, Bt. (1773–1851)**, an ambitious but troublesome officer who as a colonel was the Peninsula army's QMG 1811–12, until sent home on the excuse of bad health.

1. *Gazette*, 22 June 1815.

GOUGH, Field Marshal Hugh, Viscount (1779–1869)

Chiefly remembered for colonial service, notably as CinC during the First China War (1841–2) and in India 1843–9 (including victories in the Gwalior and First Sikh Wars), he had also had a distinguished record in the Napoleonic Wars. Born in County Limerick, he was commissioned in 1794, served at the Cape, and commanded the 87th with great distinction during the Peninsular War, most notably at Barrosa, and was wounded at Talavera and Nivelle. A brave officer and typical 'fighting general', his preferred tactic was to rush upon the enemy, leading to criticism of causing unnecessary casualties; at Chillianwalla (1849) it was said that he 'fancied himself at Donnybrook Fair, and was in the

thick of it, in the mêlée, and lost to sight!'.[1] He became viscount in June 1849 and field marshal in November 1862. His father, George Gough (1750–1836), was lieutenant-colonel of the Limerick City Militia and two of his brothers served in the army: Major George Gough who was with the 28th in Egypt and Major William Gough, 68th, who was wounded at Vittoria and drowned off Kinsale Head in 1822.

1. *Illustrated London News*, 1 March 1849.

Rait, R. S. *The Life and Campaigns of Hugh, 1st Viscount Gough*. London, 1903

HUGH, VISCOUNT GOUGH
(ENGRAVING BY STODART)

GOUJON, Jean-Marie-Claude-Alexandre (1766–95)

After a career at sea, he entered the French Convention as one of the more moderate members of the Mountain'; he served as a representative with the forces of the Rhine and Moselle, but suffered from his sympathy with the attempted insurrection of May 1795, though there was no evidence of his complicity in its organisation. One of six Deputies condemned to death, he was involved in the suicide pact by which they intended to escape the guillotine; three, including Goujon, stabbed themselves to death, but the others, only wounded, were dragged to execution (17 June 1795).

GOURGAUD, General Gaspard, baron (1788–1852)

One of Napoleon's most faithful aides, he was born in Versailles, where his father was a musician in the royal chapel. In 1802 he was commissioned in the artillery, served at Austerlitz, in Spain and in the Danube campaign of 1809, and in 1811 was appointed to Napoleon's staff as *officier d'ordonnance*. Ennobled as baron after the 1812 campaign, he was distinguished at Dresden and Leipzig, may have saved Napoleon by killing the leader of a Cossack party which was approaching the emperor's tent near Brienne, and was wounded at Montmirail. Although he took service under the Bourbons, he rejoined Napoleon as his aide in 1815, was the bearer of the abortive plea to the Prince Regent to allow Napoleon asylum in England, and accompanied Napoleon to St. Helena. A prickly character – Bunbury described him as 'a youngish man, with a smart genteel air, and somewhat of a coxcomb'[1]– he fell out with Las Cases and challenged Montholon to a duel, and the atmosphere became so unpleasant that he

returned to France in 1818 to plead (unsuccessfully) for an improvement in Napoleon's conditions. (Basil Jackson, however, found him 'a gentlemanly man, and possessed of much propriety of feeling'.)[2] Gourgaud produced a number of significant publications, perhaps the best known being *La Campagne de 1815* (London and Paris, 1818), and a critique of Ségur's work on the 1812 campaign, which led to a duel in which Ségur was wounded. Gourgaud returned to military service in 1830, was one of those who brought back Napoleon's body from St. Helena, and became a Deputy in 1852. His St. Helena journal was published posthumously.

1. Bunbury, *Memoirs*, p. 307. 2. *CUSM*, 1844, vol. I, p. 420.

Gourgaud, G. *Journal inédit de Sainte-Hélène*. Paris, 1899; *Napoleon and the Grand Army in Russia, or a Critical Examination of the Work of Count Ph. de Ségur*. London, 1825; *Mémoires pour servir à l'histoire de France sous Napoléon*. Paris, 1823

GOUVION SAINT-CYR, Marshal Laurent, marquis de (1764–1830)

The son of a butcher, born in Toul, Saint-Cyr adopted that name in his youth, after the mother who deserted the family in his infancy. He studied to be an artist and failed as an actor, but after entering the army in 1792 became *général de division* in less than two years. He served under Moreau in 1796, succeeded Massena as commander of the Army of Rome in 1798, led Jourdan's left wing 1798–9 and won a notable victory at Biberach with the Army of the Rhine under Moreau. Even at this early stage of his career he had a reputation for being a difficult colleague, cold, sullen, morose and introverted with unsociable habits (hence his nickname 'le

LAURENT GOUVION ST. CYR
(LITHOGRAPH AFTER DELPESCH)

hibou' the owl); trusted but never liked by his men, he was incorruptible (hence his despising of looters like Massena) and had firm principles including a dislike of political involvements, which caused Napoleon to distrust him. After a brief retirement from mid 1800, after falling out with Moreau, he served as ambassador at Madrid (1801–3) and Naples (1803–5), but was omitted from the first creation of the Marshalate for refusing to sign the proclamation supporting Napoleon's elevation to emperor, regarding it as a political act in which soldiers should not become involved. In August 1808 he was appointed to command French forces in Catalonia, being recalled under a cloud for failing to take Gerona; but his undoubted talents led to his recall in 1812 as commander of VI Corps. He performed so well at Polotsk that he was finally awarded his Marshal's baton (27 August 1812), but at the end of October was invalided by a severe wound in the foot. He returned in 1813 to lead XIV Corps, notably at Dresden, but was forced to surrender in November when his corps was besieged in that city. He accepted the Bourbon restoration, remained at home during the Hundred Days and in July 1815 became royal war minister, but was forced from office two and a half months later by ultra-royalists, and his attempts to gain clemency for Ney were unsuccessful. In June 1817, however, he became minister of marine, and war minister in September, having been ennobled as a marquis; the reforms he introduced transformed and revitalised the French Army, but he retired in 1819 to spend his time with his family (he was a devoted husband), writing and agriculture. Despite the less appealing traits of his character, he was described as 'an ill-used and neglected officer ... everywhere accounted, and especially in Spain, an honourable and upright man, who scorned to violate the humanities of civilized warfare',[1] and his military talents were prodigious, as even Napoleon realised. Marbot, who thought Saint-Cyr a jealous and uncaring man who was employed only out of necessity and from whom colleagues could expect little co-operation, nevertheless was clear about his abilities: 'one of the most able soldiers in Europe ... I never knew anyone handle troops in battle better ... he was of tall stature, but looked more like a professor than a soldier ... It was impossible to find a calmer man; the greatest danger, disappointments, successes, defeats, were alike unable to move him. In presence of every sort of contingency he was like ice ...'[2]

1. Anon., p. 270. 2. Marbot, vol. II, p. 530.

Ainval, C. d'. *Gouvion St. Cyr.* Paris, 1981; Coates-Wright, P. 'The Owl: Gouvion St. Cyr', in *Napoleon's Marshals*, ed. D. G. Chandler. London, 1987 (contains an extensive bibliography); Gouvion St. Cyr, L. *Journal des Opérations de l'Armée de Catalogne en 1808 et 1809.* Paris, 1821; *Mémoires pour servir à l'histoire militaire sous le Directoire, le Consulat, et l'Empire.* Paris, 1831; *Mémoires sur les campagnes des Armées de Rhin et de Rhin-et-Moselle de 1794 à 1797.* Paris, 1829

GOYA Y LUCIENTES, Francisco de (1746–1828)

The great Spanish artist became principal painter to the King of Spain in 1786, but this did not lead him to glamorise the deeply unattractive royal family in his most perceptive portraits, nor stop his penetrating observations on Spanish life. The etchings of 1810–13, *The Disasters of War*, are the most horrifying images not only of the Peninsular War but form the most devastating commentary on the nature of war in general since Callot's *Misères et Malheures de Guerre* of the Thirty Years War. Goya's most famous military works are those concerning the Madrid uprising and its brutal suppression ('2 May' and '3 May 1808'), his work being more an impression of atmosphere than a faithful record of uniform and equipment. His colourful personal life included brawls, stabbings, the abduction of a nun, banishment from court because of his liaisons, the production of twenty children, and increasing ill-health, including deafness and insanity, which was reflected in the dark nature of his later work. Having remained in royal employment despite his portraits making the subjects appear idiots, Goya worked for Joseph Bonaparte (his equestrian portrait of Wellington was originally one of that monarch!), and again for the restored Bourbon monarchy, but being a liberal he disapproved of absolutism and in 1824 moved to Bordeaux, where he died.

Adhemar, J. *Goya.* Paris, 1948; López-Rey, J. *Francisco de Goya.* London, 1950; Harris, E. *Goya.* London, 1969

GRAHAM, General Sir Thomas, 1st Baron Lynedoch (1748–1843)

SIR THOMAS GRAHAM, LORD LYNEDOCH (PRINT AFTER HOPPNER)

His career is surely one of the most unusual of any general officer of the Napoleonic Wars, in that he did not embark on a military career until late in life. A Scottish gentleman and landowner, interested in country pursuits (he made most runs in the first Scottish cricket match for which the scores are recorded), he was married to 'the beautiful Mrs Graham' immortalised by Gainsborough. After she died in the South of France in 1792, her coffin was desecrated by French national guards and drunken ruffians searching for contraband; this, and despair at events in France, caused Graham to pursue a career as a soldier, with the sole intention of overthrowing the regime in France. After service as an unpaid volunteer on Lord Mulgrave's staff at Toulon, he raised the 90th Foot (Perthshire Volunteers); in 1796 he was British commissioner with the Austrians in Italy and escaped from the siege of Mantua (in uniform and not, as reported, in disguise: see his own account in Aspinall-Oglander, pp. 98–9). His position as Whig MP for Perthshire (1794–1807) did not

hibit his military career; in 1798
  was at Minorca and Sicily, at
  e capture of Malta, went to Egypt
  o late to take part in any fighting,
  ccompanied his friend Sir John
  oore to Sweden and Spain as
  olunteer aide, was at Moore's
  de when he received his mortal
  ound, and (he believed at
  oore's dying wish) was finally
  ven permanent rank in the army
  major-general, his lieutenant-
  olonelcy of the 90th having been
  nly a provisional appointment.
  ieutenant-general at Walcheren,
  raham was then sent to
  ommand British forces at Cadiz,
  nd there won his great victory at
  arrosa; but his angry remarks
  oout the conduct there of his
  panish allies precluded his
  urther service with them, so he
  ansferred to Wellington's army.
  e had never been in favour of
  Vellington on political grounds,
  ut their association turned
  raham into an unashamed
  dmirer. Commanding the 1st
  ivision from August 1811, he
  ent home in July 1812 for treat-
  nent to an eye, returned in 1813 to
  ommand Wellington's left wing,
  xecuted the critical flanking-
  novement at Vittoria and super-
  ised the siege of San Sebastian.
  lis independent command in The
  etherlands was not a success,
  nd he retired in the same year
  1814); rewarded with the barony
  f Lynedoch, he became a general
  1 1821. Beloved and admired by
  ll ranks, the Guards whom he led
  ersonally in a charge at Barrosa
  resented him with an address
  vhich called him 'our Father and
  ur Friend', and the universal
  pinion was articulated by Wil-
  am Warre: 'one of the most excel-
  ent, worthy men I know
  nywhere, and like Hill beloved by
  verybody ... a most excellent
  ealous soldier, and a most
  miable worthy man. I know none
  have a higher respect and vener-
  tion for.'[1]

1. Warre, pp. 273, 277.

Aspinall-Oglander, C. *Freshly Remembered: The Story of Thomas Graham, Lord Lynedoch*. London, 1956; Brett-James, A. *General Graham, Lord Lynedoch*. London, 1959; Delavoye, Captain A. M. *Life of Thomas Graham, Lord Lynedoch*. London, 1880; Lynedoch, Lord. *Life and Letters of Sir Thomas Graham, Lord Lynedoch*, ed. A. M. Delavoye. London, 1868

GRANT, Lieutenant-Colonel Colquhoun (1780–1829)

One of the most efficient intelligence officers of the period, he was an officer of the 11th Foot from 1795, was captured with them in the Ostend débâcle of 1798, and during the Peninsular War was detached from his regiment to become the best of Wellington's 'observing officers', in effect his chief of intelligence. Operating behind enemy lines, always in uniform, his knowledge of Spain, its dialects and the network of agents he established, made him an invaluable source of information; he had direct and immediate access to Wellington himself, who declared Grant worth a brigade. In April 1812 he was betrayed and captured at Idanha Nova, near the Portuguese–Spanish border; but he escaped at Bayonne, gathered information in France and returned home via Paris, disguised as a sailor in a Breton fishing boat. As AQMG (and lieutenant-colonel from May 1814) he fulfilled the same intelligence role in the Waterloo campaign, and commanded a brigade in the First Burma War. He died at Aix-la-Chapelle. One of his brothers, Sir James Robert Grant, was head of the medical staff during the Waterloo campaign and was later Inspector-General of Hospitals; another was General Sir Lewis Grant, Governor of the Bahamas (1820–9) and of Trinidad (1831–3); their brother-in-law was James

McGrigor, Wellington's chief medical officer in the Peninsula, who married their sister Mary in 1810. Colquhoun Grant should not be confused with his namesake, below.

Haswell C. J. D. *The First Respectable Spy: The Life and Times of Lt. Col. Colquhoun Grant 1780–1829*. London, 1969

GRANT, Lieutenant-General Sir Colquhoun (c.1764–1835)

Not to be confused with the above, Sir Colquhoun Grant is remembered chiefly as a leader of light cavalry. He served with the 25th Light Dragoons in India, was wounded as lieutenant-colonel of the 72nd at the Cape, and in August 1808 was appointed to command the 15th Hussars, leading them with distinction in the Corunna campaign (notably at Sahagun) and again in the Peninsula from April 1813. He commanded the hussar brigade April–July 1813 (including at Morales and Vittoria) and commanded another brigade September–November; as major-general he led the 5th Cavalry Brigade at Waterloo, where he had five horses shot from under him. He rose to the rank of lieutenant-general and was MP for Queenborough (1831).

GRASSINI, Giuseppina (1773–1850)

The star of the Milan opera, she was one of Napoleon's mistresses. She left La Scala and, in Paris in 1814, was seen in the company of the Duke of Wellington, so that there were unproven rumours that she was intimate with him as well, perhaps arising from his possession of her portrait.

GRATTAN, Henry (1746–1820)

This great Irish statesman and orator (Fox called him 'the Irish Demosthenes') played only a limited role in the politics of the Napoleonic Wars, his great

HENRY GRATTAN

concerns being the independence of the Irish legislature and Catholic Emancipation, neither of which were influenced greatly by the wider military events of the period; though the 1798 rebellion was the catalyst for the 1801 union, to which Grattan was implacably opposed (at the time of the rebellion he sought sanctuary for his family in North Wales). He entered the Westminster parliament in 1805 but refused office under Fox and Grenville in 1806 and, as a supporter of the struggle against France, finally broke with the Whigs over his support for the prosecution of the war against Napoleon.

Gwynn, S. *Life and Times of Henry Grattan*. 1939

GRAVINA, Admiral Don Federico Carlos de (1756–1806)

The senior Spanish commander of the Franco–Spanish 'combined fleet' at Trafalgar, for which he is best remembered, he was an experienced, respected and capable officer who had participated in the great siege of Gibraltar and had been 2i/c of the Spanish fleet which co-operated with the British at Toulon. He was not happy to co-operate with Villeneuve in 1805 and wisely advocated delay, but to no avail. At Trafalgar he fought his flagship, the 112-gun *Principe de*

Asturias, with gallantry, but after he was wounded it fell to his chief of staff, Rear-Admiral Don Antonio Escaño, to continue the fight. After Villeneuve was captured, command of the combined fleet devolved upon Gravina, and it was he who gave the signal for those ships still able to rally and make for Cadiz, a realistic course of action given the circumstances. His wound proved fatal and he died from its effects in the following year, remarking that he hoped he was going to join Nelson.

GREENOCK, Lord: the title of Charles Murray Cathcart, see CATHCART, 1st Earl

GREGOIRE, Bishop Henri (1750–1831)

One of the most significant ecclesiastical personalities of the Revolutionary period, Grégoire began his political career as a member of the States-General in 1789; the first to take the oath under the civil constitution of the clergy, he was elected Bishop of Blois, which position he held until 1801. Although an ardent republican (he served as President of the Convention), he supported leniency towards the king and vehemently refused to follow Gobel in his rejection of religion and office; after the fall of Robespierre he was the first to speak in favour of re-opening the churches, and was much concerned with the welfare of the arts, sciences and education. He became a member of the Council of Five Hundred and of the Senate, but resigned his bishopric out of opposition to the Concordat, and voted against the establishment of the empire; nevertheless, he was ennobled by Napoleon and awarded the *Légion d'honneur*. During Napoleon's reign he travelled in Great Britain and Germany; hated by the Bourbons, he was forced into retirement at the second restoration, and his

election to the parliament in 181[ ] was annulled. The remainder ɑ his life was spent in retiremen[ ] largely concerned with literar[ ] matters, and to the end h[ ] remained true to his religion an[ ] to republicanism.

GRENVILLE, William Wyndham, Baron (1759–1834)

Son of the British chief ministe[ ] George Grenville (1712–70[ ] brother of Earl Temple, late[ ] Marquess of Buckingham, an[ ] cousin of William Pitt, he entere[ ] parliament in 1782, became Hom[ ] Secretary in 1789 and Foreig[ ] Secretary in 1791; he was enno[ ] bled as Baron Grenville in 1790. H[ ] resigned with Pitt in 1801, but grev[ ] away from his erstwhile leader an[ ] declined office upon Pitt's retur[ ] in 1804 when Pitt refused t[ ] include Fox in the government. O[ ] Pitt's death Grenville headed th[ ] 'ministry of all the talents[ ] (February 1806–March 1807[ ] which collapsed over the king'[ ] refusal to countenance Catholi[ ] Emancipation. Grenville neve[ ] again held office, and while gener[ ] ally supporting the Whigs in parlia[ ] ment, remained an advocate of th[ ] maintenance of the war agains[ ] France. Though industrious, h[ ] appears to have had no ambitio[ ] for the highest office, and hi[ ] austere manner tended to mak[ ] him unpopular; Liverpoo[ ] remarked that his judgement wa[ ] flawed because he never consid[ ] ered all the implications of [ ] subject. He was distinguished i[ ] the literary field, however, notabl[ ] in editing the letters of his uncle[ ] the elder Pitt, Lord Chatham.

Jupp, A. *Lord Grenville 1759– 1834*. Oxford, 1985

GREY, Charles, 2nd Earl (1764–1845)

This distinguished British statesman is best remembered as the Prime Minister (1830–4) under whose administration the Reform

CHARLES, 2ND EARL GREY

ill was passed; but he also held ffice during the Napoleonic Wars. e became Whig MP for Northumerland in 1786, and became nown for his attacks on Pitt and r opposition to the war with rance. He was First Lord of the dmiralty and then Foreign Secreary during the 'ministry of all the alents' but opposed Grenville's var policy and returned to opposion in 1807 when the ministry fell; aking the traditional view that rance should choose its own eaders, he split with Grenville in 815 when the latter supported the var against Napoleon. Perhaps ronically for one who denounced overnment policy, his father was ne of those who in the Revoluonary Wars carried it out with ome success: **General Charles, st Earl Grey (1729–1807).** His nilitary career included service on he staff of Ferdinand of Brunswick ne was wounded at Minden) and n the War of American Indepenlence, when his orders to attack Mad Anthony' Wayne's command t Paoli in September 1777 using nly the bayonet led to his nickame 'No-Flint Grey'. Lieutenanteneral in 1782, general in 1796, he erved in The Netherlands in 1793 nd in the following year had great uccess in capturing French ossessions in the West Indies. He

commanded the Southern District during the threat of French invasion (1798–9) and was ennobled as Baron Grey of Howick, Northumberland (1801), advanced to Viscount Howick and Earl Grey in April 1806; before inheriting the earldom, the 2nd Earl was consequently styled Lord Howick. Other sons of the 1st Earl included General Sir Henry George Grey (1766–1845) and Lieutenant-Colonel William Grey (1777–1817), and his daughter Hannah married Captain Bettesworth, RN, who nine months after their marriage was killed in action against the Danes at Bergen, when in command of HMS *Tartar* (16 May 1808).

Smith, E. A. *Lord Grey 1764–1845.* Oxford, 1990

GRIBEAUVAL, General Jean-Baptiste Vacquette de, comte (1715–89)

Although he died before the beginning of the Revolutionary Wars, he deserves inclusion here by virtue of his complete reformation of the French artillery, and the 'system' of ordnance which he designed, and which was used throughout the Napoleonic period, and, despite the introduction of a new pattern from 1803, was re-introduced in 1818. He also re-organised administration and training, to produce a superb force of artillery which served France well during the subsequent conflicts. During the Seven Years War, Gribeauval had been attached to the Austrian army, which at that time had the best artillery in Europe, and this must have inspired the work of reform in his own country.

GRIMALDI, Honoré-Gabriel, Prince Honoré V of Monaco (1778–1841)

The Genoese family of Grimaldi, which had held the principality of Monaco for many centuries, attained a French aspect following

the marriage of the heiress, Princess Louise-Hippolyte (1697–1731) to the Norman family of Goyon, comtes de Matignon. Monaco was annexed by France in 1793; Honoré V served with the French Army, including Hohenlinden, in Germany in 1806 and in the Peninsula, and became equerry to Josephine. Monaco was restored to the family by the Treaty of Paris (1814) but it was Honoré's brother Florestan (1785–1856), who succeeded in 1841, who went there to rule in person; he had served as an ordinary soldier in the French Army and had been captured in Russia in 1812. Their father, Honoré IV (1758–1819) also served in 1806 and was wounded severely in 1807. They should not be confused with Charles Philippe Auguste, marquis de Grimaldi (1775–1846), who emigrated and served with the *Armée de Condé*, later as an officer in Dillon's Regiment in British service, and became a general in the French Army after the restoration.

GROLMANN, General Karl Wilhelm George von (1777–1843)

Perhaps best remembered for his contribution to the Prussian council of war after Ligny, he was a native of Berlin who entered the Prussian army as a boy and was commissioned in 1795. He served with distinction in the War of 1806 and as a close associate of Scharnhorst was much involved in the reconstruction of the Prussian army. His desire to oppose France at a time when Prussia was officially that nation's ally led him to serve as a staff officer in the Austrian army, and then to go to Spain, where he assisted in the defence of Cadiz and was present at Albuera; captured later, he escaped and rejoined Prussian service in 1813. Wounded at Kulm and present at Leipzig, he became major-general after the 1814 campaign and as Blücher's QMG in 1815 played a significant part in directing the operations of the army; most notably in supporting Blücher in the decision that, against Gneisenau's inclinations, they should support Wellington immediately instead of retiring to re-organise, which decision proved a turning-point in the campaign. Subsequently Grolmann held important staff positions, including CinC in Poland, and was promoted to General of Infantry in 1837. Wellington's comment on his ally was somewhat obtuse: 'I was acting on the very best terms with Müffling and Blücher, indeed not otherwise with any of them. I did not much admire Gneisenau, and Grollman (*sic*) was the worst of all, but I was always on good terms with all ...'[1]

1. Ellesmere, p. 188.

Conrady, E. von. *Leben und Werken des Generals der Infanterie ... Carl von Grolman*. Berlin, 1894–6

GROS, Antoine-Jean, baron (1771–1835)

The son of a miniaturist, he studied painting under David from 1785, and became both his friend and inheritor of his mantle as leader of the classical school. From 1793 he was in Italy, and via Josephine made the acquaintance of Napoleon, with whom he was closely associated thereafter. Gros was present at Arcola (of which he produced a notable picture showing Napoleon brandishing the flag of the *51st Demi-brigade*), and followed it with a number of great canvases depicting events from the Napoleonic 'myth', perhaps most famously his *Battle of Eylau* (1808) and his picture of Napoleon visiting the plague victims at Jaffa. These received official approval: Napoleon appointed him *inspecteur aux revues* which enabled him to accompany the army. In 1797 he was part of the commission which selected

works of art to be taken from Italy to France, and he was ennobled as baron in 1808. His later work failed to capture the vigour, and public acclaim, of his earlier paintings, and though ennobled by Charles X (proof that he survived his close association with the Napoleonic regime), the apparent diminution in his own powers and the rising popularity of Romanticism, coupled with unhappy personal circumstances, led him to drown himself in the Seine in June 1835.

GROUCHY, Marshal Emmanuel, marquis de (1766–1847)

EMMANUEL GROUCHY (ENGRAVING BY H. WOLF AFTER J. S. ROUILLARD)

The last of Napoleon's Marshals to be appointed, he was also different from most of his fellows in being a genuine aristocrat who had served in the French Army 1781–7 (including in the Scottish Company of the *Gardes du Corps*). As a supporter of the Revolution he rejoined as a lieutenant-colonel in 1791, in 1793 was dismissed because of his aristocratic background, but was restored a year later and became *général de division* in 1795. Hoche's 2i/c for the abortive expedition to Ireland – in which Wolfe Tone remarked especially upon his spirit – he led Joubert's left at

Novi but was wounded an captured, commanded a divisio at Hohenlinden, but as an asso ciate of Moreau and one wh objected to the creation of th Consulate, he was excluded fror Napoleon's circle of favoure subordinates. In 1805 he con manded a division under Mai mont and from 1806 made hi name as a cavalry commander, a Eylau and Friedland; as Governo of Madrid he suppressed th rising of 2 May 1808, and in 180 served with Eugène in Italy, and a Wagram. Although he receive rewards – he was a count of th empire from January 1809 – h was denied the marshalate, an for a time went into semi-retire ment, but led III Cavalry Corps i the Russian campaign of 1812 although wounded at Borodino he led the 'sacred battalion' o officers in the final stages of th retreat. He retired temporarily i 1813 (on grounds of ill-health, an was disappointed in not receivin a desired command), but re turned in 1814 and was wounde at Craonne. Grouchy accepte office under the Bourbons bu rallied to Napoleon in 1815, an in April finally received hi Marshal's baton after dispersin Angoulême's royalists. In th Waterloo campaign he le Napoleon's right wing at Ligny and Wavre, attracting much criti cism (some surely unjustified) fo following orders instead o marching towards the sound o the major battle. He withdrew hi command in good order, and t escape Bourbon anger emigrate to Philadelphia, but wa permitted to return to France i 1820 with the retired rank of lieu tenant-general; not until 1831 wa his marshal's rank restored (b Louis-Philippe), and in th following year he was restored t the Chamber of Peers. He expended much effort in later lif endeavouring to vindicate hi nduct in the Waterloo campaign.

Grouchy, Marquis de (the arshal's son): *Mémoires de aréchal de Grouchy*. Paris, 73–4; Grouchy, Marshal. *Obsertions sur la relation de la mpagne de 1815 par le Général Gourgaud*. Philadelphia and ris, 1818 (one of a number of ritings intended to justify his nduct in 1815); Lunt, Major-neral J. D. 'The Odd Man Out: rouchy', in *Napoleon's Marshals*, l. D. G. Chandler. London, 1987

UADET, Marguerite Elie 758–94)

lawyer from Bordeaux and a illed orator, he was a leader of e Girondins who voted for the eath of the king, but for a delay nding an appeal to the people. e refused to be reconciled with anton and 'the Mountain' and so ared in the fall of the Girondins; rested at Caen, he was guil-tined at Bordeaux in June 1794, rotesting that the rolling drums revented his dying declaration om being heard by the crowd. is father, brother and aunt were xecuted shortly after.

UDIN DE LA SABLONNIERE, eneral Charles-Etienne, comte 768–1812)

n aristocrat who had served in e royal guard of the *ancien gime*, he prospered during the evolutionary Wars: he served at an Domingo and as Gouvion aint-Cyr's chief of staff, became *énéral de brigade* in 1799 (*de division* July 1800); served in Switzer-nd and Germany 1799–1800, and ommanded a division in Davout's orps from 1805, when that forma-on was regarded as the élite of e army. Wounded at Auerstädt nd Wagram, he served also at ylau and Eckmühl, and in 1812 ommanded the 3rd Division of Davout's I Corps in Russia; while ading the 7th *Légère* of Gérard's

brigade at Valutina, Gudin was mortally struck by a roundshot which broke both legs.

GUIBERT, General Jacques-Antoine-Hippolyte, comte de (1743–90)

Although he died before the beginning of the Revolutionary Wars, by his writings he exerted considerable influence on subsequent military affairs. At the age of 13 he accompanied his father, Charles-Benoît, comte de Guibert (1715–86), Marshal de Broglie's chief of staff, on campaign in Germany. Although the younger Guibert himself became a general in the French Army, his writing was more celebrated than his service record; he came to prominence from his technical military works, or military philosophy, with the publication of *Essai général de tactique* (1770), followed by *Défence du système de guerre moderne* (1779); he also wrote about the Prussian system following long discussions with Frederick the Great. Guibert's work influenced Napoleon greatly; he treated the art of war as more than the glorified drill-book implied by some treatises, but considered the widest economic and social implications as well as military. He predicted that as standing armies were insufficient to achieve a truly comprehensive victory, success could only be gained by creating a 'national army', adumbrating the 'citizen armies' of the revolutionary period; and advocated both the creation of a permanent divisional system as experimented with by Broglie, and the use of column and line combined, the former for manoeuvre and the latter for maximising fire-potential. All of these became key features in Napoleon's art of war. In 1775 Guibert began to co-operate with comte de St. Germain in the reform of the French Army, but

this did not progress beyond the latter's fall from favour in 1777; thereafter Guibert wrote in retirement until recalled to the war ministry shortly before his death. His other writings included a journal of travels and a tragedy.

GURWOOD, Colonel John (1790–1845)

Commissioned as ensign in the 52nd Light Infantry in 1808, as a lieutenant he led a 'forlorn hope' at Ciudad Rodrigo, and despite a head injury carried on to take Governor Barrié prisoner, being presented with that officer's sword by Wellington. He served throughout the Peninsular War, latterly as a staff officer, and as a captain in the 10th Hussars was wounded at Waterloo while serving as ADC to Sir Henry Clinton. He became brevet-colonel, deputy-lieutenant of the Tower and Wellington's private secretary, but is best remembered as the editor of Wellington's dispatches, of which Lord Brougham commented: 'You have published a book which will live when we are dust and forgotten.'[1] Worn down by over-work and the effects of his wounds, Gurwood took his own life at Brighton in December 1845. An obituary lamented that so brave a soldier should meet such an end, and that all his experience 'should have proved unavailing against the delusions of a harassed and distempered mind'; and that the collation of the dispatches with its 'drudgery and excitement ... acting on a brain rendered more susceptible of irritation by a wound in the head, received at the Storming of Ciudad Rodrigo, no doubt occasioned the desponding state of mind which led to the fatal result ... Colonel Gurwood was endeared to all his friends by his frank and generous character; he was an upright gentleman and a brave soldier.'[2]

1. Ellesmere, p. 140. 2. *CUSM*, 1846, vol. I, p. 298.

GUSTAVUS IV, King of Sweden (1778–1837)

GUSTAVUS IV, KING OF SWEDEN
(MEDALLIC PORTRAIT)

He succeeded to the Swedish throne on the assassination of his father, Gustavus III, in 1792, with Duke Charles of Sudermania, the young king's uncle, acting as regent until he came of age. On attaining majority, from November 1796 he ran the state as an autocracy, with a foreign policy characterised by fanatical hatred of Jacobinism and later of Napoleon, and signs of his mental instability becoming increasingly evident. Gustavus' position on foreign affairs led to war with Russia and Denmark after the Treaty of Tilsit (both acting against Sweden under French pressure), and in February 1808 the Russians invaded the Swedish territory of Finland. The British government sent a force to Sweden's aid, under Sir John Moore, but the king's mental condition and his outrageous plans made co-operation impossible; he seemed determined to model himself on the great Charles XII, and so irrational was his behaviour that he even tried to arrest Moore for non-co-operation. Such was his mismanagement of affairs that on 13

March 1809 a conspiracy of army officers arrested him, declared his family incapable of ruling Sweden, and on 5 June 1809 the previous duke-regent was elected as King Charles XIII, with a liberal constitution. Gustavus went into exile in December 1809 and lived under the titles of Count of Gottorp, or Colonel Gustafsson; he finally settled in Switzerland. Having rejected a union with Grand-Duchess Alexandra of Russia because of her Orthodox religion, in October 1797 he had married Frederica Dorothea, daughter of Grand-Duke Charles Frederick of Baden, but they were divorced in 1812.

GUYOT, General Claude-Etienne, comte (1768–1837)

One of the generals associated closely with Napoleon's Imperial Guard, he enlisted as a *chasseur* in 1791 and was commissioned in 1793. After service in Italy and Germany he transferred to the Consular Guard (1802), and after Austerlitz became 2i/c of the *Chasseurs à Cheval* of the Guard. He served at Eylau, was ennobled as baron (May 1808) accompanied Napoleon to Spain (where he succeeded to command of the *Chasseurs* after Lefebvre-Desnouëttes' capture), was promoted to *général de brigade* after Wagram (August 1809) and in the following March became chamberlain to Napoleon's household. Back in Spain, he fought at Fuentes de Oñoro, in 1812 was present with the *Chasseurs* who formed Napoleon's escort, was wounded at Lützen and captured at Kulm, but was swiftly exchanged and fought at Leipzig. Advanced to comte, in December 1813 he moved to the *Grenadiers à Cheval* of the Guard, but his handling of larger formations of cavalry at La Rothière and Vauchamps was so undistinguished that Napoleon

removed him from comman appointing him instead to l escort. Guyot retained comma of his *Grenadiers* (re-titled as tl *Corps Royal des Cuirassiers France*) after the Bourbon restor tion, but rejoined Napoleon 1815 and led the Guard hea cavalry at Waterloo. He retired 1816, but was re-employed in staff position by Louis-Philip (1830–3).

GYULAI, General Ignatius (Ignaz), Count (1763–1831)

He was a distinguished cor mander of the Austrian Arm probably best known for h participation in the later can paigns, though he had served wi distinction at Hohenlinden. In 18 he was not only milita commander but *Ban* (Governor) Croatia, and was entrusted wi independent command: I succeeded in raising the blockac of Graz (25 June) but his forc were unable to break the Frenc 84th Line in the famous actic which won for that unit the mott '*un contre dix*'. In the 1813 can paign Gyulai commanded I Corps (actually officially style *Armee-Abteilung*) of the Army Bohemia, and at Leipzig wa charged with the capture of tl villages of Lindenau and Plagwit to sever Napoleon's route retreat (16 October); but afte initial success, he was repelled by heavy counter-attack and, havir received no reinforcements, wa unable to block the escape-rout of the French. Gyulai commande his corps in France in 1814, and i 1823 was appointed Governor Bohemia. He should not b confused with Feldmarscha Leutnant Albert, Count Gyula who in 1809, like Ignatiu commanded Austrian force under the overall authority of th Archduke John.

HALKETT, General Sir Colin (1774–1856); and HALKETT, General Hugh, Freiherr von (1783–1863)

Son of Major-General Frederick Halkett, Colin's first military experience was in Dutch service. From 1800 he was in British pay; in 1803 he joined the King's German Legion, rising to command the 2nd Light Battalion. He served in the expedition to Hanover (1805), the Baltic (1808) and in the Peninsula (1808–14, with a break for Walcheren). Major-general from 4 June 1814, he led the 5th British Brigade of the 3rd Division in the Waterloo campaign with considerable distinction, being wounded at Waterloo and having four horses shot from under him. He became lieutenant-general in 1830, general in 1841, served as CinC Bombay 1831–2 and was Governor of the Royal Hospital, Chelsea, 1849–56. As a tribute to his KGL service he held the honorary rank of general in the Hanoverian Army. His younger brother, **Hugh Halkett**, served with the Scotch Brigade (later 94th Foot, with which their father had been associated) in India (1798–1801), then joined Colin's 2nd Light Battalion of the KGL, rising to command it at Albuera and in 1812. In April 1813 he joined the Hanoverian army in north Germany, commanding a brigade at Göhrde, and through to 1814. In the Waterloo campaign he led the 3rd Hanoverian Brigade of the 2nd Division, composed of *Landwehr*, and personally apprehended Cambronne in the later stages of the battle. He retained his British lieutenant-colonelcy (dating from 1 January 1812), albeit on half-pay, but transferred to Hanoverian service after the end of the Napoleonic Wars, becoming general and Inspector-General of infantry, and commanding X Corps in the Danish War of 1848.

Knesebeck, E. von dem. *Leben des Freiherr H. von Halkett*. Stuttgart, 1865

HALLOWELL (later CAREW), Admiral Sir Benjamin (1760–1834)

Of American birth (his father was the last Commissioner of the American Board of Customs), he was another of the Royal Naval officers who formed Nelson's 'band of brothers'. A huge, strong man, renowned for good-humour and kindness, he served in the War of American Independence but came to notice in the Mediterranean during the Revolutionary Wars. Ashore when his ship HMS *Courageux* was wrecked near Gibraltar in December 1796, he was aboard HMS *Victory* as a passenger at St. Vincent. He commanded HMS *Swiftsure* at Aboukir Bay and was captured when that ship was battered into surrender by Ganteaume's fleet (June 1801); released on parole, he was appointed commodore on the West African station (1802), served in the West Indies and took over Sidney Smith's old ship, HMS *Tigre*, in the Mediterranean in 1804. He sailed

SIR BENJAMIN HALLOWELL

with Nelson to the West Indies, but as part of Louis' squadron sent away to re-provision, he missed

Trafalgar. In 1807 he commanded the naval forces in the Egyptian expedition, became rear-admiral in 1811, and had risen to admiral by 1830; in 1828, on inheriting a family estate, he adopted the name Carew.

HAMILTON, Emma, Lady (*c*.1765–1815)

Forever associated with Great Britain's greatest naval hero, she was born Amy or Emily Lyon, the daughter of a Cheshire blacksmith, probably in 1765. After her father's death she entered domestic service, but her mother apparently encouraged her to exploit her great beauty, which captivated the artist George Romney, who painted many pictures of her, and it served as an introduction to high society. After being an attraction in Dr Graham's notorious quack medicine show in London, she became the mistress of Captain John Willet Payne, RN (a friend of the Prince of Wales), then of Sir Harry Featherstonehaugh (who rejected her when she became pregnant), and then of the Hon. Charles Greville, MP, who from 1782 set her up in a house and employed her mother, who was now calling herself Mrs Cadogan. In 1786 Greville passed her to his uncle, Sir William Hamilton, then British Ambassador to Naples, and in September 1791 she married him. Lady Hamilton created a considerable stir at Naples – not least for posing in artistic 'attitudes' – and was much in favour at court; indeed,

EMMA HAMILTON (ENGRAVING BY G. ZOBELL
AFTER G. ROMNEY)

such was her influence that she claimed to have been of material help in the execution of British government policy with Naples, notably (according to Nelson) for help in having the fleet re-provisioned in 1798, and in transmitting vital intelligence in 1796. She became famous, however, through her association with Horatio Nelson, whom she met in 1793, but it was after his triumph at Aboukir Bay that they became mutually devoted. The affair damaged Nelson's reputation and dragged him into Neapolitan politics, and resulted in a curious *ménage à trois* with Sir William Hamilton, who was as well-disposed towards Nelson as was his wife. This relationship continued after Hamilton's recall from Naples in 1800, and after his death in 1803 Emma lived openly with Nelson at his home, Merton Place; their child, Horatia, had been born in January 1801. On Nelson's death Emma received some financial consideration and the house, but the codicil to Nelson's will (written shortly before the commencement of the battle of Trafalgar, which described her services to her country while at Naples and made a plea that she be supported by the nation) was not acted upon. Thus

ignored and always extravagant, Emma ran seriously into debt and died at Calais in 1815, seeking refuge from her creditors. It was a melancholy end to one of the most famous love affairs in history.

Anon. *Memoirs of Lady Hamilton*. London, 1905; Fraser, F. *Beloved Emma: Emma, Lady Hamilton*. 1986; Nelson, Admiral. *Letters of Lord Nelson to Lady Hamilton*. London, 1814; Russell, J. *Nelson and the Hamiltons*. London, 1969; Sichel, W. *Emma, Lady Hamilton*. London, 1905. She also features in all biographies of Nelson.

HAMILTON, Sir William (1730–1803)

SIR WILLIAM HAMILTON
(PRINT BY H. HUDSON AFTER REYNOLDS)

Although best known as the husband of Lord Nelson's mistress, he had a quite distinguished career in art, science and diplomacy. The son of Lord Archibald Hamilton and grandson of the Duke of Hamilton, he served in the 3rd Foot Guards 1747–58, leaving after his marriage to Catherine Barlow, a Welsh heiress who died in 1782. A great friend of the king (Hamilton's mother had been governess to the Prince of Wales's children, so that Hamilton and George III were childhood playmates – his obituary even

described him as the king's foster-brother), Hamilton was appointed Ambassador to Naples in 1764 and held that position for 36 years. A courtly, intelligent man, Sir William (KB from 1772) found a perfect niche in Naples, with minimal diplomatic duties and sufficient income to entertain and study the arts and sciences; a member of the Royal Society from 1766, he published valuable treatises on earthquakes and volcanoes, but is better know as a collector of antiquities, notably for the two greatest collections of Greek vases ever to leave Italy, one of which enriched the British Museum (the Portland Vase, named after its purchaser, had belonged to Hamilton). His second collection was lost on passage to England with the sinking of HMS *Colossus* in 1798. In 1791 he married his nephew's ex-mistress, Emma, through whom his fame now resides. His diplomatic tasks increased from 1793 with the spread of conflict in Europe, and his health began to break down; and such was his devotion to his beautiful young wife that he acquiesced in her very public affair with Horatio Nelson, to whom he seems to have been almost equally devoted. Recalled from Naples in 1800, Sir William died at his London house in April 1803, 'a man of most extraordinary endowments, and his memory will be dear to the literary world, by the indefatigable exertions which he made through life to add to our stock of knowledge ... His whole life, indeed, was devoted to studies connected with the arts, and he made every interest contribute to the passion of his soul.'[1]

1. *Gent's Mag.*, April, 1803, p. 390.

Fothergill, B. *Sir William Hamilton, Envoy Extraordinary*. London, 1969; Russell, J. *Nelson and the Hamiltons*. London, 1969. Hamilton also features in all biographies of Nelson, and the story of the loss of his second collection is recounted in Morris, R. *HMS* Colossus: *The Story of the Salvage of the Hamilton Treasures*. London, 1979.

HAMILTON SMITH, Lieutenant-Colonel Charles, see SMITH

HAMPTON, Major General Wade (1751 or 1752–1835)

One of the less successful US commanders of the War of 1812, he was a Virginian who had fought in the War of American Independence, had served in the House of Representatives and become a brigadier general in the US Army in 1809. In 1812 he commanded at Norfolk, Virginia, was promoted to major general in March 1813 and was made commander of the forces around Lake Champlain in July. Blamed by Wilkinson for the failure of the campaign against Montreal, Hampton resigned on 16 March 1814; though he was not an effective general, not popular and the object of much criticism, the War Department did not endorse the censure. Subsequently Hampton made a huge fortune (at his death he was reputedly the richest planter in America); his grandson was the Confederate general Wade Hampton (1818–1902).

HARDENBERG, Karl August von, Prince (1750–1822)

He entered the civil service of his native Hanover in 1770, was well received by George III and in 1778 became count and privy councillor, but left after his wife became romantically involved with the Prince of Wales. In 1782 he entered the Brunswick civil service and in 1792 was appointed administrator of Anspach and Bayreuth, recently ceded to Prussia. His abilities were recognised and thereafter he filled a number of increasingly significant posts; in 1795 he was Prussian Plenipotentiary at Basle and signed

KARL AUGUST VON HARDENBERG
(PRINT AFTER VON GEBAUER)

the peace treaty of that name. He became a trusted adviser to Frederick William III, deputising for Haugwitz as Foreign Minister in 1803 and succeeding him in April 1804; he tried to counter-balance the 'war party' and achieve Prussia's aims through diplomacy, but lost his position through pressure from Napoleon, and although he served again as Foreign Minister in 1807, Napoleon again insisted upon his removal from office. In June 1810, however, he was appointed Chancellor in succession to Stein and began to reconstruct the country in all aspects; he was regarded as the statesman who had done most to foster the movement of national regeneration and thus enable Prussia to make an effective contribution in the 'War of Liberation'. He helped influence the king to support Yorck's desertion of the French alliance, and after signing the Peace of Paris on behalf of Prussia, Hardenberg was elevated to the rank of prince. He represented Prussia at the Congress of Vienna, and though he may have been less effective and in Metternich's shadow, his liberal inclinations having to be suppressed in line with the beliefs of the Prussian monarchy, his reputation for the

reform of Prussia remained. He died at Genoa shortly after the close of the Congress of Verona. (His cousin's son was the poet and novelist Friedrich Leopold, Freiherr von Hardenberg, 1772–1801, known to literature by the pseudonym 'Novalis'; Karl offered him a post in Prussian government service, but Friedrich's father declined it, apparently fearing the influence of Karl's loose life-style upon the young man!)

Ranke, L. von. *Hardenberg und die Geschichte des Preussischen Staats von 1793–1813*. Leipzig 1879–81; Thielen, P. G. *Karl August von Hardenberg 1750–1822*. Cologne and Berlin, 1967

HARDINGE, Field Marshal Sir Henry, Viscount (1785–1856)

SIR HENRY, VISCOUNT HARDINGE
(ENGRAVING BY STODART)

The son of a clergyman, he is remembered as a distinguished Governor-General of India. He entered the army as an ensign in the Queen's Rangers in 1799. After training in staff duties under General Jarry at High Wycombe, his first active service (as a captain in the 57th) was as deputy AQMG at Vimeiro, where he was wounded. He was at Moore's side when the general received his fatal injury (Hardinge attempted to staunch the blood with his sash), and then served throughout the Peninsular War as deputy QMG of the Portuguese Army. His great moment came at Albuera when on his own initiative he persuaded Lowry Cole to advance to relieve the beleaguered troops on 'the heights', which proved the turning-point of the battle. Wounded at Vittoria and a lieutenant-colonel from May 1811, during the Waterloo campaign he served as British commissioner with the Prussian headquarters, losing his left hand at Ligny. Wellington praised his effectiveness in this role and presented him with a sword that had belonged to Napoleon, which Hardinge later carried in action in India. He remained a firm friend of the Duke, on whose recommendation he became Governor-General of India in 1844, serving as 2i/c to Gough in the First Sikh War and asserting his authority to curb the latter's injudicious ardour. At the end of the war Hardinge was ennobled as Viscount Hardinge of Lahore and King's Newton (Derbyshire) (2 May 1846). He was less successful as CinC (1852–6) at the time of the Crimean War, resigning on health grounds shortly before his death; he had become field marshal in 1855. Wellington's appraisal was accurate: 'a plain, straightforward, just and excellent man of business'.[1] Two of Hardinge's brothers served in the Napoleonic Wars: Captain George Nicholas Hardinge (1781–1808), who was killed commanding HMS *San Fiorenzo* when capturing the French frigate *La Piedmontaise*; and Major-General Richard Hardinge (1790–1864), who served in the Peninsula from the battle of Vittoria to Toulouse, and as a lieutenant in the Royal Horse Artillery acted as Henry's assistant during the Waterloo campaign, carrying his last report from Prussian HQ to Wellington after Henry had been wounded.

1. Griffiths, p. 304.

Hardinge, C. *Viscount Hardinge and the Advance of the British Dominions in the Punjab*. London, 1900

HARDY, Vice-Admiral Sir Thomas Masterman, Bt. (1769–1839)

SIR THOMAS HARDY
(ENGRAVING BY H. ROBINSON AFTER R. EVANS)

Typical of the solid, capable sea officers who formed the backbone of the Royal Navy, and forever associated with his friend Lord Nelson, he was the son of a Dorsetshire small landowner, went to sea in 1781 and was commissioned in 1795. He came to Nelson's attention as a lieutenant in the frigate HMS *Minerve*, when captured in command of a Spanish prize. After exchange he continued to serve with distinction and in 1798 was appointed captain of Nelson's flagship, HMS *Vanguard*; he commanded HMS *St. George* at Copenhagen and in 1803 became captain of HMS *Victory*. This post ensured that he would forever be associated with Nelson, playing an important role in the Battle of Trafalgar and in the well-known story of Nelson's death. Perhaps Nelson's closest friend, he was the antithesis of the admiral: a large, calm and unflappable man with no great conversational or literary abilities but a

wise and cool head and a most experienced seaman, a perfect foil for the more volatile Nelson. In 1806 he received a baronetcy in recognition of Trafalgar, commanded HMS *Triumph* on the North America station 1806–9 (and married the daughter of his commander, Sir George Berkeley), served as his father-in-law's flag-captain on the Lisbon station (1809), and commanded HMS *Ramillies* during the War of 1812. He commanded on the South America station from 1818, when his diplomatic tact at a time of difficulty won many plaudits, and in 1826 commanded the naval contingent which took the expeditionary force to Portugal. Rear-admiral in 1825, vice-admiral 1837, on the recommendation of William IV he was appointed First Sea Lord (1830) and in 1834 Governor of Greenwich Hospital. He died at Greenwich in 1839 and was buried in the hospital, with a miniature of Nelson in his coffin.

Broadley, A. M., and Bartelot, R. G. *Nelson's Hardy: his Life, Letters and Friends*. London, 1909; Gore, J. *Nelson's Hardy and his Wife*. 1935

HARISPE, Marshal Jean-Isidore, comte (1768–1855)

One of Napoleon's lesser subordinates, he is probably best known for his career in the Peninsular War. *Général de brigade* from 1808, *de division* 1810, comte 1813, he commanded a division under Suchet in 1811, including Saguntum, defeated O'Donnell at Castalla (July 1812), served under Suchet at Castalla in April 1813, and in December 1813 was transferred to Soult's command in the hope that he could inspire support from the inhabitants of the Basque region, being of Basque origin himself. He led his division at Orthez and Toulouse, where he lost his foot to a roundshot. Together with others who might not, under the Empire, have expected the coveted promotion to Marshal, he received this great honour in 1851.

HARRIS, Benjamin Randall (1781–1858)

'Rifleman Harris' was the author of one of the most famous memoirs of the Peninsular War. Covering his service in the 95th Rifles, it was one of the earliest accounts of life in the ranks and is justly regarded as a classic; although it has been thought that Harris was illiterate, and certainly Lieutenant Henry Curling helped him with it, or wrote it entirely from Harris' dictation, Harris had letters published under his own name in the *United Service Journal*. A native of Hampshire, he was discharged in 1814 and took up the trade of shoemaker, which he had followed in the army, and as he worked in his shop in Soho he recalled his Peninsula service as the only part of his life which seemed worthy of remembrance, recollecting the comrades, who, 'long mouldered to dust, I see again performing the acts of heroes'. He died in a Westminster workhouse, where he was described as being insane.

Harris, B. *The Recollections of Rifleman Harris*, ed. H. Curling. London, 1848 (several reprints); Stratfull, J. 'Rifleman Harris', in *Journal of the Orders and Medals Research Society*, 1995, vol. 34, pp. 63–4

HARRIS, General George, 1st Baron (1746–1829)

Although not engaged in the Napoleonic Wars, he was an important commander in the British Army during the period. The son of a clergyman, he was commissioned in 1760, served in the War of American Independence and at St. Lucia, but made his name in India, initially in the Third Mysore War. Major-general from 1794, he was Governor of

GEORGE, BARON HARRIS
(PRINT AFTER DEVIS)

Madras 1797–9 and CinC Madras until 1800, commanding the army which captured Seringapatam. Being offered only an Irish peerage, Harris declined it, and was pursued by the East India Company for six years over his share of the Seringapatam prize money, until it was confirmed to him by the Privy Council. He saw no more service after his return home in 1800, but rose to general in 1812, and finally (August 1815) was ennobled as Baron Harris of Seringapatam and Belmont, Kent.

Lushington, Rt. Hon. S. *Life of Lord Harris*. London, 1840

HARRISON, Major General William Henry (1773–1841)

WILLIAM HENRY HARRISON

Best known as the ninth President of the USA, he enjoyed a not inconsiderable military career. An army officer 1791–8 (ADC to Wayne in the Fallen Timbers campaign), Governor of Indian Territory 1801–12, his military reputation was established by his victory at Tippecanoe (7 November 1811); on the outbreak of the War of 1812 he was appointed major general of Kentucky Militia, and in August 1812 a regular brigadier general. Given command of forces in the north-west (promoted major general in March 1813), his offensive intent was checked by Wilkinson's defeat at Raisin River (January 1813) and he was forced to remain on the defensive until advancing in the autumn, when he won a notable victory at the Battle of the Thames (5 October 1813). Regarded as one of the most capable commanders in the army, Harrison seemed destined for higher command, but felt himself undermined by Secretary of War John Armstrong, who apparently disliked him. In despair Harrison offered his resignation; President Madison was absent from Washington and before he learned of it, Armstrong had accepted the resignation (May 1814), an unprecedented assumption of authority which deprived the United States of a capable general who might have progressed to greater things. Later in 1814 Harrison was employed by Madison to negotiate with the Indian peoples of the north-west; he was himself inaugurated President of the USA in March 1841, but survived in office for only a month, dying on 4 April.

HASTINGS, Francis Rawdon, 1st Marquess of, Earl of Moira (1754–1826)

Remembered principally as a distinguished Governor-General of India, the son of Sir John

FRANCIS RAWDON HASTINGS, EARL OF MOIRA
(ENGRAVING BY H. BOURNE AFTER M. A. SHEE)

Rawdon of Moira, Bt., later Earl of Moira, Francis (known as Lord Rawdon) joined the army in 1771, and after distinguished service in the War of American Independence was ennobled as Baron Rawdon in 1783. In 1789 his mother (Elizabeth Hastings, daughter of the Earl of Huntingdon) succeeded to the barony of Hastings, whereupon Rawdon changed his name to Rawdon-Hastings, and in 1793 he succeeded his father as Earl of Moira. In 1794 he commanded the force sent to reinforce the Duke of York in The Netherlands; general from September 1803, in that year he was appointed CinC Scotland, and as a supporter of the Fox–Grenville ministry, was Master-General of the Ordnance 1806–7. He made a notable political contribution via the House of Lords and was a trusted adviser of the Prince of Wales; Governor-General and CinC India 1813–23, his conduct of the Nepal War was rewarded by advancement to Marquess of Hastings (February 1817). As a testimony to the honesty of his conduct, even after so long in India he was still in need of employment, and served as Governor of Malta 1824–6.

Ross of Bladensburg, J. F. G. *The Marquess of Hastings*. Oxford, 1893

HATZFELD, General Franz Ludwig, Prince (1756–1827)

This Austrian-born Prussian soldier and diplomat is known for an incident which occurred in the immediate aftermath of Jena. As Governor of Berlin, he headed the deputation which surrendered the city to Napoleon; but he had written an account of recent events to Frederick William III which included information about the dispositions of the French Army. The dispatch was intercepted and taken to Napoleon; whereupon Hatzfeld was accused of being a spy and arrested for trial by court-martial. His doom seemed certain, but his wife begged for his life in an audience with Napoleon; Napoleon handed her the incriminating letter and indicated the fire, so that she was able to burn the only evidence of her husband's guilt. Apparently Rapp, Berthier, Caulaincourt and Duroc all appealed to Napoleon to spare Hatzfeld, and it is unlikely that there was anything of importance in the document; indeed, the whole affair may have been a ploy to enhance Napoleon's standing with the Prussians, and it was remarked that never was such a reputation for clemency earned by the sparing of an innocent man! From 1822 Hatzfeld served in the important post of Prussian Ambassador to Vienna.

HAUGWITZ, Christian August Heinrich Kurt, Count von, Freiherr von Krappitz (1752–1831)

Born in Silesia of ancient family, he entered the Prussian diplomatic service, served as minister at Vienna, and entered the cabinet. Not an ardent opponent of the French Revolution, he accepted Prussia's early opposition but was influential in the policy which led to Prussia's separate peace with France in 1795. French successes deflected him from his policy of neutrality, but the king ignored his advice and in 1804 Haugwitz retired, to be replaced by Hardenberg. In 1805, with increasing concern over French intentions, he was restored as Foreign Minister as Hardenberg's colleague. But when in late 1805 he was charged with delivering an ultimatum to France he procrastinated until the war was decided by Austerlitz, Prussia having delayed too long to play any role in the campaign. Instead of threatening support for Austria and Russia, Haugwitz signed the Treaty of Schönbrunn; but the humiliation of the Prussian minister was only completed in February 1806 when he went to Paris for ratification of the treaty. Here he was forced to accept even tougher terms, Prussia being faced with compliance or a war for which she was not prepared militarily. Haugwitz remained in office until after Jena, then retired to his estates in Silesia, and because of declining health went to Italy in 1820. Although a polished intellectual with a charming manner, he probably lacked the determination to become a statesman of the highest order.

HAUTPOUL, General Jean-Joseph-Ange, comte de (1754–1807)

Remembered as a general of cuirassiers, he was a member of an old, noble family, joined the French Army as a volunteer in 1771 and was commissioned in 1777. After service in command of a regiment during the early Revolutionary Wars, he was almost deprived of his rank because of his noble blood (1794), but his men threatened revolt if he were removed (despite his noble background he had a bluff manner and uncomplicated speech which enhanced his popularity with his soldiers). He served at Fleurus, became *général de brigade* (1795) and *de division* (1797); especially distinguished at Altenkirchen 1796, where he was wounded) he was blamed by Jourdan for the defeat at Stockach (March 1799) but was exonerated by court-martial. He served as a cavalry general under Moreau, notably at Hohenlinden, and in 1805 led the 2nd Heavy Cavalry Division at Austerlitz with especial distinction; he temporarily resigned his command on being appointed a senator but was reinstated for the war against Prussia, and fought at Jena. Participating in the great cavalry charges at Eylau, he was hit in the right thigh by grapeshot; attended by two of the greatest medical experts, they offered conflicting advice. Although the femur was fractured, Percy believed the limb could be saved; Larrey recommended amputation to save his life. D'Hautpoul took Percy's advice, kept his leg, but died three days later. The loss of so great a general of heavy cavalry was felt severely.

HAWKESBURY, Baron, see **LIVERPOOL**

HAXO, General François-Nicolas-Benoît, baron (1774–1838)

Born into a military family – his uncle and namesake died as *général de brigade* in the Vendée in March 1794 – he was commissioned in the French Army in 1792. His association with the engineers, which established him as an expert on sieges and fortifications, endured for his entire career. He played an important part in the crossing of the Alps in 1800, and remained in Italy until in 1807 he went with Sébastiani to the Ottoman Empire, to advise on the defences of the Dardanelles. As *chef de bataillon* he commanded the attack on the right flank during the second siege of Saragossa, was appointed chief engineer to the Army of Aragon and was appointed *général de brigade* (June 1810), an imperial aide (March 1811) and a baron. For the Russian campaign of 1812 he was chief engineer of I Corps, and became *général de division* in December; in 1813 he was Governor of Magdeburg before becoming commandant of the Guard engineers, and was wounded and captured at Kulm. He accepted the restoration and accompanied the king into exile on Napoleon's return, but turned back at the border and rejoined his old commander; he served bravely at Ligny and Waterloo and was appointed by Davout to open negotiations with the king, whose return he favoured. His reputation as a fortification expert ensured his continued employment (from February 1816), in both administrative and active duties; probably his most important work was done at this time, during his tenure as Inspector-General of Fortifications, in reconstructing the old fortifications which had failed to deter the Allies in 1814 and 1815. Chief engineer of the Army of the North in 1831, the capture of Antwerp established him as the leading military engineer of the day; in that year he was appointed to the Council of State, became a peer of France in 1832 but retired on grounds of ill-health in 1833. One of the best engineers of the period, only his transfer of allegiance between imperial and royal masters in 1814–15 tended to mar his reputation.

HAY, Major-General Andrew (1762–1814)

One of comparatively few British generals to be killed in action during the Napoleonic Wars, he was commissioned in 1779, led the 3/1st in the Corunna campaign and a brigade of Graham's division at Walcheren. From September 1810 he commanded a brigade of the 5th Division in the Peninsula (and at times in 1813 the whole division), and was major-general from June 1811. He was killed resisting the sortie from Bayonne (14 April 1814); his obituary described him as 'a most zealous and able officer, whose whole life was spent in the service of his country, and who in every situation entitled himself to the esteem of his commanders, to the friendship of his brother officers, and to the care of his men'.[1] His reputation elsewhere was different; Frederick Robinson, who held an equivalent command, described him as 'a fool and I verily believe, with others on my side, an arrant Coward. That he is a paltry, plundering old wretch is established beyond doubt … he ought not to be a General';[2] a salutary reminder of the differences evident between some published praise and reality. Hay's eldest son, Captain George Hay, 1st Foot, was killed as his ADC at Vittoria. Andrew Hay should not be confused with other noted officers of his name, including William Hay of the 52nd Light Infantry and 12th Light Dragoons, author of *Reminiscences under Wellington*; James Hay, commander of the 16th Light Dragoons at Waterloo and subsequently lieutenant-general; Lord James Hay and James, Lord Hay, both officers of the 1st Foot Guards in the Waterloo campaign, the latter killed at Quatre Bras; Sir Andrew Leith-Hay, ADC to General Leith and author of *Narrative of the Peninsular War*; and Colonel Alexander Hay, MP, who raised the 109th Aberdeenshire Highlanders in 1794.

1. *Gent's Mag.*, May, 1814, p. 517. 2. 'A Peninsular Brigadier', ed. C. T. Atkinson, in *Journal of the Society for Army Historical Research*, 1956, vol. XXXIV, p. 168.

HAYNAU, General Julius Jacob, Freiherr von (1786–1853)

One of those whose fame was established by services subsequent to the Napoleonic Wars, he was a natural son of Wilhelm IX, Landgrave and later Elector of Hesse–Cassel. He began his military career in the Austrian Army in 1801 and saw much service during the Napoleonic Wars, notably at Wagram (wounded) and in Italy 1813–14. Although *Feldmarschall-Leutnant* by 1847, his violent temper caused trouble with superiors, and he was also renowned for his hatred of revolutionaries. When acting (very effectively) against the revolutionary outbreaks of 1848–9, notably at Brescia and in Hungary, he gained a reputation for brutality; and though attaining the rank of *Feldzeugmeister*, he resigned in 1850 after a quarrel with the Minister of War. His reputation preceded him when travelling abroad: attacked by a mob in Brussels; when visiting the brewery of Barclay and Perkins in Southwark he was assaulted by the draymen who evidently thought that pitching him into the Thames would be an appropriate way of registering their disapproval!

HEATH, William (d.1840)

This artist (who described himself as ex-captain of Dragoons but apparently was not) was best known for his many vivid battle-scenes, published in *Martial Achievements of Great Britain* (1814), *Campaigns of Wellington* (1818), *The Wars of Wellington* (1818) and, in collaboration with others, in Orme's *Historic Military and Naval Anecdotes*; his battle-scenes are impressive, sometimes frenetic, though the minutiae of costume-detail (especially those of foreign troops) is not exact. He also produced several series of uniform prints of the post-Napoleonic era, was also known for topographical and sporting prints, and was a noted caricaturist and satirist, under his own name and as 'Paul Pry'; some of his caricatures of Wellington are renowned.

HEBERT, Jacques-René (1757–94)

Born at Alençon, the son of a goldsmith, but who lived in Paris in great poverty, he became known for his vehement revolutionary agitation, expressed through his journal *Père Duchesne* (1790–4), which title also became his nickname. On 10 August 1792 he became a member of the revolutionary Commune, and in May 1793 he was arrested over the vehemence of his attacks on the Girondins, but released thanks to pressure by the mob. He was especially brutal in his criticisms of the royal family, and his suggestions about the morals of Marie-Antoinette disgusted even the most ardent anti-monarchists; he attempted, with Chaumette, to institute the worship of Reason, but his attack on Robespierre led to the arrest and execution of the Hébertist faction. He was guillotined on 24 March 1794; his wife, an ex-nun, was executed some three weeks later.

Walter, G. *Hébert*. 1939

HEGEL, George Wilhelm Friedrich (1770–1831)

The great German philosopher had no very personal involvement in the Napoleonic Wars, but was an admirer of Napoleon, and did not regard the defeat of Prussia in the same way as many of his contemporaries, who thought it a disaster. Hegel was resident in Jena in 1806 and saw Napoleon at the time of the battle; he regarded the emperor as a force for transformation, of reason and freedom. He wrote of Napoleon as the 'world-soul' (*Weltseele*), a single man, astride a single horse, at a single point, yet reaching out to dominate the world, the *Zeitgeist* or spirit of the time; this sight of Napoleon impressed him immensely and represented to him an embodiment of change.

HELY-HUTCHINSON, General John, see **HUTCHINSON**

HENRIOT (or Hanriot), François (1761–94)

A leading orator and Parisian revolutionary, he came to prominence at the time of the September massacres (1792), and from mid-1793 was commandant of the armed forces of Paris, a position of great power. A supporter of Robespierre, upon the coup of 9 Thermidor (27 July 1794) he endeavoured to mobilise his troops to rescue Robespierre, but, the Convention having outlawed him, his gunners refused to obey his orders to fire upon the Convention. Henriot attempted to escape but was discovered and bayoneted by the troops who apprehended him; dreadfully wounded, he was guillotined together with Robespierre on the following day.

HERAULT DE SECHELLES, Marie-Jean (1759–94)

Parisian-born and of noble blood, Hérault de Séchelles was a lawyer who embraced the Revolution; President of both the Legislative Assembly and the Convention, he was also employed on other duties, notably missions to Alsace (1791) and to organise the *département* of Mont Blanc during the king's trial (though absent, he expressed a preference for a capital sentence). He prepared the 1793 Constitution, and as a member of the Committee of Public Safety went on a mission to Alsace (October–December 1793) which made others suspicious of him, notably Robespierre;

accused of treason, he was condemned and executed on 5 April 1794. He was remarked upon for the care of his dress and love of literature – in which he was considerably skilled – which would have been more appropriate to the *ancien régime* but which elicited sarcastic comments from some of his revolutionary colleagues.

HEUDELET DE BIERRE, General Etienne, comte (1770–1857)

Perhaps best remembered as the commander of one of the most costly attacks delivered during the period, he was commissioned in 1792, served with distinction with the Army of the Rhine and at Zurich and Hohenlinden. *Général de brigade* from February 1799, at Austerlitz he led the 1st Brigade of Friant's 2nd Division of Davout's III Corps and was promoted to *général de division* in the same month. He commanded the 2nd Division of Augereau's VII Corps at Jena, and with his fellow divisional commander Jacques Desjardins led the catastrophic attack of Augereau's corps at Eylau. Blinded by driving snow, it veered from its intended route and marched into the mouth of Russian artillery; the entire formation was devastated, Desjardins killed and Heudelet wounded. Ennobled as comte in 1808, Heudelet was sent to the Peninsula; from November that year he led the 3rd Division of Junot's VIII Corps, which later became the 4th Division of Soult's II Corps. In Soult's absence he took command of II Corps, and led its 2nd Division at Busaco; he returned home on sick leave in June 1811 and in the 1812 Russian campaign commanded the 30th Division of XI Corps. He was besieged with Rapp in Danzig and captured upon its surrender; having rallied to Napoleon in 1815 he was posted to the Army of the Rhine under Rapp, but was unengaged. He retired from active service after the Hundred Days, but, although subsequently holding some relatively unimportant posts, was not retired officially until 1848.

HILL, General Rowland, 1st Viscount (1772–1842)

ROWLAND, VISCOUNT HILL

Wellington's most able and trusted subordinate, 2i/c during the later Peninsular War, he had an even more meritorious claim to celebrity: such was his kindness and concern for the ordinary troops that he was known as 'the soldier's friend' and nicknamed by them 'Daddy Hill'. Born in Shropshire, one of sixteen children of Sir John Hill of Hawkstone and nephew of the famous preacher Revd. Rowland Hill (1744–1833, joint founder of the British and Foreign Bible Society and the London Missionary Society), he was commissioned in 1790. He served at Toulon, commanded the 90th in Egypt, but made his name in the Peninsula. At Vimeiro he led the 1st Brigade, at Corunna a brigade in the 2nd Division, and then Wellington's 2nd Division (June 1809 to November 1810); and after his return from sick leave in May 1811 resumed command until March 1813 when he became virtually a semi-independent corps commander, leading the army's right wing at Vittoria and after. The victory of Arroyo dos Molinos (1811) was entirely his; lieutenant-general from January 1812 and knighted (by bestowal of the KB) in the following March, he continued as Wellington's closest deputy until the end of the Peninsular war (especially distinguished at Nivelle and Nive; at St. Pierre Wellington declared that the glory was his alone). He was rewarded with the barony of Hill of Almaraz and Hawkstone, the former named from the position he carried in May 1812; and in the Waterloo campaign he led I Corps, arriving just in time to lead Adam's brigade at the end of the battle. Second in command of the Army of Occupation in France (1815–18), he became a full general in 1825 and from 1828 until shortly before his death was CinC; he was advanced to a viscountcy upon his retirement. Although he was never to exercise command completely independent of Wellington's supervision, he was perhaps the only one to enjoy the Duke's complete trust; at his death, Wellington wrote to the nephew who succeeded him (Hill never married) that during his entire career, 'nothing ever occurred to interrupt for one moment the friendly and intimate relations which subsisted between us'.[1] Sir William Fraser stated that 'he was not, I believe, a man of very great abilities; but he had one great merit in the eyes of the Duke: who said "Hill does what he is told"';[2] but there was much more to him than that. Viscount Hill should not be confused with his namesake, Rowland Hill (1795–1879), inventor of the Penny Post.

1. Griffiths, p. 295. 2. Fraser, p. 182.

Sidney, Revd. E. *The Life of Lord Hill*. London, 1845; Teffeteller, G. L. *The Surpriser*. Newark, N. J., 1983

HILLER, General Johann, Freiherr (1754–1819)

One of the foremost Austrian commanders of the era, he entered the artillery in 1770 and gained campaign experience against the Ottoman Empire (1788–91) before embarking on his long career of fighting against the French. Evidently he was never an easy subordinate, being involved in disagreements with superiors and harbouring especial dislike of the Archduke Charles. Some conflict was evident in 1807 when, as *Feldmarschall-Leutnant* commanding the Karlstadt units of the *Grenzer* forces on the Military Border, he complained that the 1807 code covering the Border and its defences did not address the real problems experienced by his troops; to which the Archduke claimed that it was Hiller who was encouraging unrest among the *Grenzers*. For the 1809 campaign, for which Hiller is perhaps best remembered, he was given command of VI Corps, the only one not entrusted to a prince or to a member of the old aristocracy. He was involved in the defeat at Abensberg, commanded at the reverse of Ebersberg, and was involved in the attack on the extreme left of Napoleon's position at Aspern–Essling, Hiller making great efforts to capture Aspern. Having gone on sick leave after this battle, just before Wagram Hiller again left his corps on grounds of ill-health, after much complaining about the exposed position in which his corps had been placed, in expectation of French attack, perhaps evidence of internal conflicts within the Austrian command structure; he was succeeded in command by *Feldmarschall-Leutnant* Johann Klenau. Promoted to *Feldzeugmeister*, in 1813 Hiller commanded the Austrian forces opposing Eugène in Italy, his slow progress leading to criticism and in November 1813 to his replacement in command by Heinrich Bellegarde.

Rauchensteiner, M. *Feldzeugmeister Johann, Freiherr von Hiller*. Vienna, 1972

HILLIERS, General Louis Baraguey de, see BARAGUEY D'HILLIERS

HOCHE, General Lazare (1768–97)

LAZARE HOCHE
(ENGRAVING BY W. GREATBATCH)

One of the leading military personalities of the era, he was of humble birth but with natural abilities, intelligence and courage which led to rapid advancement after the Revolution. Having enrolled in the *Gardes françaises* in 1784, he was commissioned in 1792, was distinguished at Thionville and Neerwinden and, surviving suspicion over Dumouriez's defection (of which he was acquitted), became *général de brigade* in September 1793 and *de division* in the following month. At the age of only 25 he was appointed to command the Army of the Moselle (October 1793), was defeated at Kaiserslautern but then enjoyed success, until in March 1794 he was arrested on allegations of treason made by Pichegru. Released from imprisonment after the fall of Robespierre, he was appointed to suppress the rising in the Vendée, which he accomplished with great skill, defeating the royalist landing at Quiberon and by the use of mobile columns pacifying the whole of the western theatre with a humanity not previously evident in the civil war in that region. In July 1796 he was appointed to lead the expedition to Ireland, which was abandoned because of bad weather, and in February 1797 was given command of the Army of the Sambre and Meuse, and won the victory of Neuweid. In July he was made Minister of War, even though he was younger than the age allowed by the constitution (30 years), but soon resigned and returned to the army as a protest against his unwitting involvement in Barras' intrigues. Hoche suddenly became ill, perhaps with consumption (a violent cough was one of his symptoms), and died on 19 September 1797; the rapid demise of so young and vigorous a man caused suggestions of poison but these were almost certainly unfounded. Lejeune, who had been his ADC, said that 'he could only just read and sign his name but he was a fine fellow, and his courage was indomitable',[1] while Napoleon remarked that he was one of the best generals France had ever produced, and might well have enjoyed a glittering career had he lived.

1. Lejeune, vol. I, p. 12.

Bonnechose, F. P. E. B. de *Lazare Hoche ... 1793–97*. Cambridge, 1888; Charavaray, E. *Le Général Hoche*. 1893

HOFER, Andreas (1767–1810)

A Tyrolean innkeeper from St Leonhard, he was one of the most devoted supporters of Austria and its emperor. He had had some experience of campaigning against the French prior to 1805 and after the Tyrol was trans ferred from Austrian to Bavarian rule by the Treaty of Pressburg (1805), in 1808 he was one of a deputation which went to Vienna to be encouraged to revolt. This occurred with some success in April 1809, and the rebels were assured by Austria that no peace would be made which did not restore the Tyrol to Habsburg control; yet following the defeat of that year, Austria confirmed Bavaria in possession. As leader of the insurgents, Hofer had ruled the area from Innsbruck in the name of the emperor, but was now virtually abandoned; under the amnesty specified by the Treaty of Schönbrunn he and his followers submitted, but in November 1809 issued a call for renewed resistance. Unable to repeat the previous defeats of the invading forces, which arrived in overwhelming numbers, Hofer had to seek safety in the mountains, but was betrayed and captured (January 1810); he was taken to Mantua, court-martialled and shot (29 February). His death – which Napoleon said he regretted, having been impelled by his generals to sanction execution – created outrage in Germany, Austria and other states hostile to France, and caused embarrassment to Austria which was thought to have abandoned a faithful servant. A British paean of praise concluded:

Yes, gallant Chief! though tyrant hate
Awhile may blot th' historic page,
Yet shall thy virtues flourish great
Through many a distant age:
Applauding worlds shall yet revere thy name.
And wreaths of future praise immortalize thy Fame.'[1]

In belated acknowledgements of Hofer's loyalty and his victories against France and Bavaria, his family was ennobled by the emperor in 1818.

1. 'Ode to the Memory of Hoffer (sic), The Tyrolese Patriot', by 'Oscar', in *Gent's Mag.*, Aug, 1810, p. 162.

Eyck, F. G. *Loyal Rebels: Andreas Hofer and the Tyrolean Uprising of 1809*. New York, 1986; Hormayer zu Hortenburg, J. *Memoirs of the Life of Andrew Hofer*, trans. C. H. Hall. London, 1820

HOHENLOHE-INGELFINGEN, General Friedrich Ludwig, Prince of (1746–1818)

A member of a distinguished princely family from the Hohenlohe district of Franconia, son of Prince Johann Friedrich of Hohenlohe-Ingelfingen (whom he succeeded in 1796), he at first served against the Prussians at the end of the Seven Years War, but then entered their service and rose to the rank of general officer. In 1793 he was distinguished at Kaiserslautern, became one of the most popular Prussian generals, and in 1806 was given command of the Prussian left. This was not a particularly felicitous appointment: he was not in good health and unduly influenced by his chief of staff, Colonel Christian von Massenbach, whose military judgement was very seriously flawed. Following the defeat of Jena, Hohenlohe rallied part of the army and retired, but surrendered at Prenzlau on 28 October 1806, again under the influence of Massenbach, a capitulation which affected adversely the resolution of the commandants of Prussian fortresses. After two years as a prisoner of war, Hohenlohe retired to his estates; just before the outbreak of hostilities he had handed over his principality to his eldest son. Prince Friedrich Ludwig should not be confused with other distinguished soldiers who bore the name Hohenlohe. These included: **Friedrich Wilhelm, Prince of Hohenlohe–Kirchberg**, *Feldzeugmeister* in the Austrian Army, who commanded imperial forces in The Netherlands and on the German frontier (1792–4); and **Ludwig Aloysius, Prince of Hohenlohe-Waldenburg-Bartenstein (1765–1829)**, who commanded his father's regiment in the *Armée de Condé*, after a period in Dutch service entered the Austrian Army (1794), rose to the rank of general officer and was appointed Governor of Galicia. After the Bourbon restoration he entered French service, served in the Spanish campaign of 1823 and in 1827 became a Marshal and peer of France. Friedrich Ludwig's nephew, **Kraft, Prince of Hohenlohe-Ingelfingen (1827–92)**, was a distinguished Prussian general and writer on tactics, for example *Conversations on Cavalry*, London, 1897.

HOOD, Admiral Alexander, see **BRIDPORT**

HOOD, Admiral Samuel, 1st Viscount (1724–1816)

SAMUEL, VISCOUNT HOOD
(PRINT AFTER LEMUEL ABBOT)

With an active naval career mostly prior to the Napoleonic Wars, he had entered the Royal Navy in 1741 and gained much distinction. Rear-admiral and baronet in 1780, he was ennobled as Baron Hood of

Catherington in September 1782 for his part in the defeat of De Grasse off Dominica; full admiral from April 1794 and a member of the Board of Admiralty 1788–93, he was CinC Mediterranean from May 1793 to October 1794, his operations including the occupations of Toulon and Corsica. Disagreements with the military commanders, and political enmities led to his recall in October 1794, and he was not again employed at sea; his recall was greeted with dismay, notably by Nelson, who bemoaned the fact that the Admiralty had thus deprived the nation of its greatest admiral, who despite his age had the mind of a 40-year-old. Hood himself blamed Spencer who, he claimed, had not only treated him badly but had extended his prejudice to all his friends and protégés, whom he recommended not to mention their association with him, lest it blight their careers. In June 1796 he was advanced to the rank of Viscount Hood of Whitely, Co. Warwick, and in the same year became Governor of Greenwich Hospital, which post he held until his death. His younger brother was Admiral Viscount Bridport, his cousin's son was Vice-Admiral Sir Samuel Hood, and his eldest grandson, Lieutenant-Colonel Samuel Wheler Hood of the 3rd Foot Guards, was killed at Aire on 2 March 1814, serving as assistant adjutant-general to the 2nd Division.

Hood, D. *The Admirals Hood*. London, 1942; Rose, J. Holland. *Lord Hood and the Defence of Toulon*. Cambridge, 1922. An account of the Hood family appears in Cust, Sir Edward. *Annals of the Wars of the Eighteenth Century*. London, 1862, vol. V, pp. 287–9

HOOD, Vice-Admiral Sir Samuel, Bt. (1762–1814)

He entered the Royal Navy in 1776 and served under his father's cousin, Sir Samuel (later Viscount) Hood, in the West Indies and Mediterranean, including Toulon. He commanded HMS *Zealous* at Aboukir Bay, HMS *Venerable* at Algeciras, and in 1802 became commodore on the Leewards station, helping to reduce French holdings in the region, and most notably commissioned Diamond Rock as a sloop to block the approach to Martinique! Blockading Rochefort in September 1805, he lost his right arm when the French squadron trapped there were trying to escape; promoted to rear-admiral, in 1807 he commanded the operations against Madeira and the following year served in the Baltic, his flagship HMS *Centaur* with HMS *Implacable* capturing the Russian *Sevolod* (28 August 1808). After service with the fleet that evacuated the British army from Corunna, Hood returned to the Mediterranean for two years; vice-admiral in 1811, he was sent to command the East India station and died in Madras in 1814. His attitude was expressed when rescuing three drowning seamen during a West Indian hurricane: 'I never gave an order to a sailor in my life which I was not ready to undertake and execute myself.'[1] His brother, Captain Alexander Hood (1758–98), entered the Royal Navy in 1767, accompanied James Cook on his second circumnavigation, and after ill-health had prevented his serving in the early Revolutionary Wars was appointed to command HMS *Mars* in 1797; he was mortally wounded capturing the French 74-gunner *L'Hercule* on 21 April 1798.

1. Cust, vol. V, p. 287.

HOPE, General John, Earl of Hopetoun (1765–1823)

Son of the 2nd Earl of Hopetoun, he joined the army in 1784, in 1796 was adjutant-general under Abercromby in the West Indies, and

JOHN HOPE, EARL OF HOPETOUN
(PRINT BY W. WALKER AFTER RAEBURN)

served in North Holland (1799) and Egypt (wounded at Alexandria). Major-general in April 1802, lieutenant-general 1808, he served at Copenhagen, succeeded Moore in command at Corunna, commanded the reserve at Walcheren, and from October 1813 led the 1st Division in the Peninsula, replacing Graham as commander of the left wing of the army. His style of command was not especially prudent; he made an error at the beginning of the Battle of the Nive but made up for it later in the day, though hazarded himself unduly. Wellington commented: 'I have long entertained the highest opinion of Sir John Hope, in common, I believe, with the whole world ... we shall lose him, however, if he continues to expose himself in fire as he did in the last three days; indeed his escape was then wonderful. His hat and coat were shot through in many places, besides the wound in his leg. He places himself among the sharpshooters without, as they do, sheltering himself from the enemy's fire. This will not answer; and I hope that his friends will give him a hint on the subject.'[1] The Duke's prediction was accurate: Hope was wounded and captured during the sortie from Bayonne on 14 April 1814. In May 1814 he was ennobled as Baron Niddry, became a full general in 1819, and succeeded his half-brother as 4th Earl of Hopetoun in May 1817. (James, 3rd Earl 1741–1817, had raised and commanded the Hopetoun (or South) Fencibles 1793–9.) The 4th Earl should not be confused with his namesake (as below) nor with General Sir James Archibald Hope, who was ADC to Graham, carried the Barossa dispatch and served throughout the Peninsular War, latterly as Hope's ADC.

1. Wellington, 15 Dec 1813, vol. XI, pp. 371–2.

HOPE, Lieutenant-General Sir John (1765–1836)

Not to be confused with his more illustrious namesake, he served in the Dutch forces 1778–82; deputy adjutant-general in the expeditions to Hanover (1805) and Denmark (1807), he took command of the 7th Division in the Peninsula in May 1813. In this position he was undistinguished, and Wellington appears to have seized the opportunity of disposing of him: when Hope complained of rheumatism, Wellington immediately told him to go home and be cured; he left the army on 23 September 1813. He received a knighthood of the Bath in January 1815 and became lieutenant-general in 1819.

HOSTE, Captain Sir William, Bt. (1780–1828)

A protégé of Nelson, he served under him in the Mediterranean, having entered the Royal Navy in 1793; a lieutenant in HMS *Theseus* at Aboukir Bay, he became a captain in 1802 and made his name in the Mediterranean, with frigate attacks on enemy warships, merchantmen and shore establishments which also brought him a considerable fortune in prize money (most of which went to pay his father's debts). His great victory was off Lissa on 13 March 1811 when, with his flagship HMS *Amphion* and three other frigates, he engaged a squadron of three French and three Venetian frigates, and a Venetian brig, two schooners, a xebec and a gunboat. Two of the enemy frigates were taken, one destroyed and a fourth surrendered but escaped. Hoste spent the remainder of the war in the Mediterranean, latterly in poor health (a precursor of the tuberculosis which killed him), and he did not again serve at sea (though was captain of the royal yacht *Royal Sovereign*). He became a baronet in 1814. His younger brother, Lieutenant-Colonel Sir George Hoste, served at Waterloo as a captain in the Royal Engineers.

Hoste, Lady Harriet. *The Memoirs and Letters of Captain Sir William Hoste*. London, 1833; Pocock, T. *Remember Nelson: The Life of Captain Sir William Hoste*. London, 1977

HOTHAM, Admiral William, 1st Baron (1736–1813)

Son of Sir Beaumont Hotham, 7th Baronet, descendant of the Hothams executed by parliament in 1645 for correspondence with royalists, he entered the Royal Navy in 1751, served in the Seven Years War and the War of American Independence, became rear-admiral in 1787, vice-admiral in 1790 and admiral in 1795. Hood's deputy in the Mediterranean, he succeeded to command when that admiral was unfairly recalled, and fought an inconclusive action against a French squadron, in which two French ships were captured (13–14 March 1795). Nelson, whose HMS *Agamemnon* played a leading role in the action, was not alone in thinking Hotham too cautious in not pursuing, and was even more critical of the action on 13 July 1795 when Hotham's fleet was in a position to engage the French off Toulon, after a chase, only for the over-cautious admiral to signal withdrawal after one French ship had struck and then blown up. Hotham received no official censure for his timidity, but shortly afterwards returned home and in March 1797 was ennobled as Baron Hotham of South Dalton (Yorkshire). He should not be confused with other naval officers of the same name, notably his nephew (son of Beaumont the 2nd Baron, who succeeded William who had no children), Vice-Admiral Sir Henry Hotham (1777–1833), who saw much service in the Napoleonic Wars, became vice-admiral in 1825 and died at Malta commanding the Mediterranean Fleet; and another nephew, son of William's brother George, Admiral Sir William Hotham (1772–1848), who also served in the Napoleonic Wars, notably at Camperdown. The brother George (1741–1806) was a general. The grandson of the 2nd Baron, Beaumont Hotham (1794–1870) who succeeded as 3rd Baron in 1814, served in the Peninsula and at Waterloo as a lieutenant in the 2nd Foot Guards, subsequently rising to the rank of general officer.

HOWDEN, Baron, see CRADOCK

HOWE, Admiral Richard, Earl (1726–99)

'Black Dick' Howe (so called from his swarthy complexion) is one of the great figures of British maritime history. The son of 2nd Viscount Howe and Maria Sophia Charlotte von Kielmansegge (daughter of George I's Hanoverian Master of Horse and of the king's mistress, the Countess of Darlington), he went to sea in 1740 and won great distinction during the War of the Austrian Succession, Seven Years War and Jacobite

RICHARD, EARL HOWE
(ENGRAVING BY FRY AFTER DUPONT)

Rebellion. In 1758 he succeeded to the family viscountcy on the death of his brother, Brigadier-General George Augustus, 3rd Viscount, at Ticonderoga; rear-admiral in 1770, vice-admiral 1775, he played an important role in the War of American Independence both as naval commander and, because of his sympathy with the colonists, as peace commissioner; his brother, Sir William Howe (1729–1814), who succeeded as 5th Viscount, was principal military commander in America until 1778. Richard carried out the relief of Gibraltar, was First Lord of the Admiralty 1783–8 and in August of the latter year became an earl; in 1793 he took command of the Channel Fleet and led it at the crowning achievement of his career, the Battle of the Glorious First of June (1794). Although this ended his active career, he remained in nominal command until 1797, in which year he performed one of his most valuable services, intervening in the naval mutinies; despite his age he spent three days rowing round the fleet at Spithead to inform the seamen of the king's pardon, and was so well trusted by the sailors that all was settled with equanimity; not without reason was he known as 'the sailor's friend'. In addition to consummate seamanship and professional skill – Collingwood wrote that the Battle of the First of June was conducted with such skill that it was like magic – despite a taciturn and reserved demeanour, Howe had great courage and legendary calmness in times of crisis; once, when informed that his ship was on fire, he merely observed, 'If that be the case, we shall soon know it'![1]

1. Cust, vol. IV, p. 311 (which contains a brief biographical notice).

Barrow, Sir John. *The Life of Richard, Earl Howe*. London, 1838

HOWICK, Lord, see **GREY, 2nd Earl**

HUGUES, Victor (1770–1828)
Perhaps the most notable personality in the French involvement in the West Indies, he had been a businessman and commissary in San Domingo when the revolt began, then returned to France and, as an ardent supporter of the Revolution, became prosecutor for revolutionary tribunals at Rochefort. Sent in 1794 as commissioner to Guadeloupe, he conducted a skilful campaign which forced the British to abandon the island; royalist inhabitants were massacred, and so tightly did he consolidate his power that he was nicknamed 'the colonial Robespierre'. From Guadeloupe he attempted to initiate slave revolts in islands controlled by the British, which he supported with troops and supplies, and organised privateers to attack British trade. These efforts caused great trouble to the British in the region, but although confirmed in his position by the Directory, Hugues lost favour with Paris over his independence, suspected peculation and many allegations about his private life (as a menace to women). It is perhaps a measure of his style of rule that he ordered the body of General Thomas Dundas, British commander on Guadeloupe who had died of yellow fever in the spring of 1794, to be disinterred and flung away, and erected a monument to commemorate the deed. Reports of his conduct and his increasingly arrogant attitude caused the Directory to arrest him and return him to France (1798), although he was re-employed as Governor of Cayenne and held offices throughout the Empire and even after the restoration. His achievements as virtual dictator of Guadeloupe, however, had been considerable, both in waging war against the British and in pursuing a social policy wherein slavery was abolished and racial discrimination to a large extent suppressed.

HUGO, Victor-Marie (1802–85)
This great literary figure is not always associated with the Napoleonic era, despite his keen interest in Waterloo (as expressed in *Les Misérables*), yet his background was firmly rooted in the Napoleonic Wars. His father was a French general, Joseph Leopold Sigisbert Hugo (1777–1828), and his mother, Sophie Trébuchet (d.1821) a Vendéen royalist, a conflict of beliefs which led to their separation. Joseph Hugo served as aide to Joseph Bonaparte in Naples and followed him to Spain (where for a time the child Victor lived), became Governor of Avila and was ennobled as count of Siguenza. Ultimately, General Hugo was posted to Thionville, which he held until the end of hostilities in 1814.

HULL, Commodore Isaac (1775–1843)
Born in Derby, Connecticut, Hull was one of the leading American naval officers of the War of 1812. Commissioned in the US Navy in 1798, he served against the Barbary corsairs and became captain in 1806. At the beginning

ISAAC HULL

WILHELM VON HUMBOLDT
(PRINT AFTER F. KRÜGER)

of the War of 1812 he commanded USS *Constitution*, a large and excellent frigate, with which on 19 August 1812 he captured the British frigate HMS *Guerrière* in a dramatic action; and although the British ship was inferior in guns, so accustomed to victory had the British become that this defeat was an enormous shock to national prestige. Having been on the point of replacement before the action, Hull stepped down from command of *Constitution* after the victory, but his fame was established; he received a gold medal from Congress and the freedom of New York. He held commands after the war and was naval commissioner 1815–17. He was a nephew of General William Hull.

HULL, Brigadier General William (1753–1825)

The unfortunate William Hull must have been among the least competent general officers of the period. Born in Derby, Connecticut, and educated in law, he had served in the War of Independence and risen to lieutenant colonel and was regarded as a brave, capable officer. Governor of Michigan Territory from 1805, he accepted the post of brigadier general (April 1812) with some

reluctance, and command of the army which was to defend the region. Perhaps his age, lack of resources, the magnitude of the task and the unwise strategy of Dearborn conspired to produce inept leadership; his attempted invasion of Upper Canada was over in a very few days, and he was virtually bluffed into surrendering his army at Detroit by Isaac Brock (16 August 1812). Paroled in September 1812, he was court-martialled on charges of treason, cowardice and neglect of duty; Dearborn, whose plans had contributed to the defeat, was president of the court. He was absolved of treason but otherwise convicted, and a general order of 25 April 1814 announced that the rolls of the army were no longer disgraced by including his name. Sentenced to be shot, he was pardoned by the President and retired to private life, maintaining to the last that he had been right to surrender Detroit, losing his reputation but saving its inhabitants. His adopted nephew was Isaac Hull, whose great victory over HMS *Guerrière* occurred just three days after the capitulation at Detroit.

Campbell, Mrs M., and Clarke, J. F. (Hull's daughter and grandson). *The Revolutionary Services and Civil Life of General William Hull ... with the History of the Campaign of 1812*. 1814; Hull, W. *Memoirs of the Campaign of the North Western Army of the United States, A.D. 1812*. 1824

HUMBOLDT, Karl Wilhelm, Freiherr von (1767–1835)

Elder brother of the celebrated naturalist and explorer Friedrich Heinrich Alexander von Humboldt (1769–1859), he is probably most remembered as a philologist, philosopher and friend of Schiller, but he also pursued an important diplomatic career. In 1802 he was appointed Prussian Ambassador

at Rome, and after a brief meeting with Napoleon was initially an admirer, but his opinion changed after Jena and in 1809 he returned to Prussia as councillor of state and minister of public instruction. Subsequently he was minister to Vienna, and played an important role in the conclusion of the Congress of Prague, which allied Austria with Russia and Prussia against Napoleon. He attended the Congress of Vienna, was a signatory to the capitulation of Paris, and was involved in deciding the Saxon question, in which he disagreed with Hardenberg. He attended the congress at Aix-la-Chapelle but in 1819 left politics over his disagreement with repressive policies, and spent the remainder of his life in the literary work for which he is most famous.

Sweet, P. R. *Wilhelm von Humboldt, a Biography*. Columbus, Ohio, 1980

HUNTLY, Marquess of, see GORDON, Alexander, 4th Duke of

HUTCHINSON, General John Hely, Baron, 2nd Earl of Donoughmore (1757–1832)

Son of the Provost of Trinity College Dublin and Secretary of State for Ireland, as a major-general he had commanded in Connaught during the 1798 rebellion, commanding at Castlebar before Lake arrived and not especially blameworthy for the defeat. He led a brigade in North Holland in 1799 and was wounded in the thigh, but is best known as Abercromby's deputy in the expedition to Egypt. He was not a popular choice when he succeeded to command after Abercromby's death; though a student of his profession and personally brave, his manner was ungracious, appearance untidy, temper short and he had poor health and very bad eyesight. So unpopular was his command that some officers thought he should be deprived of his position and replaced by Moore, an outrageous suggestion akin to open mutiny which was silenced instantly by Moore himself. Following the successful conclusion of the campaign, he was ennobled as Baron Hutchinson of Alexandria and Knocklofty; was British commissioner at Allied headquarters in 1807 and in 1825 succeeded his brother as 2nd Earl of Donoughmore. The nephew who succeeded him as 3rd Earl was John Hely Hutchinson (1787–1851) who, as a captain in the 1st Foot Guards, was one of those who assisted the escape of Lavalette after of the Hundred Days.

JOHN HELY HUTCHINSON, EARL OF DONOUGHMORE (ENGRAVING BY W. NICHOLLS)

IBRAHIM BEY, Emir (1735–1817)

Of European birth, he had been sold as a slave but became one of the Mameluke rulers of Egypt. After the supremacy of the Ottoman Empire had been re-asserted in Egypt by the defeat in 1773 of Ali Bey, the victorious Abu'l-Dhahab appointed as his deputies in Cairo Isma'il Bey and Ibrahim Bey, while he made war on one of Ali Bey's allies in Palestine. Dhahab died in Palestine, and Isma'il Bey was driven out by Ibrahim and Murad Bey, the latter having brought back Dhahab's forces to Egypt (1775). These two installed themselves as rulers of Egypt, Ibrahim as Sheik al-Balad, or head of state, and Murad as Amir al-Hajj, the leader of the annual pilgrimage to Mecca, which positions were the symbols of rule. Ibrahim and Murad withdrew to Upper Egypt when an Ottoman expedition re-asserted control and installed Isma'il Bey as Sheik al-Balad, but when he died in the plague of 1791, Ibrahim and Murad were called to resume their government. Defeat by Napoleon ended Ibrahim's period of power; he was unable to resist the rise of Mehemet Ali, but escaped the massacres of the Mameluke leaders. The survivors went south, ultimately to New Dongola, where Ibrahim died. He should not be confused with the earlier Ibrahim, murdered in 1755, nor with Ibrahim Pasha (1789–1848), Mehemet Ali's son, who completed the destruction of Mameluke power.

INGLIS, Lieutenant-General Sir William (1764–1835)

Son of an old Roxburghshire family, he entered the army in 1781, served in The Netherlands and West Indies, but gained fame as commander of the 57th Foot, of which he had become lieutenant-colonel in August 1804. Com-

Sir William Inglis

manding the 1st Bn in the Peninsula, he led a brigade of the 2nd Division at Busaco, and at Albuera made his name when, himself wounded, he exhorted his battalion to 'Die hard, 57th, die hard!' This exploit became almost legendary in the history of the British Army and conferred upon the 57th and the Middlesex Regiment (which title was adopted in 1881 when the number was discontinued) the nickname 'Diehards', which served to inspire successive generations of the regiment. Inglis continued to serve in the Peninsula, became major-general on 4 June 1813, lieutenant-general in 1825, was knighted by virtue of a KCB (April 1815) and held the colonelcy of the 57th from April 1830 until his death at Ramsgate.

ISABEY, Jean-Baptiste (1767–1855)

A pupil of David, and notable as a miniaturist and portraitist, Isabey became official painter to Napoleon and Josephine. He helped arrange their coronation ceremonies and designed some of the costumes, but his main celebrity arises from his brilliant miniatures of contemporary personalities. Despite being patronised by Napoleon, he was retained in favour after the

restoration, by Louis XVIII, Charles X, Louis-Philippe and Napoleon III, the latter appointing him a commander of the *Légion d'honneur*. His son, Eugène-Gabriel (1803–86), was also a notable artist, originally marine and landscape but also depicting events of the reign of Louis-Philippe.

ISNARD, Maximin (1758–1825)

An affluent wholesale perfumerer at Draguignan when elected to the Legislative Assembly and Convention, he made a notable speech in November 1791 exhorting the nation not to fear conflict with other powers. A member of the Committee of General Defence, he presented the report which led to the establishment of the Committee of Public Safety; and though as an associate of the Girondins his arrest was decreed, he escaped their fate. He was recalled to the Convention in March 1795, was sent to the *département* of the Bouches-du-Rhône where he declaimed against the Terrorists, and in 1796 was elected to the Council of Five Hundred. He retired to his home town in 1797, subsequently publishing pamphlets on the immortality of the soul and in support of the empire, and upon the restoration was so ardent a royalist that he escaped proscription as a regicide.

ISTRIE, duc d', see BESSIERES

JACKSON, Major General Andrew (1767–1845)

[Se]venth President of the United [St]ates, to which office he was [el]ected in 1828, he was one of the [m]ost able commanders of the War [of] 1812. The son of parents who [ha]d emigrated from Ireland, his [ex]periences in the War of Independ[e]nce left him with a dislike of [Gr]eat Britain. A lawyer, he became [in]volved in politics from 1796, [in]itially as a representative for [Te]nnessee, though his reputation [w]as as much for a quarrelsome [na]ture, which led to a number of [du]els, than as a political or legal [lu]minary. Despite having attacked [th]e President and his administra[tio]n, upon the declaration of war [ag]ainst Great Britain Jackson [im]mediately offered himself (as [m]ajor general of Tennessee militia) [an]d his men for service. In 1813–14 [h]e conducted a successful cam[pa]ign against the Creek nation, [cu]lminating with a victory at [H]orseshoe Bend (27 March 1814) [w]hich ended resistance, and in [A]ugust 1814 a treaty was signed at [Fo]rt Jackson which deprived the [Cr]eeks of more than half their [la]nd. Jackson's military talents [w]ere recognised by his commis[si]on as brigadier general in the [re]gular army (May 1814) with [b]revet rank of major general and [co]mmand of the 7th Military [D]istrict, based at Mobile. In [N]ovember 1814 he captured [P]ensacola, the Spanish base in [F]lorida (though the invasion of [S]panish territory was without [go]vernment sanction), and then [p]repared the defences of New [O]rleans. It was there on 8 January [18]15 that he inflicted a severe [re]verse upon the British attackers, [n]either side being aware that peace [h]ad already been signed; the defeat [w]as felt severely by the British but [en]hanced Jackson's prestige and [a]ided his political career which [w]as to culminate with the highest [o]ffice.

Heidler, D. S., and J. T. *Old Hickory's War: Andrew Jackson and the Quest for Empire*. Mechanicsburg, Pa., 1996; James, M. *Andrew Jackson, Portrait of a President*, New York, 1937

JAHN, Friedrich Ludwig (1778–1852)

A student of theology, he joined the Prussian Army after Jena and conceived the idea of the regeneration of national prestige and morale through gymnastics; his writings and advocacy of physical exercise were influential in the patriotic movement which inspired the 'War of Liberation'. In 1813 Jahn helped raise Lützow's corps and commanded a battalion, and after the war was appointed state teacher of gymnastics. Known as the father of the discipline, although his liberal inclinations caused him problems in the period after the Napoleonic Wars, in 1840 he was decorated by the Prussian government for services in the war against Napoleon.

JAY, John (1745–1820)

A native of New York and an experienced lawyer and diplomat who had risen to prominence during the War of American Independence and served as Secretary for Foreign Affairs (1784–90), he was Chief Justice when in 1794 he was sent to England in an attempt to avert Anglo–US hostilities. These were threatened over British non-compliance with the 1783 treaty which required evacuation of posts in the north-west, and other grievances including British strictures on neutral merchant vessels trading with France. The so-called 'Jay's Treaty' of November 1794 succeeded in restoring friendly relations and relieved the American merchant trade of the previous constraints. France protested and domestic opposition in the USA was considerable, but it secured peace until the War of

1812. After serving as Governor of New York State (1795–1801), Jay retired from public life.

JELLACIC VON BUZIM, General Franz, Baron von (1746–1810)

Best known for his services in 1805 and 1809, this Austrian general served against the Ottoman empire in 1789, in the Revolutionary Wars on the Rhine against Moreau, and checked Oudinot at Feldkirch (7 March 1799). *Feldmarschall-Leutnant* from 1800, in 1805 he commanded some 11,000 men which when endeavouring to withdraw into Vorarlburg were overtaken and forced to surrender by Augereau's VII Corps (14 November), only his cavalry escaping. In 1809 he suffered similar ill-fortune; commanding a detached force of 7,000 men under nominal command of the Archduke John, with which he was ordered to occupy Graz until John arrived, *en route* he ran into Eugène at St. Michael near Leoben (25 May) and was defeated, only about 2,000 of his command managing to escape.

JERVIS, Admiral John, see ST. VINCENT

JOHN, Prince of Brazil, Regent of Portugal (later King John VI) (1769–1826)

Second son of Queen Maria I of Portugal, and bearing the title 'Prince of Brazil' from 1788, he assumed the reins of government in 1792 when his mother became insane following the deaths of her

QUEEN MARIA I OF PORTUGAL, WHOSE
INCAPACITY LED TO JOHN, PRINCE OF BRAZIL,
BECOMING REGENT (MEDALLIC PORTRAIT)

husband and eldest son. In 1799 he took the official title of Regent, which he held until Maria's death in 1816, when he became King John VI. A weak and indecisive character, he attempted to preserve Portuguese integrity in the face of demands from both Spain and France. Forced into concluding the Peace of Badajoz in June 1801, he attempted to placate the French without entirely acceding to the Continental System which would have severed Anglo–Portuguese trade, while assuring his erstwhile ally, Great Britain, that he was acting under compulsion. While he was prevaricating about what to do, in November 1807 he received a French announcement that the Portuguese royal house of Braganza had ceased to reign, which decided his course of action: packing up the entire royal family and court, on 29 November he set sail for Brazil, leaving the governance of the country in the hands of a council of regency. He remained in Brazil even after the successful conclusion of the Peninsular War which caused dissatisfaction resulting in the 1820 revolution which established a constitutional monarchy, to which John swore allegiance when he finally returned to Portugal in 1822. He had to suppress risings by his

son Dom Miguel in 1823–4 (who was exiled) and on his death in March 1826 was succeeded by his elder son as King Pedro IV.

JOHN, Archduke of Austria (1782–1859)

One of sixteen children of the Emperor Leopold II, he was the younger brother of Emperor Francis II (I of Austria) and of the Archduke Charles. His military position owed more to birth than to ability or experience; indeed, it has been said that his success at Sacile was due to his opponent making even more mistakes. John's first command was over the Austrian army in Germany in 1800, aged only 18; totally inexperienced, he relied heavily on his 2i/c, *Feldzeugmeister* Franz, Baron Lauer, but was defeated by Moreau at Hohenlinden. In 1805 he commanded in the Tyrol, then withdrew and united with Charles in the Alps. In 1809 he led the Army of Inner Austria and on 16 April had the better of an action against Eugène de Beauharnais at Sacile, but was defeated by him at Raab, in a period during which relations between John and his superior, his brother Charles, became strained. This factor may have affected John's conduct in the Wagram phase of the campaign, for he was slow in responding to Charles' order that he unite his forces with the main army, and his arrival was too late to swing the course of the action (Charles claimed that with proper progress his earlier arrival would have been decisive, but this must be speculation). After Napoleon's defeat in Russia, John was a leading advocate of Austria's re-entry into the war against France, and was among those who favoured supporting a revolt in the Tyrol, at a time when Austria was not prepared to be committed to the fight quite so soon.

Zweideneck-Südenhorst, H. von. *Erzherzog Johann von Oster-*

reich im Feldzug von 1809. Gra 1892

JOHNSON, Colonel Richard Mentor (1781–1850)

Vice-President of the USA 1837– and a leading political figure in l native Kentucky, he achieved son fame during the War of 1812 l raising and commanding a volu teer rifle regiment, the Kentuc Mounted Volunteers. The conce of rapidly moving, rifle-arme troops being particularly useful frontier warfare, he led them wi considerable effect, notably at tl Battle of the Thames, at whic Johnson may have been the ma who killed Tecumseh. Conspic ously mounted upon a white por he was severely wounded in the l and arm during the action and ha to leave his unit, resuming his se in Congress in the followii February although at that stage si not sufficiently recovered to l able to walk.

JOMINI, General Antoine-Henr baron (1779–1869)

One of the most influential of a military theorists, he was born i Payerne, Vaud, Switzerland, an began his military career as a officer during the Swiss revolutio after a period as a bank clerk i Paris. He returned to Paris an wrote *Traité des Grandes Oper*

ANTOINE HENRI JOMINI

ns Militaires (published 1804–5), rved as a volunteer aide to Ney, d after Napoleon recognised s abilities as a theorist on reading s views about the coming war th Prussia, Jomini served on poleon's own staff in the Jena d Eylau campaigns. In 1807 he came Ney's chief of staff and rved with him in Spain and was nobled as baron in 1808, but racted enemies, most notably rthier. He intended to enter ussian service, and actually held mmissions simultaneously in th armies, despite becoming a ench *général de brigade* in 1810; d because of the Russian nnection served only in the rear helons in the 1812 campaign, as vernor of Smolensk and Vilna. e rejoined Ney for the 1813 mpaign, served at Lützen and utzen, but was arrested on rthier's orders for failing to liver returns. He then joined ussian service, was appointed utenant-general and ADC to the ar and served as adviser to the ies, but in deference to his evious service declined to take rt in the invasions of Switzerland d France. He remained in ussian service, attended the ongresses of Vienna, Aix-la-Chap-le and Verona, was promoted to neral and appointed military tor to the Tsarevich (later cholas I), organised the Russian aff college and saw his last active rvice in the Russo–Turkish War 328). In 1829 he settled in Brus-ls where he wrote his great work écis de l'Art de Guerre (1836) hich confirmed his status and came one of the most influential all military textbooks; for ample, its use in the US Military ademy affected the thinking of any commanders of the Amer-an Civil War. During the Crimean ar he advised Nicholas II, and ally settled near Paris, where he ed. He wrote many works on ilitary technique and history, but

although their effects were profound, they were eventually overshadowed by those of Clausewitz. Next to the works mentioned above, probably his best-known publication was *Histoire Critique et Militaire des Campagnes de la Révolution*, which was originally published in 1806.

Jomini, A. H. *The Art of War*, intro. C. Messenger. London, 1996 (modern edn.); *Vie Politique et Militaire de Napoléon*. Paris, 1827 (one of his historical studies); Lecomte, F. *Le Général Jomini, sa Vie et ses écrits*. 1861

JONES, Captain George (1786–1869)

An artist best known for his many prints of Waterloo (he was nicknamed 'Waterloo Jones'), he is often referred to as 'Capt. George Jones, R. A.', which might suggest that he was a serving officer of the Royal Artillery. In fact his captaincy appears to relate to service in the Royal Montgomeryshire Militia, and the 'R. A.' to the Royal Academy. It is possible that he was for some time in the Peninsula, and perhaps with the Allied forces in the occupation of France in 1816, but his familiarity with military matters is evident from the detail and atmosphere in his prints (for example, he illustrated Kelly's *Memorable Battle of Waterloo*, London, 1817); he also painted portraits and a number of Napoleonic and later battle-scenes. He bore a remarkable resemblance to Wellington and was often mistaken for him; someone who accosted the Duke in the street with 'Mr. Jones, I believe?' prompted Wellington's famous rejoinder, 'If you believe that you will believe anything.'[1]

1. Longford, E. *Wellington: Pillar of State*. London, 1972, p. 148

Harrington, P. 'The Battle Paintings of George Jones, RA', in *Journal of the Society for Army Historical Reseach*, 1989, vol. LXVII, pp. 239–52

JONES, Major-General Sir John Thomas, Bt. (1783–1843)

One of the leading military engineers of his generation, he was commissioned in the Royal Engineers in 1798, served 1805–6 in the Mediterranean (including Maida), in 1808 was ADC to Leith with the Spanish forces, and served in the Corunna campaign (having declined appointment as British commissioner to the Spanish forces on the grounds of his youth). In 1810 he supervised the construction of the Lines of Torres Vedras, about which he wrote a valuable treatise (*Memoranda relative to the Lines thrown up to cover Lisbon*), became brevet-major for services at Ciudad Rodrigo and lieutenant-colonel for Badajoz (where he carried out much of the engineering work after Fletcher's injury). At Burgos he was attempting to signal the completion of a breach by waving his hat when he attracted the attention of a French sharpshooter, who shot him through the ankle. The injury gave him great pain for the remainder of his life and for eighteen months he was an invalid, unable to walk, but was just fit enough in 1815 to undertake a review of the defences of The Netherlands, at Wellington's behest, and superintended the construction of fortifications during the Allied occupation of France. Despite ill-health he was to undertake a number of important tasks in subsequent years, including a review of the fortifications of Gibraltar (1840); at Wellington's recommendation he became a baronet (1831), was ADC to George IV and William IV and became major-general in 1837. During his convalescence following the Burgos injury he wrote his great work, *Journals of the Sieges undertaken by the Allies in Spain*, published 1814, which he was uniquely qualified to write. His brother William became a major-general in the Royal Artillery, brother George a captain in the Royal Navy, and brother Sir Harry served with the Royal Engineers in the Peninsula, at Walcheren and New Orleans, and was chief engineer at Sebastopol in 1855.

A long memoir was published in *Colburn's United Service Magazine*, 1843, vol. II, pp. 109–15

JOSEPHINE, Empress (1763–1814)

Born Marie-Joseph-Rose de Tascher de la Pagerie (she was generally called Marie-Rose) in Martinique, the daughter of an artillery officer, Joseph-Gaspard de Tascher de la Pagerie, the future empress married Alexandre,

EMPRESS JOSÉPHINE (ENGRAVING BY T. W. HARLAND AFTER LETHIÈRE)

vicomte de Beauharnais at the age of 16. The union produced two children, Eugène and Hortense, but was unhappy, although the beauty and wit of Joséphine (as she had begun to sign herself) charmed Parisian society. After the execution of her husband, she became the mistress of a number of leading political figures, notably Paul Barras, and captivated the young General Bonaparte, whom she married in March 1796. Evidently his ardour was greater than her own, for she maintained liaisons during his absences, notably with

Captain Hippolyte Charles, so that Napoleon almost divorced her in 1799. Consequently she was disliked by the Bonaparte family, but was crowned empress (by Napoleon) in 1804; yet her extravagance was a constant source of friction and upon the grounds that she had not provided him with an heir, Napoleon divorced her in December 1809. She retired in great comfort to her house, La Malmaison, near Paris, pursuing among other interests a love of rare plants and flowers (Rédouté the celebrated flower-painter received commissions from her), and she spent some time in Italy. Relations with Napoleon remained friendly, though in exile he recalled that she 'possessed in an eminent degree the taste for luxury, gaiety, and extravagance, natural to Creoles.[1] It was impossible to regulate her expenditure; she was constantly in debt; so there was always a grand dispute when the day of payment arrived. She was frequently known to direct her tradesmen to send in only half their accounts. Even at the island of Elba, Joséphine's bills came pouring in upon me from all parts of Italy.'[2] Nevertheless, Joséphine's was the name upon Napoleon's lips in his final moments, surely testimony to his continuing regard for this fascinating woman.

1. This term was used for someone born in the French West Indies, at this time without the implication of mixed race. 2. Las Cases, vol. II, p. 185.

Bruce, E. *Napoleon and Joséphine: an Improbable Marriage*. London, 1995; Cole, H. *Josephine*. London, 1962; Epton, N. C. *Josephine: the Empress and her Children*. London, 1975; Laing, M. *Napoleon and Josephine*. London, 1973; Méneval, C. F. *The Empress Josephine*. London, 1912; Wilson, R. McN. *The Empress Josephine: the Portrait of a Woman*. London, 1929. Joséphine also

features in most biographies Napoleon, and of her children; f example, her relations with the are included in Oman, *Napoleon's Viceroy: Eugène Beauharnais*. London, 1966

JOUBERT, General Barthélemy Catherine (1769–99)

BARTHÉLEMY JOUBERT (PRINT AFTER ERIC PA AFTER F. BOUCHOT)

He ran away to join the army 1784, but was brought back continue his studies in law; so h military career proper bega during the early Revolutiona Wars. Elected an officer in 1792, l was distinguished in Italy, becan *général de brigade* in 1795, ar having attracted Napoleon's atte tion was given important suborc nate commands, notably at Rivc commanding in the second pha of the battle and followir Napoleon's orders to perfectio *Général de division* from Decembe 1796, in late 1797 he led the Army Batavia, and commanded in Ita until a dispute with the civil autho ities led to his resignation i January 1799. He was soon r employed, taking command in Ita from Moreau, whom he persuade to remain; and at Novi on 15 Augu 1799 he engaged Suvarov. Whil encouraging his men, almost at th very commencement of the battl Joubert was shot through the boc d killed on the spot; Moreau took mmand but the French were efeated. Great similarities were oticed between the careers of oubert and Napoleon, and it might ave been that Joubert would have on great fame but for his early eath. Napoleon claimed that oubert 'entertained a high venera- on for me ... had taken me for his odel, aspired to imitate my plans, d attempted to accomplish othing less than what I afterwards ffected in Brumaire [but] any ttempt of his, at Paris, would have iled; he had not yet acquired a ufficient degree of glory, of consis- ncy, and maturity. He was, by ature, calculated for all these cquirements ...'[1] Montholon served s his ADC and was also his rother-in-law, Joubert having in une 1799 married Zaphirine de lontholon, who later became lacdonald's second wife.

. Las Cases, vol. III, p. 162.

OURDAN, Marshal Jean- aptiste, comte (1762–1833)

native of Limoges, son of a urgeon, he served in the army 778–84 before becoming a cloth erchant in his home town. lected to command a volunteer orps at the outbreak of the Revo- tionary Wars, he was promoted général de brigade in May 1793,

JEAN BAPTISTE JOURDAN
(PRINT AFTER A. TARDIEU)

de division in July after service at Jemappes and Neerwinden. He led a division at Hondeschoote (and was wounded), was appointed to command the Army of the North (September 1793), won the victory at Wattignies but fell foul of political intrigue and was relieved of command. Reinstated, he led the Army of the Moselle, later the Army of the Sambre and Meuse, and was victorious at Fleurus. Resigning after defeats at Amberg and Würzburg, he was re-appointed nominally to the Army of the North, but his next duties were largely political as a member of the Council of Five Hundred, super- vising the 1798 conscription law which is sometimes styled by his name. Back on active duty in 1799, he was defeated at Stockach and succeeded by Massena; and his career went into something of an eclipse when he refused to assist in the coup of Brumaire (as he favoured republicanism more than consulate and empire). Neverthe- less, he was among the first appointments as Marshal, was chosen to lead the Army of Italy in 1804, and in 1806 became Joseph Bonaparte's military adviser at Naples. He followed Joseph to Spain, where his position was diffi- cult in the extreme, with the Marshals nominally under his command disregarding his orders and appealing directly to Nap- oleon; so that after the defeat of Talavera, for which he was blamed unfairly, he went home on grounds of ill-health. He returned in 1811, becoming Joseph's chief of staff with control over the Army of the Centre, and from March 1812 as Joseph's chief assistant, but the old problems remained, and when Joseph was defeated at Vittoria it was Jourdan who was made the scapegoat. Recalled, he was left effectively unemployed, accepted service under the Bourbons but rejoined Napoleon in 1815, though given only a minor command

(Army of the Rhine). Ennobled by the king as comte and appointed a peer of France (1819), he remained a political liberal, supported the 1830 revolution and was made Governor of Les Invalides by Louis- Philippe. An honest and capable man rather than an inspired soldier, his nickname 'the anvil' (for being so often beaten) was unfair, as the difficulties he encountered were often the responsibility of others. Napoleon recognised how unfairly he had been treated: 'This is one who has been assuredly very ill treated by me; it was, therefore, natural to conclude that he would be highly incensed against me; but I have heard with pleasure that he has behaved with great moderation since my fall. He has set an example of that elevation of mind which serves to distinguish men, and does honour to their character ... he was a true patriot, and that explains many things.'[1]

1. Las Cases, vol. IV, p. 13.

Glover, M. 'The True Patriot: Jourdan', in *Napoleon's Marshals*, ed. D. G. Chandler. London, 1987. Jourdan himself wrote: *Mémoires militaires du Maréchal Jourdan*, ed. Vicomte de Grouchy. Paris, 1899; *Mémoires pour servir à l'histoire sur la Campagne de 1796*. Paris, 1819; and *Operations de l'Armée du Danube*. 1799

JOVELLANOS, Gaspard- Melchor de (1744–1811)

Described by Wellington as 'a very clever man',[1] he earned celebrity as both author and statesman in his native Spain. A lawyer and leader of the Spanish liberals, he gained a reputation for wisdom and patriot- ism and had held ministerial office (chief minister 1797–8), but he became disillusioned with Godoy's conduct and in 1801 was impris- oned (for heresy) at Majorca. He was released in 1808, and Joseph Bonaparte tried to enlist his support to give the Bonapartist regime more legitimacy, but Jovellanos declined the ministry of the interior and instead joined the patriot party and became a member of the central *junta*. He helped re-organise the Cortes but was involved in the fall of the *junta*, and died in 1811. His writings included fiction, but most notably political and legal treatises, and he was active in the encouragement of social, agricultural, industrial and educational reform in his native province, the Asturias.

1. Stanhope, p. 5.

Jovellanos, G. M. de. *Mémoires Politiques*. Paris, 1825; Polt, J. *Gaspard Melchor de Jovellanos*. New York, 1971

JUNOT, General Jean-Andoche, duc d'Abrantès (1771–1813)

One of Napoleon's generals, who resented bitterly what he regarded as an unjust withholding of promotion to Marshal, he was a law student in Paris at the outbreak of the Revolutionary Wars. Joining a volunteer battalion, he was wounded in 1792 and 1793. As a sergeant at Toulon he came to Napoleon's notice while taking dictation; a roundshot threw up earth which covered the paper, whereupon he remarked, 'Well, I shall have no need of sand'[1] (to blot the ink). Following this evidence of coolness under fire, he served as Napoleon's aide in Italy, suffering a severe head wound at Lonato, an injury which may have contributed to his subsequent mental instability. He was promoted to *général de brigade* in Egypt (January 1799), survived much hard campaigning but was wounded in a duel, and was captured by the British when returning home. After his release he became Commandant of Paris and *général de division* (1801), and at this time married Laure Permon (1783–1834), daughter of a family well known to Napoleon (she claimed that he had once proposed to her mother). Laure was

renowned for beauty, wit and also extravagance, so that Junot was constantly burdened with financial worries, and was himself similarly spendthrift; Napoleon gave him fortunes only for them to be squandered (as Napoleon said) 'without credit to himself, without discernment or taste, and, too frequently ... in gross debauchery'.[2] Napoleon even tried to talk financial probity into Madame Junot, only for her to become angry and treat him like a child. Junot served as ambassador to Portugal, as Napoleon's aide in the Austerlitz campaign, as Governor of Parma and Piacenza and from October 1806 as Governor of Paris. Here his behaviour and liaisons (including one with Napoleon's sister Caroline) caused some disquiet – on more than one occasion he was said to have threatened to settle a creditor's bill with a sword-thrust – so, perhaps to get him out of the way, he was charged with leading the invasion of Portugal. This he accomplished with some skill, becoming duc d' Abrantès and Governor-General of the occupied country (from which he profited greatly in loot), but returned to France in some disgrace after his defeat at Vimeiro. He returned to the Peninsula as a corps commander and commanded briefly at the siege of Saragossa (where in Lejeune's opinion his natural arrogance and jealousy were developing into serious mental instability; only with difficulty and in a furious rage was he persuaded to cancel a suicidal assault intended to bring him personal glory before he could be superseded in command by a superior). In 1809 Junot commanded the reserve army in Germany, returned to the Peninsula (serving at Busaco and Fuentes de Oñoro and on 19 January 1811 being shot in the nose by a German Legion hussar during the skirmish at Rio Mayor). In the Russian campaign of

ANDOCHE JUNOT (ENGRAVING BY T. READ)

1812 he succeeded to command VIII Corps in place of Jérôm Bonaparte, but was severely criticised for mishandling the entrapment of Barclay as he withdrew from Smolensk; as Napoleon remarked, he 'gave me great caus of dissatisfaction; he was no longe the same man, and committe some gross blunders which cost u dear'.[3] In consequence, Junot wa recalled to France in January 181 and given the minor appointmen of Governor-General of Illyria, bu his dissipated lifestyle havin resulted in advanced syphili derangement overtook him com pletely and he was relieved of dut Committed to his father's house a Montbard, he died on 29 July 181 as a result of leaping from window. His wife continued he somewhat scandalous lifestyle spending much of her time ami the fashionable society of Rom and publishing entertaining bu unreliable memoirs in an un availing attempt to stave off inso vency.

1. Las Cases, vol. I, p. 99. 2. Ibid vol. II, p. 391. 3. Ibid., vol. II, p. 394

Abrantès, duchesse d'. *Mém oires de Madame la Duchess d'Abrantès*. Paris, 1893; Bearne, C *A Leader of Society at Napoleon' Court*. 1904; Gunn, P. *Napoleon 'Little Pest': the Duchess o Abrantès*. London, 1979

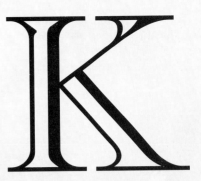

**ALKREUTH (or KALCK-
REUTH), Field Marshal
Friedrich Adolf, Graf von
(1737–1818)**

Joining the Prussian Army in 1752,
he served during the Seven Years
War, but promotion was slow
following personal differences
with Frederick the Great's
brother, Prince Henry. He served
as major-general in Holland in
1787, lieutenant-general in 1792–4,
including Valmy, Kaiserslautern
and most notably at Mainz, which
established his reputation. In 1806
he commanded the Reserve Corps
and for a time was able to cover
the retreat from Auerstädt, but did
not subsequently distinguish
himself, being persuaded from
capitulation by Blücher and others
of his mettle. However, he showed
his old skill and energy when
defending Danzig in the following
year, holding out from mid
February until 26 May; whether he
could have held longer, in hope of
relief or more realistically to tie up
French troops, is arguable, but he
was able to extract advantageous
terms (the garrison to march out
with their arms and not to serve
again for a year). Despite failing to
support the attempted relief by
Kamenskoi, which might possibly
have broken through to the
besiegers, the defence reflected
great credit upon Kalkreuth and
his garrison. Subsequently
promoted to field marshal, he
participated in the Tilsit negotiations, and at his death was
Governor of Berlin. The artists
Graf Stanislaus and his son
Leopold von Kalkreuth were
descendants.

**KAMENSKOI (or KAMENSKI),
Marshal Alexander (1731–1807)**
Despite having served with
distinction under Suvarov, it is as
commander of the Russian forces
in 1806–7 that he is best remembered. By this time he was
unsuited by age and temperament

for such a command: 75 years old
and possessed of a violent temper
which led to his murder by a
peasant. He was late in joining his
command and left his subordinates to fight at Golymin and
Pultusk, but did order a general
withdrawal to avoid his army
falling into a French trap. That he
could no longer perform the duty
required of him seems exemplified by Wilson's remark that
following the withdrawal, he went
into the streets of Grodno without
his shirt and indicated to a
surgeon all his old injuries to
extract a certificate that he was no
longer fit to serve, and he was
succeeded in command by
Bennigsen in early January 1807.
He should not be confused with
the divisional general of the same
name, best known for his unavailing attempt to relieve Kalkreuth in Danzig later in the same
campaign.

**KEITH, Admiral George Keith
Elphinstone, Viscount
(1745–1823)**

GEORGE ELNHINSTONE, VISCOUNT KEITH
(PRINT BY W. HALL AFTER HOPPNER)

Son of Charles, 10th Lord Elphinstone, he entered the Royal Navy
in 1761, and in 1767 undertook a
trading venture with the East India
Company which laid the foundations of his fortune. Captain in

1775, he served during the War of
American Independence both at
sea and at Charleston, South
Carolina; MP for Dumbarton-
shire, later Stirlingshire, he
resumed his naval career upon
the outbreak of the Revolutionary
Wars, notably at Toulon and in the
evacuation. Rear-admiral in 1794,
he participated in the capture of
the Cape, sailed to India and on
the way home captured a Dutch
squadron in Saldhana Bay. In 1797
he helped suppress mutiny at the
Nore and Plymouth, and in 1798
was appointed St. Vincent's 2i/c in
the Mediterranean; despite some
dissension among the comman
ders, and being blamed for the
escape of a French squadron, in
November 1799 he became CinC
Mediterranean. He co-operated
with the Austrians at the siege of
Genoa, landed Abercromby's
expedition to Egypt, and objected
strongly to the Convention of El-
Arish, negotiated by Sidney Smith,
which was not ratified. Admiral
from 1801, he then served as CinC
North Sea (1803–7) and of the
Channel Fleet (1812–15); ennobled in March 1797 as Baron Keith
in the Irish peerage, he was
granted an English barony in
December 1801 and in June 1814
was advanced to a viscountcy. In
1815 he conveyed the British
government's instructions to
Napoleon concerning his exile at
St. Helena, and while scrupu-
lously formal in the execution of
his duty, did not seem very
impressed by the emperor or his

complaints. Las Cases presented some of these to Keith aboard HMS *Tonnant* on 7 August 1815; Keith, 'a fine-looking old man, of highly polished manners, received me with great politeness' but tried to avoid discussing the complaints, frequently bowing to suggest that Las Cases should leave; but when he persisted Keith became impatient and even showed anger, evidently believing that as a defeated enemy Napoleon had less rights than he thought he should![1] The uncle of Keith's mother was James Keith, Frederick the Great's field marshal, killed at Hochkirch; and the admiral's daughter Margaret (who succeeded him as heir to the baronies – having no son the viscountcy became extinct) married Auguste Flahaut de la Billarderie.

1. Las Cases, vol. I, pp. 49–50.

Allardice, A. *Memoir of the Honourable George Keith Elphinstone, Viscount Keith.* Edinburgh, 1882; Perrin, W. G., and Lloyd, C. (eds.). *The Keith Papers.* London, 1927, 1950, 1955

KELLERMANN, Marshal François-Christophe de, duc de Valmy (1735–1820)

Descended from a Saxon family long settled in Strasbourg, he joined the army in 1752, served in the Seven Years War and, marked out as an able officer, rose steadily until he attained the rank of *maréchal-de-camp* in 1785. He supported the principles of the Revolution, was promoted to lieutenant-general in March 1792 and took over the Army of the Centre from Luckner in August. His great moment was at Valmy on 20 September when in concert with Dumouriez he turned back Brunswick's army by a cannonade. Nevertheless, Kellermann came under political suspicion as an officer of the *ancien régime*, was transferred to the Army of the

FRANÇOIS CHRISTOPHE KELLERMANN

FRANÇOIS ETIENNE KELLERMANN

Alps and then arrested and imprisoned for thirteen months. When finally acquitted he was restored to his command (1795) but his active career ended with the disbandment of the Army of the Alps in September 1797. Thereafter his organisational skills were used by Napoleon, who appointed him a Marshal in the first creation of 1804 and ennobled him as duc de Valmy in June 1808. Greatly skilled as an administrator, he was an invaluable asset in command of reserve formations and in organising recruits, and still played a useful role as late as 1814, despite his age. A senator from 1799, he was made a peer of France by the Bourbons and helped re-organise the army after the restoration. His son was the probably better known François-Etienne de Kellermann.

Hofschröer, P. 'The Good Officer: Kellermann', in *Napoleon's Marshals*, ed. D. G. Chandler. London, 1987

KELLERMANN, General François-Etienne, comte de, later duc de Valmy (1770–1835)

Son of Marshal Kellermann, duc de Valmy (to which title he succeeded in 1820), he is probably the better known of the two, despite not attaining the rank achieved by his father. Commis-

sioned in 1785, he served as his father's ADC (1795) and made his name as a cavalry leader in Italy, rising to *général de brigade* in May 1797. Serving under Napoleon in the Marengo campaign, at that battle he executed the decisive charge which, seconding the arrival of Desaix, turned defeat into victory. Kellermann always resented the fact that in his opinion he never received sufficient recompense for saving Napoleon; however, when in future years his unbridled looting was reported, Napoleon merely remarked that whenever his name was mentioned, he thought only of Marengo. Promoted to *général de division*, Kellermann led a division at Austerlitz, commanded Junot's cavalry in Portugal and was responsible for negotiating the Convention of Cintra. He remained in the Peninsula until returning to France on sick leave in May 1811; he was appointed to command a division in III Cavalry Corps for the 1812 campaign, but his health (never robust) precluded his serving until the spring of 1813. He fought at Lützen and Bautzen, commanded VI Cavalry Corps in 1814, remained in service under the Bourbons but rallied to Napoleon in 1815 and led III Cavalry Corps with great courage

Quatre Bras and Waterloo. Although reconciled with the Bourbons, he held only advisory posts until his retirement in 1831. Undoubtedly one of Napoleon's best cavalry generals, his opportunities for advancement were frustrated by ill-health, and his habits as a plunderer soured his reputation. De Gonneville described him as 'a little man, of unhealthy and insignificant appearance, with a clever look, but false'; as an example of his piety, he built a church near his house outside Paris, but 'It is very likely that both house and church were the result of exactions committed in Spain.'[1] As Napoleon would have agreed, however, for all his faults, 'the fact that his name is indissolubly linked in history with that of the victory of Marengo is more than a sufficient title to glory.'[2]

Recollections of Colonel de Gonneville, ed. C. M. Yonge. London, 1875, vol. I, pp. 250–1. 2. Sheppard, Captain W. E. 'The Napoleonic Cavalry and its Leaders', in *Cavalry Journal*, 1931, vol. XXI, p. 88 (includes a biog. note on Kellermann)

KEMPT, General Sir James (1764–1855)

Born in Edinburgh, he was commissioned in the army in 1783 but upon the disbandment of his regiment two years later found employment as a clerk at the army agents Greenwood, until obtaining another commission via the interest of the Duke of York. In 1799 he was ADC to Abercromby, and to him and Hutchinson in Egypt; he commanded the Light Brigade at Maida, served in Canada 1807–11, and as major-general took over a brigade of the 3rd Division in the Peninsula after the death of its commander, Mackinnon, at Ciudad Rodrigo. Kempt led it until wounded at Badajoz; from

March 1813 he led a brigade of the Light Division, and in 1815 commanded the 8th British Brigade of the 5th Division, to the command of which he succeeded upon Picton's death at Waterloo. Knighted by virtue of a KCB (2 January 1815), he served as Governor-General of Canada 1828–30 and as Master-General of the Ordnance 1830–4.

KENNEDY, General Sir James Shaw, see **SHAW KENNEDY**

KENT, Field Marshal Edward Augustus, Duke of (1767–1820)

EDWARD AUGUSTUS, DUKE OF KENT (ENGRAVING BY W. SKELTON AFTER BEECHEY)

The fourth son of George III, he was created Duke of Kent and Strathearn and made the army his career. Field marshal from September 1805, he served at Gibraltar, Quebec, the West Indies and as CinC North America and subsequently Gibraltar, earning a reputation as something of a martinet which did not enhance his popularity. He is probably best remembered as being the father of Queen Victoria.

Neale, Revd. E. *Life of HRH Edward, Duke of Kent*. London, 1850

KEPPEL, George Thomas, see **ALBEMARLE**

KERSAINT, Vice-Admiral Armand Guy Simon de Coetnempren, comte de (1742–93)

Born in Paris, the son of comte Guy François, a distinguished naval officer, he joined the navy in 1755. Despite his aristocratic background, he supported the Revolution and became a member of the Legislative Assembly and the Convention, his particular interest being naval affairs; after a spell as a representative with the Army of the Centre, he was promoted to *vice-amiral* on 1 January 1793. Although he advocated the deposition of the king, he voted against the death sentence and on 20 January, after it had been passed, he resigned from the Convention, declaring that he could no longer endure the disgrace of sitting in the same place as bloodthirsty individuals whose policies had prevailed over decency. This, and his attacks on Marat, seem to have sealed his fate; he was denied naval employment, was arrested in September 1793 and guillotined in December, on a charge of having conspired for the restoration of the monarchy and of insulting the nation by resigning his seat. His brother, Guy Pierre (1747–1822), served in the navy during the War of American Independence, but, opposing the Revolution, emigrated until returning in 1803 when his rank was restored.

KEY, Francis Scott (1779–1843)

Immortalised by his authorship of *The Star-Spangled Banner*, which was itself a result of the War of 1812, he was personally opposed to the war on moral grounds, and no supporter of conflict with Great Britain; but still entered military service in defence of his country, very briefly as a volunteer gunner in 1813, and as a lieutenant in 1814, for no more than a couple of weeks on each occasion. In August 1814, however, he volunteered to act as aide to General Walter Smith, and received some blame for the faulty disposition of the US forces at Bladensburg.

KILMAINE (originally JENNINGS), General Charles Edward Saul (1751–99)

Born in Dublin as Charles Jennings, he was taken to France by his father at the age of 11, Jennings senior having great animosity towards England and its religion; in France he changed the family name to Kilmaine, after a village in Mayo. Kilmaine junior joined the army in 1774, served as a volunteer with the navy in Senegal, and, commissioned in 1780, fought in the War of American Independence with Lauzun's corps. He embraced the principles of the Revolution, was distinguished at Jemappes as a leader of hussars, and became *général de brigade* in 1793; but his foreign birth called his loyalty into question, and he was arrested in August 1793. Reinstated in 1795, he was sent as a cavalry general to Italy where he served under Napoleon, perhaps most notably in conducting the siege of Mantua. He was appointed to command the cavalry of the 'Army of England' and with other Irish exiles entertained hopes of an expedition to that country (on St. Patrick's Day 1798, with Napper Tandy and Thomas Paine, he headed a banquet for Irish patriots in Paris), but when that plan failed to materialise, Kilmaine was offered command of the French troops in Switzerland. He declined on health grounds and was replaced by Massena; he died of dysentery on 15 December 1799.

A brief memoir appears in Grant, J. *British Heroes in Foreign Wars.* London, 1893

KINCAID, Captain Sir John (1787–1862)

Perhaps the most famous of all memorialists of the British Army of the period, he was a native of Dalbeath, near Falkirk, and joined the 2nd Battalion 95th Rifles as a second lieutenant from the North York Militia in 1809. He served with distinction during the Peninsular War, from Fuentes de Oñoro to Toulouse, perhaps most notably at Badajoz, earning nine clasps for the Military General Service Medal, and was adjutant of his battalion at Waterloo, where his horse was shot from under him. He was later knighted and became Exon of the Yeomen of the Guard; but his fame rests upon his two books: *Adventures in the Rifle Brigade* (1830) and *Random Shots from a Rifleman* (1835), exceptionally attractive and notably good-humoured volumes, deservedly regarded as among the greatest 'classics' of the Napoleonic Wars. Typical of the style is Kincaid's account of sheltering behind a tree in March 1811, to avoid French musketry: 'the cleverest method of teaching a recruit to stand to attention, is to place him behind a tree and fire balls at him ... [I] never saw any one stand so fiercely upright as I did behind mine, while balls were rapping into it as fast as if a fellow had been hammering a nail on the opposite side ...'[1]

1. Kincaid, *Adventures*, 1908 edn. p. 25.

KLEBER, General Jean-Baptiste (1753–1800)

Born in Strasbourg, the son of a mason, he trained at the Bavarian military school and was commissioned in the Austrian Army, but despairing of rising beyond the rank of subaltern, resigned in 1783. He used his earlier architectural training when appointed inspector of public buildings at Belfort, but at the beginning of the

JEAN BAPTISTE KLÉBER (ENGRAVING BY T. JOHNSON AFTER GUÉRIN)

Revolutionary Wars was elected field rank in a volunteer battalio rising to *général de brigad* (August 1793) and after succe against the Vendéen rebels to c *division*. He was recalled fo stating that the rebels should b treated leniently, but in April 179 was appointed to the Army of th Sambre and Meuse. Althoug distinguished at Fleurus and espe cially under Jourdan in 1796, h was so dissatisfied with ne receiving the recognition accord ed to others that he refuse further commands. However, h accepted a divisional comman from Napoleon for the expeditio to Egypt, but was wounded in th head at Alexandria, whic prevented further participation i the early part of the campaign. I Syria in 1799 he was especiall distinguished, however, notably a Mount Tabor, and succeeded t command of the French force when Napoleon went home. In parlous situation, he conclude the Convention of El-Arish wit Sidney Smith, but when this wa not ratified he took the offensiv and won a victory over the Ottoman forces at Heliopolis (2 March 1800) which enabled th French to re-occupy Cairo. On 1 June, however, while walking in garden in Cairo, he was stabbed t

eath by a fanatic known as
uliman of Aleppo, who was
apprehended and executed with
revolting barbarity. Although
appearing to lack self-belief,
Kléber was equally competent
with administrative affairs as on
the battlefield, and Napoleon
declared that he and Desaix had
been his best lieutenants, both
possessed of 'great and rare
merits'; Kléber's, he said, 'was the
talent of nature; Desaix's was
entirely the result of education
and assiduity. The genius of
Kléber only burst forth at particular moments, when roused by
the importance of the occasion;
and then it immediately slum-
bered again in the bosom of indo-
ence and pleasure.'[1] By a dreadful
coincidence, Desaix and Kléber
were killed on the very same day.
1. Las Cases, vol. I, p. 148.

Ernouf, E. E. *Le Général Kléber*.
Paris, 1870 (the author was the
grandson of Jourdan's chief of
staff)

KLEIN, Johann Adam
(1792–1875)

This Bavarian artist and engraver
trained in Vienna, was not
primarily however a 'military'
artist, but was an eye-witness to
the troops of the 1813–14
campaigns and painted many military uniforms, often for his own
amusement. His battle-scenes
were comparatively few, most of
his work depicting soldiers in
natural settings or off duty, with
precise uniform detail. Collections
have been published as *Oesterreichische Soldatentypen 1814–15*,
and *Bayerische Soldatentypen
1815*, Hamburg, 1985.

KLEIST, Field Marshal
Friedrich Heinrich Ferdinand
Emil, Graf von Nollendorf
(1762–1823)

Although he served in the Revolutionary Wars, and as an officer on
the general staff in the 1806

FRIEDRICH KLEIST VON NOLLENDORF

campaign, it is as a commander of
the Prussian Army in 1813–14 that
Kleist is best known. Commanding
a corps during the 'War of Liberation', he was given the task of
holding Leipzig at the time of the
battle of Lützen, and, outnumbered, was driven back; at
Bautzen he helped to hold the
Allied right flank; served at
Dresden; at Leipzig was notably
involved in the desperate fighting
around Markkleeberg in the
southern sector of the action; and
played a vital role in the defeat of
Vandamme at Kulm. In 1814 he
served under Blücher's command
in the defeat of Vauchamps, served
with distinction at Laon, and led
his corps in the advance on Paris.
In 1815 he commanded the
Prussian forces which were to
meet Napoleon, until superseded
in command by Blücher. He
should not be confused with other
Prussian soldiers of the same
name, most notably with the
superannuated, 73-year-old Governor of Magdeburg who surrendered after a feeble defence in
1806, nor with the soldier-poets
Ewald von Kleist (1715–59),
mortally wounded at Kunersdorf,
and Bernd Heinrich Wilhelm von
Kleist (1777–1811), who served in
the Revolutionary Wars, left the
army in 1799, was arrested by the
French as a spy and imprisoned

for six months in 1807, and who
died in a suicide pact.

KOBELL, Wilhelm von
(1766–1855)

The son of another distinguished
artist, Ferdinand von Kobell,
Wilhelm was a Bavarian landscape
and military artist, known for
several series of splendid uniform-
and battle-paintings, many aquatinted by Bartsch. Apart from the
artistic merit, his work has the air
of being that of an eye-witness,
with detailed uniform-observation
and 'character'.

KORNER, Karl Theodore
(1791–1813)

Son of a notable Saxon legal expert
and a friend of Schiller, he is
remembered as a young poet
whose work was suffused with the
patriotic enthusiasm engendered
before and by the 'War of Liberation'; indeed, he was compared
with the Greek poet of the 7th
century BC, Tyrtaeus, whose
verses inspired the soldiers of
Sparta. Körner put his beliefs into
practice: forsaking his literary
career in Vienna in 1813, he joined
Lützow's corps, and having
already been wounded, was killed
in action near Gadesbusch in
Mecklenburg on 26 August 1813.
His most famous works were
probably *Lützow's Wild Hunt* and
Song of the Sword (*Schwertlied*),
which was only completed on the
morning of the day of his death.

KORSAKOV, General Alek-
sander Mikhailovich
(1753–1840)

Although he served in The Netherlands in 1794, and in Persia in
1796, it is for his service in
Switzerland in 1799 that the
Russian general Korsakov is best
known. In the autumn of that year
he was given command of the
Allied forces in that country, to
cover and support the advance of
Suvarov's main army from Italy,

and intended to drive Massena's French from the region. Part of the Allied force in Switzerland, however, under the Archduke Charles, was directed to cause a diversion on the Rhine to support the Allied expedition to North Holland. Before he left, Charles collaborated with Korsakov in an attack upon the French, which failed (17-18 August 1799); and once Charles' army had gone, Massena pressed his offensive and routed Korsakov's army at the third battle of Zurich (25 September), which stalled Suvarov's advance and led to the final dismissal of that great commander. Korsakov's defeat overturned all Allied plans, and was followed by the Tsar's withdrawal from the coalition. Subsequently Korsakov served as Governor of Lithuania for almost thirty years, being recalled only at the time of the Polish insurrection (1830–1). He is sometimes referred to with the additional name of Rimski.

KOSCIUSZKO, General Tadeusz Andrej Bonawentura (1746–1817)

This great Polish soldier and patriot played only a peripheral role in the Napoleonic Wars. After receiving his military education primarily in Poland and France, he served with distinction in the US Army during the War of Independence, becoming brigadier general and being granted American citizenship. Major-general in Polish service, he stalled a Russian invasion at Dubienka (July 1792) before retiring to Leipzig in dismay at the surrender, and attempted unsuccessfully to elicit French assistance. He joined the 1794 rebellion against the Russo–Prussian forces and was appointed dictator, but despite some successes the revolt failed, and he was wounded and captured in the defeat of

Maciejowice (10 October) which preceded the Third Partition of Poland. Kosciuszko remained imprisoned in Russia until the accession of Paul I, then lived in Philadelphia until moving to Paris in May 1798. Napoleon endeavoured to gain his support, but he refused to become involved in Napoleon's plans unless they included a guarantee of Polish independence. Thus uncommitted throughout the remainder of the Napoleonic Wars, and having finally failed in his entreaties to the Tsar at the Congress of Vienna, he retired to Switzerland. As befitted so steadfast a patriot, his remains were taken to his homeland for burial in the cathedral at Cracow. His fame as a symbol of freedom spread far, for example prompting Thomas Campbell to write: 'Hope, for a season, bade the world farewell/And freedom shrieked – as Kosciusko (*sic*) fell.'

Gardner, M. M. *Kosciuszko*. London, 1920; Haiman, M. *Kosciuszko in the American Revolution*. New York, 1943; *Kosciuszko, Leader and Exile.* New York, 1946

KRAY, General Paul, Freiherr Kray von Krajova (1735–1804)

One of the most respected Austrian commanders of his time, born in Késmárk, Hungary, he joined the Austrian Army at the age of 19 and after service in the Seven Years War, in the suppression of an insurrection in Transylvania and against the Turks, he attained the rank of general officer in 1790. During the French Revolutionary Wars he was distinguished in The Netherlands, when commanding the Allied advanceguard, and in 1796 played an important part in the victories of Archduke Charles' army at Wetzlar, Amberg and Würzburg. He had less success in 1798, but in 1799 temporarily commanded in

Italy, won the victory of Magnano and recaptured Mantua, for which he was promoted to *Feldzeug meister*. In Germany in 1800 he was defeated several times by Moreau (second Stockach, Mösskirch, Ulm and Höchstadt) but managed to avoid total defeat and retire. By late June 1800 it was decided that he had to be replaced and he was succeeded by Lauer. Acknowledged as a courageous, chivalrous and capable general even by his opponents, Kray spent the remainder of his life in retirement.

KUTUZOV (or KUTUSOV), Field Marshal Mikhail Larionovich Golenishchev-Kutuzov, Prince of Smolensk (1745–1813)

MIKHAIL KUTUZOV
(ENGRAVING BY T. BLOOD)

One of the outstanding Russian soldiers of the era – though perhaps not given his due in his own time – he was born in St. Petersburg, son of a military engineer, and enrolled as a cadet in the engineer school at the age of 12. Somewhat unusually for a Russian officer, he was well-educated and could speak French, German, Polish, Swedish, English and Turkish in addition to his native tongue. He saw much active service in Poland (1764–9) and in the Crimea against the Turks

1770–4), where he was shot in the head and lost an eye. A general officer from 1784, he was Governor-General of the Crimea in 1787 and he won considerable fame in the Turkish War (1788–91) under Suvarov, whose heir in some respects he became. After a variety of administrative and diplomatic duties, in 1805 he commanded the Russian Army in the Danube theatre; he attempted to prevent the Austro–Russians fighting at Austerlitz, but was hindered by the presence of the Tsar and Emperor, yet though wounded managed to extricate the Russian survivors. He was never popular with the Tsar (though regarded with great affection by the army), so between 1806 and 1811 was employed only in administrative posts, but returned to field command with effect against the Turks in 1811, and reluctantly the Tsar was forced to recall him in 1812 to command against Napoleon instead of either Barclay de Tolly or Bagration. He continued the strategy of withdrawal initiated by these two subordinates and permitted Moscow to be captured; but despite criticism, it was a policy that ensured the destruction of the *Grande Armée*. He was also criticised for lethargy in the pursuit, but this permitted Napoleon's force to be destroyed by exertion and the climate, with little cost to the Russians, and the plan to trap the survivors at the Berezina only just failed. For his success, Kutuzov was appointed field marshal and Prince of Smolensk; but, ill and ageing, he was relieved of command by the Tsar and died shortly after, at Bunzlau in Silesia, on 28 April 1813. Clausewitz wrote that at Borodino Kutuzov was 'almost a nullity. He appeared destitute of inward activity, or any clear view of surrounding occurrences, of any liveliness of perception, or independence of action', but admitted that his 'cunning and prudence' were superior to those of his rivals.[1] Sir Robert Wilson, one of his fiercest critics, reported that he was so 'corpulent and unwieldy' that he had to command from a droshky, but found him 'polished, courteous, shrewd as a Greek, naturally intelligent as an Asiatic and well instructed as a European'.[2] Wilson also thought that 'he died most opportunely for his fame',[3] but criticisms are mostly unfair. A shrewd, capable commander with a gift of inspiring the ordinary Russian soldiers, and like his old master Suvarov putting effectiveness in combat before appearance and parade-ground drill, Kutuzov's command in 1812 was perhaps the most important factor in the defeat of the invasion, from which Napoleon's downfall stemmed.

1. Clausewitz, p. 141. 2. Wilson, *Narrative*, p. 131. 3. Wilson, *Diaries*, vol. I, p. 356.

Parkinson, R. *The Fox of the North: The Life of Kutuzov.* London, 1976

LA BEDOYERE, General Charles-Angélique-François-Huchet, comte de (1786–1815) Although an aristocrat, La Bédoyère was a Bonapartist of literally fatal ardour. He entered the Imperial Guard as a member of the *Gendarmes d'Ordonnance* (a corps restricted to those of good breeding who could afford to equip themselves), and became ADC to Lannes, later to Eugène; he carried the order to Mortier for applying the *coup de grâce* to the Russian Army at Friedland, and was among the first to lead the escalade at Ratisbon. He served in the Russian campaign of 1812 and in 1813–14, and as commander of the 7th Line was among the first to defect to Napoleon upon his return in 1815; appointed general and ADC to Napoleon, as bearer of orders he was held partially responsible for d'Erlon's confusion on 16 June. After Waterloo he continued to speak with vehemence in favour of Napoleon, loyalty which proved fatal: court-martialled for treason by the Bourbons, he was executed by firing-squad on 19 August 1815.

LA BISPAL, Count of, see **O'DONNELL**

LAFAYETTE, General Marie-Joseph-Paul-Yves-Roch-Gilbert du Motier, marquis de (1757–1834) Possessed of a large fortune (his father was killed at Minden), and having influential connections from an early age, he entered the French Army in 1771. He is probably best remembered for his participation in the War of American Independence, first as a young volunteer commissioned as an American major general, later as an intermediary between the USA and the French expedition which aided them. His American experiences probably reinforced his liberal opinions, so that he played an important role in the early stages of the French Revolution. A member of the States-General, in July 1789 he was appointed commander of the National Guard and in October marched to Versailles to rescue the royal family from the Paris mob. He supported many reasonable reforms and sanctioned the apprehension of the king at the time of the flight to Varennes, but became increasingly concerned at the more extreme policies which were gaining influence. Appointed lieutenant-general in June 1791, in December he was given command of the Army of the Centre, transferred to the Army of the North in July 1792, but viewing with alarm the growing power of the Jacobins he planned to take the king to the safety of his army, or to march on Paris to secure a form of limited monarchy. Neither occurred: on 19 August the Assembly declared him a traitor, and with his staff he crossed the frontier and arrived in Liège. Instead of being welcomed by the Allies, he was held prisoner until his release was included by Napoleon in the terms of the Treaty of Campo Formio (1797); Lafayette was allowed to return to France in 1799 but lived in retirement, declining employment and the *Légion d'honneur* and

MARQUIS DE LAFAYETTE
(ENGRAVING BY W. GREATBATCH)

objecting to the titles of consul for life and emperor adopted by Napoleon. He re-entered politics after the restoration, was a deputy from 1824, took command of the National Guard in 1830 and supported the duc d'Orléans. Jefferson stated that he had 'a canine appetite' for fame and popularity, but he never abused it, and was respected, even revered, in both France and the USA. The debt felt to Lafayette by the Americans led to one of the most famous exclamations of the First World War, when an American colonel (Stanton) remarked, on the arrival of the American Expeditionary Force in France, '*Lafayette, nous voici!*' ('Lafayette, we are here!'), repaying by American succour to France that which Lafayette had brought to the United States 140 years before. His son, Georges Washington Motier de Lafayette (1779–1849), served in the French Army, was ADC to Grouchy 1805–7, but retired in the latter year, believing that Napoleon's distrust of his father would inhibit his chance of advancement.

Buckman, P. *Lafayette*. London, 1977; Gottschalk, L. R.: *Lafayette and the Close of the American Revolution*. Chicago, 1935; *Lafayette between the American and French Revolutions*. Chicago, 1950; *Lafayette Comes to America*. Chicago, 1935; *Lafayette joins the American Army*. Chicago, 1937; La Fayette, marquis de. *Mémoires, Correspondances et Manuscrits de La Fayette*. Paris, 1837–8

LAKE, General Gerard, 1st Viscount (1744–1808)

Although best known for his campaigns in India, he also served in Europe. Entering the Foot Guards in 1758, he served in the Seven Years and American Wars, became major-general in 1792, commanded the Guards Brigade in The Netherlands 1793–4 and in 1797 was promoted to lieutenant-general. He succeeded Abercromby as commander in Ireland and in the 1798 rebellion defeated the rebels at Vinegar Hill, and once Cornwallis had taken overall command, brought about the French surrender at Ballinamuck. CinC India in 1801 and full general from 1802, he achieved success commanding in the northern sphere in the Second Maratha War, most decisively at Laswaree (1 November 1803), and in the second phase of the war, against Holkar of Indore, won a victory at Furruckabad (17 November 1804) and captured Deig. Superseded by Cornwallis in 1805, he resumed command after the latter's death and pursued Holkar into the Punjab until he surrendered. Lake remained as CinC India until 1807 and became a viscount; after returning home, he was taken ill while serving on the Whitelocke court-martial and died on 20 February 1808, thus being spared the knowledge of the death of his son, Lieutenant-Colonel George Lake, killed leading the 29th at Rolica.

Pearse, H. *Memoir of the Life and Services of Viscount Lake*. London, 1908

LALLEMAND, General François-Antoine, baron (1774–1839)

Born in Metz, François (also referred to as Charles) enrolled in the artillery in 1792, served at Valmy, transferred to the cavalry, served in Italy and Egypt, was commissioned and graduated from Bonaparte's Guides to Napoleon's staff in the Marengo campaign. He served with the cavalry at Austerlitz, Jena and Friedland, was ennobled as baron in 1808, served in the Peninsula where he achieved a victory over the incompetent 'Jack' Slade at Llerena in June 1812, and was *général de brigade* from August 1811. Withdrawn from Spain in 1813, he commanded the cavalry of Macdonald, then Davout, with whom he was besieged in Hamburg. He rallied to Napoleon in 1815, served with the *Chasseurs à Cheval* of the Imperial Guard in the Waterloo campaign, and accompanied Napoleon into exile (Bunbury saw him aboard HMS *Bellerophon* and described him as 'a thick-set man, coarse in his appearance, and sullenly determined in his looks'.[1] Lallemand was not permitted to go to St. Helena but was sent as a prisoner to Malta and then, under proscription, was instrumental in the establishment of the abortive colony of French veterans at Champ d'Asile in Texas. After that collapsed he wandered between Europe and America, returning to France after the 1830 revolution, when his rank was restored and he received staff appointments. His brother was **General baron Henri-Dominique Lallemand (1777–1823)**, who also had a distinguished military career. Commissioned in the French artillery in 1797, he served in Egypt, in 1806 transferred to the Guard artillery with which he served in the campaigns until 1814 (including Spain), becoming *général de brigade* in March 1814. He was imprisoned briefly with his brother for implication in the latter's plot to raise the northern garrisons in support of Napoleon in 1815, commanded the Guard artillery in the Waterloo campaign and became overall artillery commander after the death of Desvaux. Under sentence of death like his brother, he fled to Hungary and then America, and was involved in the settlement at Champ d'Asile. In October 1817 he married Henriette-Marie (known as Harriet) Girard (1800–80), niece of Stephen Girard, a French emigrant who had become one of the richest men in America. They settled near Philadelphia; Henri died of dysentery in September 1823.

1. Bunbury, *Memoirs*, p. 307.

LAMBALLE, Marie-Thérèse-Louise de Savoy–Carignan,

PRINCESSE DE LAMBALLE
(ENGRAVING BY W. GREATBATCH)

princesse de (1749–92)

Fourth daughter of Louis Victor de Carignan, Louise of Savoy (as she called herself) was married in 1767 to Louis-Alexandre-Stanislaus de Bourbon, prince de Lamballe, who died in the following year. Noted for her beauty and gentleness, she became a close friend of Marie-Antoinette, which was her only 'crime'; imprisoned in the Temple and La Force by the French Revolutionaries, on 3 September 1792, having refused to swear hatred of the king and queen, she was most hideously murdered by the mob and her body dismembered, her head being borne through the streets on a pike to taunt the royal family. Small wonder that the British officer J. F. Neville, who saw this ghastly sight, remarked 'How grateful should I not be to the Almighty, for not having made me a Frenchman!'[1]

1. Neville, J. F. *Leisure-Moments in the Camp and in the Guardroom*, York, 1812, p. 160.

Bertin, G. *Madame de Lamballe*. Paris, 1888

LAMBERT, General Sir John (1772–1847)

Perhaps best known for succeeding Pakenham in command of the British forces at New Orleans, Lambert also saw much service in Europe. Commissioned in the 1st Foot Guards in 1791, he served in the Peninsula from 1808, at Walcheren, and in the Peninsula again from 1811, becoming major-general on 4 June 1813 and commanding a brigade of the 6th Division from that July. At Waterloo he commanded the 10th British Brigade of the 6th Division. After New Orleans he appointed Harry Smith as his military secretary, and as Smith remarked, 'From that moment to the present, dear General Lambert has ever treated me as one of his own family';[1] and Smith was the only one to discover, by accident, that at Waterloo Lambert had received a violent blow on the right arm which turned it black from shoulder to wrist, but refused even to consult a surgeon. Knighted by virtue of receiving the KCB in January 1815, he became lieutenant-general in 1825 and general in 1841.

1. Smith, pp. 243–4.

LAMOIGNON-MALESHERBES, Chrétien-Guillaume de, see MALESHERBES

LANGERON, General Louis-Alexandre-Arnault de, count (1763–1831)

A distinguished commander of the Russian Army, he was one of many foreigners who attained high rank in the Tsar's service. A member of an ancient French family, he had served in the War of American Independence and then emigrated, entering Russian service under Suvarov. Attaining the rank of lieutenant-general, he led the 2nd Column at Austerlitz and fought against the Turks, but is probably best known for his service in 1812–14 and for the memoirs he wrote. In 1812 he commanded a division of Chichagov's army, but most notably led a corps of Blücher's Army of Silesia in 1813–14, especially distinguished at Leipzig and in the 1814 campaign. Blücher and Langeron did not especially esteem each other and there were some difficulties about Langeron serving under Prussian command, but he proved a valuable subordinate. He was not a typical Russian general; despite his long service and understanding of the Russian language, he retained a marked French accent, and was noted for his French manners, appearance and wit (he loved puns and riddles). He behaved with great kindness to those under his command and was thus loved by his troops. Experienced and with a cool bearing in battle, he was a talented commander even though he was regarded as a somewhat eccentric and absent-minded character.

Langeron, L. A. A. *Mémoires de Langeron, Général d'Infanterie dans l'Armée Russe, Campagnes de 1812, 1813, 1814*. Paris, 1902

LANNES, Marshal Jean, duc de Montebello (1769–1809)

Probably none of the Marshals was so esteemed as a colleague and friend by Napoleon as was he. The son of a farmer and livery-stable keeper at Lectoure, he had little education and was apprenticed to a dyer, but in June 1792 enlisted in the 2nd Gers volunteer battalion and, his military talents

JEAN LANNES
(ENGRAVING BY KRUELL AFTER GUÉRIN)

becoming evident, had risen to command his battalion by 1795. He came to Napoleon's notice when serving with the Army of Italy, was several times wounded and became *général de brigade* in March 1797. From Arcola especially he became not only Napoleon's most loyal subordinate but also a true friend; he accompanied him to Egypt, was severely wounded in the neck at Acre and again at Aboukir, was one of the few chosen to accompany Napoleon back to France, and assisted in the coup of Brumaire. As *général de division* and commander of the Consular Guard, Lannes led the advance-guard in the 1800 campaign, winning the victory of Montebello and playing an important role at Marengo. A period as ambassador to Lisbon was less successful (Lannes was not best-equipped to be a diplomat) and he relinquished command of the Guard after unauthorised expenditure upon it, but he was among the first creation of the Marshalate in 1804, and as commander of V Corps in 1805 played an important part in the campaign of Austerlitz, holding Napoleon's left flank. In 1806 he won the action at Saalfeld and served valuably at Jena; a wound at Pultusk and illness kept him out of action for some months, but he returned to serve at Heilsberg and Friedland. Ennobled as duc de Montebello in 1808, in the Peninsula he won the action at Tudela and brought a successful conclusion to the siege of Saragossa; summoned to the German front, he led the storming of Ratisbon (even threatening to be first up the scaling-ladders), and led the defence of Essling. In this dreadful action he was talking to his old friend and mentor General Pierre Pouzet when a roundshot struck off the general's head; Lannes wandered off and sat on a bank to recover his composure, and a cannon-ball smashed one knee and tore the ligaments behind the other. One leg was amputated and it seemed as though he might recover, but infection set in and he died on 31 May. Napoleon was stricken with grief, not only for the loss of perhaps his only true friend, but also of an exceptionally brave and skilled general; rough and uncultured Lannes might have been, but as a subordinate carrying out Napoleon's directives he was probably unmatched. Napoleon commented that 'He was assuredly one of the men on whom I could most implicitly rely ... courage at first predominated over judgement; but the latter was every day gaining ground ... he had become a very able commander at the period of his death ... I found him a dwarf, but I lost him a giant.'[1]

1. Las Cases, vol. I, p. 251; vol. II, p. 395.

Horward, D. W. 'Roland of the Army: Lannes', in *Napoleon's Marshals*, ed. D. G. Chandler, London, 1987; Lannes, C. L. M. *Le Maréchal Lannes, duc de Montebello*. Tours, 1900; Thoumas, C. *Maréchal Lannes*. Paris, 1891; Wilette, L. *Le Maréchal Lannes, un D'Artagnan sous l'Empire*. Paris, 1979

LAPISSE, General Pierre-Bellon, baron de Sainte-Hélène (1762–1809)

Perhaps best known for his participation in the Peninsular War, he was born in Lyons, served in the army during the War of American Independence and was commissioned before the Revolution. After service in Germany he became *général de brigade* in October 1799, commanded a brigade under Augereau in VII Corps in 1805 and at Jena, and was promoted to *général de division* in December 1806. In the early stages of the Peninsular War he commanded the 2nd Division of Victor's I Corps, making the decisive attack at Espinosa; in 1809 he was sent to subdue southern Leon, and was then ordered to advance into Portugal, but with insufficient forces he performed lethargically and the task was never even begun. He rejoined Victor's corps and fought with it at Talavera, and was killed urging on his men to the attack.

LA REVELLIERE-LEPEAUX, Louis-Marie de (1753–1824)

A lawyer from the Vendée, whose family name was La Révellière (he adopted the 'Lépeaux' from a property they owned), he was a member of the States-General and Convention and was known as a good speaker and as an honest, industrious man. Although he voted for the death of the king, he was not an extremist, and was forced into hiding upon the proscription of the Girondins. His position restored, he was a member of the Committee of Public Safety and became President of the Directory, acting to preserve unanimity between Directors who hated one another; he was especially close to Rewbell and hated Carnot. Unseated as a Director, he retired into private life (30 June 1799), refusing even to accept the money that was his

due. While in office he had favoured the moral and philosophical 'religion' of theophilanthropy, which attracted some criticism, but he retained great respect. Napoleon remarked on his unimpeachable honesty, but thought him 'not qualified to occupy any higher station than that of an inferior magistrate'; he, his wife and daughter, said Napoleon, 'were three paragons of ugliness'.[1]

1. Las Cases, vol. II, p. 258.

La Révellière-Lépeaux, L. M. de. *Mémoires*, ed. R. D. d'Angers. Paris, 1895

LA ROCHEJAQUELEIN, Henri, comte de (1772–94)

HENRI, COMTE DE LA ROCHEJAQUELEIN (ENGRAVING BY W. GREATBATCH)

Heir to an ancient Vendéen family, and his only military experience being as a member of the king's constitutional guard, despite his youth he was chosen as CinC of the royalist insurrection in the Vendée. The undisciplined nature of this army reduced its commander's authority, but he was an inspiration by virtue of his bravery and adherence to the royalist cause; his most famous exhortation was: 'If I advance follow me; if I retreat, shoot me; if I am killed, avenge me.' 'His courage was ardent and rash, which acquired him the title of *The Intrepid*. In battle he had a just and quick eye; his measures were prompt and able, and he always inspired the soldiers with ardour and confidence; but he was blamed for exposing himself to danger without necessity, going too far, often engaging in personal combat ... He was thought to attend too little to the discussions of the council of war. In reality, he found them often idle and useless, and was apt to fall asleep after having delivered his opinion. To these charges he only answered, "Why was I made a general? My only wish is to be a hussar, that I may have the pleasure of fighting!" Notwithstanding ... he was full of gentleness and humanity; and the battle over, felt nothing but pity for the vanquished.'[1] On 4 March 1794, during a skirmish at Trémentines-sur-Nuaillé, he attempted to save the lives of two enemy soldiers, but one of them shot him in the head and killed him on the spot. He was greatly lamented: 'To this day the peasants speak with love and pride of his great courage, his modesty, his affability; that easy careless good humour of a soldier which distinguished him. There is not a Vendéen whose countenance does not brighten when he tells of his having served under M. Henri!'[2] His father, Henri-Louis-Auguste, marquis de La Rochejaquelein, *maréchal de camp* in the French Army, emigrated with his second son, entered British service and died at San Domingo in 1802. This son, Louis, who inherited the title as marquis, was in the *Armée de Condé* and then British service; he returned to France under the Consulate, and in 1801 married the marquise de Lescure, widow of another leader of the Vendéen revolt, whose memoirs form a valuable commentary on the subject. In 1814 they both took part in the royalist movement in

the Bordeaux region, and Louis was killed on 4 June 1815 in a skirmish with Napoleon's troops at Pont des Marthes.

1. La Rochejaquelein, pp. 113–14.
2. Ibid., p. 475.

La Rochejaquelein, marquise de. *Memoirs of the Marchionness de Larochejaquelein* (sic). Edinburgh, 1816

LA ROMANA, General Pedro Caro y Sureda, marquis of (1761–1811)

Reckoned by many as one of the best Spanish commanders of the Napoleonic Wars, and certainly most popular with his allies, he was born in Majorca and began his career in the navy, before transferring to the army. He served against France 1793–5 and in 1807 was appointed to lead the Spanish division 'lent' to Napoleon for service in Denmark and northern Germany. He was instrumental in arranging for the defection of these troops, who escaped from Denmark in British ships (thanks also to the efforts of the British intelligence agent James Robertson, alias 'Brother Gallus'). La Romana was appointed a member of the Seville *junta* and in 1810 became commander of the Spanish army which collaborated with Wellington, whom he supported fully. D'Urban described him as 'wild and fantastic in all his measures',[1] but Surgeon Boutflower articulated the general opinion: 'He is most devoted to his Country, and I really believe determined not to survive the extinction of her liberty. His appearance proves that a very great soul does sometimes inhabit a very mean body'.[2] La Romana was lamented universally when he died unexpectedly (apparently of an aneurism of the heart) on 23 January 1811; at his funeral the band of the 79th Highlanders played *To The Land of the Leal*, an appropriate tune for such

a champion of Spanish liberty. Wellington wrote that in him, 'the Spanish Army has lost their brightest ornament, his country their most upright patriot, and the world the most strenuous and zealous defender of the cause in which we are engaged; and I shall always acknowledge with gratitude the assistance which I received from him, as well by his operations as by his counsel'.[3] He esteemed him less as a general, however, remarking later that La Romana was 'the worst of all – a good man – a very good excellent man, but no general ... a good-natured excellent man, most easy to live with – and very clever too – knew all about the literature and poetry of his country more than any Spaniard I ever knew, but he knew nothing of troops at all. I never in my whole life saw a man who had acted at all with troops understand so little about them'.[4]

1. D'Urban, 1930, p. 92. 2. Boutflower, C. *The Journal of an Army Surgeon during the Peninsular War*. private pubn., n.d., p. 50. 3. Wellington, vol. VII, p. 190. 4. Stanhope, pp. 10, 23

LARPENT, Francis Seymour (1776–1845)

A lawyer by profession, he joined the British Army in the Peninsula as deputy JAG, responsible for the superintendence of courts-martial, from 1812 until the end of the war, and is remembered for the account he wrote of his duties and experiences. He was not entirely removed from the fighting despite being a non-combatant, civil officer; he found it necessary to remove his black plume to avoid being mistaken for a surgeon, so as not to be thought uncaring when surrounded by wounded men pleading for assistance which he had no ability to give, and he was even apprehended by the enemy at San Marcial. Subsequently he occupied a number of important legal and civil service positions.

Larpent, F. S. *The Private Journal of Judge-Advocate F. S. Larpent, attached to the Head-Quarters of Lord Wellington ...*, ed. Sir George Larpent. London, 1853

LARREY, Dominique-Jean, baron (1766–1842)

DOMINIQUE-JEAN LARREY

Although his father was a shoemaker, the family included a number of medical practitioners, so it was appropriate that Larrey became one of the greatest surgeons, and humanitarians, of the age. Although he took part in the storming of the Bastille, medical matters rather than politics came to dominate his life; from 1792 he served as a surgeon with the French Army, on the Rhine, in Italy from 1797, and in Egypt. He was not only a gifted surgeon but an innovator and organiser, devising a 'flying ambulance' for the better evacuation of casualties from the battlefield, and in Egypt utilising camels with panniers for the same purpose. Popular throughout the army for the great concern he showed for his patients, he was appointed chief surgeon to the Imperial Guard and to the *Grande Armée*. After the campaigns of Austerlitz, Jena and Eylau, he went to Spain

in 1808 (where he almost died from typhus), and after Aspern–Essling (where he amputated Lannes' shattered leg) and Wagram he was ennobled as baron. He was the army's senior medical officer in the 1812 campaign in Russia, and at Waterloo was wounded and captured by the Prussians who were about to shoot him when he was recognised and saved by a Prussian surgeon who had attended lectures he had given in Berlin. After the wars Larrey held a number of important posts, none more to his liking than that of chief surgeon to the Invalides, though old rivalries and jealousies led to his dismissal in 1836. To the end of his life he was worshipped by the army to which he had devoted his life and energies. Napoleon's tribute is appropriate: 'To science he united, in the highest degree, the virtue of active philanthropy: he looked upon all the wounded as belonging to his family; every consideration gave way before the care which he bestowed upon the hospitals ... [he was] the most virtuous man that I have known.'[1]

1. Las Cases, vol. IV, pp. 8–9.

Larrey, D. J. *Mémoires de Chirurgie Militaire* (trans. as *Memoirs of Military Surgery*). Paris, 1812–17; he wrote many other works and papers; Richardson, R. G. *Larrey: Surgeon to Napoleon's Imperial Guard*. London, 1974; Triaire, P. *Napoléon et Larrey*. Paris. 1902

LASALLE, General Antoine-Charles-Louis, comte (1775–1809)

Often held to have been the archetypal hussar, and cultivating that image, he was born of noble family in Metz, was commissioned in the army but was deprived of his rank at the Revolution, so enlisted as a trooper. He came to prominence by his ability and

ANTOINE CHARLES, COMTE DE LASALLE (ENGRAVING BY FORESTIER AFTER GROS)

bravery, notably in Italy, became *général de division* in February 1805, but his opportunity for real distinction came in the pursuit after Jena when, with an insignificant force of cavalry, he bluffed and threatened Stettin into surrender. After service at Golymin he became *général de division* (December 1806); at Heilsberg when commanding the 1st Cavalry Division he saved the life of, and was then saved by, Murat. In Spain in 1808 he won further distinction, notably at Medina del Rio Seco and especially Medellin; ennobled as comte, he was recalled from the Peninsula to command the 1st Division of Light Cavalry in the Danube campaign of 1809, including the desperate fighting at Aspern–Essling. Lasalle once remarked that any hussar who wasn't dead by the age of thirty was a blackguard; he only just failed to meet this target, for while leading the pursuit at Wagram he was shot through the head and killed on the spot. Despite his flamboyant appearance – his trademark was hussar uniform and a pipe – and wild reputation, as a general of light cavalry he was a true expert, both on the battlefield and in reconnaissance work, so that his loss was a severe blow to the army.

Marbot described him as the best light cavalry leader, but was less impressed by his manner: 'although well educated, he adopted the fashion of posing as a swashbuckler. He might always be seen drinking, swearing, singing, smashing everything', and although he trained his troops to perfection, Marbot considered that he did harm by providing a model for others who thought that they too had to 'become, like him, a reckless, drinking, swearing rowdy';[1] in other words, they copied his faults but were unable to emulate his great merits.

1. Marbot, vol. II, pp. 381, 383.

De Lisle, General H. de B. 'Great Cavalry Leaders: Lasalle', in *Cavalry Journal*, 1912, vol. VII, pp. 78–83; Hourtoulle, F. G. *Le Général Comte Charles Lasalle 1775–1809*. Paris 1979; Sheppard, Captain E. W. 'The Napoleonic Cavalry and its Leaders', in *Cavalry Journal*, 1930, vol. XX, pp. 451–7 (biography of Lasalle)

LAS CASES, Emmanuel-Augustin-Dieudonné-Martin-Joseph, comte de (1766–1842)

A French aristocrat with a hereditary title, he was a naval officer before emigrating at the beginning of the Revolution; he served against the republicans (surviving the expedition to Quiberon) and lived in London until returning to France under the Consulate. He became a supporter of Napoleon, came to the emperor's attention from 1810, and was appointed chamberlain and a count of the empire. He returned to England at the first restoration but rejoined Napoleon in 1815, and for the early part of his exile was one of his closest confidants. He conducted negotiations with the British, and accompanied Napoleon to St. Helena; Bunbury described him as 'not far removed from being a little old quiz; nervous and fidgety'.[1] His sojourn

EMMANUEL, MARQUIS DE LAS CASES
(ENGRAVING BY R. COOPER)

on St. Helena was relatively short: in December 1816 he was ordered to leave for 'corrupting the fidelity of an inhabitant of the island, so far as to render him, in a criminal and underhand way, the bearer of secret and clandestine letters for Europe'.[2] He returned to Europe via the Cape, but, forbidden to enter France, lived in Brussels until allowed back to Paris after Napoleon's death. While at St. Helena he had taken notes of conversations and events concerning Napoleon, and published them in 1823 as *Mémorial de Sainte-Hélène*, which enjoyed great success; his memoirs had been published in Brussels in 1818. From 1830 he sat as a Deputy under Louis-Philippe.

1. Bunbury, *Memoirs*, p. 307. 2. Las Cases, vol. IV, p. 227.

Las Cases, comte de. *Mémoires d'Emmanuel-Dieudonné, comte de Las Cases*. Brussels, 1818; *Memoirs of the Life, Exile and Conversations of the Emperor Napoleon*. London, 1834 (one of a number of editions of the *Mémorial de Sainte-Hélène*)

LA TOUR D'AUVERGNE, Théophile-Malo Corret de (1743–1800)

One of the French Army's most famous lower-ranking personali-

ties, he was born in Brittany, the son of a lawyer, and gained a commission in 1767 under the name of Corret de Kerbaufret, which he changed in 1771 to La Tour d'Auvergne, this being the name of the great Turenne (from whose illegitimate half-brother Corret was descended). A supporter of the Revolution, he earned a reputation for great bravery in the early campaigns of the period, notably in the Pyrenees, but his health declined and he retired in 1795. Captured by the British *en route* (by sea) to Brittany, he was held for two years, and after his release, in 1797 he volunteered again in the place of the conscripted son of a friend. After service as a captain on the Rhine and in Switzerland (1798–9), Napoleon styled him 'the first grenadier of France' (April 1800); but he was killed at Oberhausen on 27 June 1800. Such an impression had been made by his bravery that his heart was carried on the belt of a grenadier NCO in his regiment (46th Line), and on Napoleon's order his name remained on the roll, which when called was answered with '*Mort au champ d'honneur*', a practice which continued even after the heart was laid-up at Paris in 1883.

LAURISTON, Marshal Jacques-Alexandre-Bernard Law, marquis de (1768–1828)

The son of the French General Jacques-François Law de Lauriston (1725–85), he was born in Pondicherry in India; he was great-nephew to John Law (1671–1729) of Lauriston near Edinburgh, who in the early 18th century had brought financial chaos to France with his 'Mississippi scheme', his Royal Bank, the *Compagnie des Indes* and the issue of paper money. Commissioned in the artillery, Jacques Alexandre supported the Revolution and served in the early campaigns

JACQUES-ALEXANDRE LAURISTON (ENGRAVING BY T. JOHNSON AFTER GÉRARD)

until resigning in 1796. He re-entered service in 1800 as ADC to his friend Napoleon, and served at Marengo; a skilled gunner, he was given charge of the artillery school at La Fère, but was then employed on diplomatic duties, as envoy to Denmark, and to England where he carried details of the Peace of Amiens. *Général de brigade* from September 1802, *de division* from February 1805, he sailed with Villeneuve to Martinique and was present in the action off Cape Finisterre; in 1806 he took Ragusa, in 1807 was Governor of Venice, was ennobled as comte in 1808, and commanded the Guard artillery in Spain. In the 1809 campaign he commanded the artillery at Wagram; in 1811 he became ambassador to Russia, joined the *Grande Armée* during the 1812 campaign (when he was sent on an abortive attempt to negotiate with the Tsar), at Lützen and Bautzen commanded V Corps but was taken prisoner at Leipzig and held for the remainder of the war. He remained loyal to the Bourbons during the Hundred Days and prospered: he became a marquis in 1817, a Marshal in 1823, in that year commanded the corps in Spain which took Pamplona, and was Minister of State from 1824.

LAVALETTE, Antoine-Marie Chamans, comte de (1769–1830)

One of Napoleon's most valuable friends and subordinates, he was a Parisian who became close to Napoleon while an officer in the Army of Italy. Courageous and intelligent, he was a faithful aide and undertook delicate missions, accompanied Napoleon to Egypt and returned with him, assisted in the coup of Brumaire, and was even connected to him by marriage: before leaving for Egypt Lavalette married Emilie de Beauharnais (1781–1855), daughter of François, marquis de Beauharnais (1756–1847), Josephine's brother-in-law. Lavalette remained close to Josephine even after her divorce, but continued to serve Napoleon with undiminished loyalty; ennobled as comte, he served as councillor of state, was Postmaster-General during the Consulate and Empire, and provided a useful source of intelligence. He assisted Napoleon's escape from Elba and during the Hundred Days was again in control of posts, and upon the second restoration was sentenced to death, an unjust verdict unpopular, it was said, even with the king. Lavalette's escape was dramatic: on the eve of execution he walked out of the Conciergèrie prison after exchanging clothes with his wife, and his friends concealed him in the foreign ministry until he was smuggled out of France in British uniform by Sir Robert Wilson, Captain John Hely-Hutchinson and the idealistic British traveller and sometime lover of Lady Hester Stanhope, Michael Bruce. (All three were convicted of helping his escape and spent six months in a French gaol). Lavalette escaped to Bavaria, where he received help from Eugène de Beauharnais and lived under the alias of 'M. Cossar' with the connivance of the king, and later returned to France to care for his wife, who had lost her reason after being imprisoned for helping his escape. She recovered and Lavalette was pardoned in 1822.

Lavalette, comte de. *Mémoires et Souvenirs de comte de Lavalette*. 1831; translations include White, L. A. *The Adventurous Life of Count Lavalette, Bonaparte's Aide-de-Camp and Napoleon's Postmaster-General*. 1936; Bruce, I. *Lavalette Bruce: his Adventures and Intrigues before and after Waterloo*. 1953 (concerns one of his rescuers who received 'Lavalette' as a nickname)

LAVOISIER, Antoine-Laurent (1743–94)

The great French chemist, perhaps most noted for his work on overturning the phlogistic theory, held a number of public posts during the early Revolutionary period, in which his scientific skills were put to good effect, notably in the commission appointed to ensure uniformity of weights and measures. He fell victim to the Revolution's excesses, however: arrested on ridiculous charges, he was guillotined on 8 May 1794, his appeal for a delay in sentencing to enable him to complete some experiments being rejected; it was said that the president of the tribunal, Jean-Baptiste Confinhal, remarked that the Republic had no need of scholars.

LAWRENCE, Captain James (1781–1813)

One of the heroes of the War of 1812, he was born in Burlington, New Jersey, and forsook a career in the law to join the US Navy (1798). Having served against Tripoli, at the beginning of the War of 1812 he commanded the USS *Hornet*, sinking the sloop HMS *Peacock* off Demerara (24 February 1813); but his name is always associated with USS *Chesa-*

JAMES LAWRENCE

peake, to which he was appointed captain in May 1813. Joining the ship at Boston, he responded to the challenge issued by Captain Philip Broke of HMS *Shannon* and engaged that ship on 1 June 1813; *Chesapeake* was devastated by British gunnery and captured by boarding, though Lawrence's conduct became almost legendary. Wounded in the leg, he stayed at his post until hit more severely, when he was taken below, making his famous declaration 'don't give up the ship'. The wound proved mortal and he died on 4 June.

Gleaves, A. *James Lawrence*. New York and London, 1904

LAWRENCE, Sir Thomas (1769–1830)

The son of a Bristol innkeeper, he was a child prodigy who became the most popular portraitist of his time. In 1792 he succeeded Reynolds as painter to the king; elected to the Royal Academy in 1794 he was knighted in 1815 and became President of the RA in 1820. His reputation spread throughout Europe: in 1818 he went to Aix-la-Chapelle to paint the personalities at the Congress, and visited Rome and Vienna, his courtly manner impressing the sovereigns and statesmen who sat for him. A notable collection of his work was deposited in the Waterloo Chamber at Windsor, depicting Allied participants of the Napoleonic Wars, painted for George IV. Although the quality of his work is mixed (his vast outpouring resulted in some pictures having a somewhat superficial quality), his best bear the hallmark of greatness, for example his portraits of Wellington (that showing the Duke holding the Sword of State, and the half-length used later to decorate the British £5 bank note). He also formed one of the finest of all collections of Old Master drawings, part of which was bought for the Ashmolean, Oxford.

Gower, Lord. *Sir Thomas Lawrence*. 1900; Levey, M. *Sir Thomas Lawrence*. National Portrait Gallery, 1979; Williams, D. E. *Life and Correspondence of Sir Thomas Lawrence*. 1831

LEBRUN, Charles-François, duc de Plaisance (1739–1824)

A lawyer, he entered public life in the 1760s, notably as inspector-general of crown lands and as an adviser to the French Chancellor René Maureou (1714–92), being eclipsed with him in 1774. Lebrun then turned to literature, including a translation of *The Iliad*, but re-entered politics at the outset of the Revolution. A Deputy in the Constituent Assembly, he survived imprisonment during the Terror and in 1795 was elected to the *Conseil des Anciens*. He supported Napoleon in the coup of Brumaire and was appointed Third Consul, working on the re-organisation of finances and internal administration, in 1804 became arch-treasurer (*Architré-sorier*) of the empire, was Governor-General of Liguria (1805–6) and in 1808 (with some reluctance) accepted the dukedom of Plaisance (Piacenza). He administered the ex-kingdom of Holland after its annexation (1811–13), and somewhat unenthusiastically accepted the Bourbon restoration and was made a peer of France by Louis XVIII. Rallying to Napoleon in 1815, his peerage was suspended until 1819. Throughout his career he was known as an able and prudent official, experienced yet forward-thinking and liberal. Although also known for his literary endeavours, he should not be confused with the two French poets of the same name, both of whom produced works in honour of Napoleon and his army: Echouard Lebrun (1729-1807) and Pierre Lebrun (1785–1873). The son of the duc de Plaisance was **General Anne-Charles Lebrun (1775–1859)**, who entered the French Army in 1799 and was at Desaix's side when that general was killed at Marengo. He served as Napoleon's aide in 1805, with the cavalry at Jena and Eylau, then as *général de brigade* rejoined Napoleon's staff for Friedland (wounded), Spain and the campaigns of 1809 and 1812–14; he was employed by the Bourbons but rejoined Napoleon in 1815. Subsequently he was admitted to the reserve of the general staff, succeeded his father as duke in 1824 and became a senator in 1852. He was married to the daughter of Director Barbé-Marbois.

LECLERC, General Charles-Victor-Emmanuel (1772–1802)

Perhaps best remembered as Napoleon's brother-in-law, he joined the army and was commissioned in 1791. After service at Toulon, with the Armies of the North, Rhine and Italy in a variety of staff duties, and being known to the Bonaparte family as a capable soldier and a man of means (heir to a flour-merchant), he was accepted as a suitor for the hand of Pauline Bonaparte. They were married on 14 June 1797 at

CHARLES VICTOR LECLERC
(PRINT BY M. HAIDER AFTER F. KINSON)

Mombello, near Milan, Leclerc having become *général de brigade* in the previous month. He was appointed chief of staff to the forces intended to invade Ireland, later England, and in August 1799 became *général de division*. He assisted in the coup of Brumaire, then led a division with the Army of the Rhine and a corps sent to assist Spain against Portugal (1801), being recalled to command the expedition to San Domingo. He was accompanied by Pauline and their child, Dermide (1798–1804), arrived at San Domingo in late January 1802 and succeeded in arresting Toussaint l'Ouverture, but soon became unwell and died of fever on 2 November. Pauline, who in San Domingo had enjoyed her usual social life of balls and soirées, returned home with her son and the body of her husband (with some of her hair sealed in his coffin); the child died in Italy in 1804.

Leclerc, C. V. A. *Lettres du Général Leclerc*, ed. P. Roussier. Paris, 1937

LEFEBVRE, Marshal François-Joseph, duc de Danzig (1755–1820)

The son of a miller, born in Rouffach, Alsace (and never losing the Alsacian accent), he enlisted in the

Gardes Françaises in 1773 and had risen to the rank of sergeant by the beginning of the Revolution. This provided the opportunity of advancement: elected an officer in the Paris National Guard in 1789, his experience and competence led to promotion to *général de brigade* in December 1793, *de division* in the following month. Although a republican, he was no extremist, and as a regimental officer had several times helped protect members of the royal family. His courage and calmness in action continually attracted notice when serving with the Army of the Moselle, later Sambre and Meuse, notably at Fleurus, and this continued on the German front 1795–7 and when leading a division of the Army of the Danube in 1799. While recuperating from a severe wound in the right arm sustained at Ostrach, he was given command of the Paris military district, in which office he was of great help at the coup of Brumaire, in which he favoured Napoleon; in reward he became a senator (April 1800) and was among the first creation of the Marshalate in 1804. Despite bad health, he requested active employment; in 1806 he led V Corps briefly and in that October received command of the Old

FRANÇOIS LEFEBVRE
(PRINT BY FORESTIER)

Guard infantry. In 1807 he commanded the forces besieging Danzig, from which he took the title of his dukedom, and in 1808 was given IV Corps in Spain. Although he defeated Blake at Espinosa, in other respects he failed to follow orders and was removed in January 1809, Napoleon realising that he was not suitable for independent command, remarking that he 'commits nothing but follies; he cannot read his instructions. It is impossible to entrust him with the command of a corps, which is a pity, as he shows great bravery on the field of battle'.[1] However, in 1809 he was given command of VII Corps, and after Wagram pacified the Tyrol. In the 1812 campaign he commanded the Old Guard, then retired briefly before returning to service in 1814, when he was attached to headquarters and fought with distinction, notably at Montmirail and Montereau. Although loyal to Napoleon, Lefebvre advised abdication; and, created a peer by the Bourbons, remained in retirement in 1815 while accepting the appointment of senator from Napoleon (for which he was penalised at the second restoration, only being restored to his rank in 1819). He died on 14 September 1820; 'To his eminent qualities as a soldier, he united many of the virtues of the citizen, a simplicity of manners which never left him, a noble disinterestedness, and great modesty.'[2] In 1783 he had married an Alsatian laundry-woman, Catherine Hübscher, and the couple remained mutually devoted, neither attempting to alter their plain manners. The duchess in particular attracted some ridicule for her unpolished demeanour, but on learning of her kindness and philanthropy, like that of Lefebvre himself, Napoleon remarked that 'I no longer entertained towards her any other feeling than that of profound respect. I eagerly advanced to take her hand whenever I met her at the Tuileries, and I felt proud in escorting he through the drawing-room, in spite of the sneers that were buzzing around me.'³ Only the fate of their children marred the Lefebvres' personal happiness: of fourteen, the last surviving, Marie-Xavier-Joseph, was killed as a *général de brigade* in the 1812 campaign.

1. Napoleon, 9 Jan 1809, vol. II, p. 11. 2. Anon., p. 297. 3. Las Cases, vol. II, p. 182

Rothenberg, G. E. 'The Honest Soldier: Lefebvre', in *Napoleon's Marshals*, ed. D. G. Chandler, London 1987; Wirth, J. *Le Maréchal Lefebvre, duc de Dantzig.* Paris, 1904

LEFEBVRE-DESNOUETTES, General Charles, comte (1773–1822)

The son of a Parisian draper, he ran away to the army three times before making it his career. Commissioned in the 5th Dragoons in February 1793, after much service he came to Napoleon's notice in the Army of Italy, serving as his ADC in the Marengo campaign. He was with the cavalry in the 1805 campaign, became *général de brigade* in September 1806, was Jérôme Bonaparte's ADC, later Grand Equerry, and led his cavalry in the 1807 campaign. Appointed colonel of the *Chasseurs à Cheval* of the Imperial Guard, and allied to the imperial family by his marriage to Napoleon's second cousin, he was ennobled as comte in March 1808, went to Spain as Bessières' chief of staff, initiated the siege of Saragossa but returned to France after being wounded at that place. *Général de division* from August 1808, he returned to Spain in command of the Guard *Chasseurs*, but was captured at Benavente by Corporal Levi Grisdale of the

British 10th Hussars (who subsequently ran an inn at Penrith named the 'General Lefebvre'!). Lefebvre-Desnouëttes was held on parole at Cheltenham until 1812 when, with the assistance of his wife, he escaped to France; resuming command of the Guard *chasseurs*, he led them in the Russian campaign (wounded at Vinkovo) and in 1813 commanded the 1st Guard Cavalry Division. He fought in the 1814 campaign in command of a Young Guard cavalry division (twice wounded at Brienne), retained command of the ex-Guard *chasseurs* (re-titled *Corps Royale des Chasseurs à Cheval de France*) under the Bourbon restoration, but was an active plotter in gathering support for Napoleon's return. During the Hundred Days he commanded the Guard Light Cavalry division, and was wounded at Waterloo. Sentenced to death as a diehard Bonapartist, he fled to America until his hopes were dashed by Napoleon's death, and sailed for Europe after being offered a pardon; but the ship (*Albion*) foundered off the coast of Ireland on 22 April 1822 with the loss of all aboard, a melancholy end for a brave and talented leader of light cavalry who was utterly loyal to his emperor and in return much esteemed by him.

LEGENDRE, Louis (1752–97)

This Parisian butcher and ex-seaman became one of the leading orators and advocates of the Revolution. A member of the Jacobin and Cordeliers' Clubs, he was involved in the attacks on the Bastille and Tuileries, as a Parisian Deputy voted for the death of the king, went on a mission to Lyons in 1793 and was a member of the Committee of Public Safety. Initially violent in his beliefs, he was later accused of becoming more moderate; as a follower of Danton, he at first defended him

but then withdrew his support. After the fall of Robespierre he assisted in the closure of the Jacobin club and the impeachment of Carrier. He served as president of the Convention and was elected to the *Conseil des Anciens*, but died in 1797, leaving his body to medical science. He should not be confused with **General baron François-Marie-Guillaume d' Harvesse Legendre (1766–1828),** who served in the army of the *ancien régime*, in the Vendée and Italy (including Marengo) and was *général de brigade* from December 1805, but whose career was blighted by his service as Dupont's chief of staff, the disgrace of Bailen virtually ending it until after the Bourbon restoration.

LEGRAND, General Claude-Juste-Alexandre-Louis, comte (1762–1815)

One of Napoleon's best divisional commanders, he enlisted in 1777 and rose to the rank of sergeant-major; in 1790 he joined the National Guard and rose rapidly in rank, becoming *général de brigade* by September 1793. His service included Fleurus and, as *général de division*, Stockach and Hohenlinden; in the 1805 campaign he served with distinction as commander of the 3rd Division of Soult's IV Corps, and similarly at Jena and Eylau. Ennobled as comte in 1808, in the following year he commanded the 1st Division of Massena's IV Corps, most notably at Aspern–Essling, Wagram and Znaim; on the night of the evacuation of Aspern, Lejeune, carrying the order which instituted it, found him in a very bad temper: Legrand swore at him for disturbing the sentries, the ill-humour perhaps arising from the fact that he had taken a cannon-ball through his hat during the battle! In the 1812 campaign Legrand commanded the 6th Division of II Corps, serving at Polotsk and being severely wounded at the Berezina; on his return home he became a senator, but returned to service in 1814, defending Chalon-sur-Saône. At the restoration he was appointed a peer of France, but died in January 1815 from the effects of his Berezina injury.

LEITH, Lieutenant-General Sir James (1763–1816)

SIR JAMES LEITH

One of the soundest of Wellington's divisional commanders, he was educated at Aberdeen and at a private military academy at Lille; commissioned in 1780, he served at Toulon, as ADC to Sir David Dundas, and as major-general from April 1808 led a brigade of Hope's 2nd Division in the Corunna campaign. Leith commanded the 5th Division of the Peninsula army from autumn 1810 to February 1811, and in 1812 until wounded at Salamanca; he returned in 1813 but after a couple of days in command was wounded again, at San Sebastian (1 September). Lieutenant-general from June 1813, he was appointed to command in the West Indies, and was Governor of Antigua in 1814 and of Barbados from 1815 until his death there on 16 October 1816; he was buried in

Westminster Abbey. His nephew and ADC, Sir Andrew Leith Hay, was the author of *Narrative of the Peninsular War*, and an account of Leith's career.

Hay, Sir Andrew Leith. *Memoir of the late Lieut. Gen. Sir James Leith ... with a précis of some of the most remarkable events of the Peninsular War*. London, 1818 (2nd edn.), originally pubd. in Barbados

LEJEUNE, General Louis-François, baron (1776–1848)

Perhaps best known as one of the most important of contemporary battle-painters, his impressive pictures have the stamp of authenticity that one would expect of an artist who not only understood his subject, but who was present on many Napoleonic battlefields. Born in Alsace of affluent parents who lived at Versailles, Louis combined precocious artistic talent with a military career: commissioned in the artillery, later engineers, in the early Revolutionary Wars, from his time as Berthier's ADC in the Marengo campaign he was associated with the highest ranks in the French Army, though evidently regretted that his imperial staff duties detracted from his painting. He served in the campaigns of Austerlitz, Jena, Eylau and Friedland, as an engineer at the siege of Danzig and was employed in many important missions at the personal instruction of Napoleon. He served at Somosierra, as an engineer at the siege of Saragossa, in the 1809 Danube campaign (carrying Napoleon's order for the evacuation of Aspern–Essling), was taken prisoner in Spain and escaped from captivity in England, served through the 1812 campaign and in 1813 commanded a brigade of VII Corps. On the day after the Battle of Hanau he was seriously wounded when a piece of shell hit him on the forehead, causing his

retirement from military service. In addition to his painting, he was the first to introduce lithography into France, having learned that technique from its inventors, the Senefelder brothers, in 1806. The meticulous nature of his paintings was exemplified by his comment which implied criticism of short-cutting by other artists: 'Not depending as so many did on my art work for my daily bread, I was never afraid of giving too much time to details'.[1] Lejeune's memoirs give an excellent account of his adventures.

1. Lejeune, vol. II, p. 29.

Lejeune, L. F. *Memoirs of Baron Lejeune: Aide-de-Camp to Marshals Berthier, Davout and Oudinot*, trans. Mrs. A. Bell. London, 1897

LE MARCHANT, Major-General John Gaspard (1766–1812)

A member of an old Guernsey family, he was born in Amiens at the family seat of his maternal grandfather; his middle name was chosen in memory of his ancestor, Gaspard de Coligny (1519–72), admiral of France and Protestant leader, murdered in the St. Bartholomew's Day massacre. Le Marchant followed his father into the British Army, commissioned in 1781 and becoming one of the most far-sighted and intelligent officers of his generation. Service with the Queen's Bays in The Netherlands convinced him of the superiority of the Austrian cavalry and of the need for reformation of the British; the result was his design of a new sabre which became the 1796 light cavalry pattern, and in December 1796 his instructional manual *Rules and Regulations for the Sword Exercise of Cavalry* was issued officially. Even more significant was his plan for the reformation of officers' instruction by the establishment of schools at High Wycombe and Marlow, which were the foundation of the world-renowned academy at Sandhurst. Le Marchant was in control from 1799 until his promotion to major-general in June 1811, when he was sent to the Peninsula to command a cavalry brigade; he chose to remain there even though his wife had died in childbirth shortly after he left England, leaving eight children (who were cared for by his brother-in-law). It was thought that he would have made an outstanding cavalry leader, but having led a decisive charge at Salamanca he was shot through the body and killed on the spot, while harrying some retreating French infantry. This tragic loss of a potentially fine general was due in part to his own enthusiasm, for he had cut down six men himself, and William Tomkinson remarked pointedly that 'his conduct before he fell was much spoken of as particularly forward',[1] and he was unduly conspicuous by continuing (for reasons of economy) to wear his old blue uniform of the 7th Light Dragoons, which contrasted markedly with the red of his brigade. Although an obituary remarked that he had not 'seen much service of an active kind',[2] his importance as a reformer and educator of the British Army could hardly be over-stated, and his family received a generous pension. His eldest son, Carey (1791–1814) was an officer of the 1st Foot Guards, served as his father's ADC in the Peninsula and was mortally wounded at the Nive; the second son, Sir Denis, Bt. (1795–1874) had a distinguished political career, and the third, Sir John Gaspard (1803–74) became a general.

1. Tomkinson, p. 189. 2. *Gents Mag.*, October, 1812, p. 398.

Le Marchant, Sir Denis. *The Memoirs of the late Major-General Le Marchant*. London, 1841;

Thoumine, R. H. *Scientific Soldier: A Life of General Le Marchant 1766–1812*. London, 1968

LEON, comte, see **DENUELLE**

LEOPOLD II, Emperor (1747–92)

EMPEROR LEOPOLD II
(MEDALLIC PORTRAIT)

Third son of the Empress Maria Theresa and Emperor Francis I, he succeeded to the grand-duchy of Tuscany upon the death of his father in 1765 and became emperor upon the death of his elder brother, Joseph II, in 1790. His short reign was dominated by the upheavals in France, where his sister, Marie-Antoinette, was queen; and while he at first tried to avoid entanglement, in August 1791 he and the King of Prussia issued the Declaration of Pillnitz, which signified their readiness to intervene in France if required. Leopold died on 1 March 1792, before the first hostilities; he was succeeded by his son, Francis II (later I of Austria), and among his other children were the noted military leaders the Archdukes Charles and John.

LEOPOLD, GEORGE FREDERICK, Prince of Saxe–Coburg–Saalfeld (later Leopold I, King of the Belgians) (1790–1865)
Third son of Francis, Duke of Saxe–Coburg–Saalfeld, he entered

LEOPOLD, PRINCE OF SAXE-COBURG-SAALFELD
(ENGRAVING BY H. MEYER AFTER BURNEY)

Russian military service at the age of 18 and attended the Tsar at the Congress of Erfurt, but was forced to relinquish his position by Napoleon, Saxe–Coburg–Saalfeld being part of the Confederation of the Rhine. In 1813, however, he rejoined the Russian army as a cavalry general, serving at Lützen, Bautzen, Leipzig and in the 1814 campaign. In May 1816 he married Princess Charlotte Augusta (1796–1817), heir to the Prince of Wales, and was created Duke of Kendal; and continued to live in England after her tragically early death in November 1817. He is best known as the first King of the Belgians, which throne he accepted in June 1831, and as the uncle and adviser of Queen Victoria; his intelligence and wisdom were valued by many sovereigns and statesmen. By his second marriage, in August 1832 to Louise, daughter of Louis-Philippe, he ensured his family's succession to the Belgian throne.

LEPELLETIER DE SAINT-FARGEAU, Louis-Michel (1760–93)
Born in Paris of a prominent and wealthy family, he became President of the *parlement* of Paris and was a Deputy to the States-General; embracing the Revolu-

tion, he served as President of the Constituent Assembly and became Secretary to the Convention. He voted for the death of the king, and on the eve of the execution was accosted in a restaurant in the Palais Royale by one Paris, a member of the king's bodyguard, who asked if he were the villain Lepelletier who had voted for the king's death. When answered in the affirmative, Paris ran him through with a sword and killed him on the spot; the assassin escaped to Normandy but shot himself when about to be arrested.

LEPIC, General Louis, comte (1765–1827)

Best remembered for his personal bravery and perhaps as the subject of a memorable painting, he rose from the rank of corporal in Louis XVI's Constitutional Guard to become commanding officer of the *Grenadiers à Cheval* of Napoleon's Imperial Guard in December 1805. He led them with great distinction at Eylau, almost missing the action because of an attack of rheumatism in the knees; and, as they sat immobile under galling artillery fire, he uttered his immortal exhortation, 'Heads up, by God! Those are bullets, not turds!'[1] The incident formed the subject of Detaille's famous painting titled with the French version of his exclamation: '*Haut les têtes! La mitraille n'est pas de la merde*' (exhibited at the Salon of 1893, it appears on the cover of the study of the artist's work, *Edouard Detaille: l'Héroïsme d'un Siècle*, J, Humbert, Paris, 1979). Lepic led his troopers in the great French cavalry charges which saved the day for Napoleon, but was late in returning, having penetrated the Russian lines, declined a call to surrender and cut his way back. Napoleon greeted his arrival with a remark that he had feared Lepic

captured; no, answered Lepic, the only report he would ever receive would be of his death, never of his capture! He served subsequently as a general with the Guard in the Peninsula, in 1809 (notably at Wagram), in Russia, and in 1813 was honoured by the bestowal of the colonelcy of the 2nd *Gardes d'honneur* of the Guard.

1. This translation is that given in Lachouque, H., and Brown, A. S. K. *The Anatomy of Glory*. London, 1962, p. 88

LESCURE, Louis-Marie-Joseph, marquis de (1766–93)

Cousin of Henri de La Rochejaquelein, he had served in the French cavalry before emigrating in 1791; but returned in 1792, took part in the defence of the Tuileries, and became a leader of the Vendéen royalists. Militarily he was the best educated of them, and fluent in German, English and Italian; and in action both brave and composed. 'Although so much loved and respected, he was thought tenacious of his opinions. But in his humanity, there was something angelic and wonderful! In a war in which the generals were soldiers, and fought frequently man to man, no one ever received death from the hand of M. de Lescure. Never did he allow, when in his power to prevent it, a prisoner to perish or be ill treated ... The number of lives he saved was astonishing, and his memory is cherished and venerated by all parties throughout La Vendée. Of all those who distinguished themselves in this war, none acquired a purer glory.'[1] Hence he was known as 'The Saint of Poitou'. Indeed, he went into action carrying an ancient sword tied to his wrist as a badge of office, and armed only with a whip. On 15 October 1793 he was shot in the head during an action near the château de la Tremblaye, and

died on 6 November. His wife, Marie Louise Victoire de Donnissan (1772–1857), whom he married when she was 17, was closely connected to the court and shared his adventures in the Vendéen war. In 1801 she married Louis, marquis de La Rochejaquelein, and wrote a memorable account of the period of the Vendéen revolt.

1. La Rochejaquelein, pp. 114–16.

La Rochejaquelein, marquise de. *Memoirs of the Marchioness de Larochejaquelein* (sic). Edinburgh, 1816

LETORT, General Louis-Michel, comte (1773–1815)

A cavalryman of great élan, he entered the army in 1791, served in a number of campaigns and survived serious injuries before joining the Dragoons of the Imperial Guard in 1806. Wounded at Jena, he served in Spain in 1808, in the 1809 Danube campaign, in Russia, in 1813 (especially distinguished at Leipzig) and became *général de brigade* in January 1813, *de division* and comte in February 1814, subsequently leading a division of Guard cavalry. At the restoration he remained with his regiment, as deputy to Ornano, and in 1815, following the latter's injury in a duel, Letort led the Guard Dragoons in the Waterloo campaign. On the evening of 15 June Napoleon ordered him to attack some retiring Prussian infantry; in typical fashion he led the charge himself, was struck in the breast by a musket-ball, was borne away to a house in Charleroi but died on the night of 17 June. Napoleon felt his loss severely (and left 100,000 francs to Letort's children in his will), and he was much lamented; his reputation as a dashing cavalry leader is exemplified by the sobriquet bestowed after his heroism in 1814, 'Letort the Brave'.

LEWIS, Major General Morgan (1754–1844)

A native of New York, he rose to the rank of colonel in the US Army during the War of Independence (chief of staff to Gates at Saratoga), and his political career culminated with the Governorship of New York (1804–7). On 3 April 1812 he was appointed brigadier general and QMG, and on 2 March 1813 became major general, relinquishing the QMG post later in the month. In summer 1813 he succeeded Dearborn in field command, and after service on the Niagara frontier he commanded in the New York City area, prior to honourable discharge in June 1815.

L'HERITIER, General Samuel-François, baron (1772–1829)

The son of a baker, L'Héritier joined the army in September 1792 and was commissioned in May 1794; after staff appointments with the Army of the Rhine, he served on the staff of the Army of Reserve and was wounded in the thigh at Marengo. Thereafter he commanded heavy cavalry, leading cuirassiers at Austerlitz, Jena, Eylau, Aspern–Essling and Znaim (wounded in the last three of these actions), and was ennobled as baron in April 1808 and promoted to *général de brigade* in July 1809. In the 1812 campaign he commanded a brigade (consisting of just the 7th Cuirassiers) in the 3rd Heavy Cavalry Division of III Cavalry Corps, the division serving with Oudinot's II Corps. *Général de division* from March 1813, he commanded the 5th Heavy Cavalry Division of V Cavalry Corps, leading the corps at Leipzig after its commander, Pajol, was wounded. Continuing to lead heavy cavalry in 1814, he incurred Napoleon's disfavour after an unduly slow pursuit after Montereau, but having been employed at the first restoration, rallied to Napoleon in

1815. He commanded the 11th Heavy Cavalry Division of III Cavalry Corps in the Waterloo campaign, being wounded in the shoulder, and as a consequence of his support for Napoleon received little employment before he retired in 1828.

LIGNE, Field Marshal Charles Joseph, prince de (1735–1814)

Born in Brussels of a princely family of the Austrian Netherlands, he entered the Imperial Army and was considerably distinguished in the Seven Years War, becoming *Feldmarschall-Leutnant*. A trusted friend and adviser of Joseph II, he returned to active service as *Feldzeugmeister* during the War of the Bavarian Succession, accompanied Catherine the Great on her tour of the Crimea, was appointed field marshal in Russian service and was present at the siege of Belgrade (1788). He declined to lead the Belgian revolutionary movement, in which many of his kinsmen (including a son) were involved, and lived in Vienna after his Netherlands estates were overrun in the early Revolutionary Wars; his eldest son was killed in September 1792. He remained in retirement during the Napoleonic Wars, though was given the honorary rank of field marshal in 1809 and was captain of the emperor's *Trabanten Leibgarde*. Much interested in literature and science, he was an influential and prolific writer on military theory. Lejeune met him in 1809, when the old man was full of life and spirits, though moved to tears when he saw a likeness between Lejeune and the son who had been killed in action.

Ligne, prince de. *Mélanges Militaires, Littéraires et Sentimentaires.* Dresden, 1795–1802; among other editions of his work is *Lettres et Pensées du Maréchal prince de Ligne*, ed. Madame de Staël, 1809, and *Fragments de*

l'Histoire de ma Vie, ed. F. Leuridant. Paris, 1928

LINDET, Jean-Baptiste-Robert (1749–1825)

A lawyer born in Bernay, he gained some prominence as a Deputy to the Convention; although initially regarded as a moderate, he voted for the death of the king and assisted in the downfall of the Girondins. As a member of the Committee of Public Safety, he used his administrative skills to good effect on the problem of food supplies, acted with moderation when sent to suppress provincial unrest, and in September 1794 was the committee member who presented to the Convention their report on the state of France, urging a return to national unity, internal peace and the release of those unfairly imprisoned, his speech and the proposed measures being greeted with applause. He was the only member of the Committee of Public Safety not to sign the order condemning Danton and his supporters, opposed the Thermidorian reaction and defended Billaud-Varenne and Collot d'Herbois. He was himself denounced in May 1795 but escaped by virtue of the amnesty of that October; after which he declined public office until, with reluctance, out of patriotic duty and because he was trusted universally, he served as finance minister under the Directory from June to November 1799. Proscribed as a regicide in 1816, he returned to France only shortly before his death.

LINIERES, baron de, see **TURREAU**

LIVERPOOL, Robert Banks Jenkinson, 2nd Earl of (1770–1828)

The son of Charles Jenkinson, 1st Earl of Liverpool (1729–1808, who occupied a number of govern-

ROBERT JENKINSON, 2ND EARL OF LIVERPOOL
(ENGRAVING BY J. THOMPSON AFTER WIVELL)

mental positions including presidency of the Board of Trade 1786–1801), he followed his father into Parliament as MP for Appleby in 1790, as a supporter of Pitt and later of the war against France. He was appointed Foreign Secretary in 1801, conducted the negotiations of the Treaty of Amiens, and was Home Secretary 1804–6 as Baron Hawkesbury, a title originally bestowed upon his father. Declining to form a ministry after Pitt's death, he led the opposition until Portland took office, when he resumed his position as Home Secretary, until Perceval appointed him Secretary for War and the Colonies in 1809 (he had succeeded his father as Earl of Liverpool in 1808). In this office he was a noted supporter of Wellington and his army, and became Prime Minister after Perceval's murder in May 1812. He was a sound, rather than inspired, head of the government, and it has been said that his greatest feat was in keeping his colleagues in order and ensuring that the wheels of government ran reasonably smoothly. He continued the war against France until victory, but had less success in domestic policies in the difficult economic circumstances which followed the Napoleonic Wars, and remained

as Prime Minister until forced to retire in February 1827 following a severe stroke from which he never recovered. He was no stranger to military affairs: his paternal grandfather had fought with the Royal Horse Guards at Dettingen and commanded that regiment at Fontenoy, and in May 1794 Robert himself raised and commanded the Cinque Ports Fencible Cavalry. As Lord Warden of the Cinque Ports from 1806, he was colonel of the Cinque Ports Local Militia; but despite this experience, he was described as not possessing a military bearing, having a somewhat unkempt appearance and a rather slouching posture as well as one of the longest necks in England. Appearance notwithstanding, as remarked at the time, he was a perfectly honest, upright man, if not the most gifted of politicians.

Gash, N. *Lord Liverpool: The Life and Political Career ...* London, 1984; Petrie, Sir Charles. *Lord Liverpool and his Times.* London, 1954; Yonge, C. D. *The Life and Administration of Robert, Second Earl of Liverpool.* London, 1868

LOBAU, comte de, see MOUTON

LOISON, General Louis-Henri, comte (1771–1816)

He is probably best remembered as the one-armed general who was especially hated in Portugal, and who spent much of his career in the Peninsula. Commissioned in 1791, he had become *général de brigade* by 1795, assisted Napoleon in the suppression of the attempted coup of 13 Vendémiaire (and presided over the subsequent courts-martial), and was promoted to *général de division* in 1799 after good service in Switzerland. In the 1800 campaign he commanded at the siege of Fort Bard, in 1805 led a division of VI Corps at Elchingen and in 1807 conducted the siege of Colberg (where Lejeune recalled him in

the trenches, flapping his empty sleeve in the face of heavy fire from the defenders, as if taunting them to hit it instead of the troops who were suffering around him). In the invasion of Portugal, Loison commanded the 2nd Division of Junot's corps and led the reorganised division at Vimeiro; returning under Soult after Cintra, he became thoroughly hated for his behaviour towards the local people. Foy was almost murdered in Oporto, where Loison was especially execrated, when mistaken for him in March 1809 (Foy saved himself by holding up both hands, thus proving that he was not 'Maneta' 'the one-armed one', as Loison was known). Loison's relations with Soult were hardly any better: he hated the Marshal, who suspected him not only of incompetence but treachery at the time of the Argenton plot. Loison does seem to have been involved in some dissent, but perhaps only arising from suspicions of Soult's supposed ambitions and in loyalty to Napoleon. At Busaco he commanded a division of VI Corps, and succeeded Ney in command of the corps in March 1811; he led it at Fuentes de Oñoro where he was blamed for a mishap involving one of his units, the Hanoverian Legion, whose brigadier requested that they be allowed to wear their greatcoats to conceal their red uniforms. Loison refused, and consequently they were attacked by their own side who mistook them for British troops in the smoke of battle. Loison was sent back to France upon Marmont's assumption of command of the Army of Portugal in 1811; in 1812 he was Governor of Königsberg and defended Vilna, but in the 1813 campaign his active career was virtually ended when he was disciplined by Napoleon for failing to lead his division to the front, and he was retired officially in 1815.

LONDONDERRY, 2nd Marquess of, see **CASTLEREAGH**

LONDONDERRY, 3rd Marquess of, see **STEWART, General Charles William Vane**

LONGA, General Francisco (1770–1831)

Originally a gunsmith, he achieved fame during the Peninsular War as a leader of irregulars in the region of Cantabria, although he was much more than simply a guerrilla commander. Like Porlier, his forces had more the organisation of regular troops; Longa was commissioned as a colonel in the regular army and by early 1813 his command, regularly organised, had been so successful as to overshadow Porlier's reputation. As well as operating independently, they served with Graham at Vittoria, behaved equally well at Tolosa, shared in the Spanish victory at San Marcial, and served at Nivelle. Their disciplinary record was among the worst, however, and their excesses contributed to Wellington's decision to send back to Spain all except Morillo's division.

LOUIS XVI, King of France (1754–93)

The unfortunate Louis XVI, whose downfall and execution to a considerable extent was the trigger for the entire Napoleonic conflict, was the son of Louis the Dauphin and grandson of Louis XV, whom he succeeded on 10 May 1774. National finances were not sound from the outset, and his dismissal of capable statesmen such as Anne Robert Jacques Turgot (1727–81), and involvement in the War of American Independence, served to compound the financial difficulties. This led to the meeting of the States-General, from which the Revolution developed; Louis was unable to provide

LOUIS XVI (ENGRAVING BY T. W. HARLAND AFTER CALLET)

the firm leadership required at this juncture, and was increasingly powerless in the hands of a political establishment which became ever more radical. On 21 June 1791 he and the royal family attempted to flee to the Austrian Netherlands, but were arrested at Varennes and returned to Paris; this may have been the critical act which turned the balance against the monarchy. Louis was maintained as a constitutional king – he took the oath on 13 September 1791– but the pressure for his deposition grew as foreign troops marched into France. On 10 August 1792 the Tuileries palace was stormed by a mob and the royal family had to seek sanctuary at the Convention; on 21 September the latter abolished the monarchy and in the following January convicted the king of treason. He was guillotined on 21 January 1793, behaving at the end with great fortitude, contrasting with his somewhat ineffectual conduct earlier in the revolution. In 1770 he had married Marie-Antoinette, who became his queen and subsequently shared his fate; their two surviving children (the eldest son had died in June 1789) at the time of the Revolution were Louis-Charles the Dauphin, known as Louis XVII, and Marie-

Thérèse-Charlotte (1778–1851) who married her cousin Louis, duc d'Angoulême (son of Charles X) in 1799.

Hardman, J. *Louis XVI*. London, 1992

LOUIS XVII, King of France (1785–95)

LOUIS XVII
(ENGRAVING BY W. GREATBATCH)

The son of Louis XVI and Marie-Antoinette, born at Versailles on 27 March 1785, Louis-Charles, Duke of Normandy, became Dauphin and heir to the French throne upon the death of his elder brother in June 1789. He was never crowned nor did he reign, but he was recognised as Louis XVII by supporters of the monarchy following the execution of his father on 21 January 1793. The unfortunate child was held in the Temple prison from 13 October 1792, latterly in conditions of appalling squalor and neglect, and died on 8 or 9 June 1795, apparently of a fever arising from scrofula, but caused by the shameful ill-treatment he received. The circumstances of his death being shrouded in mystery, a number of claimants came forward in later years, stating that they had been smuggled out by royalists (who certainly did plot his release), but although a few of these gained some notoriety, it was accepted that the dauphin died in captivity at the age of 10.

LOUIS XVIII, King of France (1755–1824)

LOUIS XVIII
(ENGRAVING BY HOLL AFTER ISABEY)

Third son of Louis the Dauphin, grandson of Louis XV and brother of Louis XVI, Louis-Stanislas-Xavier, comte de Provence, was heir to the French throne until the birth of a child to Louis XVI in 1781. At the time of the flight to Varennes, he made his escape (unlike the king and queen, successfully), reached Brussels and then went to Coblenz, where he became leader of the royalist emigrant movement. A violent opponent of the Revolution, his pronouncements and deeds probably made the plight of the king and queen more parlous; upon the execution of the king he declared himself regent, and when the death of his nephew, Louis XVII, was announced, he became king-in-exile, recognised by the royalists as Louis XVIII. He continued to support royalist agitation during his wanderings, from Westphalia to Verona, in April 1796 to Condé's army on the German border, thence to the Duke of Brunswick, and from 1797 to Mittau and Warsaw. After Tilsit

he was forced to quit the Tsar's territory, and from 1807 lived in England. He returned to France as king in 1814 and accepted the terms of the Treaty of Paris, but his reign was bedevilled by vehement reactionaries among the returned royalist *émigrés*. Forced to flee to Ghent during the Hundred Days, at the second restoration he had to accept harsher terms imposed by the second Treaty of Paris, and though the ministry under duc de Decazes was reasonably liberal, under his successor, duc de Richelieu, the most extreme royalists gained power, the so-called 'White Terror' doing nothing to unite French society. Obese and infirm even when he began to reign, Louis' health deteriorated so that his more extreme brother, Artois, became more influential. Louis was extremely unpopular with large sections of French society, and many foreigners; the Duke of Wellington observed that 'I had a very bad opinion of Louis XVIII – he was selfish and false in the highest degree. I always thought better of Charles X [Artois], but you see where he came to at last!' He also recalled Louis' very poor health in a story told him by comte de Villèle, Prime Minister from 1822: Louis 'was a walking sore – a perfect walking sore – not a part of his body was sound ... Villèle told me he found him with his head resting on the table, and his voice so low that to converse with him Villèle was obliged to get under the table and speak from thence. Yet, weak as he was, Villèle assured me that he gave a most clear and precise answer ... and gave such directions that ... it was not found necessary to alter one single word.'[1] In 1771 Louis had married Louise-Marie-Joséphine of Savoy; she died in 1810 and they had no children so Louis was succeeded by his brother Artois as King Charles X.

1. Stanhope, pp. 32, 36.
    Mansell, P. *Louis XVIII*. Londor 1981

LOUIS FERDINAND, General, Prince of Prussia (1773–1806)

Nephew of the king, son of Princ Ferdinand of Prussia an described as 'the Alcibiades of Prussia', he was said by Clause witz to have had the potential of becoming a great general, and th leading Prussian commander of his time. A man of accepted mil tary and administrative ability, h was involved in the reforms intro duced by King Frederick Williar III (in which he believed progres was not sufficiently rapid), an with Queen Louise was a leader of the court 'war party'. He was th youngest of the principal Prussia commanders in the war of 180 and as *Generalleutnant* led th advance-guard division of Hohen lohe–Ingelfingen's Prusso–Saxo army. Whatever military distinc tion would have been his due, i was cut off by the action at Saalfel on 10 October 1806, four day before Jena and Auerstädt, whe his comparatively small forc engaged Lannes' V Corps and wa defeated; leading a cavalry charg in an attempt to stem the Frencl advance, he was killed by Quarter master Guindet of the French 10tl Hussars, having refused to sur render even though wounded. Hi loss was felt severely by Prussia though Napoleon commented tha it resulted from his promotion of the war.

LOUIS-PHILIPPE, King of France, duc d'Orléans and de Chartres (1773–1850)

Son of Louis-Philippe-Josep (Philippe Egalité), duc d'Orléans and descended from Louis XIV, h was known as duc de Valois unt 1785, when he took the title duc d Chartres. Like his father, h supported the Revolution witl enthusiasm, and as lieutenant

THE DEATH OF LOUIS FERDINAND OF PRUSSIA AT SAALFELD
(PRINT AFTER F. DE MYRBACH)

LOUIS PHILIPPE, KING OF FRANCE, RECEIVED AT WINDSOR BY QUEEN
VICTORIA, 1844; THE DUKE OF WELLINGTON IS IN ATTENDANCE AT EXTREME
LEFT. (PRINT AFTER W. H. OVEREND)

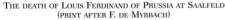

General served at Valmy and Jemappes. Alienated by the increasing extremism of the Revolution, however, he plotted with Dumouriez to overthrow the government, and fled with him to the Austrians when the plan was discovered. Following the execution of his father in November 1793 he became duc d'Orléans, and though a potential leader of the royalist movement, he agreed to go to America in 1796 in return for the Directory's offer to release from confinement his mother Louise-Maria-Adelaide de Bourbon) and his brothers (duc de Montpensier and comte de Beaujolais). The three brothers lived at Philadelphia until 1800 when Louis-Philippe returned to Europe for a reconciliation with the exiled Louis XVIII, but declined to take up arms against republican France and lived in retirement at Twickenham until 1807, when Montpensier died of consumption. Beaujolais was afflicted similarly, so Louis-Philippe took him to Malta for his health, where he died in May 1808. Louis-Philippe then went to Sicily, where he married Princess Marie Amélie Thérèse (1782–1866), daughter of Ferdinand IV, and remained there until the restoration. He supported the liberal opposition in France (to the extent that he had to return to Twickenham for two years in exile), but only became really prominent during the 1830 revolution, when he was proclaimed king in succession to the deposed Charles X. His policies brought about a decline in support, however, and he was himself deposed in 1848, escaping to England, where he died in August 1850. Wellington's opinion is of interest: 'His conduct during the Revolution was bad – very disgraceful indeed ... He is a monstrous able fellow, much abler than is commonly supposed, but a **** ... [he] combines the pretensions of the French Revolution with the pretensions of Louis XIV ... all the views and ambitions of a Bourbon combined with all the popular support of a Radical'.[1]

195

It was probably the former losing the support of the latter which cost him his throne.

1. Stanhope, pp. 36–7, 271.

Howarth, T. E. B. *Citizen King: The Life of Louis-Philippe, King of the French*. London, 1961

LOUISE, Queen of Prussia (1776–1810)

QUEEN LOUISE OF PRUSSIA

The daughter of Prince Charles of Mecklenburg–Strelitz and his wife, Frederika of Hesse–Darmstadt, Auguste Wilhelmine Amalie Luise was born in Hanover (where her father was in the army) and met the crown prince of Prussia, later King Frederick William III, at Frankfurt in 1793. He was smitten by her beauty and intelligence; they were married on Christmas Eve of the same year, and she duly became Queen of Prussia and greatly beloved by the Prussian people. Her graceful appearance concealed an iron will, however, and she became one of the leading members of the 'war party' opposed to Napoleon (who dubbed her 'the only man in Prussia'!). In the negotiations after the 1806–7 campaigns she attempted to charm Napoleon into making concessions, but he resisted. (Coignet of the Imperial Guard, no impressionable youth, was not so resistant; standing

guard when Napoleon entertained the Prussians at Königsberg, he saw Louise and recalled that he would have given one of his ears to change places with Napoleon!). Louise supported the beginnings of the movement to reform Prussia and reconstruct the army, but she died tragically early, on 19 July 1810, while visiting her father at Strelitz.

Lonke, A. *Königin Luise von Preussen*. Leipzig, 1903; Sorel, A. A. E. *Louise de Prusse*. Paris, 1937; Wright, C. *Louise, Queen of Prussia*. London, 1969

L'OUVERTURE, Toussaint, see TOUSSAINT l'OUVERTURE

LOWRY COLE, General Sir Galbraith, see COLE

LOUVET DE COUVRAI, Jean-Baptiste (1760–97)

Born in Paris, a bookseller's clerk and author of novels and plays, his writings brought him to prominence at the beginning of the Revolution. Elected to the assembly, he gravitated towards the Girondins and in 1792 published a bi-weekly journal, *La Sentinelle*, and became editor of the *Journal des Débats*. He became famous for attacks on Robespierre and Marat, in print and notably in a speech to the Convention in October 1792, and at the trial of Louis XVI supported the idea of an appeal to the people. He defended the Girondins and had to go into hiding upon their fall, but was restored to the Convention after the end of Robespierre. He helped prosecute Carrier for the outrages at Nantes, became a member of the Committee of Public Safety, and under the Directory was Secretary to the Council of Five Hundred; but his political views caused unpopularity, his bookshop was attacked and he was insulted in the streets. Compelled to leave

Paris, the Directory appointed him consul at Palermo, but he died in August 1797 before he could begin the job. He was described as resembling a short-sighted, untidy weakling, but this appearance disguised literary talent, courage, wit and sincerity, though it was said he had a somewhat petulant and credulous disposition. He wrote his memoirs while in hiding.

Louvet de Couvrai, J. B. *Mémoires de Louvet de Couvrai*, ed. F. A. Aulard. Paris, 1889

LOWE, Lieutenant-General Sir Hudson (1769–1844)

SIR HUDSON LOWE

Napoleon's 'gaoler' was born in Ireland, son of an army surgeon and was commissioned at the age of 12. He served during the early Revolutionary Wars in Gibraltar (not at Toulon, as has been stated) and became a 'Mediterranean expert' after service at Corsica and Minorca, fluent in all the languages of the area, Greek excepted. He commanded the Corsican Rangers in Egypt, reformed them after the Peace of Amiens and led them in Sicily; he commanded the garrison of Capri until forced to evacuate (October 1808) and thereafter served as Governor of Cephalonia, Ithaca and Santa Maura. Early in 1813 he as sent to Sweden to inspect the rming Russo–German Legion, d accompanied the Allied mies in the 1813–14 campaigns, aving made the acquaintance of ernadotte, the Tsar and the King f Prussia. He served with ücher's headquarters at Leipzig d carried news of Napoleon's dication to England, where he as rewarded with a knighthood d promotion to major-general June 1814). He was appointed MG to the British forces in The etherlands and was there at the ginning of the Hundred Days, t Wellington rejected his rvices and he was appointed to mmand British forces at Genoa stead. He was sent to St. Helena s governor and Napoleon's custo- ian, a period of much argument; apoleon and his supporters eaped calumnies upon him, ccusing him of vindictiveness, spicion and almost brutality; d during the whole of Nap- leon's confinement, Lowe met im only four times. Certainly he ems to have lacked tact and nown little concern for the ignity of his prisoner (who was, ter all, a defeated enemy), but e criticisms he endured were eyond fairness. When he eturned from St. Helena in 1821, owe intended to sue O'Meara for e critical remarks in his book, t the application for damages as submitted too late. In 1825–30 e commanded the forces in eylon, and became lieutenant- eneral in 1830; his three legiti- ate children were born at St. elena; his natural daughter and on were born before his arriage, during his Mediter- anean service. He was not a olished man; Sir James Fraser nought him 'though not a bad oldier ... wanting in many of the ssentials of a Gentleman',[1] and eing notably inarticulate he gave e impression of taciturnity. Wellington thought him a bad

choice of governor of St. Helena: 'He was a man wanting education and judgement ... I knew him very well. He was a stupid man [but] not an ill-natured man. But he knew nothing at all of the world, and like all men who know nothing of the world, he was suspicious and jealous'; but regarding the criticism Lowe endured, 'I must say that I think he has been shamefully used about this business – shamefully.'[2] But Lowe's friend, Major Basil Jackson, who served with him on St. Helena, wrote that he 'admired and respected his character, while I truly loved the man. I knew him to be a kind, indulgent, affec- tionate husband and parent, a warm and steady friend, a placable, nay, generous enemy, and an upright public servant'; and as for the 'unmerited oppro- brium' he received for his deal- ings with Napoleon, Jackson recalled how Montholon had admitted that 'an angel from heaven could not have pleased us, as Governor of St. Helena'.[3]

1. Fraser, p. 209. 2. Stanhope, pp. 67, 105, 326. 3. Jackson, Major B. 'A Slight Tribute to the Memory of Sir Hudson Lowe', in *CUSM*, 1844, vol. I, pp. 417, 420 (a long biography appeared in this publication, 1844, vols. I and II).

Gregory, D. *Napoleon's Jailer: Lieutenant-General Sir Hudson Lowe*. London, 1996; Seaton, R. C. *Napoleon's Captivity in relation to Sir Hudson Lowe*. London, 1903; Seaton, R. C. *Sir Hudson Lowe and Napoleon*. London, 1898

LUCCHESINI, Girolamo (1751–1825)

Born in Lucca, the eldest son of Marquis Lucchesini, he entered Prussian service as a diplomat in 1779, and accomplished many important missions and negotia- tions. In 1789 he was appointed Prussian ambassador to Poland, in 1792 accompanied the king in the

invasion of France (though personally he opposed the war and the alliance with Austria), and in 1794 became ambassador at Vienna, being recalled in 1797 after objections to his anti- Austrian bias. He was ambassador in Paris from 1800 until just prior to the 1806 war, favouring Franco–Prussian friendship but warning of Napoleon's perceived intentions. He negotiated for an armistice after Jena, terms which the king refused to ratify, and upon rejoining the Prussian court at Königsberg he received no further employment. He then took service with Elisa Bonaparte in Tuscany, retiring after Napoleon's fall.

LUDWIG, Crown Prince of Bavaria (later King Ludwig I) (1786–1868)

CROWN PRINCE LUDWIG OF BAVARIA
(ENGRAVING BY RAUSCHMAYR AFTER HAUBER)

Son of Maximilian I Joseph, the Crown Prince Ludwig (some- times styled Louis in English- language works) succeeded to the throne of Bavaria as King Ludwig I on 12 October 1825 and is best remembered for his reign, the political troubles arising from his association with the dancer Lola Montez, his interest in artistic matters and for his abdication in March 1848 in favour of his son;

but he also played a considerable role in the Napoleonic Wars. In contrast to his father, Ludwig hated Napoleon and the French alliance, but nevertheless served in Napoleon's army, notably in 1809 when he commanded the 1st Division of Lefebvre's VII Corps. The king had hoped that Ludwig might have commanded the corps (composed of Bavarians), but Napoleon was uncompromising, stating that whatever his other qualities, Ludwig was militarily inexperienced and had to be content with a divisional command; and aided by a reliable chief of staff, General Clemens von Raglovich, he acquitted himself well. Relations between the Crown Prince and Napoleon never improved (Ludwig stated that if Satan were to take human form the result would be Napoleon), and the conflict between the Bavarian military and Lefebvre (which resulted in the latter's replacement by d'Erlon after the Bavarians had become almost insubordinate) led Napoleon to ask what was prevent him from shooting a crown prince? As a leader of the anti-French party, Ludwig was among those who supported Bavaria's change of allegiance in 1813.

LUMLEY, General Sir William (1769–1850)

Seventh son of the 4th Earl of Scarborough (and brother of the 5th, 6th and 7th Earls), he was commissioned in 1787, led the 22nd Light Dragoons in the Irish rebellion and Egypt, became major-general in 1805, served at the Cape, in South America and the Mediterranean, but is best known for his service in the Peninsula. He was sent there upon the recommendation of Sir

Henry Bunbury, Adjutant-General Torrens reporting that 'I never thought him a clever man, but he is zealous, active, obedient, and brave as a lion',[1] if unsuited for commanding anything greater than a brigade. This was an accurate assessment, for Lumley proved a most capable cavalry commander; posted to lead a brigade of the 2nd Division in September 1810, he commanded the cavalry at Albuera with considerable skill, and proved his talents again in the remarkably successful cavalry action at Usagre (25 May 1811). He went home ill from the Peninsula in August 1811; subsequently he rose to the ranks of lieutenant-general (June 1814) and general (January 1837).

1.Fortescue, vol. VII, p. 419.

LUTZOW, General Ludwig Adolf Wilhelm, Freiherr von (1782–1834)

LUDWIG VON LÜTZOW
(PRINT AFTER G. LONGHI)

Having entered the Prussian Army in 1795, Lützow served at Auerstädt and Colberg but retired as a major in 1808, disgusted by the terms extracted from Prussia after the defeat. He took part in the revolt of his old commandin officer Schill in 1809 but w. wounded, rejoined the army 1811 and in February 1813 orga ised a *Freikorps*, bearing h name, recruited initially from th territories west of the Elbe lost l Prussia in 1807. On 17 June, Kitzen, the corps was all but ann hilated (not aware of th armistice, they were caught i French territory), but Lützo escaped (though wounded) ar began recruiting anew until th corps (infantry, cavalry ar artillery) numbered some 3,6(men. Subsequently the un served with distinction at Göhrc (where he was again woundec and against Denmark, he himse being captured in 1814. Lützow *Freikorps* attracted much atter tion by virtue of the patrioti motives that prompted its raisin, and because of the presence in i ranks of many intellectuals ar upper-class volunteers, includir the poets Theodore Körner ar Joseph von Eichendorff, and th philosopher and educationa reformer Friedrich Froebel. I March 1815 the unit was broke up, its elements going to forr parts of the 25th Infantry, 6t Uhlans and 9th Hussars. Durir the Hundred Days, Lützow led th 6th Uhlans, was captured at Ligr but escaped two days later; h challenged Blücher over perceived slight in his dispatcl but nothing came of it. Promote to colonel in 1815, Lützov became *Generalmajor* in 1822 an *Generalleutnant* upon his retire ment in 1830.

Jagwitz, Freiherr von. *Gesch ichte des Lützow'schen Freikorp:* Berlin, 1892; Lützow, K. von. *Ado Lützows Freikorps.* Berlin, 1884

LYNEDOCH, General Baron, se GRAHAM, Sir Thomas

MACDONALD, Marshal Jacques-Etienne-Joseph-Alexandre, duc de Tarente (1765–1840)

JACQUES-ETIENNE MACDONALD

Napoleon's 'Scottish' Marshal was the son of Vall Macachaim of South Uist, a Jacobite who went into exile in France following the 1745 rebellion, entered the French Army and changed his name to the better-known Macdonald, the Macachaims of Uist being a sept of the Macdonalds of Clanranald. Jacques Macdonald spoke no English, but when visiting his father's relations in 1825 was able to converse with them in Gaelic, his father's native tongue. Having served in the Dutch forces in 1785, he entered Dillon's Regiment of the French Army, supported the Revolution, served as ADC to Dumouriez and refused to desert with him; he became *général de brigade* in August 1793, *de division* in November 1794. After service in The Netherlands and on the Rhine, he succeeded to command of the Army of Italy in place of Championnet, despite having fallen out with that general (he was not the easiest of comrades: Macdonald sued Moreau for defamation and was intractable in a row with Talleyrand). He was severely wounded in June 1799 and severely handled at the Trebbia; he blamed Victor, who continued to harbour a grudge over the rebuke. Macdonald acquiesced, or even assisted, in the coup of Brumaire, then commanded in Switzerland and served as envoy to Denmark, but in 1803 was caught up in the accusations against Moreau and retired into private life. He was recalled only in March 1809, because of the shortage of capable generals, was sent to provide an experienced hand to guide Eugène de Beauharnais in Italy, and marching to join Napoleon commanded the formation which made the crucial attack at Wagram, for which he received his Marshal's baton, actually on the battlefield. In December 1809 he was ennobled as duc de Tarente (Tarentum), commanded the Army of Catalonia 1810–11 and in 1812 led X Corps, which protected the extreme left flank of the *Grande Armée*'s advance into Russia. There he suffered the defection of Yorck's Prussian contingent, and leading XI Corps in 1813, after service at Lützen and Bautzen, was routed by Blücher at the Katzbach, admitting his errors at the time (though not in his memoirs); Marbot thought that this enabled him to retain the trust of his subordinates, but believed that the enterprise was too large for what he considered to be Macdonald's limited talents. Macdonald fought a bitter rear-guard action at Leipzig, escaping by swimming the Elster, and in subsequent campaigns obeyed his orders loyally while arguing with Napoleon over the course to be taken. He was among those who persuaded Napoleon that the fight was lost, and with Ney and Caulaincourt was appointed to negotiate terms of abdication with the Allies; only then, it appears, did Napoleon fully appreciate his worth, remarking that those whom he had loaded with honours had deserted him, while Macdonald, for whom he had done little, had remained faithful. Regretting that he was no longer in a position to reward him, Napoleon presented him instead with the sword of Murad Bey. Accepting the Bourbon restoration (though disagreeing with many of their actions, for which the king nicknamed him 'his Outspokenness'), Macdonald remained loyal to them in 1815, attempting to prevent the army's defection to Napoleon and then escorting the king to safety. His final active command was in disbanding the last of the Napoleonic forces; he sat as a moderate liberal in the house of peers. His first wife died in 1797, his second (Joubert's widow, whom he married in 1802) died in 1804, and his third, who finally provided a male heir, he married in 1821, but she died in 1825. If militarily he was not the most talented of the Marshals, none was more loyal or honourable.

Hankinson, A. 'His Outspokenness: Macdonald', in *Napoleon's Marshals*, ed. D. G. Chandler, London, 1987; Macdonald, Marshal. *Recollections of Marshal Macdonald*, ed. C. Rousset, trans. S. L. Simeon. London, 1892

MACDONELL, General Sir James (c.1781–1857)

'The bravest man at Waterloo' was the son of Duncan Macdonell of Glengarry, and was commissioned in 1796; he served at Maida and in

SIR JAMES MACDONELL.

the Peninsula from Salamanca, but it was his service at Hougoumont which made his name. A lieutenant-colonel in the 2nd (Coldstream) Guards, he was sent to defend the château which was crucial to the security of Wellington's position at Waterloo; a large, powerful and determined Highlander, he was evidently selected especially for the task, for when Müffling queried the weakness of the detachment sent to hold Hougoumont, Wellington remarked, 'Ah, you do not know Macdonell.' Although not in overall command, he held the position throughout the day, personally helping to close the north gate when it was penetrated by the French; and when asked to name 'the bravest man in England' to receive a legacy, Wellington remarked that 'The success of the battle ... turned upon the closing of the gates of Hougoumont.'[1] Characteristically, Macdonell shared the legacy with Sergeant James Graham, who had aided him at the time. He was promoted to major-general in July 1830, lieutenant-general in November 1841 and general in June 1854, and was CinC Canada 1838–41. His eldest brother, Colonel Alexander Macdonell, was the model for 'Fergus MacIvor' in Scott's *Waverley*.

1. Cotton, E. *A Voice from Waterloo*. Brussels, 1900, p. 278 (9th edn.; orig. pubd. 1849)

MACDONOUGH, Captain Thomas (1786–1825)

Born in Delaware, the son of a physician who had been an officer in the US Army, he entered the US Navy as a midshipman, served in the Mediterranean (notably with Decatur in the destruction of the captured *Philadelphia*), but made his name in the War of 1812. Commanding the American flotilla on Lake Champlain, he achieved a notable victory over a British force under Captain George Downie (11 September 1814); he was rewarded with a gold medal from Congress and land-grants which made him a wealthy man, but his health was afflicted by consumption and he died in November 1825.

McGRIGOR, Sir James, Bt. (1771–1858)

One of the great medical experts and humanitarians of the age, he came of an old Scottish family; the son of a merchant, he joined the army as surgeon of the 88th Foot in September 1793. He served in The Netherlands 1794–5, the West Indies (1796, returning home in a ramshackle hulk of a merchantman with a drunken crew, navigated by an army officer), in India (1798) and with Baird's expedition to Egypt. Deputy Inspector-General of the Medical Department from June 1805 and Inspector-General in August 1809, after service at Walcheren he went to the Peninsula in January 1811 and until the end of the war served as head of the Medical Department with Wellington's army. An energetic and capable man, he made great improvements in the treatment of the sick and wounded, notably in the evacuation of casualties, and his introduction of portable,

prefabricated hospitals mad treatment more rapid and mu have saved thousands of live Wellington trusted him con pletely, though he made it clea that military considerations cam before humanitarian: when afte Salamanca McGrigor reporte that he had diverted commis sariat resources from the rout planned by Wellington, the latte turned on him in fury: 'Who is t command the army? I or you? . As long as you live, sir, never do s again; never do anything withou my orders.'[1] This outburst was s violent that it astonished Goya, fo whom Wellington was sitting a that moment; but the rage abate immediately and McGrigor wa invited to dinner! That the Duk appreciated McGrigor's qualitie is evident from his statement i 1814 that he was one of the mos able, industrious and successfu public servants he had eve encountered. Appointed Director General of the Medical Depart ment on 13 June 1815, McGrigo missed Waterloo; he retained th post until 1851, making man important reforms. Knighted i 1814, he became baronet i September 1831, small enoug reward for one of the greates figures in the field. In June 181 he married Mary Grant, sister o both Colquhoun Grant, the intel ligence expert, and Sir Jame Robert Grant, who was head o the medical staff in the Waterlo campaign.

1. McGrigor, *Autobiography*, a below, p. 302.

Blanco, R. L. *Wellington' Surgeon General: Sir Jame McGrigor*. Durham, North Carol ina, 1974; McGrigor, Sir James *The Autobiography and Services o Sir James McGrigor, Bart., late Director-General of the Army Medical Department*. London 1816; *Sketch of the Medical History of the British Armies in the Penin sula ... 1816*

MACK VON LEIBERICH, General Karl, Freiherr (1752–1828)

KARL MACK VON LEIBERICH
(PRINT AFTER J. MÜLLER)

Born in Bavaria, in 1770 he joined an Austrian regiment in which his uncle was an officer, and was himself commissioned in 1777. Selected for staff duty during the War of the Bavarian Succession, he served under Lacy and Loudon, became ADC to the emperor, and was greatly distinguished in the Turkish War, notably at the storming of Belgrade, and was severely wounded in the head. Chief of staff to Saxe–Coburg in 1793, he helped arrange the defection of Dumouriez and was wounded at Famars; though held in high regard as a strategist, he fell into some disfavour when part of the blame for the Allied failure in The Netherlands was ascribed to him. In 1797 he became *Feldmarschall-Leutnant* and at the emperor's request took command of the Neapolitan army; a hopeless task given the character of the troops, and to escape his mutinous soldiers he fled to the French (telling Macdonald that one attempt had been made to poison him, and another to assassinate him). After two years as a prisoner he escaped from Paris in disguise,

and despite his mixed reputation in 1804 was given the position of what amounted to chief of army staff, to reform tactics and influence Austria's strategic planning. Although necessary, the reforms were introduced so soon before the 1805 campaign that they caused confusion; and as effective commander on the Danube front, Mack was completely outmanoeuvred by Napoleon and forced to surrender at Ulm. After the war he was court-martialled and was sentenced to death, commuted to two years' imprisonment and deprivation of all his titles and honours. Released in 1808, at Schwarzenberg's request in 1819 he was restored to rank and to membership of the Order of Maria Theresa (awarded for service against the Turks). He was certainly incompetent, and Horatio Nelson went further: 'let not General Mack be employed; for I knew him at Naples to be a rascal, a scoundrel, and a coward.'[1] Napoleon would have concurred, for he remarked that Mack was the most mediocre man he ever knew, full of conceit, believing himself capable of anything, but possessed of no talent and unlucky besides.

1. Clarke, J. Stanier, and McArthur, J. *Life and Services of Horatio, Viscount Nelson.* London, 1809; 1840 edn., vol. III, p. 117.

MACKENZIE, Major-General John Randoll, see FRASER, Lieutenant-General Alexander Mackenzie

MACLEOD, Lieutenant-Colonel Charles (1784–1812)

One of the most respected members of the British Army in the Peninsula, he was the son of Lieutenant-General Sir John Macleod, who commanded the artillery at Walcheren and became colonel-commandant of the Royal Horse Artillery. One of

CHARLES MACLEOD

four brothers who all became soldiers, Charles was commissioned in 1799, served as ADC to Cornwallis in India (1805), and in May 1807 joined the 43rd Light Infantry, serving in the Danish and Corunna campaigns. From 1810 he commanded the regiment's 1st Battalion, gaining a reputation for ability and bravery in the Peninsula, notably at the Coa, and he became popular and respected throughout the army. At Badajoz he led the forward elements of the Light Division in the assault on the breaches, continuing even after a wounded man behind him ran his bayonet into his back. Harry Smith found Macleod in the ditch, holding his breast and declaring that he was mortally wounded by a musketshot; Smith helped him out of the ditch but the wound was fatal. He was buried near his regiment's camp, all the mourners overcome with grief, and even the privates who carried his coffin were openly in tears. His friend William Napier described Macleod as a young man 'whose feeble body would have been quite unfit for war, if it had not been sustained by an unconquerable spirit',[1] and Wellington described him as 'an ornament to his profession'.[2] Perhaps more telling was a remark by one of his men,

Sergeant Thomas Blood: 'There was not a man in that corps [the 43rd] but would have stood between him and the fatal ball that struck him dead, so esteemed was he by all.'[3] His brother-officers erected a monument to his memory in Westminster Abbey, sculpted by Joseph Nollekens.

1. Napier, W. vol. IV, p. 425. 2. Wellington, vol. IX, p. 44. 3. Biography (as below), p. 114.

A biography appears in *The Oxfordshire Light Infantry Chronicle*, 1895, vol. IV, pp. 97–115

MACOMB, Major General Alexander (1782–1841)

Born in Detroit, he served with the US Army on the frontier and at the beginning of the War of 1812 was colonel commanding the 3rd Regiment of Artillery. Brigadier General from January 1814, he commanded in the victory of Plattsburg, for which he was awarded a gold medal by Congress. In 1821 he was appointed chief engineer, and upon the death of Jacob Brown became major general commanding-in-chief of the US Army; as the monument over his grave recorded, he served his country for more than forty years 'without stain or blemish upon his escutcheon'.

MADAME MERE, see BONA-PARTE, Letizia

MADISON, President James (1751–1836)

For all his abilities the fourth President of the United States was hardly an effective leader for the war which dominated his presidency. Born in Virginia, his distinguished political career included service as Jefferson's Secretary of State (1801–9) before winning election as President for the Republican party, defeating the Federalist C. C. Pinckney in 1808. President from 1809, he was re-

JAMES MADISON

elected after defeating De Witt Clinton in 1812, and remained President until March 1817. His administration during the War of 1812 was weak, and indeed he was pushed into hostilities by a section of his own party; his leadership during the war was unimpressive, even inept, but in fairness much of the military leadership was equally poor, and the nation was unprepared in terms of military resources. Madison was present at the Battle of Bladensburg and had to flee, the subsequent burning of some of the capital's public buildings by the British being the nadir of his presidency, though the conclusion of the war restored some of his lost popularity. His wife, Dorothy Payne Todd (1772–1849), was almost as famous, as a society hostess whose beauty contrasted with the small and somewhat unimpressive appearance of her husband. As the British approached Washington, she had the determination and presence of mind to delay her departure until a portrait of George Washington and the Declaration of Independence were carried to safety from the presidential mansion.

Brant, I. *The Fourth President*. London, 1970 (abridgement of the author's 6-volume biography)

MAHMUD II, Sultan of Turkey (1785–1839)

Sultan of the Ottoman Empire for the second half of the Napoleonic era, he succeeded his brother Mustafa IV, who was murdered in 1808, having reigned only from the previous year, when he had been installed as Sultan in place of their cousin Selim III, who had reigned since 1789. Although nominal overlord of the empire, Mahmud's power and ability to reform were limited; his chief supporter and Grand Vizier, Mustafa Baïrakdar, was attacked by the Janissaries and blew himself up in the arsenal at Constantinople, and revolt (or at least the establishment of semi-autonomous states) occurred in the provinces, most notably in Egypt. Although after Tilsit the Ottoman Empire remained neutral in the Napoleonic Wars, hostilities with Russia were only concluded by the Treaty of Bucharest (28 May 1812), by which the empire kept Moldavia and Wallachia but Russia took Bessarabia. Mahmud was beset with more difficulties later in his reign, notably defeat by Russia (1828–9) leading to the Treaty of Adrianople, and at his death he was involved with the revolt in Syria. Personally brave, energetic and humane, his inclination to reform was frustrated by circumstances, internal opposition and an empire which was breaking up from within.

MAISON, Marshal Nicolas-Joseph, marquis de (1771–1840)

One of Napoleon's able subordinates, who did not achieve the highest rank until long after the Napoleonic Wars, he began his military service in the National Guard during the Revolutionary Wars, survived suspension for political reasons, collected many wounds and served on the Rhine and in Italy under Bernadotte. His

ssociation with that Marshal ontinued, serving in the Austertz campaign and becoming *énéral de brigade* in February 806. In 1807 he was Victor's chief f staff, serving at Friedland; ennoled as baron in 1808, he served nder Victor in Spain and led the ital attack which routed Blake at spinosa (11 November 1808). In ie Russian campaign of 1812 Maison served under Oudinot, ucceeding to command II Corps fter the wounding of Oudinot and egrand; *général de division* from ugust, he was greatly distinuished under Ney during the etreat. Advanced to comte in 813, in 1814 he commanded I Corps based originally in The Netherlands; greatly outnumered, he served with distinction nd near Courtrai on 31 March von a notable victory over Thielnann, which proved him to be 'a nan of ability and solid character',[1] according to Marbot. He iccepted the restoration and emained loyal to the Bourbons in 815, becoming marquis in 1817; n 1828 he led the French expedi-ion which supervised the Turko–gyptian evacuation of Greece and n February 1829 was appointed a Marshal of France. A supporter of Louis-Philippe, he served as imbassador to Austria and Russia, 'oreign Minister, and finally 1835–6) Minister of War.
. Marbot, vol. II, p. 676.

MAITLAND, General Sir Peregrine (1777–1854)

oining the 1st Foot Guards in 1792, he became lieutenant-colonel in that regiment in June 1803, served at Corunna and commanded the 1st Guards Brigade at the Nive, but is best emembered as the major-general who led the 1st British Brigade (1st Foot Guards) at Waterloo, and as he recipient of Wellington's order to counter-attack, 'Now Maitland, now's your time!' He received a

knighthood of the Bath in June 1815 and was subsequently CinC Madras (1836–8) and at the Cape (and Governor, 1843–7). He should not be confused with General Frederick Maitland who served at Martinique and in 1812 led the expedition from Sicily to Catalonia.

MALESHERBES, Chrétien-Guil-laume de Lamoignon de (1721–94)

This distinguished French lawyer and statesman enjoyed a promi-nent legal and political career prior to his retirement in 1776, with a brief return at the king's request in 1787. As the Revolution progressed he retired to Switzer-land, but returned to France in 1792 to conduct the king's defence, even though (as Louis remarked) he knew he was risking his life in what he believed to be a hopeless cause. His efforts proving unavailing – Malesherbes broke down during his speech of mitiga-tion before the Convention – he was the one who carried news of the sentence to the king. He then retired to the country, but Louis' fears for his safety proved sadly justified: Malesherbes was arrest-ed in December 1793 and on 23 April 1794 was executed, as was his entire family (for no other reason than their relationship to him). A notably popular and entirely good man, Malesherbes was also a leading figure in literary and scientific circles, being espe-cially learned in botany.

MALET, General Claude-François de (1754–1812)

He is remembered less for his military career than for his mad attempt to overthrow Napoleon. Of noble descent, he had served in the *Maison du Roi* of the *ancien régime* and as an officer during the early Revolutionary Wars. Suspended in 1793 for his aristo-cratic background, he was

recalled and became *général de brigade* in 1799. He opposed the election of Napoleon as Consul for Life, and the formation of the empire, and was arrested finally in 1807 for republican agitation. After imprisonment he was permitted to live in a mental institution, from which he escaped on 22 October 1812. 'An officer without renown, connection, or support, without any other resource than his imagination and audacity',[1] he attempted a republican *coup d'état* by means of a false report that Napoleon had died in Russia. With a few associates he requisi-tioned a unit of the National Guard by convincing their commandant, Colonel Soulier, of the authenticity of his forged documents, then released from La Force prison Generals Lahorie (formerly Moreau's chief of staff) and Guibal (a Jacobin involved in previous plots), and arrested Minister of Police Savary and Police-Prefect Pasquier, whom he committed without resistance to La Force. The Prefect of the Seine, Frochot, was also fooled, but Malet was less successful with General Hulin, Governor of Paris and a re-doubtable Imperial Guardsman. When Hulin resisted arrest, Malet shot him (but not, as has been stated, fatally: Hulin survived to assist in the defence of Paris in 1814); but a staff officer recognised Malet as a madman, had him seized, and the coup was over hours after it began. On the following day Malet was tried by a military tribunal and together with Guibal, Lahorie, Soulier and eight others (mostly innocent dupes) was condemned and executed by firing-squad. Malet was allowed to command it himself, and met his end with incredible composure, giving the squad its orders and even making them re-commence its drill when it was less than perfect first time. The first volley dropped his associates but missed Malet, whereupon he went through the same process with the reserve firing-squad and was killed by the second volley. Ridiculous though his plot had been, the amount of credence put upon the announcement of Napoleon's death (at a time before the disaster in Russia had been reported, or was even complete) demonstrated that the emperor's hold was not as firm as might have been expected. This was what most disturbed Napoleon: 'I was ... far less incensed at the attempt of the criminal than at the facility with which those who appeared most attached to me had been prevailed on to become his accomplices ... so accustomed were they to changes and revolutions, that all were perfectly resigned to the establishment of a new order of things ... I said ... "where were your oaths to the King of Rome? What became of your principles and doctrines? You make me tremble for the future."'[2]

1. L'Ardeche, Laurent de. *History of Napoleon*. London, 1841, vol. II, p. 146. 2. Las Cases, vol. IV, pp. 64–5.

Artom, G. *Napoleon is Dead in Russia*. New York, 1970; Sérignan, A. M. *Le Général Malet*. Paris, 1925

MARAT, Jean-Paul (1743–93)

One of the most significant personalities of the Revolution, he was born in Neuchâtel, his father a native of Sardinia and his mother of Geneva. He gained a high reputation as a scientist and philosopher, practised as a physician (he was made an MD of St. Andrews), was an expert on optics, experimented with electricity, and was in great demand as a doctor among the French aristocracy. At the beginning of the Revolution his career turned to politics and he gained great notoriety for his journal *L'Ami du Peuple*; he attacked almost everyone in

JEAN-PAUL MARAT
(ENGRAVING BY H. W. EGLETON)

power and was denounced, at times sheltering in London and at others hiding in cellars and sewers where he contracted a skin disease. Eventually elected to the Convention, he continually opposed those in power, was one of the chief antagonists of the Girondins, and was acquitted by a revolutionary tribunal before which they sent him. One of the most extreme of the contemporary politicians, he was blamed for helping to instigate the September massacres, and advocated the extermination of opponents (it was said that he calculated how 260,000 people might be killed in a day). His exhortations were greatly influential, but his career ended abruptly when, sitting in the bath which alleviated his skin condition, he was stabbed to death by Charlotte Corday on 13 July 1793, while requesting the names of disloyal Deputies at Caen whom he could have guillotined. The murder created a sensation and he was mourned intensely (David's painting of his body contributing to the cult created around him); his ashes were transferred to the Pantheon in September 1794 and thrown out in the following February when public and political opinion decided he was a butcher, and his

busts were overthrown from their positions of honour in the public places. His reputation suffered accordingly, from his insistence on the death penalty for those not sufficiently extreme; for example Scott described his political writing as the howl of a blood hound for murder, and that he resembled a wolf whose blood lust was never appeased! His appearance perhaps contributed to this opinion: a small and ugly man latterly very infirm.

Gottschalk, L. R. *Jean Paul Marat: a Study in Radicalism*. 1927

MARBOT, General Jean-Baptiste-Antoine-Marcellin, baron de (1782–1854)

JEAN-BAPTISTE MARBOT

The author of one of the most famous of soldiers' accounts of the Napoleonic Wars, he was the son of General Jean-Antoine de Marbot who died of typhus during Massena's defence of Genoa (1800). Young Marbot joined the army as his father's aide in 1799 and, having proved his worth as an officer, served as ADC to Augereau in the campaigns of 1806–7. At Eylau he was severely wounded while (by his own account) attempting to rescue the 'Eagle' of the 14th Line, then served in the Peninsula on the staffs of Murat and Lannes, and as

ADC to the latter in 1809 helped (though wounded himself) to carry the stricken Marshal from the field of Aspern–Essling. Wounded again at Znaim, he returned to Spain under Massena, and in Russia in 1812 commanded the 23rd *Chasseurs à Cheval* with great distinction. He fought through the 1813 campaign, commanded at Mons in 1814, led the 7th Hussars in the Waterloo campaign and received a lance-wound in the side. Exiled by the Bourbons, he returned to France in 1818, was given command of the 8th *Chasseurs* in 1829, and as a general in 1830 became ADC to the duc d'Orléans; he was at the siege of Antwerp in 1832, was shot in the knee in Algiers, became a peer of France in 1845 and retired in 1848. While in exile in Germany he wrote a criticism of General Rogniat's *Considérations sur l'Art de Guerre*, which had been critical of Napoleon's handling of Aspern–Essling; this defence of the emperor earned Marbot a bequest in Napoleon's will (100,000 francs for 'guarding the glory of the armies of France and confounding their slanderers and apostates.'[1] More important were Marbot's *Memoirs*, vivid if not the most self-effacing; they have been criticised for accuracy (for example, his version of the 14th at Eylau), but the work remains a classic and was the inspiration for Sir Arthur Conan Doyle's *Brigadier Gerard*. Both Marbot's brothers served in the army: the elder, General Antoine-Adolphe Marcellin de Marbot (1781–1844) was ADC to Bernadotte, survived arrest for complicity in a republican plot, served in the 1806–7 campaigns and in the Peninsula, was captured in Russia in 1812, was ADC to Davout in 1815 and attained the rank of general officer under Louis-Philippe. Marbot's younger brother, Felix, died of an infected wound caused by

duelling with compasses while a cadet at the military school at Fontainebleau.

1. *Napoleon's Last Will and Testament*, ed. J. P. Babelon and S. d'Huart, trans. A. de Jonge, New York and London, 1977, p. 40.

Edwards, Major T. J. 'The Cavalryman of Romance: Brigadier Gerard in Real Life', in *Cavalry Journal*, 1930–1, vols. XX, XXI (a précis of Marbot's memoirs but confirming by Conan Doyle's testimony the inspiration for 'Brigadier Gerard'); Marbot, General. *The Memoirs of Baron de Marbot*, trans. A. J. Butler. London, 1913 (orig. trans. 1901)

MARCEAU-DESGRAVIERS, General François-Séverin (1769–96)

One of the 'fallen heroes' of the Revolutionary Wars, he was born in Chartres and was intended for his father's legal profession, but enlisted in the infantry at the age of 16, and while on leave took part in the storming of the Bastille. Commissioned in the National Guard, then the regular army, and having survived a period of imprisonment for being politically suspect, Marceau was sent to oppose the Vendéen rising, where

he became a friend and protégé of Kléber. Appointed *général de brigade* and *de division* in the autumn of 1793, he temporarily succeeded to the chief command prior to the arrival of Turreau de Linières (November–December 1793), but was exhausted by the campaign in the Vendée and retired to Paris for the winter. He next served under Jourdan, at Fleurus and was especially distinguished at Aldenhoven and Coblenz, and in the following year with Kléber at Neuweid and Sulzbach. In 1796 he covered Jourdan's retreat, fought the actions on the Lahn, but at Altenkirchen (19 September) was mortally wounded by an Austrian skirmisher. The retiring French found it impossible to move him, so he was abandoned to the Austrians; he was found by Kray and the Archduke Charles, who visited him on 20 September, and directed that after his death (21 September) his body was to be returned to the French with all due solemnity and honour. At his funeral French and Austrian artillery shared the mourning-salute. Marceau's ashes were placed under a pyramid designed by his friend Kléber, and was

MARCEAU MORTALLY WOUNDED AT ALTENKIRCHEN (PRINT AFTER LEJEUNE)

removed to the Pantheon in Paris in 1889.

Johnson, T. G. *François-Séverin Marceau 1769–1796*. 1896

MARCH, Earl of, see **RICH-MOND, Charles, 5th Duke of**

MARCHAND, General Jean-Gabriel, comte (1765–1851)

One of Napoleon's reliable divisional commanders, he was trained as a lawyer but entered the army at the time of the Revolution. From 1792 he was in Italy, served as ADC to Joubert when that General was killed at Novi, and became *général de brigade* in October 1805. In that year he served at Haslach and Durrenstein; *général de division* from December 1805, he led the 1st Division of Ney's VI Corps at Jena, and continued to serve under Ney in 1807, including Friedland. Comte from 1808, he went to the Peninsula with the 1st Division of Ney's corps, was defeated by Del Parque at Tamames (18 October 1809), led the French attack on the left at Busaco, commanded the rearguard of Massena's retreat in March 1811 and led his division at Fuentes de Oñoro. In the Russian campaign of 1812 he fought at Smolensk and Borodino as commander of the 25th (Württemberg) Division of Ney's III Corps, and in 1813 served at Lützen, Bautzen and Leipzig. He accepted the Bourbon restoration and in 1815 unsuccessfully attempted to oppose Napoleon at Grenoble, for which he was court-martialled at the second restoration, but acquitted; he retired in 1825.

MARESCOT, General Armand-Samuel, marquis de (1758–1832)

A skilful and industrious engineer, he was one of those French officers whose career was blighted by the Peninsular War. Commis-

sioned in 1778 and distinguished in the Revolutionary Wars, notably at Toulon and in The Netherlands, he became *général de brigade* and *de division* in 1794; in 1800 he was chief engineer in the Army of Reserve and showed typical diligence in the passage of the Alps (advocating, for example, that to prevent avalanches artillery should be fired to bring down the threatening snow), and served at Marengo. After service in Austria in 1805, and a comte from 1808, he served in Spain and helped negotiate the surrender at Bailen, being the senior French signatory to the capitulation. After repatriation he was imprisoned for his part in the disaster and not reinstated until 1814; he retired in 1815 and was made marquis by the Bourbons in 1817.

MARET, Hugues-Bernard, duc de Bassano (1763–1839)

HUGUES MARET (ENGRAVING BY T. JOHNSON AFTER LEFEVRE)

Born in Dijon, he was a lawyer of moderate views who supported the Revolution. He helped create the *Bulletin de l'assemblée*, which was incorporated into the *Le Moniteur Universel*; in 1792 he entered the foreign ministry and went on a fruitless mission of peace to Pitt, which failed because of the execution of the king and

the subsequent declaration of war. Appointed ambassador to Naples, he was captured by the Austrians en route and was held for thirty months until on Christmas Day 1795 he was one of those (with Sémonville) exchanged for the daughter of Louis XVI, later duchesse d'Angoulême. (Originally he was held in a dungeon in Mantua, but was removed to a healthier place of confinement after the intercession of Mantuan academics who respected Maret's father, an eminent surgeon and scientist). In 1799 he became Napoleon's secretary, then editor of *Le Moniteur* (which became the official journal of the state from 1800); as a minister from 1804 he was involved in diplomatic affairs and in the composition of treaties and constitutions, including that intended for Spain. His loyalty to Napoleon was rewarded with appointment as comte in 1809 and the dukedom of Bassano in 1809; he accompanied Napoleon on campaign to dispense advice and assistance. Much in favour of an Austrian alliance and Napoleon's marriage to Marie-Louise, in 1811 he replaced Champagny as Foreign Minister and went on the Russian campaign, but in November 1813 was replaced by Caulaincourt (who was thought to be more devoted to peace and more acceptable to the Tsar). Maret remained as Napoleon's private secretary, however, and served throughout the 1814 campaign; appointed Minister of the Interior and Secretary of State during the Hundred Days, he was present at Waterloo. He was exiled at the second restoration and emigrated to Graz, but was permitted to return to France in 1820, and Louis-Philippe made him a peer. One of the most devoted of all Napoleon's servants, it has been said that his servility was against Napoleon's best interests (Fouché remarked that Maret saw and heard only with the eyes and ears of his master), and that the position of foreign minister was too onerous for his abilities (Talleyrand supposedly remarked that 'In all France I know but one greater ass than Maret and that is the duc de Bassano',[1] and Savary said that he was less fitted for the job than a man just fallen from the clouds); but whatever the case, his unswerving loyalty to Napoleon must have counted for a great deal.

1. Anon., p. 184.

Ernouf, Baron A. A. *Maret, duc de Bassano*. Paris, 1878

MARIE-ANTOINETTE, Queen of France (1755–93)

MARIE-ANTOINETTE (ENGRAVING BY T. W. HARLAND AFTER BENEZACK)

The tragic queen of Louis XVI was the ninth child of the Empress Maria Theresa and Emperor Francis I, and married Louis on 16 May 1770. From the beginning she attracted the hostility of those opposed to an Austrian alliance and her extravagances (though exaggerated) also aroused much criticism. Queen of France from Louis' accession on 10 May 1774, she overshadowed her somewhat apathetic husband, both personally and in terms of the court. Her regal

appearance was doubtless a contributory factor; the artist Louise Vigée-Lebrun declared that she was not only beautiful and dignified, but was the most graceful woman in France, while Burke compared her to the morning star. She had four children: Marie-Thérèse-Charlotte, later duchesse d'Angoulême, born 1788; the dauphin Louis-Joseph-Xavier-François, born 1781 and died 1789; Louis-Charles, Duke of Normandy, born 1785, later dauphin and uncrowned Louis XVII; and Sophie-Hélène-Beatrix, born 1786 and died 1787. Marie-Antoinette's involvement in matters of state began relatively early, because she arranged places for her favourites, but the degree of her influence can be over-stated; at the Revolution she took a leading part in the negotiations involving the royal family and maintained correspondence with supporters outside the country. The declaration of war upon Austria forced her into definite opposition to the Revolution and into support for foreign intervention. With her husband executed, separated from the dauphin and herself imprisoned, she showed great courage and dignity despite declining health; accused of betraying her country, she was convicted and guillotined on 16 October 1793. Such 'betrayal' was the result of her support for the French royalist cause rather than for a foreign power, her ambition always being to preserve the position of her husband, and later her son.

Goncourt, E., and Goncourt, J. *Histoire de Marie-Antoinette*. Paris, 1859; Haslip, J. *Marie-Antoinette*. London, 1987; Hearsey, J. *Marie-Antoinette*. London, 1972; Seward, D. *Marie-Antoinette*. London, 1981

MARIE-LOUISE, Empress (1791–1847)

Napoleon's second wife was the daughter of Emperor Francis II (I

EMPRESS MARIE-LOUISE (ENGRAVING BY T. BLOOD AFTER J. GODEFROY)

of Austria) and his second wife, Maria Theresa, daughter of Ferdinand IV of Naples. She was chosen by Napoleon as empress, in place of Josephine, to cement the association between France and Austria, although the idea came at first from Austria, particularly from Metternich, to prevent Napoleon from contracting a marriage with a Russian princess. The wedding – to which Marie-Louise did not object – was carried out by proxy at Vienna on 11 March 1810, with Berthier standing in for Napoleon. The new empress was escorted to France by Caroline Murat, the civil and religious contracts taking place in Paris in the following month, Napoleon having been so impatient to see his bride that he drove out to meet her carriage. He became genuinely attached to her, and on 20 March 1811 she produced the heir for which he had longed, the King of Rome. Marie-Louise found some little difficulty in adjusting to life as empress, particularly until she became fluent in French, but in January 1814 was appointed regent of France in Napoleon's absence on campaign. After the abdication of 1814 she returned to her father in Vienna, and never saw Napoleon again; awarded the duchies of Parma, Piacenza and Guastalla by the Congress of Vienna, even before Napoleon's death she was living with Count Adam von Niepperg, whom she married subsequently and to whom she bore a son. She went to Parma without the King of Rome, who was placed under the guardianship of the emperor, his grandfather, though she visited him in Vienna, including at the time of his last illness; and she remained as ruling Duchess of Parma until the 1831 revolution, that state coming under Austrian rule upon her restoration. Very young when she married Napoleon, Marie-Louise was said to possess the charm of modesty and innocence, and a demeanour which impressed those who met her as much as her beauty and perfect complexion; affectionate in nature and genuinely attached to Napoleon, she provided him with some real happiness. In addition to all her other attributes, she was an excellent billiards player.

Masson, E. *The Private Diaries of the Empress Marie-Louise, Wife of Napoleon I.* New York, 1922; Méneval, C. F. *Napoléon et Marie-Louise*, Paris, 1843; Palmstierna, C. F. *My Dearest Louise: Marie-Louise and Napoleon*, trans. E. M. Wilkinson. London, 1958; Stoeckl, A. de. *Four Years an Empress: Marie-Louise, Second Wife of Napoleon.* London, 1962; Saint-Armand, I. de. *Memoirs of Empress Marie-Louise.* 1886; Turnbull, P. *Napoleon's Second Empress: A Life of Passion.* New York, 1972

MARMONT, Marshal Auguste-Frédéric-Louis Viesse de, duc de Raguse (1774–1852)

Born in Châtillon-sur-Seine on 20 July 1774, the son of an ex-officer, of minor nobility, he was commissioned from the artillery school at Châlons in September 1792.

AUGUSTE MARMONT (ENGRAVING BY T. JOHNSON AFTER J. B. P. GUERIN)

Distinguished at Toulon, he became a close friend of Napoleon, was appointed his aide, served in Italy and Egypt and became *général de brigade* after capturing the banner of the Knights of St. John at Malta. He served as Commandant of Alexandria during Napoleon's absence in Syria, accompanied him on his return to France, assisted in the coup of Brumaire, and after commanding the artillery at Marengo (making a notable contribution towards that victory) was promoted to *général de division* in September 1800. He introduced important reforms after his appointment as Inspector-General of Artillery (1802), including the *An XIII* system of ordnance, but in 1805, as commander of II Corps, later I Corps, of the Army of Italy had little opportunity for distinction. As Governor-General of Dalmatia (July 1806–April 1811) he was conspicuously successful both in securing Napoleon's hold on the territory and in improving conditions for the inhabitants, and was ennobled as duc de Raguse (Ragusa, now Dubrovnik). During this period he led the Army of Dalmatia (XI Corps of the *Grande Armée*) in the 1809 campaign, and in July of that year was promoted to Marshal, though Napoleon told

him that it was an award made more out of affection than on the basis of talent, as he still lacked complete military ability. In 1811, however, he was appointed to succeed Ney as commander of VI Corps in the Peninsula, and shortly after was given command of the Army of Portugal in succession to Massena. He manoeuvred against Wellington's advance of 1812 with considerable skill, but was defeated massively at Salamanca, though he had some excuse, having been severely wounded at the beginning of the action, his right arm and two ribs being shattered by a shell. By March 1813 he had recovered sufficiently to lead VI Corps at Lützen, Bautzen, Dresden and Leipzig and in subsequent actions, but was blamed for the rout of his corps at Laon which aroused Napoleon's wrath. If this strained their friendship, it was broken entirely when Marmont negotiated a truce which allowed the Allies to enter Paris (31 March 1814) and on 5 April surrendered his entire corps, which finally ended Napoleon's ability, and will, to resist. This was regarded as an act of betrayal and was never forgotten – the colloquial verb *raguser*, to betray, was taken from his title – but his old adversary Wellington was more understanding, remarking that everyone was beginning to negotiate with the Allies, 'and Marmont being nearest to Paris, treated first. That was all.'[1] The Bourbons gave him a peerage and other honours, but he was never fully trusted and held no further field command. Marmont remained loyal to the Bourbons in 1815, and as Governor of the military district of Paris attempted to defend the monarchy in 1830, but despite his efforts, the duc d'Angoulême had him arrested and asked if he were preparing to betray them, as he had betrayed Napoleon, so bitter were the memories. He went into exile with the king and never returned to France, settled in Vienna, became tutor to the Duke of Reichstadt (the ex-King of Rome, Napoleon's son), wrote a number of travel, military and historical works and died in Vienna in March 1852. His countrymen never forgave him, and the suspicion remains that he achieved the highest rank more from his friendship with Napoleon than from his abilities; and yet he was a talented general. Wellington commented: 'Ah, Marmont was a great tactician. Very clever in handling his troops; but he was too theatrical ... and while he was manoeuvring he lost his opportunities, and I caught him.'[2] Marmont supposedly wrote one of the most illegible hands of the period; when he wrote orders himself in 1815, fearing a traitor on his staff, it was said that the duc de Mortemart (commanding the royal rearguard) took so long in attempting to understand the document that he was captured!

1. Stanhope, p. 8. 2. Bunbury, *Memoirs*, p. 295.

Christophe, R. *Le Maréchal Marmont, duc de Raguse*. Paris, 1968; Marmont, Marshal. *Mémoires du Maréchal Marmont, duc de Raguse, de 1792 à 1841*. Paris, 1857 (Marmont's other writings include *Voyage en Hongrie* (1837), *Voyage en Sicile* (1838) and *Esprit des Institutions Militaires* (1845)); Pimlott, J. L. 'Friendship's Choice: Marmont', in *Napoleon's Marshals*, ed. D. G. Chandler. London, 1987

MARRYAT, Captain Frederick (1792–1848)

This popular and prolific author was one of those who drew upon his own experiences for his writing, in such well-known works as *Mr. Midshipman Easy*. Son of the agent for the Island of Grenada, at the age of 14 he was

permitted to enter the Royal Navy, having already run away to sea several times. As a midshipman he saw much service under Thomas Cochrane, including Basque Roads and Walcheren; senior naval officer at Rangoon during the First Burma War (1824), he retired in 1830 to pursue his successful literary career. His father, Joseph Marryat (1757–1824), was MP for Horsham and Sandwich in a parliamentary career which lasted from 1808 until his death, and was one of the original committee members of the Patriotic Fund at Lloyd's, of which he was chairman from 1811.

MASSENA, Marshal André, duc de Rivoli, prince d'Essling (1758–1817)

ANDRÉ MASSENA

One of the best of Napoleon's Marshals, he was born in Nice, the son of a wine merchant in a small way of business, perhaps of Jewish origin; that area being part of the kingdom of Sardinia, he was officially Italian by birth (his first name was also rendered as Andrea, and his surname may be found with the accented spelling of Masséna). Orphaned and raised by an uncle, he went to sea as a cabin boy but in 1775 enlisted in

the army, becoming sergeant-major before taking his discharge. After a career as a fruit-seller and even smuggler, he was elected lieutenant-colonel of the 3rd Var Volunteers in 1792, and his obvious talents won him promotion to *général de brigade* in August 1793, *de division* in December. He won great renown in Italy, notably at Loano, and was one of Napoleon's most trusted subordinates, winning especial laurels at Rivoli (from where in 1808 he took the title of his dukedom); it was there that Napoleon described him as 'dear child of victory' ('*l'enfant chéri de la victoire*', though apparently he actually used the word 'gâté', i.e., 'spoiled'). In 1798 Massena led the Army of Switzerland and won his greatest triumph at the second Battle of Zurich (26 September). Transferred to command the Army of Italy, he was besieged in Genoa and compelled to surrender after enduring appalling privations, before Napoleon could relieve him; he was then allowed temporary retirement to recover his health (though his reputation was somewhat clouded by the unashamed plundering in which he indulged throughout his career). One of the first Marshals in 1804, in 1805 he led the Army of Italy, in 1807 V Corps of the *Grande Armée*, but his health suffered from the Polish climate and he took sick leave; in 1808 he lost the sight of his left eye in a shooting accident (Napoleon was the culprit but Berthier took the blame). In 1809 he commanded IV Corps and won great distinction at Aspern– Essling, holding the former village as long as possible and helping to cover the army's withdrawal; because the battle was generally known to the French as Essling, that was the princely title granted him in January 1810 even though he had not been involved in the fighting around Essling village. His bravery and inspirational presence was never more apparent than on this occasion, as Lejeune recorded: 'Throughout this awful struggle Massena stood beneath the great elms on the green opposite the church, calmly indifferent to the fall of the branches brought down upon his head by the showers of grape-shot and bullets, keenly alive to all that was going on, his look and voice, stern as the *quos ego* of Virgil's angry Neptune, inspiring all who surrounded him with irresistible strength.'[1] Seriously unwell after a fall from his horse, he commanded later in the campaign (including Wagram) from his carriage. In April 1810 he was appointed to lead the Army of Portugal when possibly past his best (as his ADC Marbot believed), and distracted by his mistress Henriette Leberton, who accompanied his staff dressed as an officer; while some of his subordinates were either not especially co-operative, or downright obstructive. Massena was defeated at Busaco, compelled to retreat from Portugal when his path was blocked by the Lines of Torres Vedras, and defeated again at Fuentes de Oñoro. He was relieved of command in April 1811, which ended his active career, though from April 1813 he was Governor of the Toulon military district, a post he continued to hold under the Bourbons. He was virtually uncommitted during the Hundred Days, but his reticence in finally declaring for Napoleon and ultimate desertion of the Bourbons, satisfied neither side; he was appointed to command the Paris National Guard by the provisional government after Waterloo. He objected to sitting in judgement on Ney (despite his bad relations with that Marshal in the Peninsula), fell into great disfavour with the royalists, and died on 4 April 1817. Marbot described him as being

below medium height, lean and with 'a highly expressive Italian face', uneducated, with a tendency to bear malice, harsh and avaricious (the latter was certainly true) but a 'natural' general, brave and tenacious, though 'as he grew old he pushed caution to the point of timidity, in fear of compromising the reputation he had earned'.[2] Napoleon remarked that Massena's lack of military education (he hated reading) caused him not to know what to do when he arrived on a battlefield, but instinct determined his course of action; he was 'endowed with extraordinary courage and firmness, which seemed to increase in excess of danger. When conquered, he was always as ready to fight the battle again as though he had been the conqueror.'[3] Wellington had no doubt about his abilities: 'When Massena was opposed to me I could not eat, drink or sleep. I never knew what repose or respite from anxiety was. I was kept perpetually on the alert';[4] 'I found him oftenest where I wished him not to be.'[5] Massena reciprocated when he met Wellington after the war: "*Ah, Monsieur le Maréchal, que vous m'avez fait passer des mauvais momens!*" And he declared to me that I had not left him one black hair on his body; he had turned grey, he said, all over. I answered that I thought we had been pretty even – things nearly balanced between us. No, he said, how near you were to taking me two or three times!'[6] For all Massena's reputation for insatiable looting, his reputation as a general was immense; indeed, Wellington remarked that 'the ablest after Napoleon was, I think, Massena'.[7] Massena had two sons and a daughter: both sons in due course succeeded to his title, Captain Prosper Massena accompanying his father on campaign as his ADC;

the daughter married General Reille.

1. Lejeune, p. 271. 2. Marbot, vol. II, p. 483. 3. Las Cases, vol. I, p. 189. 4. *Wellington Anecdotes*, London n.d., p. 36. 5. Bunbury, *Memoirs*, p. 295. 6. Stanhope, pp. 162–3. 7. Ibid., p. 20.

Amic, A. *Histoire de Massena.* Paris, 1864; Marshall-Cornwall, General Sir James. *Massena.* Oxford, 1965; 'Dear Child of Victory: Massena', in *Napoleon's Marshals*, ed. D. G. Chandler. London, 1987; Massena, Marshal. *Mémoires de Massena*, ed. General J. B. F. Koch. Paris, 1850; Valentin, R. *Le Maréchal Massena 1758–1817.* Paris, 1960

MASSENBACH, Colonel Christian Karl August Ludwig von (1758–1827)

Born in Schmalkalden and educated at Stuttgart, he entered the Württemberg Army in 1778 and transferred to Prussian service in 1782, where he gained a reputation as a military theorist and mathematician (he taught the latter subject at the engineer school and as tutor to Prince Louis). He served as an engineer at Valmy and in the 1793–4 campaigns, but his main work was in re-organising the staff system, including the formulation of elaborate but wholly impracticable plans to be followed in the event of war; yet he made no provision for hostilities against France and instituted no method of transmitting orders other than the time-wasting process of formation commanders or their chiefs of staff reporting in person to headquarters to receive orders verbally. Massenbach's plans were intended to cover every eventuality, giving generals little scope for individualism or the taking account of conditions. With his great reputation, as chief of staff to Hohenlohe he exercised an even more pernicious influence in the 1806 campaign once the war with France (which he had opposed) began; he persuaded Hohenlohe not to attack first at Jena, and was a major factor in his surrender. His malign influence on the Prussian conduct of the war was such that there were even suggestions of disloyalty, and he retired to his estates to write; he tried to obtain but was denied staff employment in the 'War of Liberation', and after an unsuccessful foray into Württemberg politics he was arrested at Frankfurt and sentenced by the Prussians to fourteen years' imprisonment for publishing state secrets in his memoirs. He was released under an amnesty in 1826. He has been called 'the evil genius' of Prussia, which is perhaps unfair, von der Golz's description as a fantastic and unstable man being more accurate, and his superiors must take responsibility for following his advice.

MAXIMILIAN I JOSEPH, King of Bavaria (1756–1825)

MAXIMILIAN I JOSEPH, KING OF BAVARIA
(MEDALLIC PORTRAIT)

The son of Count Palatine Friedrich of Zweibrücken-Birkenfeld, he was one of Napoleon's most loyal allies and rose to the rank of general officer in French service. At the outbreak of the Revolution he transferred to Austrian service, participating in the early Revolutionary Wars,

succeeded his brother Karl II as Duke of Zweibrücken in April 1795, and became Elector of Bavaria in February 1799 upon the death of the incumbent, Charles Theodore. Francophile in outlook, Maximilian and his minister Montgelas introduced many beneficial, French-style reforms both internally and in the army, and though initially compelled by the presence of Austrian troops to oppose France, after Hohenlinden he concluded a peace with France, much to Bavaria's advantage. This resulted in the acquisition of territories which compensated for those lost by the Treaty of Lunéville, and as the most staunch of Napoleon's allies Bavaria supported France in the campaigns of 1805, 1806, in the Tyrol and Danube theatres in 1809, in 1812 and in Saxony in 1813; Maximilian was rewarded by the title of King of Bavaria (assumed on 1 January 1806) and by the marriage of his daughter Auguste Amélie to Eugène de Beauharnais. His son Ludwig, the crown prince, however, was very anti-French, and in October 1813 Maximilian yielded to pressure to join the Allied camp in the 'War of Liberation', on condition that the integrity of his kingdom be guaranteed. After the war he continued to support the principle of independence for Bavaria and of the sovereignty of German princes, and in May 1818 he granted his kingdom its first liberal constitution. A kindly man, regarded with affection by his subjects, he was succeeded by Ludwig upon his death on 13 October 1825. He was married twice: to Princess Wilhelmine Auguste of Hesse–Darmstadt (mother of the crown prince) (1785), and to Princess Caroline Frederike of Baden (1797).

Söltl, J. M. *Max Joseph, König von Bayern*. Stuttgart, 1837

MEHEMET (or MOHAMMED) ALI (1769–1849)

The great viceroy and ultimately hereditary ruler of Egypt, who achieved that position by his own efforts, he began his military career during the Napoleonic Wars. An Albanian, born in Kavala on the frontier of Thrace and Macedonia, he became an officer in an irregular unit recruited in that part of the Ottoman Empire for service against the French in Egypt in 1798. He served at Aboukir (25 July 1799) and, was among those who managed to swim to their ships when broken by the French attack; it was said that he was saved by Sidney Smith's gig. He returned to Egypt in 1801 and was distinguished at Ramaniyeh, and in succeeding years, supported by his Albanian troops, sided with the Ottoman Empire against the Mamelukes. After much bloodshed he was appointed Pasha in 1805, and having destroyed Mameluke power by massacre in 1811 he confirmed his position as ruler of Egypt, officially under Ottoman suzerainty but in effect as an autonomous sovereign. He created an army and navy on European lines, the latter begun with the assistance of French officers in 1808, which gave him a great advantage over the less disciplined forces which he encountered in subsequent operations and which enabled him to expand his territory.

MEISSONIER, Jean-Louis-Ernest (1815–91)

Although not contemporary with the Napoleonic Wars, he was arguably the greatest of French historical painters, including in his work a large number of Napoleonic scenes, meticulous in detail and capturing the spirit of the subject in a remarkable manner. Based on research and the study of extant relics, his work includes many of the best-known and most impressive images of the soldiers and campaigns of the First Empire, perhaps most notably his great *1814: La Campagne de France*, showing Napoleon in the snow, at the head of his exhausted staff, reproduced many times under the impression that it represents the retreat from Moscow.

Guilloux, P. *Meissonier: Trois Siècles d'Histoire*. Paris, 1980

MELAS, General Michael Friedrich Benedikt, Freiherr von (1729–1806)

Born in Radeln, Transylvania, he entered the Austrian Army in 1746 and served throughout the Seven Years War. In 1799, as *Feldzeugmeister*, he was appointed to command Austrian forces in Italy, and enjoyed early successes in conjunction with Suvarov at Cassano, the Trebbia and Novi, and on his own against Championnet. In 1800, though he forced Massena's capitulation at Genoa, he was heavily defeated at Marengo by Napoleon, a battle which he appeared to have won until the arrival of Desaix. Tired, elderly and slightly wounded, and believing himself to be victorious, Melas prematurely handed command of what he believed would be the pursuit to his chief of staff, General Zach, and returned to his headquarters at Alessandria. When Zach was captured in the early part of the French counter-attack, the Austrians were deprived of leadership at a critical moment, and much of their army was routed. On the following day Melas was forced to conclude an armistice, and subsequently withdrew Austrian forces from north Italy; as a token of esteem for his conduct, Napoleon presented him with a sabre which he had brought as a trophy from Egypt. Melas retired from active duty in 1803.

MELVILLE, Viscount, see DUNDAS, Henry

MENEVAL, Claude-François de, baron (1780–1842)

Few of Napoleon's servants can have been as valuable to him as de Méneval, his principal private and cabinet secretary. Recommended by Joseph, whose secretary he had been, he was appointed secretary to Napoleon when he was First Consul; by which, as Napoleon himself said, he acquired a treasure, 'a man of gentle and reserved manners, very discreet, working at all times and at all hours. The Emperor never had reason to be dissatisfied or displeased with him, and was very much attached to him.'[1] He handled all Napoleon's correspondence and was even entrusted with writing some replies himself, and was indefatigable in his exertions on Napoleon's behalf. He also served Marie-Louise in a similar capacity, and used his unique position to write interesting memoirs.

1. Las Cases, vol. III, pp. 332–3.

Méneval, C. F. *Memoirs to serve for the History of Napoleon I from 1802 to 1815*, trans. R. H. Sherard. London, 1894; *Napoléon et Marie-Louise*. Paris, 1843

MENOU, General Jacques-François de Boussay, comte (1750–1810)

Best known for his assumption of command of the French forces in Egypt, he was the son of a marquis and had served in the army from 1766. Having sat in the States-General, he supported the Revolution, became *général de division* in 1793 and served in the Vendée, but retired after reverses and a wound. From July 1795 he was commander of the Army of the Interior, but was censured (though acquitted) for failing to quell the unrest preceding the attempted coup of Vendémiaire

(which Napoleon settled by his 'whiff of grapeshot'). Nevertheless, he accompanied the expedition to Egypt and was given a divisional command when Baraguey d'Hilliers had to return home because of ill-health. Menou was not an imposing or military-looking figure, somewhat corpulent, balding and apparently looking much older than his years, and after he was wounded at Alexandria he relinquished command of his division when Napoleon appointed him Governor of Rosetta. In Egypt he took the very unusual step of converting to Islam, taking the name Abdallah, perhaps to improve French relations with the local people but more likely so as to marry Zobeida, the daughter of a Rosetta bath-keeper. Upon Kléber's assassination, he succeeded to command of the army, but although a capable administrator, his reputation as a general was not great; he was defeated by Abercromby at Alexandria, an injudicious battle which he handled badly, and was reportedly condemned as incompetent by General Lanusse, who was mortally wounded in the action. Having surrendered the French forces, Menou returned to France and was subseqently employed in administrative posts, including the governance of Tuscany and Venice, and was elevated to comte in 1808.

Rigault, G. *Le Général Abdallah Menou et la dernière phase d'Expédition d'Egypte*. Paris, 1911

MERCER, General Alexander Cavalié (1783–1868)

Remembered as the author of one of the most famous accounts of Waterloo, Cavalié Mercer (as he apparently preferred to style himself) was the son of a General Mercer of the Royal Engineers, and was commissioned in the Royal Artillery in 1799. Captain from December 1806, he served in South America, missed the Peninsular War entirely, but made his name, via his book, as commander of G Troop, Royal Horse Artillery, in the Waterloo campaign. His account of the battle is memorable and colourful, but, as he admitted, was written for his own amusement, long after the event though from journals kept at the time, and thus contains some errors and concentrates upon the aspects of events which most interested him. Promotion after the battle was slow and Mercer believed himself insufficiently rewarded (he did not become colonel until 1846 and major-general in 1854), which he attributed to jealousy among his brother-officers. It is clear that Waterloo was the single most significant episode in his life, to which he often referred, and while he believed himself unjustly ignored, his name has subsequently become famous by virtue of his account of the battle.

Mercer, A. C. *Journal of the Waterloo Campaign*. Edinburgh, 1870; his letters on the subject appear in Leathes, H. M. *Reminiscences of Waterloo*. London n.d.; a brief memoir and commentary on Mercer's account, by the present author, appears in the 1995 New York edition of the *Journal*

MERLIN, Antoine-Christophe (1762–1833)

Known as 'Merlin of Thionville' to distinguish him from 'Merlin of Douai', he was a native of Thionville who became a lawyer and municipal officer of that town. A member of the Legislative Assembly and National Convention, he advocated the execution of the king but was absent on a mission to the army at the time of the trial. (In an interview with the royal family in 1792, he had shed tears; Marie-Antoinette remarked

that he was weeping to see his king and queen treated so unfairly, to which Merlin replied that he wept over the plight of a beautiful, kind mother, but not one tear for the king and queen, as he hated all royalty). During the defence of Mainz Merlin exhibited great courage, and after the fall of Robespierre sat in the Council of Five Hundred, which he left in 1798. He retired at the creation of the Consulate.

MERLIN, Philippe-Antoine, comte (1754–1838)

A lawyer who espoused the Revolution, he took his nickname 'Merlin of Douai' when elected Deputy to the States-General for that town, and to distinguish him from 'Merlin of Thionville'. An industrious, moderate and conscientious man, largely devoid of personal ambition, he served as President of the Convention and was a member of the Committee of Public Safety after the fall of Robespierre, working to prevent any return to earlier tyranny, and advocating the re-admission to the Convention of the surviving Girondins. He worked on matters of foreign policy, was partially responsible for an important liberal report on the law and penal system, in October 1795 became Minister of Justice and was a Director from September 1797 to June 1799 (in the voting for which place he beat both Massena and Augereau). Under Napoleon he was a councillor of state, remained involved in legal affairs and was ennobled as comte; and as a regicide was banished at the restoration, returning to France only in 1830. His son, General Antoine-Eugène Merlin (1778–1854), also styled 'Merlin de Douai', saw much service during the Napoleonic Wars and was colonel of the 2nd (Young Guard) *Chasseurs à Cheval* of the Imperial Guard.

METTERNICH-WINNEBURG-BEILSTEIN, Prince Clemens Wenzel Lothar von (1773–1859)

CLEMENS VON METTERNICH (ENGRAVING BY T. W. HARLAND AFTER LAWRENCE)

One of the greatest European statesmen of the 19th century, he was born of noble family in Coblenz on 15 May 1773; his father, Graf Franz von Metternich-Winneburg zu Beilstein, was at that time Austrian Ambassador to the Electors of the Rhineland. Clemens' education, at Strasbourg and Mainz, was interrupted by the events of the French Revolution and the wars it engendered, arousing his suspicions of liberal or innovative political systems. He began his diplomatic career as assistant to his father, was ambassador to The Netherlands, and prospered in terms of influence by his marriage in 1795 to Countess Eleonore von Kaunitz, grand-daughter of the great Austrian chancellor of that name. In January 1801 Metternich became Austrian Ambassador to Saxony, to Prussia in November 1803 and to France in August 1806, endeavouring to bring about friendly relations between Austria and Napoleon, though at the outbreak of war in 1809 he was held for exchange for two French diplomats arrested in Hungary. Present at Wagram, Metternich advocated sueing for peace; but his negotiations dragged on so long that the Emperor opened talks with Napoleon direct, leading to the Treaty of Schönbrunn, Metternich thus having no responsibility for this humiliating document even though he had been appointed Foreign Minister shortly before its conclusion. This position he held for the next four decades. He tried to improve Austro–French relations, suggesting the marriage of Marie-Louise to Napoleon, against the opposition of influential anti-French voices in the establishment. Napoleon's defeat in Russia convinced him that a change in policy would be to Austria's interest and he negotiated with skill (meeting Napoleon at Dresden in June 1813), ensuring that Austria would remain neutral and not threatened by France until in a position militarily to join the Allies. Throughout the succeeding campaigns, Metternich was not so determined on Napoleon's destruction as were other members of the alliance, being suspicious of increasing Russian power and of a united Germany; hence the comparatively generous terms offered to Napoleon (but rejected). When it became clear that Napoleon would not consent to being 'saved' by his father-in-law (and thereby indebted to Austria), Metternich joined the others in agreeing to Napoleon's complete removal and the restoration of the Bourbons. The Allied triumph pushed him to the zenith of his reputation; in October 1813 he had been created an hereditary prince of the empire, and was now accorded the singular honour of quartering his arms with those of the house of Austria–Lorraine. The Congress of Vienna sealed his reputation, and until 1848 his was the most influential presence in Europe,

every matter of foreign policy throughout the continent being affected by his diplomacy and intrigue. He opposed all liberalism and movements which to him were reminiscent of revolution, but the upheavals of 1848 caused him to retire, after an unprecedented career as a statesman. From March 1848 until October 1849 he lived in retirement in England, then moved to Brussels, and returned to Austria only in September 1851. Much praise and much obloquy has been bestowed upon him by those who admired or hated him; but whatever the opinion all would admit that his diplomatic talents were prodigious and his influence vast. Three times married, he was not a faithful husband but was devoted to his children.

Buckland, C. S. B. *Metternich and the British Government from 1809 to 1813*. London, 1932; Cecil, A. *Metternich*. London, 1933; Grunwald, C. de. *Metternich*. London, 1953; Krahe, E. E. *Metternich's German Policy*. 2 vols., Princeton, 1963, 1983; Metternich, Prince. *Memoirs*, ed. Prince Richard Metternich (Clemens' eldest son). London, 1880–2; Palmer, A. *Metternich*. London, 1972

MIDDLETON, Admiral Charles, see BARHAM

MILHAUD, General Edouard-Jean-Baptiste, comte (1766–1833)

Although perhaps best known as a cuirassier general at Waterloo, he enjoyed a long career in the army. A farmer's son, he was commissioned in the National Guard and sat with the most extreme faction in the Convention; a friend of Marat, he spoke against the Girondins and voted for the death of the king. After service as a representative with the army, he resigned from the

Convention in 1795 and pursued a military career, developing into a skilled cavalry commander even though his original appointment was essentially political. Promoted to *général de brigade* in January 1800 after assisting in the coup of Brumaire, he led a dragoon brigade in the campaign of 1800 (being detached from Napoleon's army he missed Marengo), commanded a light cavalry brigade at Austerlitz and Jena, became *général de division* in December 1806 and commanded the 3rd Dragoon Division at Eylau. Comte from March 1808, he led his 2nd Dragoon Division at Talavera and with more success at Ocaña, where it participated in the vital charge which destroyed the Spanish army. In independent command (of cavalry and infantry), he routed Blake's army at Baza (4 November 1810), served on the staff in Russia in 1812 but reverted to leading cavalry in 1813 including leadership of Pajol's corps after its commander was wounded. Milhaud took service under the Bourbons at the restoration, but was retired when they realised what his revolutionary career had been; and rallying to Napoleon in 1815, he led IV Cavalry Corps (composed entirely of cuirassiers) in the Waterloo campaign. After the abdication he was among the first to advocate negotiation with the Allies, but despite his undoubted skill as a cavalry general and his expressions of support for the Bourbons he was again forcibly retired because the extreme republicanism of his early career could hardly be overlooked; indeed, he only escaped banishment as a regicide by a personal appeal for clemency. He was recalled to the reserve after the 1830 revolution but retired on grounds of ill-health after barely a year.

MILLER, Brigadier General James (1776–1851)

A native of New Hampshire, he was commissioned in the US Army's 4th Infantry as major in July 1808; lieutenant colonel in 1810, he served in the Tippecanoe campaign, was breveted colonel in August 1812 for service near Detroit, and subsequently led the 6th Infantry on the Niagara front, transferring to the 21st in March 1814. He served at Chippewa, Lundy's Lane and Fort Erie, and became renowned for his reply when ordered by Brown to capture a battery at Lundy's Lane: 'I'll try, Sir,' a modest remark which gained great approval and fame. For service in this campaign he was breveted as brigadier general and received a gold medal from Congress which included the inscription 'I'LL TRY'; in May 1815 he transferred to the 5th Infantry in which he had served 1810–12, a unit which adopted his famous exclamation, for example using it upon their Distinctive Insignia. Miller left the army in 1819 when appointed Governor of Arkansas Territory, which post he held until March 1825.

MILORADOVICH, General Mikhail Andreivich, Count (1770–1825)

Best known for his service in 1812, he came to prominence under Suvarov in campaigns against the Ottoman Empire and Poland, and in Italy and Switzerland in 1799 where he earned distinction in command of advance-guard formations. As lieutenant-general he was in joint command of the 4th Column of the Austro–Russian army at Austerlitz, was distinguished against the Turks in 1807 and was promoted to general in 1810. At Borodino he commanded a wing of the Russian Army and covered the evacuation of Moscow. He defeated Murat at Tarutino and was further distin-guished in 1813–14, notably at Kulm. Eugène of Württemberg, his subordinate in 1812, wrote affectionately of him, describing him as a knight in the proper sense of the word, courteous, calm and outstandingly brave. Unruffled in even the most dire circumstances, his good humour and ready wit never left him, his only chastisement being by satire; such was his consideration that when the fighting began he would leave the commander on the ground to act as he thought, and allow him to consider his general as a guest.[1] In 1818 he was appointed Governor of St. Peters-burg, which position he held at the time of the Decembrist revolt in 1825; when some of the Guard battalions mutinied he attempted to talk to the insurgent leaders but was shot in the back and killed.

1. A translation is in Brett-James, A. *1812*. London, 1966, pp. 160–1

MINA, General Francisco Espoz y (1781–1836)

Born in Navarre, of yeoman stock, Francisco Espoz Ilundain enlisted in the loyalist forces upon the French invasion of Spain, and from there entered the guerrilla band of his nephew, Xavier Mina. After the latter's capture in 1810, some of his men elected to follow Francisco, who decided that the name made famous by Xavier should be perpetuated, so hence-forward styled himself Espoz y Mina. He assembled a formidable force in the border region between Aragon and Navarre, was confirmed in command of the guerrillas of the area by the Regency, and consolidated his position by shooting a principal rival, the bandit Echeverria, who had been terrorising the popu-lace. With his command varying from a handful to 3,000 men, he not only inflicted damage on the French but kept many thousands of them occupied by his raids; he boasted that at one time no less than six generals and their armies were hunting him, without success. At times he collaborated with others; in August 1811, for example, he advanced with Longa and Porlier into Dorsenne's region based on Burgos, and in 1812 co-operated with Home Popham's British naval forces and the guer-rillas of Longa and 'El Pastor' on the Biscayan coast. In the field he defeated General Abbé, com-manding in Navarre, near Pamplona in early 1812, and in March 1813 destroyed two battal-ions at Lerin; Clausel defeated him heavily in May but he re-grouped and was back harrying the French the following month. In 1813–14 Wellington placed especial trust in him, and he made a valuable contribution to Allied success in the Pyrenees, even carrying oper-ations into France. A most capable strategist and organiser, he trained his troops and formed them into proper military units, and paid them regularly by means of a levy derived from customs-duty on goods entering Spain; even the French customs-post at Irun, on the Bidassoa, paid him a monthly contribution. Generally his campaigns were conducted with more humanity than those of some other guerrillas, and in 1812 he came to an accommodation to end the cycle of mutual reprisal and execution of prisoners. A democrat and radical, after the war he attempted to raise a liberal revolt and was forced into exile; the 1820 revolution allowed him home, and he made effective but ultimately unsuccessful resistance to the French intervention in 1823, until escaping to England. In 1830 he participated in an unsuccessful revolt against the king, returning again to Spain to serve against the Carlists in 1835 until forced to resign because of ill-health.

Iribarren, J. M. *Espoz y Mina.* Madrid, 1965–7; Mina, F. E. *A Short*

Extract from the Life of General Mina, published by Himself. London, 1825 (his full memoirs, *Memorias*, were posthumously published, Madrid 1851–2)

MINA, Xavier (1789–1817)

Sometimes known as 'Mina Junior' to distinguish him from his more famous uncle, and, at the time, 'the Student', Xavier Mina Larrea was one of the earliest and most effective guerrilla leaders of the Peninsular War, operating on the borders of Navarre and Aragon. Skilled despite his youth, he executed raids and undertook more extensive combat (on one occasion he stormed Tarifa and chased its garrison into the castle), but on 31 March 1810 his success in evading pursuing French columns ended with his capture. His uncle Francisco took over leadership of the guerrillas with even greater effect, while Xavier was imprisoned at Vincennes until 1814. After his release he had to flee Spain because of conflict aimed at forcing the king to accept a constitutional government, and deciding to continue the fight in the colonies, he attempted to raise a revolt in Mexico with the assistance of American adventurers. When they abandoned him he was again forced to become a guerrilla, but was caught and shot as a rebel.

MINTO, Earl of, see ELLIOT, Gilbert

MIOT DE MELITO, André-François, comte (1762–1841)

One of Napoleon's most trusted diplomats, he is probably best remembered for the memoirs he wrote in retirement after the second restoration. He had served as French Minister to Tuscany and Sardinia, administered Corsica, and served his friend Joseph Bonaparte as Minister of the Inte-rior at Naples, and as head of his household in Spain.

Miot de Melito, A. F. *Memoirs of Count Miot de Melito, Minister, Ambassador, Councillor of State ...* ed. T. Fleischmann. 1881

MIRABEAU, André-Boniface-Louis Riqueti, vicomte de (1754–92)

The younger brother of the 'great' Mirabeau, he served in the army and took part in the War of American Independence, and was elected to the States-General by the noblesse of Limoges. Unlike his brother, he was a vehement defender of the existing political system, yet was proud of the comte even though he attacked his liberal ideals. In 1790 he emigrated and formed a unit for the *Armée de Condé*, styled the *Légion de Mirabeau* or the *Légion Noire*, but he died in September 1792, probably of a heart attack brought about by indulgence in liquor and resulting corpulency, which had gained him the nickname 'Mirabeau Tonneau' ('the Barrel'; the term is used colloquially for 'drunkard'). He was also a writer of verse.

Berger, E. *Le Vicomte de Mirabeau (Mirabeau Tonneau) 1754–1792.* 1904; Sarrazin, J. *Mirabeau Tonneau: ein Condottiere aus der Revolutionszeit.* Leipzig, 1893

MIRABEAU, Honoré-Gabriel Riqueti, comte de (1749–91)

The eldest surviving son of Victor Riqueti, marquis de Mirabeau (1715–89) who had served in the army but enjoyed most fame as a political economist, Honoré had an early career in the army but his life at that time was one of recklessness, extravagance, exile and imprisonment – even sentence of death – mainly the result of romantic entanglements (despite being very ugly after a disfiguring attack of smallpox). His liberal

HONORÉ GABRIEL MIRABEAU
(ENGRAVING BY H. B. HALL)

ideas and political writings made him unpopular with his fellow-aristocrats, but he was elected to the States-General by the 'Third Estate' of both Aix and Marseilles. From then until his death he was perhaps the most important political figure in France, though his aim of creating a constitutional monarchy of British style, with a strong governing ministry, was not to be fulfilled. The king at first rejected his advice and the queen openly disliked him, leading to thoughts that the duc d'Orléans might be more suitable as a constitutional monarch; but latterly his object was to strengthen the monarchy by ending absolutism and creating a different but more stable form of kingship. In foreign affairs he worked to prevent foreign intervention; he was elected to the Convention and served as its president, but his health broke down from a combination of the pressures of his work and his youthful excesses. He died on 2 April 1791, amid suspicions that he had been poisoned, because he was only in early middle age. At the time his death was greatly mourned and was a serious blow, most of all to the court; but despite a huge funeral, in November 1793 his ashes were removed from the

Pantheon at the order of the Convention, which now regarded him as a traitor to the republic and a friend of the royal family. Had he lived it is possible that the course of the Revolution might have been very different.

Dumont, E. *Souvenirs de Mirabeau.* 1832, trans. by E. R. Seymour as *The Great Frenchman and the Little Genevese,* 1904; Mirabeau, comte de. *Mémoires biographiques, littéraires et politiques de Mirabeau,* ed. L. de Montigny (Mirabeau's adopted son). Paris, 1834–5; Warwick, C. F. *Mirabeau and the French Revolution.* 1905; Welch, O. J. G. *Mirabeau.* 1951

MIRANDA, General Francesco (*c.*1754–1816)

This Spanish-American soldier was born in Caracas and served with the French in the War of American Independence, but his subsequent career was concerned with attempts to win independence for the Spanish colonies in South America, and he was forced into exile on the discovery of schemes to instigate revolution. He travelled in Europe, eliciting sympathy but no material assistance; he met Pitt and the Whig opposition and in April 1792 went to France, where his friendship with Jérôme Pétion de Villeneuve led to his appointment as a general in the French Army. After service at Valmy, Dumouriez appointed him to command the siege of the citadel of Antwerp, which he took on 29 November 1792, in February 1793 commanded at the siege of Maastricht, and led the French left wing at Neerwinden. Although he had warned of Doumouriez's defection, he was arrested in its wake and imprisoned for a period. In 1797 he went to England to seek assistance for his South American schemes, but neither there nor in the USA did help materialise; after

returning to France he was expelled by Napoleon in the interests of good relations with Spain. His influence was felt in the scheme which involved Britain in the disastrous South American expedition, and in 1806, with the assistance of Admiral Sir Alexander Cochrane, he landed near Caracas and proclaimed a republic, but with little success. He tried again in 1811, established a republic of Venezuela and New Granada (Colombia) and was proclaimed dictator, but on 26 July 1812 surrendered to the Spanish governor on condition that he would be deported to the USA. This agreement was not honoured and he was imprisoned, dying at Cadiz on 14 July 1816. His nickname 'el Precursor' ('the forerunner') is an accurate reflection of his significance as one of the originators of South American independence which was achieved by Bolivar and others. The vehemence of his opinions is evident from Wellington's comment of how he, when Secretary for Ireland, was appointed to tell Miranda that the British government would have nothing to do with his schemes: 'I thought it best to walk out in the streets with him and tell him there, to prevent his bursting out. But even there he was so loud and angry, that I told him I would walk on first a little that we might not attract the notice of everybody passing.'[1]

1. Stanhope, p. 69.

MIREUR, General François (1770–98)

A medical student before he joined the National Guard in 1789, he made quite rapid progress in the army during the Revolutionary Wars, serving on Bernadotte's staff in the Army of the Sambre and Meuse, and in Italy in 1797. *Général de brigade* from April 1797, he commanded a cavalry

brigade in Egypt, where he died on 9 July 1798, in circumstances which are recorded variously. Nicolas Devernois (who was not present) stated that Mireur had been so critical of Napoleon in a council of war that he had blighted his chance of advancement and rode out into the desert to shoot himself; alternatively he may have ridden out and been killed by Bedouins, the official version of his death.

MISSIESSY, Amiral Edouard-Thomas de Burgues, comte de (1756–1837)

He went to sea with his father, a naval officer, at the age of 10, and progressed through the ranks of the French Navy, serving in the War of American Independence and becoming rear-admiral in 1793, when he was suspended on suspicion of having noble blood, but was reinstated two years later. He is probably best remembered as commander of the Rochefort squadron (1804) which was sent to the West Indies – as part of the plan to decoy the Royal Navy from the intended descent on England – to rendezvous with Villeneuve and Ganteaume thereby forming a huge fleet which would return to Europe and cover the invasion. This did not happen and Missiessy returned to Rochefort, having inflicted some damage upon the British in the West Indies but having failed to capture Diamond Rock off Martinique. Napoleon was especially angry at this element of Missiessy's failure, writing that he almost choked with indignation when he heard of it. From 1808 Missiessy commanded the squadron in the Scheldt, helping to oppose the Walcheren expedition and to defend Antwerp in 1814; in the former operation he exhibited his tactical wisdom by withdrawing his ships up-river to Antwerp rather than risk attack by a force of overwhelming superiority. Ennobled as comte in 1811, he accepted the restoration and served until 1832.

MOIRA, Earl of, see **HASTINGS**

MOLITOR, Marshal Gabriel-Jean-Joseph, comte (1770–1849)

Perhaps most famous for his part in the desperate fighting at Aspern–Essling, he was commissioned in 1791, served in Germany and Switzerland and became *général de brigade* in 1799, *de division* in the following year. In 1805 he served in Italy (including Caldiero), was Governor of Swedish Pomerania from April 1807 and was ennobled as comte in June 1808. In 1809 he commanded the 3rd Division of Massena's IV Corps, and at Aspern–Essling made a most heroic fight in an attempt to hold Napoleon's left flank by possession of the village of Aspern. Its defence was one of the great epics of the period, made the more desperate by the great disparity in numbers and the fact that few reinforcements could be transported across the Danube; and it was only with reluctance that Molitor's four shattered regiments were eventually pulled back when fresh troops were able to replace them. Despite their losses, on the second day of the battle his men resisted the Austrian attempts to break through to the south of Aspern, which would have severed Napoleon's army from its route of withdrawal across the Danube. Subsequently he led his division at Wagram, and from 1810 held various appointments in northern Europe, making a skilled withdrawal through The Netherlands with the 4,000 men of his 'Corps of Observation of Holland' in 1814 against some 50,000 men under Bülow and Wintzingerode. In 1815 he served under Rapp, and his

services were retained by the Bourbons; having commanded a corps in Spain in 1823, he was promoted to Marshal.

MOLLENDORF, Field Marshal Richard Joachim Heinrich von (1724–1816)

A distinguished Prussian soldier of the later 18th century, he became a page of Frederick the Great in 1740, and made his name in the wars which followed; as a captain he won perhaps his greatest fame leading the 3rd Battalion of the Garde at Leuthen, especially in the storming of the churchyard. He was further distinguished at Hochkirch, Torgau and (as major-general commanding a brigade) at Burkersdorf. He was a lieutenant-general in the War of the Bavarian Succession, became Governor of Berlin in 1783, general of infantry in 1787 and *Generalfeldmarschall* in 1793. In 1794 he commanded the Prussian army on the Rhine, and played an important advisory role in 1806, being present with the king at Auerstädt though not holding the command of any formation. He arranged for the withdrawal from Erfurt of some of the fugitives from the Jena–Auerstädt defeat, and might have persuaded the commandant of that place not to surrender as soon as he did, but Möllendorf's age and severe wound caused him to faint during the negotiations and the fortification surrendered.

MOLLIEN, Nicolas-François, comte (1758–1850)

The son of a merchant, he was one of the longest-serving of Napoleon's ministers. During the *ancien régime* he entered the finance ministry where he proved to be extremely capable. He emigrated to England after having been hauled before a Revolutionary tribunal in 1794, only resuming his employment at the finance ministry after the estab-

lishment of the Consulate. Napoleon recognised his abilities, made him a councillor of state, head of the treasury and in 1808 comte, but did not always heed his advice, such as Mollien's belief that the Continental System could not succeed. Honest and industrious, he remained at the Treasury until the restoration, returned during the Hundred Days and was offered the same position by Louis XVIII, but could not be tempted out of retirement. He was made a peer of France in 1819.

Mollien, comte. *Mémoires d'un Ministre du Trésor Public 1780–1815*. Paris, 1845

MONCEY, Marshal Bon-Adrien-Jeannot de, duc de Conegliano (1754–1842)

Born near Besançon, the son of a lawyer named Jeannot (the name Moncey was adopted only in 1789, from the family estate), he three times forsook his legal studies in favour of the army, twice being bought out and once discharged, before he secured a commission in 1779. Having taken until 1791 to become a captain, distinguished service in the Pyrenees led to his promotion to *général de brigade* in February 1794, *de division* in June, and in August he took command of the Army of the Western Pyrenees. Dismissed in October 1797 for suspected royalist sympathies, he was reinstated shortly before the coup of Brumaire (of which he approved) and in 1800 was sent to Switzerland, from where he co-operated with Napoleon's Marengo campaign. After holding commands in Italy he retired from active service in August 1801, becoming Inspector-General of Gendarmerie, but was among the first creation of the Marshalate, presumably largely a political appointment. He returned to campaign service at the beginning of the Peninsular War, with little success, failing to take Valencia; in September 1808 he took command of III Corps of the Army of Spain, serving at Tudela under Lannes, but being adjudged to have conducted the siege of Saragossa too slowly, and perhaps for treating his Spanish opponents with undue consideration, he was recalled in January 1809. He had become duc de Conegliano in July 1808. His subsequent employment was in internal commands, not campaigns, though as commandant (from January 1814) of the Paris National Guard he served with gallantry at the defence of the Clichy Gate. Moncey was one of those who advocated Napoleon's abdication, took service under the Bourbons and was made a peer of France, and though taking no active part in the Hundred Days was dismissed and imprisoned for declining to serve on Ney's court-martial. Reinstated in July 1816, he led IV Corps in Spain in 1823, retired from active duty in 1830, and as Governor of the Invalides (from 1833) received Napoleon's body when it was brought home in 1840. Courage and honour, rather than military genius, were the dominant features of his career; he refused to wage war with the ruthlessness of some of his companions, notably in Spain, so that when refusing Moncey's call to surrender Saragossa, Palafox referred to 'the wisdom which characterises him so well, and which has earned him the name Bon',[1] while the *junta* of Oviedo declared that they would welcome him if he changed sides: 'We offer him the tribute of truth and honour ... if the respect which he pays to the mandates of nature do not permit him to take up arms against his unworthy companions, yet he shall be considered by us as a just and honourable man, and our love and our esteem shall follow him wherever, in the vicissitudes of life, his lot shall be cast.'[2] Such remarks from his enemies are eloquent testimony to his character.

1. Belmas, J. *Journaux des Sièges faits ou soutenus par les Français dans la Péninsule, de 1807 à 1814.* Paris, 1836, vol. II, p. 355. 2. Anon., p. 332.

Beckett, I. F. W. 'An Honest Man: Moncey', in *Napoleon's Marshals*, ed. D. G. Chandler. London, 1987; Conegliano, duc de. *Le Maréchal Moncey.* Paris, 1902

MONGE, Gaspard, comte de Péluse (1746–1818)

Despite his political career, he is best remembered as a mathematician and scientist. Born in Beaune, the son of an artisan, his talent for mathematics led to his appointment as tutor at the engineer school at Mézières, where he became professor of mathematics in 1768 and of physics in 1771. Here he developed the science of descriptive geometry, and having moved to Paris in 1780, collaborated with Lavoisier and published significant scientific papers. He supported the Revolution, became Minister of Marine in 1792 but in April 1793 left office to use his scientific skill for the benefit of the nation, writing two important treatises, *Description of the Art of Manufacturing Guns* and *Advice to Ironworkers on the Manufacture of Steel.* He was instrumental in the foundation of the Ecole Polytechnique, went to Italy in 1796 to advise on the appropriation of works of art, and to Rome in 1797–8 to head the commission investigating the murder of General Duphot, and unofficially to replace papal authority with the Roman Republic. Monge met Napoleon in Egypt and became a devoted admirer, was appointed to head the Egyptian Institute, remained close to Napoleon during the campaign, and accompanied him to Syria and back to France. On his return he resumed his scientific and tutorial duties, became a member of the senate and was ennobled as comte de Péluse (Pelusium, an ancient port at the mouth of the Nile), but was deprived of his honours on Napoleon's fall. Napoleon remarked that although he was a violent republican, Monge was so mild a man that he would not have allowed a chicken to be killed if he had had to do it himself or see it done; yet at the fight between French and Mameluke gunboats at Shubra Khit in July 1798, he helped reload the cannon, evidently putting to practical use his theoretical knowledge of gunfounding.

Aubry, P. V. *Monge: le Savant Ami de Napoléon Bonaparte.* Paris, 1954; Jomard, E. F. *Souvenirs sur Gaspard Monge.* Paris, 1853

MONROE, James (1758–1831)

The fifth President of the United States, he was a Virginian who had become a lieutenant colonel in the US Army during the War of Independence and had entered politics in the Virginia Assembly in 1782. US envoy to France (1794–6), he was welcomed as an ardent republican and persuaded the Directory not to initiate a break with the USA. In January 1803 his close friend Jefferson appointed him envoy to France and Spain to assist in the negotiation of the Louisiana Purchase, and in that April to be US minister to Britain, where attempts to solve Anglo–American maritime disagreements were largely unsuccessful, despite the Britain–Pinkney Treaty (named also after William Pinkney who assisted him). In 1811 Monroe became Secretary of State under Madison, an office he held until March 1817, and was also Secretary at War September 1814–March 1815, succeeding the ineffective John Armstrong. In these positions Monroe was much concerned with the War of 1812, notably in the direction of foreign policy, and at Bladenburg he assisted in directing the deployment of US forces before Winder arrived to take command, having already helped to reconnoitre the British advance. The commander of the troops already on the ground, General Tobias Stanbury, was unimpressed by Monroe's moving of troops without informing him, and this interference was blamed in part for the loss of the action. Monroe was elected President in 1816 and again in 1820, from which period dates his greatest renown, notably in the expression in 1823 of what came to be termed the 'Monroe Doctrine' concerning the non-interference by European powers in the Americas, which was to have an enduring effect upon US foreign policy.

Bond, B. W. *Monroe's Mission to France 1794–1796.* Baltimore, 1907; Gilman, D. C. *James Monroe.* Boston, 1883

MONTBRUN, General Louis-Pierre, comte (1770–1812)

One of the best known of Napoleon's cavalry generals, he enlisted in the cavalry in 1789, was commissioned in 1794 and became *général de brigade* after Austerlitz. Ennobled as baron in 1808, in that year he was sent to Spain but fell temporarily into disfavour by exceeding his leave of absence to protect the lady he was to marry. His reputation was restored by Somosierra (he led the charge and was the first to dismount and begin to pull down the Spanish palisade), and he was promoted to *général de division.* He led the light cavalry division of

LOUIS MONTBRUN

Davout's III Corps in the 1809 campaign, notably at Eckmühl, and was made comte in August of that year. In 1810 he returned to the Peninsula as commander of the cavalry of Massena's Army of Portugal; his cavalry was in reserve at Busaco, he served at Fuentes de Oñoro and with especial distinction at E1 Bodon. In January 1812 he failed in an attempt to capture Alicante, his superior Marmont claiming that he was so anxious to distinguish himself in independent command that he acted unwisely and diverted a considerable part of the Army of Portugal until too late to prevent the fall of Ciudad Rodrigo, though it would be unfair to place the blame for this upon Montbrun's actions. He was given command of II Cavalry Corps for the Russian campaign, but at Borodino was mortally wounded in the stomach by a shell fragment; he exclaimed 'Good shot!' before he fell, and died that evening, a sad loss to the army. Not only brave and capable, he even looked the part, as Marbot recalled: 'Montbrun was a splendid man, in the same style as Murat; lofty stature, a scarred face, a black beard, of soldierly bearing, and an admirable horseman.'[1]

1. Marbot, vol. I, p. 276.

MONTEBELLO, duc de, see LANNES

MONTESQUIOU-FEZENSAC, General Anne-Marie, marquis de (1739–98)

Raised among the children of the French king, he entered the army in 1754, attained the colonelcy of the *Régiment Royal-Vaisseaux* in 1761 and became a general officer in 1780; a man of literary as well as military accomplishments, he was admitted to the Academy in 1784. In 1789 he was elected to the States-General by the *noblesse* of Paris, supported liberal principles and became President of the Constituent Assembly in 1791. Lieutenant-general from May 1791, in 1792 he was given command of the Army of the South, occupied Savoy, and in November of that year was denounced for royalist sympathies and for having sought to favour the King of Sardinia; he fled to Switzerland and took with him the military chest by way of compensation for property abandoned in France. In 1795 the accusation was lifted and he returned to France, dying in Paris in December 1798. He should not be confused with others of his family name, notably **Raymond de Montesquiou, duc de Fézensac**, who joined Napoleon's army in 1804, occupied staff positions and came to prominence during the Russian campaign of 1812, which he began as ADC to Berthier, and took command of the 4th Line in September 1812, leading it throughout the retreat, about which he left a valuable memoir. He attained the rank of lieutenant-general. The comtesse de Montesquiou was selected by Napoleon to be the governess of the King of Rome, a duty which she discharged with great fidelity.

Fézensac, duc de. *A Journal of the Russian Campaign of 1812,* ed. and intro. Colonel. W. Knollys.

London, 1852; Fézensac, duc de. *Souvenirs militaires de 1804 à 1815*. Paris, 1863

MONTFORT, comte de, see **BONAPARTE, Jérôme**

MONTGAILLARD, Jean-Gabriel-Maurice de Roques, comte de (1761–1841)
From a family of minor nobility, he was born in Montgaillard, whence the name of his title was derived; after military service in the West Indies he came to the notice of the comte de Provence (later Louis XVIII) and became a diplomatic agent in Bourbon service. He liaised with Francis II and Pitt in 1794, secured Austrian intervention on behalf of the imprisoned future duchesse d'Angoulême, and was involved in negotiations with Pichegru. In 1796 he went to Italy in an attempt to open negotiations with Napoleon, and on his return was regarded with suspicion by the royalists, disclosed confidential documents concerning Pichegru, and by indicating support for Napoleon hoped to receive favour from that quarter. Instead he was imprisoned, but later was employed by Napoleon as diplomatic and political adviser (despite a somewhat untrustworthy reputation) because of his shrewd insight into politics and knowledge of foreign courts, and was retained in this position after the Bourbon restoration. He wrote a number of historical and political works (his earliest influential treatise, *Etat de France au moi de Mai 1794* was translated by Burke), and somewhat unreliable memoirs.

Montgaillard, comte de. *Mémoires diplomatiques*, ed. C. de Lacroix. 1896

MONTGELAS, Maximilian Josef Garnerin, Graf von (1759–1838)
Jean Sigismund Garnerin, baron Montgelas, was a Savoyard nobleman who served as an officer in the army of Maximilian Josef III, Elector of Bavaria; his son, Maximilian Josef, also entered Bavarian service (1779) but in a civilian capacity. He was driven from office by his association with the anti-clerical *Aufklärung* ('Enlightenment') movement and found employment as secretary to Maximilian Joseph, brother of the Duke of Zweibrücken. When Maximilian succeeded to the duchy in 1795, Montgelas became his minister, and upon Maximilian's succession as Elector of Bavaria, he became the most influential statesman in that country; he was raised to count in 1809. As half-Savoyard and more fluent in French than in German, he might have been expected to favour a French alliance, but the fact that he did was probably equally a matter of pragmatism, to protect Bavaria from the conflicting aims of Austria and Prussia. He presided over the enlargement of Bavaria and its transformation into a kingdom, and remained a staunch supporter of the alliance with Napoleon, in which he endeavoured to secure for Bavaria the status of a junior partner rather than a puppet. Bavaria's break with Napoleon was urged by the crown prince and Wrede more than by Montgelas, but Bavarian interests being his concern, he would have had no sentimental attachment to Napoleon once the fall of the emperor became inevitable. His domestic policy included secularisation and administrative reforms, reminiscent of his association with the *Aufklärung*. In 1817 the king was persuaded by Montgelas' opponents to dismiss him, after which he lived in retirement.

Eckart, D. *Bayern unter dem Ministerium Montgelas*. Munich, 1894; Montgelas, Graf L. von. *Denkwürdigkeiten des bayr. Staatsministers Maximilian Graf von Montgelas*. Stuttgart, 1887; Döberl, L. *Maximilian von Montgelas und das Prinzip der Staatssouverenität*. Munich, 1925

MONTHOLON, General Charles-Tristan, comte de (1783–1853)
A French aristocrat, he served as a staff officer from an early age, acting as ADC to Joubert, Augereau, Macdonald and Berthier, and became an imperial chamberlain in 1809. He fell into disfavour with Napoleon after leading a delegation to Würzburg in 1812, when he married Albine de Vassal, a twice-divorced lady whom Napoleon though unsuitable. In 1814 Montholon was accused of embezzling military funds, and it has been suggested that he exaggerated his military prowess, but offered his services to Napoleon after the second abdication and accompanied him to St. Helena, with his wife (who later returned to France). He made many enemies among Napoleon's staff in exile, but although several departed, he remained there until the end. Bunbury described him as 'rather insignificant',[1] but Basil Jackson, who knew him at St. Helena, thought him 'a man of talent, possessing many excellent qualities, and for whom I have ever felt a sincere regard'.[2] Montholon had obvious royalist connections (his stepfather – perhaps his natural father – was comte de Sémonville, a close aide of comte d'Artois), and it has been suggested that he was implicated in a Bourbon plot to murder Napoleon, and that he actually administered poison to the ex-emperor; there are conflicting opinions. Montholon was shown consideration by the monarchy, notably by Louis-Philippe, but was imprisoned for seven years for implication in the attempted coup by Louis Napoleon (later Napoleon

III) in 1840. From his somewhat unreliable writings, *Mémoires de Napoléon à St.-Hélène* and *Récits de la Captivité de Napoléon à St.-Hélène*, he made considerable sums, and after his release he was elected to the National Assembly. Napoleon at least had no doubts about the value of his services, because he left Montholon two million francs in his will, 'as proof of my satisfaction for the filial attentions he has paid me during six years, and as an indemnity for the losses his residence in St. Helena have occasioned him'.[3]

1. Bunbury, *Memoirs*, p. 307. 2. *CUSM*, 1844, vol. I, p. 419. 3. Las Cases, vol. IV, p. 401.

Montholon, C. T. de *History of the Captivity of Napoleon at St. Helena*. London, 1846; *Memoirs of the History of France during the Reign of Napoleon*. London, 1823–4. Among the works which consider the poisoning of Napoleon are those by B. Weider and S. Forshufvud, notably *The Assassination at St. Helena Revisited*. New York, 1995.

MONTMORIN DE SAINT HEREM, Armand-Marc, comte de (1743–92)

One of Louis XVI's closest aides when dauphin, he was appointed Foreign Minister in 1787. A supporter of Necker, he later became a supporter of Mirabeau, who virtually took over his duties. Montmorin cleared himself of accusations of complicity in the flight to Varennes, but resigned shortly after. He remained a close adviser to the king, and after his denunciation in July 1792 took refuge in the house of a washerwoman in the Faubourg St. Antoine. He was discovered, it was said, when she was seen carrying in delicacies suitable for an aristocrat to eat; he was interrogated at the bar of the National Assembly and conveyed to the Abbaye prison, apparently on the grounds

that possession of a bottle of laudanum implied guilt of some crime. Shortly after his incarceration he was murdered in the September massacres.

MOORE, Lieutenant-General Sir John (1761–1809)

SIR JOHN MOORE
(ENGRAVING BY TURNER AFTER LAWRENCE)

The most famous British soldier (after Wellington) of the period, he was described by the latter as the only general (apart from himself) in whom the army had complete confidence; as he once said to Sir John, 'you are the man, and I shall with great willingness act under you'.[1] The son of a Scottish doctor with high connections, he was commissioned in 1776, having already declined a commission in the Austrian Army. He served in the War of American Independence, sat as MP for Lanark, Selkirk, Peebles and Linlithgow (in the interest of his friend the Duke of Hamilton), and although his Whig affiliations must have hindered advancement, he purchased command of his old regiment, the 51st, in 1790. He led them in the Mediterranean in 1794, but, having become close to Corsican patriots like Paoli, had a blazing row with the Viceroy, Sir Gilbert Elliot, and was sent home in disgrace. Retaining the confi-

dence of Pitt and the Duke of York, as brigadier-general he served in the West Indies, was further distinguished as major-general in Ireland in 1798 and led a brigade in North Holland in 1799, where he was shot in the head with no permanent effect. He was his friend Abercromby's most valuable subordinate in Egypt (wounded at Alexandria), and in 1803 commanded at Shorncliffe, where he trained what was to evolve into the Light Division (the 43rd, 95th and his own 52nd, the colonelcy of which he had been granted in May 1801) in the light infantry skills which were to make them probably the most expert light troops in Europe. Moore did not invent light infantry tactics, but was a perfecter of existing drills and a refiner of theories, and in this regard his influence was immense; a charismatic leader, he was regarded by his officers with a devotion verging upon idolatry. In 1804 he became a knight of the Bath, lieutenant-general in 1805, and went to the Mediterranean as deputy to General Henry Fox, whom he succeeded in command, before being sent to the Baltic in the abortive mission to support Sweden, which failed thanks to the insanity of the Swedish king. Moore had to escape in disguise, and was immediately sent to the Peninsula as subordinate to Burrard and Dalrymple, a slight for one who had held an important independent command, but one which Moore accepted without demur. After Cintra he succeeded to command all British forces in the Peninsula, advanced into Spain to concert action with the Spanish, but was compelled to undertake the appalling retreat to Corunna and Vigo, turning at bay to defeat Soult at Corunna, allowing the British forces to be evacuated by sea. Terribly wounded by a roundshot in the left shoulder, Moore died during the night and was buried on the ramparts of Corunna: 'We carved not a line, and we raised not a stone/But we left him alone with his glory', in the words of Charles Wolfe's poem; but Soult raised the first monument to him. Much controversy surrounded the Corunna campaign, but Moore's situation had been fraught with probably insurmountable difficulties; and it is as a trainer and inspirer of men that he is perhaps best remembered, in which field he had few if any equals. Despite attempts by political opponents to damage his reputation, the general impression was that recorded by George Napier: 'In Sir John Moore's character we have a model for everything that marks the obedient soldier, the persevering, firm, and skilful general; the inflexible and real patriot who sacrificed all personal feeling to his country's weal; the truly virtuous and honourable man; the high-minded, finished, and accomplished gentleman.'[2] One of Sir John's brothers was Admiral Sir Graham Moore (1764–1843), who entered the Royal Navy in 1771, helped escort the Portuguese Royal family to Brazil (for which he received the Order of the Tower and Sword), was knighted by bestowal of the KCB in 1815, was a Lord of the Admiralty 1816–20, CinC Mediterranean (1820–3) and Plymouth (1839–42); and became an admiral in 1841.

1. Stanhope, p. 244. 2. Napier, G., pp. 77–8.

Brownrigg, B. *The Life and Letters of Sir John Moore*. London, 1921; Moore, Sir John. *The Diary of Sir John Moore*, ed. Sir J. F. Maurice. London, 1904; Moore, J. C. (Moore's brother). *The Life of Lieutenant-General Sir John Moore*. London, 1934; Oman, C. *Sir John Moore*. London, 1953; Parkinson, R. *Moore of Corunna*. London, 1976

MORAND, General Charles-Antoine-Louis-Alexis, comte (1771–1835)

One of the most capable of the second rank of Napoleon's generals, he abandoned his father's law practice to enlist in 1792, and his education and intelligence gained him rapid promotion. After distinguished service on the German and Italian fronts he became *général de brigade* in Egypt in September 1800. In the Austerlitz campaign he commanded a brigade (consisting of the 10th *Léger*) in the 1st Division of Soult's IV Corps, and following its important role in the battle he was promoted to *général de division* (December 1805). From February 1806 until early 1813 he led the 1st Division of Davout's corps; especially distinguished at Auerstädt, he served at Eylau, Abensberg, Eckmühl and Wagram. He was ennobled as comte in 1808 but thought Davout had blocked further promotion in order to keep so capable a subordinate under his command; but continued to serve under the Marshal, even after being severely wounded by a shell-splinter in the jaw at Borodino. After recuperation he was posted to lead the 12th Division of IV Corps, serving at Lützen, Bautzen, Leipzig and Hanau, and though elevated to command the corps spent the remainder of the war besieged in Mainz. He rallied to Napoleon in 1815 and was appointed colonel of the *Chasseurs à Pied* of the Imperial Guard in which capacity he commanded that part of the Guard infantry at Waterloo, notably in the desperate fighting around Plancenoit. Exiled at the second restoration, Morand was sentenced to death for having conspired to overthrow the king, but this decision was reversed and his rank was restored in 1820. Although he returned from exile in Poland, he held no military appointment until after the 1830 revolution; he was made a peer of France in October 1832.

Rivollet, G. *Général de Bataille Charles-Antoine-Louis-Alexis Morand, comte d'empire (1771–1835)*. Paris, 1963

MORARD DE GALLES, Vice-Amiral Justin-Bonaventure, comte de (1741–1809)

Having joined the navy in 1757, de Galles (whose name can be found rendered as 'Morard-de-Gallis') saw much service before rising to flag rank at the beginning of the Revolutionary Wars (rear-admiral January 1792, vice-admiral January 1793). After war against England had begun, he was given command of a fleet of 21 ships of the line at Quiberon Bay, but in November of the same year was arrested and expelled from the navy because of aristocratic connections. Liberated and reinstated in March 1795, after commanding the Brest fleet he was ordered to lead Hoche's expedition to Ireland. Seventeen ships of the line, 19 frigates and smaller vessels and seven transports left Brest on 15 December 1796 and enough of them arrived at Bantry Bay on 20 December to make a landing feasible, but Morard and Hoche were aboard one of the ships that had gone astray, and by the time they rejoined the main body on 29 December bad weather had driven some from the projected landing-point and the remainder had sailed after them. The enterprise was abandoned with the loss of five ships lost or destroyed to prevent capture, and six more taken by British frigates from Cork. De Galles later held the shore command at Brest, became a senator in 1799 and comte in 1808.

MOREAU, General Jean-Victor-Marie (1763–1813)

One of the most able French generals of his era, he was born in

223

JEAN VICTOR MOREAU
(ENGRAVING BY H. B. HALL AFTER GUERIN)

Morlaix in Brittany and trained in his father's legal profession, but having been elected a lieutenant-colonel of volunteers in 1791 achieved rapid promotion, becoming *général de division* by April 1794, his qualities having been recognised by Carnot. He succeeded Pichegru as commander of the Army of the North and in 1796 led the Army of the Rhine and Moselle, conducting its eventual forced retreat with such skill that his reputation was undamaged. His attempts to defend Pichegru and conceal that general's treacherous correspondence with Condé led to his temporary dismissal, even though he had denounced Pichegru as a traitor; but he was brought back in desperation as commander of the Army of Italy and then of the Army of the Rhine. He remained in Italy, however, taking command again after the death of his successor, Joubert, at Novi. Dissatisfied with the Directory, he assisted Napoleon in the coup of Brumaire, was rewarded with command of the Army of the Rhine and won his great victory of Hohenlinden. At this stage he was a popular rival to Napoleon, but his poor political judgement and the ambitions of his wife led to his downfall. Madame Moreau (a

Creole and member of Joséphine's circle) encouraged the association of malcontents in the so-called 'Moreau club', and although unwilling to countenance royalist intrigue, Moreau was perhaps not unwilling to be considered as a potential military dictator to restore the republic of which he was a committed supporter (despite the fact that his father had been guillotined during the Terror). Napoleon had Moreau arrested and condemned for complicity in the Pichegru and Cadoudal plot, and though innocent he was banished; from 1804 to 1813 he lived at Morrisville in New Jersey. Upon news of Napoleon's disasters in 1812, probably at the instigation of his wife and at Bernadotte's recommendation, he allowed himself to be appointed military adviser to the Tsar, perhaps in the hope of being named republican administrator of France after Napoleon's defeat. The opportunity never arose, for he was mortally wounded at the Tsar's side at Dresden by a cannon-ball which smashed his right knee, went through his horse and mangled the other leg; the ball was evidently fired on Napoleon's order, having seen enemy staff officers in conference. Moreau survived a double amputation (smoking a cigar throughout) and appeared to be recovering, but died at Laun five days later (2 September 1813), having been exhausted by a long council of war. He was buried at St. Petersburg and his wife received a Russian pension. Napoleon described him as an ideal divisional commander, calm and brave under fire, but too indolent and unwilling to study to make a great army commander. Moreau's friend, General Lamarque, remarked that if Moreau and Napoleon had led opposing armies, once in place he would

have favoured Moreau whose army was 'sure to be managed with the utmost regularity, precision, and calculation. On these points, it was impossible to excel or even to equal, Moreau. But if the two armies had to approach from points a hundred leagues distant from each other, the Emperor would have routed his adversary three, four, or five times over, before the latter could have had the time to look about him.' Moreau's last words, 'Rest easy gentlemen, it's my destiny', seem to epitomise his career; militarily skilled but unfulfilled, ending in opposition to the forces of the country he loved, which led to his condemnation as a traitor in some quarters. He should not be confused with others of similar name. **Médéric-Louis-Elie Moreau de Saint Méry** (1750–1819) was a kinsman of Josephine, born in Martinique, who became Deputy for that island in the Assembly but was forced to flee to the USA in 1792 because of his moderate views. He returned to France in 1799, was employed in naval and colonial administration, became a councillor of state and was administrator of Parma, Piacenza and Guastalla 1802–6 before his dismissal for leniency. **General Jean-Claude Moreau** (1755–1828) came to prominence as the commandant of Soissons in 1814, when he repulsed an Allied attack with his small garrison on 2 March, but then allowed himself to be cajoled and threatened into abandoning the place without further resistance, a grievous blow to Napoleon's plans. Napoleon ordered him to be tried and shot in public, but before this could happen the empire fell and Moreau escaped a fate which many would have regarded as well-deserved. At the restoration he was given command of a *département*.

1. Las Cases, vol. II, p. 357.

Philippart, Sir John. *Memoirs of General Moreau*. London, 1814; vinine, P. *Some Details Concerning General Moreau*. London, 814

IORILLO, General Pablo, onde de Cartagena (778–1837)

prominent Spanish commander in the Peninsular War, he ad served as a marine at St. incent and Trafalgar, at Bailen, nd came to prominence leading ying columns under Castaños. e made a notable raid in La 1ancha in January 1812, but is best known for his service leading a division with Wellington's army, at Vittoria and in subsequent operations. His was the only Spanish division which Wellington kept with him when the others were sent back to Spain over fears of looting and indiscipline, although in December 1813 Morillo was the recipient of a stern note from Wellington to the effect that: 'I warned you repeatedly of the misconduct of your troops, in direct disobedience of my orders [which] really must be obeyed, and strictly carried into execution; and if I cannot obtain obedience in one way, I will in another, or I will not command the troops which disobey me.'[1] Nevertheless, Morillo and his men were such doughty fighters that they remained an important contingent of the army until almost the end of the war in the Peninsula, until tasked with investing Navarrenx, which deprived Wellington of the use of them with the field army. Subsequently Morillo participated in the Spanish campaigning in South America.

1. Wellington, vol. XI, p. 391.

MORNINGTON, 2nd Earl of, see WELLESLEY, Richard

MORTIER, Marshal Edouard-Adolphe-Casimir-Joseph, duc de Trévise (1768–1835)

The son of a cloth merchant at Cateau-Cambrésis, he was unique among Napoleon's Marshals in that he was half-English (by his mother Marie-Anne) and spoke that language. Educated at the English College at Douai, he was destined for a mercantile career, but joined the National Guard at the Revolution and became a captain in his uncle's volunteer battalion in September 1791. A large, imposing and popular man, he was distinguished in the early campaigns and became *général de brigade* in October 1799, following noteworthy service in Switzerland. A close supporter of Napoleon, he exercised his administrative skills as commander of the Paris region, occupied Hanover in 1803, became colonel-general of the Artillery and Seamen of the Consular (later Imperial) Guard, and was among the first creation of the Marshalate in 1804. In 1805 he won the action of Dürrenstein and after Austerlitz took over Lannes' V Corps; in 1806 he led VIII Corps, and at Friedland led the left wing of Napoleon's army. Duc de Trévise (Treviso)

EDOUARD MORTIER
(PRINT BY LACOSTE AFTER DEMORAINE)

from July 1808, later in that year he led V Corps in Spain, participating in the siege of Saragossa and under Soult playing a major role in the victories of Ocaña and Gebora. In May 1811 he was recalled to France, led the Young Guard with distinction in the Russian campaign (where he was appointed Governor of Moscow), and continued to lead the Guard with great skill in 1813–14, culminating with the vain attempt to defend Paris. Having accepted a command from the king at the restoration, he did not rally to Napoleon until the king had been escorted safely out of France. Both sides found his conduct beyond reproach, but though Napoleon had intended him to lead the Young Guard in the Hundred Days campaign, Mortier was laid low by sciatica and was unable to mount a horse, let alone take the field. An unwilling member of the military court assembled to try Ney (but which declared itself invalid), he was briefly in disgrace, but though his title was not restored until 1819, he was given command of the Rouen military district as early as January 1816. He continued to enjoy royal favour, assisting in the coronations of Charles X and Louis-Philippe, was Ambassador to Russia in 1830 and 1832 and briefly Minister of War (1834–5). On 28 July 1835 he was attending the National Guard review with Louis-Philippe when he was killed by the terrorist Fieschi's bomb cum musket battery device. Greatly distinguished as an administrator, and no inconsiderable general in a subordinate role (notably in defensive and rearguard situations), it was as an honourable, honest and loyal man that his reputation was unsurpassed. His nickname 'the big mortar' was a pun on his name, coined by Napoleon himself.

Despréaux, J. C. E. Frignet. *Le Maréchal Mortier*. Paris, 1913–20;

Gray, R. 'The Big Mortar: Mortier', in *Napoleon's Marshals*, ed. D. G. Chandler. London, 1987; Moreel, L. *Le Maréchal Mortier, duc de Trévise*. Paris, 1958

MOSCOWA, prince de la, see **NEY**

MOUTON, Marshal Georges, comte de Lobau (1770–1838)
The subject of Napoleon's well-known pun, '*Mon Mouton est un lion*' ('My sheep is a lion'), Georges Mouton was the son of a Lorraine baker, commissioned soon after his enlistment in 1792. From early in his career he gained experience of staff duties, serving as Joubert's ADC in Italy, and at Genoa was desperately wounded by a shot through the body. *Général de brigade* from February 1805, and having attracted Napoleon's attention by his courage and ability, he was appointed an imperial aide in March 1805, served at Austerlitz, Eylau and Friedland (wounded), and in October 1807 became *général de division*. In Spain in 1808 he held a divisional command under Bessières and Soult, and was distinguished at Medina del Rio Seco and Burgos, before returning to ADC duties with Napoleon for the 1809 Danube campaign. One of his great exploits – which brought forth the 'lion' pun – occurred at Landeshut, when he led the 17th Line in a charge over the bridges spanning the Isar; the second was at Aspern–Essling, when he led the counter-attack which, with Rapp's assistance, secured possession of Essling. For this action Mouton received the title of comte de Lobau, the name of the island which formed the crossing-point of the Danube and which Napoleon made his base. He served as Napoleon's aide at Wagram and throughout the Russian campaign; distinguished at Lützen, he took command of I

Corps at Dresden and was take[n] prisoner on the fall of that cit[y]. Although he accepted employ[?]ment under the Bourbons, h[e] rejoined Napoleon in 1815 and le[d] VI Corps in the Waterlo[o] campaign, notably at Plancenoi[t]; he was captured on the day aft[er] the battle and was sent as a pri[s]oner to England. Proscribed b[y] the Bourbons, he lived in Belgiu[m] until permitted to return [to] France in 1818; entering politics a[s] a liberal, he played a significa[nt] role in the revolution of 1830 an[d] supported Louis-Philippe thoug[h] he had favoured a return to [a] republic. He took command of th[e] Paris National Guard in Decembe[r] 1830 and suppressed unrest in th[e] following year; a peer of Franc[e] from June 1833, he had become [a] Marshal in July 1831 an[d] continued a political and militar[y] career until his death in 183[8], occasioned by the re-opening [of] his old Genoa wound. His comb[i]nation of great bravery wit[h] prudence was recalled by Marbo[t,] who was once mildly repri[?]manded by Mouton for riskin[g] injury unnecessarily; he remarke[d] that it was useless to be killed o[r] crippled without advantage t[o] one's country, a lesson whic[h] Marbot said he never forgo[t.] Mouton also had a somewha[t] blunt and honest manner whic[h] was appreciated by Napoleon.

MUFFLING, General Philipp Friedrich Carl Ferdinand, Frei[?]herr von (1775–1851)
Born in Halle, the son of an office[r] of Saxon minor aristocracy, h[e] entered the Prussian Army i[n] 1788, served in the earl[y] campaigns of the Revolutionar[y] Wars, and by 1804 was serving o[n] the general staff, initially occupie[d] in surveying as assistant to th[e] astronomer Franz-Xaver von Zac[h] (1754–1832), and later to Hohen[?]lohe and Blücher, with whom h[e] served in 1806. After th[e]

irrender he entered the civil
ervice of the Duke of Weimar;
ejoining the Prussian staff in
313, he served with Blücher and
ecame major-general at the end
 the year; later he was chief of
aff to Barclay de Tolly and Kleist
on Nollendorf. Müffling is best
nown, however, for his role as
russian liaison officer with
ellington during the Waterloo
ampaign, ensuring close and
iendly relations between that
eneral and Blücher. He was
elected for this post perhaps for
is knowledge of English (though
e admitted that his knowledge of
ie language had not progressed
r beyond the ability to read
oldsmith's *Vicar of Wakefield*!),
nd although initially not enthusi-
stic about the appointment he
roved to be an most valuable
iember of the Allied staff, liked
nd respected by Wellington.
ater he served as Governor of
aris during the occupation,
ecame chief of general staff at
erlin in 1821, performed much
nportant cartographic, survey
nd diplomatic work, and was
overnor of Berlin 1838–47. He
as a prolific author on military
nd historical subjects, some of
is writing being published under
ie initials 'C von W' ('Carl von
eiss'), and the English edition of
is history of the 1815 campaign
ppeared under the initials 'C de
'.

Müffling, General. *History of the
ampaign ... in the Year 1815*, ed.
ir John Sinclair, Bt. London,
316; Müffling, General. *Passages
 My Life; together with Memoirs
 the Campaign of 1813 and 1814*,
1. Colonel P. J. Yorke. London,
353 (the German version was *Aus
einem Leben*. Berlin 1851, and
ie latest edition, entitled *The
lemoirs of Baron von Müffling, a
russian Officer in the Napoleonic
'ars*. London, 1997, has a
iographical introduction by P.
ofschröer)

MULGRAVE, General Henry Phipps, 1st Earl (1755–1831)

Third son of Constantine, 1st
Baron Mulgrave, he succeeded his
brother, Captain Constantine, 2nd
Baron (1744–92), a distinguished
naval officer, as Baron Mulgrave of
New Ross; the English barony of
Mulgrave, created for Constantine
in 1790, became extinct at his
death but was re-created for
Henry in 1794. He sat as an MP
1784–94 and as a colonel in 1793
went to Italy as an envoy to the
Austrian and Sardinian military;
he commanded the British forces
in the expedition to Toulon (where
he introduced Thomas Graham to
military service), and in 1794 led
the brief expedition to Flushing. A
general from October 1809, he
subsequently acted as military
adviser to Pitt, was Foreign Secretary (1805–6), First Lord of the
Admiralty (1807–10) and Master-
General of the Ordnance
(1810–18). In September 1812 he
was created 1st Earl of Mulgrave
and Viscount Normanby; his son,
Constantine Henry (1797–1863),
who succeeded as 2nd Earl in
1838, was advanced to the rank of
Marquess and was a distinguished
statesman and diplomat. The 1st
Earl's brother Edmund (1760–
1837) was also a general officer.

MURAD BEY (1750–1801)

Originally a Circassian slave who
became a Mameluke, he shared
with Ibrahim the governance of
Egypt after the death of Abu'l
Dhahab, Murad bringing back the
latter's forces from the Palestinian
expedition to Egypt (1775).
Possessed of great wealth by
virtue of his marriage to the
widow of Ali Bey, the virtually
independent ruler of Egypt
1763–73, Murad rose to the position of Amir al-Hajj, leader of the
annual pilgrimage to Mecca.
Described as unjust and cruel, yet
with a taste for music and literature, he shared in Ibrahim's vicis-

situdes, being displaced by the
Ottoman attempt to regain Egypt
which foundered with the death
of Isma'il Bey in 1791, when
Murad and Ibrahim returned to
power. They were finally dispos-
sessed by the French invasion of
1798; Murad, who commanded at
the Battle of the Pyramids, had
little tactical skill although he had
established the Mameluke Nile
flotilla and the Cairo arsenal and
arms manufactory. After his
defeat he declined Napoleon's
offer of the governorship of an
Upper Egypt province and,
pursued by Desaix, was defeated
at Sediman (7 October 1798).
Unwilling to submit to his
nominal Ottoman overlords,
however, Murad agreed to change
sides and join the French,
concluding an alliance with
Kléber. He died of plague in May
1801, whereupon his successor,
Osman Bey, took his forces into
the Anglo–Ottoman camp. Although the French believed that
Murad remained loyal to his
agreement with them, Osman Bey
and the British suggested that he
was contemplating another
change of allegiance, if via the
British an accommodation could
have been arranged to prevent
any reprisals against him by the
Ottoman authorities.

MURAT, Marshal Joachim, King of Naples, Grand Duke of Berg (1767–1815)

The most flamboyant of all
Napoleon's subordinates, the
archetypal *sabreur*, he was born
in La Bastide, the son of an
innkeeper, whose full family
name was Murat-Jordy. He abandoned his religious training and
to escape his creditors enlisted in
the cavalry, but was dismissed in
1790 for idleness or insubordination. After a brief period in Louis
XVI's Constitutional Guard he was
commissioned in his old regiment
in October 1792; he was almost

JOACHIM MURAT
(ENGRAVING BY BOSSELMAN)

purged for his Jacobin views but was appointed as Napoleon's aide, having proved his mettle by securing the guns with which Napoleon delivered his 'whiff of grapeshot'. In Italy and Egypt he established his reputation as a daring cavalry commander, was *général de brigade* from May 1796, *de division* in October 1799, and was severely wounded by a pistol-shot in the jaw at Aboukir. He returned to France with Napoleon, assisted in the coup of Brumaire and joined the Bonaparte family by his marriage to Napoleon's sister Caroline on 20 January 1800. He commanded the cavalry at Marengo, was created a Marshal in 1804 and a prince in February 1805; after Austerlitz Napoleon bestowed upon him the grand-duchy of Berg (15 March 1806). Murat commanded the cavalry at Jena and Eylau (where he led the great charges which saved the day), and in 1808 received overall command of the French armies in Spain. The height of his career came with his appointment as King of Naples (1 August 1808) in succession to Joseph Bonaparte, but the acquisition of a throne seems to have turned his head; taking his regal status more seriously than had been intended, he came into

conflict with Napoleon (even blaming him for the failure of his own attack on Sicily in 1810), and only war with Russia in 1812 prevented a complete break. In the campaign he led the cavalry with his usual dash, but though ideal for inspiring a charge he was not best suited for a larger command, and when Napoleon turned over to him the remnant of the *Grande Armée* he returned to Naples, fearing that Napoleon was intending to dethrone him. To guarantee his kingdom he negotiated in secret with Austria and Britain although he fought alongside Napoleon in 1813 until after Leipzig. Having received Austrian guarantees of retaining his kingdom, he changed sides and in 1814 engaged the French, but when it became obvious that neither Austria nor Britain was prepared to allow him to remain in power, he attempted to instigate a movement of Italian national resistance against foreign occupation. Murat was defeated by the Austrians at Tolentino (2 May 1815) and fled to France in an endeavour to regain Napoleon's favour, but the returned emperor would not even receive him. Virtually a fugitive, Murat landed at Pizzo in Calabria with a small band of followers; he was apprehended, tried by a court-martial which he claimed (with much reason) was illegal, and was executed by firing-squad on 13 October 1815. Whatever his merits as a king (he had many, especially in his desire to improve the lot of his subjects), he will always be remembered as the most handsome, dashing and gallant cavalry leader of his or perhaps any age. A man of great vanity, he delighted in wearing the most outrageously ostentatious uniforms (the public called him 'King Franconi' after the director of a Paris theatre), but this very flamboyance served to inspire his

own troops, and even his enemies: in 1812 he was as popular with the Cossacks against whom he fought as he was with his own men. Napoleon remarked that these costumes gave him the appearance of 'a quack operator or a mountebank', and stated that 'Murat was endowed with extraordinary courage and little intelligence. The too great disproportion between these two qualities explains the man entirely ... the fault is originally mine. There were several men I had made too great; I had raised them above the sphere of their intelligence.'[1] In action, however, he was the *sabreur* supreme; Wolfe Tone's son, who served with him noted that: 'His eyes would sparkle at the random discharge of a tirailleur's carbine. Without counting the enemy, he would cry, "Chassez-moi ces canaille la!" (Drive off that rabble!) nor could he refrain, covered in gold and feathers, and remarkable as he was by his singular and theatrical dress, from dashing in among the sharp-shooters. He was an admirable swordsman and when he singled out some wretched Cossack, would dart on him like a falcon on his prey.' Awaiting execution, Murat reflected on how his fortune had been expended in the interests of his subjects: 'Both in court and camp, my only object was the national good. I employed the public revenues solely for public purposes; I did nothing for myself. At this hour of my death, I have no other wealth than that of my actions. They are all my glory and my consolation.'[3] By Queen Caroline, Murat had two sons, Napoléon-Achille (1801–47), Prince Royal of the Two Sicilies during his father's reign, who emigrated to the United States, where he died; and Napoléon-Lucien-Charles (1803–78), created Prince of Ponte Corvo in 1813, who also

ent to America but returned to
France, and from 1849 until 1878
held a number of political and
diplomatic posts. He was recognised as a royal prince, under the
title Prince Murat, by Napoleon
I.

Las Cases, vol. II, pp. 394–7. 2.
Anon., p. 361. 3. Ibid., p. 375.

Atteridge, A. H. *Joachim Murat,
Marshal of France and King of
Naples*. London, 1911; Cole, H. *The
Betrayers: Joachim and Caroline
Murat*. London, 1972; Dupont, M.
*Murat: Cavalier, Maréchal de
France, Prince et Roi*. Paris, 1980;
Espitalier, A. *Napoleon and King
Murat*. London, 1912; Pickles, T.
'Prince Joachim: Murat', in
Napoleon's Marshals, ed. D. G.
Chandler. London, 1987; Shep-
pard, Captain W. E. 'The
Napoleonic Cavalry and its
Leaders: Part IV: Murat', in *Cavalry
Journal*, 1931, vol. XXI, pp. 277–85

MURRAY, General Sir George (1772–1846)

SIR GEORGE MURRAY
(PRINT AFTER LAWRENCE)

One of the best professional staff
officers of the period, second son
of Sir William Murray, 5th Baronet
of Ochtertyre (1746–1800), he was
commissioned in 1789, served
with the 3rd Foot Guards in The
Netherlands 1793–5, and then
entered the Quartermaster-

General's Department. He served
in The Netherlands in 1799
(wounded in the ankle), Egypt,
West Indies (1802–3), in the expeditions to Hanover and Copenhagen,
and went with Moore to Sweden
and then to the Peninsula. With
local rank of major-general from
December 1811, he proved an
invaluable assistant to Wellington,
his efficiency making his department more significant than that of
the Adjutant-General. He retired
home in late 1811 to recover his
health, but at Wellington's request
returned to the Peninsula in the
spring of 1813, where he took on
increasing responsibility; having
been sent to Canada with the local
rank of lieutenant-general, he
returned too late for Waterloo, but
was Wellington's chief of staff
during the occupation of France.
Subsequently he held a number of
administrative appointments including Governor of the Royal
Military College (1819–24), CinC
Ireland, Colonial Secretary during
Wellington's administration,
Master-Generalship of the
Ordnance (1834–5, 1841–6). He
rose to the rank of general in 1841,
but his career was perhaps not
helped by his marriage; from 1819
he lived with Lady Louisa Erskine,
wife of Lieutenant-General Sir
James Erskine, Bt. (sister of the
Marquess of Anglesey) and only
married her at Erskine's death in
1825, a liaison somewhat frowned
upon by polite society.

Anon. *Description of the British
and Foreign Orders and Decorations Conferred on Rt Hon. General
Sir George Murray 1772–1846*.
London, 1910 (includes biographical detail); Ward, S. G. P. 'General
Sir George Murray', in *Journal of
the Society for Army Historical
Research*, 1980, vol. LVIII

MURRAY, General Sir John, Bt. (1768?–1827)

He is best known for his less than
impressive performance in the

Peninsula, though he had also
served in India, under Wellington,
and remained there as QMG until
promoted to major-general in
1801. He commanded a brigade in
the Oporto campaign, with no
distinction, and left the army
rather than risk having to take
orders from Beresford, his junior,
but returned to the Peninsula to
command the forces operating on
the east coast. His attempt to take
Tarragona was a fiasco, and he
abandoned the enterprise, leaving
18 siege-guns behind. Wellington's
comment is appropriate '... what I
cannot bear is his leaving his guns
and stores, and strange to say not
only does he not think he was
wrong in so doing, but he writes of
it as being rather meritorious, and
says he did it before ... The best of
the story is, that all parties ran
away ... Sir John Murray ran away;
and so did Suchet ...'[1] Murray was
court-martialled after the war but
was acquitted of all charges save
that of abandoning his guns, for
which he was reprimanded. He
should not be confused with his
namesake, **John Murray**, who
was Wellington's Commissary-
General in the Peninsula 1809–10.
The son of Sir Robert Murray, 6th
Baronet of Clermont, Sir John
inherited the family baronetcy in
1811 from his half-brother, **Lieutenant-General Sir James
Murray**, who had himself inherited in 1771, and who upon his
marriage in 1794 assumed the
name of Murray Pulteney. Sir
James was a more distinguished
soldier than his half-brother: after
service in the West Indies he was
the Duke of York's Adjutant-
General in The Netherlands in
1793 (in effect chief of staff to assist
the inexperienced duke), held a
senior post in the 1799 campaign
in North Holland, commanded at
Ferrol and in the expedition to
Portugal. MP for Weymouth and
Melcome Regis from 1790, he was
Secretary at War 1807–9 and died

from the effects of losing an eye by the explosion of his powder-flask in April 1811. He was experienced and capable, but had a diffident manner, lacked self-confidence and according to Bunbury was 'dreamy'; until close acquaintance, 'the kindness of his nature, the extent of his knowledge, and the largeness of his views remained hidden under a grotesque and somewhat repulsive exterior'.[2] Wounded in the arm on the day of the landing in Holland in 1799, he went off for treatment mumbling and chuckling to himself (as was his habit) to the effect that he had completed a 'set', having during his care[er] been shot in all four limbs!

1. Wellington, 8 Aug 1813, vol. . pp. 616–7. 2. Bunbury, *Narrative* pp. 30–1

Anon. *The Trial of Lieu[t.] General Sir John Murray. Bart. .* London, 1815

NANSOUTY, General Etienne-Marie-Antoine-Champion, comte de (1768–1815)

One of Napoleon's finest commanders of heavy cavalry, he was born of a noble family in Bordeaux and followed his father into the army at the age of 17. Promoted to lieutenant-colonel in 1792, he achieved a fine reputation as a cavalry commander with the Army of the Rhine, becoming *général de brigade* in 1799, *de division* in March 1803. He led the 1st Heavy Cavalry Division in the Austerlitz campaign and continued to serve with distinction in the campaigns of 1806 and 1807 (most notably at Friedland), after which he was appointed comte and first equerry to Napoleon. He continued to lead his division in the 1809 campaign, notably at Eckmühl and Aspern–Essling, and at Wagram his command was mauled so severely that it was unable to support Macdonald as intended. On being quizzed by Napoleon about this matter, Nansouty tried to explain, but, not being understood, turned away and remarked, 'After all, there is nothing Your Majesty can teach me about the handling of cavalry!'[1] In 1812 he led I Cavalry Corps, where the sarcastic wit which aroused some anger against him was again in evidence: when Murat complained about the poor physical state of the horses in his command, Nansouty remarked, 'they have no patriotic instincts'![2] At Borodino he was wounded in the knee, which ended his active service until July 1813, when he took command of the Guard cavalry, an honour as great as his appointment as Colonel-General of Dragoons. He led the Guard cavalry with distinction in the campaign, most notably at Hanau, but was blamed for errors in 1814, at La Rothière and Vauchamps, which though surely redressed by his conduct at Montmirail led to his being informed that he was so unwell he must leave his command, at the moment that the action at Craonne was about to begin. He replied politely that he could still do his duty, led his troops in the action, and then retired, ending his active service. Under the restoration he was appointed aide to the comte d'Artois and was given a command in the Maison du Roi, but his health declined and he died at Paris in February 1815.

1. Sheppard, Captain W. E. 'The Napoleonic Cavalry and its Leaders', in *Cavalry Journal*, 1931, vol. XXI, p. 91. 2. Ibid.

NAPIER, Admiral Sir Charles (1786–1860)

Son of Captain Charles Napier, RN, of Merchiston Hall, Stirlingshire, and grandson of 6th Baron Napier, he was thus cousin to the military Napiers: Charles James, George and William. He became a midshipman in the Royal Navy in 1800 and had risen to captain by 1809, but after much service at sea was put on half-pay. 'Being too active and enterprising a fellow to remain at home idle',[1] he joined his cousins as an 'amateur' in the Peninsular War and made a nuisance of himself on the day before Busaco, when he appeared 'most fantastically dressed' in naval uniform, with a cutlass and pistols, and spent the day urging Captain Thomas Brotherton of the 14th Light Dragoons, commanding the advanced posts, to charge everything in sight.[2] Charles borrowed a conspicuous white pony from his cousin George, 'notwithstanding I told him it was very foolish for most certainly he would get hit, being the only person on horseback ... in less than half an hour he got shot in the calf of the leg, but very slightly; and I was delighted at it, the obstinate dog, he deserved it well ... he was very good-humoured and laughed as much as anyone at his own folly.'[3] Nevertheless, he was back in time for the battle of Busaco on the morrow. Returning to the navy, he served in 1811 in the Mediterranean and in 1813 in North American waters, and after a period in retirement returned to duty in 1827, having been ruined by a steamship venture. Entering Portuguese service in 1833 as commander of the queen's fleet in the civil war, he destroyed a naval force of the rival Miguel off Cape St. Vincent (5 July 1833), captured Lisbon and held it against the Miguelites. Ennobled as Count St. Vincent in the Portuguese peerage, he returned to British service in 1836, was distinguished

ADMIRAL SIR CHARLES NAPIER
(ENGRAVING BY H. W. HUNT)

in the Syrian expedition as 2i/c to Admiral Stopford, commanded the Channel Fleet 1846–8 and in

1854 in the Baltic, though by declining to attack Cronstadt received much criticism (he had been involved in quarrels with the Admiralty throughout his career). He received no further command after his return in December 1854. He had been a Liberal MP for Marylebone 1842–6 and continued to sit for Southwark from 1855 until his death. His brother, General Sir Thomas Erskine Napier (1790–1863), served with the 52nd in the campaigns of Copenhagen and Corunna, and as a staff officer in the Peninsula from 1811, losing his left arm at the Nive when a captain in the Chasseurs Britanniques and ADC to Sir John Hope.

1. Napier, G., p. 146. 2. Brotherton, Captain T. *A Hawk at War*, ed. B. Perrett, Chippenham, 1986, pp. 28–9. 3. Napier, G., p. 147.

Napier, Major-General E. *Life and Correspondence of Admiral Sir Charles Napier KCB*. London, 1862

NAPIER, Lieutenant-General Sir Charles James (1782–1853)

SIR CHARLES JAMES NAPIER

He was probably the most distinguished member of a distinguished family: of the sons of Colonel George Napier (1751–1804, son of the 6th Baron Napier), and his second wife, Lady Sarah Lennox, daughter of the 2nd Duke of Richmond, George and William became generals, Henry Edward Napier (1789–1853) became a captain in the Royal Navy and wrote a learned *Florentine History*, and Charles James became best known as the conqueror of Sind. Commissioned at the age of 12 (and then going on half-pay to enable him to return to school!), he served as an ADC in Ireland from 1797, joined the Rifle Corps in 1800 and left after quarrelling with William Stewart in 1803, became ADC to General Henry Fox in Ireland and via the influence of his grandfather, the Duke of Richmond, and of his cousins, the Foxes, rose in rank through the Royal Staff Corps and the Cape Regiment to a majority in the 50th, with which he served in Denmark and at Corunna. In the latter action he made his name by leading a charge with Major Edward Stanhope, causing Moore to call out, 'Bravo Fiftieth! Well done my majors!'; but the charge progressed too far, Stanhope was killed and Napier shot in the ankle and bayoneted and clubbed while lying wounded, only being saved from death by a French drummer who would not see a helpless man murdered. Napier was so well treated in captivity by Soult and Ney that ever after he held them (and Napoleon) in the highest regard, and indeed Ney allowed him to return home to his old mother long before an official exchange was arranged. When this was completed he returned as a volunteer with the Light Division, had his jaw broken by a ball at Busaco and rejoined the army when barely recovered. When appointed to command the 102nd (a notoriously ill-disciplined and mutinous regiment, the ex-New South Wales Corps) he improved it out of all recognition, led it in America in 1813 and then exchanged back into the 50th, joining the army as a volunteer on half-pay in 1815 in time to be present at the capture of Cambrai. His subsequent career was marked by great success and continual conflict with those in authority (his temperament was difficult), and by great humanitarian and liberal principles which he demonstrated as Governor of Cephalonia (1822–30) and commander of the Northern District at the time of Chartist agitation. He won his great fame in Sind in 1843, returned home in 1847 after difficult relations with those in authority, but was regarded so highly as a general that he was appointed to succeed Gough after Chillianwalla, only for that general to end the war before Napier could arrive. Predictably his last period of Indian service ended with a quarrel with the Governor–General. Napier also had a literary career, embracing a translation of de Vigny, treatises on colonisation and even a historical romance (*William the Conqueror*, published posthumously). For all his difficult temperament, he was beloved by the ordinary soldiers under his command, and as Hardinge commented: 'In his whole conduct there was displayed every quality which could adorn public and private life: bravery, humanity and Christian feeling; nor could the honour of the British Army be in better hands.'[1]

1. *CUSM*, 1844, vol. I, p. 459.

Bruce, W. N. *Life of General Sir Charles Napier*. London, 1855; Holmes, T. R. E. *Sir Charles Napier*. Cambridge, 1925; Lawrence, Lady Rosamond. *Charles Napier, Friend and Fighter*. London, 1952; Napier, Sir William. *Life and Opinions of General Sir Charles James Napier*. London, 1857. A number of other biographical studies concentrate upon Napier's activities in India

NAPIER, General Sir George Thomas (1784–1855)

SIR GEORGE NAPIER
(ENGRAVING BY J. G. STODART AFTER KIRKUP)

Second of the Napier brothers, George rejected careers in the navy and church because of his dislike of the sea and of Latin, and instead obtained a commission in the 24th Light Dragoons (1800). From there he progressed to a captaincy in the 52nd, where he came under the influence of Sir John Moore, 'that great and good soldier [who] treated me like a son. I was never from under his command, and I am proud, most proud, to say I never received the slightest reproof from his lips, and was with him through all his subsequent difficulties and sufferings till that dreadful night when I saw him to whom I looked up as the first of men, a bloody corpse.'[1] He served as Moore's ADC, was slightly wounded at Busaco, suffered a shattered right wrist at Casal Nova (14 March 1811) and leading the stormers at Ciudad Rodrigo had his right elbow smashed by grapeshot. The arm was amputated by Staff-Surgeon Guthrie, whose 'instruments were blunted, so it was a long time before the thing was finished, at least twenty minutes, and the pain was great. I then thanked him for his kindness, having sworn at him

like a trooper while he was at it, to his great amusement ...'[2] Napier returned to England to recuperate but returned to the Peninsula in early 1814, being appointed to command the 71st in March. Subsequently he was Governor of the Cape (1838–44), was knighted in 1838, declined command of the forces in India and of the Sardinian Army in 1849, became full general in 1854 and died at Geneva in the following year. Two of his sons became generals in the British Army: Major-General George Thomas Conolly (1816–73) and General Sir William Craig Emilius (1818–1903). The third son, John Moore Napier (whose forenames demonstrate George's devotion to his old commander) (1817–46) was a captain in the 62nd and served on Sir Charles James Napier's staff, married the daughter of Sir Charles' second wife, and (with his infant daughter) died of cholera in Sind in July 1846.

1. Napier, as below, pp. 11–12. 2. Ibid., p. 219.

Napier, Sir George. *Passages in the Early Military Life of General Sir George T. Napier KCB*, ed. General W. C. E. Napier, London, 1884

NAPIER, General Sir William Francis Patrick (1785–1860)

The younger brother of Charles James and George Napier, he attained the rank of general but is best known as a historian. First commissioned in 1800, at Moore's suggestion he joined the 52nd in 1803 and obtained a company in the 43rd in 1804, and like his brothers became a devoted friend and admirer of the General. He served in the Denmark and Corunna campaigns, and on his return to the Peninsula after duty as ADC to the Duke of Richmond in Ireland suffered from an attack of pleurisy on the march to Talavera, a wound on the Coa, and

at Casal Nova a bullet lodged near the spine which could not be extracted and gave him pain for the rest of his life. An attack of ague forced him home in 1811 but he returned for Badajoz, commanded the 43rd in the Salamanca campaign and served with them from Nivelle (where he was especially distinguished) until the end of the war, being wounded again at the Nive. Lieutenant-colonel from November 1813, he served with the army of occupation in France until 1819 and then went on half-pay. To support his family (in March 1812 he had married Caroline, daughter of General Henry Fox and niece of Charles James, and they had a large family) he taught himself to write fluently and undertook his immortal *History of the War in the Peninsula and the South of France*, originally to defend Moore's reputation. He received much help and encouragement from sources as diverse as Wellington and Soult, and the multi-volume study, published between 1828 and 1840, established his reputation as the greatest British military historian, but produced much controversy, notably with Beresford, and a furious war of pamphlets and in the press. Despite any failings, the importance of the work can hardly

WILLIAM NAPIER
(ENGRAVING AFTER 'MISS JONES')

be over-emphasised in terms of its influence at the time and since; Napier's account of the attack of the fusilier brigade at Albuera is arguably the most renowned piece of prose in military writing, for the style and spontaneity of the language, and the author's obvious intense concern for his subject. As a supporter of political reform, Napier was offered the chance to enter parliament, but declined; major-general from November 1841, he was Lieutenant-Governor of Jersey 1842–7 and continued his literary career, notably defending his brother Charles James' conduct in Sind, with two books and much correspondence in the press. Lieutenant-general from November 1851, he became full general four months before his death in February 1860. He was reckoned by many to be the most handsome man of the age, six feet tall (and, it was said, able to jump six feet into the air), and resembling a classical portrayal of a god of war (in 1811 one lady said his black hair and moustache made him resemble a young Venetian by Titian!); but it is by his literary endeavours that he will be best remembered. The name of his only son, John Moore Napier (1816–67), like one of George's sons, recalled the family reverence for their friend and general.

Bruce, H. A. *Life of General Sir William Napier, KCB.* London, 1864

NAPLES, King of, see **MURAT**

NAPOLEON I (Napoleon Bonaparte), Emperor of the French, King of Italy (1769–1821)
It is, of course, impossible to cover adequately the career and achievements of Napoleon Bonaparte in so short a summary. That he dominated the period in which he lived is evident from the name assigned to that age, 'Napoleonic'. Arguably no other historical char-

NAPOLEON AS FIRST CONSUL
(ENGRAVING BY MERET AFTER AFTER APPIANI)

acter has left so clear a mark upon the terminology of his era; even 'Alexandrian' can relate to the place or its school of philosophy as much as to Alexander himself, and 'Augustan' may refer equally to any perceived 'golden age' as to the period of Augustus. No such ambivalence attaches to 'Napoleonic': the word defines the period in which Europe's most influential, powerful, revered and reviled personality was Napoleon Bonaparte.

His career followed a course which might be taken as an allegory of human endeavour and human frailty: of one who rose to the highest level, but in reaching even higher fell to earth and paid an awful price for his ambition; as Sir John Seeley commented, he stooped to pick up a crown, but having held it in his hands, dropped it.[1] The events of his career, his abilities, achievements and failings, have been recounted and dissected innumerable times, so only a brief outline is necessary here. Born on 15 August 1769 in Ajaccio, Corsica, the second son of a lawyer of minor aristocratic background and little fortune, Napoleone Buonaparte (as his name was spelled originally) embarked upon a military career, and owed his early successes not

only to the political and social conditions which facilitated his rise, but, above all, to his own abilities, ambition and willingness to undertake endless toil. Although in many ways fortunate in the conditions he encountered conducive to his progress – which mirrored his own belief that in addition to talent a general needed luck – it was his own abilities which led to his advancement. Educated at Brienne and the Military School in Paris, he was commissioned into the French artillery, a 'technical' service which not only suited his aptitude in mathematics and science but one which was less the province of the aristocracy and more that of the dedicated, educated professional. The Revolution gave him the opportunity to display his talents at an early age; coming to notice at Toulon, his progress was interrupted by the political ferment of the time, which led even to his arrest, but his fortunes were restored by his defence of the Convention with his 'whiff of grapeshot'. With the support of Barras and the Directory he was appointed to command the Army of Italy, and married Barras' ex-mistress, Joséphine de Beauharnais.

Napoleon's victories in Italy established his reputation as a general of immense talents, and one with a charismatic personality which throughout his career he used to inspire idolisation among his followers. So high was his reputation that the Directory feared his powers and sanctioned his expedition to Egypt partially on strategic grounds and partially to remove him as a threat to their own existence. Despite the eventual failure of the enterprise, and Napoleon's abandonment of it in mid-campaign, his reputation was unaffected and by the *coup d'état* of Brumaire he was one of three Consuls appointed to replace the orrupt and unpopular Directory. Those who engineered the establishment of the Consulate probably intended him as a figurehead, but his own political skills, not to say cunning and ruthlessness, soon established him as First Consul and effectively as master of France, an exceptional rise from obscurity in less than five years.

Confirming his position by the victory of Marengo and the peace which followed, it was a short step from his proclamation as Consul for Life to Emperor of the French, as Napoleon I (2 December 1804), the attainment of which position confirmed that his political skills matched his military ability. Many aspects of his reign were beneficial to his country, notably the reform of administration and economy, and perhaps his most enduring achievement, the *Code Napoléon*; and by removing the spectre of internal turmoil and bringing peace to Europe after a decade of conflict, had the Peace of Amiens endured Napoleon might have been regarded as a revered statesman of world significance. However, a combination of his own ambitions and the threat which he was perceived to pose to his enemies, made peace impossible.

Upon the renewal of war, at first he enjoyed spectacular success, with his army probably at its peak in the 1805 campaign which was decided by the manoeuvre of Ulm and the Battle of Austerlitz, military achievements among the greatest in history. The defeat of Prussia in 1806, the construction of a satellite confederation of German states and the peace forced upon Russia at Tilsit confirmed his position of pre-eminence, but his most implacable enemy, Great Britain, remained unpacified. Napoleon's attempt to ruin British trade by the Continental System resulted instead in the beginning

of his own ruin, for although he defeated Austria again in 1809, in the course of it he sustained his first serious military reverse, and the attempt to establish a Bonapartist dynasty in Spain led to the 'running sore' of the Peninsular War which exerted a continual drain upon his resources, and when conflict again arose in eastern Europe presented him with the insupportable problem of having to fight a war on two fronts. The first signs of a decline in Napoleon's own powers, and the collapse of the Empire, were evident even before he undertook the disastrous expedition to Russia in 1812. After this massive defeat, his allies deserted (including Austria, whose compliance he had endeavoured to cement by marriage to an Austrian princess, Marie-Louise, following his divorce from Josephine), the 'War of Liberation' overthrew his barrier of satellite states, and France was invaded. Napoleon defended France with much of his old vigour in 1814, but the odds were overpowering, his marshals turned against him, and he was forced to abdicate on 6 April 1814, having failed to preserve his dynasty by having his infant son recognised as his successor. After chafing with boredom on his new 'kingdom' of Elba, in 1815 he made a last attempt to regain his old position, but his enemies were implacable and his defeat at Waterloo consigned him to a second abdication and a miserable exile on the inhospitable rock of St. Helena, where he lived for the last six years of his life in bitter contemplation of what might have been. He died on 5 May 1821.

As a general, his reputation is unquestioned. Less of an innovator than a developer of a system already in vogue, he honed the existing 'minor tactics' to perfection and utilised them in a

NAPOLEON AS EMPEROR
(PRINT AFTER HORACE VERNET)

Blitzkrieg style of strategy. He identified an objective (usually the destruction of the enemy's field army rather than acquisition of territory) and pursued it ruthlessly, his army and subordinates moving like a proficient machine which took its orders from a single source, the Emperor himself. Herein lay both its strength and its weakness: the 'unity of command' which was both decider of policy and the means to carry it out, but handicapped by a lack of subordinates capable of independent action, so that things began to go awry when undertakings became too large for Napoleon to supervise every detail in person, let alone conduct a war on two fronts. Yet his successes did not depend entirely upon his administrative, tactical and strategic genius; his charismatic hold over his followers must also have been a factor in the excellence of his army and its willingness to hazard all for him. It is a sad reflection that the object of such reverence was the cause of the deaths of countless thousands of his most loyal followers, which at times he claimed to lament while continuing to pursue his goals none the less.

It was this element of his character which caused his enemies to regard him as 'the Corsican ogre', and few personalities in history can have been the recipient of such calumny as Napoleon, from expressions of hatred born out of fear to wilder accusations which identified him as the Antichrist or the Beast of the Book of Revelation whose number was 666! Such criticisms did not take hold in France except among the extreme Royalist faction; indeed the 'Napoleonic legend' which grew after his death (doubtless reinforced by the melancholy nature of his end) found expression in the solemn return of his body to France in 1840, attended by many of the surviving veterans, and the final deposition of his remains in Les Invalides. From that time the facts concerning the historic figure of Napoleon have been interwoven with the heroic image of 'Le Tondu', 'L'Empereur'. The effects of Napoleon's career were profound, not only upon his own country; while it might be debatable to regard him as the originator of the concept of a unified continent, the wars begun by the Revolution and which he continued changed Europe fundamentally. It is perhaps slightly ironic that much of this change, for example the growth of movements for German and Italian unity and national regeneration, were more the result of the reaction against Napoleon than anything he did directly himself. It could be argued that the spread of liberal ideas arising from the Revolution would have occurred irrespective of Napoleon; but it is worth remarking that it was under him that they *did* happen, and it would be as misleading not to recognise that and to deny his contribution as it would be to accord him sole credit for all the beneficence which occurred during his reign. Whether the

results would have been accompanied by so many years of war and so much bloodshed had France been led by another, is an insoluble question. At a purely personal level, as different from his wider influence, Napoleon's career must be seen as a failure, for he created no ruling dynasty and ended his life in exile; as Seeley remarked, 'All that he built at such a cost of blood and tears, was swept away before he himself ended his short life.'[2]

Opinions about Napoleon are probably as divided now as they were in his own time, from the creator of a golden age of enlightenment and triumph to the perpetrator of aggressive and ruthless tyranny; but even those who favoured the latter perception of him recognised his unique status. Wellington's view would find some sympathy: 'Napoleon was the first man of his day on a field of battle, and with French troops. I confine myself to that. His policy was mere bullying, and, military matters apart, he was a Jonathan Wild,'[3] an allusion to the notorious organiser of robberies and receiver of stolen property who was hanged at Tyburn in 1725. Yet whatever the opinions on Napoleon's merits or failings, his unique place in history is assured.

1. Seeley, Sir John, *A Short History of Napoleon the First*. London, 1895, p. 30. 2, Ibid., p. 322. 3. Ellesmere, p. 100.

Biographical works on Napoleon are countless: for a bibliography and critical essay, see Connelly, O. 'Napoleon and his Family: Lives and Careers', in the invaluable *Napoleonic Military History: A Bibliography*, ed. D. D. Horward, London 1986. A selection of works, including significant modern studies, follows: Aubry, O. *Napoleon*. London, 1964; Baring Gould, S. *The Life of Napoleon Bonaparte*. London, 1897; Barnett, C. *Bonaparte*. London, 1978;

Collins, I. *Napoleon, First Consul and Emperor of the French*. London, 1986; Chandler, D. G. *The Campaigns of Napoleon*. London, 1967 (a most influential military study); Connelly, O. *Blundering to Glory: Napoleon's Military Campaigns*. Wilmington, Delaware, 1987; Cronin, V. *Napoleon*. London, 1971; Herold, J. C. *The Age of Napoleon*. London, 1963; Las Cases, Count de. *Memoirs of the Life, Exile and Conversations of the Emperor Napoleon*. London, 1836; Lyons. M. *Napoleon Bonaparte and the Legacy of the French Revolution*. London, 1994; Markham, F. *Napoleon*. New York, 1963; Marshall-Cornwall, Sir James. *Napoleon as Military Commander*. London, 1967; Rosebery, Lord. *Napoleon, the Last Phase*. London, 1900; Sloane, W. M. *The Life of Napoleon Bonaparte*. New York, 1906; Schom, A. *Napoleon Bonaparte: A Life*. London, 1997; Thompson, J. M. *Napoleon Bonaparte*. Oxford, 1952; Tulard, J. *Napoleon: the Myth of the Saviour*. London 1984

NAPOLEON II (Napoléon-François Joseph-Charles Bonaparte), King of Rome, Duke of Reichstadt, Prince of Parma 1811–32)

Napoleon's only legitimate child, perhaps best known by his title, King of Rome, bestowed by his father, was born at the Tuileries on 20 March 1811 to Napoleon I's second wife, Marie-Louise. The event was one of great joy for the Bonapartist regime as it appeared to secure the dynasty by providing the heir for which Napoleon had longed. The birth was not easy and Napoleon was so troubled over the health of the Empress that the child was put to one side after the delivery as all attended to the mother, and indeed it seemed at first that the child was dead, but to Napoleon's great relief this was not the case. Napoleon proposed

NAPOLEON II, KING OF ROME
(ENGRAVING BY M. HAIDER AFTER LAWRENCE)

that he be educated among the princes of allied nations so that those who would inherit their thrones would know one another from childhood, but the fall of the empire intervened. Napoleon abdicated in favour of his son, who to Bonapartist supporters thus became Napoleon II, but this was only a fleeting attempt to secure a fallen dynasty. When Napoleon went to Elba, Marie-Louise and her son went to Austria where the child came under the guardianship of his grandfather, Francis I. From his mother's Italian territories, young Napoleon received the title Prince of Parma, but after a renewed attempt to proclaim him as Napoleon II (as which he was recognised by the Council of Five Hundred upon Napoleon I's abdication after Waterloo), the Allied powers stood against his having any involvement in Parma. Marie-Louise went there alone, leaving the 4-year- old in Austria, where he became something of a political pawn. It was decided that he should not inherit Parma and at his mother's insistence an alternative title was found for him, Duke of Reichstadt (22 July 1818). The young duke (nicknamed 'L'Aiglon', 'the eaglet') showed a liking for military affairs as he grew, but was never allowed

to correspond with his father, and was never in robust health. Schemes were floated of making him a king (Modena actually proclaimed him king of Italy), and even of his returning to France upon the 1830 revolution, but nothing came of them, and any chance of his active involvement in European politics ended with his death from tuberculosis on 22 July 1832, some four months after his 21st birthday. That he died in the room in which his father had dictated peace terms to the Austrians was the final irony of a sad life. His place in the Bonaparte dynasty as Napoleon II was the reason why Louis Bonaparte's son styled himself Napoleon III upon his assumption of the imperial mantle on 1 December 1852.

Aubry, O. *The King of Rome, Napoleon II*. London, 1932; Castelot, A. *King of Rome: a Biography of Napoleon's Tragic Son*. New York, 1960; Montbel, comte de. *Le Duc de Reichstadt*. Paris, 1832; L'Hérault, G. de. *Histoire de Napoléon II*. Paris, 1853; Wertheimer. E. de. *The Duke of Reichstadt*. London, 1905; Wilson, R. McN. *The King of Rome*. London, 1932

NARBONNE-LARA, General Louis-Marie-Jacques-Amalric, comte de (1755–1813)

Born in the duchy of Parma, where his mother was a lady-in-waiting to the Duchess and his father a Spanish aristocrat, he was raised at Versailles in company with the royal children; he was commissioned in the French Army in 1771, became *maréchal-de-camp* in 1791 and from that December until March 1792 was Minister of War. He was regarded as too moderate and, although he joined the Army of the North, he soon emigrated, returning to France only in 1801 after spending time in Britain, Switzerland and Germany. He was granted the rank

of *général de division* but remained on the retired list until 1809, when he was appointed Governor of Raab and employed as minister-plenipotentiary at Munich. Napoleon was very attached to him and tried to appoint him to Marie-Louise's staff, only for the Empress to reject him (it was said because her other staff feared his influence), so he was appointed ambassador to Vienna. Napoleon stated that of all his ambassadors, only Narbonne truly deserved the title, being especially fitted by the advantages 'not only of his talents, but of his old-fashioned morals, his manners, and his name,'[1] for in negotiating with the old aristocracy, he said, one needed to employ a member of that same class. Although Narbonne's mission was unsuccessful, in that Austria defected from the French alliance, Napoleon said that Narbonne had discerned their intentions, and their knowledge that he had had hastened their decision. Narbonne survived this by only a short period, dying of typhus at Torgau, where he was Governor, on 17 November 1813.

1. Las Cases, vol. II, p. 89.

Dard, E. *Le Comte de Narbonne 1755–1813*. Paris, 1943

NECKER, Jacques (1732–1804)

Born in Geneva, son of a professor of law of Pomeranian origin, he went to Paris in 1747 to begin a career in finance. With another Genevese he established the bank of Thellusson & Necker, superintending its operations in Paris and Thellusson in London. (Isaac de Thellusson was ambassador from Geneva to the court of Louis XV; his son Peter (d.1797) made his fortune in London, his son Peter (1761–1808) being ennobled as 1st Baron Rendlesham, whose second son George (1791–1813) was killed at Vittoria as a lieutenant in the 11th Light Dragoons). With the

JACQUES NECKER

encouragement of his wife, Suzanne Curchod, Necker aspired to public office, his financial skills bringing him to notice; so after serving as Genevan representative in Paris, he transferred his holding in the bank to his brother Louis and in October 1776 became French Minister of Finance. The national finances could not be resolved quickly, and though he made some progress, he was dismissed in 1781; recalled in 1788 he supported the Assembly of the States-General and as such was regarded as a cause of the upheaval by the court, and in July 1789 he was ordered to leave France. Recalled by public pressure, he again proved deficient in statesmanship and unable to solve the financial problems; in September 1790 he resigned and retired to his estate at Coppet, near Geneva, where he would die in April 1804. There Napoleon met him but was unimpressed; he thought Necker far below his reputation and claimed that he had only the narrow views of a banker, confirming the lack of political aptitude which he had demonstrated when in office. Necker's only child, Anne, better known as Madame de Staël, wrote his biography, *Mémoires sur la Vie Privée de M. Necker*, which was published in 1818, and Necker's

own prolific works were collected and republished under the editorship of his grandson, Auguste de Staël-Holstein, in Paris in 1820–1.

NEILLY, Vice-Admiral Joseph-Marie, baron (1751–1833)

A distinguished French naval officer, Neilly (whose name is also found spelled 'Nielly') was the son of a merchant captain; he went to sea at the age of 7 and was wounded in the action off Belle-Isle. After merchant service (including capture in 1778 and escape from Jersey) he was commissioned in the navy in the same year and rose to the rank of rear-admiral in 1793. He is probably best known for his command of a squadron from Rochefort, sent to escort Admiral Pierre-Jean Vanstabel's grain fleet, and which joined Villaret-Joyeuse for the Battle of the First of June, when he flew his flag in the 110-gun *Républicain*. (It was fortunate for Neilly that when his squadron joined the main fleet he transferred from his original flagship, the 80-gun *Sans-Pareil*, as that was one of those captured in the action.) Neilly's other outstanding exploit occurred on 6 November 1794 when he led a squadron of five 74-gun ships out of Brest and encountered two British 74s, HMSs *Alexander* and *Canada*; two of Neilly's ships chased *Canada*, which escaped, while the other three caught and battered *Alexander* into submission, Captain Rodney Bligh fnally striking his colours. This was one of very few French successes against a British ship of such size during the entire Revolutionary Wars (although *Alexander* was later recovered). In 1796 Neilly participated in the Bantry Bay expedition, became maritime prefect at Dunkirk in 1800 and retired in September 1803. He became baron in 1814 and *vice-amiral* in 1821.

NELSON, Vice-Admiral Horatio, 1st Viscount, Duke of Brontë (1758–1805)

Few commanders have imprinted their reputation and personality upon their Service to the degree which Horatio Nelson did upon the Royal Navy; he remains the best known and greatest of British naval heroes. Not only the dominant naval commander of the Napoleonic era, he was one of the greatest naval tacticians and strategists, and is still one of the most famous of all Englishmen. The son of a Norfolk clergyman and of the grand-niece of Sir Robert Walpole, he entered the navy via the influence of a maternal uncle, Captain Maurice Suckling (1725–78) and became proficient in every aspect of his trade; appointed lieutenant in 1777, he attained the rank of post-captain at the remarkably early age of 20. Patronage played little part in his advancement, his abilities and personality establishing his reputation. After service in the West Indies (where he married the widow Frances Nisbet, 1761–1831), in November 1793 he was appointed to the 64-gun HMS *Agamemnon*. His subsequent service was greatly distinguished; at Calvi (Corsica) in 1794 he lost the sight of his right eye when struck by debris thrown up by the impact of a cannon-shot, and in 1797, when commanding HMS *Captain*, he was largely responsible for Jervis' victory at St. Vincent by preventing the escape of the Spanish fleet and personally capturing two ships by boarding, in recognition of which he received a knighthood. Later in the same year he lost his right arm in an unavailing attack at Santa Cruz (Tenerife) and was invalided home; but by April 1798 he was back in the Mediterranean as rear-admiral. His brilliant victory of Aboukir Bay, or 'Battle of the Nile' on 1 August 1798 at a stroke

HORATIO NELSON (ENGRAVING BY T. W. HARLAND AFTER LEMUEL ABBOT)

doomed to failure Napoleon's oriental expedition, and earned for Nelson a barony and the status of the greatest national hero of his time. His Mediterranean service had another profound conse-quence; he made the acquain-tance of the British ambassador to Naples, Sir William Hamilton, and his wife, Nelson's subsequent affair with Emma Hamilton becoming one of the most famous romances in history, though the cause of some considerable scandal at the time. His conduct at Naples after Aboukir was less glorious than his victory, when he fell under the influence of the queen and Lady Hamilton; and when in 1800 he returned home, despite his popularity, he was somewhat estranged from the Admiralty and, by his liaison with Emma, from polite society. Despite this relationship he remained on the best of terms with Sir William Hamilton, estab-lishing a curious *ménage à trois*; but his estrangement from Lady Nelson was complete. Awarded the Neapolitan dukedom of Brontë, on 1 January 1801 he became vice-admiral by seniority, and in the same year was sent as deputy to Sir Hyde Parker in the operations against Denmark. By disobeying Parker's orders he won

the Battle of Copenhagen, earning himself (22 May 1801) the viscountcy of Nelson of the Nile and of Burnham Thorpe, Norfolk (his birthplace), and an even greater reputation. Later that year he returned home, continuing to live with Emma, who gave birth to their daughter, Horatia; Sir William Hamilton died in April 1803. On the renewal of the war, Nelson was appointed to command in the Mediterranean; he pursued Villeneuve's break-out to the West Indies and back, and destroyed French aspirations by the shattering victory of Trafalgar (21 October 1805). During the action, while pacing the quarter-deck of his flagship HMS *Victory*, he was shot through the spine by a sharpshooter from the French ship *Redoutable*, and died on the evening of the battle. His was a devastating loss to his nation; universally mourned, he received a state funeral at St. Paul's and his nearest male relative, his only surviving brother (of seven), the Revd. William Nelson (1757–1835) was created Earl Nelson of Trafalgar and Merton (the latter Nelson's home with Emma in Surrey), on 20 November 1805. The dukedom of Brontë passed via the Earl's daughter to another great naval family, the Hoods, to the barony, later viscountcy, of Bridport. Nelson's character was complex, embracing not only courage, resolution and kindness but vanity and a desire for popu-larity. His charismatic personality served him well, so that he was genuinely revered not only by his immediate subordinates – the 'band of brothers' who were his captains – but by the ordinary seamen, and to this was added supreme capability as a seaman and commander. His personal bravery was evident in such actions as St. Vincent, his tactical audacity at Aboukir, and his inno-vative genius at Trafalgar, where

his attack in two columns broke the enemy line and brought about the 'pell-mell' battle he desired. He was not the first to use such tactics, but none had so perfected them, and the absolute trust engendered in his subordinates carried them through perfectly. Such aspects of his character overcame criticisms of his highly unconventional life with the Hamiltons, and raised the morale of his officers and seamen to the highest level. His popularity in the country at large, and the lamenta-tion at his death, is reflected in the closing paragraph of Clarke and McArthur's biography: '... he acted on a superior principle: in every work ... which he undertook, in the service of his king and country, he did it, in the language of the sacred historian, *with all his heart, and prospered*. The fame of Nelson will endure as long as the name of his country shall be pronounced, in new ages of the world, by future generations of men. Let posterity consecrate his memory by emulating the perfec-tion of his public character, and the disinterested zeal of his conduct; and should the time arrive, when on our native land we shall be called to protect the tomb of Nelson, and the liberties which he died to save, may his immortal spirit hover around us, and with the blessing of God's providence lead us to victory.'[1]

1. 1840 edn., vol. III, pp. 211–12.

Biographical works on Nelson are legion, including: Clarke, J. Stanier, and McArthur, J. *The Life and Services of Horatio, Viscount Nelson, from his Lordship's Manu-scripts*. London, 1840 (orig. 1809), on which Robert Southey's classic *Life of Nelson*. London, 1813, is based; Deuchar, S., Lavery, B., and Morriss, R. *Nelson: An Illustrated History*. London, 1995; Hibbert, C. *Nelson: A Personal History*. London, 1994; Mahan, Captain A. T. *The Life of Nelson, the Embodi-*

ment of the Sea Power of Great Britain. London, 1897; Nicolas, Sir Nicholas (ed.). *The Despatches and Letters of Vice-Admiral Lord Viscount Nelson.* London, 1844–6; Oman, C. *Nelson.* London, 1947; Pocock, T. *Horatio Nelson.* London, 1987; Warner, O. *A Portrait of Lord Nelson.* London, 1958; White, C. (ed.). *The Nelson Companion.* Stroud, 1995

NESSELRODE, Karl Robert, Count (1780–1862)

One of the most important figures in Russian diplomacy in the first half of the 19th century, he came from a Westphalian family long settled in Livonia. He was born in Lisbon where his father was Russian ambassador, was baptised as a member of the Church of England in the British embassy there, and educated in Berlin when his father became ambassador to Prussia. He entered the Russian navy, transferred to the army and then to the diplomatic service; in 1806–7 he served with field headquarters, was present at Eylau and helped negotiate the Treaty of Tilsit. On the staff of the Russian ambassador to France, he helped increase understanding between Talleyrand and the Tsar, and was involved in much diplomatic activity at about the time of the fracture in Franco–Russian relations. He joined the Tsar's headquarters in 1812 and although Rumiantzov was officially Foreign Minister, the direction of policy was largely Nesselrode's. He accompanied the Russian forces in the Leipzig campaign and in the invasion of France, helped negotiate the capitulation of Paris and signed the Treaty of Chaumont. His relations with Talleyrand were significant in the diplomatic activity following the end of the war; he was present at the Congress of Vienna and retained his influence after the appointment of Capodistrias as

Foreign Minister in August 1816. The latter was influential as long as Alexander I retained liberal principles, but Nesselrode's importance increased as the Tsar began to adopt Talleyrand's ideas, and in 1822 he replaced Capodistrias as Foreign Minister. A supporter of Alexander's advocacy of a 'Holy Alliance', he remained in office under Nicholas I, and only retired after the conclusion of the Treaty of Paris in 1856.

Nesselrode, A. de. *Lettres et Papiers du Chancelier Comte de Nesselrode.* Paris, 1904–7

NEUCHATEL, Prince de, see BERTHIER

NEY, Marshal Michel, duc d'Elchingen, prince de la Moscowa (1769–1815)

MICHEL NEY
(ENGRAVING BY R. G. TIETZE AFTER GÉRARD)

Known as 'le Rougeaud' from his red hair, his character was summarised by another sobriquet, 'the bravest of the brave'. The son of a cooper of Saarlouis, he enlisted as a hussar in 1787; commissioned in 1792, he became known as an officer of great courage, and became *général de brigade* in August 1796, *de division* in March 1799 after distinguished service under Massena in Switzerland. Although he had served

under Kléber, Hoche and Moreau (at Hohenlinden), he had not served with Napoleon, but though earlier a committed republican, he became an ardent supporter of the future emperor; the wife whom he married in May 1802, Aglaé Auguié, was reputedly chosen for him by Josephine. One of the few officers of the old Army of the Rhine to become a trusted lieutenant of the Emperor, he was appointed Marshal in the first creation of 1804 and for the next several years led VI Corps of the *Grand Armée* with great distinction, perhaps most notably at Elchingen in 1805, from which victory he took the title of his dukedom in 1808. He was somewhat lucky to escape after making a premature attack at Jena, and by another foray provoked the Russian response which led to the Eylau campaign, but his arrival on the Russian right helped swing the course of that battle. At Friedland he was again distinguished (commanding Napoleon's right), but such success was not repeated in his involvement in the Peninsula. He was present at Busaco, but his relations with Massena so deteriorated that he was guilty of absolute insubordination, whereupon Massena relieved him of his command; such was his following in the army that it was suggested that Ney might forcibly replace Massena, but he declined this invitation to mutiny and returned to France. Commanding III Corps in the Russian campaign of 1812, his bravery and determination raised him to the status of almost a legend. Leading the rearguard at a most desperate period, he defied the climate and the pursuing enemy and, having been thought lost, cut his way free: 'I would have given everything rather than lose you,'[1] was Napoleon's remark on his reappearance. Ney's efforts in Russia gained him not only fame as the saviour of what remained of the *Grande Armée* (and by his own account for being the last Frenchman to quit Russia and firer of the last shot over the Niemen at Kovno), but the title 'Prince of the Moscowa' and nickname 'bravest of the brave', both bestowed by Napoleon. He commanded III Corps in 1813, serving at Lützen, Bautzen, Dennewitz (where he suffered a notable reverse) and Leipzig; wounds suffered in this campaign caused him to return home to recover, but he served throughout the 1814 campaign. His adherence to Napoleon weakened, however, and he was in the forefront of those who advocated abdication. Ney accepted the Bourbon restoration and upon Napoleon's return in 1815 demonstrated his fidelity to the king by declaring that he would apprehend the ex-emperor and put him in an iron cage; yet he defected to his old chief and was given one of the most important commands for the Waterloo campaign. His conduct has been criticised variously, ranging from lethargy at Quatre Bras to impetuosity at Waterloo; but he demonstrated again his personal courage if not any great tactical ability. This perhaps exemplifies Ney as a general: an ideal corps commander for performing a given task and for inspiring his subordinates (admiration for him was unbounded), but less fitted for independent command or, as at Waterloo, for conducting a major action without supervision. The aftermath of Waterloo was melancholy; Ney made no further attempt to assist Napoleon, considered flight, expected to be allowed to retire quietly, but was arrested by the Bourbons, tried for treason and shot on 7 December in the Luxembourg Gardens, the result of a desire for revenge by the most vehement royalist elements. It was said that even the king wished to avoid such an outcome, and the execution was regarded by many as a scandalous stain upon the

reputation of all involved. Ney faced death with customary courage, but perhaps it would have been better had he fallen at Waterloo, where he was said to have exclaimed, 'Come and see how a Marshal of France dies,' only to escape death on that occasion. The tragic circumstances of his death perhaps helped give rise to the rumour that he had escaped to America.

1. Lejeune, vol. II, p. 226.

Atteridge, A. H. *The Bravest of the Brave: Michel Ney.* London, 1912; Bonnal, General E. *La Vie militaire du Maréchal Ney.* Paris, 1910–14; Compton, P. *Marshal Ney.* London 1937; Horricks, R. *Marshal Ney: The Romance and the Real.* Tunbridge Wells, 1982 (repr. as *Military Politics from Bonaparte to the Bourbons: Life and Death of Michel Ney)*; Hourtoulle, Dr. F. G. *Ney, le Brave des Braves.* Paris, 1981; Kurtz, H. *The Trial of Marshal Ney; His Last Years and Death.* London, 1957; Young, Brigadier P. 'The Bravest of the Brave: Ney', in *Napoleon's Marshals*, ed. D. G. Chandler. London, 1987. Ney's own memoirs were not completed, but those for the period up to Elchingen were published as *Mémoires du Maréchal Ney, publiées par sa Famille.* Paris, 1833 (English edn., London, 1833). Another publication of Ney's was *Military Studies ... Written for the Use of his Officers*, trans. G. H. Caunter, intro. A. James. London, 1833

NIGHTINGALL, Lieutenant-General Sir Miles (1768–1829)

One of the least effective of Wellington's subordinates, he was commissioned in 1787, served in the 3rd Mysore War, the West Indies, San Domingo, as ADC to Cornwallis in Ireland and as assistant adjutant-general in the expedition to The Netherlands in 1799, and returned to India to serve under Lake, including Laswaree.

He led a brigade at Roleia and Vimeiro, and as major-general from July 1810 commanded a brigade of the 1st Division, being wounded at Fuentes de Oñoro. He appears to have been something of a defeatist and probably a hypochondriac, and was clearly unhappy with his lot as he bemoaned his fear of a return of rheumatism, which he thought would be alleviated by a command in India. In June 1811 he duly left the Peninsula, serving subsequently as CinC Java; lieutenant-general from June 1814, he received a knighthood of the Bath in January 1815, and after commanding at Bombay returned home in 1819.

NORTHESK, Admiral William Carnegie, 7th Earl of (1758–1831)

WILLIAM CARNEGIE, 7TH EARL OF NORTHESK (ENGRAVING BY H. COOK AFTER H. PATTERSON)

Son of Admiral George, 6th Earl of Northesk (1716–92), he followed his father into the Royal Navy at the age of 13, and on the death of his eldest brother in 1788 took the title Lord Rosehill. He succeeded to the earldom upon his father's death in 1792. He is best remembered, when rear-admiral, as third in command behind Nelson and Collingwood at Trafalgar, when he flew his flag in Captain

Charles Bullen's 100-gun HMS *Britannia*, a notoriously slow sailer but thanks to Northesk's determination was able to keep up and play her part at Trafalgar. He rose to the rank of admiral and became CinC Plymouth; he married a niece of Earl St. Vincent and his eldest son, George, Lord Rosehill, was lost in his sixteenth year when HMS *Blenheim* was wrecked on Rodriguez Island in the Indian Ocean in 1807.

NUGENT, Field Marshal Laval, Prince (1777–1862)

This Austrian commander had a military career of remarkable length: entering the service in 1793, he was present at Solferino in 1859. Rising to the rank of field marshal and becoming a prince of the empire, he was noted for serving in Hungary in 1849 but mostly for service in 1813–14, when as *General-Major*, serving under *Feldmarschall-Leutnant* Paul von Radivojavic, he recovered the Military Border and Croatia from its previous French control. Of Irish origin, his family was that which held the earldom of Westmeath, and thus he was a distant kinsman of the British field marshal Sir George Nugent, Bt. (1757–1849) who served in The Netherlands, as CinC Jamaica 1801–6 and India 1812–13, and who attained the rank of field marshal in November 1846.

O'DONNELL, General Henry Joseph, count of La Bispal (or Abispal) (1769–1834)

A product of the Jacobite diaspora, Henry (Enrique José) O'Donnell was one of a number of distinguished soldiers of that name who fled Ireland after the Battle of the Boyne, one of the most famous being General Carl O'Donnell (1715–71) who was an important figure in the Austrian Army. Henry was an officer in the Spanish (Irish) Regiment 'Ultonia' and came to prominence in October 1809 when he fell upon the French siege-camp at Gerona, for which he was promoted to major-general. In January 1810 he was given command of the Army of Catalonia, and, undismayed by reverses (notably a failed attempt to relieve Lerida in April), in September of that year defeated and captured a brigade of Confederation of the Rhine troops at La Bispal (or Abispal), from which victory he took his title; though he was wounded in the foot and had to retire to recover. Having survived gangrene, in January 1812 he became a member of the council of regency, and in the same year took over the Army of Andalusia. Given the task of blockading Pamplona (July 1813), in the following month he came into conflict with Wellington; he had a somewhat quarrelsome disposition and when his proposal that all Spanish troops should be united under a single leader (presumably himself) was rejected, he went on sick leave on account of his old wound. Wellington wrote on this matter that 'Of all the officers that I have yet had to deal with [he] is the most difficult ... the most impracticable temper that I have yet met with in any country ... I sent him word, that I had not lately heard of any Spanish troops acting together as one corps that had not been destroyed; and that the last that

had so acted had been destroyed by half their numbers.'[1] As the latter referred to the defeat of O'Donnell's brother at Castalla it is hardly surprising that he asked for leave two days later! He returned in December, however, resuming command from his successor Giron. Following the restoration of Ferdinand VII, he was appointed captain-general of Andalusia and Governor of Cadiz; at the time of the French invasion of 1823, however, he fled to France where he was interned, and died in exile.

Henry O'Donnell should not be confused with other members of his family who served during the Peninsular War, notably his brother Joseph, who commanded a division at La Cuadra in August 1811, and, captain-general of Murcia in 1812, was routed at Castalla in July of that year. Charles, later Count O'Donnell, was another brother who served as a divisional commander under La Romana, was appointed captain-general of Valencia in 1811, and had his troops routed at Saguntum; in 1823 he was captain-general of Old Castile and a leading commander on the royalist side. Another brother, Alexander O'Donnell, served with La Romana's expedition to the Baltic, and with Napoleon's *Grande Armée* in the Russian campaign, returning to Spain via the Royal Navy. Henry O'Donnell's second son Leopold, Duke of Tetuan (1809-67) was a leading Spanish general and statesman.

1. Wellington, 16 Aug 1813, vol. XI, pp. 5–6.

O'MEARA, Barry Edward (1782–1836)

Originally an assistant-surgeon in the British Army, he had to resign his commission after acting as second in a duel at Messina in 1808; he then obtained a post in the Royal Navy, and encountered Napoleon when serving aboard

HMS *Bellerophon*. He served as physician to Napoleon on St. Helena, but was removed by Hudson Lowe, on Bathurst's instructions, in July 1818. He subsequently published *A Voice from St. Helena* which was extremely critical of Lowe and his treatment of Napoleon. He was succeeded as physician to Napoleon by James Roche Verling (1787–1858) who served with the Royal Artillery; but Napoleon would not consent to see him, Verling refusing a bribe made by Montholon to act in Napoleon's interest instead of in Lowe's.

O'Meara, B. E. *Napoleon in Exile, or, A Voice from St. Helena*. London, 1822

OMPTEDA, Colonel Christian Frederick William von, Baron (1765–1815)

One of the most distinguished Hanoverian officers of the period, he entered the Royal Corps of Pages at Hanover in 1777, progressing to a commission in the Hanoverian Guards. He served in The Netherlands in 1793–5 (and was orderly to the Duke of York), but was wounded and suffered the first of his mental breakdowns. One of the early members of the King's German Legion, he commanded the 1st Line Battalion, and was exchanged after being shipwrecked on the Dutch coast in 1807. He sailed for the Peninsula in 1808 but a further bout of mental instability led to his retirement; he lived in Germany for some time, his friend Scharnhorst helping his recovery, until he rejoined the Legion as commander of the 1st Light Battalion in 1812, serving through the remainder of the Peninsular War. In the Hundred Days campaign he commanded the 2nd K. G. L. Brigade, which included his own 5th Line Battalion; at Waterloo, ordered by the Prince of Orange and Alten to make a suicidal attack, he calmly drew his sword, asked a friend to try and save his nephews, and rode off at the head of his men. As he had realised, the order resulted in the near destruction of his battalion, but he carried it out without hesitation and was last seen surrounded by French troops. Shot through the neck, his body was recovered and buried near the gate of La Haye Sainte. His family suffered severely in the fight against Napoleon: his brother, Lieutenant-Colonel Ferdinand, his health shattered by service with the K.G.L., fell dead in 1815; brother Captain Augustus died in Portugal in 1811, cousin Captain Ferdinand died in Britain in 1809, victim of illness contracted in the Peninsula, and his brother Louis' step-son, Count Carl zu Solms–Sonnenwalde, an officer of the 1st Prussian Guards, was twice wounded at Bautzen and killed by a shot through the head at Montmartre.

Ompteda, Baron. *In the King's German Legion: Memoirs of Baron Ompteda ...* London, 1894

ORANGE William Prince of, later King William II of The Netherlands (1792–1849)

The son of William Frederick, Prince of Orange (later King William I of The Netherlands), Prince William left his homeland as a child when his family was driven out by the French. Educated at Berlin and Oxford, he served as ADC to Wellington in the

WILLIAM, PRINCE OF ORANGE
(PRINT AFTER J. ODERAERE)

later Peninsular War, and became a major-general in the British Army in December 1813, lieutenant-general in July 1814. When commenting on the possibility of the prince leading an insurrection in Holland, Wellington stated that he 'appears to me to have a very good understanding, he has had a very good education, his manners are very engaging, and he is liked by every person who approaches him: such a man may become any thing; but, on the other hand, he is very young, and can have no experience in business, particularly in the business of revolutions; he is very shy and diffident.'[1] (He even took two tutors with him to the Peninsula, one of whom, a Mr. Johnson, was disliked by the Duke after he once questioned Wellington's statement that rats could squeeze through the necks of wine bottles!) In 1815, as heir to the throne, the prince commanded I Corps of the Anglo–Allied army and was nominally Wellington's deputy, despite his youth, limited experience and dangerous enthusiasm; indeed, John Colborne stated that the government wrote to him 'begging me to prevent the Prince from engaging in any affair of his own before the combined operations'.[2] This lack of experi-

ence caused the prince to receive some criticism for tactical errors committed during the campaign, 'the fatal self-sufficiency of military ignorance'[3], as Ompteda's biographer stated; but in fairness even this source admits that the unwise order which led to the death of the subject of the memoir was issued by the prince in consultation with Alten, who had the experience which the prince lacked. The prince behaved with great courage at Waterloo until forced to retire after being wounded. In 1816 he married the Tsar's sister Anna, having earlier been jilted by Princess Charlotte of Wales. He became very popular in The Netherlands and but for his father's intransigence might have brought about a peaceful settlement to the 1830 Belgian revolt. After a period of friction with his father, during which the prince lived in England (he was a noted Anglophile), he commanded the Dutch forces which invaded Belgium in 1831 and probably would have succeeded but for French intervention. He became King William II upon his father's abdication in 1840, and although never an advocate of democracy he supported electoral reform and the establishment of a constitutional monarchy, so his country escaped unrest in 1848. In July 1845 he was appointed a field marshal in the British Army.

1. Wellington, 18 May 1813, vol. X, p. 390. 2. Moore Smith, p. 213. 3. Ompteda, Baron: *In the King's German Legion: Memoirs of Baron Ompteda*. London, 1894, p. 311

ORANGE, William Frederick, Prince of, see William I, King of The Netherlands

ORDENER, General Michel, comte (1755–1811)

Perhaps best known as commander of the *Grenadiers à*

Cheval of Napoleon's Imperial Guard, he joined the cavalry in 1773 and was commissioned in 1792. He was distinguished at Lodi and when serving with the forces of the Helvetian Republic became almost a legend by virtue of his many wounds (eleven on one occasion: three from bullets, one from an artillery round and the rest from sabres). Having been a major in the 10th *Chasseurs*, he was appointed to the horse grenadiers of the Consular Guard in July 1800, becoming *général de brigade* in August 1803. He commanded the force which seized the duc d'Enghien, and in 1805 led the *Grenadiers à Cheval* at Austerlitz, where he was wounded. Later in the same month he was promoted to *général de division*, and retired in the following year on account of his injuries; subsequently he served as a senator, became Josephine's equerry and was made comte in 1808. His son, also Michel Ordener, also became a general officer; he served with his father at Austerlitz, where he was wounded, and earned considerable distinction commanding the 7th Cuirassiers at the Berezina.

ORLEANS, Louis-Philippe, duc d', see LOUIS- PHILIPPE, King of France

ORLEANS, Louis-Philippe-Joseph, duc d' (known as 'Philippe Egalité') (1747–93)

The son of Louis-Philippe, duc d'Orléans (1725-85), Louis-Philippe-Joseph was known as duc de Montpensier until 1752, then duc de Chartres, until succeeding to the dukedom of Orleans upon his father's death. He had a reputation as a libertine, but entered the navy and served in the battle off Ushant (27 July 1778); never popular at court, he was denied further

LOUIS-PHILIPPE, DUC D'ORLÉANS ('PHILIPPE EGLALITÉ')(ENGRAVING BY W. GREATBATCH)

active service. Visits to England and British friends encouraged his liberal beliefs, which increased his estrangement from the court; he was exiled twice to his estates at Villers-Cotterets, but his public popularity was undiminished, and even enhanced by his expenditure of part of his immense fortune upon the needy. He was among the most liberal of the nobility in the States-General, and from July 1790 sat in the National Assembly, but although viewed by some as a pretender to the throne, in January 1792 he attempted a reconciliation with the royal family. Though he spoke at length with the king, he was greatly insulted – even spat upon – by courtiers, which inevitably coloured his future perception of the situation. In the summer of that year he was present with the army, with his sons, the ducs de Chartres and Montpensier, then returned to Paris and was elected to the Convention, his adopted name 'Egalité' being representative of his beliefs. He voted for the death of the king, but then fell under suspicion after the duc de Chartres defected with Dumouriez, and was arrested in April 1793. He was tried on 6 November and guillotined,

meeting his fate with great composure. He attracted much blame from all sides, although much of the ambition and intrigue for which he was criticised were exercised by his supporters. Upon his death the duc de Chartres succeeded to his title, and subsequently became King Louis-Philippe.

Nettement, A. *Philippe-Egalité*. Paris, 1842 (one of a number of early histories)

ORNANO, Marshal Philippe-Antoine, comte d' (1784–1863)

A cousin of Napoleon, he was born in Ajaccio; an officer in the 9th Dragoons at the age of 15, he served as ADC to Leclerc in San Domingo, later to Berthier, was present at Austerlitz and Jena, and became commander of the 25th Dragoons in January 1807. Appointed comte in November 1808, *général de brigade* after Fuentes de Oñoro, *de division* after Borodino, in the Russian campaign he commanded a brigade of the 4th Heavy Cavalry Division in II Cavalry Corps. Severely wounded at Krasny, in February 1813 he was given command of the *Dragons de l'Impératrice* of the Imperial Guard. He served in the campaigns of 1813–14, including Dresden, Leipzig and Hanau, leading the Guard Heavy Cavalry Division, and in 1814 was made commander of the Guard in Paris. At the restoration he retained his regimental command of the re-named *Dragons de France*, but rallied to Napoleon in 1815; yet missed Waterloo after being seriously wounded in a duel. Surviving arrest at the second restoration, he married Marie Walewska in 1816 and thus became step-father to Napoleon's illegitimate son, Alexandre Walewski. In April 1861 he became the last of Napoleon's old comrades to be given the rank of Marshal, and was Governor of the Invalides; he died on 13 October 1863.

OSTERMANN-TOLSTOI, General Ivan, Count (1770–1837)

A reliable divisional and corps commander of the Russian Army, he was the grandson of Tsar Paul I's Chancellor Ostermann. He was distinguished in a number of actions: in December 1806 he led the force which disputed the passage of the Ukra against the French, at Eylau commanded a division on the left-centre of Bagration's army, and was wounded at Guttstadt (5 June 1807). In 1812 he led the Russian IV Corps, at Borodino holding a position on the right-centre of Kutuzov's army; but he is perhaps best remembered for his role in defeating Vandamme at Kulm, in conjunction with Friedrich Kleist von Nollendorf, an action in which he was severely wounded.

OTRANTE, duc d', see FOUCHE

OTT, Feldmarschall-Leutnant Peter Carl, Baron (1738–1809)

A distinguished member of the Austrian Army, he served during the Turkish war in 1789 and in The Netherlands in 1793–4. In Italy in 1796 he commanded the imperial cavalry and in 1797 was promoted to *Feldmarschall-Leutnant*. In 1799 he held a divisional command under Suvarov in Italy and served at Novi. In 1800 he commanded the force which besieged Massena in Genoa and compelled his surrender, then rejoined Melas' army for Marengo, at which battle he commanded the left wing which drove the French from Castel Ceriolo; but the rout of the Austrian centre compelled him to retire, back into Alessandria, despite his own successes on his wing. It was his last active field command.

OUDINOT, Marshal Nicolas-Charles, duc de Reggio (1767–1847)

NICOLAS OUDINOT
(ENGRAVING BY H. WOLF AFTER R. LEFEVRE)

The dauntless Oudinot was probably the most frequently wounded senior commander of the period, suffering injury on at least 22 occasions; such was his disregard for personal safety that his servant prepared the medical kit before every action in the expectation that his master would be struck! The son of a brewer at Bar-le-Duc, he enrolled in the army in 1784, but seeing no opportunity for advancement left after three years. He returned with the advent of the Revolution; elected captain of a company formed at Bar-le-Duc in 1789, he rose to command the 3rd Meuse Volunteers in September 1791 and served with distinction in the Armies of the Rhine and Moselle. *Général de brigade* from June 1794, *de division* from April 1799, he won further laurels in Switzerland, latterly as Massena's chief of staff, and shared with him the tribulations of the siege of Genoa. In 1805 he led the élite 'combined grenadier' division known to posterity as the *Grenadiers d'Oudinot*, surviving further injury and commanding them at Friedland. Incapacitated for some time after breaking a leg

when his horse fell, he returned to lead Massena's advance-guard in 1809, and assumed command of II Corps after Lannes' death at Aspern–Essling. He played a vital role at Wagram (despite advancing contrary to orders) – where he almost had an ear shot off – and won his Marshal's baton; having been comte from July 1808, he was advanced to the dukedom of Reggio. In 1812 he commanded II Corps, was wounded and missed part of the campaign, but returned to play an important part in the defence of the army's line of retreat at the Berezina, was wounded again and while being evacuated, even as an invalid, led his escort when it was ambushed by Cossacks. He fought through the 1813–14 campaigns, commanding XII and VII Corps and collecting more injuries, but accepted the Bourbon restoration and remained loyal to them in 1815, declining service under Napoleon. His loyalty was rewarded at the second restoration, when he received joint command of the Royal Guard and was appointed Minister of State, and in 1823 commanded I Corps in the invasion of Spain. His last appointment was as Governor of Les Invalides. He made no pretence of being a tactical genius – Napoleon remarked that he was brave but not very bright – but he did possess organisational skills, as Massena had reported: he 'knows how to apply his fiery energy to clerical labour ... he has followed me in everything, and has made a perfect second in command'.[1] A story which epitomises Oudinot's greatest attribute, however, is the time when Napoleon remarked, 'And yet there always comes a moment when the bravest man is afraid for at least once in his life.' 'Sire,' replied Oudinot, 'I have never had time for that.'[2] His progeny included a number of distinguished soldiers. By his first wife, Charlotte Derlin, his six children included Charles-Nicolas-Victor (1791–1863), known as Victor, who saw much hard service from 1809 as a cavalryman, remained loyal to the Bourbons in 1815 (when it was reported that he fired a pistol at the first of his men who shouted *Vive l'Empereur!*'), succeeded his father as second duc de Reggio, and as a lieutenant-general commanded the expedition to Rome in 1849; he retired after the coup of 1851, which he tried to resist. His brother Auguste (1800–35) was killed as a colonel leading his 2nd *Chasseurs d'Afrique* at La Macta in Algeria. Oudinot's first wife having died in 1810, in 1812 he married an 18-year-old aristocrat from Bar, Eugénie de Coucy, an intrepid and loyal young woman who even joined the 1812 campaign to nurse him. His two sons by her, Colonel Charles (1819–58) and General Henri (1822–91) both served under Victor in the expedition to Rome, and three of Oudinot's grandsons also became general officers. In all he had eleven children.

1. Memoirs, as below, p. 22. 2. Ibid., p. 440.

Austin, P. B. 'The Father of the Grenadiers: Oudinot', in *Napoleon's Marshals*, ed. D. G. Chandler. London, 1987; Stiegler, G. *Memoirs of Marshal Oudinot, duc de Reggio*, trans. A. de Mattos. New York, 1897, orig. pubd. as *Le Maréchal Oudinot, duc de Reggio*. Paris, 1894, and including the memoirs written by the Duchess Eugénie

PACK, Major-General Sir Denis (1772–1823)

SIR DENIS PACK (PRINT AFTER SANDERS)

Son of the Dean of Ossory, he was commissioned in 1791, and commanded the 71st in South America; but is best known as a general officer in the Peninsular and Waterloo campaigns. Major-general from June 1813, he commanded the 6th Division in July, but was wounded at Sorauren; thereafter he reverted to his original brigade command in the division, and was again wounded at Toulouse. He received a knighthood of the Bath in January 1815, and in the Waterloo campaign commanded the 9th British Brigade. He was known to have a temper – a rhyme referring to his being freed after the surrender in South America stated: 'The devil break the gaoler's back/That let thee loose, sweet Denis Pack' – but he was very popular with his men, one of whom described him in the Peninsula as 'a very forward and bold officer; one of those who says, "Come, my lads, and do this", and who goes *before* you to put his hand to the work'.[1] Pack married Elizabeth Louise Beresford, daughter of George, 1st Marquess of Waterford; their second son became Beresford's heir and assumed his name.

1. Anon., *Personal Narrative of a Private Soldier who served in the Forty-Second Highlanders*. London, 1821, pp. 200–1.

Pack-Beresford, D. *Memoir of Major-General Sir Denis Pack*. Dublin, 1908

PAGET, General Sir Edward (1775–1849)

Fourth son of the 1st Earl of Uxbridge, and brother of Henry William, 2nd Earl, he was appointed lieutenant-colonel of the 28th Foot in 1794 and commanded them in The Netherlands and Egypt. He led the 'Reserve Division' in the Corunna campaign and was sent back to the Peninsula as second in command under Wellington. Leading the troops which forced the passage of the Douro, he was severely wounded, losing an arm; when he returned to the Peninsula in 1812 he took command of the 1st Division (11 October) but was captured on 17 November. He rose to the rank of general, served as Governor of Ceylon (1820–2) and CinC India (1822–5); in parliament he sat for Carnarvon

Borough (1796–1806) and succeeded his brother Henry as MP for Milborne Port, 1810–20. He was popular with his men and appreciated the importance of morale, as shown by his regimental order of 1803 to a newly raised battalion of the 28th: 'He wished every individual at once to consider himself an old soldier; and he will find that he is already more than half become so ...'[1]

1. Daniell, D. S. *Cap of Honour: The Story of the Gloucestershire Regiment*. London, 1951; 1975 edn., p. 87.

Paget, E. *Letters and Memorials of General Hon. Sir Edward Paget*. London, 1898

THE CAPTURE OF SIR EDWARD PAGET
(PRINT BY M. DUBOURG AFTER J. A. ATKINSON)

PAGET, Henry William, see **UXBRIDGE, Earl of**

PAILLETERIE, General Thomas-Alexandre Davy de la, (see **DUMAS, General Thomas-Alexandre**)

PAINE, Thomas (1737–1809)
One of the most important political writers of his era, he now enjoys a considerably higher reputation than he did in his own time, especially in his native land. Born at Thetford, the son of a stay-maker, he spent his early career in a number of occupations, none with great success, including some time at sea and in the excise service, from which he was twice discharged for neglect of duty. During this time he educated himself and produced a pamphlet on the grievances of excisemen; but the most crucial event of his life was his meeting with Benjamin Franklin in London. With recommendations from Franklin he went to America in 1774, and in January 1776 published his pamphlet *Common Sense* which, in understandable, plain language, advocated American independence; it sold in huge quantities and was very influential. When the War of Independence began he produced tracts entitled *The Crisis*, the first of which (December 1776) began with the famous lines, 'These are the times that try men's souls. The summer soldier and the sunshine patriot will, in this crisis, shrink from the service of their country; but he that stands it *now*, deserves the love and thanks of man and woman.' His efforts were recognised by the US authorities with various employment during the war and by the grant of an estate in New Rochelle (though he had to resign as secretary to the committee for foreign affairs after disclosing confidential matters relating to France). In 1787 he

returned to Europe to promote an iron bridge he had invented, and, still an advocate of change, wrote against the British government; but it was his *Rights of Man* (1791), written in reply to Burke's *Reflections on the French Revolution*, which propelled him again into the forefront of political debate. It provoked a furious reaction. Paine was indicted for treason and outlawed *in absentia*, he having gone to France where he was elected to the Convention. His influence there was somewhat limited by his ignorance of the language, but he spoke against the execution of the king; following the fall of the Girondins he retired from active politics, but in December 1793 was arrested. Released from detention following the fall of Robespierre, he resumed his seat in the Convention until October 1795. Two further publications alienated him even from his supporters in America: *The Age of Reason*, which attacked organised religion, and *Letter to George Washington*, which attacked that hero's military and presidential record. Paine returned to America in 1802 and spent the remainder of his life there, but without influence, having lost sympathy by such publications and by his intemperance. Though his reputation is now much enhanced, the obituary in *The Gentleman's Magazine* (July and August 1809, pp. 679, 781) articulates a common contemporary view in his own country: 'the *notorious* Thomas Pain [sic]; whose death is an admonitory event; may the lesson that it inculcates be impressive! He was not of the saturnine order of the ambitious, who are content with reversionary fame; he wished to bequeath a legacy of confusion to posterity; but still he wished for an usufructary enjoyment, at least, in his own works. He plunged hard to carry his purpose, but in vain:

all his praises on the French, and his obloquies on British liberty have preceded him to the grave; and British liberty yet survives the enmity and the existence of the first of its modern calumniators .. He had lived long; and had done a little good, and much harm.' His body was later returned to Britain by William Cobbett.

Aldridge, A. O. *Man of Reason: the Life of Thomas Paine*. London, 1960; Edwards, S. *Rebel! A Biography of Thomas Paine*. London, 1974; Hawke, D. F. *Paine*. London, 1974; Keane, J. *Tom Paine: A Political Life*. London, 1996; Powell, D. *Tom Paine: the Greatest Exile*. London, 1985; Truelove, E. *The Complete Works of Thomas Paine* ... London, 1850 (also many other later editions); Williamson, E. *Thomas Paine: His Life, Work, and Times*. London, 1973

PAJOL, General Claude-Pierre, comte (1772–1844)

CLAUDE PAJOL

One of the best light cavalry leaders of the period, he was born in Besançon and forsook his father's profession of the law for a military career. Commissioned in 1792, he served as ADC to Kléber 1794–7 and gained considerable distinction when commanding the 6th Hussars in the Army of the Rhine. He served in the 1805 campaign, became *général de brigade* in March 1807, and after service at Güttstadt and Heilsberg became a baron in March 1808. He held a brigade command in 1809 (notably at Wagram) and in Davout's I Corps during the invasion of Russia in 1812; promoted to *général de division* in August, he was given command of the 2nd Light Cavalry Division of II Cavalry Corps which he led at Borodino, but was wounded severely two days later. He returned in the spring of 1813 as commander of the 10th Light Cavalry Division and served with distinction at Dresden, and was advanced to command of V Cavalry Corps in September, but again had to retire after breaking an arm when his horse was brought down at Wachau in October. Comte from November 1813, he was sufficiently fit to resume command of a light cavalry division in early 1814, was distinguished at Montereau but again had to retire with injury following a fall from his horse. He accepted service under the Bourbons but rallied to Napoleon in 1815 and led I Cavalry Corps at Ligny and Wavre. Dismissed from the service, he became involved in anti-royalist intrigues, assisted in the 1830 revolution and was rewarded by Louis-Philippe with the restoration of his military career; he was appointed a peer of France in November 1831, was Governor of Paris until 1842, and died as a result of a fall from his horse. By his marriage to Elise Oudinot, the Marshal's eldest daughter, he produced two sons who became generals, Eugène (1817–85) and Charles-Paul-Victor (1812–91) who in addition to a distinguished military record was also a sculptor and author of his father's biography.

Pajol, General comte C. P. V. *Pajol: Général en Chef.* Paris, 1874

PAKENHAM, Major-General Sir Edward Michael (1778–1815)

Second son of Edward Michael, 2nd Baron Longford (1743–92), he was commissioned in 1794, and rose to the rank of major-general in January 1812. His service included Martinique and Fuentes de Oñoro, but he came to prominence commanding the 3rd Division at Salamanca; he led the 6th Division January–June 1813, was then appointed adjutant-general, but took over again after Sorauren until early August 1813. He is best remembered as commander of the British force defeated at New Orleans, where he was killed. He was Wellington's brother-in-law; his brother, Lieutenant-General Sir Hercules Robert Pakenham (1781–1850), saw much service in the Peninsula, initially as an officer of the 95th Rifles and later as assistant adjutant-general, notably at Badajoz.

PALAFOX Y MELZI, General José de, Duke of Saragossa (1780–1847)

He is one of those commanders whose name is forever associated with a single great action: the siege of the city from which he took the title of his dukedom. A kinsman of the bishop Juan de Palafox de Mendoza (1600–59), noted for his protests against cruelty to the natives of Mexico, he was a member of an aristocratic Aragonese family with close connections to the Spanish throne, his mother having been one of the queen's attendants. An officer of the royal bodyguard and devotedly loyal to the royal family, he had plotted to rescue them from their detainment in France, but had returned home when the scheme proved impossible. In May 1808, by popular acclamation, he was appointed Captain-General of Aragon, and organised resistance against the French occupation of Spain from Saragossa (Zaragoza).

Attempts to defeat the French in the field proved futile: his brother Luis, Marquis of Lazan, was defeated at Tudela on 8 June 1808, as was Palafox himself at Alagon. Wounded in the arm, he withdrew into Saragossa with his remaining troops, but had no great optimism for the security of the city; when the French appeared on 15 June he left the city, ostensibly to raise reinforcements but probably intending to continue the fight irrespective of the fate of Saragossa. He returned when the French attack failed, and the successful defence, by civilians as well as military, he characterised as a beacon for the rest of Europe. He then collaborated with Castaños, but after the rout at Tudela (23 November 1808) the siege of Saragossa was resumed, and became one of the most bitter and horrifying events of the war. With disease decimating the besieged as much as the combat, his leadership proved crucial, if his tactical awareness was poor (he never attempted to detach part of his large command to harry the French outside the city walls, which would have been the most effective policy). Palafox himself fell ill and thus avoided having to negotiate the surrender of the city (21 February 1809), which had resisted for longer and with more spirit than could ever have been anticipated. He was imprisoned in France for the remainder of the war, and after his release was confirmed as captain-general of Aragon, but was forced to retire over his support for the liberal constitution against the king for whom he had fought so hard. Queen Maria Christina accorded him the title Duke of Saragossa, and from 1836 he was again captain-general of Aragon, supporting the infant Queen Isabella II when the Carlist Wars began. His significance in the defence of Saragossa has been questioned: William Napier, for example, regarded him as a mere figurehead, a tool of 'a stern band of priests and plebeian-leaders'[1] who did not entirely trust him (presumably because of his aristocratic background) while Wellington recalled that 'there was nothing in him – all parties agreed that he was a poor creature';[2] but he was surely more than that, and even if he were to some extent merely articulating public sentiment, he was truly the head of the resistance of Saragossa. His brother Francisco also attained some fame as a leader of the resistance against France.

1. Napier, W., vol. I, p. 72. 2. Stanhope, p. 10.

Garcia Mercadal, J. *Palafox, Duque de Zaragoza 1775–1847.* Madrid, 1948

PALM, Johann Philipp (1768–1806)

Born in Württemberg, he was the proprietor of his father-in-law's book-selling business in Nuremberg when in 1806 he handled a pamphlet entitled 'Germany in Deep Humiliation', which was extremely critical of Napoleon. Being unable to discover the identity of the author, Napoleon ordered the arrest and conviction of Palm, who was tried at Braunau on 25 August 1806 and shot next day, thereby becoming a martyr to the cause of German independence.

Schulteis, F. *Johann Philipp Palm.* Nuremberg, 1860

PALMERSTON, Henry John Temple, 3rd Viscount (1784–1865)

One of the great statesmen of the mid 19th century, he succeeded his father as 3rd Viscount Palmerston in 1802, an Irish peerage which allowed him to sit in the House of Commons, which he entered as MP for Newport, Isle of Wight, in June 1807. Although his years of

HENRY, 3RD VISCOUNT PALMERSTON
(ENGRAVING BY T. W. HUNT)

greatness occurred after the Napoleonic era, during that period he did play a part in national affairs. Appointed a Lord of the Admiralty in 1807, his maiden speech (in support of the expedition to Denmark) was so impressive that in 1809 Perceval offered him the chancellorship of the exchequer. Palmerston declined, preferring the post of Secretary at War (though declined a seat in the Cabinet), which position he held until 1828. He became involved in a dispute over jurisdiction with the CinC, Dundas, which was resolved only after the Duke of York resumed office; it was decided that the Secretary-at-War should not be subordinate to the CinC, but that he should not issue orders to the army without consulting the CinC, with disputes to be settled by the Prime Minister. Palmerston served as Lieutenant-Colonel-Commandant of the South-West Hants. regiment of Local Militia; his brother William Temple was a captain in the same regiment.

Bourne, K. *Palmerston: the Early Years.* London, 1982; Dalling, Lord. *The Life of Henry John Temple, Viscount Palmerston.* London, 1870–4 (completed by E. Ashley); Guedalla, P. *Palmerston.* London, 1931; Ridley, J. *Lord Palmerston.* London, 1970

PAOLI, General Pasquale (1725–1807)

PASQUALE PAOLI
(ENGRAVING BY R. G. TIETZE AFTER DRELLING)

Originally something of a hero to the young Napoleon, he was the champion of Corsican independence during the 18th century. Born in Corsica, he was educated by his father Giacinto Paoli, 'a man of learning, religion, and bravery, well qualified to serve his Country either in politicks or war', and who formed in Pasquale 'his taste for letters, and inspired him with every worthy and noble sentiment'.[1] A leader of the Corsican independence movement against Genoa, Giacinto was forced into exile, Pasquale entering Neapolitan service. In 1755, at the suggestion of his brother Clemente who had himself led the independence movement, Pasquale was invited to assume command of their forces, was elected a general and established independent rule over most of the island. France established a military presence in 1764, and following renewed Corsican successes Genoa sold sovereignty to France in 1768; Paoli resisted but without the help from Britain for which he had hoped, French success could not be averted, and in June 1769 Pasquale and Clemente and their followers quit the island. Pasquale took refuge in England, but was recalled from exile by the National Assembly, returned to Corsica in 1790 and in 1792 was appointed lieutenant-general of the forces and Governor of Corsica by the French government; but he had no sympathy with the new regime in France and in May 1793 declared a revolt. The Corsican *consulta* (assembly) elected him president, but he received only limited support (the Bonapartes, for example, hitherto his friends, rejected the concept of a break from France), and Paoli had to appeal for British assistance. By mid 1794 they succeeded in possessing the island, and in June the assembly offered sovereignty to George III; but after some two years (during which administration of the island was carried out by Sir Gilbert Elliot) France repossessed Corsica and the British presence ended. Paoli had left already: his presence was not thought expedient and he returned to London in 1796, 'the safest and most honourable asylum for persecuted Virtue',[2] where he lived on a pension until his death. During his exile in London he became a noted figure in society; Samuel Johnson, for example, loved to dine at Paoli's because of both the food and the company, and upon first meeting Paoli in 1769 remarked that not only did he admire his intellect, but that he had the loftiest bearing of any man he had ever seen.

1. *Gent's Mag.*, Feb, 1807, p. 188. 2. Ibid.

Thresher, P. *Pasquale Paoli, an Enlightened Hero, 1725–1807.* London, 1970

PARKER, Admiral Sir Hyde (1739–1807)

Second son of Vice-Admiral Sir Hyde Parker, Bt. (1714–82), who shortly after inheriting the family baronetcy was lost at sea when his

SIR HYDE PARKER
(PRINT BY J. WALKER AFTER ROMNEY)

flagship HMS *Cato* disappeared en route to the East Indies, Hyde Parker jun. went to sea at an early age and received his first command at the age of 23. After much service he was awarded a knighthood in 1779 and in the same year survived the wrecking of HMS *Phoenix* on the coast of Cuba (he entrenched with his crew on the hostile shore until help arrived). Despite his experience and influential contacts he was still not given command of anything larger than a frigate, and in command of another served with his father's force in the inconclusive action at Dogger Bank (5 August 1781). In 1783 he went on half-pay, rising by seniority to rear-admiral in February 1793; recalled to service in the Mediterranean, he served under Hood and promoted to vice-admiral in 1795 became third in command to Hotham. He commanded at Jamaica 1796–1800, and in all these positions exhibited an earnest attitude but no inspiration, and despite lack of experience commanding a fleet was appointed to lead the expedition against the Armed Neutrality, initially against Denmark, a task obviously beyond him. The victory of Copenhagen was won by his deputy Nelson in spite of Parker

rather than with his assistance; he was censured for his prevarication during the campaign and in May 1801 was ordered to hand over the fleet to Nelson and return home. He received no further employment, a competent if unspectacular career having been ended by the allocation of a task beyond his abilities. Twice married (the second time in 1800 to Frances, the 18-year-old daughter of Admiral Sir Richard Onslow, Bt.), all four of his sons went into the service of their country; the eldest, Hyde, became a vice-admiral, two became generals (John Boteler and Richard), and the third son, Harry, was killed at Talavera while serving as a subaltern in the Cold-stream Guards.

PARMA, Prince of, see NAPOLEON II

PARTOUNEAUX, General Louis, comte (1770–1835)

Most remembered for the loss of his division in 1812, he was commissioned in 1791, served at Toulon and with the Army of Italy, became *général de brigade* in April 1799, *de division* in August 1803, and having been captured at Novi was exchanged for the Austrian general Zach. After service with Eugène at Caldiero and Massena at Naples, for the Russian campaign he was given command of the 12th Division of Victor's IX Corps. At the Berezina this formed part of the force tasked with holding back the Russian advance; ten days before, Partouneaux had asked to be relieved of command because of physical weakness (he was probably considerably despondent) but had been told to continue. Ordered to leave his position around Borisov and retire upon Studianka, to rejoin the remainder of IX Corps, he made no use of scouts to keep contact with the main body, and at least according to Marbot relied upon information from a local peasant whose language he could not understand. Inadequate reconnaissance saw him taking the wrong road when he set off at about 3 a.m. on 28 November, an error (or lack of common sense in Marbot's opinion) compounded when he and his staff went out to reconnoitre and were captured by Wittgenstein's army. His command, thus deprived of leadership, held its ground until daybreak revealed that it was entirely surrounded, when it surrendered (except for one unit which broke out by following what was surely obviously the correct road). The loss of some 4,000 excellent infantry, 500 cavalry and four guns was a severe loss under the circumstances, and aroused Napoleon's anger; upon his return Partouneaux received no further employment until after the Bourbon restoration, when he became comte and enjoyed a renewed military and political career until his retirement in 1832.

PASKEVICH, Field Marshal Ivan Federovich, Count of Erivan, Prince of Warsaw (1782–1856)

One of the leading Russian commanders of the mid 19th century, he is best known for his command in the Persian War (1826–8, where he gained his title as Count of Erivan), against the Ottoman Empire (after which he became field marshal), and against the revolts in Poland (1831) and Hungary (1848), the former success bringing the title of Prince of Warsaw; but he also saw considerable service during the Napoleonic Wars. From an ancient family, he was commissioned in the Russian guards in 1800 and became ADC to the Tsar; he served at Austerlitz, against the Ottoman Empire 1807–12 and as a general

officer commanded the 26th Division of VII Corps in the 1812 campaign. He was considerably distinguished at Borodino, where his men held the vital Raevsky Redoubt, and served throughout the 1813–14 campaigns, becoming lieutenant-general after Leipzig (still commanding the 26th Division). A most influential figure in the Russian Army, his last service was as commander of the Army of the Danube in 1854, but he was forced (by threat of Austrian intervention) to raise the siege of Silistria, and an injury compelled him to retire from active service; he died at Warsaw in February 1856. He also held the appointment of field marshal in Austrian and Prussian service.

PASLEY, General Sir Charles William (1780–1861)

He is remembered chiefly as a most influential writer and administrator in the subject of military engineering, his knowledge founded upon practical experience during the Napoleonic Wars. He was commissioned in the Royal Artillery in 1797, but transferred to the Royal Engineers in 1798, and as a captain from 1 March 1805 served at the defence of Gaeta (1806), Maida, Copenhagen (1807) and in the Peninsula under Baird and Moore, where his knowledge of Spanish was a great asset. After service at Corunna, with the Walcheren expedition he was severely injured while leading a storming party near Flushing on 14 August 1809, by a bayonet-wound in the thigh and a musket-ball which damaged the spine. He saw no further active service, but spent the remainder of his career perfecting a system of military engineering and re-organising the corps, becoming very influential by virtue both of his duties and of his publications. He held such positions as head of the en-

gineering school at Woolwich (1812), inspector-general of railways (1841–6) and colonel-commandant of the Royal Engineers (1853), becoming a general in 1860

PASQUIER, Etienne-Denis, duc de (1767–1862)

Originally a lawyer, he is remembered chiefly in a Napoleonic context as the Prefect of Police who was flung into La Force prison during Malet's attempted coup in 1812. He had been associated with the *parlement* of Paris before the Revolution, and survived imprisonment shortly before the fall of Robespierre to enter the civil service under Napoleon. He became a baron in 1809 and was appointed a councillor of state and Police Prefect in 1810; he resigned the police post after the restoration but was still employed by the Bourbons, serving as Minister of the Interior after the second restoration. Ever a moderate, he declined to support the extreme royalists of Charles X, but after the 1830 revolution became President of the Chamber of Peers, which office he held until his retirement upon the fall of Louis-Philippe in 1848; he was given a dukedom in 1842.

Pasquier, E. D. *Mémoires du Chancelier Pasquier.* Paris, 1893–5 (English trans. as *A History of My Time: Memoirs of Chancellor Pasquier 1789–1815*)

PAUL I, Tsar (1754–1801)

His reputation is perhaps characterised by his sobriquet 'the Mad Tsar', and it was stated during his lifetime that his 'conduct we could wish to attribute to insanity; but every thing forbids us to interpret so charitably of him ... a series of transactions that must render him odious in the mind of every impartial person'.[1] He was the son of Empress Catherine the Great and her husband Peter III, but she

TSAR PAUL I
(MEDALLIC PORTRAIT)

implied that as Peter was impotent the father was actually Prince Soltykov; such rumours evidently affected Paul's mind and made him determined to demonstrate his legitimacy. He was neglected as a child and became convinced that his mother wanted him dead (perhaps not an unreasonable fear, the assassins of Catherine's husband being not unknown to her), but in reality she probably only wished to exclude him from succession in favour of his son Alexander. (Paul's first wife, Wilhelmina of Hesse–Darmstadt, re-named in Russian Nathalie Alexeevna, died in childbirth in 1775; Alexander was his son by his second wife, Sophia Dorothea of Württemberg, re-named Maria Feodorovna). In 1783 Catherine gave Paul an estate at Gatchina, where he kept a miniature army drilled in Prussian fashion; and although evidence of his mental instability was obvious, Catherine failed to ensure that young Alexander would be her successor, so upon her death (November 1796) Paul inherited the throne. In foreign policy especially, his reign was eccentric; he loathed the principles of the French Revolution, but his declaration of war was prompted by Napoleon's occupation of Malta, of whose Knights of St. John he had become Grand Master. Having

greatly damaged the Russian Army by imposing upon it the outdated strictures as used by his Gatchina corps, he sent armies to fight in The Netherlands, Italy and Switzerland, and despite the skill of old Suvarov and early successes, they were ultimately unsuccessful. Angered by the British occupation of Malta, Paul then left the anti-French coalition, showing more sympathy towards Napoleon. Domestically, even the higher classes stood in fear of ill-treatment and exile at the hands of a ruler of increasing instability, and the result was a court conspiracy led by Count Pahlen, his trusted Governor-General of St. Petersburg, with the complicity of Alexander (who became involved on the condition that Paul should not be harmed). On 23 March 1801 the Tsar was attacked in his bedroom at the Mikhailovsky Castle and during the struggle was throttled by a paperweight pressed against his throat; it was announced that he had died of apoplexy and Alexander succeeded. An obituary published in Britain laid part of the blame for his sad condition upon his mother under whose neglect he had grown up 'uninstructed, ignorant, and frivolous in his pursuits ... checked, slighted and overawed by a parent ... he became habitually jealous, resentful, and unjust. Yet, his heart was not naturally a bad one; and he seems to have acted commonly with as much rectitude of intention as was possible for an understanding so uninformed and perverted.'[2]

1. *Gent's Mag.*, Dec, 1800, p. 1195.
2. Ibid., April, 1801, p. 374.

McGrew, R. E. *Paul I of Russia 1754–1801*. Oxford, 1992; Ragsdale, H. (ed.). *Paul I: a Reassessment of his Life and Reign*. Pittsburgh, 1979

PEACE, Prince of the, see **GODOY**

PEEL, Sir Robert, Bt. (1788–1850)

SIR ROBERT PEEL
(ENGRAVING BY J. W. COOK AFTER LAWRENCE)

One of the most important political figures of the second quarter of the 19th century, Prime Minister 1834–5 and 1841–6, he entered the House of Commons as MP for Cashel in 1809 (later Chippenham) and made his maiden speech in defence of the Walcheren expedition. During the Napoleonic Wars he served as Under-Secretary for War and the Colonies from 1810, and from 1812 was Secretary for Ireland. His father Robert (1750–1830) was a prominent and very rich textile manufacturer in Bury, Lancashire, and was MP for Tamworth 1790–1818; an ardent supporter of Pitt, he was rewarded with a baronetcy in November 1809. He was lieutenant-colonel commandant of the Bury Loyal Association, which he led with a paternal attitude as expressed in his speech made upon the presentation of Colours to his corps: 'avoid bad company; and having raised yourself to a situation commanding respect, preserve it by good behaviour ... I wish to be considered rather as your parent than Commander; and in cases of sickness and distress, I shall ever feel happy in affording assistance to yourselves and families.'[1] Robert Peel junior succeeded to the baronetcy upon his father's death. His third son, Captain Sir William Peel (1824–58) was a most distinguished leader of the naval brigades in the Crimea (where he won the Victoria Cross) and in the Indian Mutiny, who died of smallpox while recuperating from an injury sustained at Lucknow.

1. *Morning Chronicle*, 29 Oct 1798.

Gash, N. *Mr. Secretary Peel: the Life of Sir Robert Peel to 1830*. London, 1961; Parker, C. S. *Sir Robert Peel*. London, 1981

PELET-CLOZEAU, General Jean-Jacques-Germain, baron (1777–1858)

Perhaps best known as a commander of the Imperial Guard in Napoleon's later campaigns, and as the author of an interesting Peninsula history, he joined the Army in 1799 and was commissioned as an engineer two years later. On Massena's staff in 1805, he served (and was wounded) in the Danube campaign of 1805 (of which he wrote an account), and was aide to Massena in the Peninsula 1810–11. (He carried to Napoleon the dispatch in which Massena explained his dismissal of Ney; Marbot was not altogether complementary about the advice Pelet gave to the Marshal). In the Russian campaign of 1812 Pelet was considerably distinguished, and was wounded severely leading a charge at Krasny. *Général de brigade* from April 1813, he was given a brigade command in the Young Guard, then became the Guard's adjutant-general, and commanded the *Chasseurs à Pied*. He retained this command under the Bourbon restoration, but joined Napoleon in 1815, and fought with great courage as commander of the 2nd *Chasseurs* in the forlorn attempt to hold Plancenoit; his conduct in rallying

his *Chasseurs* around their Eagle with cries of '*A moi, Chasseurs! Sauvons l'aigle ou mourons autour d'elle!*' was held up as a heroic example even by his enemies, and was praised by Siborne. From 1818 he held a number of significant staff positions, including the director-generalship of military stores, and head of the staff college, rising to the rank of lieutenant-general. In addition to his prolific writings, he entered politics, survived a bomb explosion, became a peer of France and only retired in 1848.

Pelet, J. J. G. *The French Campaign in Portugal 1810–1811* (trans. and ed. D. D. Horward). Minneapolis, 1973; *Histoire des Campagnes ... en 1805 ... 1806 et 1807... en 1809*. Paris, 1843; *Mémoires sur la Guerre de 1809*. Paris, 1824–6; *Mémoires sur les Guerres de Napoléon depuis 1796 jusqu' en 1815*. n.d.; *Des Principales Opérations de la Campagne de 1813*. Paris, 1827

PELLEW, Admiral Sir Edward, see EXMOUTH

PELUSE, comte de, see MONGE

PEPE, General Guglielmo (1783–1855)

One of the heroes of the struggle for Italian independence who came to most prominence in the post-Napoleonic age, he was a Calabrian who joined the Neapolitan Army at an early age, but became involved in the republican movement. An officer by the age of 17, he served with Napoleon in the Marengo campaign (on one occasion Napoleon remarked that he could tell Pepe was a Neapolitan by the appearance of his nose!). he served under Joseph Bonaparte and Murat in their Neapolitan army, and commanded the 8th Line Regiment in the Peninsula, returning to Italy in 1813 as a general officer, to re-

organise the Neapolitan Army. He was one of those who endeavoured to persuade Murat to grant a constitution to save his throne, but served with him in 1815 and retained his rank after the restoration of Ferdinand IV. He played a major role in the Neapolitan revolution of 1820–1, leading an army against the king's Austrian allies and in support of the liberal constitution, and went into exile after the defeat. He continued political agitation and maintained links with the Carbonari movement, and in 1848 returned to command the Neapolitan Army; when the king changed his mind on the matter of supporting Piedmont against the Austrians, Pepe resigned and took a corps of volunteers to fight them anyway. His final command was in Venice with Daniele Manin; he went into exile when the city was starved into surrender by the Austrians. He wrote his memoirs and accounts of events in 1820–1 and 1848–9.

Pepe, General G. *Memoirs of General Pepe*. 1846

PERCEVAL, Spencer (1762–1812)

Having the melancholy distinction of being the only British prime minister to die by assassination, he was the fourth son of John, 2nd Earl of Egmont. He pursued a legal career before entering parliament as MP for Northampton in 1796, and came to prominence by speeches in support of Pitt; Solicitor-General in 1801 and Attorney-General in the following year, in the latter office he had the unusual task of prosecuting one Jean Peltier, a French *émigré* for a libel on Napoleon (this during the Peace of Amiens). On the death of Pitt he left office and became a leading member of the opposition, returning to government as Chancellor of the Exchequer in 1807, and in 1809 he succeeded Port-

and as Prime Minister. His task was not easy: he had to deal with the political repercussions of the Walcheren expedition, the regency crisis following George III's incapacity, and the Peninsular War, for which he was criticised for providing insufficient support. Unassisted, like Mr. Pitt, by men of superior talents, he had borne the chief weight of government through a period of difficulty and danger,' but was an accomplished parliamentary orator: 'Nothing could exceed his acuteness, his adroitness, and dexterity in debate, but the gentlemanlike suavity of his demeanour, his very sarcasms even being softened down by the irresistible sweetness of his countenance, which took away all appearance of malignity.'[1] Sadly for a man of whom it was said 'gave offence to none – in his private life was an example to all; and who, however firm and unbending in his principles, yet conducted political conflicts in a way that seemed to disarm them of their characteristic bitterness',[2] he was shot dead through the heart in the lobby of the House of Commons on 11 May 1812 by a bankrupt maniac, John Bellingham, who had been unable to gain redress by seeking the prime minister's help. He was convicted of murder and executed on 16 May.

. Gent's Mag., June, 1812, p. 593.
. Ibid., May, 1812, p. 482.

Gray, D. Spencer Perceval 1762–1812: the Evangelical Prime Minister. Manchester, 1963; Walpole, S. The Life of Rt. Hon. Spencer Perceval. London, 1874

PERCY, Pierre-François, baron (1754–1825)

One of the outstanding military medical officers of the period, he was inspector-general of military hospitals and Surgeon-in-Chief of the French Army. He joined the service in 1776, in 1792 was consultant surgeon to the Army of the North, and in 1799 introduced the medical würst-wagen, a caisson with a padded top on which medical staff sat, to transport them (and their equipment contained therein) to the battlefront to hasten the treatment of casualties. A brave and skilful surgeon, he made significant attempts to improve the medical service, which he thought should be an independent corps, but did not enjoy the success of his better-known colleague Larrey, with whom there was a measure of jealousy: Larrey appears to have resented Percy's attempt to copy his own 'flying ambulances' and resented having to spend time on duties which he thought were Percy's responsibility. Percy showed signs of heart problems in Spain and saw no further active service after 1811, until appointed (instead of Larrey and to the latter's dismay) as Surgeon-in-Chief for the 1815 campaign, though he became unwell at Ligny where he performed his last active duties.

Percy, P. F. Journal des Campagnes du Baron Percy, Chirurgien en chef de la Grande Armée. Paris, 1904

PERIGNON, Marshal Dominique-Catherine, marquis de (1754–1818)

Perhaps the least known of Napoleon's Marshals, he came from a family of minor nobility in the Toulouse region, and was commissioned in 1780. His career was unspectacular; in 1789 he was appointed lieutenant-colonel in the National Guard and in 1791 was elected to the Legislative Assembly, but in May 1792 relinquished his political career for military service in the Pyrenees, where he was distinguished, rising to général de division by December 1793. After the death of Dugommier (November 1794) he was appointed CinC, and achieved his greatest success with the capture of Rosas (February 1795), but was replaced by Schérer in May. He then resumed a political career, election to the Council of Five Hundred being followed by appointment as ambassador to Spain (1795–7), where he was a considerable success. He then commanded French troops in Liguria but was severely injured and captured at Novi. In April 1801 he became a senator, and was one of four honorary appointments at the first creation of the Marshalate in 1804. From September 1806 he was appointed Governor-General of Parma and Piacenza, and became comte in March 1808. He saw no further active service, accepted the Bourbon restoration and refusing to support Napoleon in 1815; under the Bourbons he held several offices, rising to the rank of marquis in 1817; he was among those who voted for the death of Ney. His eldest son, Pierre, was killed in Napoleon's service at Friedland.

Osterman, G. 'The Unknown Marshal: Pérignon', in Napoleon's Marshals, ed. D. G. Chandler. London, 1987

PERREE, Vice-Amiral Jean-Baptiste-Emmanuel (1761–1800)

A native of Picardy, Perrée went to sea at the age of 12 and in 1793 began a successful career as a captain in the navy, capturing a number of prizes when in command of the frigates Proserpine and Minerve, most notably in March 1795 when participating in the capture of the British 74-gunner, HMS Berwick, in the Mediterranean. In June 1795, however, Minerve was captured by HMSs Dido and Lowestoft. Promoted to commodore in June 1796, he commanded part of Brueys' fleet for the Egyptian expedition, winning considerable distinction in command of a flotilla of light vessels which operated on the Nile in collaboration with the army. Leading the flotilla from the xebec *Le Cerf,* after a stiff fight he defeated a Greek-manned Mameluke flotilla at Shubra Khit, a shot from his boat blowing up the enemy flagship; he was wounded in the left arm but was promoted to rear-admiral. He conveyed the French siege-train to Jaffa, but was less successful in the operations against Acre, declining to risk his ships putting into port to evacuate the French wounded. On his way home he was captured by the Royal Navy, but exchanged. In 1800, aboard his flagship *Généreux,* he was sent to run supplies to the French garrison of Malta, but on 18 February was intercepted by a squadron under Nelson. Chased by HMS *Alexander* and engaged by the frigate *Success,* in the interchange of fire he was wounded by a splinter in the eye but refused to go below, and then was struck by a round-shot on the right thigh. When Nelson's HMS *Foudroyant* came up and fired two shots, *Généreux* surrendered, Perrée having died shortly before. Despite some accounts to the contrary, the fight was evidently not very protracted, Lord Keith (Nelson's superior) reporting that *Généreux* 'had surrendered without any Action',[1] evidently an exaggeration because *Success* reported one man killed and nine wounded in the fight. Perrée's death was mourned not only by his own side: 'he was also highly esteemed and respected by all the British officers whom he had met in the course of his career, either as enemies or friends'.[2]

1. Dispatch, 20 Feb, 1800, *Gazette* 29 Mar 1800.
2. Cust, vol. V, p. 285.

PERRIN, Marshal Claude-Victor, see VICTOR

PERRY, Commodore Oliver Hazard (1785–1819)

OLIVER HAZARD PERRY

A native of Rhode Island, in 1799 he entered the US Navy in which his father, Christopher Perry (1761–1818), was a captain. After service against the Barbary pirates he was commissioned as a lieutenant in 1810 and was in command of a gunboat flotilla at Newport when selected for command of a flotilla on the Great Lakes. Collaborating with Chauncey, he took command of the forces on Lake Erie in March 1813. Commanding from his flagship, the brig *Lawrence* (named after the captain of USS *Chesapeake,* whose exhortation 'Don't give up the ship' was displayed on Perry's battle-flag), on 10 September 1813 he defeated a British squadron under Captain Robert Barclay in the Battle of Lake Erie. Although *Lawrence* was so devastated that she struck her colours after Perry had transferred to *Niagara,* the victory was complete, and he was able to write his famous dispatch, 'We have met the enemy and they are ours: Two Ships, Two Brigs one Schooner & one Sloop.' The victory had important consequences, especially for American morale, and Perry received a gold medal from Congress. Subsequently he com-

manded the frigate *Java* in the Mediterranean, and in 1819 led a squadron in the West Indies, to protect American shipping from piracy; there he fell victim to yellow fever and died at Port-of-Spain, Trinidad, on his 34th birthday. In 1862 his remains were transferred in great state from there to Rhode Island. His brother Matthew Calbraith Perry (1794–1858) also served as a naval officer during the War of 1812, but is best remembered for his negotiation in 1854 of the first treaty between the USA and Japan.

Lyman, O. H. *Commodore O. H. Perry and the War on the Lakes,* New York, 1905

PETION DE VILLENEUVE, Jérôme (1756–94)

A lawyer from Chartres, Pétion achieved some fame as a writer and became a leading radical during the Revolution. He was elected Deputy for Chartres to the States-General and had risen to be President of the National Assembly by December 1790. One of the three commissioners sent to bring back the king from Varennes, he vied with Robespierre for popularity, and in November 1791 was elected Mayor of Paris. First President of the Convention, he agitated for the deposition of the king, but a hatred grew between him and Robespierre, and he became associated with the Girondins. He voted for the execution of the king and for an appeal to the people, and in March 1793 became a member of the first Committee of Public Safety, but his feud with Robespierre proved fatal when he was accused of prior knowledge of Dumouriez's treason. A decree of accusation was passed on him on 2 June 1793, and he was outlawed on 25 July for having escaped from his own house; he was one of those who fled to Caen to attempt insurrection, but when that failed e sought refuge in the Gironde. A fugitive, he killed himself there and was found in a field, his body half-eaten by animals; a strange end to one who only two years before had been termed 'Father of the People'.

PFULL (or PHULL), General Ernst von (1779–1866)

One of the Prussian officers who entered Russian service as a reaction against Prussia's alliance with Napoleon, Colonel (later General) von Pfull became a trusted adviser to the Tsar, and exerted some influence upon the planning to resist Napoleon's invasion in 1812. He was not, however, a particularly adept strategist, and was described as living in a world of his own, a pedantic crank who managed to trip over every straw that lay in his path.[1] Clausewitz, who worked with him, described him as 'a man of much understanding and cultivation, but without a knowledge of actual things; he had, from the earliest period, led a life so secluded and contemplative that he knew nothing of the occurrences of the daily world ... he had framed for himself a one-sided and meagre system of war, which could stand the test neither of philosophical investigation, nor historical comparison ... The author never saw a man who lost his head so easily, who, intent as he ever was on great things, was so soon overwhelmed by the least of little realities.' Clausewitz noted that in six years' residence in Russia, Pfull had never tried to learn the language or involved himself in the management of civil or military affairs, so that the Tsar considered him as an 'abstract genius' who should fill no role but that of 'friend and adviser to the Emperor *pro forma*'. For all these weaknesses, however, Clausewitz noted that 'to the honour of his integrity we must say that no

better heart, no more disinterested character could be imagined than he on every occasion displayed'.[2]

1. Duffy, C. *Borodino and the War of 1812*. London, 1972, p. 54. 2. Clausewitz, pp. 5–9.

PHELIPEAUX, Colonel Louis-Edmond le Picard de (1768–99)

Different spellings of his name may be encountered, for example, 'Philippeaux'. He was of aristocratic birth, and was a classmate of Napoleon's at the *Ecole Militaire* in Paris. The relationship was one of mutual loathing (it was said they would try to kick each other beneath their desk), and Phélipeaux was the better student, graduating higher than Napoleon. Both were commissioned in the artillery, but thereafter their careers diverged. A captain from 1789, Phélipeaux emigrated in 1791, served in the *Armée de Condé* and returned to France in 1795 to assist comte de Rochecotte and others in organising an insurrection in the province of Berri, but this was crushed in 1796 and both fled. He left France briefly in 1797 but returned to resume his counter-revolutionary activities, and by impersonating a police commissioner helped Sir Sidney Smith escape from the Temple prison. Smith's influence gained Phélipeaux a British colonelcy, and he accompanied Smith to Acre in 1799. An expert military engineer, he improved the city's defences, and his efforts helped to confound Napoleon's attempt to take the place; it was somewhat ironic, perhaps, that he should be frustrated by an old classmate, and one with whom there existed such bitter dislike. He was unable to enjoy his triumph; shortly before the siege was lifted he died, either of exhaustion (as Smith believed) or of the plague.

PHILIPPON, General Armand, baron (1761–1836)

His name may be found spelled 'Phillipon', but 'Philippon' is the version given in early sources. One of the personalities whose fame rests upon a single incident, he enlisted in the French Army in 1778 and was commissioned after the Revolution; he served in Spain (1793–5), in the Danube region, Italy, Switzerland, Germany and at Austerlitz. From 1808 he served in Spain, including Talavera, becoming *général de brigade* and a baron in 1810. From March 1811 he was Governor of Badajoz, rising to *général de division* in July after having resisted the first Allied siege. If not especially distinguished in the field, his talents were demonstrated in the second siege of 1812; skilled and resourceful, his presence was probably the single most important factor that made the task of capturing the fortress so costly. The obstacles he put in the way of the attackers – presumably planned in concert with Colonel Lamare, his chief of engineers – made the breaches impregnable and cost the attackers terrible casualties. Only the unexpected success of Wellington's diversionary attack, by escalade, led to the fall of the fortress, upon which Philippon retired across the River Guadiana to the San Christobal fort, but without provisions he was forced to surrender next morning. He and his two daughters were conveyed to safety by two British officers with drawn swords, through the rampaging mob of drunken Allied soldiers, but this did not see the end of his trials; at Lisbon he was recognised by a 'populace ... very much enraged, and several stones were thrown at him, but fortunately they had no effect'.[1] He was sent as a prisoner of war to Oswestry, but in July 1812 broke his parole, accompanied by an officer named Garnier who, it was conjectured, had been taken for his ability to speak English. These 'disgraceful fugitives' were described in the press: 'Philippon himself is a tall man, being nearly six feet in height, of a stout frame, with a fair complexion, and having a scar over his left eye.'[2] But with the aid of a miller who guided them from Oswestry, the postmaster of Rye, and two smugglers, they reached France safely. Philippon resumed active service in Germany, and commanded the 1st Division of Vandamme's I Corps when it was almost destroyed at Kulm, but retired in the following month. Although his later service was undistinguished – he accepted the Bourbon restoration – he will always be remembered for his great defence of Badajoz, his efforts probably meriting the adjective 'heroic'.

1. *Edinburgh*, 11 May 1812. 2. Ibid., 9 July 1812.

PICHEGRU, General Charles (1761–1804)

CHARLES PICHEGRU
(ENGRAVING BY W. GREATBATCH)

A great hero of the early Revolutionary Wars, yet dying in ignominy, he was the child of a poor family but received a good education by courtesy of the monastery of his native Arbois. He

joined the artillery, served in the War of American Independence, was commissioned and, as leader of the Jacobins in Besançon, was appointed lieutenant-colonel of a volunteer battalion in 1792. With the support of Saint-Just, by his own abilities he rose to the rank of *général de division* in 1793 and achieved considerable success in command of the Army of the Rhine, later Army of the North, improving the discipline, morale and tactics of his command. Most notably, he occupied Holland and captured the icebound Dutch fleet, and after a period as commandant of Paris (when he acted against the Terrorists), in command of the Armies of the North, Sambre and Meuse, and Rhine, crossed the Rhine in 1795. By this time, however, his sentiments had swung in favour of the royalists, and he became active in their interest; his plans were suspected and when he offered his resignation to the Directory in October 1795, to his surprise it was accepted. In May 1797 he was elected to the Council of Five Hundred, where he led the royalist party, but on 18 Fructidor (4 September 1797) he was arrested in the purge and exiled to Cayenne. After some months he escaped to Surinam and from there travelled to England, where he was welcomed. In the 1799 campaign he accompanied Korsakov's staff, and in 1803 returned to France as one of the leaders, with Cadoudal, of the intended royalist insurrection. He was betrayed by a friend (an act which even Napoleon, the target of the conspiracy, condemned as 'truly a disgrace to human nature'),[1] arrested (28 February 1804) and taken to the Temple gaol. In April he was found in his cell, strangled by a handkerchief wrapped around his neck and twisted with a stick like a tourniquet. Napoleon was blamed for

having him murdered – Bourr enne asserted that it was nece sary to prevent his speaking out his trial – but Napoleon consi ered the accusation absurd, an there was little to contradict th theory of suicide. As Napoleo said, it was a sad end for th conqueror of Holland, and for general of considerable militar talents. Sir Gilbert Blane, wh attended Pichegru during h recovery from the rigours of h banishment, found him 'we educated, both classically an mathematically ... subjects science were familiar to him. H was by nature a humane an moderate man, and had muc more the appearance an manners of a Swiss than of Frenchman.'[2] Added to his mil tary talents were a captivatin manner and a strong constitutio (he claimed that on campaign h managed on one hour's sleep night!), though he was political unskilled, as proven by th intrigues against the Director which led to his loss of commanc

1. Las Cases, vol. II, p. 222. Anon., pp. 399–400.

Gassier, J. M. *Vie du Généra Pichegru.* Paris, 1815

PICTON, Lieutenant-General Sir Thomas (1758–1815)

One of Wellington's most capabl (and eccentric) subordinates, h was a bluff, uncompromisin Welshman who was commis sioned in 1771. After the War American Independence he live in retirement on his father's estat until he went to the West Indies i 1794 as aide to Sir John Vaughar and rose to the rank of lieutenan colonel. After service under Aber cromby he was appointe Governor of Trinidad and becam brigadier-general in 1801, but th nature of his rule aroused objec tions, and he resigned. On hi return home (1803) he wa arraigned for permitting the inter

SIR THOMAS PICTON
(ENGRAVING AFTER M. A. SHEE)

ogation of a Mulatto woman under duress (according to Spanish law which had not been replaced in Trinidad), which case dragged on to a trial before Lord Ellenborough in 1806, the technically guilty verdict being overturned in 1808. As major-general he was appointed Governor of Flushing during the Walcheren expedition (from which he was invalided home), and then, upon Miranda's recommendation, was requested by Wellington for a Peninsula command. Wellington was not disappointed: 'I found him a rough foul-mouthed devil as ever lived, but he always behaved extremely well; no man could do better in the different services I assigned to him.'[1] Although Wellington never gave him an independent command, he was a splendid subordinate, leading the 3rd Division with distinction; that formation's nickname 'the Fighting Division' might equally have been applied to its leader. Picton was especially distinguished at Fuentes de Oñoro, Badajoz (where he was wounded in the escalade which captured the city, returning home to recover until spring 1813) and Vittoria; he received seven votes of thanks from the House of Commons and a knighthood of the Bath (February

1813, advanced to GCB in January 1815) but no peerage, probably a legacy of the Trinidad troubles. A lieutenant-general from June 1813, he commanded the 5th Division at Quatre Bras, concealing a wound to enable him to lead it at Waterloo, where he was killed by a shot through the head. His rough manner was exemplified by the story in which he was said to have threatened to hang a commissary if rations did not arrive in time (also told of Craufurd), and his reaction to a discussion on Lowry Cole's impending marriage. Cole said that he did not intend to do an imprudent thing, as his intended was not very young; whereupon Picton exclaimed, 'Well, when I marry I shall do a d ***** imprudent thing, for I mean to marry the youngest tit I can find!'[2] He was also known for eccentricity of dress, frequently wearing civilian clothes and a round hat; Mercer recalled how on the eve of Waterloo 'a man of no very prepossessing appearance came rambling amongst our guns ... dressed in a shabby old grey great-coat and rusty round hat. I took him at the time for some amateur from Brussels ... and thinking many of his questions rather impertinent, was somewhat short in answering him',[3] and was astonished to learn that it was Picton. At Vittoria Kincaid described him as wearing a round hat and swearing as much as if he had two cocked ones, at Busaco he wore his nightcap, and his dress-sense being imitated by his aides, from that and his imposing physical presence he was nicknamed 'the Bear and ragged staff'.

1. Stanhope, p. 69. 2. Ibid., p. 323. 3. Mercer, *Journal of the Waterloo Campaign*, Edinburgh and London, 1870, vol. I, p. 284.

Harvard, R. *Wellington's Welsh General*. London, 1996; Myatt, F. *Peninsular General*. Newton Abbot, 1980; Robinson, H. B.

Memoirs and Correspondence of Lieutenant-General Sir Thomas Picton. London, 1836

PIKE, Brigadier General Zebulon Montgomery (1779–1813)

Born in New Jersey, the son of an officer in the US Army, he entered the army himself and was commissioned in 1799. He achieved great fame as an explorer in 1805–7, in what was then wilderness, first in an expedition to the head waters of the Mississippi, and then into what is now Kansas, Nebraska and Colorado; the mountain Pike's Peak bears his name. By 1812 he was a colonel, and deputy QMG April–July 1812; in March 1813 he was appointed brigadier general and commanded the troops at York (now Toronto) on 27 April 1813, where he was mortally wounded. He was conversing with a British prisoner when the British blew up the powder magazine, and he was struck on the back by a lump of masonry; he survived long enough to receive a captured British flag. Two of his aides and the prisoner were also killed.

PILS, Grenadier François (1785–1867)

One of the most remarkable artists of the period, he was an Alsacian who joined the 51st *Demi-brigade* at the age of 16, and became valet to Oudinot whom he served with great loyalty, accompanying the Marshal into the places of greatest danger with medical kit at hand to bind up the injuries of that most wounded general. 'As he had a great natural talent for drawing, he liked to plant himself in a corner of the battle-field, take from his pocket a note-book and pencil, and calmly sketch the scene of the action and the action itself with ingenuous awkwardness but striking precision,' according to Oudinot's memoirs; this decries

Pils' book, *Journal de Marche du Grenadier Pils*, Paris, 1895, as comprising 'daubs', 'of no literary value, but sincere and refreshing in their very simplicity'.[1] Pils' attempt to study under Horace Vernet was unsuccessful, and though his drawings are hastily executed and 'sketchy' in the extreme, to modern eyes perhaps more attuned to freer drawing, they have great vigour and are especially significant in being perhaps the most immediate eye-witness sketches of Napoleon and his generals. Pils' son Isadore, himself a competent painter (his most famous work was *Rouget de l'Isle for the first time declaiming the Marseillaise*), remarked that his father was a greater artist than he, and by modern standards the elder Pils was indeed more of an artist than many of his time who had a higher reputation.

1. *Memoirs of Marshal Oudinot*, ed. G Stiegler, trans. A. Teixeira de Mattos, New York, 1897, pp. 28–30

PINKNEY, William (1764–1822)
Born in Maryland, the son of a Loyalist, he pursued a legal and political career in the United States, with some distinction. As commissioner in England 1796–1804, he superintended the claims of American merchants under Jay's Treaty, and returned to Britain in 1806 to assist Monroe in negotiations over the capture of neutral ships. He returned home in 1811, from that December to January 1814 was US Attorney General, and was wounded at Bladensburg. From 1816 to 1818 he was US Minister to Russia, and to Naples where he tried to negotiate reparations for seizures from American merchants under Murat's rule. He should not be confused with members of the distinguished Pinckney family of South Carolina, including Charles (1757–1824) US Minister to Spain 1801–5; Major General Charles

Cotesworth (1746–1825), Minister to France in succession to Monroe; and his brother, Major General Thomas (1750–1828), who was Ambassador to Great Britain 1792–6 (where, like his brother, he had spent his youth and where he was educated), during which time he concluded 'Pinckney's Treaty' with Spain, and as a major general in the War of 1812 served in a region where no hostilities occurred (Southern Department).

PIRCH, Lieutenant-General Georg Dubislaw Ludwig (1763–1838)
He is best remembered for his service as *Generalmajor* in command of the Prussian II Corps of Blücher's army in the Waterloo campaign. A native of Magdeburg, he was appointed to this command in May 1815 following the mutiny of the Saxon troops in the army, led it with distinction at Ligny, and two days later formed part of the Prussian force which fell upon Napoleon's right flank at Waterloo. He is often referred to as 'Pirch I', the use of roman numerals being used in Prussian service to distinguish officers of the same name, in this case from his brother, seven years his junior, **Otto Karl Lorenz,** who commanded the 2nd Division of Zieten's I Corps in the same campaign, and who is often styled 'Pirch II'. Georg Pirch was promoted to *Generalleutnant* after the Waterloo campaign, retired in 1816 and died in 1838.

PIRE-HIPPOLYTE, General Marie-Guillaume, comte de (1778–1850)
Perhaps best known as a cavalry commander at Waterloo, Piré is also remarkable as being one of those who fought on both sides during the Revolutionary and Napoleonic era. An aristocrat, born in Rennes, he emigrated with his family and saw his first military

service in opposition to the French republican regime, most notably as an officer of Rohan's Regiment at Quiberon (where he was wounded) and the Ile d'Yeu. Returning to France under the amnesty to *émigrés*, he joined Napoleon's army as a staff officer with the cavalry, serving at Austerlitz, in the 1806–7 campaigns, in Spain and, as *général de brigade* from March 1809, led a light cavalry brigade under Lasalle at Wagram. In 1812 he led the same regiments (8th Hussars and 16th *Chasseurs*) in a brigade of the 1st Light Cavalry Division, receiving a divisional command after promotion to *général de division* in October 1813. He rallied to Napoleon in 1815 and led the 2nd Cavalry Division in II Corps in the Waterloo campaign. Proscribed at the second restoration, he went to Russia until 1819, but on his return received no important employment until after the 1830 revolution.

PITT, General John, see **CHATHAM**

PITT, Thomas, see **CAMELFORD**

PITT, William (1759–1806)
The second son of the great British Prime Minister, William Pitt the elder, 1st Earl of Chatham (1709–78), the younger Pitt was a precocious talent; called to the bar in 1780, he became an MP (for Appleby) in the same year, and in his maiden speech in the Commons (26 February 1781) spoke with such authority and grace that Burke, comparing him to the Elder Pitt, was moved to tears and remarked that it was not a chip off the old block, but the old block itself. Aided by his talents as an orator, Pitt's rise was meteoric; he became Chancellor of the Exchequer in Shelburne's administration in July 1782, and after the

WILLIAM PITT
(ENGRAVING BY H. B. HALL AFTER HOPPNER)

brief hiatus of the Fox–North coalition he was appointed Prime Minister and Chancellor in December 1783, and won a resounding victory in the 1784 election. He governed for the next seventeen years, spending much time in reforming finances, instituting the Sinking Fund, and emerging in triumph from the regency crisis of 1788. The second part of his administration was dominated by the French war, in which he proved not to be as great a war-leader as his father. His policies were much criticised, both by the opposition at the time and since, both for his handling of the strategy and for the overall direction. Some colonial acquisitions and successes at sea hardly compensated for failures on land, especially those involving Great Britain's allies, and the consequences of the conflict were felt severely at home; intended reforms were suspended, there was a measure of political restraint (involving even the suspension of Habeas Corpus), and there were severe economic difficulties. Income tax was among the fiscal measures adopted to defray the great expense of the war, but despite the confounding of his schemes, Pitt's position in parliament strengthened; he was a

skilled party manager and the opposition was reduced to a rump as many of his previous political foes gave him their support. Despite the ineffective attempt to maintain forceful coalitions against France, and the great costs these involved, it was not the French war which led to Pitt's fall. The plan for unifying Ireland with mainland Britain was carried through, but the associated plan of relieving Roman Catholics from restrictions proved impossible, the king believing that such would be a violation of his coronation oath; and on 4 March 1801 Pitt resigned over it. He supported his successor, Addington, and the Peace of Amiens, and after the renewal of the war compelled a change of ministry, Pitt was entrusted with its formation. The king's opposition to Fox precluded his idea of a national coalition, and thus his second administration began on 12 May 1804 in not the most auspicious of circumstances. Pitt was able to construct the Third Coalition, but it had no more success than its predecessors, and the reverses helped undermine his health. Always frail in appearance, and used to drinking considerable quantities (advocated originally for the sake of his health), he became somewhat despondent and the news of Ulm and Austerlitz was a crushing blow. Worn down by cares of state, he died on 23 January 1806. His last public utterance, at the Lord Mayor's dinner, was perhaps his most memorable. Coming two days after news of Trafalgar, the Lord Mayor proposed his health as the saviour of England and the future saviour of Europe; Pitt replied: 'Let us hope that England, having saved herself by her energy, may save Europe by her example'; Wellington, who was present, described it as 'one of the best and neatest speeches I ever heard in my life ... he was scarcely

up two minutes – yet nothing could be more perfect'.[1] Opinions as to Pitt's reputation varied from vehement opposition to adulation: 'To do justice to his talents, would require eloquence equal to his own; and to attempt to enumerate the various acts of his political life, which entitle him to the admiration of mankind, would be to give the history of Europe for the last 20 years.'[2] Napoleon regarded him as an inveterate enemy, blaming him for much of the warfare of the time: 'Posterity will brand him as a scourge; and the man so lauded in his own time will hereafter be regarded as the genius of evil. Not that I consider him to have been really wicked, or doubt his having entertained the conviction that he was acting right.'[3] More venomous remarks came from his own country: 'Where'er he walk'd, all nature died / Whene'er he spake, assertion lied; / Whate'er he plann'd went still amiss ...'[4] A fairer assessment might be that he was a man of great talents, liberal inclinations, honest and a capable manager of finances, but who was assailed with the problems of war over which he never triumphed, even though he did hold together the opposition to France. A contemporary assessment stated, 'Till it shall be proved, that the evils, which even this country has suffered from the French revolution, would not have been a thousand times worse by flattering and yielding to it, surely nothing is proved against the wisdom of Mr. Pitt's administration.'[5] As Lord Warden of the Cinque Ports, Pitt was colonel of the Cinque Ports Volunteers, and paid considerable attention to the duties this entailed.

1. Stanhope, p. 118. 2. *Gent's Mag.,* Feb, 1806, p. 125. 3. Las Cases, vol. IV, p. 79. 4. *The Age, or The Consolation of Philosophy*, quoted in *The Courier,* 12 Feb, 1811. 5. *Gent's Mag.*, suppl., 1811, vol. I, p. 677.

Coupland, R. *The War Speeches of William Pitt the Younger*. Oxford, 1916; Ehrman, J. *The Younger Pitt: The Years of Acclaim, The Reluctant Transition, The Consuming Struggle*. London, 1969, 1983, 1996 respectively; Reilly, R. *Pitt the Younger*. London, 1979; Rose, J. H. *William Pitt and the Great War*. London, 1911; Stanhope, Earl. *Life of William Pitt*. 1862

PIUS VI, Pope (1717–99)

POPE PIUS VI
(MEDALLIC PORTRAIT)

Giovanni Angelo Braschi was elected to the papacy in 1775, and had to face the upheavals of the Revolution. Strictures against the Church in France, and a charge of complicity in the murder of a French agent in Rome in 1793, led him to join the coalition against France; but having lost some territory (including Avignon) in 1791, Napoleon's triumphs in Italy and the defeat of the papal forces caused him to sue for peace. By the Peace of Tolentino (19 February 1797) he surrendered some territorial claims, paid an indemnity to France and agreed to disband his army, but the French encouraged republican agitation in Rome, and the death of the French General Duphot in a scuffle (28 December 1797) provided the pretext for invasion. Berthier's army entered Rome unopposed in February 1798, proclaimed a republic and when the pope declined to renounce his temporal powers he was taken into custody and removed to Siena; he was finally deposited at Valence, where he died on 29 August 1799.

PIUS VII, Pope (1740–1823)

POPE PIUS VII
(ENGRAVING BY T. JOHNSON AFTER DAVID)

Luigi Barnaba Chiaramonti, a Benedictine monk (known as Gregorio), who was appointed cardinal and to the see of Imola in 1785, was elected pope on 14 March 1800. His relations with France and Napoleon were at first cordial; his election had been facilitated by the French Cardinal Maury, he concluded the Concordat (ratified 14 August 1801) and was persuaded to crown Napoleon as emperor. Relations deteriorated, however, and were exacerbated by friction over the dissolution of Jérôme Bonaparte's American marriage; in February 1808 Rome was occupied by a French army, in the following month Napoleon annexed some papal territory to the Kingdom of Italy, and in May 1809 declared the union of the Papal States with France. Pius retaliated by excommunicating the invaders, whereupon he was arrested and taken to Grenoble and then to Savona. In May 1812 he was taken to Fontainebleau and in January 1813 was compelled to assent to a new Concordat, the terms of which were so demeaning that in March he abrogated it, and persisted in his defiance of Napoleon by declaring invalid the acts of the new French bishops to whose institution he had been compelled to assent. In January 1814 Napoleon ordered that he be returned to Savona, but the collapse of the empire led to his return to Rome (May). The Congress of Vienna restored almost all the lost papal territory, and the pope's secretary of state, Ercole Consalvi, who had assisted in his election and had represented him at the Congress, negotiated treaties with all the important Roman Catholic powers, save Austria. Pius VII died on 20 August 1823.

Allies, M. H. *Pius the Seventh*. London, 1897

PLAISANCE (Piacenza), duc de, see LEBRUN

PLATOV, General Matvei Ivanovich (1751–1818)

One of the most colourful of military leaders, at least in public perception, he was born in Azov, served with distinction under

MATVEI IVANOVICH PLATOV

Suvarov, but achieved fame as leader of the Don Cossacks, whose *Hetman* he became in 1801. The value of these splendid light horsemen became evident in the 1812 campaign, when they virtually harried the *Grande Armée* to destruction. Such was their reputation that they were effective even though their style of warfare rarely led them to engage formed troops in a regular manner. An exception was the mauling Platov inflicted upon Sébastiani at Inkovo, and though Platov's manoeuvrings on Napoleon's left flank at Borodino were criticised at the time (for not pressing the attack), his presence caused such paralysis in the French ranks that it bought valuable time for the beleaguered Russian army. Platov served at Leipzig and led his Cossacks into Paris in 1814. Among his own troops he was something of a legend, and his fame (doubtless enhanced by the exotic and colourful nature of the troops he led) spread to the civilians of the Allied nations; 'Platov caps' became fashionable for ladies in Britain, though few would be as splendid as that which he wore when welcomed to London's Guildhall in June 1814, which sported a plume decorated with diamonds said to be worth £10,000.

PONIATOWSKI, Marshal Josef Anton, prince (1763–1813)

Napoleon's Polish Marshal was a member of a most distinguished princely family, originally of Italian–Lithuanian descent. Born in Vienna, he was the son of André Poniatowski (1735–73), brother of the elected King Stanislaus II of Poland (1732–98) and himself a general officer in Austrian service. After his father's death, his education was supervised by Stanislaus, and he was encouraged to think of himself as a Polish prince despite being commissioned in the

JOSEF ANTON PONIATOWSKI
(ENGRAVING BY C. STATE)

Austrian Army in 1780. He served against the Turks in 1788 (distinguished and wounded at Sabac) but in the following year was called to Poland, where he was appointed a general officer. After the proclamation of the constitution he commanded the Polish forces in the Ukraine, won an action at Zielence (18 June 1792) against the Russian invaders, but resigned in dissatisfaction with the king and the peace terms he accepted, and was banished for his criticisms. In the 1794 rising led by Kosciuszko (who had been his deputy in 1792), he refused a command but fought as a volunteer, until persuaded to take over a division, which he relinquished after a reverse. After the collapse of the rebellion he lived in Vienna, later Warsaw, courted by both the Tsar and the King of Prussia, but was unwilling to participate in public life, maintaining his beliefs as a liberal reformer and national patriot. The arrival of the French in Poland after their defeat of Prussia gave him hope that through them an independent Poland might be established, so despite his mistrust of Napoleon he accepted from him the appointment as War Minister (January 1807) and in the following October became com-

mander of the army of the Grand Duchy of Warsaw. His reforms produced an excellent army despite the financial strictures under which he had to work, and in 1809, following a reverse at Raszyn in April, his counter-offensive overran Galicia, captured Cracow and forced the Austrians to abandon Warsaw. Although Napoleon regarded him as a somewhat dangerous subordinate because of his undiminished national aspirations and status as national hero, for the 1812 campaign he was given command of V Corps of the *Grande Armée* and led it with distinction, notably on the right wing at Borodino, the Polish troops forming one of the finest elements of the army but sustaining terrible losses. Ignoring Austrian and Russian overtures, Poniatowski considered that his honour demanded adherence to Napoleon despite the lack of progress towards Polish independence, so he raised a new army and took command of Napoleon's VIII Corps in 1813. Again he was distinguished, and on 15 October 1813 he received the appointment of Marshal of the Empire. Next day the Battle of Leipzig began; Poniatowski remained in command, despite having suffered a number of wounds, and when the premature demolition of the bridge marooned him on the far bank of the Elster he refused to contemplate surrender and attempted to swim across on his horse. Already weakened by his injuries, he was swept to his death. He was mourned even by his enemies, and despite his failure to achieve the independence for Poland which he desired, his reputation as a patriot endured, his conduct having been determined not by any enthusiasm for Napoleon but by aspirations for his country and from his own code of personal honour. Appropriately, his remains were laid beside

Kosciuszko and Jan Sobieski in Cracow Cathedral.

Lee, N. de. 'Tragic Patriot and Reluctant Bonapartist: Poniatowski', in *Napoleon's Marshals*, ed. D. G. Chandler, London, 1987; Askenazi, S. *Le Prince Joseph Poniatowski, Maréchal de France*. Paris, 1921 (orig. pubd. in Polish, Warsaw, 1905)

PONSONBY, Major-General Sir Frederick Cavendish (1783–1837)

SIR WILLIAM PONSONBY
(PRINT AFTER G. MAILLE)

Best known for a graphic account of his tribulations after being wounded severely at Waterloo, he was the second son of Frederick, 3rd Earl of Bessborough (1758–1844). Commissioned in the 10th Light Dragoons in 1800, he rose to take command of the 23rd Light Dragoons after its desperate action at Talavera, remaining in the Peninsula as assistant adjutant-general after his regiment was withdrawn. He served at Busaco and Barossa and in June 1811 was appointed (as lieutenant-colonel) to command the 12th Light Dragoons, which he led for the remainder of the war, minus a short break in 1811 to convalesce from recurrent fever which continued to afflict him but which he tried to conceal. He carried the

news of Napoleon's abdication to Wellington, riding 150 miles in 19 hours, and led his regiment at Waterloo where he was wounded seven times and lay unattended on the field for some eighteen hours; when he returned to duty his right arm was virtually useless. Major-general from May 1825, in that December he became Governor of Malta, from which post he resigned on grounds of ill-health in 1836. His eldest son Henry was a distinguished general officer who served in the Crimea, but is best known as Queen Victoria's private secretary; Frederick's eldest brother, John William, Viscount Duncannon (later 4th Earl of Bessborough, 1781–1847), was lieutenant-colonel commandant of the Royal York Marylebone Volunteers from 1803.

Collins, Major R. M. 'Colonel the Hon. Frederick Cavendish Ponsonby, 12th Light Dragoons', in *Journal of the Society for Army Historical Research*, 1968, vol. XLVI. Ponsonby's account of his Waterloo experiences appears, for example, in Sir Edward Creasey's *Fifteen Decisive Battles of the World* (1877 edn., pp. 610–14), but the story had appeared as early as in T. Kelly's *The Memorable Battle of Waterloo*. London, 1817, p. 93, and in R. Batty's *An Historical Sketch of the Campaign of 1815*, London, 1820

PONSONBY, Major-General Sir William (1772–1815)

Second son of William, 1st Baron Ponsonby of Imokilly, Co. Cork, he came to prominence commanding the 5th Dragoon Guards (lieutenant-colonel from February 1803). The regiment joined the Peninsula army in autumn 1811, and Ponsonby succeeded to command of Le Marchant's brigade after the latter's death at Salamanca. Major-general from June 1813, he led it until January 1814, and was knighted by

bestowal of the KCB in January 1815. In the Waterloo campaign he commanded the 'Union Brigade' (2nd Cavalry Brigade); after leading their charge his horse became stuck in heavy ground and, unable to get free, he was overtaken and killed by French lancers. Seeing his approaching fate, he handed over his watch and a miniature to an aide (presumably his brigade-major, Captain Thomas Reignolds of the 2nd Dragoons) for delivery to his wife, but both were killed by the lancers. His son, born posthumously, succeeded as 3rd Baron Ponsonby.

PONTE CORVO, Prince of, see BERNADOTTE

PONTECOULANT, Louis-Gustave Le Doulcet, comte de (1764–1853)

The son of a French general officer, he was commissioned in 1778 and, as a moderate supporter of the Revolution, was elected Deputy to the Convention for Calvados in 1792, and served with the Army of the North. He voted for the imprisonment and exile of the king, and as a supporter of the Girondins had to go into hiding after being outlawed; he was sheltered by a bookseller, Madame Lejay, whom he married. He returned to the Convention in March 1795, served as its president and on the Committee of Public Safety, and was elected to the Council of Five Hundred. A senator from 1805 and comte from 1808, he organised the National Guard in the *Franche Comté* in 1811 and supervised the defence of the north-east frontier in 1813. He was appointed a peer of France at the first restoration, and by Napoleon during the Hundred Days.

Pontécoulant, comte. *Souvenirs Historiques Parlementaires*. Paris, 1861–5

POPHAM, Rear-Admiral Sir Home Riggs (1762–1820)

A member of a remarkably large family (his mother's 21st child), he was the son of the British consul at Tetuan (Morocco). He entered the Royal Navy in 1778, and from 1787 busied himself in the merchant trade; in 1793, with a loss of £70,000, his ship *Etrusco* was seized for carrying contraband and infringing the East India Company monopoly; the case lasted until 1805 when he finally received £25,000 compensation. He resumed his naval career upon the commencement of the French war, and as an expert on inland navigation, gun-boats and pontoons, won the confidence of the Duke of York under whom he served in Flanders, and of the ministers he encountered while delivering dispatches. Captain from 1795, as an acknowledged expert in amphibious warfare, he devised and commanded the naval contingent in the disastrous raid on Ostend in 1798, and served in the Red Sea when transporting the Indian expedition to Egypt. He was unpopular with elements of the naval establishment, including St. Vincent, which complicated his case when he was charged over the expense of ship-repairs in Calcutta; he brought the case before parliament and was vindicated. He commanded the naval force which conveyed Baird's expedition to the Cape in 1806, whom he persuaded to detach a battalion for an unauthorised foray to South America where, persuaded by Miranda, Popham believed there was a triumph for the taking. He was recalled and court-martialled for thus instigating the disastrous South American expedition; his defence was based on the premise that officers operating far from home should be permitted latitude of action, and his character witnesses included Henry Dundas. Although

found guilty of abandoning his post, he received only a severe reprimand, and his reputation hardly suffered; from the City of London he received a sword in gratitude for his attempts to open new markets in South America, and he was appointed captain of the fleet in the expedition to Copenhagen. Ever an advocate of amphibious warfare, he commanded forces on the coast of Spain from mid 1812, collaborating with guerrillas and keeping French forces occupied; his capture of Santander was especially valuable in providing an important base. Rear-admiral from 1814, he received the KCB in 1815 and commanded at Jamaica 1817–20, until his health broke down; he died at Cheltenham. For all his involvement in the South American fiasco, he was an expert in army–navy combined operations, was one of the navy's most scientific officers, undertook much useful survey work and devised a code of signals adopted by the Admiralty in 1803. His brother William (*c.*1740–1821) rose to the rank of lieutenant–general and served mainly in India, most notably at Seringapatam.

Popham, H. *A Damned Cunning Fellow: the Eventful Life of Rear-Admiral Sir Home Popham.* Tywardreath, 1991

PORLIER, General Juan Diaz, Marquis of Matoarosa (1783–1815)

Having served at Trafalgar and in the early campaigning against the French at the beginning of the Peninsular War, he was one of those Spanish commanders who in 1809 was authorised to begin irregular warfare with elements of the regular Spanish forces; in his case the order came from La Romana and the Oviedo *Junta*, his sphere of operations being in the Asturias. From that time he

became one of the most effective guerrilla leaders and being La Romana's nephew was known as *El Marquesito*, 'the little Marquis'. His reputation was based upon perseverance, courage and audacity; the latter was demonstrated in summer 1810 when he collaborated with British ships in raiding the Biscay coast. With support from the British by sea, and collaborating with such commanders as Home Popham, he not only tied up large numbers of French troops but made daring raids such as his capture of Santander in 1811, withdrawing to the safety of the hills when the French reacted and poured in more troops. He collaborated with Popham in the capture of Santander in August 1812, and although his forces were reduced in size later as other guerrilla commanders came to prominence, he collaborated in the actions around Tolosa (June 1813) and San Marcial. His active service did not end with the expulsion of the French from Spain; one of those disillusioned with the restored monarchy, he led the first Liberal insurrection at Corunna in September 1815, but failing to get support was captured and executed. His brother-in-law was José Maria de Savaria, Count of Toreno (1786–1843), a noted politician and historian, who was involved in framing the 1812 Constitution and served briefly as Prime Minister in 1834.

PORTALIS, Jean-Etienne-Marie (1746–1807)

A lawyer before the Revolution, in 1795 he was elected to the Council of Ancients where he became a leader of the moderates opposed to the Directory; he was one of the most vehement opponents of the law which confiscated the property of relatives of emigrants, contending that any crimes were personal. Proscribed after the coup of Fructidor, he escaped to Switzerland and returned under the Consulate. Napoleon made him a councillor of state in 1800, and as head of the department concerned with religious affairs was entrusted with much work in formulating the Concordat; but his most influential work was probably on the *Code Napoléon*. In 1804 he became a minister and in 1805 a grand officer of the *Légion d'honneur*. His treatise 'On the Duties of Historians' gained a prize at the Stockholm Academy in 1800.

PORTER, Commodore David (1780–1843)

Born in Boston, the son of a US naval officer, he is perhaps best remembered as commander of the frigate USS *Essex* during her destructive cruise of 1812–14, when she inflicted considerable damage on British shipping in the Atlantic and Pacific. He first sailed with his father in 1796, had escaped from British impressment, and was promoted to lieutenant after gallant conduct in the action between USS *Constellation* and *L'Insurgente* (1799). After service in the Tripoli war (when he was taken prisoner) he became captain in 1812. When *Essex* was finally defeated by HMSS *Cherub* and *Phoebe* at Valparaiso (28 March 1814) he was permitted to return home on parole. Subsequently he served in the West Indies on anti-piracy duty, was suspended for six months for exceeding his authority when dealing with the Spanish colonial authorities, resigned in 1826 and until 1829 commanded the Mexican navy. He was appointed US Consul General at Algiers in 1830, and from 1831 was US representative at Constantinople; he wrote an account of the cruise of the *Essex*. His four sons all pursued military or naval careers, most notably Admiral David (1813–91) who rendered distinguished service during the American Civil War, as did Commodore William (1809–64) and Henry (1823–72), while Theodoric (1817–46) was the first US Army officer to be killed in the Mexican War. He also adopted David Farragut (1801–70), a most distinguished admiral, who despite his youth accompanied Porter on the cruise of the *Essex*. Porter's monument at Philadelphia described him as 'among the bravest of the brave'.

Porter, Admiral D. D. *Memoir of Commodore David Porter*. Albany, 1875

PORTER, Major General Peter Buel (1773–1844)

A native of Connecticut, he was a lawyer who entered Congress and served as chairman of the Foreign Relations Committee during the period preceding the War of 1812. Governor Tompkins appointed him Major General of New York Volunteers upon the outbreak of that war; disgusted by Smyth's conduct after he had taken command on the Niagara frontier from Stephen Van Rensselaer, Porter fought a bloodless duel with Smyth (he had earlier challenged Solomon Van Rensselaer, but that did not end in a duel). For his effective services at Chippewa, Niagara and Erie, he was awarded a gold medal by Congress; he subsequently resumed a political career, including a year as John Quincy Adams' Secretary of War, before he retired to private life in 1829.

PORTER, Sir Robert Ker (1777–1842)

Son of an army surgeon, his was a precocious artistic talent; trained under Benjamin West, his fame was established by his immense (120-foot) painting *The Storming of Sepingapatam*. He travelled widely becoming historical painter to the Tsar in 1804, received a Swedish knighthood in 1806, and accompanied Moore in the Corunna campaign, after which, using the *nom de plume* 'an officer', he wrote (and illustrated) his book *Letters from Portugal and Spain, written during the March of the British Troops under Sir John Moore*, London, 1809. In 1811 he returned to Russia, where he married a Russian princess, and in 1813 published *A Narrative of the Campaign in Russia During the Year 1812*. He produced valuable archaeological illustrations during a trip through Persia, wrote accounts of his travels, and in 1826 became British consul in Venezuela. He went on leave in 1841 but died during a return visit to St. Petersburg, his demise being attributed to the change of climate, after so long in South America, which brought on a fit of apoplexy. He was a major in the Royal Westminster Militia. His sisters Jane (1776–1850) and Anna Maria (1780–1832) were both successful novelists.

PORTLAND, William Henry Cavendish Bentinck, 3rd Duke of (1738–1809)

One of the least impressive of British prime ministers, he succeeded his father (William, 1709–62) as 3rd Duke of Portland. He had been a Member of Parliament from 1761, but his political career was spent almost entirely in the House of Lords, his advancement owing more to his position and acknowledged integrity than to any noted brilliance. At first a Whig, he served as Rockingham's Lord Chamberlain (1765–6) and Lord-Lieutenant of Ireland (April–September 1782), declined to serve under Shelburne but accepted the post as nominal head (as Prime Minister) of the

hort Fox–North coalition (April–
December 1783). His opinions
changed with the advent of the
French Revolution, and he
served as Home Secretary under
Pitt, 1794–1801, Lord President of
the Council under Addington and
remained in the Cabinet during
Pitt's second administration. He
again accepted the position of
nominal head of the government
from 1807 until a stroke caused
him to resign shortly before his
death (30 October 1809); during
his second term as Prime
Minister he was notably ineffectual, and is perhaps better
remembered for giving his name
to the famous Portland Vase
which he bought from Sir
William Hamilton.

POZZO DI BORGO, General Carlo Andrea, Count (1764–1842)

Born into a noble Corsican family,
he was an early associate of the
Bonaparte family, though after
service as a Deputy for Corsica in
the National Assembly, upon his
return home he found his right-
leaning politics in conflict with
those of his erstwhile friends. He
was head of the civil government
during Paoli's rule, and president
of the council of state during the
British governance of Corsica, but
had to leave upon the French
assumption of power. In 1798 he
accompanied Lord Minto (who as
Sir Gilbert Elliot had governed
Corsica) to Vienna, where he lived
for six years and became known
for his vehement opposition to
Napoleon. In 1804 he joined the
Russian diplomatic service, serving as commissioner with the
Anglo-Neapolitan army in 1805
and with the Prussian in 1806, but
after a mission to the Ottoman
Empire the Franco–Russian
treaty caused him to retire, and
he sought refuge in England. The
collapse of Franco–Russian relations in 1812 led to his recall by
the Tsar, and he helped gain the
co-operation of Bernadotte; at the
restoration he became Russian
Minister in France, assisted at the
Congress of Vienna and accompanied Louis XVIII to The Netherlands during the Hundred Days.
At Waterloo he rode with
Wellington's staff and was
unhorsed; Wellington wrote in
his dispatch that along with other
Allied observers, 'General Pozzo
di Borgo … rendered me every
assistance in [his] power,' and
that he had 'received a contu-
sion',[1] His later service as Russian
ambassador was marked by a
pro-French and pro-Liberal attitude. His influence declined
under the reactionary rule of
Charles X, but increased under
Louis-Philippe; in 1835 he was
transferred to London, probably
for being thought too pro-French,
but his health declined, he left the
diplomatic service in 1839 and
spent the remainder of his life
back in Paris. He had been ennobled as count and peer of France
in 1818.

1. Wellington, XII p. 484

McErlean, J. M. P. *Napoleon
and Pozzo di Borgo in Corsica and
After, 1764–1821: Not Quite a
Vendetta*. Lewiston, N. Y., 1996

PRIESTLEY, Joseph (1733–1804)

This great chemist was one of
those whose political sympathies
cost him dearly during the
upheavals of the Revolutionary
period. Living in Birmingham,
where he was a Nonconformist
minister, a dinner of the Birmingham Constitutional Society,
held to celebrate the second
anniversary of the fall of the
Bastille, gave rise to a riot in which
a mob burned his chapel and
pillaged his house because of his
known sympathies with the Revolution. This destroyed the work of
years; he then moved to London
until in 1794 he emigrated to
America, where he spent the rest
of his life.

Priestley, J. *Autobiography of
Joseph Priestley*, intro. J. Lindsay.
Bath, 1970

PRINA, Giuseppe (1768–1814)

A Piedmontese lawyer who
became a devoted follower of
Napoleon, he was appointed
Finance Minister of the Kingdom
of Italy; when Eugène became
viceroy, Napoleon told him that
Prina was the only man who really
mattered and who could be relied
upon to do his duty assiduously.
Being responsible for the collection of taxes to fund Napoleon's
campaigns, he became highly
unpopular. After Napoleon's abdication he made the suggestion, on
behalf of other supporters, that
Eugène be appointed ruler of an
independent Italy; this was the
trigger for great violence in which
a mob took the opportunity for
revenge and beat him to death in a
quite appalling manner, and then
dragged his remains through the
streets.

PROVENCE, comte de, see LOUIS XVIII

PROVERA, General Johann, Marquis (1740–1804)

Born in Pavia, he attained high
rank in the Austrian Army, serving
against the Turks and rising to
Feldmarschall-Leutnant in 1792,
when he served with the Army of
the Alps; in 1794 he served with
the Piedmontese when Austria
supplied a corps to assist them. He
is best known, however, for his
service during Napoleon's Italian
campaigns of 1796–7; he
commanded the force which was
forced to surrender at Cossaria
castle, after his release leading
one of the columns which
marched to the relief of Mantua.
He served at Arcola, and in
January 1797 attempted to force
his way into Mantua via Padua and

Legnano, while Napoleon was occupied with Alvintzi at Rivoli. The attempt failed, and he was forced to surrender at La Favorita: 'A braver or better general than Provera was not in the ranks of the enemies of the Republic; never- theless adversity is sometimes the fate of military commanders, and this was the second time within the same twelvemonth that General Provera had given up his sword to the French.'[1] Subse- quently he was given command of the papal troops, but French pres- sure compelled his removal (1798).

1. Cust, vol. V, p. 86.

PULTENEY, Sir James Murray, see **MURRAY, General Sir John**

RABAUT SAINT-ETIENNE, Jean-Paul (1743–93)

A lawyer and Protestant pastor, Rabaut (who took the additional name Saint-Etienne from a small property near his native Nîmes) was an assiduous worker on behalf of his religion and entered politics as a Deputy to the States-General. Although a supporter of the Revolution, he opposed the trial of the king, voted only for his confinement and subsequent banishment. President of the Convention in 1793, he was a member of the Girondin group and was thus proscribed; betrayed by an old friend with whom he had tried to find sanctuary, he was guillotined on 5 December 1793. He was the author of a history of Greece which gained him much literary renown. He should not be confused with his father, Paul Rabaut (1718–94), also a pastor; he was vice-president of the National Assembly but having refused to renounce his title as pastor, was imprisoned at Nîmes for some weeks and died shortly after his release.

RADETZKY, Field Marshal Josef Wenzel Anton, Graf zu Radetz (1766–1858)

One of the best-known Austrian commanders of the 19th century, his great fame rests upon his career in old age, but he was also an influential figure in the Napoleonic Wars. Born in Bohemia of a noble family of Hungarian descent, he joined the Austrian Army in 1785 and gained experience in the Turkish War and during the Revolutionary Wars in The Netherlands, on the Rhine and in Italy. Originally a cuirassier, he won a reputation for personal bravery (with a small detachment he once rescued Beaulieu from amidst the enemy), served under Wurmser in the operations around Mantua, and was distinguished at the Trebbia, Novi and

JOSEF RADETZKY
(PRINT AFTER MANSFELD)

especially at Marengo, where he received five wounds. He also gained a reputation for tactical and organisational ability (as a colonel of the staff, he tried to modify the Austrian plan which led to defeat at Marengo), became *General-Major* in 1805 and served notably in the Caldiero campaign. In 1809 he served first with V Corps, was promoted to *Feldmarschall-Leutnant* and led a division of IV Corps at Wagram. After the war he served as chief of general staff and assisted in the programme of reform, and in 1813 served as Schwarzenberg's chief of staff. With a pleasant and lively personality, he was much in favour with the Allied command, and worked easily with the staff of other armies; such was his popularity that when he almost collapsed from over-work in 1813, and was advised that the restitution of his health depended upon drinking mulled Bordeaux at noon every day, the Tsar arranged for a bottle to be carried to him by a Cossack orderly daily, no matter what the state of the campaign! Radetzky received great credit for his assistance in conducting the campaigns of 1813–14, and during the Congress of Vienna helped smooth relations between the Tsar and Metternich. As chief of

general staff 1815–29, his attempts at reform were thwarted and earned him enemies, but in 1834 he succeeded Frimont in command in Italy and became field marshal in 1836. His greatest renown was earned in 1848–9, when despite his age he conducted a brilliant campaign which led to the victories of Custozza (24–5 June 1848) and Novara (23 March 1849). Although best remembered as a skilled and victorious general, his administrative and reforming work was also of the highest value, and his kindly attitude earned him the nickname 'Vater Radetzky', bestowed by his troops who idolised him. He is also remembered by the march composed in his honour by Johann Strauss the Elder.

Heller von Hellwald, F. A. *Der K.K. Oesterreichische Feldmarschall Graf Radetzky*. Stuttgart, 1858; Herre, F. *Radetzky*. Cologne, 1981; Regele, O. *Feldmarschall Radetzky: Leben, Leistung, Erbe*. Vienna and Munich, 1957

RAFFET, Denis-Auguste-Marie (1804–60)

Originally a porcelain-decorator, this French artist achieved fame as a lithographer. He produced a number of works on military uniforms, but is best known for his scenes of Napoleon and his troops, which are both vigorous and unashamedly patriotic and admiring. His output was prodigious; in the military field he illustrated Fieffé's *Napoléon et La*

Garde Impériale, produced lithographs of the siege of Rome in 1849 (at which he was present), and produced *Episodes de la campagne d'Italie de 1859*. One of the most typical of his Napoleonic subjects is *The Awakening*, in which, to the beat of a drum, the dead rise from the battlefield and prepare to follow the Emperor again, a sentimental subject but typical of the Napoleonic 'legend'.

RAGLAN, Field Marshal Fitzroy James Henry Somerset, Baron (1788–1855)

FITZROY SOMERSET, BARON RAGLAN (ENGRAVING BY W. J. EDWARDS)

Best known as the commander of the British Army in the Crimea, Raglan also enjoyed considerable fame as a staff officer during the Napoleonic Wars. The eighth and youngest son of Henry, 5th Duke of Beaufort (1744–1803), he joined the army in 1804, served on the embassy to the Ottoman empire in 1807, and was attached to Sir Arthur Wellesley's staff for the Copenhagen expedition. He became perhaps the closest of all Wellington's staff, serving as aide in the Peninsula and from January 1811 as military secretary; Wellington remarked that he valued Fitzroy so much because although he had no special talents, he could always be relied

upon to tell the truth and carry out orders to the letter. He was wounded at Busaco, and at Badajoz, accompanied only by one companion and a Portuguese drummer, demanded and received Philippon's surrender; after which he was promoted to lieutenant-colonel by brevet. After the war he became Secretary at the British embassy at Paris, and (as a colonel in the 1st Foot Guards) served again as Wellington's military secretary in the Waterloo campaign. Towards the end of the battle he was hit in the right arm by a musket-ball, an injury so serious as to necessitate amputation; he endured the operation with astonishing stoicism and then called for the limb to be returned so that a ring could be removed from the finger! In 1819 he became secretary to Wellington as Master-General of the Ordnance, and served as Military Secretary at the Horse Guards from 1827 until the Duke's death; his friendship and close working relationship with Wellington was strengthened by his marriage to the Duke's niece Emily, daughter of the Earl of Mornington, in August 1814. He then served as Master-General of the Ordnance and was ennobled as Baron Raglan in October 1852; in 1854 he was promoted to general and given command of the expedition to the Crimea, where he died of dysentery on 28 June 1855, having become field marshal in November 1854. His period of command was marked by severe criticism for matters of general mismanagement, and he became the scapegoat for many ills not of his making. His brothers included General Charles Henry Somerset (1767–1831), General Robert Edward Henry (1776–1842, q.v.), and Colonel John Thomas Henry (1787–1846); Raglan's eldest son, Arthur William Fitzroy (1816–45) was mortally wounded at Feroze-

shah while a major, serving as Hardinge's military secretary.

Sweetman, J. *Raglan: from the Peninsula to the Crimea*. London, 1993

RAGUSE, duc de, see MARMONT

REGGIO, duc de, see OUDINOT

RAINIER, Admiral Peter (1741?–1808)

A native of Sandwich, he entered the Royal Navy in 1756, made post-captain in 1778 and rose to the ranks of rear-admiral (June 1795), vice-admiral (February 1799) and admiral (November 1805). Commanding in the East Indies to 1804, his most notable services included the capture of Trincomalee (1795), Amboyna and Banda Neira (1796); the former was kept in British possession but the latter were returned to the Dutch by the Treaty of Amiens. Rainier was MP for Sandwich, and by his services in the east he accumulated a fortune computed at almost a quarter of a million pounds; by his will he gave one-tenth of his property to the Chancellor of the Exchequer to help reduce the National Debt, as an acknowledgement that this enormous wealth, 'which has exceeded my merit and pretensions'[1] had resulted from his naval career. His nephew, Captain John Sprat Rainier, RN, succeeded to his parliamentary seat.

1. *Gent's Mag.*, May, 1808, p. 457.

RAMPON, General Antoine-Guillaume, comte (1759–1842)

Entering the army in 1775, he was commissioned in 1792, served (and was captured) in the campaign in the Pyrenees in 1793, but only came to prominence from late 1795 in Italy. Commanding the 32nd *Demi-brigade*, he held a position at Montelegino (10 April 1796) with

ANTOINE RAMPON AT MONTELEGINO (PRINT AFTER BERTHON)

The Netherlands in 1814. He supported Napoleon in 1815 and became a peer of France, which position was restored in 1819 despite his support for his old commander.

RAMSAY, Major William Norman (1782–1815)

One of the great heroes of the Royal Horse Artillery, he was the eldest of three sons of a retired Scottish naval officer. He joined the army in 1798 and served with the artillery in Egypt, but gained universal fame with Bull's Troop of the RHA in the Peninsula. His great exploit, celebrated by Napier, occurred at Fuentes de Oñoro when, commanding two guns, he was cut off by a force of French cavalry and saved his guns by charging through them; it was certainly audacious, but Napier exaggerated it by imagining that Ramsay had a whole troop, and underestimated the assistance he received from British cavalry. At Vittoria he disobeyed an order of Wellington's and went into action at his own discretion, for which he was put under arrest, and the brevet and mention-in-dispatches which he thought he deserved were withheld. To the delight of the army, however, he was restored to duty three weeks later,

notable gallantry, which brought him to Napoleon's attention. In the same month he was promoted to provisional *général de brigade*, served throughout the Italian campaign (notably at Arcola), in Switzerland in 1798, in Egypt (notably at the Pyramids and Aboukir) and became *général de division* in 1800. He retired from active duty after his return to France, entered the senate in 1802 and became comte in 1808, served in a number of administrative roles and with reserve formations, and was taken prisoner in

NORMAN RAMSAY SAVING HIS GUNS AT FUENTES DE OÑORO (PRINT AFTER R. CATON WOODVILLE)

273

and received his brevet majority in November 1813. He commanded 'H' Troop , RHA, at Waterloo, where he was killed by a musket-ball; buried on the field of battle, his body was subsequently re-interred at Inveresk.

RAPP, General Jean, comte (1771–1821)

JEAN RAPP

One of the best known of Napoleon's aides, he chose a military career instead of the intended calling. as Protestant minister. He joined the cavalry in 1788 and was commissioned in 1794, and as a lieutenant in the 10th *Chasseurs à Cheval* attracted the notice of Desaix in 1794–5 and became his aide. He served with him in Egypt, and after Desaix's death at Marengo, evidently having impressed Napoleon, was appointed his aide. He became one of Napoleon's most valuable subordinates, though his position on the staff in no way inhibited his desire to be in the thick of the fighting, and he was wounded many times. *Général de brigade* from 1803, he was promoted to *de division* in December 1805 after leading a famous charge of the Guard cavalry at Austerlitz; his dramatic return to Napoleon to announce his success, with broken sabre and bloody from a sabre-cut to the head, formed the subject of Gérard's famous painting. In the Jena campaign he was wounded for the ninth time in his left arm; when Napoleon remarked on his remarkable propensity for collecting injuries, Rapp replied that it was no wonder as they were always fighting! He was appointed Governor of Danzig, but served again in 1809, notably at Essling where he disobeyed his orders to cover Mouton's withdrawal and mounted a counterattack which saved the position, and for which disobedience Napoleon actually commended him. Rapp missed Wagram after suffering three broken ribs and a dislocated shoulder in the overturning of a carriage three days before the battle, and fell into disfavour with Napoleon for showing sympathy with Josephine after the divorce, and (when sent back to Danzig) for not enforcing trading restrictions with which he disagreed. He returned to field service in 1812, however, and at Borodino took over the 5th Division of I Corps after its commander, Compans, was wounded; while leading it he was wounded four times, three grazes and a ball in the left hip, which he computed was his 22nd injury. He survived the retreat from Moscow and Battle of the Berezina, defended Danzig in 1813 and was imprisoned in Kiev until the end of the war. In 1815 he rejoined Napoleon and commanded the small Army of the Upper Rhine, winning a small action on 28 June and holding on in Strasbourg until the end of the war. He accepted the Bourbon restoration and became a member of the house of peers. He died in 1821.

Rapp, General J. *Memoirs of General Count Rapp, First Aide-de-Camp to Napoleon*. London, 1823

RECAMIER, Jeanne-Françoise-Julie-Adélaide (1777–1849)

One of the most famous of Parisian society hostesses, Madame Récamier was the most celebrated beauty of the age, as Gérard's stunning portrait shows. The daughter of a Lyons lawyer named Bernard, at the age of 15 she married a banker, Jacques Rose Récamier, much older than she and whose relationship with her was semi-paternal. Her salon in Paris attracted many political and literary celebrities, especially those of royalist leanings, and such was her beauty and charm of manner that her appearance in the streets caused crowds to gather. 'The divine Juliette' had many admirers, notably Benjamin Constant and Lucien Bonaparte, she entertained Bernadotte, Moreau and Massena, and formed a very close friendship with Madame de Staël (whose son, like so many others, fell in love with her). On a visit to Madame de Staël at Coppet, she met Prince August of Prussia, and it was suggested that they marry; but she felt unable to divorce her husband. He went bankrupt and Juliette came under suspicion because of her friendships with Madame de Staël and others of dubious loyalty to Napoleon, and from her refusal to be lady-in-waiting to Josephine, and Napoleon exiled her from Paris. Subsequently she visited the Murats in Naples. After Napoleon's fall she remained a figure in Paris society and fell in love with Chateaubriand, going to Italy for some eighteen months during his infatuation with Cordélia de Castellane, but their friendship was renewed upon Juliette's return to Paris in May 1825, and they remained close for the rest of Chateaubriand's life.

Herriot, E. *Madame Récamier.* 1906; Levaillant, M. *The Passionate Exiles: Madame de Staël and Madame Récamier*, trans. M.

Barnes. London, 1958; Williams, H. *Madame Récamier*. 1901

REGNAULT DE SAINT-JEAN D'ANGELY, Michel-Louis-Etienne, comte (1761–1819)

He was a lawyer, elected to the States-General for Saint-Jean d'Angély; his moderation, especially at the time of the flight to Varennes and the trial of the king, and in articles published in the *Journal de Paris* and *Ami des Patriotes*, led to his arrest, but he escaped. After the fall of Robespierre he was appointed administrator of military hospitals, and became a good friend to Napoleon, supporting him in the coup of Brumaire. As a councillor of state he was a staunch supporter, exercised considerable influence in the establishment of Napoleon as emperor, and was rewarded with important appointments and elevated to comte. He was dismissed at the restoration but resumed his offices during the Hundred Days; proscribed at the second restoration he escaped to America, returning only on the amnesty of 1819, but died on the day of his arrival in Paris. His son, Auguste-Michel-Etienne (1794–1870) was an army officer dismissed at the restoration, but after service with the Greeks in their War of Independence was re-admitted to the French Army in 1830, served in the Crimea and Italy, and was appointed a Marshal after Magenta.

REICHSTADT, Duke of, see NAPOLEON II

REILLE, Marshal Honoré-Charles-Michel-Joseph, comte (1775–1860)

A native of Antibes, he volunteered for the army in 1791, was commissioned in 1792 and in the following year became Massena's aide, serving with him in Italy, Switzerland and during the siege

HONORÉ REILLE

of Genoa. *Général de brigade* from August 1803, he served as Lauriston's deputy with the troops which accompanied Villeneuve's fleet; he was present in the action off Finisterre but missed Trafalgar when he was sent to Paris with dispatches. In 1806 he commanded a brigade of Suchet's 1st Division of V Corps against Prussia, became *général de division* in December 1806 and served as chief of staff to V Corps in 1807. Appointed an imperial aide in May 1807, comte in June 1808, he served at Friedland, was sent to report on Brune's conduct in Pomerania, was involved in the political manoeuvrings which led to Ferdinand VII's detention, and led the force which relieved Duhesme in Catalonia. He captured Rosas in December 1808 but was relieved of duty in May 1809; in the Danube campaign of that year he served on Napoleon's staff, including Aspern–Essling and Wagram, and was then sent to Antwerp to report on the Walcheren expedition (but probably also to watch the suspect Bernadotte). In May 1810 he returned to Spain as Governor of Navarre, then transferred to command II Corps of Suchet's Army of Aragon, and from February 1812 took command of the new 'Army of the Ebro'. In

November 1812 he was appointed to lead the Army of Portugal, with which he served at Vittoria, and upon Soult's return was given command of the 'Lieutenancy of the Right' (or right wing), which he led for the remainder of the war. His relationship with Soult was latterly uneasy, Reille objecting to sharing command at Bayonne with its governor, and temporarily quit the army until the matter was decided in his favour. He accepted employment under the Bourbons, and cemented his relationship with his old commander when he married Massena's daughter Victoria. He rallied to Napoleon in 1815 and led II Corps in the Waterloo campaign, attracting some criticism for his failure to curb Jérôme Bonaparte's dissipation of resources in the fruitless attacks against Hougoumont, which as his superior Reille could have stopped. He was restored to favour in 1819 when he became a peer of France, and subsequently occupied a number of administrative and advisory posts. Having shown genuine support for the Bourbons, his influence waned after 1830, but he managed to work his way back into favour, was appointed a Marshal in September 1847 and became a Senator in January 1852; and supported Napoleon III for the remainder of his life.

REMUSAT, Claire-Elisabeth-Jeanne Gravier de, comtesse de (née De VERGENNES) (1780–1821)

Madame de Rémusat is best remembered for her memoirs, published by her grandson Paul (1831–97), which throw interesting light upon the Napoleonic court, which she observed as lady-in-waiting to Josephine from 1802. From an aristocratic background (her father was a royal court official and was guillotined), she married Auguste Laurenant, comte de Rémusat (1762–1823), a nobleman from Toulouse. He became Napoleon's chamberlain but supported the restoration and became a prefect, first of Haute Garonne, then of Nord. In addition to the memoirs, her reputation was founded upon her correspondence (published 1881), and shortly after her death by an *Essai sur l'éducation des Femmes*. Their son Charles-François-Marie, comte de Rémusat (1797–1875) was an active politician (he became Foreign Minister in 1871) and a significant literary personality, writing most prolifically on philosophy and history; his son Paul also became distinguished as a writer and, to a lesser degree, as a politician.

Rémusat, C. E. J. G. *Memoirs 1802–1808*, ed. P. L. E. de Rémusat, 1880

REPNIN, Field Marshal Prince Nikolai Vasilievich (1734–1801)

A member of an ancient, Russian princely family, he enjoyed a most distinguished career as a soldier and diplomat in the later 18th century, latterly gaining a reputation second only to Suvarov in the Turkish war of 1787–92, and succeeded Potemkin as CinC in 1791. Promoted to field marshal in 1796, he was sent by Paul I on a diplomatic mission to Berlin and Vienna in 1798 in an attempt to bring about an alliance between Prussia and Austria against France, and was dismissed when he could not accomplish his master's designs. He should not be confused with General Prince Nikolai Grigorievich Repnin-Volkonski (1778–1845), who is best remembered as the commander of the Russian Chevalier Guard who was taken prisoner on their defeat at Austerlitz; in 1814 he was Russian Governor of Dresden, and attended the Congress of Vienna.

REWBELL, Jean-François (1747–1807)

Born in Colmar, he was a lawyer of some distinction when elected to the States-General, and in successive parliamentary bodies came to prominence by reason of his oratory, legal knowledge and integrity. He was a zealous supporter of the republic and an advocate of the king's trial (he declared that the queen should be arraigned under the same decree), but was absent at the time of the king's condemnation. After Robespierre's fall his moderate views won considerable support; he served on the Committee of Public Safety and the Council of Five Hundred, and was appointed a member of the Directory on 1 October 1795. He became its President in 1796 but was heartily disliked by, and disliked in return, both Barras and Carnot. Despite his personal integrity, the employment of his considerable fortune brought him into contact with men of business, which provided a route of attack for his enemies, as did tales of alleged extortions committed by his brother-in-law, the Directory's agent in Switzerland, which Barras used to raise suspicions of his own probity. In 1799 he was selected by ballot to retire as a Director – which was unfortunate because he was the most able member – but he was elected to the Council of Ancients from where he was able to reply, successfully, to his calumniators. After the coup of Brumaire he retired from public life. Napoleon remarked that 'he possessed that kind of intelligence which denotes a man skilled in the practice of the bar – his influence was always felt in deliberations – he was easily inspired with prejudices – did not believe much in the existence of virtue ... he displayed great energy in the assemblies ... and was fond of a life of application and activity ... Like all lawyers, he had imbibed

from his profession a prejudice against the army'.[1]

1. Las Cases, vol. II, p. 259.

REY, General Louis-Emmanuel, baron (1768–1846)

Entering the army in 1784 and receiving a commission in 1792, he became *général de brigade* in 1796, after four years with the Army of the Alps. He commanded the camp at Boulogne 1805–8 and became a baron in 1808, but is best remembered for his service in the Peninsula. After serving as Saint-Cyr's chief of staff, he was appointed Governor of San Sebastian two days before the battle of Vittoria; he worked wonders in improving its defences and held it with courage and resolution, making notable sorties on 3 and 27 July which drove back the besiegers in the first, unsuccessful, siege. He was not so fortunate in the second siege, which commenced in the following month, his attempt to hold the outer defences being frustrated by the explosion of a magazine on 31 August, and his system of internal barricades failed because he had insufficient troops to hold them. He withdrew into the castle and continued to defy the attackers until his defences were destroyed on 8 September; three days earlier a council of war of his senior officers had already declared that further resistance was impossible. Rey's defence had so impressed the besiegers that he was permitted to send a courier to Soult, explaining what had happened, before the garrison surrendered; but the British did not especially admire Rey as a person, finding him fat, coarse, sulky, of brutal manner and vulgar expression. As a tribute to his gallant and skilful defence Napoleon promoted him to *général de division* in November 1813 even though he was then a prisoner. He returned home in

May 1814, served as Governor of Valenciennes during the Hundred Days, but had no further employment before a brief recall in 1830. He should not be confused with another French general of the same name, Jean Pierre Rey, who commanded a brigade of Conroux's 4th Division of the Army of the South at Vittoria, and the same at the Nivelle, Orthez and Toulouse.

REYNIER, General Jean-Louis-Ebenézer, comte (1771–1814)

JEAN LOUIS REYNIER
(PRINT AFTER GUERIN)

A native of Lausanne, he was one of the most famous Swiss soldiers of his generation. Originally a civil engineer, he joined the French Army in 1792, served at Jemappes and became *général de brigade* in January 1795, *de division* after acting as Moreau's chief of staff. He commanded a division in the Egyptian expedition, notably at the Pyramids and in the Syrian campaign; but, evidently always a difficult subordinate, he quarrelled violently with Menou to whom he was second in command after Kléber's murder. Menou had him arrested and sent to France for trial; Reynier replied in a scathing letter to Menou, which said he was relieved to be free of a commander he despised

and who had wrecked the army. Although exonerated of Menou's charge of treason, this affair (and Reynier's killing of General Destaing in a duel) led to his eclipse and even banishment from Paris; but he was re-employed in Italy, suffered defeat at Maida but was appointed Minister of War and Marine for the Kingdom of Naples in 1808. In the 1809 campaign he took command of the force which held Lobau after the evacuation of Aspern and Essling, and continued in that command during the Wagram campaign, later taking command of the Saxon corps after Bernadotte's recall. In March 1810 he took command of II Corps of Massena's Army of Portugal, which he led at Busaco, Fuentes de Oñoro and Sabugal, and like the other corps commanders was highly critical of his chief. Comte from May 1811, he commanded the Saxon VII Corps in the 1812 Russian campaign, and in 1813, including Bautzen, Dresden and Leipzig. After the defection of the Saxons in the latter battle he was taken prisoner, and declined to accept the offered Russian commission (as a Swiss it was imagined that his loyalty to France would not be strong). He was exchanged in February 1814 but died shortly after his return to Paris, from exhaustion and fatigue (though gout was also blamed). Napoleon acknowledged that he was a great loss, an honest man and a loyal servant despite his reputation for insubordination and a taciturn demeanour.

Reynier, J. L. E. *Mémoires de Comte Reynier*. Paris 1827

RIALL, General Sir Phineas (1775–1850)

Although attaining the rank of general and a KCH, he is best remembered for his defeat in the War of 1812. A native of Tipperary, he was commissioned in the army

in 1794, served in the West Indies and, as lieutenant-colonel in the 69th Foot, was promoted to major-general in June 1813. In December 1813 he was appointed to command forces on the Niagara frontier as deputy to Lieutenant-General Gordon Drummond, who was given civil and military command of Upper Canada. At Lundy's Lane (Drummond in overall command) Riall was wounded and taken prisoner by accident; after nightfall he and some aides rode into an American force which they mistook for British, someone called out to make way for the general, the Americans obliged and then surrounded the party, which had to surrender. In 1816 Riall was appointed Governor of Grenada and attained the rank of general in 1841; he was described as a brave officer but not possessed of any great military skill.

RICARD, General Etienne-Pierre-Sylvestre, comte (1771–1843)

Perhaps most remembered for his part in the supposed scheme to make Soult king of Portugal, he was born in Castries, only a short distance from Soult's own birthplace. Commissioned in 1791, he served as Suchet's aide in the Army of Italy, became *général de brigade* in December 1806 after distinguished service at Jena, and baron in 1808. He went to the Peninsula as Soult's chief of staff, where he was responsible for a letter dated 19 April 1809, circulated to all French generals, which asked for their co-operation and stated that if Soult were to assume royal powers it would not be disloyalty to Napoleon; and Ricard supported his master in soliciting addresses of support from towns in northern Portugal. When Napoleon received a copy of the letter he was understandably furious, berated Soult for allowing his chief of staff to suggest such a thing, and the unfortunate Ricard was recalled for a personal reprimand. He did not remain in disfavour permanently, however, and after good service in Russia became *général de division* (September 1812), and led a division of III Corps in 1813, including Lützen, Bautzen and Leipzig. He commanded a division of VI Corps in 1814 and was wounded before Paris, but accepted service under the Bourbons and remained loyal to them in 1815; he became comte in 1817, in 1823 led a division in Spain and from 1829 to 1831 his last active duty was as head of the Royal Guard infantry.

RICHELIEU, General Armand-Emmanuel-Sophie Septemanie du Plessis, duc de (1766–1822)

He is best remembered as Prime Minister of the restored Bourbon monarchy, but also spent much time in Russian service. The son of duc de Fronsac, he was grandson of Louis-François, duc de Richelieu (1698–1788), a Marshal of France and grand-nephew of the great Cardinal Richelieu. Until he succeeded to the dukedom in February 1791 he was known as comte de Chinon. He was a member of the French court until he emigrated in 1790, taking service with Russia, and returned there after a further brief spell at the French court. He served originally as a volunteer under Suvarov (having a narrow escape when participating in the storming of Ismailia), and became a general officer in the Russian Army. In 1803 he was made Governor of Odessa, his authority extending to 'New Russia' (including the Cheronese and the Crimea) in 1805; commanded a division in the war of 1806–7 against the Ottoman Empire, and participated in a number of expeditions to the Caucasus. He returned to France in 1814, accompanied Louis XVIII

to Lille in 1815 and then rejoined the Russian Army, which he believed would be the best way he could serve the Bourbons. At the second restoration he was a great supporter of the monarchy but lacked the resentment harboured by many returned *émigrés*, and as a friend of the Tsar had important contacts with the Allies which he employed when he succeeded Talleyrand as premier. He resigned in December 1818 but returned to office February–December 1821, resigning when his moderate position became untenable from attacks by both 'Ultras' and Liberals.

RICHERY, Vice-Admiral Joseph de (1757–99)

Noted for an exploit against British merchant shipping in 1795, he joined the French Navy in 1774 after some years in the mercantile marine; he rose to the rank of captain in 1793, was suspended because of noble birth, but in 1795 was restored to duty. On 7 October of that year, commanding a force from Toulon with six ships of the line and three frigates, he fell in with a British merchant convoy and naval escort off Cape St. Vincent. Thirty-two merchantmen escaped, but 31 were captured, as was the escort HMS *Censeur* (74 guns but jury-rigged and armed *en flûte*). The prizes were taken to Cadiz but some of Richery's crews mutinied when denied the spoils of the capture. Promoted to rear-admiral, he raided the British fishing grounds off Newfoundland with seven ships of the line and three frigates, causing considerable havoc in the colony and against the fishing-fleets (September 1796). On his return to France he was blockaded in Rochefort, and his last command at sea was as part of the abortive expedition to Bantry Bay. He should not be confused with *Lieu-*

tenant-de-vaisseau Richer, commander of the French frigate *Bayonnaise*, who scored a notable success when he captured the 32-gun frigate HMS *Ambuscade* off Bordeaux in December 1798.

RICHMOND, General Charles Lennox, 4th Duke of (1764–1819)

CHARLES LENNOX, 4TH DUKE OF RICHMOND (PRINT AFTER JOHN KAY)

The son of General George Henry Lennox, he inherited the dukedom from his father's brother, the 3rd Duke of Richmond and Lennox, on 29 December 1806. He joined the army and gained some fame by fighting a duel on Wimbledon Common with the Duke of York in 1789 (which served to increase the Duke's popularity), and from 1790 until inheriting the title, he sat as MP for Sussex. Lieutenant-general from 1805, general from 1814, he served as Lord-Lieutenant of Ireland 1807–13 (Arthur Wellesley was his Chief Secretary in 1807), and despite lack of command experience he offered to serve under his friend Wellington in the Peninsula, a request which was declined. He is best remembered, with his wife Charlotte (daughter of Alexander, 4th Duke of Gordon), for hosting the famous ball at Brussels on the

CHARLOTTE, DUCHESS OF RICHMOND.

eve of the Waterloo campaign. Richmond duly turned up on the field of Waterloo, and only with great difficulty was persuaded to return to Brussels after Wellington reminded him that as the father of a large family he should not expose himself to danger, but he stayed to observe at least half the battle. Two of his sons fought in the battle (the Earl of March, later 5th Duke, q.v., and Lieutenant Lord George (John George) Lennox, 9th Light Dragoons (1793–1873), ADC to Wellington). A third son, Cornet Lord William Pitt Lennox, Royal Horse Guards (1799–1881), had intended to serve as ADC to Peregrine Maitland, but had been injured severely by a fall from his horse, breaking his right arm and losing the sight of his right eye. Despite having his arm in a sling, and aged only fifteen, he accompanied his father to the battle and remained there until their return to Brussels; at the time of the charge of the Union Brigade, Richmond was heard to shout 'Now's your time!' in encouragement! In May 1818 Richmond was appointed Governor-General of Canada, and died there on 28 August 1819, of hydrophobia after having been bitten by a fox. His third son, Henry Adam (1797–1812) lost his life while serving in

the Royal Navy when he fell overboard from the 74-gunner, HMS *Blake*.

RICHMOND, Colonel Charles, 5th Duke of (1791–1860)

The son of the foregoing, he inherited the title upon his father's death in 1819; prior to that date he was known as the Earl of March, which name is familiar in the history of the Napoleonic Wars. Commissioned in 1809, he served as ADC to his father in Ireland, and in July 1810 joined Wellington as ADC in the Peninsula. During this time he was an officer in the 13th Light Dragoons, 92nd Highlanders and 52nd Light Infantry, a captain from July 1812, brevet-major from June 1815 and lieutenant-colonel in July 1816 when he went on half-pay. With Wellington he proved to be a most gallant and fearless man, and also, as Gronow recalled, a very hard worker. With Fitzroy Somerset and the Prince of Orange he joined the stormers of the 52nd at Ciudad Rodrigo (and received a mild reproof from Wellington for risking himself unnecessarily), carried home the duplicate dispatch announcing the victory of Salamanca, joined the 52nd in the fight at the crossing of the Bidassoa, and at Orthes was desperately wounded by a shot through the lungs. At Waterloo he was ADC to the Prince of Orange, and joined Wellington after the prince was wounded. Subsequently he was one of the foremost advocates of a medal to reward the services of Peninsular veterans, and following the institution of the Military General Service Medal many of those who received it subscribed 1,500 guineas for a magnificent piece of plate to commemorate his efforts on their behalf. Married to the eldest daughter of the Marquess of Anglesey (Caroline, said to be the greatest beauty of the age), in 1836

he changed his name to Gordon-Lennox following the death of his maternal uncle, George, 5th Duke of Gordon; his eldest son, who succeeded to the dukedoms of Richmond and Lennox, was himself created Duke of Gordon in 1876.

Lennox, Lord W. P. *Memoir of Charles Gordon-Lennox, 5th Duke of Richmond*. London, 1862

RIOU, Captain Edward (1758?–1801)

EDWARD RIOU
(ENGRAVING BY HEATH AFTER SHELLEY)

One of the foremost junior officers of the Royal Navy, he entered the service at an early age, became lieutenant in 1780 and came to prominence in 1789 taking a cargo of prisoners to Botany Bay in HMS *Guardian*. She struck an iceberg and began to sink; Riou evacuated as many of the crew as could be accommodated in five boats (one of which reached safety) but stayed aboard with a volunteer crew (including Lord Camelford, then a midshipman), and with an average of 16 feet of water in the hold, miraculously reached Cape Town after nine weeks of pumping. Promoted captain in 1791, he served in the West Indies under Jervis and, commanding the frigate HMS *Amazon*, led a small squadron of frigates attached to Nelson's division at Copenhagen. He helped Nelson plan his attack, was wounded in the early part of the action, and with the greatest reluctance obeyed Parker's signal to retire (which Nelson ignored); he remarked, 'What will Nelson think of us?' when he was hit by a chain-shot and killed on the spot. Parliament commemorated his memory by a memorial at St. Paul's, but 'he still lives in the lively regret of a very large circle of friends. Lord Nelson most appropriately styles him the gallant and the good.'[1] His sister was the wife of Lieutenant-Colonel Lyde Browne of the 21st Foot, who was killed by rebels in Dublin at the time of Emmot's abortive rising.

1. *Gent's Mag.*, April, 1801, p. 379.

RIPLEY, Major General Eleazer Wheelock (1782–1839)

A New Hampshire lawyer (and lineal descendant of Miles Standish), he was Speaker of the Massachusetts Legislature; he entered the US Army as lieutenant colonel in March 1812, became brigadier general and was subsequently breveted as major general. He served at Chippewa and Lundy's Lane, his tardy conduct attracting much censure from General Jacob Brown, who believed that Ripley, though personally brave, feared the responsibility of command, and the quarrel continued after the war. Ripley was severely wounded at Fort Erie, and resigned from the army in 1820, subsequently representing Louisiana in Congress; he was voted a gold medal by Congress in November 1814.

RIVOLI, duc de, see MASSENA

ROBESPIERRE, Augustin-Bon-Joseph de (1763–94)

Younger brother of Maximilien, he was a lawyer at Arras before the Revolution, and as a member of the Convention gave unreserved support to his brother. The duchesse d'Abrantès described him as an agreeable young man without any bad feelings, who claimed that he thought his brother was being influenced by a pack of wretches. He was sent on a number of missions during which he encountered the young Napoleon Bonaparte, was greatly impressed by his pamphlet *Le Souper de Beaucaire* and pressed for his advancement, a factor in Napoleon's rise to prominence. Augustin shared the fate of his brother; he was taken to the guillotine despite the injuries sustained in attempting to kill himself by jumping from a window in the Hôtel de Ville.

ROBESPIERRE, Maximilien-François-Marie-Isidore de (1758–94)

MAXIMILIEN DE ROBESPIERRE
(ENGRAVING BY W. H. EGLETON)

Perhaps the best-known personality associated with the French Revolution, he too was a lawyer at Arras, like his father and grandfather. Elected to the States-General, the next five years saw him become the most powerful and feared man in France. Possessed of strong democratic ideals, his integrity and sense of purpose led to his nickname 'the incorrupt-ible'; he became a leading figure in the Jacobin faction, but turned to republicanism only slowly. He opposed the war against Austria, took no part in the overthrow of the monarchy, and opposed the September massacres; and despite his limited influence at the time his popularity was such that he was elected first Deputy for Paris to the National Convention, and was a member of the Commune. He spoke (he said with regret) in favour of the execution of the king not on personal grounds but as a matter of national necessity; and was a leading figure in the fall of the Girondins. He became the most important and influential voice in the Committee of Public Safety, and supported (though did not invent) the Terror as a necessary means of preserving the nation. The Hébertists were regarded as a threat, and were destroyed in March 1794, and at the end of that month the Dantonists (who had opposed the Terror) were apprehended, and executed in April. Robespierre supported the festival and doctrine of the Supreme Being, while the Terror increased in ferocity; and his enemies multiplied in number. On 26 July 1794 he delivered an address to the Convention in which he stated that the Terror should be ended, that those Deputies who had exceeded their authority should be punished, and that the Committee of Public Safety should be purified, as if he had not been a member. The reaction came next day – 9th Thermidor in the Revolutionary calendar – when he was branded a tyrant and an order was given for his arrest and for that of his followers. He was released by the troops of the Commune and taken to the Hôtel de Ville, whereupon the Convention passed a degree of outlawry upon the released men and the Commune; national guardsmen under Barras apprehended him, Robespierre receiving a shot in the lower jaw during the struggle. Next day, injured as he was and watched by a baying crowd of the relatives and friends of his victims (or at least those of the Terror), he and his followers were guillotined in the Place de la Révolution, an event which ended the Terror and removed from the scene one of the great figures of the Revolutionary era. Robespierre was no sans-culotte but a cultured, articulate man who wore powdered hair and silk stockings to the end, honest and respectable in his private life; his power came not through the supreme authority of a dictator but from his membership of the Committee of Public Safety, and while not initiating the Terror, he not only acquiesced to it but increased it as a method of establishing his theories of government. Napoleon believed him 'destitute of talent, energy, or system', and to be merely 'the scapegoat of the Revolution, sacrificed as soon as he endeavoured to arrest it in its course ... the Terrorists and their doctrine survived Robespierre; and if their excesses were not continued, it was because they were obliged to bow to public opinion. They threw all the blame on Robespierre ...' Napoleon recalled seeing letters from Robespierre to his brother in which he condemned the tyranny and atrocities being perpetrated, and how Cambacérès had described Robespierre's condemnation as 'a sentence without a trial'; and that he believed Robespierre's intention was, 'after subduing the unbridled factions which he had to oppose, to restore a system of order and moderation'.[1] Not all commentators viewed his actions with such charity.

1. Las Cases, vol. I, p. 221.

Carr, J. L. *Robespierre*. London, 1972; Hamel, E. *Histoire de Robe-*spierre d'après des papiers de famille ... Paris, 1865–7; Hampson, N. *Life and Opinions of Maximilien Robespierre*. London, 1974; Jordan, D. P. *The Revolutionary Career of Maximilien Robespierre*. London, 1986; Rudé, G. *Robespierre: Portrait of a Revolutionary Democrat*. London, 1975; Thompson, J. M. *Robespierre*. 1939

ROBINSON, Henry Crabb (1777–1867)

Probably best known for his literary connections (a friend of Wordsworth, Coleridge, Lamb and Southey), he forsook a legal career to travel in Europe, and was appointed foreign correspondent of *The Times* at Altona (on the right bank of the Elbe, west of Hamburg), from where he sent reports in 1807. In 1808 he was sent to the Peninsula as that paper's war correspondent – perhaps the first in that occupation – and, based at Corunna from July 1808, reported on Moore's campaign and the Battle of Corunna itself. On his return to England he again took up law.

Morley, E. J. *Life and Times of Henry Crabb Robinson*. 1935

ROCHAMBEAU, Marshal Jean-Baptiste-Donatien de Vimeur, comte de (1725–1807)

This French general, who won great renown commanding the army sent to assist the United States in the War of American Independence, played only a minor role in the Revolutionary Wars. He had retired on health grounds in 1789 but was recalled to command the Army of the North in September 1790, and in December 1791 became a Marshal of France. He fell out with Dumouriez and resigned command in 1792; arrested during the Terror, he escaped execution only narrowly, and subsequently received a pension from Napoleon. His son, **General**

Donatien-Marie-Joseph de Vimeur, vicomte de Rochambeau (1750–1813), entered the Army in 1767, accompanied his father to America and became lieutenant-general in July 1792. Sent to the West Indies, he was forced to surrender Martinique in March 1794 (the garrison being shipped home rather than being taken into custody); he was subsequently appointed Governor of San Domingo, was recalled and imprisoned by the Directory, and then returned and took command there as general-in-chief of the French forces following Leclerc's death. Rochambeau acted harshly in this position and was given the nickname 'Robespierre', but opposed by both the British and Dessalines' insurgents, surrendered to the former in December 1803. Kept a prisoner by the British until 1811, after his exchange he rejoined the French Army and commanded a division of Lauriston's corps in the 1813 campaign, and was killed at Leipzig in the fighting at Probstheida.

ROCHEJAQUELEIN, Henri, comte de, see LA ROCHEJAQUELEIN

RODGERS, Commodore John (1771–1838)

Born in Maryland, he was commissioned in the US Navy in March 1798, served aboard USS *Constellation* when the French frigate *Insurgente* was taken, and succeeded to command in the Mediterranean, but is best known for his actions in May 1811 when in command of USS *President* he defeated the British sloop HMS *Little Belt*, an event debated by the nations involved and which was regarded as one of the provocations that led to the War of 1812. When that war began he was the first to begin maritime hostilities when he engaged the British frigate HMS *Belvidera*, but abandoned the pursuit after one of his own guns burst, breaking his leg when the explosion flung him into the air. In September 1813 he captured the schooner HMS *Highflyer* by a stratagem (pretending to be HMS *Seahorse* and inviting *Highflyer*'s captain aboard); and relinquished command of *President* to Decatur. He served subsequently on the board of navy commissioners (1815–37, less time commanding a squadron in the Mediterranean, 1824–7). His brother Commodore George Washington Rodgers (1787–1832), brother-in-law of Oliver Hazard Perry, also served in the US Navy during the War of 1812 as a lieutenant, and died in command of a squadron at Buenos Aires.

ROEDERER, Pierre-Louis, comte (1754–1835)
A lawyer from Metz, he became involved in politics before the Revolution, expressing moderate liberal views, and was elected to the States-General. As a member of the tax committee of the Constituent Assembly, he worked on the new system of taxation, but opposed more radical policies. It was upon his advice on 10 August 1792 that the king took refuge with the Legislative Assembly; the queen opposed the move. asking for guarantees of safety, to which Roederer replied that all he could promise was to die by the king's side. He went into hiding during the Terror but re-appeared after the fall of Robespierre, becoming one of the leading political journalists. He supported Napoleon at the time of the Brumaire coup and remained close to him thereafter, despite disagreements, Napoleon using his advice and services on matters relating to the press. His influence was considerable and, being also an able economist, he served as Joseph Bonaparte's

finance minister in Naples in 1806 and as Administrator of Berg. He was created a peer of France during the Hundred Days, and although the Bourbons deprived him of his privileges and offices, he recovered his rank in 1832.

Roederer, P. L. *Journal du Comte P. L. Roederer, Ministre et Conseiller d'Etât*, ed. M. Vitrac. Paris, 1909; *Oeuvres de Comte Pierre Louis Roederer*. Paris, 1853–9

ROGNIAT, General Joseph, baron (1776–1840)
An outstanding military engineer, he was commissioned in 1794, performed well in the Revolutionary Wars (including Hohenlinden) and served in the campaigns of 1805–7, but came to prominence in the Peninsula. He succeeded to command of the engineers during the second siege of Saragossa after General Lacoste's death and performed with great skill, for which he was promoted to *général de brigade*; he became a baron after service with II Corps in the 1809 Danube campaign. Back in Spain, he was Suchet's chief engineer in the Army of Aragon from the spring of 1810, winning further distinction at Tortosa and Tarragona; *général de division* from July 1811, he was recalled in January 1813 to command the engineers with Napoleon's army in Germany. He accepted service under the Bourbons but with some hesitation joined Napoleon in 1815 and led the engineers in the Waterloo campaign, despite doubts over his adherence to the Emperor. Because of this and his outstanding engineering skills his services were retained at the second restoration; he also wrote technical and historical studies, including some criticism of Napoleon.

Rogniat, General J. *Considerations sur l'Art de Guerre*. Paris, 1816; *Relation des Sièges de*

Saragosse et Tortose par les Français. Paris, 1814

ROGUET, General François, comte (1770–1846)
One of Napoleon's most reliable divisional generals, 'Old Man Roguet' was a man of great courage, who never lost touch with or neglected his ordinary soldiers. The son of a Toulouse locksmith, he joined the army in 1789 but deserted when he failed to gain promotion, joining a volunteer unit instead. Commissioned in 1793, after much hard service and wounds he became *général de brigade* in August 1803. Leading a brigade in Ney's VI Corps in 1805 he was distinguished at Elchingen, served at Jena and was captured after being wounded in the foot at Guttstadt. Released after Tilsit and ennobled as baron (March 1808), he led a brigade of IV Corps in Spain 1808–9 and then transferred to the Imperial Guard, with which he was associated for the rest of the Napoleonic Wars. His Young Guardsmen performed prodigies at Aspern–Essling, but then endured two years of frustration in anti-guerrilla duties in Spain; but as *général de division* (from 1811) he and his Guardsmen were recalled in 1812 for the Russian campaign. Leading the 2nd Guard Division, he became almost a legend in the retreat from Moscow, sharing the privations of his troops and maintaining morale by his presence, toughness and indomitable spirit. In 1813 he led the Old Guard division, and from that August the 4th Young Guard division, with equal fortitude (being badly bruised by a spent ball at Dresden); and in 1814 commanded the Guard division in The Netherlands, including the siege of Antwerp, from which he broke out. Advanced to comte in February 1814, he took service under the Bourbons but rejoined Napoleon in 1815 and com-

manded the 3rd and 4th Grenadiers in the Waterloo campaign. He received no further active employment until after the 1830 revolution, when he held a number of staff posts until his retirement in 1839; he became a peer of France in 1831. His son, *chef de battalion* C. M. Roguet, wrote the important history *De la Vendée Militaire*, Paris, 1833.

Roguet, General F. *Mémoires Militaires du Lieutenant-General Comte Roguet*. Paris, 1862–5

ROLAND DE LA PLATIERE, Jean-Marie (1734–93)

An acknowledged expert in matters of commerce and industry, he served as inspector of manufactories at Amiens, later at Lyons, and became involved in politics at the start of the Revolution. Although a man of talent, it was said that much of his prominence was due to his wife, Manon-Jeanne, née Philipon (1754–93), a woman of great knowledge, learning and charm, to whom he was devoted. Both became involved in politics in Paris, where they were sent by the council of Lyons on matters concerning the city's debts, Madame Roland hosting a salon where many of the foremost political figures gathered. They sided with the Girondins, and on 23 March 1792 Roland was appointed Minister of the Interior, but his middle-class background sat uneasily with the court (on his first official visit he was at first refused entry because his shoes were fastened with laces rather than buckles!). In June 1792 he was dismissed for impertinence when he wrote to the king regarding his position (as with everything else it was influenced by his wife; Condorcet remarked that whenever he looked at Roland he saw only petticoats!), but after the August insurrection he was restored to office. He considered that the Revolution was going too

far, came into conflict with Robespierre and his supporters, and proposed that the king be sentenced by the whole population, not just the Convention; and resigned two days after the king's execution. The reaction came on 1 June 1793 when Madame Roland was arrested; Roland himself evaded capture and hid at Rouen. During her detention, Madame Roland wrote her memoirs, which were first published in 1820; but on 8 November 1793 she was guillotined, the occasion of her famous remark, 'O Liberty! What crimes are committed in thy name!' When Roland learned of her death he was so heartbroken that he left his refuge, wrote a note expressing his horror at current events and declaring that he had no wish to survive his beloved wife, and sitting beside a tree on the Paris road ran a swordstick through his heart.

ROME, King of, see NAPOLEON II

ROSS, Field Marshal Sir Hew Dalrymple (1779–1868)

Cousin of Sir James Clark Ross, the Polar explorer, he was one of the foremost artillerymen of the period. Commissioned in the Royal Horse Artillery in 1795, he served in Ireland in 1798 and as a captain from 1806 commanded 'A' Troop (known as 'The Chestnut Troop') throughout the Peninsular War. He won great renown attached with his troop to the Light Division, becoming brevet major in December 1811 and brevet lieutenant-colonel after Vittoria; he was wounded at Badajoz. He commanded his troop with equal distinction in the Waterloo campaign; subsequently he served as CRA in the Northern District at a time of civil unrest, and from 1840 until his retirement in 1858 contributed greatly to the efficiency and improvement of the service. He became a general

officer in 1841 and was the first artilleryman to become field marshal (1 January 1868). *Memoir of Field Marshal Sir Hew Dalrymple Ross*. Woolwich, 1871

ROSS, Major-General Robert (1766–1814)

ROBERT ROSS
(PRINT AFTER W. TOMLINSON)

A native of Rosstrevor, Co. Down, he was commissioned in 1789, became major in the 20th Foot in 1799, was wounded in The Netherlands in that year, served in Egypt, and having succeeded to command of the regiment fought with great distinction at Maida. He was with his regiment in the Corunna and Walcheren campaigns, and returned to the Peninsula in 1812. On 4 June 1813 he was promoted to major-general and led a brigade of the 4th Division until wounded at Orthes; his wife rode for five days through appalling weather to nurse him. Barely recovered, he accepted the command of a brigade sent to America, winning the action at Bladensburg for which he is most famous, after which the public buildings of Washington were burned. Following this brilliant exploit, Ross marched to attack Baltimore; but when passing through heavily wooded country he was shot by an American rifleman, receiving a ball through the right arm which then penetrated his breast, and he died after commending his beloved wife and children to the protection of his country. His death, it was said, left the expedition as crippled as a watch without its mainspring, and when news spread to the troops, an involuntary groan rose from the ranks. As stated in parliament, 'his goodness of heart, coupled with a peculiar kindness and urbanity of manner, secured the regard and esteem of all who knew him. Never was an officer so universally and sincerely lamented by those under his command. He possessed the happy skill of conciliating by his disposition, and instructing by his example ... his foresight and example in the field were such as to excite the enthusiasm and reverence of those whom he led to victory.'[1] Deprived by death of the honours he would have received, the Prince of Wales accorded his family the unique distinction of the name 'Ross of Bladensburg'.

1. Smyth, as below, p. 349.

A memoir appears in Smyth, B. *A History of the XX Regiment 1688–1888*, London, 1889 pp. 340–50

ROSSLYN, General James St. Clair Erskine, 2nd Earl of (1762–1837)

Entering the army in 1776, he rose to the rank of general in 1814, and was a Member of Parliament from 1782 until he succeeded his uncle, Alexander Wedderburn (Pitt's Lord Chancellor 1793–1801) upon his death in January 1805 as 2nd Earl of Rosslyn. He commanded at Minorca in 1799 and served under Cathcart in the Copenhagen expedition of 1807, but is best known for his command of the Light Division in the Walcheren expedition, and for his later career in government as Lord Privy Seal (1829–30) and Lord President of the Council

(1834–5). He was colonel of the 9th Light Dragoons from 1801 until his death.

ROSTOPCHIN, General Feodor Vassilievich, Count (1763–1826)

FEODOR ROSTOPCHIN
(ENGRAVING BY F. MAYER AFTER GEBAUER)

Perhaps the most famous incendiary in history, he came to prominence under Tsar Paul I, who made him a Count (1799) and gave him a number of important posts, including adjutant-general and Minister of the Interior. He fell from favour in 1801 over opposition to the French alliance with Russia, but by 1810 was restored and was appointed to the important post of Military Governor of Moscow. In 1812, when the city's evacuation became imperative upon Napoleon's approach, although Rostopchin denied having ordered it to be burned, it is likely that the destruction of much of the city was a deliberate act to deny its use to the invaders; certainly he removed the fire-fighting apparatus, making the destruction easier, and it was accepted that he was responsible. Undoubtedly he did burn his own country palace at Woronowo, applying the torches himself (hesitating only at igniting his marriage-bed), and leaving a

message for the approaching French which was recorded variously: Wilson said that it contained the lines, 'I voluntarily set the house on fire, that it may not be polluted by your presence. Frenchmen, I abandoned to you my two houses at Moscow, with their furniture and contents worth half a million roubles. *Here* you will find only *ashes*.'[1] Rostopchin attended the Congress of Vienna with the Tsar, but again fell from favour and moved to Paris, his daughter Sophia having married Eugène de Ségur.

1. Wilson, *Narrative*, p. 180.

Narichkine, Madame. *1812: Le Comte Rostopchine* [sic] *et son Temps*. St. Petersburg, 1912; Ségur, A. de (Rostopchin's grandson). *La Vie du Comte Rostopchine* [sic]. Paris, 1871

ROTHSCHILD, Nathan Mayer, baron (1777–1836)

The great banking family of Rothschild was founded by Mayer Anselm Bauer (1743–1812), who established his financial business at the sign of the red shield (Rothschild) in his native Frankfurt-am-Main. In 1802, when he was not only a prominent banker but agent for the Landgrave of Hesse–Cassel, he negotiated his first great government loan (for Denmark), and he established his sons in the chief capitals of Europe. The eldest, Anselm (Amschel) (1773–1855) took over the Frankfurt office, the second son Salomon (1774–1826) that at Vienna, where he became a close friend of Metternich; the third son, Nathan Mayer, went to England, initially to Manchester and later London; the others, Charles (1788–1835) and Jacob James Mayer (1792–1865), ran the Naples and Paris offices respectively. Nathan was perhaps the greatest financial genius, the family's great influence dating from a deal involving the British government in 1810, and in the later Napoleonic Wars the loans which enabled the Allies to finance the conflict, of great significance in the pursuance of the war against Napoleon, were largely negotiated through the Rothschild company. Nathan employed fast boats and carrier-pigeons to bring him news, and by receiving word of the victory of Waterloo before anyone else reputedly was able to make a huge profit on stocks. Like his brothers he became a Baron of the Austrian Empire in 1822, his son Anthony became a British baronet in 1847, and his grandson a British baron in 1885.

Corti, Count. *The Rise of the House of Rothschild.* London, 1928

ROTTENBURG, Lieutenant-General Sir Francis de, Baron (1757–1832)

One of the major influences on the development of light infantry tactics, he was born in Danzig when that city was under Polish jurisdiction. In 1782 he was commissioned in the French Army, seconded to Neapolitan service in 1787 to assist with the re-organisation of that army, in 1791 commanded a Polish battalion during Kosciuszko's rebellion, and after its defeat joined Hompesch's *Chasseurs* in British service. He was appointed to command the 5th Battalion, 60th Royal Americans, on 30 December 1797, the first regular rifle battalion in British service, and the manual he wrote, *Regulations for the Exercise of Riflemen and Light Infantry, and Instructions for their Conduct in the Field* (1799), was very influential in the evolution of the principles of light infantry service under Sir John Moore. In 1808 he was given a brigade command, and as a major-general in 1811 took command of the forces in Lower Canada. After good service in the War of 1812 he was knighted (1818) and rose to the rank of lieutenant-

general in 1819. He died in 1832 and was buried in Portsmouth.

ROUGET DE LISLE, Claude Joseph (1760–1836)

His fame rests upon his composition of *La Marseillaise*, which was not only a noted song of the Revolutionary period but became the national anthem of France. Born at Montaign, near Lons-le-Saulnier, he was a captain of engineers in the French Army when he composed both words and music at Strasbourg in 1792, at the instigation of the mayor of that city, Philippe Frédéric, Baron de Dietrich, who required a patriotic song for a musical evening, enunciating the sentiments then common. Its original title was *Chant de Guerre de l'Armée du Rhin*, and only received its more familiar name after it was sung by the volunteers from Marseilles who were involved in the storming of the Tuileries. The author profited little from his composition; a moderate, he was imprisoned for refusing to swear an oath of allegiance to the new constitution, although he rejoined the army and was wounded in the Vendée. He retired to his native village where he lived in some poverty, with only a small pension from Louis XVIII and later Louis-Philippe. Although he wrote more songs and other literary works, nothing equalled the impact of his most famous composition, which though decreed a national song in 1795 did not officially become the national anthem until 1879. The commissioner of *La Marseillaise* was even more unfortunate: having emigrated, he returned, was arrested and executed in 1793.

ROUSSEL D'HURBAL, General Nicolas-François, vicomte (1763–1849)

Although he was one of those officers who served on both sides during the Napoleonic Wars, his career was rather unusual in that

it did not result from emigration from his native land for political reasons. Born in Lorraine, of noble descent and German origin, he entered the Austrian Army in 1782, and served in the Austrian Netherlands during the insurrection, and in Germany during the Revolutionary Wars, from 1785 with the cavalry. After service in the 1805 campaign he was promoted to *Generalmajor* on 23 May 1809 after serving with distinction at Aspern–Essling, and led a cuirassier brigade in Hessen–Homburg's division at Wagram. Unemployed at the end of the 1809 campaign, he decided to further his career elsewhere, and entered the French Army as *général de brigade* in July 1811; he commanded a brigade of the 1st Light Cavalry Division of I Cavalry Corps in Russia in 1812, was wounded at Borodino and promoted to *général de division*. He led a division in 1813, was wounded at the Katzbach, became a baron, served in 1814 with a dragoon division, but accepted the Bourbon restoration and was employed by them. He rallied to Napoleon in 1815 and led the 12th Cavalry Division of Kellermann's III Cavalry Corps in the Waterloo campaign; yet was recalled to service in June 1816 and prospered under the Bourbons, rising to vicomte in 1822 and commanding a cuirassier division in Spain in 1823. He retired in 1832. He should not be confused with General François Roussel, chief of staff of the Imperial Guard, who was killed when hit by a shell at Heilsberg.

ROUSTAM RAZA (1780–1845)

One of the most familiar and colourful members of Napoleon's entourage, he was an Armenian kidnapped by a slave dealer at the age of 7, taken to Cairo and sold to Salih Bey, the Amir al-Hajj. On the return from a journey to Mecca,

ROUSTAM (EXTREME RIGHT) IN HIS USUAL PLACE AS ONE OF NAPOLEON'S CLOSEST ATTENDANTS
(ENGRAVING BY C. TURNER AFTER MASQUERIER)

learning of the French expedition to Egypt, Salih went to Acre to confer with his old enemy, Djezzar Pasha, who poisoned him. Now without a master, Roustam made his own way to Cairo and entered the service of Sheik el-Bekri, and when that dignitary grew tired of him he gave Roustam as a present to Napoleon in June 1799. From then until shortly before the abdication, he was one of Napoleon's closest attendants, bodyguard and valet, always dressed in his Mameluke costume (an exotic appearance which ensured that he was portrayed in many pictures with his master), and even slept at the doorway of Napoleon's room. The distinctive costume must have appeared so remarkable that when in 1810–11 Roustam was given an assistant, Louis Saint-Denis, the young Frenchman adopted the same style of dress and called himself Ali. Roustam made himself wealthy by selling influence, finally deserting his master (though Ali remained loyal); he married a French girl, wrote unreliable memoirs, spent some time in London and was among those who welcomed Napoleon's body back to France in 1840.

Roustam Raza. *Souvenirs de Roustam, Mamelouck de Napoléon Ier*, ed. P. Cottin. Paris, 1911

ROVIGO, duc de, see SAVARY

ROWLANDSON, Thomas (1756–1827)

Born in London, he began his artistic career as a classical painter, but became famous as a caricaturist and engraver after his inherited fortune had been dissipated by gambling. Although his fame resides with his cartoons and caricatures – his great creation was Dr. Syntax – his military art was considerable, notably the magnificent *Loyal Volunteers of London & Environs* (London 1798–9) depicting both the manual exercise and the uniforms of the various corps, most of which assisted in the production of the work, presumably ensuring its accuracy. His military and caricature work overlaps in such works as *The Military Adventures of Johnny Newcome* (1815) which illustrates humorously the vicissitudes of a subaltern's life.

Gregg, J. *Rowlandson the Caricaturist*. 1880; Hayes, J. *Rowlandson*. 1972

RUCHEL, General Ernst Philipp von (1754–1823)

A Pomeranian, he entered the Prussian Army in 1771, served in the early campaigns of the Revolutionary Wars, attained the rank of general in 1794, was present at Kaiserslautern and in the French attacks in the Vosges in July 1794. He is best remembered, however, as commander of the detached corps (sometimes termed an army) which seconded Hohenlohe's army at Jena. He was not present at the commencement of the action but at Weimar, and although he set off to join Hohenlohe as soon as he received an order to that effect, no urgency was implied because Hohenlohe claimed the battle was going well. Subsequently he received a plea for urgent help, but the battle was over before he arrived and criticisms of his slow approach are unjustified. Instead of using Rüchel's 15,000 men to cover the retreat, Hohenlohe then ordered him to attack, and near Gross Romstedt he was overwhelmed by the victorious French; he was severely wounded near the heart but refused to quit his post until his command had been broken. Subsequently he was found by Soult, apparently mortally wounded; Soult ordered his surgeon and a guard to attend him, but he made off before they arrived, and survived to serve subsequently in Poland.

RUFFIN, General François-Amable, comte (1771–1811)

Best known for his service in the Peninsular War, he enrolled in the French Army in 1792 and was elected as an officer almost immediately. He served in the Army of the North, in Germany and on the Danube, including as aide to Jourdan and chief of staff to Ney in 1799; *général de brigade* from February 1805, at Austerlitz he commanded a brigade in Oudnot's élite division of grenadiers. Promoted to *général de division* after service in Poland (including Friedland), the rest of his career was spent in the Peninsula. In 1808 he commanded the 1st Division of Victor's I Corps, served at Talavera, and remained with Victor until Barrosa, where he commanded the French force which occupied the Cerro del Puerco and which was defeated by Graham's counter-attack. Ruffin was shot through the neck by a rifle-ball, which hit the spine and caused paralysis, and he was captured. William Surtees described him as 'an immense and fine-looking man, about six feet two inches or six feet three inches high, and ate enormously'[1] Graham showed him every consideration and sent him dishes from his own table every day, but on 15 May Ruffin died aboard the transport *Gorgon*, within sight of the Isle of Wight, while being taken to England as a prisoner: 'He had spent the day in good spirits, and repeatedly expressed his satisfaction at coming to England, and his escape from the Spaniards. He seemed to suffer but little from his wound, till about ten minutes before his death. After having eaten a hearty dinner, he was suddenly seized with pain, which terminated in his death.'[2] It was recorded that he possessed a considerable landed property at Havre-de-Grace, and he was buried with full honours at Portsmouth on 18 May.

1. Surtees, W. *Twenty-Five Years in the Rifle Brigade*. London, 1833, pp. 126-7. 2. *Gent's Mag.*, June, 1811, p. 602.

RUFFO, Cardinal Fabrizio (1744–1827)

Born in Calabria, the son of Litterio, Duke of Baranello, he benefited from the influence of his uncle, Cardinal Thomas Ruffo, finding favour with Pope Pius VI and entering the papal civil service, rising to the office of Treasurer-General and Minister of War. He never entered the priesthood but in September 1791 became a cardinal after his removal from the treasurership, and went to Naples. Upon the French invasion in 1798 he fled to Palermo with the royal family, and because of his family influence in that region was chosen to lead the royalist movement in Calabria; in January 1799 he was named as vicar-general. On 8 February he landed with eight companions and raised the 'Christian Army of the Holy Faith' (*Esercito Cristiano della Sante Fede)* which included soldiers, bandits like 'Fra Diavolo' and even Russians and Turks, which ravaged the Parthenopean Republic and persuaded the French to leave under an armistice. Ruffo appears to have lost the king's favour, however, for his tendency to show mercy towards the republicans ('We must not drive the principal Jacobins at Naples to despair, but must rather leave them the means of escape. The anarchy, after all, is not so great as some people may imagine.').[1] He resigned the vicar-generalship and during the subsequent French possession of Naples lived quietly, though returned to favour after the restoration of the Bourbons, was consulted on matters of state and even briefly held office. He was not especially esteemed by his allies; some accused him of corruption when in papal service; as head of the Army of Holy Faith he was described as a coward, Nelson thought him 'a swelled-up priest',[2] and one of Nelson's subordinates styled him 'that worthless fellow ... who was endeavouring to form a party hostile to the interests of his sovereign'.[3] He should not be confused with Paul Ruffo, the Neapolitan Prince Castelcicala, later Neapolitan ambassador to

Britain, but who served as a lieutenant in the 6th (Inniskilling) Dragoons at Waterloo.

1. Clarke, Revd. J. S., and McArthur, J. *The Life and Services of Horatio, Viscount Nelson*. London, 1840, vol. II, p. 257. 2. Oman, C. *Nelson*. London, 1947, p. 349. 3. Clarke and McArthur, *op. cit.*, p. 264

RUMFORD, Sir Benjamin Thompson, Count (1753–1814)

A scientist of considerable distinction, he was a native of Massachusetts who found favour first with Governor Wentworth of New Hampshire, and later with Lord George Germain, with whom it was rumoured (though not proven) he had a homosexual relationship. He was given government appointments, was elected a Fellow of the Royal Society in 1779 as a result of his scientific interests, and after the fall of North's ministry made a brief return to North America as an officer (he attained the rank of lieutenant colonel). His reputation was such that he was welcomed into Bavarian civil and military service, serving for eleven years as adjutant-general, Minister of War and of Police, and grand chamberlain; during his tenure he changed the appearance of the Bavarian Army radically and introduced a new fieldpiece, the 'Rumford 3pdr'. Given a British knighthood, in 1791 he was created a Count of the Holy Roman Empire, taking his title 'Rumford' from the old name of Concord, New Hampshire, where his wife was still living (she died in 1792). Rumford conducted much important scientific work in Bavaria, improving industry and the conditions of its employees, and although principally famous as a chemist he had considerable skills as an inventor, notably his devising of a smokeless fireplace designed when in London in 1790, which brought him considerable wealth. Recalled to Bavaria when Munich was threatened by French and Austrian forces, he negotiated its safety; but was refused accreditation as Bavarian Ambassador to Great Britain ostensibly because he was a British citizen, but perhaps on grounds of character. He resided in London (and was one of the founders of the Royal Institution in 1800), and in 1802 moved to Paris where he married the widow of the chemist Lavoisier; the union was unhappy and he moved to Auteuil where his daughter (from his first marriage) kept house for him. He continued his scientific interests (he invented the coffee percolator), but his chief recreations in retirement were enjoyment of his garden and playing billiards against himself. He died of a 'nervous fever' in August 1814 when on the point of returning to England. He was especially proud of advancing the careers of the Bavarian General Wrede and Sir Humphrey Davy, whom he appointed lecturer in chemistry to the Royal Institution.

Brown, S. C. *Benjamin Thompson, Count Rumford*. 1979; Sparrow, W. J. *Knight of the White Eagle: Sir Benjamin Thompson*. New York, 1964; Thompson, J. A. *Count Rumford of Massachusetts*. New York, 1935. Rumford's complete works were published 1870–5 (with a memoir by Revd. G. Ellis), and his principal publications were listed in a long memoir in *Gent's Mag.*, Oct, 1814.

SACKEN, General Fabian Gottlieb von der Osten, Count (1752–1837)

Born in Kiev of an old Pomeranian family, Fabian von der Osten-Sacken (who is generally styled 'Sacken') was a distinguished Russian commander who gained much experience under Suvarov in campaigns against the Turks and Poles, but who came to real prominence during the later Napoleonic Wars. He commanded a division at the left-centre of Bennigsen's position at Eylau, in 1812 commanded that part of the 3rd West Army which faced the Austrian and Saxon force, and in 1813 was one of the three corps-commanders in Blücher's Army of Silesia, together with Langeron and Yorck (and was probably the easiest to get along with, despite a reported tendency towards intrigue). He was engaged very heavily at Leipzig, and led his corps in the 1814 campaign. His son Dmitri (1790–1881) also served at this time, rose to become a general and is probably best known as commander of Sebastopol during the Crimean War. The family name is also familiar from its relationship with the life of Leo Tolstoy, Countess Osten-Sacken being his aunt.

SAINT-ANDRE, André Jeanbon (1749–1813)

Also known as Jean-Bon Saint-André, this French politician and administrator was born in Montauban, the son of a fuller, and became a Protestant minister. Elected to the Convention, he supported the tenets of the Revolution, was allied with the more radical factions, voted for the death of the king and opposed punishment for the perpetrators of the September massacres. In July 1793 he became a member of the Committee of Public Safety, and, having been to sea, was appointed maritime commissioner. At Brest and Cherbourg he re-organised the naval establishment, but his reforms were not entirely beneficial. He promulgated the decree that any officer who surrendered before his ship was sinking should suffer death, so that French commanders had to justify their actions; abolished the distinction between seamen and gunners on the grounds that to differentiate them would be to create an 'aristocracy', ignoring advice that it was necessary to give specialist training in gunnery; and advocated boarding instead of seamanship as the way to win battles. His interference even extended to accompanying Villaret-Joyeuse aboard his flagship *Le Montagne* at the Battle of the First of June, though when battle was joined Saint-André went below (it was announced that he had been injured when a block fell on his arm!). After he showed moderation on a subsequent mission he was arrested (May 1795) but was later released, served as consul at Algiers and Smyrna (1798) and was held prisoner by the Turks for three years. Subsequently he became Prefect of the *département* of Mont-Tonnerre (1801), commissary-general of the *départements* on the left bank of the Rhine, and was Prefect of Mainz at his death in 1813.

St. CLAIR, Major-General Thomas Staunton (1785–1847)

A member of a Scottish military family (his father and three brothers were all in the service), he was born at Gibraltar, commissioned in the 1st Foot in 1803 and served in British Guyana (1806–8), Walcheren, and in the Peninsula from 1810, mostly with the Portuguese Army, latterly as lieutenant-colonel commanding the 5th *Caçadores*. He remained in Portuguese service until 1818, served in the British Army until he went on half-pay in 1828, became a major-general in 1844 and a Knight of Hanover in 1834. He is best known, however, as an artist, notably for a series of aquatints of Peninsular War scenes engraved by Charles Turner (1812–13), *A Series of Views of the Principal Occurrences of the Campaign in Spain and Portugal*, which are among the most accurate views of the period. He also wrote and illustrated a valuable study, *A Residence in the West Indies and America, with a Narrative of the Expedition to the Island of Walcheren*, London, 1834.

Feibel, R. M. 'Major-General Thomas Staunton St. Clair', in *Journal of the Society for Army Historical Research*, 1970, vol. XLVIII, pp. 29–34

SAINT-CYR, General Claude Carra, see **CARRA SAINT-CYR**

SAINT-CYR, Marshal Laurent Gouvion, see **GOUVION SAINT-CYR**

SAINT-ETIENNE, Jean-Paul Rabaut, see **RABAUT SAINT-ETIENNE**

SAINT-FARGEAU, Louis-Michel Le Pelletier de, see **LE PELLETIER DE SAINT-FARGEAU**

SAINT-HILAIRE, General Louis-Vincent-Joseph le Blond, comte de (1766–1809)

'The pride of the army, as remarkable for his wit as for his military talents',[1] he joined the army in

1777, was commissioned in 1783 and saw extensive service in Italy during the Revolutionary Wars, becoming provisional *général de brigade* in September 1795 and suffering several wounds, including the loss of two fingers at Loano. *Général de division* from 1799, at Austerlitz he commanded the 1st Division of Soult's IV Corps with great distinction, notably in the counter-attack on the Pratzen Heights, led the same formation at Jena and Eylau, where his division mounted the great but costly attack on the Russian centre. Comte from 1808, in 1809 he led the 3rd Division of Lannes' II Corps and was mortally wounded at Aspern–Essling. Such was his devotion to Napoleon (which was reciprocated) that, according to Lejeune, he had been serving despite a serious open wound, and when Lannes' advance stalled and had to withdraw, Saint-Hilaire's staff was hit by a blast of grape-shot which smashed his foot; Marbot, injured at the same time, carried news of the catastrophe to Lannes and Napoleon, both of whom, he said, felt Saint-Hilaire's loss keenly. He was borne away and died at Vienna a fortnight later.

1. Lejeune, vol. I, p. 281

SAINT-JUST, Antoine-Louis-Léon de Richebourg de (1767–94)

As might be suggested by his nickname 'the Apocalyptic', he was one of the most ardent and visionary of the more extreme French revolutionaries. Born in Decize, he was elected an officer of the National Guard of the Aisne and entered politics. He became a friend and supporter of Robespierre, and as a Deputy to the Convention for the *département* of the Aisne and became known for the extreme, cold and gloomy nature of his pronouncements, which were reflected by his

ANTOINE SAINT-JUST
(PRINT AFTER DAVID)

austere and resolute conduct. He exercised considerable influence in the Committee of Public Safety, reporting to the Convention on the Girondins and Hébertists, and assisting in the fall of Danton; his proposal was accepted that the Convention, through its committees, should control and direct all military concerns and all facets of government. The same inflexible, even ruthless, principles he applied to military affairs, when sent to Strasbourg and to the Army of the North, weeding out those of suspicious loyalty and threatening commanders with trial if they were unsuccessful. He returned to Paris to support Robespierre, and on 9th Thermidor it was his speech (delivering to the Convention his report of the committees of Public Safety and General Security) which was interrupted, ending with the arrest of Robespierre and his followers, including Saint-Just. On the following day (28 July), he was guillotined in the Place de la Révolution, together with Robespierre and his friends; he showed the same courage and resolution which had characterised his actions of the past several years.

SAINT-LEU, comte de, see BONAPARTE, LOUIS

SAINT-PRIEST, General Guillaume-Emmanuel (1776–1814)

He was one of the many foreign commanders who served in the Russian Army. He was the eldest son of François-Emmanuel-Guignard, comte de Saint-Priest (1735–1821), a distinguished French statesman and diplomat who served in Necker's ministry, resigned in December 1790 and emigrated, serving the comte de Provence as minister of the household and living in various countries until the restoration. Guillaume rose to the rank of general officer in Russian service, commanding a brigade at Lützen and then a division in Langeron's corps of the Army of Silesia, including Leipzig. In 1814 he commanded the force which occupied Rheims on 12 March, but was attacked heavily by Napoleon on the following day; as he was organising his withdrawal he was mortally wounded by a roundshot, which Napoleon claimed was fired by the same gunner who had killed Moreau. Saint Priest's brother, Armand-Emmanuel-Charles (1782–1863) also entered Russian service and became Governor of Odessa, and the third brother, Emmanuel-Louis-Marie-Guignard (1789–1881), a godson of Marie-Antoinette, also participated in the 1814 campaign, and enjoyed a distinguished diplomatic and military career until the 1830 revolution, becoming lieutenant-general, vicomte de Saint-Priest and Spanish Duke of Almazan.

SAINT-SULPICE, General Raymond-Gaspard de Bonardi, comte de (1761–1835)

Best known as a commander of heavy cavalry who came to prominence in the later campaigns, he was commissioned in 1777 and

rved extensively in the Revoluonary Wars despite a suspension
two years because of noble
rth. *Général de brigade* from
03, in the following year he
ecame Josephine's Master of
orse; at Jena he commanded a
rigade (of the 10th Cuirassiers) in
Hautpoul's 2nd Cuirassier Divi-
on, was wounded at Eylau and
the same month was advanced
général de division and took
ver d'Hautpoul's command.
omte from 1808, he led the 2nd
eavy Cavalry Division at Aspern–
ssling; when Arrighi took over
e division of Espagne, killed at
at battle, he replaced Arrighi as
olonel of the Dragoons of the
nperial Guard, which he led in
ussia in 1812. Worn out by the
ampaign, he asked to be relieved,
as succeeded as colonel by
rnano and became Governor of
ontainebleau. He became col-
nel of the 4th *Gardes d'honneur*
the Imperial Guard in April
313, and after some staff duty
etired in October 1815.

T. VINCENT, Admiral John ervis, Earl of (1735–1823)

nown as 'Old Jarvie', he was the
on of an Admiralty solicitor and
reasurer of Greenwich Hospital.
ntering the Royal Navy in 1749,
e became one of its most
enowned figures. He served at
uebec in 1759, through the
even Years War and the War of
merican Independence; he
ecame rear-admiral in 1787,
ice-admiral in 1793, and admiral
n his return from the West
ndies, where (1793–5) he assisted
n the taking of Martinique and
uadeloupe. In November 1795
e was appointed CinC Mediter-
anean, but the entry of Spain
nto the alliance with France led
o the British evacuation of that
egion, Jervis taking his fleet to
he coast of Portugal, from where
e could watch the Spaniards in
Cadiz. On 14 February 1797,

JOHN JERVIS, EARL OF ST. VINCENT
(ENGRAVING BY G. COCHRAN AFTER J. KEENAN)

thanks in part to the actions of
Horatio Nelson, commanding
HMS *Captain*, Jervis won a very
notable victory at Cape St.
Vincent. For all his abilities and
the confidence they inspired,
however, he was not universally
popular; a dour man with a
temper and hatred of inefficiency,
he was a stern, even savage disciplinarian who led not only by
force of personality but fear of
punishment (though it should be
added that the improvements in
efficiency and discipline were
greatly beneficial to the combat
ability of the navy). Perhaps
remembering his own extreme
penury when first in the navy, he
disliked patronage and those who
exploited it, treating his officers
as severely as the seamen, though
supporting those of obvious merit
(Nelson in particular was a great
favourite and beneficiary of
Jervis' ability to recognise talent).
A Whig (and thus an opponent of
Pitt, despite the fact that he
received employment under that
ministry), Jervis was elected MP
for Launceston in 1782, Yarmouth
1784; he was also devoted to the
king (who styled Jervis his 'old
oak') and the Church, and had a
hearty dislike of Dissenters. The
victory at St. Vincent secured his
fame, and in June 1797 he

became Earl St. Vincent. He
remained in command, sending
Nelson back into the Mediterranean, and when Sir John Orde
objected to Nelson having been
appointed over him, Nelson's
senior, St. Vincent, ordered him
home. Orde was so hurt that he
requested a duel, and the criticism thus provoked, and ill-
health, led to St. Vincent's
resignation in June 1799. In the
following year, however, he took
over the Channel Fleet, and from
1801 was First Lord of the Admiralty, in which he did much to
reform the corruption in the
naval dockyards, but was criticised for not strengthening the
navy in preparation for the
renewal of the war. He stood
down from the post when Pitt
resumed office, declining to
resume command in the
Channel, but did so in 1806–7
after Pitt's death, with temporary
rank of admiral of the fleet, which
was only made permanent upon
the coronation of George IV in
1821. He finally retired to his
house in Essex in 1810. For all his
unpopularity in certain quarters,
he was acknowledged as one of
the greatest and most capable
admirals of his time.

Berckman, E. *Nelson's Dear
Lord: A Portrait of St. Vincent.*
London, 1962; Brenton, E. P. *Life
and Correspondence of John, Earl
of St. Vincent ...* London, 1838;
Sherrard, O. E. *Life of Lord St.
Vincent.* London, 1933; St. Vincent,
Earl. *The Letters of Lord St.
Vincent*, ed., D. Bonner-Smith.
London, 1922–7; Tucker, J. S. (the
son of St. Vincent's secretary).
*Memoirs of Admiral Rt. Hon. the
Earl of St. Vincent.* London, 1844

SALICETI, Antoine Christophe (1757–1809)

Born in Saliceto, Corsica, of a
Piacenzan family, he was a lawyer
before he was elected to the
States-General. An advocate of the

union of Corsica with France, he was a Jacobin in the Convention (where he voted for the death of the king), and was sent to Corsica to oppose the counter-revolutionaries (it was upon his motion that Paoli and his followers were declared outlaws). Saliceti was then sent to Marseilles and Toulon on the same errand; he already knew his compatriot Captain Napoleon Bonaparte and showed the latter's paper *Le Souper de Beaucaire* to Robespierre junior, who was *en mission* with him, which for Napoleon proved a vital rung on the ladder of success. It was Saliceti who had Napoleon appointed to command the artillery at Toulon, had him arrested and then released after the fall of Robespierre, and when attached to the Army of Italy gave his support to General Bonaparte in his dealings with the Directory. In 1797 Saliceti was elected to the Council of Five Hundred and held several offices under the Consulate, and was subsequently Minister of War and Police at Naples under Joseph Bonaparte (1806–9). Greatly appreciated by Napoleon, he did not find universal favour (his jaundiced complexion, dark and glaring eyes and pallid lips reminded the duchesse d'Abrantès of a vampire, and his face haunted her dreams), and upon his death at Naples on 23 December 1809 it was alleged that he was the victim of poison.

SALTOUN, Lieutenant-General Alexander George Fraser, 16th Baron (1785–1853)

Son of Alexander, 15th Baron Saltoun (whom he succeeded in 1793), he served in the British Foot Guards; he was present in Sicily in 1806, in the Corunna campaign, Walcheren and again in the Peninsula 1811–14, but his greatest moment occurred at Waterloo,

ALEXANDER, 16TH BARON SALTOUN

when as captain and lieutenant-colonel (the unique 'double rank' system of the Guards) of the 1st Foot Guards he commanded the light companies deployed to hold the orchard and gardens of Hougoumont. Here his stubborn gallantry earned him undying fame; Wellington described him as 'a *thorough* soldier', and 'a pattern to the army both as man and soldier'.[1] He rose to the rank of lieutenant-general and commanded a brigade in China in 1842; he was married to Catharine, natural daughter of Lord Chancellor Thurlow. As a boy, the war correspondent Archibald Forbes encountered Saltoun in old age and found a gruff if affable character prepared to entertain with stories of Hougoumont, if not resembling a hero: 'a very queer-looking old person, short of figure, round as a ball, his head shrunk between very high and rounded shoulders, and with short stumpy legs ... curiously attired in a whole-coloured suit of grey [with] a droll-shaped jacket the great collar of which reached far up the back of his head'.[2]

1. Dalton, C. *The Waterloo Roll Call*. London, 1904, p. 100. 2. Forbes, A. *Camps, Quarters and Casual Places*. London, 1896, p. 155

SAN JUAN, General Benito (*d.*1808)

He is perhaps most remembere for suffering the most extrem sanction for a defeat. In Novembe 1808, as an officer of good repute he was entrusted with the 12,00 Spanish troops available for th defence of Madrid, though he wa not personally in overall command, that role being dispute between General Eguia and th Marquis of Castelar. When Egui attained supremacy he ordere San Juan to defend the Somc sierra Pass. Having unwisel divided his forces, they wer pushed aside by Napoleon in th famous action of 30 Novembe San Juan himself receiving tw sword-cuts to the head from Polish *chevau-léger* as h attempted, unsuccessfully, to ral his disintegrating reserve for stand. He assembled some of hi men and marched toward Madrid, where it was known tha the *Junta* was debating surrende San Juan paused to consider (December 1808) when his troop mutinied, and insisted that the continue; but a short while late they received news of Madrid's fa and panicked. After bolting fo about sixty miles, some of then were rallied at Talavera on December, but when San Jua attempted to re-assert his com mand the soldiers declared that h was intent on leading them t surrender; he tried to escape th mutineers by climbing through window, but was shot and the hanged from an elm tree jus outside the town. Napier wa outraged by this appalling exampl of mutiny; he described the action of San Juan's troops as 'intolerabl villainy' made worse 'by murderin their unfortunate general, an fixing his mangled body to a tree after which, dispersing, the carried dishonour and fear int their respective provinces'.[1]

1. Napier, W., vol. I, p. 403.

SANSON, Charles-Henri (b.1739)

Charles Sanson (whose name is sometimes rendered as 'Samson') was hereditary public executioner of Paris 1788–95, and as such was much concerned with the guillotining of important personages during the Revolution, including the king and queen; it was remarked of him that he seemed quite insensible of the actions he was committing. He was succeeded in his post by his son Henri, who had been his assistant, and subsequently by his grandson.

SANTERRE, General Antoine-Joseph (1752–1809)

A Parisian brewer of revolutionary sympathies, he gained great popularity in the Faubourg St. Antoine by his commanding appearance and speech, led that area's National Guard and took part in the attacks on the Bastille and the Tuileries. He protected the royal family, however, and even attempted to bring about a reconciliation. He was made CinC of the National Guard and appointed warder of the king, whom he treated with compassion; he was present when Minister of Justice Garat informed the king of his condemnation, and at the execution. Promoted to general officer, he temporarily handed over command of the National Guard to go to the war in the Vendée, where his command was undistinguished and the republican forces were defeated (though he was in supreme command only briefly). Like the Nantes chemist Proust who tried (unsuccessfully) to devise an asphyxiating bomb, Santerre proposed the use of chemical warfare (a poisonous smoke) against the Vendéen rebels, but nothing came of the idea. He returned to Paris amid criticisms of his conduct, and the nature of his report aroused suspicions of royalism; he was imprisoned until after the fall of Robespierre. He resigned from public life and returned to business, but the brewery was ruined and he died in poverty.

Carro, A. *Santerre, Général de la République Française*. Paris, 1847

SAUERWEID, Alexander Ivanovich (1783–1844)

A Russian painter and aquatinter who worked in Dresden until 1814, he produced battle-paintings for the Tsar from that year, but is perhaps better known for uniform-studies of the Saxon, Westphalian, Polish and Russian armies (1810–14). He also painted British subjects in great detail, but many were apparently derived from prints like those of Hamilton Smith, and thus not of the greatest reliability.

SAUMAREZ, Admiral James, 1st Baron (1757–1836)

JAMES, 1ST BARON SAUMAREZ
(PRINT AFTER CARBONNIER)

A member of an old Guernsey family, he followed two uncles and an elder brother into the Royal Navy at the age of 13; commissioned lieutenant in 1776 after displaying bravery at Charleston, he saw much service, including the Battle of the Saints, and was knighted for the capture of the French frigate *La Réunion* (20 October 1793) off Cherbourg, while commanding HMS *Crescent*. As commander of HMS *Orion* he fought in the action off Lorient (22 June 1794) and at St. Vincent, for which he thought he did not receive his due; it was said he was not the easiest of companions, with a very formal manner which probably caused Nelson not to like him especially. He served in the blockade of Cadiz (1797–8) and was 2i/c at Aboukir Bay, with *Orion*, where he was wounded; he did not achieve his baronetcy until June 1801. After serving with HMS *Caesar* on the blockade of Brest (1799–1800) he became rear-admiral, and in July 1801 was at first repulsed off Algeciras but then defeated a Franco–Spanish squadron (including the capture of the 74-gunner *St. Antoine*), for which he received the Order of the Bath and in 1803 a pension of £1,200 p.a. Occupied in the Channel and on the blockade of Brest 1803–7, in 1808–13 he commanded in the Baltic, where his diplomatic skills were demonstrated; he was decorated by Bernadotte. Admiral from 1814, he was ennobled as Baron Saumarez in 1831, having commanded at Plymouth 1824–7. His brother, General Sir Thomas Saumarez, was equerry to the Duke of Kent and CinC New Brunswick in 1813.

Ross, Sir John. *Memoirs and Correspondence of Admiral Lord de Saumarez*. London, 1838; Saumarez, Admiral. *The Saumarez Papers*, ed. A. N. Ryan. London, 1968

SAVARY, General Anne-Jean-Marie-René, duc de Rovigo (1774–1833)

More of a diplomat than a soldier (though distinguished as such), he was born in Marcq in the Ardennes and joined the army as a volunteer in 1790, quickly attaining a commission and serving with the Army of the Rhine 1792–7. In

ANNE-JEAN-MARIE SAVARY (ENGRAVING BY A. E. ANDERSON AFTER R. LEFEVRE)

October 1797 he became Desaix's ADC, serving in Egypt and at Marengo, and after Desaix's death became ADC to Napoleon. In July 1801 he organised the élite legion of gendarmes for Napoleon's protection and subsequently became colonel of the *Gendarmerie d'Elite* of the Imperial Guard into which this unit evolved. *Général de brigade* from August 1803 (de *division* from February 1805), he became involved in matters of intelligence and security, most notably the suppression of the Cadoudal–Pichegru plot and in the execution of the duc d'Enghien (commanding the troops at Vincennes and being accused of preventing the dispatch to Napoleon of a plea for mercy). Attached to Napoleon's staff in 1805, he carried a message to the Tsar before Austerlitz which aided Napoleon's tactical plan; in 1806 he showed great daring in the cavalry pursuit after Jena, and in command of V Corps won the victory at Ostrolenka in 1807. After Tilsit he was appointed French Ambassador to Russia, then was recalled to serve in Spain, where he helped persuade Prince Ferdinand to go to Bayonne, and in June 1808 took command of French forces in Spain after Murat went home. Ennobled as duc de Rovigo (a town

in Venetia) in May 1808, he led the Guard Fusiliers at Somosierra, and accompanied Napoleon in the 1809 Danube campaign. From 1810 to April 1814 he served as Minister of Police in succession to Fouché, being arrested in his bed and imprisoned by the Malet conspirators, which damaged his reputation. He rallied to Napoleon in 1815 and was appointed inspector-general of gendarmerie and a peer of France, and accompanied Napoleon into exile aboard HMS *Bellerophon*, where Bunbury found him 'a handsome man, but with something sinister in the working of his countenance. His manner restless, and betokening the fears which were excited by the knowledge that he was one of those proscribed by Louis XVIII.'[1] Savary was not permitted to accompany Napoleon to St. Helena, but was interned for some months in Malta; thereafter he lived in Smyrna, Austria and London, before returning to France in 1819, and later settled in Rome. The 1830 revolution returned him to favour and he commanded the French Army in Algeria 1831–2 before returning home on health grounds; he died in Paris in June 1833. Napoleon described him as a kind, good-natured man entirely devoted to him (Napoleon), if self-interested, and said that criticism of him was unjust; by being present at the execution of Enghien, stated Napoleon, he was only obeying orders.

1. Bunbury, *Memoirs*, p. 307.

Savary, A. J. M. R. *Mémoires du duc de Rovigo*. Paris, 1828; English edn. London, 1828

SAXE–COBURG–SAALFELD, Ernst Anton Karl Ludwig, Duke of (later **Ernst I of Saxe–Coburg–Gotha**) (1784–1844)

At the time of the death of Duke Francis (Franz) of Saxe–Coburg–Saalfeld in 1806, his heir Ernst was

a serving soldier, and only cam[e] into possession of his state afte[r] the peace of Tilsit, its bankru[pt] finances having been admini[s]tered by a commission. The sta[te] entered the Confederation of th[e] Rhine, but Ernst, having aided th[e] Prussians in 1806, continued o[ut] of favour with Napoleon an[d] supported the 'War of Liberation[';] after Leipzig he was give[n] command of a corps and reduce[d] Mainz. An enlightened ruler an[d] patron of the arts and sciences a[s] well as a competent soldier, h[e] became Duke of Saxe–Cobur[g] –Gotha in 1826 when that state wa[s] created by a redistribution o[f] territory following the death of th[e] last duke of Saxe–Gotha–Alten[-] burg, Saalfeld being exchanged fo[r] Gotha. Ernst became one of th[e] most influential rulers of th[e] smaller German states; his so[n] Albert married Britain's Quee[n] Victoria.

SAXE–COBURG–SAALFELD, Prince Leopold George Frederick of, see **LEOPOLD George Frederick**

SAXE–WEIMAR, Duke of, and SAXE–WEIMAR, Prince Bernhard of, see **CHARLES AUGUST Duke of Saxe–Weimar–Eisenach**

SCHARNHORST, General Gerhard Johann David von (1755–1813)

One of the most significant mili[-] tary figures of the era, he neve[r] exercised an important fiel[d] command; yet his influence wa[s] immense. Born in Hanover o[f] farming stock, he educate[d] himself and in 1778 was commis[-] sioned in the Hanoverian cavalr[y] transferring to the artillery i[n] 1783. Appointed to the artiller[y] school, he made most of his livin[g] by writing on military theory an[d] publishing a military journal. H[e] served in The Netherlands i[n]

GERHARD JOHANN DAVID VON SCHARNHORST
(PRINT AFTER J. G. BRÜCKE)

1793–4 with distinction, writing a book on Menin (*Vertheidigung der Stadt Menin*, Hanover, 1803), which with his *Die Ursachen des Glücks der Franzosen im Revolutionskrieg* is perhaps his best-known work. Becoming a major on the staff, his reputation as a military theorist led to other offers of employment, and in 1801 he transferred to Prussian service as a lieutenant-colonel, with a patent of nobility and double his previous salary. Employed at the War Academy in Berlin (where Clausewitz was a pupil), in 1806 he was Brunswick's chief of staff, was slightly wounded at Auerstädt, served with Blücher in the final stages of the campaign, and exchanged following the surrender, played a leading part with L'Estocq's corps serving with the Russians. For service at Eylau he received the coveted decoration *Pour le Mérite*. (Scharnhorst's practical abilities in the field proved that he was more than just a theorist; his shy manner, said Clausewitz, gave the impression that he was more a scholar than a soldier, but for all his intellectual gifts this was far from the truth). He was promoted to major-general and appointed head of the commission to reconstruct the Prussian Army. Despite Nap-

oleon's obstruction, this work was of vital consequence; Scharnhorst's influence extended beyond just organisation and tactics to the concept of a 'national' army. The patriotic fervour which characterised the Prussian armies of 1813–14, the enabling of commoners to gain commissions, and the foundation of the *Landwehr* and all that it entailed were due to him; it might be said that he was the creator of the 1813 army and in the widest sense one of the founders of German nationalism. Forced into retirement by pressure from Napoleon, he passed his time writing a work on firearms, and in 1813 returned to serve as Blücher's chief of staff. At Lützen he received a wound in the foot, which became infected and proved mortal; he died at Prague on 8 June 1813, where he had been sent to negotiate Austria's entry into the war, having recently been promoted to *Generalleutnant*. He did not live to see the success of his policy and reforms, but his reputation endures.

Clausewitz, C. 'Uber das Leben und den Charakter des General v. Scharnhorst', in Leopold von Ranke's *Historisch-politischer Zeitschrift*, 1832; Lehmann, M. *Scharnhorst*. Leipzig, 1886–8; White, C. E. *The Enlightened Soldier: Scharnhorst ...* New York, 1989

SCHERER, General Barthelémy-Louis-Joseph (1747–1804)

Best known for his command of French forces in Italy during the Revolutionary Wars, he had enjoyed a long and varied military career before coming to prominence. He served in the Austrian Army during the Seven Years War, then transferred to the French artillery; in Netherlands service 1785–90, he returned to the French Army in 1792, becoming

général de brigade in September 1793 and *de division* four months later. In July 1794 his forces captured the fortresses of Quesnoy, Landrecy, Valenciennes and Condé, and he subsequently commanded the right wing of Jourdan's army, crossing the Ourthe and driving back the enemy (from 18 September). After briefly commanding the Army of Italy, he replaced Pérignon in command in the Pyrenees (spring 1795), and after conclusion of hostilities there again took over in Italy (October 1795), achieving success at Loano. Deprived of the resources he requested, and ordered to accomplish more than was feasible by a stream of impracticable instructions from France, which he regarded as intolerable interference, he asked to be relieved of command; his resignation was accepted in March 1796 and Napoleon was appointed in his place. This did not end his career, however; his most important subsequent appointment was as Minister of War (1797–9), in which he became unpopular because of attempts to introduce stricter discipline and order. Early in 1799 a new commander was required for the Army of Italy, a post that was turned down by the more obvious candidates, so Schérer was appointed despite his protestations of age, poor health and unpopularity; it was even suggested that Barras proposed him as a way of removing him from his ministerial position, in which he was proving troublesome. This period of his command was unsuccessful, including the defeat of Magnano, the subsequent retreat and deployment of his army in an injudicious fashion which contributed to the defeat at Cassano (27 April), though that was fought by his successor, Moreau, who took over on that day following Schérer's resignation, to the approval of the army. Schérer was not again employed.

SCHILL, Major Ferdinand Baptista von (1776–1809)

Born in Silesia, he entered the Prussian cavalry in 1789 and was still a subaltern in 1806. He was wounded at Auerstädt but gained considerable fame in the subsequent operations as a cavalry leader, raiding from Colberg, being promoted to major after Tilsit and appointed to command the 2nd Brandenburg Hussars. His patriotism brought him into contact with other German nationalists, and into a brave but somewhat unrealistic attempt to free Prussia from French domination by raising a rebellion at the time of Napoleon's war with Austria in 1809. In late April he led his regiment out of Berlin, ostensibly for manoeuvres, and then announced his intentions, permitting those unwilling to follow him to depart. He attracted some limited support, but mostly found opposition from the Saxon and Westphalian garrisons he encountered on his ride through those territories, notably in a skirmish at Dodendorf, south of Magdeburg, on 5 May. With the Prussian

authorities condemning his actions, and with the failure of Dörnberg's attempted revolt, Schill was left without hope of support; he marched north to Stralsund where he hoped he might receive help from the Royal Navy. Dutch troops under General Gratien and Danish under von Ewald stormed his position at Stralsund on 31 May; Schill's small command put up a considerable fight but was overwhelmed, and Schill himself was killed in the market square, where a last stand was made. The circumstances of his death are not entirely clear, but the Danish version averred that he had been wounded in the street-fighting, surrendered but was cut down and shot by a Danish hussar, Jasper Crohn, who feared that he would escape. A small number of Schill's hussars escaped, but most of the survivors were captured; eleven officers were court-martialled and shot. Although Schill's rebellion failed, it caused much consternation in north Germany, and he became a hero for the subsequent 'War of Liberation'. His head was cut off and taken to Holland, where it remained until 1837. His name

was commemorated in the German Army by the title of the Hussar Regiment No. 4 (1st Silesian), Von Schill's.

Binder von Kriegelstein, C *Ferdinand von Schill*. Berlin, 1902

SCHLEGEL, August Wilhelm von (1767–1845)

Like his friend, Madame de Staël, the German poet, critic and translator, born in Hanover, was no admirer of Napoleon (whom he termed the *Landerverwüster*, 'country-devastator'), and was hostile to France even before the advent of the Empire. He wrote patriotic works and was expelled from France with Madame de Staël, and briefly entered an active political career as secretary and adviser to Bernadotte, upon her recommendation. In return for his services, and writings like his condemnation of the Continental System, he was appointed a privy councillor of Sweden. His younger brother, Karl Wilhelm Friedrich von Schlegel (1772–1829), a major literary figure in his own right, also had a connection with the Napoleonic Wars through his appointment as secretary to Archduke Charles' headquarters (1809).

SCHWARZENBERG, Field Marshal Karl Philipp, Prince zu (1771–1820)

He came from an ancient and distinguished family of Franconian origin, elevated to princely status in 1670, whose members included the Imperial General Adolf von Schwarzenberg (1547–1600) and Johann, Freiherr von Schwarzenberg und Hohenlandsberg (1463–1528), the jurist and friend of Luther. Karl joined the Austrian Army in 1788, served against the Turks, but won his first real fame in The Netherlands in 1794. Despite his youth, he was given command of a force of Allied cavalry to repel a French

DEATH OF FERDINAND VON SCHILL AT STRALSUND (PRINT AFTER R. KNÖTEL)

KARL PHILIPP SCHWARZENBERG
(ENGRAVING BY J. W. MANSFELD)

SIR WALTER SCOTT
(PRINT AFTER RAEBURN)

attempt to raise the siege of Landrecies, and succeeded spectacularly in the action of Le Cateau-Cambresis or Beaumont (26 April), for which he received the Cross of the Order of Maria Theresa. After service at Amberg and Würzburg he attained the rank of *Feldmarschall-Leutnant* in 1799, saved the Austrian right wing from defeat at Hohenlinden, and with a divisional command in 1805 under Mack was among those who cut themselves free from the encirclement at Ulm. Sent as an envoy to the Tsar in 1808, he returned to command a cavalry division at Wagram, and after the peace was sent as ambassador to Paris to negotiate Napoleon's marriage to Marie-Louise. During a ball at his house in the Rue de Montblanc, a fire led to the deaths of many guests, among whom was his sister-in-law, Princess Pauline Schwarzenberg, who was killed by the falling roof when she plunged back into the fire to seek her daughter. (Pauline's daughter, the wife of Field Marshal Prince Alfred Windischgrätz (1787–1862) was killed in the Prague revolt of 1848). Highly esteemed by Napoleon, Schwarzenberg commanded the Austrian Reserve Corps for the Russian campaign

of 1812; promoted to field marshal, in 1813 he was appointed to command the Army of Bohemia. This he led in the campaigns of 1813–14 with considerable distinction, and though accused of timidity his task was made difficult by the conflict of opinions between the various Allied nations, and though in command at Leipzig the three Allied monarchs were present to overshadow his actions. Greatly honoured after the war and appointed President of the *Hofkriegsrath*, he suffered partial paralysis after a stroke in 1817, and died after another stroke on 15 October 1820, while visiting the scene of his greatest success at Leipzig. His three sons all became general officers (the eldest, Friedrich, 1800–70, also served in the Carlist War and with the French in Algeria), and his nephew Felix (1800–52) was not only a soldier but more importantly a statesman, who led the ministry with considerable success from November 1848, at a time a great tension.

Kerchnawe, H., and Veltzé, A. *Feldmarschall Karl, Fürst zu Schwarzenberg*. Vienna, 1913

SCOTT, Sir Walter, Bt. (1771–1832)

The Scottish literary genius was not involved to any great degree in the Napoleonic conflict, but apart from his acquaintance with personalities who were, and his production of a life of Napoleon (1827), his work was highly popular with many of the participants, and its consequences occupied much of his time as a volunteer. A lawyer by profession, Scott served as secretary, quartermaster and paymaster of the Royal Edinburgh Light Dragoons (raised 1797); it was not a duty, according to Lord Cockburn, but an 'absolute passion' with him, and he infused the members of

the corps with his zeal. This was evident in sabre practice, when he would chop at the target – a turnip mounted atop a pole, representing a Frenchman – muttering to himself, 'Cut them down, the villains, cut them down!'. Such duties had an effect on his work; apart from his poem *War Song of the Edinburgh Light Dragoons*, written shortly after the unit's formation and reprinted as a patriotic exhortation in *The Anti-Gallican* (1803, p. 71), it was said that a whole canto of *Marmion* was written when on duty with the Midlothian Yeomanry in October 1807, the martial atmosphere evidently providing inspiration for his verses on Flodden, much of which he composed in his mind while galloping alone at the edge of the sea on the drill-ground at Portobello sands. At the time, Scott's popularity was as a poet; although he had begun *Waverley* tentatively in 1805, it was not published until 1814, and then anonymously. His baronetcy was conferred in 1820.

Lockhart, J. G. *Memoirs of the Life of Sir Walter Scott*. Edinburgh, 1837–8; Oman, C. *The Wizard of the North: The Life of Sir Walter Scott*. London, 1973

SCOTT, General Winfield (1786–1866)

One of the premier American soldiers of the first half of the 19th century, most noted for his successful command in the Mexican–American War, he was considerably distinguished in the War of 1812. A Virginian, he commenced a legal career but joined the army at the time of the war scare with Great Britain; commissioned an artillery captain in 1808, he survived suspension over criticism of General James Wilkinson, and as a lieutenant colonel was captured at Queenston after making himself greatly conspicuous by his exhortations to the troops as well as by his bearing (he was a huge and imposing figure). Exchanged in January 1813, he became brigadier general in March 1814 and brevet major general in July; he was further distinguished at Chippewa and Lundy's Lane, being severely wounded at the latter by a bullet through the shoulder. It took him some time to recover, but he was sufficiently fit to take command of the 10th (Washington) Military District in October 1814. Congress voted him a gold medal in the following month (it was actually presented a decade later), and in an extremely distinguished subsequent career he became commanding general of the US Army and retired only in 1861.

Elliott, C. W. *Winfield Scott: the Soldier and the Man*. New York, 1937; Mansfield, E. D. *Life and Services of General Scott*. New York, 1862; Scott, General W. *Memoirs of Lieutenant General Scott*. New York, 1864

SCOVELL, General Sir George (1774–1861)

Commissioned in 1798, he served during the Peninsular War in the adjutant-general's department, while an officer in the 57th Foot, and was commandant (1813) of the Staff Corps of Cavalry. He served at Corunna, and was with Wellington's headquarters 1809–14, where he was a most valuable staff officer and code-breaker, who unravelled the 'Great Paris cypher'. He was assistant QMG at Waterloo, attained the rank of full general in 1854 and held the colonelcies of the 4th Dragoons and 7th Dragoon Guards. 'The Scovell Cyphers' is in Oman, Sir Charles, *History of the Peninsular War*, London, 1914, vol. V, pp. 611–18.

SEATON, Field Marshal Lord, see COLBORNE

SEBASTIANI, Marshal Horace-François-Bastien, comte (1772–1851)

HORACE SÉBASTIANI (ENGRAVING BY J. W. EVANS AFTER M. F. WINTERHALTER)

Of Corsican birth and intended for the priesthood, Sébastiani was instead commissioned in the French Army in 1789. His early service with the Army of the Alps included the campaigning on his native island, and with the Army of Italy under Napoleon including Dego and Arcola. He supported Napoleon at the coup of Brumaire and served at Marengo, and undertook his first diplomatic mission (to Turkey and Egypt) before becoming *général de brigade* on his return in 1803. At Austerlitz (where he was wounded) he led a brigade of the 2nd Dragoon Division, was promoted to *général de division* after the battle and in the following year became ambassador at Constantinople where he helped persuade the Ottoman Empire to declare war on Russia and assisted in the defence of the Dardanelles against Duckworth's British fleet. Recalled after the deposition of Selim III reduced the French influence, in August 1808 he went to the Peninsula to command the 1st Division of Lefebvre's IV Corps and early in 1809 replaced the latter in command of the corps. He led it at Talavera and defeated the Army of La Mancha at Almonacid (11 August 1809), assisted in the conquest of Andalusia and defeated Blayney's incompetent landing at Fuengirola in October 1810. He continued to lead IV Corps (in Soult's Army of the South), but was recalled to lead the 2nd Light Cavalry Division of Montbrun's II Cavalry Corps in the Russian campaign, taking over the corps after Montbrun's death. His unfortunate reputation, exemplified by his rough handling at Vinkovo, led to the nickname 'General Surprise'; Marbot described him as brave enough in action, but so careless at reconnaissance that he spent his time in his slippers, reading Italian poetry, even when the enemy was near, so that he was only noted for his mediocrity. He continued to command cavalry in 1813 (wounded at Leipzig) and 1814, notably at Rheims and Arcis-sur-Aube. He accepted the Bourbon restoration but rejoined Napoleon in 1815, but was given only a National Guard command. Retiring from the army, he entered politics, became Minister of Marine (1830), Foreign Minister (1830–2), Minister without Portfolio (1832), ambassador to Naples (1833) and London (1835–40), and upon his retirement in the latter year was appointed a Marshal of France; he was also a leading figure in Paris society. In a notable scandal, his daughter was murdered by her husband, the duc de Praslin, who then poisoned himself in gaol. Sébastiani's brother, Jean André Tiburce Sébastiani (1786–1871) also served in the French Army from 1806, including the Peninsula, Russia and subsequent campaigns; he participated in the Greek War of Independence and as a lieutenant-general commanded the Paris district from 1842, retiring to Corsica after the 1848 revolution.

SECHELLES, Marie-Jean-Hérault de, see HERAULT DE SECHELLES

SEELE, Johann Baptist (1775–1814)

Born in Mörsburg, this artist became court painter and director of the grand-ducal art gallery at Stuttgart in 1804. He produced notable illustrations of Austrian troops in campaign dress in the late 1790s, and in 1813 a series of uniform-prints of the Württemberg Army in conjunction with the engraver L. Ebner.

SEGUR, General Philippe-Paul, comte de (1780–1873)

He was a member of a most distinguished French aristocratic and literary family; his grandfather was Marshal Philippe-Henri, marquis de Ségur (1724–1801), his father Louis-Philippe, comte de Ségur (1753–1830). The latter served in the War of American Independence but gained most fame as a diplomat (notably as minister to Russia), served as a member of the council of state and a senator under Napoleon, was deprived of his offices for supporting Napoleon in 1815, but was reinstated in 1819. He was also a noted writer and historian. Philippe-Henri the Marquis had a distinguished military career, losing an arm at Lauffeld (1747), served as Necker's Minister of War and became a Marshal of France in 1783; imprisoned during the Terror, he received a pension from Napoleon in the year before his death. Of the two sons of Louis-Philippe, Philippe-Paul was the more famous. He enlisted in the French cavalry in 1800 and was soon commissioned, served as ADC to Macdonald and through the influence of Duroc gained a post on Napoleon's staff. In 1805 he was party to the negotiations for Mack's surrender, served in Naples in 1806, was taken prisoner in Poland in 1807 and freed after Tilsit, and wounded at Somosierra, which earned him promotion to colonel. He served with Duroc in 1809 and became comte, and after important diplomatic missions was promoted to *général de brigade* (February 1812). He served in Russia in 1812 and, as a notable author, his best-known work was a history of that campaign (published 1824); its unsympathetic tone with regard to Napoleon led him to fight a duel with Gourgaud, in which Ségur was wounded. He served in the campaigns of 1813 (notably at Leipzig and Hanau) and 1814 (wounded at Rheims), accepted the Bourbon restoration but was retired for rejoining Napoleon in 1815. After the 1830 revolution he was restored to favour, becoming a peer of France and lieutenant-general in 1831, but retired again in 1848. His literary work was extensive; in addition to the history of the 1812 campaign he wrote his memoirs and among other historical works continued the history of France begun by his father. Philippe's brother Octave-Henri-Gabriel de Ségur (1778–1818) also served in the French Army, and while leading a squadron of the 8th Hussars was captured near Vilna at the commencement of the 1812 campaign; his unhappy domestic life led him to drown himself in the Seine in August 1818. His elder son, Eugène, who succeeded his grandfather Louis-Philippe in the peerage in 1830, married Sophie Rostopchine (1799–1894), daughter of the famous governor of Moscow at the time of the 1812 campaign. She attained great fame as a writer of children's books, notably *Malheurs du Sophie* and *Mémoires d'un âne*; their son Louis-Gaston-Adrien (1820–81) became a bishop and wrote a number of religious works, and another son, Anatole-Henri-Philippe (1823–1902) became a councillor of state, his writings including a biography of his grandfather Rostopchin.

Ségur, A. de. *Le Maréchal de Ségur 1724–1801*. Paris, 1895 (contains material on the family in general); Ségur, P. P. de. *An Aide-de-Camp of Napoleon*, trans. H. A. Patchett-Martin. London, 1895 (English edn. of Ségur's memoirs); *History of the Expedition to Russia undertaken by the Emperor Napoleon in the Year 1812*. London, 1825 (English edn. of *Histoire de Napoléon et de la Grande Armée pendant l'année 1812*. Paris, 1824)

SELIM III, Sultan (1762–1808)

The son of Sultan Mustafa III, he succeeded his uncle Abd-ul-Hamid I as Sultan of Turkey in 1789. A capable and energetic ruler, he was determined to implement reforms in the Ottoman Empire and was willing to learn from abroad; but at the time of his accession the empire was engaged in war against Austria and Russia, which only ended in January 1792. Napoleon's expedition to Egypt required another major military effort and temporarily broke the old relationship with France, but the necessary internal reforms instituted by Selim were the cause of even more problems, including revolts in the provinces. The creation of a regular military force (*Nizam-i-jedid*) aroused the hostility of the Janissaries and their revolt caused a temporary halt to reforms. Disputes over Wallachia, Moldavia and Bessarabia in late 1806 led to the empire's declaration of war on Russia (encouraged by France via her ambassador Sébastiani), and the latter helped the repulse of Duckworth's British fleet which attempted to penetrate the Dardanelles. During the war with Russia internal unrest spread, and with the Janissaries again proving hostile, Selim was unable to cope; he attempted to appease them but was deposed and imprisoned, his nephew being placed on the throne as Sultan Mustafa IV (reigned 1807-8). The Treaty of Tilsit suspended hostilities with Russia and a reform-minded supporter, Mustafa Bairakdar, gathered his forces and marched to restore Selim to the throne; however, Selim was strangled before he could be freed, and in vengeance Mustafa IV was killed, Bairakdar being appointed Grand Vizier to the new sultan, Mahmud II (who reigned 1808-39), the sole survivor of the imperial family.

SEMONVILLE, Charles-Louis Huguet, marquis de (1759–1839)

A notable French diplomat, Sémonville came to prominence as French envoy at Genoa (1790-1), and was one of those (with Maret) seized by the Austrians in 1793 while en route to Florence on a mission; he was released only in December 1795 in a prisoner exchange for Louis XVI's daughter. In 1799 he went to the Hague to

cement the Franco–Batavian alliance, and was involved in the diplomacy around Napoleon's second marriage; he became comte in 1808. He was valued equally by the restored Bourbon monarchy, supported Louis XVIII and took no part in the events of Napoleon's return in 1815. He was elevated to marquis in 1819 and, opposing the extremism of Charles X, tried without success to secure that monarch's throne by persuading him to moderate his policy.

SENARMONT, General Alexandre-Antoine Hureau de, baron (1769–1810)

One of the most distinguished artillerymen of the period, Senarmont was born in Strasbourg, the son of an artillery officer. He was educated at the artillery school at Metz and commissioned in the artillery in 1785. He saw considerable active service during the Revolutionary Wars, and in 1800 won great distinction by his conduct in transporting the artillery of the Army of Reserve over the Alps and in handling his guns at Marengo. He served at Austerlitz, became *général de brigade* in 1806 and commander of the Metz school, and in the campaigns of 1806-7 was a corps artillery commander. He won his greatest fame with his celebrated artillery 'charge' at Friedland, which proved that a concentration of artillery (or 'massed battery' fire) was a potent offensive weapon in its own right, as well as serving as a support for the other arms. Ennobled as baron, he was appointed artillery chief of Victor's I Corps in Spain, where he served at Somosierra and became *général de division*. He again employed the massed-battery tactic to good effect at Ocaña, but his career was sadly terminated in October 1810 when he was killed by a shell at Cadiz.

SERURIER, Marshal Jean-Mathieu-Philibert, comte (1742–1819)

JEAN MATHIEU SÉRURIER
(ENGRAVING AFTER J. L. LANEUVILLE)

One of the least well known of Napoleon's Marshals, he spent most of his career as a regimental officer. Born in Laon of middle-class or minor provincial nobility, he entered the militia as an officer in 1755, and having transferred to the regular army spent the next 34 years as a company officer. He served in the Seven Years War (wounded in the jaw at Warburg, which left him scarred), in Portugal (1762) and Corsica (1770-4), and not until 1789 did he become a field officer. Promotion was more rapid thereafter; an experienced and proficient officer, he survived arrest after the Revolution because of his background and suspected royalist sympathies (he was reinstated through the influence of Barras), and at the instigation of the same became *général de brigade* in June 1793, *de division* provisionally in December. For the remainder of his active career he served in Italy, where he proved to be one of the young General Bonaparte's staunchest supporters. Although he served in a subordinate capacity throughout, the victory of Mondovi was attributed to him, and he was entrusted with the conduct of the siege of Mantua. He fell ill with malarial fever while in command at Mantua, shortly before Castiglione, and was invalided home; but early in 1797 was back in command of the investment, defeated Provera's attempted relief at La Favorita, and was accorded the honour of accepting the subsequent surrender of Mantua. He was esteemed universally both as a soldier who combined strict discipline with fairness, and as an upright man with a spotless reputation for integrity, hence the nickname bestowed by his soldiers, 'the Virgin of Italy'. This reputation led to his appointment as Governor of Venice (1797), and he returned to field command in Italy in 1799 under Schérer, in circumstances entirely inauspicious; and was compelled to surrender his command at Verderio (April 1799). Paroled and allowed to return home, he assisted Napoleon in the coup of Brumaire and was rewarded with vice-presidency of the Senate (1802), Governorship of Les Invalides and in 1804 by a Marshalcy, one of four honorary appointments. Comte from 1808, he accepted the Bourbon restora-

tion and was appointed a peer of France, which Napoleon confirmed during the Hundred Days, but for having supported Napoleon in 1815 he was deprived of his rank and appointments, his Marshalcy only being restored in January 1819; he died on the following 21 December. The successes he had enjoyed were more the consequence of integrity and application than military genius, as Napoleon remarked: he 'retained the manners and severity of an old major of infantry, was an honest and trustworthy man; but an unfortunate general',[1] which was perhaps a shade ungenerous.

1. Las Cases, vol. I, p. 189.

Rooney, D. S. 'The Virgin of Italy: Sérurier', in *Napoleon's Marshals*, ed. D. G. Chandler. London, 1987; Tuetey, L. *Un Général de l'Armée d'Italie: Sérurier*. Paris, 1899

SHAW, Corporal John (1789–1815)

Perhaps the best-known 'other rank' in the British Army at the time, he was born in Nottingham and first made his name as a prize-fighter of great distinction. He continued his sport, with

much encouragement, after his enlistment in the 2nd Life Guards in 1807. His pugilistic skill must have been considerable – he employed the 'retreating tactics' of Cribb – and even defeated Molyneux in a bout with gloves. He was regarded as a contender for the championship of England, but sadly the Waterloo campaign intervened. At the battle he was said to have slain a number of Frenchmen, finally lashing out with his helmet after his sword broke, until he collapsed from multiple wounds and, it was reported, crawled away to die from loss of blood upon a dunghill.

Knollys, Major. *Shaw the Life Guardsman*. London, 1885

SHAW (later SHAW KENNEDY), General Sir James (1788–1865)

Born in Kirkcudbrightshire, the son of an officer, James Shaw was educated at the Military College at Marlow and was commissioned in the 43rd Light Infantry in 1805. He served at Copenhagen and in the Corunna campaign, contracting a fever from which he never fully recovered, but returned to the Peninsula, served as regimental adjutant and in 1809 became Craufurd's ADC, suffering a severe wound in the left elbow at Almeida. When recovered, still with Craufurd, he carried the mortally wounded General from the glacis at Ciudad Rodrigo; and cnducted himself with conspicuous bravery at Badajoz, where he was observed at the Santa Maria breach, standing amid the carnage and the enemy's shot, unable to proceed but unwilling to retire, and calmly consulting his watch while remarking that the position could not be carried that night. After service at Salamanca and the retreat from Burgos, he was again stricken by fever and had to go home, embarking again for active service only in 1815,

JOHN SHAW (RIGHT) AT WATERLOO.

when (as a captain) he served as deputy assistant QMG to the 3rd Division in the Waterloo campaign. At the battle he organised the disposition of the division (in chequerboard fashion) to considerable effect, and was rewarded with a brevet majority. He was commandant at Calais during the occupation of France, and for nine years AAG at Manchester at a time of considerable unrest. In 1820 he married Mary Kennedy and upon succeeding to her estates in 1834 took her name, hence 'Shaw Kennedy'; two years later he re-organised and trained the Royal Irish Constabulary, commanded them for two years as Inspector-General, and after ten years in retirement briefly commanded at Liverpool during the Chartist unrest. Major-general from 1846, lieutenant-general in 1854, he held the colonelcy of the 47th Foot from 1854 until his death in May 1865. He is perhaps best known for his writings, including a memorandum on countermeasures to be taken against civil disorder, but most famously for *Notes of the Battle of Waterloo*, London, 1865, which includes an autobiographical notice (pp. 3–46).

SHERBROOKE, General Sir John Coape (1764–1830)

Best known as Wellington's 2i/c for part of the Peninsular War, he was commissioned in the 4th Foot in 1780, and was 2i/c of the 33rd when Arthur Wellesley was CO in The Netherlands. Sherbrooke led the battalion when Wellesley was commanding the brigade, and by his own account it was his actions at Boxtel, rather than Wellesley's, which repelled the French cavalry charge which threatened the position. He went to India with the 33rd, rising to command a brigade, and led the right column at the storming of Seringapatam, but further advancement in India

was curtailed by poor health. Major-general from January 1805, he served in Sicily and was appointed to command the 1st Division of Wellington's Peninsula army from June 1809 to April 1810, replacing Edward Paget as Wellington's 2i/c . A knight of the Bath from September 1809, he returned home for reasons of ill-health in June 1810, but as lieutenant-general (4 June 1811) he was appointed Lieutenant-Governor of Nova Scotia, which position he held during the War of 1812. In 1816 he became Governor and CinC of Canada; the town of Sherbrooke was named after him. Wellington described him as 'a very good officer, but the most passionate man I think I ever knew'; when attending a funeral in Sicily, and being offered a huge candle to carry (intended as an honour and mark of respect), he was so indignant at the gesture that he seized the candle and with it felled the man who had offered it. Wellington also recalled his disagreement with a Portuguese interpreter, Sherbrooke telling the man that he (Sherbrooke) had his hands behind his back, and advised him to make himself scarce before he moved his hands forward, when he intended 'to break every bone in your skin!'[1]

1. Stanhope, pp. 190, 323.

SHERIDAN, Richard Brinsley Butler (1751–1816)

The great playwright also enjoyed a long career in parliament, and is best known as an ally of Charles James Fox and an influential friend of the Prince of Wales. He supported Fox on the question of non-interference in the French Revolution, but later spoke eloquently about the need to defeat Napoleon; he also spoke in parliament in support of strong measures against the Nore mutineers. In 1806 he became Treasurer of the Navy; he succeeded

RICHARD BRINSLEY SHERIDAN (ENGRAVING AFTER REYNOLDS)

Fox as MP for Westminster, but failed to succeed him as leader of his party, lost his seat in 1807, sat briefly for Ilchester but as financial pressures overtook him was unable to afford a seat in 1812.

Moore, T. *Memoirs of the Life of the Rt.Hon. Richard Brinsley Sheridan*. 1858; Morwood, J. *Life and Works of Richard Brinsley Sheridan*. Edinburgh, 1985

SHRAPNEL, Lieutenant-General Sir Henry Scrope (1761–1842)

An officer of the Royal Artillery who served in the 1793 Netherlands campaign, he was the inventor of the artillery projectile known as 'spherical case-shot', a hollow sphere filled with musket-balls and a bursting charge which when correctly fused exploded over the heads of enemy troops. It was something of a British 'secret weapon' during the Napoleonic Wars, first used at Surinam in 1804 and with great effect during the Peninsular War, at Waterloo (where Sir George Wood claimed it helped save the day), and at sea. It came to be called after the name of its inventor, but was only applied officially in 1852 after Shrapnel's son requested the Board of Ordnance that his name be commemorated. The term hrapnel' has since been used – technically incorrect – to describe the flying fragments of shell-casing which are properly styled splinters. From 1804 Shrapnel was assistant inspector of artillery, was a major-general at his retirement in 1825, and became lieutenant-general in 1837. He was notoriously ill-rewarded for his invention, and was aggrieved by his treatment; the Board of Ordnance even forbade the royalty of 6d. per shell which the East India Company wanted to pay him! He died on 13 March 1842; the date 1849 upon the family memorial in the parish church of his native Bradford-upon-Avon was engraved incorrectly.

SIBORNE, Captain William (1797–1849)

He served in the same regiment (the British 9th Foot) as his father, Benjamin Siborn (c.1772–1819; the 'e' was added to the family name by William), who was severely wounded at Nivelle and died from the consequences, though continuing to serve. William is remembered not for his own military career (which continued with staff appointments) but as one of the earliest serious historians of the Waterloo campaign, his study of the battle being published in 1844. It arose from his detailed surveys of the battlefield of Waterloo and from his construction of remarkable and huge representations of the action in model form, the larger now residing in the National Army Museum at Chelsea and the smaller at Dover Castle. His account of the battle, and the disposition of troops on the model, were criticised from a relatively early date, and notably in modern times; but the history was probably no more biased or inaccurate than others of its genre, and if he did not make the fullest use of his sources, he took great

pains in the research, which involved circulating a questionnaire to many surviving participants (extracts of which were published by his son, Major-General Herbert Siborne). While criticism is justified, he did a great service to posterity by eliciting these recollections, and it is most unfortunate that he lost a considerable sum from the immense undertaking of constructing his models, which by any standards are quite remarkable.

Chandler, D. G. 'Captain William Siborne and his Waterloo Models', in *The Road to Waterloo*, ed. A. J. Guy, Stroud and London, 1990, pp. 184–96; Siborne, Major-General H. T. *The Waterloo Letters*. London, 1891; Siborne, Captain W. *History of the War in France and Belgium in 1815*. London, 1844 (the London 1990 reprint is entitled *History of the Waterloo Campaign*)

SIDMOUTH, Viscount, see ADDINGTON

SIEYES, Emmanuel-Joseph (1748–1836)

EMMANUEL SIÈYES
(ENGRAVING BY MAUDUISON)

Born in Fréjus, the Abbé Sieyès entered the church despite his preference for liberal political ideals rather than theology; but

advanced to become vicar-general and chancellor of the diocese of Chartres. His political activity began before the Revolution, when he gained much notoriety with his pamphlet *What is the Third Estate?*, and was elected to the States-General. He became involved with the Jacobin Club but maintained a low profile in the Convention, concentrating upon self-preservation and surviving the internal conflicts and the Terror; he voted for the death of the king. In 1795 he helped draw up the Franco–Batavian treaty, but not approving the constitution which established the Directory, declined to serve as a Director himself; but after a diplomatic mission to Berlin in 1798 (which failed to secure a Franco–Prussian alliance) his fame was such that he was elected a Director in place of Rewbell in May 1799. Even though a member, he disapproved of the system and worked for its replacement by a system not unlike the Consulate, which did come about. At first he courted Joubert to be the military member of the planned ruling body, but after his death turned to Napoleon Bonaparte instead. Having worked towards the coup of Brumaire, his plan for what should follow was altered radically by Napoleon, and he retired from the post of consul which he had occupied since the coup. He became a senator, but played little part in subsequent political affairs, having become considerably wealthy (Napoleon claimed that he appropriated 600,000 francs from the sum set aside for retiring Directors). As a regicide, he left France at the Bourbon restoration, but returned in 1830. Napoleon said of him, 'Sieyès was always attached to me, and I never had any cause to complain of him. He was probably vexed to find that I opposed his metaphysical ideas; but he was at length convinced that it was necessary for France to have a ruler, and he preferred me to any other. Sieyès was, after all, an honest and a very clever man; he did much for the Revolution.'[1]

1. Las Cases, vol. III, pp. 391–2.

Neton, A. *Sieyès d'après Documents Inédits*. Paris, 1900

SINCLAIR, Colonel Sir John, of Ulbster, Bt. (1754–1835)

One of the leading financial and agricultural experts of the period, Sir John Sinclair of Ulbster (Co. Caithness), who received a baronetcy in 1780, was among the many distinguished in other fields whose careers involved military affairs at the time of the Revolutionary and Napoleonic Wars. A Member of Parliament 1780–1811 (with few interruptions), he is perhaps best known for supervising the *Statistical Account of Scotland* (1791–9), but also achieved fame as an influential financier, economist and agriculturalist (first President of the Board of Agriculture). In 1794 he raised and commanded the Rothsay & Caithness Fencibles (disbanded 1802), and among his writings were articles on military subjects, including *Hints Respecting the State of the Camp at Aberdeen*, and *Cursory Observations on the Military System of Great Britain*, the latter including a very sensible plea for the creation of light infantry. Sinclair believed that trews, not the kilt, was the real ancient dress of the Highlanders and clothed his regiment accordingly as shown in his famous portrait by Raeburn. He maintained his interest in military affairs, visited Waterloo shortly after the battle and edited the English edition of Müffling's history of the campaign.

Mitchison, R. *Agricultural Sir John*. 1962

SMITH, Lieutenant-Colonel Charles Hamilton (1776–1859)

Born in Flanders of a Protestant family originally named Smet, he was educated in England and at the Austrian artillery and engineer school at Louvain. Having served as a volunteer in the British 8th Light Dragoons in 1794, he was commissioned lieutenant in December 1797; he served with Hompesch's hussars, with the 60th in the West Indies, as an engineer in Jamaica and as Deputy Quartermaster-General in the Walcheren expedition. A major from December 1813, he served in The Netherlands 1813–14 and in 1816 undertook an intelligence mission in North America, resulting in a plan for the defence of Canada. He went on half-pay (15th Foot) in October 1821, became brevet lieutenant-colonel in July 1830 and a Knight of Hanover in the same year. His fame, however, is as an artist; a prolific sketcher of natural history and of historical and military costumes, he is best known for his *Costume of the Army of the British Empire*, a series of plates aquatinted by J. C. Stadler and published by Colnaghi of London in 1812–15, depicting the 1812 regulation uniforms, the most famous study of the subject. Smith wrote other works – including the military part of William Coxe's *Memoirs of the Duke of Marlborough* (London 1818–19) – and produced a vast number of illustrations, many of which he deposited at the Athenaeum in Plymouth, where he settled, and which were destroyed in an air raid in 1941, although others survive, notably in the Victoria & Albert Museum and the Houghton Library at Harvard. He is often listed as if his surname were 'Hamilton Smith', but in the *Army List* he appears as 'C. H. Smith'.

Chartrand, R. 'The United States Forces of 1812–1816 as drawn by Charles Hamilton Smith, Officer and Spy', in *Military Collector & Historian*, 1983, vol. XXXV, pp. 142–50; Sumner, Revd. P. 'Hamilton Smith's Drawings', in *Journal of the Society for Army Historical Research*, 1941, vol. XX, pp. 85–92

SMITH, Lieutenant-General Sir Henry George Wakelyn, Bt. (1787–1860)

SIR HARRY SMITH
(ENGRAVING BY J. W. EDWARDS)

'Harry' Smith (the name he used throughout his life) achieved his greatest fame in India and South Africa, but was also one of the best-known members of the British Army in the Peninsula. The son of a Whittlesey surgeon, he was commissioned in the 95th Rifles in 1805, served in the South American expedition and in the Peninsula from 1808 until the end of the war. He was shot through the ankle at the Coa, and trouble with the wound led to a long staff career, as aide and brigade-major with the Light Division, though such duties never took him out of danger. His most famous exploit was at Badajoz when, having taken part in the storming of the breaches, he was resting with his friend Kincaid when they were approached by two Spanish ladies, seeking protection from the sack of the city. Smith fell hopelessly in love with the younger of the two, who was barely 14 years old, and married her. Juana Maria de los

Dolores de Léon (1798–1872) was the pillar of his life from that moment, accompanying him throughout his campaigning; for her beauty, courage and kindly nature she became adored throughout the Peninsular army, and theirs is one of the most famous true love-stories of the era. Smith next served in the War of 1812, including Bladensburg and New Orleans, and at Waterloo was brigade-major to Sir John Lambert. Breveted lieutenant-colonel after Waterloo, he became deputy QMG at the Cape in 1828, commanded a division in the Sixth Frontier War, served with great distinction in the First Sikh War (winning the battle of Aliwal when in independent command, for which he received a baronetcy), returned to the Cape as Governor 1847–52, crushed the Orange River rebellion at Boomplaats, but was recalled before the conclusion of the Eighth Frontier War. Major-general from November 1846, lieutenant-general from June 1854, his subsequent service was at home, and he retired in 1859. Three towns were named for him, in South Africa: Aliwal North, Harrismith and, most famously, Ladysmith, after his devoted Juana. His brothers also served in the 95th: Thomas Lawrence Smith (d.1877), who served in the Peninsula and was adjutant of the 2nd Battalion at Waterloo, and Charles Smith (d.1854), a volunteer with the 1st Battalion at Waterloo.

Harington, A. L. *Sir Harry Smith, Blundering Hero*. Cape Town, 1980; Lehmann, J. H. *Remember you are an Englishman: A Biography of Sir Harry Smith*. London, 1977; Moore Smith, G. C. (ed.). *The Autobiography of Sir Harry Smith*. London, 1902

SMITH, Admiral Sir William Sidney (1764–1840)

A mercurial and colourful character, he was the son of an officer

SIR WILLIAM SIDNEY SMITH
(ENGRAVING AFTER J. OPIE)

and entered the Royal Navy in 1777; he achieved rapid promotion to captain (October 1782) after much hard service in the War of American Independence. After the end of hostilities he spent two years in France, was naval adviser to the King of Sweden (1790–2) which earned him a Swedish knighthood, then went in a similar capacity to Turkey, and after the outbreak of the French war served at Toulon while officially on half-pay. While serving in the Channel he was captured when attempting to rescue a lugger at Le Havre (19 April 1796) and imprisoned in the Temple at Paris. He escaped by means of a forged document and made his way back to England, was appointed to command HMS *Tigre* and was sent to the Mediterranean. Ever a man to boost his own importance, he took upon himself powers which were not rightfully his, and with the engineer Louis Phélipeaux, who had helped him escape from gaol, organised and inspired the defence of Acre, which frustrated Napoleon's schemes. He was showered with rewards by the Ottoman Empire and received an annuity from the British; but the convention of El-Arish, which he concluded by convincing Kléber that he had plenipotentiary

powers, was not surprisingly disowned by his CinC. Wounded at Aboukir leading the naval detachment under Abercromby, he returned home, was elected MP for Rochester, and as rear-admiral from November 1805 subsequently returned to the Mediterranean. There he performed useful service (including the capture of Capri and against the Turks under Duckworth in 1807), but was probably responsible for the failure to relieve Gaeta. He was instrumental in embarking the Portuguese royal family for South America, was CinC in South American waters until he quarrelled with the British minister at Rio, became vice-admiral in July 1810 and in the following year returned to the Mediterranean as 2i/c to Pellew. His active service ended in 1814; in the following year he received a KCB, was present as a spectator in the Waterloo campaign, and became an admiral in 1821. His final years were spent in Paris, where he died. In his extraordinary career he came into conflict with a number of his contemporaries, his vanity, boasting and self-belief not being well-received. He did not get on with Nelson, Wellington thought that of all people of reputation he had met, Smith deserved his fame least, being 'silly' and a 'vapourizer'; and Napoleon, acknowledging the damage Smith had done him at Acre, described him as 'a chatterer and an intriguer, and tries only to deceive',[1] though admitted later than his opinion of Smith had risen. Despite his unfortunate manner, however, Smith remained one of the most daring and colourful (if independent) naval officers of the period. He should not, of course, be confused with his contemporary, the Revd. Sydney Smith (1771–1845), the writer and wit.

1. Napoleon, 19 May 1806, vol. I, p. 115.

Barrow, J. *The Life and Correspondence of Admiral Sir William Sidney Smith*. London, 1848; Howard, E. *Memoirs of Admiral Sir Sidney Smith*. London, 1839; Pocock, T. *A Thirst for Glory*. London, 1996; Russell of Liverpool, Lord. *Knight of the Sword: Life and Letters of Sir Sidney Smith*. London, 1964; Shankland, P. *Beware of Heroes: Admiral Sir Sidney Smith's War against Napoleon*. London, 1975

SMYTH, General Alexander (1765–1830)

A Virginian of Irish origin, he was one of the least effective US generals of the War of 1812. A member of the Virginia legislature, he was colonel of the Rifle Regiment from July 1808, and was inspector general when appointed deputy to Van Rensselaer in 1812. Evidently resentful of being subordinated to a northern militia general, he was somewhat impertinent towards Van Rensselaer, and having succeeded him in command of the Niagara frontier in late October 1812 issued pompous proclamations critical of his predecessor and of Hull, which caused some ridicule. His own attempt at an offensive against Canada in late November 1812 was undermined by mistrust of Smyth among his subordinates and by his own indecision, and it was abandoned; he was even accused of treachery, fired at by his own men, and fought a bloodless duel with General Peter Porter. Early in 1813 Smyth was removed from the Army List, and his petition to Congress for his reinstatement was ignored. Although vilified for his conduct, he was subsequently elected to Congress. He should not be confused with Brigadier General Thomas A. Smith, a regular officer promoted to that rank on 24 January 1814, who served on the Canadian border and was retained as colonel of the

Rifle Regiment after the war; he resigned shortly before his death in 1818.

SOMERSET, Fitzroy, see RAGLAN

SOMERSET, General Lord Robert Edward Henry (1776–1842)

LORD EDWARD SOMERSET

The fourth son of Henry, 5th Duke of Beaufort, and elder brother of Fitzroy Somerset, Lord Edward Somerset (as he was known) joined the 15th Light Dragoons in 1793 and served as ADC to the Duke of York in The Netherlands. He received command of the 4th Dragoons in 1801 and led them in the Peninsula, including Talavera, Busaco and Salamanca, and from July 1812 commanded the hussar brigade, becoming major-general in June 1813. At Waterloo he was especially distinguished in command of the 1st Cavalry Brigade (Household), subsequently commanding the British cavalry during the occupation of France, and became general in 1841. He was MP for Monmouth Boroughs (1799–1802), Gloucestershire (1802–31) and Cirencester (1834–7). His ADC at Waterloo, Lieutenant (later Lieutenant-General Sir) Henry Somerset (1794–1862) of the 18th Hussars,

was the nephew both of Lord Edward and of his wife Louisa, daughter of 2nd Viscount Courtney, whose sister was Henry Somerset's mother.

SOUHAM, General Joseph, comte (1760–1837)

Born in Loubersac, he served in the ranks from 1782, but achieved rapid promotion after the Revolution. Elected to command a volunteer battalion in 1792, by September 1793 he was *général de division*. He was distinguished in The Netherlands, notably at Tourcoing, but fell under suspicion from 1799 for suspected royalist sympathies; having served closely under Moreau, after that general's disgrace he was arrested (1804) and received no further employment until 1807. His rehabilitation began with service in Italy and, more importantly, in the Peninsula. He commanded the 1st Division of Gouvion Saint-Cyr's VII Corps, including at the siege of Gerona, and defeated O'Donnell at Vich (February 1810) where he was wounded severely in the head, and for which he was made comte. After service in Italy and Germany he returned to the Peninsula in summer 1811 in command of a new division for the Army of Portugal; he was on leave in France at the time of Salamanca, and on his return succeeded Clausel in command of the army (September 1812), who had commanded temporarily since Marmont's injury. Souham was regarded as having been overcautious in his operations and in November 1812 was superseded, so in 1813 served on the German front, leading a division of Ney's III Corps. He won the action at Weissenfels, served at Lützen, Bautzen and Leipzig, where he was severely wounded leading III Corps. He recovered to serve at the defence of Paris in 1814, but accepted the Bourbon restoration nd remained loyal to them in 315; after the second restoration e held a number of appoint- nents, including Governorship of trasbourg, and retired in 1832.

OULT, Marshal (Nicolas) ean-de-Dieu, duc de Dalmatie (769–1851)

NICOLAS JEAN-DE-DIEU SOULT
ENGRAVING BY E. FINDON AFTER H. GREVEDON)

ean-de-Dieu Soult – commonly alled Nicolas though it was not his baptismal name – vies with Davout and perhaps Massena as Napoleon's most capable Marshal. Born in St. Amans-la-Bastide, the on of a notary, he enlisted in 1785 fter his father's death. Commis- ioned in 1792, he served with distinction at Fleurus, became *énéral de brigade* in October 794, *de division* in 1799 after ervice in Germany, then served under Massena in Switzerland nd was wounded and captured at Monte Creto during a foray from he besieged Genoa (1800). He erved in Naples after gaining his reedom, and although having erved under Moreau (whose ubordinates Napoleon generally disliked) he was named as one of he commanders of the Consular Guard, and was among the first reation of the Marshalate in 1804. Commanding IV Corps he was greatly distinguished at Austerlitz,

led it at Jena, fought at Eylau but missed Friedland while occupied by the taking of Königsberg. In June 1808 he became Duke of Dalmatia, and was sent to Spain, initially in command of II Corps. He was defeated by Moore at Corunna and outmanoeuvred by Wellesley at Oporto, but gained a victory at Ocaña. His career in the Peninsula, however, did not match his earlier successes; his reputa- tion was damaged by rumours that he had planned to make himself king of Portugal, and though enjoying considerable power as Joseph Bonaparte's senior commander and leader of the Army of the South, relations with his fellows deteriorated very badly, resulting in lack of co-oper- ation. Although in 1810 he reduced Andalusia (except for Cadiz), his attempt to relieve Badajoz resulted in defeat at Albuera, a battle which in all prob- ability he should have won. Finally, such were the internal conflicts that Soult was recalled from Spain at Joseph's request, and in 1813 he commanded IV Corps at Lützen and Bautzen; but the deteriorating situation in Spain led to his recall with unprecedented powers, French forces (but for Suchet's army) being unified at last under a single commander. By then the situation was not salvageable, but Soult performed with great distinction in the most difficult of circum- stances, and though he was defeated several times by Wellington, the campaign in defence of the French frontier probably showed his military talents to their best advantage. The actions in the Pyrenees, Nivelle, Nive, Orthez and Toulouse provided a stern test for his oppo- nents and led William Napier to comment: 'I take this opportunity to declare that respect which I believe every British officer who has had the honour to serve

against him feels for his military talents. By those talents the French cause in Spain was long upheld, and after the battle of Salamanca, if his counsel had been followed by the intrusive monarch, the fate of the war might have been changed.'[1] Soult accepted the Bourbon restoration and became Minister of War in 1814; but rejoined Napoleon in 1815 and served as chief of staff in the Waterloo campaign, surely a waste of his talents as a field commander. At the second restoration he was proscribed and emigrated to Germany, but returned in 1819, and his Marshalcy was restored in 1820. Although appointed a peer of France in 1827, not until after the 1830 revolution did he again become prominent: Minister of War 1830–4 and 1840–4, and ambassador to London for the coronation of Queen Victoria. He retired from active duty in September 1847, and was appointed to the rank of Marshal- General of France, previously accorded only to Turenne, Saxe and Villars. Whether this was entirely justified is debatable, though he was a commander of great skill; as Napoleon declared: 'I account you the ablest tactician in the empire.'[2] Wellington remarked that although he was most skilful in bringing his troops up to the battlefield, he was not quite sure how to use them, and told Bunbury that 'Soult is a very able man – excellent as an *admin- istrateur*; but in the field he is apt to doubt and hesitate, and to lose the proper moment for acting'; and told Pakenham that 'Master Soult is a very clever fellow, but now he will take time to consider and look about him ...'[3] Soult's reputation has also suffered from his ambition, liking for plunder and unwillingness at times to co- operate, but he remains one of the great commanders of the era, revered by the nation and the army. From his dukedom he was known to the British as 'the Duke of Damnation' or 'Old Salt'.

1. Napier, W., vol. I, p. viii. 2. Anon., pp. 406–7. 3. Bunbury, *Memoirs*, pp. 295–6.

Griffith, P. 'King Nicolas: Soult', in *Napoleon's Marshals*, ed. D. G. Chandler. London, 1987; Grozelier, A. *Le Maréchal Soult*. Castries, 1851; Hayman, Sir Peter. *Soult: Napoleon's Maligned Marshal*. London, 1990; Soult, Marshal. *Mémoires du Maréchal-Général Soult*, ed. N. H. Soult (Napoléon-Hector, the Marshal's son). Paris, 1854

SOULT, General Pierre-Benoît, baron (1770–1839)

This younger brother of the Marshal served with him for much of his career and owed him his advancement. Enlisting in 1788, he served as his brother's unofficial ADC from January 1794, but was commissioned only in April 1796. Taken prisoner in Switzerland, then exchanged, he was again captured with his brother in 1800. In 1805 he was in the Army of Italy (with Mermet's dragoons), served at Jena and Eylau and was wounded at Heilsberg; he became *général de brigade* in July 1807. His progress owed more to his brother's successes than to any great natural talent for command; he led the light cavalry of his brother's II Corps in Spain, was wounded in the leg at Busaco and served at Sabugal. In February 1812 he took over the 3rd Cavalry Division of the Army of the South, was wounded at Alba de Tormes, then took command of a dragoon division until in March 1813 he was promoted to *général de division* and given command of the Army of the South's light cavalry, despite Joseph Bonaparte's suggestion that he was so unskilled that Marshal Soult was loath to let

him operate without close supervision. Pierre continued in his command after his brother's recall, and served under him again in the last stage of the war; the Marshal had to blame him for the loss of the bridge at Croix d'Orade near Toulouse. He accepted the Bourbon restoration and was employed by them, but returned to Napoleon in 1815 even though his loyalty was considered questionable, and during the Waterloo campaign he commanded the 4th Division of I Cavalry Corps. Unemployed thereafter, he retired officially in 1825 but returned after the 1830 revolution, occupying some staff positions until 1836.

SPENCER, General Sir Brent (1760–1828)

Best known as Wellington's deputy for part of the Peninsular War, he was commissioned in 1778 and rose to lieutenant-colonel in 1794. He was distinguished in the West Indies, notably at San Domingo in 1794 (though later enjoyed less success in that troubled island), and served in the expeditions to North Holland (1799), Egypt, and (as major-general from January 1805) Denmark. He was Wellington's 2i/c at Rolica and Vimeiro, having arrived from Andalusia with his division to support Wellington; a KB from April 1809, he returned to the Peninsula and commanded the 1st Division from June 1810 to July 1811. He went home ostensibly on health grounds, but actually was resentful of Graham's appointment as commander of Wellington's left wing, instead of himself. Wellington was not sorry to see him go; though coolness personified under fire, he was regarded (by Wellington and others) as unfit for the role of 2i/c, unable to be depended upon from the fickleness of his opinions and lack of resolution. Wellington

described him as 'exceeding puzzle-headed' and he apparent had difficulty with names, refering, for example, to the Tagus 'the Thames'. (Wellington's confidential assessment of him is to b found in Oman's *History of th Peninsular War*, vol. IV, p. 552 Lieutenant-general from Jun 1811 and general in 1825, he wa MP for Sligo 1815–18.

SPERANSKI, Mikhail Mikhailovich, Count (1772–1839)

Mikhail Speranski rose to grea eminence in the Russian goverr ment from a relatively humbl origin, the son of a village pries An intellectual of the highes order, he accompanied Alexande I to Erfurt where he negotiate with Napoleon who was muc impressed by him. He was largel the architect of Alexander' internal reforms, especially i matters of local government, an as a personal friend of the Tsa became in effect his chief ministe in the 1809–12 period. Th reforms, and the policy wit regard to relations with France attracted much criticism, an both Speranski and his maste attracted unpopularity; anc having unsettled the Tsar by hi proposals to reform freemasonr in Russia, he was used as some thing of a scapegoat and dismisse in March 1812. Although re instated in 1816, becomin Governor-General of Siberia, h never recovered his previou influence.

Raeff, M. *Michael Speransk Statesman of Imperial Russia*. Th Hague, 1957

STADION, Johann Philipp Karl Joseph, Count (1763–1824)

One of the leading Austria statesmen of the era, he entere the diplomatic service in 1787 serving as ambassador to Londo 1790–3. In 1800 he went as envoy t

JOHANN PHILIPP STADION
(ENGRAVING BY FLEISCHMANN AFTER J. ENDER)

the Prussian court, where he failed to persuade that nation to re-enter the conflict against France, and in 1803 was succeeded by Metternich. Stadion was transferred to the embassy at St. Petersburg, where he negotiated the convention between Russia and Austria for joint action against Napoleon. Early in 1806 he was recalled to become Foreign Minister, and in his vital position was part of the 'war faction' which prepared for yet another conflict against France. An advocate of both internal reform and of a crusade against France, he supported the 1809 war and resigned upon Austria's defeat. In 1813 he was recalled as envoy to Austria's allies, notably to the Russo–Prussian military headquarters, and as Metternich's deputy chaired the Châtillon conference. On Austria's behalf he signed the Treaty of Fontainebleau, attended the Congress of Vienna, and then as Finance Minister worked hard to re-organise the empire's economy.

STAEL, Anne-Louise-Germaine, née Necker, baronne de Staël–Holstein (1766–1817

One of the great figures of literary and society life of the period, she was the daughter of the Bourbon Finance Minister, Jacques Necker, and had already established herself as a society figure and author before her brief and unsuccessful marriage to the Swedish diplomat Eric Magnus, Baron Staël–Holstein, which took place in January 1786, and from which her universally familiar title 'Madame de Staël' was taken. An acknowledged literary personality from 1788 (her earlier work had been published anonymously), she became known as a hostess around whom political moderates gathered, though she also resided for a time in Surrey and at the family's Swiss estate at Coppet, which she was later to make famous by her residence there. Returning to Paris after the fall of Robespierre, her salon assumed some political importance; she enjoyed relationships with both Narbonne and Benjamin Constant, and a considerable feud developed between her and Napoleon, with whose rule she had become disillusioned. Her husband died in 1802 (they had separated formally in 1797) and also in 1802 her literary credentials were established fully by the publication of her novel *Delphine*. Forbidden by Napoleon to reside within forty leagues of Paris, she travelled in Germany and Austria, maintaining Coppet as her base. Her most famous work, *Corinne*, was published in 1807, but literary distinction exerted no influence upon Napoleon; he condemned her subsequent book, *De l'Allemagne*, and exiled her from France. She went to Coppet, lived with and married a French hussar officer of Swiss extraction, Albert de Rocca, who had been wounded in the Peninsular War (and who wrote an account of his experiences in Spain), and finally escaped from Napoleon's influence by returning to England, where she was lionised in the season of 1813. She returned to Paris after the Restoration, in 1815 went to Italy in an attempt to cure de Rocca's consumption, returned to Coppet and finally to Paris, where increasing ill-health ended in her death in July 1817; de Rocca survived her by barely six months. She had three children by the Baron: Auguste-Louis, baron de Staël, who edited her complete works (Paris 1820–1) and died in 1827; Albert, the second son, who entered the Swedish Army and was killed in a duel arising from gambling; and Albertine, who married Victor, duc de Broglie in February 1816, and was thus the wife and mother of distinguished statesmen. A woman of great intelligence, Madame de Staël was one of the leading cultural figures of her day. Although never a great beauty, she fascinated many whom she encountered: Byron was impressed by her work but less by her personality, but Wellington, a warm friend, described he as 'a most agreeable woman, if you only *kept her light*, and away from politics. But that was not easy. She was always trying to come to matters of State. I have said to her more than once: "*Je déteste parler politique*," and she answered, "*Parler politique pour moi c'est vivre*."[1]

1. Stanhope, p. 218.

Herold, J. C. *Mistress to an Age: A Life of Madame de Staël*. New York, 1958; Levaillant, M. *The Passionate Exiles: Madame de Staël and Madame Récamier*, trans. M. Barnes. London, 1958; Staël, Madame de. *Oeuvres Complètes de Madame la Baronne de Staël*, ed. A. L. G., baron de Staël–Holstein. Paris, 1820–1; Wilson, R. M. *Germaine de Staël, the Woman of Affairs*. London, 1931

STEIN, Heinrich Friedrich Karl, Freiherr (1757–1831)

One of the most important Prussian personalities of the period, he was born near Nassau,

HEINRICH FRIEDRICH KARL VON STEIN
(LITHOGRAPH AFTER VON HENNE)

the ninth child of Karl Philipp, Freiherr von Stein, of an old and aristocratic family. He studied in Hanover (becoming an admirer of Great Britain and her system of politics and government), and though intended for the law or imperial civil service, entered the Prussian civil service instead, arising from his admiration for Frederick the Great. His success from 1787 in important posts involving commerce, mining, internal navigation, administration and from 1796 presidency of the Westphalian chamber of trade gained him a considerable reputation and led in 1804 to his appointment as Minister of Finance. An opponent of cooperation with France, he declined the offer of the foreign ministry after Jena, and was dismissed after pressing the case for Hardenberg in too outspoken terms. After Tilsit, however, the king relented and made Stein virtually chief minister, whereupon he embarked upon sweeping reforms which transformed not only the ruined economy but also society; the abolition of serfdom and other restrictions altered the class system radically, municipal reform transformed local government, and he assisted Scharnhorst in military reforms. So

fundamental were the improvements which he instituted that he might be regarded as the civil counterpart of the army reformers; but he was so openly hostile to France that Napoleon demanded his dismissal, branded him an enemy of France and the Confederation of the Rhine and confiscated his property in the latter region. In January 1809 Stein fled from Berlin and lived for three years in Austria, then went to Russia to assist and encourage the Tsar in his resistance to Napoleon. Having assisted in the construction of the coalition against France, in 1813 he was appointed by the Allies as administrator of the liberated territories, and although he was regarded as a great German patriot, his relations were closer with the Tsar than with Frederick William III. His vision of a powerful and united Germany, administered on constitutional lines, was frustrated at the Congress of Vienna, and he retired from public life, disillusioned by the postponement of the representative system of government which had been promised by Frederick William. In retirement he devoted most of his time to the study and encouragement of history. His wife Wilhelmine, whom he married in June 1793, was the daughter of Field Marshal Count Johann von Wallmoden–Gimborn, a natural son of King George II of Great Britain. Although Stein's ideas of a strong federal Germany governed by a liberal system of politics was unfulfilled, and although the reforms he instituted in Prussia were assisted by others, his influence was immense.

Grunwal, C. de. *Baron Stein: Enemy of Napoleon*. London, 1940; Seeley, Sir John. *The Life and Times of Stein*. Cambridge, 1878

STENDHAL, see BEYLE

STEWART, Rear Admiral Charles (1778–1869)

Born in Philadelphia of an Irish family, he joined the US Navy as lieutenant from the merchant trade in 1800, served in the war against Tripoli and became captain in 1806. He rejoined the merchant service in 1808 but returned to the Navy in 1812, commanded the USS *Constellation* and succeeded Bainbridge as commander of USS *Constitution*. His greatest success occurred on 22 February 1815 when he captured the British ships HMS *Levant* and *Cyane* (22 and 20 guns respectively) off Cape St. Vincent, for which he received a gold medal from Congress. He continued to serve in the Navy, retiring only in 1855, and became a rear admiral in 1862. His daughter Delia married John Henry Parnell; her son Charles Stewart Parnell (1846–91), the famous Irish politician, was given his first names from his distinguished grandfather.

STEWART, General Charles William (Vane), 3rd Marquess of Londonderry (1778–1854)

CHARLES STEWART, 3RD MARQUESS OF LONDONDERRY (ENGRAVING BY W. J. COLLS AFTER LAWRENCE)

Half-brother to Viscount Castlereagh (their father, the 1st

Marquess of Londonderry, having married Frances, the eldest daughter of 1st Earl Camden in 1775, some five years after the death of his first wife), he joined the army and served in The Netherlands, the Irish rebellion, in the North Holland and Corunna campaigns, but was most distinguished as Wellington's adjutant-general 1809–13. He was a valuable staff officer, but having been a cavalryman was too eager to get into the fighting, even though (as Wellington reported) he was deficient in both sight and hearing, which prevented him from fully comprehending what was going on around him. In January 1813 Wellington had to write to him that 'although it might be more agreeable to you to take a gallop with the Hussars, I think you had better return to your office';[1] and on another occasion he burst into tears as he was being scolded by Wellington. Stewart was then sent by his brother as British representative to the Allied headquarters in Europe, where he was never afraid to speak his mind, even to the commanders-in-chief, and gained a reputation for eccentric behaviour; and also became involved in the fighting as well as the diplomatic side of his duty. In 1814 he was ennobled as Baron Stewart of Stewart's Court and Ballylawn (Co. Donegal), and as ambassador to Vienna assisted his brother in the Congress. He succeeded his brother as 3rd Marquess of Londonderry in 1822, having adopted the name of Vane from his second wife's family in 1819. He was the author of *Narrative of the Peninsular War from 1808 to 1813*, London 1828, and *Narrative of the War in Germany and France in 1813 and 1814*, London, 1830.

1. Wellington, vol. X, p. 19.

Alison, A. *Lives of Lord Castlereagh and Sir Charles Stewart, Second and Third Marquesses of Londonderry*. Edinburgh, 1861

STEWART, Lieutenant-General Sir William (1774–1827)

Fourth son of John, 7th Earl of Galloway, he was commissioned in 1786, was wounded in the West Indies in 1794, served on the staff in the Quiberon expedition and after duty in San Domingo obtained leave to serve with the Allies in 1799, being present at the Battle of Zurich. Returning to duty, he was instrumental (with Coote Manningham) in the formation of the first regular rifle corps in British service, commanding them at Ferrol (wounded) and Copenhagen; his friendship with Nelson in the latter campaign led him to christen his son Horatio (1806–35, a captain in the Rifle Brigade). In December 1806 Stewart led a brigade in Sicily, served in the Egyptian expedition, and as major-general from April 1808, went to the Peninsula in 1810; he was present at Busaco in an unofficial capacity, and commanded a brigade of the 2nd Division, then the division itself, from August 1810. His impetuosity was held to be partially responsible for the near-destruction of his division at Albuera, where he was wounded, and he went home to recuperate. He returned in November 1812 to lead the 1st Division, transferring to the 2nd in March 1813, commanding it until the end of the war; he was wounded again in the Pyrenees. His health undermined by hard service, he saw no further active duty, and in 1816 resigned the parliamentary seat (Wigtonshire) which he had held since 1796. Popular with his command, he was nicknamed 'Auld Grog Willie' from his issue of extra allowances of rum. He was a superb battalion commander, full of good intentions, but as Wellington reported in 1812, he was incapable of following orders and needed supervision, as apparently confirmed by his brave but unimpressive performance at Albuera and Maya. His brother George, 8th Earl of Galloway (1768–1834), rose to the rank of admiral.

STOFFLET, General Jean-Nicolas (1751–96)

The grandson of a German settled in Lorraine, he enlisted in the French Army in 1770, served for eight years and then became gamekeeper to one of his officers, comte de Maulévrier (who, it was said, had also been impressed by Stofflet's sister). In the Vendée rising, he became a leader of the royalist party, and demonstrated a natural talent for command. He became one of the leaders of the Army of Anjou and Haut-Poitou, and was greatly distinguished in action. Following the death of Cathelineau he was perhaps the obvious candidate as overall commander, but his humble and foreign background and dominating character might have proved difficult for his aristocratic comrades to accept, so d'Elbée was appointed instead. The same strictures applied after d'Elbée was wounded, even though Stofflet was promoted to the rank of major-general. Despite his efforts, Vendéen reverses and divisions in their command (Stofflet proclaimed Charette a traitor and put him under sentence of death) in May 1795 forced him to accept the terms of the treaty of La Jaunaye. However, at the instigation of royalist agents he took up arms again (December 1795), but was betrayed, seized and shot at Angers in February 1796; his last words were '*Vive la réligion! Vive le Roi!*' Madame La Rochejaquelein described him as 'A large and muscular man, forty years of age. The soldiers did not like him, because he was harsh and absolutely brutal, but they obeyed him better than any other officer ... He was active, intelligent, and brave, and the generals had great confidence in him ... he was devoted to the cause without thinking of himself'; but later, she wrote that he gained a reputation for 'selfishness, vanity and ambition. That prudence, judgment, and talent, he had shewn to attain his end, forsook him entirely afterwards.'[1]

1. La Rochejaquelein, pp. 112–13, 484.

STRACHAN, Admiral Sir Richard John, Bt. (1760–1828)

The 4th Baronet Strachan is known for two important actions, one conspicuously more successful than the other. Commanding a small squadron, as captain of HMS *Caesar*, on 4 November 1805 he captured four French ships-of-the-line (*Duguay-Trouin*, *Formidable*, *Mont Blanc* and *Scipion*) commanded by Admiral Dumanoir, which had escaped from Trafalgar. For this success he was much celebrated, awarded the Order of the Bath and a pension (he was already a hereditary baronet), but the promotion to rear-admiral which followed immediately was in the ordinary course of seniority. No such success attended his command of the naval forces in the expedition to Walcheren; his relations and co-operation with Chatham, the army commander, were not good, and deteriorated as the campaign progressed. The whole unsuccessful enterprise prompted the famous anonymous rhyme:

'Great Chatham with his sabre
    drawn
Stood waiting for Sir Richard
    Strachan;
Sir Richard, longing to be at 'em,
Stood waiting for the Earl of
    Chatham'.

A brave and energetic man, he was also somewhat impulsive; 'headstrong in his zeal' was how William Hotham described him.[1]

1. Fortescue, vol. VII, p. 57.

STRAFFORD, Earl of, see BYNG

STRANGWAYS, Brigadier-General Thomas Fox (1790–1854)

One of the most famous officers of the Royal Artillery, he was a nephew of Henry, 2nd Earl of Ilchester (1747–1802), and came to prominence when he succeeded to command of the rocket troop after the death of its commander, Richard Bogue, at Leipzig. He was rewarded for his conduct by a Russian knighthood of the Order of St. Anne, bestowed by the Tsar. He served in Whinyates' rocket troop at Waterloo, and was severely wounded. As brigadier-general he was killed at Inkerman; with great irony, it was said that he was wearing his Russian order at the time of his death at the hands of the nation which had so honoured him.

STRATFORD DE REDCLIFFE, Stratford Canning, Viscount (1786–1880)

Ennobled in 1852, he was one of the leading British diplomats of the mid 19th century, and is especially associated with the Ottoman Empire. Cousin of George Canning, his significance during the Napoleonic Wars was founded upon his appointment in 1808 as first secretary, later *chargé d'affaires*, at the British embassy at Constantinople, where he was allowed to operate entirely at his own discretion following the transfer to Vienna of the ambassador, Robert Adair, in 1810. He was successful in dissuading the Turks from pursuing close relations with France (using a copy of Napoleon's plans which envisaged the partition of the empire), and

STRATFORD CANNING, VISCOUNT
STRATFORD DE REDCLIFFE

was instrumental in the negotiation of the Treaty of Bucharest (May 1812) which brought peace between Turkey and Russia, allowing the latter to concentrate its military resources against Napoleon for the 1812 campaign. Canning left Constantinople in July 1812, but returned as ambassador in 1824 after serving as minister to Switzerland and the USA.

Poole, S. Lane. *Life of Lord Stratford de Redcliffe.* London, 1888

STUART, Lieutenant-General Sir Charles (1753–1801)

Described by Sir John Fortescue as one of the most able British officers of the period,[1] he is best remembered for his command in the Mediterranean during the Revolutionary Wars. Fourth son of the ex-prime minister John Stuart, 3rd Earl of Bute (1713–92), he entered the army at the age of 15 and served with distinction in America, before being appointed to command all the troops in the Mediterranean (save Gibraltar), and as lieutenant-general of Corsica in 1794. Despite friction with Hood, he improved relations between army and navy and secured Corsica, and in 1797 led the expedition in support of Portugal. He returned to England

1 June 1798, but on St. Vincent's advice was sent back to the Mediterranean in command of the attack on Minorca; St. Vincent claimed that he was England's best general, who could deal with Frenchmen better than any other, and who the British troops would follow to hell. He captured the island with considerable skill, and in March 1799 landed a force which secured Sicily. In December 1799 he presented a plan for British operations against any part of the Mediterranean coast, using Minorca as a base, to open a second front to assist the Austrians in Italy; but the government so reduced his plans, and were so dilatory, that this, together with Stuart's disobeying the instructions to restore the governance of the Knights of St. John in Malta, led to his resignation early in 1800. He died in May 1801, his potential unfulfilled. He was much admired by those with whom he served; Hudson Lowe, for example, spoke of 'his high and chivalrous character, his daring enterprise, the art he possessed of cheering with a word, and rewarding with a look, the generous encouragement he gave to merit, the decision with which he could repress insubordination, the kindness and generosity he evinced for all under his command'.[2] His son, **Charles Stuart (1779–1845)**, earned considerable distinction as a diplomat, notably in Spain in 1808, when he worked with Moore, and subsequently as ambassador to France; he became Baron Stuart de Rothesay in 1828.

1. Fortescue, vol. IV, p. 777. 2. *CUSM*, 1844, vol. I, p. 592.

Fortescue, Hon. Sir John. *Six British Soldiers*, London, 1928

STUART, Lieutenant-General Sir John, Count of Maida (1759–1815)

Born in Georgia, the son of Colonel John Stuart, Superinten-

SIR JOHN STUART
(ENGRAVING AFTER W. WOOD)

dent of Indian Affairs for the South from 1762 (and a survivor of Anson's expedition of circumnavigation), the younger John Stuart entered the 3rd Foot Guards in 1778. He served in the War of American Independence and under the Duke of York in The Netherlands, as a brigadier-general was with Charles Stuart's expedition to Portugal in 1796, was at Minorca, and in Egypt commanded the 5th Brigade, being commended for his actions at Alexandria. As major-general he went to the Mediterranean, succeeding to command in Sicily upon Craig's return home in April 1806; he led the expedition to Calabria and won his great victory at Maida (4 July 1806), though his contribution to the success is questionable. Although not untalented, he was described as a vain and ambitious man, and Bunbury stated that he appeared more like a spectator than a commander at Maida, so that his deputies had to fight the battle. Stuart, he claimed, spent his time declaring how wonderful it was and imagining the fame which would come to him as a result, and was so busy composing his victory dispatch that he neglected to organise a pursuit. None the less, the success was significant and among other

rewards he received a KCB and, from the Neapolitan regime established in Sicily, the title of Count of Maida; but when Henry Fox and Moore were sent to supersede him in command in the region, he resigned and went home. As lieutenant-general (from April 1808) he returned to the Mediterranean and commanded in Sicily from that year until he returned home again in 1810, repelling Murat's attempts at offensive warfare but failing to hold Capri.

SUBERVIE, General Jacques-Gervaise, baron (1776–1856)

He was elected lieutenant in his native region (Gers) in 1792, and after service in the Pyrenees became ADC to his friend Lannes in September 1797. He accompanied him on the Egyptian expedition, but ill-health forced him to remain at Malta (as Vaubois' ADC) until its surrender; he rejoined Lannes when the latter was ambassador to Portugal, and in the 1805 campaign. In December 1805 he took command of the 10th *Chasseurs à Cheval*, led them at Jena and Friedland, and from 1808 served in Spain. After service under Lasalle, including Medellin, he was promoted to *général de brigade* (August 1811; he had become baron in 1809), and transferred to Suchet's staff. Recalled from Spain in 1812, he led the 2nd Light Cavalry Division of II Cavalry Corps in Russia, but a splinter-wound in the thigh at Borodino prevented further service until August 1813. From then he served with Piré's 9th Light Cavalry Division, including Brienne, Champaubert and Montereau, and was wounded in the defence of Paris. He was promoted to *général de division* immediately before Napoleon's abdication, but although the rank was confirmed by the Bourbons he rejoined Napoleon to lead the 5th Cavalry Division of I Cavalry

Corps in the Waterloo campaign. He was retired in 1825 and entered politics, playing a significant part in the 1830 revolution, was employed by Louis-Philippe and served briefly as War Minister in the provisional government of 1848. He retired in that year but was recalled by Napoleon III to advise on military affairs.

SUCHET, Marshal Louis-Gabriel, duc d'Albufera (1770–1826)

LOUIS GABRIEL SUCHET (ENGRAVING BY R. A. MULLER AFTER J. B. P. GUERIN)

One of the best of Napoleon's subordinates, especially in independent command, he was the son of a silk merchant in Lyons; he enrolled in the National Guard in 1791 and by 1793 was a lieutenant-colonel. He came to Napoleon's notice at Toulon, commanded a battalion of the 18th *Demi-Brigade* in Italy (including Arcola and Rivoli), was Brune's chief of staff in Switzerland (1798), became *général de brigade* in that March, and survived an attempt to discredit him on the grounds of political opinions, aristocratic background and alleged plundering to become Massena's chief of staff in Switzerland. Promoted to *général de division* in 1799, he was Joubert's chief of staff in Italy, and in 1800 was given his own

command, defending southern France along the Var. Never one of Napoleon's closest companions, in 1805–6 he held only a divisional command (3rd Division, V Corps in the Austerlitz campaign, 1st Division of the same at Jena), but in 1807 succeeded to command of the corps. Comte from March 1808, he was next sent to Spain, where unlike that of the majority of his fellows, his reputation was enhanced; before he left for Spain his marriage to Honorine St. Joseph, twenty years his junior and a niece of Désirée and Julie Clary, linked him to the families of both Joseph Bonaparte and Bernadotte. In Spain he first commanded a division, then succeeded Junot in command of III Corps (April 1809, later the Army of Aragon). In Aragon he proved to be a success in his civil capacity (governor) as well as military; the most successful of all French administrators in Spain, his humane attitude won the respect even of the Spanish. Having defeated Blake, his honourable treatment of the population discouraged much of the resistance which would have resulted from more draconian measures. In 1810 he failed to take Valencia for want of resources, but captured Lerida, Tortosa and Tarragona, for which he was awarded his Marshal's baton (July 1811). He defeated Blake at Saguntum (where he was wounded in the shoulder), and in January 1812 captured Valencia, for which he was created duc d'Albufera. Although defeated by Murray at Castalla, he forced the Allies to lift their siege of Tarragona, and in August 1813 was named as Governor of Catalonia as well as commanding the Armies of Aragon and (from April 1813) Catalonia. A further mark of imperial favour was his appointment as colonel-general of the Imperial Guard in succession to Bessières; and when Soult was restored in

command of the unified French forces in Spain, Suchet's command was excluded and remained under his own direction. Despite his best efforts, and last victory at Molina del Rey (January 1814), the situation elsewhere in the Peninsula made his position untenable, and he conducted a successful withdrawal. He accepted the Bourbon restoration and was honoured by them, but supported Napoleon in 1815, his command of the Army of the Alps perhaps not the best way of utilising his talents; and after Napoleon's defeat he concluded an armistice with his Austrian opponents. He then retired into private life, but was restored as a peer of France in 1819 (having initially been deprived of his titles and offices); but upon his death (3 January 1826) he received a unique tribute, when a Mass was said for him in the cathedral at Saragossa, the erstwhile centre of his governance, which demonstrates the respect felt for him even by those who had been his enemies. Although perhaps not rewarded as fully as he deserved during his military career, he was named by Napoleon as among the most skilled of his subordinates; he remarked that with two Marshals of such sound judgement, military and administrative skills and bravery, he could have won the Peninsular War.

Barault-Rouillon, C. H. *Le Maréchal Suchet, duc d'Albufera.* Paris, 1854; Ojala, J. A. 'Peninsular Marshal: Suchet', in *Napoleon's Marshals*, ed. D. G. Chandler. London, 1987; Rousseau, F. *La Carrière du Maréchal Suchet, duc d'Albufera.* Paris, 1898; Suchet, Marshal. *Memoirs of the War in Spain, from 1808 to 1814.* London, 1829

SUDERMANLAND, Charles, Duke of, see CHARLES XIII, King of Sweden

SUHR, Christophe (1771–1842)

A German genre painter (later professor of the Berlin Academy), he produced an important series of uniform-illustrations depicting the troops who visited Hamburg 1808–15, which were produced as prints by his brother Cornelius. These are among the most valuable depictions of troops on active service, if slightly naive; the coverage of La Romana's Spaniards is particularly significant. They were reprinted (Paris 1899, Leipzig 1902) under the sobriquet by which Suhr is best known, *Manuscrit du Bourgeois de Hambourg.*

SULKOWSKI, Jozef (*d.*1798)

This young Polish nobleman (whose date of birth is uncertain: either 1770 or 1773) saw military service against the Russians in Poland, and after leaving his country after the third partition, was commissioned in the French Army in 1796. After distinguishing himself in Italy he was appointed an ADC by Napoleon; but although he was acknowledged as a soldier of great potential, Napoleon perhaps did not entirely trust him, because he was supported by Carnot and others and might even have been regarded as a rival for Napoleon's position. An idealist whose ambition was directed towards Polish independence, he became somewhat disillusioned with Napoleon's own ambition, but remained the most loyal of subordinates, serving more from a sense of honour than affection. For the Egyptian campaign he proved most useful; a Knight of Malta, he was familiar with the area, spoke Arabic and Turkish, and as an intellectual was most interested in the work of the Institute, notably the archaeological investigations as well as his own political economy section. For whatever reason, Napoleon was slow to promote him, until he again distinguished himself in action, notably at Alexandria and the Battle of the Pyramids. Despite not having recovered from several wounds, Napoleon ordered him to undertake a reconnaissance mission during the Cairo insurrection; his horse fell during an ambush and he was hacked to death. Napoleon, it was said, showed distress at his loss, though some suspected that he was not sorry at the removal of a potential rival.

Saint-Albin, H. R. C. *J. Sulkowski: Mémoires historiques.* Paris, 1832; Zamoyski, A. 'Napoleon's Polish Aide-de-Camp', in *History Today*, July 1973 (includes detailed bibliography)

SULIMAN EL-HALEBI, or 'Soliman of Aleppo' (1773–1800)

Suliman, or Soliman, is perhaps one of the best-known assassins of the era. A public writer at Aleppo, he was evidently a pious young man, claiming to have spent three years at Mecca; and in early 1800 went to Jerusalem to obtain redress over exactions upon his merchant father. In return for help on this matter, after much cajoling, he agreed to attempt to murder the French commander in the Orient. Friends at Cairo, where he arrived about the middle of May, attempted to dissuade him, but on 14 June he attacked Kléber who was strolling in a garden. The architect friend who was walking with Kléber was also attacked, though not fatally, and beat Suliman over the head with his stick; but the knife-blows delivered against Kléber, most seriously in the chest and abdomen, led to his death within minutes. Suliman was apprehended shortly after; his interrogation (by torture), trial and execution were carried out by the French authorities, but not according to French standards or law. The punishment was permitted by local custom but was an appalling method of dispatching a condemned man: the hand which struck the blow was burned off and the prisoner was then impaled alive. The three friends to whom he had announced his intention were regarded as accessories and were beheaded.

SUVAROV, Field Marshal Alexander Vasilievich, Count Suvarov–Rimniksky, Prince Italysky (1729–1800)

ALEXANDER VASILIEVICH SUVAROV
(ENGRAVING BY A. ROFFE AFTER HAMPE)

This great Russian general served for only a short time during the Revolutionary Wars, although with great effect; yet his fame was already established. Born in Moscow of distant Swedish descent, he served in the Seven Years War and against the Poles (1762–72), but as a general officer his real fame resulted from campaigns against the Ottoman Empire, first in 1773–4. He helped to suppress Pugachev's serf revolt (1775) and then served in the Caucasus and Crimea, rising to the rank of general of infantry by 1783. In the Turkish War of 1787–91 he was immensely distinguished, notably for his victories at Focsani and on the Rimnik (1788), taking his title from the latter (and being appointed a Count of the Holy Roman Empire, Austrian forces participating in the victory). In December 1790 he stormed Ismailia in Bessarabia, the sack of which was conducted with great barbarity; and similar cruelty occurred when taking Warsaw during the Third Partition of Poland. A great favourite of Catherine the Great, who appointed him field marshal, he went into eclipse under her successor Paul I; dismissed from service, he retired (though continued to criticise the politics of the new Tsar) until recalled in 1799. His command in Italy was at first a series of spectacular triumphs, including Cassano, the Trebbia and Novi, which undid most of Napoleon's successes of 1796–7, and won for Suvarov his title of 'Prince of Italy' from the Tsar; but reverses against the Allies, notably Korsakov's defeat by Massena in Switzerland, forced Suvarov to retire from north Italy into Austria. The old general returned to St. Petersburg in disgrace; the Tsar refused to see him, and he died a few days later, on 18 May 1800. The insult perpetrated by his sovereign, however, was not repeated elsewhere; though sometimes regarded as ill-educated, uncompromising and even brutal, he was beloved by his soldiers and his reputation was undiminished, both as a general of great skill and as a personification of Russian military spirit, bravery and tenacity, exemplified by his advocacy for the offensive in military operations. An obituary published in England articulated the sentiments of many: 'his heart [was] afflicted with the grief of finding his important services repaid by unaccountable caprice and ingratitude ... The man so lately the theme of Royal panegyric ... was absolutely abandoned in the struggles of sickness and death ... Posterity will render him that justice which his contemporaries refused him; and we are not afraid to express its language beforehand, by paying this homage to the great talents and virtues of a hero, whose actions will maintain a distinguished rank in the history of the 18th century.'[1] Suvarov's son Arkady (1783–1811) also became a general officer in the Russian Army, but with terrible irony was drowned in the River Rimnik in 1811.

1. *Gent's Mag.*, June, 1800, p. 592.

Anthing, J. F. *History of the Campaigns of ... Suwaroff (sic).* London, 1799 (a translation of the original *Versuch einer Kriegsgeschichte des Grafen Suworow.* Gotha, 1796–7; Blease, W. F. *Suvarof.* London, 1920; Longworth, P. *The Art of Victory: the Life and Achievements of Field-Marshal Suvorov.* London, 1965; Macready, E. N. *A Sketch of Suwarow, and his Last Campaign.* London, 1851; Spalding, Lieutenant-Colonel. *Suvorof.* London, 1890

TALLEYRAND-PERIGORD, Charles-Maurice de, prince de Benavente (1754–1838)

One of the great statesmen of the age, he was at least as distinguished in the area of self-preservation, so that he enjoyed a period of influence surely unrivalled. Born in Paris, the son of Lieutenant-General Charles-Daniel de Talleyrand-Périgord, his was an old and aristocratic family; his great-great-aunt was the marquise de Montespan, mistress of Louis XIV. A fall in childhood crippled his foot and prevented his expected military career; so he entered the church and rose to become bishop of Autun in March 1789, but he was never particularly noted for great piety. Politics became his occupation instead; after entering the States-General he accepted the civil constitution of the clergy and in January 1791 resigned his see to concentrate on politics. From early 1792 he was employed in the diplomatic service as assistant to the ambassador to Great Britain; unsuccessful in his attempts to keep the British neutral, he was expelled upon the outbreak of war and went to the United States, returning to Paris only in

CHARLES-MAURICE DE TALLEYRAND (ENGRAVING BY W. H. EGLETON AFTER GÉRARD)

September 1796, having avoided the worst upheavals of the Revolu-

tion. His abilities and diplomatic skills recommended him to the Directory, and in July 1797 he was appointed Foreign Minister. Recognising the potential of General Bonaparte, he shifted his loyalties in that direction and helped bring about the coup of Brumaire, having resigned his portfolio on 20 July 1799, probably in anticipation of the imminent collapse of the Directory. In December 1799 he was reinstated as Foreign Minister and held the post until 1807, exercising a profound influence on Napoleon's policy. He was in sympathy with the Concordat, and in June 1802 the Pope removed from him the ban of excommunication proclaimed in 1791; and in September 1803, partly under pressure from Napoleon, he married his companion of some years, Madame Grand. He was able to profit personally, to a considerable degree, from his position; but was not able to direct Napoleon in his favoured direction. He disapproved of the execution of the duc d'Enghien, and was unable to deflect Napoleon from actions which he believed were unwise or counter-productive. He accepted the office of Grand Chamberlain of the Empire, and in July 1806 the dukedom of Benavente (in Neapolitan territory); but after Tilsit resigned his portfolio. Thereafter, although he remained an adviser and retained influence, he was largely a spectator to the events which led to the collapse of the empire; he disagreed with the war in Spain, but it was to his estate at Valençay that the Spanish royal family were taken during their enforced exile. In his own interests, and in what he believed to be those of France, Talleyrand maintained secret relations with the Bourbons and the Allies, and was thus in a position of influence when Napoleon's reign ended. He supported the abdication, was head of the provisional government and,

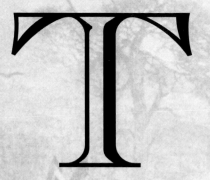

having used his influence to secure the best terms for France, represented his country at the Congress of Vienna. He helped to form the secret alliance of France, Austria and Great Britain which modified Russian and Prussian claims for annexation of Poland and Saxony respectively, and escaped the events of the Hundred Days by remaining at Vienna. Again he was influential in presenting France's case, but resigned the post of Foreign Minister (held since July) in September 1815, Louis XVIII appointing him as chamberlain. In 1830 he encouraged Louis-Philippe to accept the throne, declined the foreign ministry but accepted the post of ambassador to Great Britain, in which office he played an important part in the negotiations which established the kingdom of Belgium. He resigned in late 1834, ending a remarkable political and diplomatic career which had established him as not only one of the most important diplomats of the era, but a remarkable survivor in his ability to serve so many regimes. Talleyrand's moral character and capacity for self-enrichment were greatly criticised, as was his changeable loyalty and intrigue. Napoleon's description of him, 'a lump of dung in a silk stocking', is well known; less colourfully, his aloof demeanour, exaggerated by his limp, earned the comparison of 'death in red velvet'. Lady Frances Shelley thought his appearance diabolical, and his laugh fiendish, but many ladies found him an enchanting companion, and he had numerous liaisons; it was believed that the painter Eugène Delacroix (1798–1863) was his natural son (officially the artist's father was Charles Delacroix, or Delacroix de Contaut, 1741–1805, Foreign Minister under the Directory). Although using Talleyrand's talents, Napoleon had no illusions about him; perceptively, he remarked that Talleyrand 'was always in a state of treason; but it was in partnership with fortune. His circumspection was extreme; he treated his friends as if they might in future become his enemies; and he behaved to his enemies as if they might some time or other become his friends.'[1] The diplomat supreme, he would give away nothing; 'so skilful in his evasions and ramblings that, after conversations which lasted several hours, he has gone away, frequently avoiding the explanations and objects I expected to obtain from him,'[2] recalled Napoleon. Despite a witty and ironic form of conversation, so impassive was his manner that Lannes and Murat joked that if he were kicked while speaking he would betray not a sign of it, and Wellington recalled that though his conversation was neither lively nor pleasant, 'now and then he comes out with a thing that you remember all the rest of your life'.[3]

1. Las Cases, vol. II, p. 64. 2. Ibid., vol. III, p. 119. 3. Stanhope, p. 5.

Bernard, J. F. Talleyrand: a Biography. London, 1973; Blennerhasset, Lady. Talleyrand. London, 1894; Dard, E. Napoleon and Talleyrand. London, 1937; Dwyer, P. G. Charles Maurice de Talleyrand. 1995; Lacour-Gayet, G. Talleyrand. Paris, 1928–31; McCabe, J. Talleyrand, a Biographical Study. London, 1906; Talleyrand, C. M. de. Memoirs of the Prince de Talleyrand, ed. duc de Broglie, trans. A. Hall. London, 1891–2

TALLIEN, Jean-Lambert (1767–1820)

Son of the marquis de Bercy's porter, he was born in Paris and educated by his father's employer as a lawyer's clerk. An enthusiastic supporter of the Revolution, he worked on the printing of *Le Moniteur*, and his Jacobin news-sheet *Ami des Citoyens* brought him to prominence. One of the leaders in the attack on the Tuileries, he was appointed secretary to the Paris Commune on 10 August 1792. He defended the September massacres, was elected to the Convention, voted for the death of the king and assisted in the fall of the Girondins. Sent on missions to the provinces, notably Bordeaux (September 1793) to duplicate the Terror, he acted with vigour, but his actions were softened by Thérèse, comtesse de Fontenay, née Cabarrus, whom he saved after she was arrested at Bordeaux, and under whose spell he fell. She so moderated his revolutionary zeal that, from the lives saved by her efforts, she became known as 'Notre Dame de Thermidor'. Tallien subsequently led the Convention against Robespierre, was elected to the Committee of Public Safety, was active in suppressing the Revolutionary Tribunal and Jacobin Club, and attacked Carrier. Married to Tallien in December 1794, Thérèse became a leader of Parisian society, but became also somewhat notorious for scandal and infidelity. Tallien was present at Quiberon (ordering the execution of the émigrés), but his influence declined, and as a member of the Council of Five Hundred he was unpopular with both moderates and extremists. He accompanied Napoleon to Egypt with the Economic Section of the Scientific Commission, but on his way home was captured by the British and taken to London, where he was well-received by the Whigs. On his

THÈRESE, MADAME TALLIEN
(PRINT AFTER GÉRARD)

return to Paris in 1802 he divorced his wife, but was left without employment until appointed consul at Alicante (1806), where he remained until he lost an eye from fever. He lived on half-pay in Paris thereafter, was excused the exile accorded to regicides after the restoration, but died in poverty. Madame Tallien remarried in 1805, becoming the wife of comte de Caraman, later prince de Chimay.

Houssaye, A. *Notre Dame de Thermidor*. Paris, 1866

TANDY, General James Napper (1740–1803)

'I met with Napper Tandy, and he took me by the hand, Saying, how is old Ireland? and how does she stand?' Thus is Napper Tandy immortalised in the ballad *The Wearing of the Green*. Born in Dublin, a small tradesman who turned to politics, he was a leading personality in the nationalist movement in Ireland. One of the most vehement in his opinions, he co-operated with Wolfe Tone in founding the Society of United Irishmen in 1791, of which he became secretary, and his extreme views, influenced by the ideals of the French Revolution, brought him to the attention of the government. In 1792 he evaded arrest after challenging to a duel John Toler, he Solicitor-General (afterwards st Earl of Norbury, 1745–1831), ho had insulted him; but when reatened with prosecution for king the oath of the Defenders, andy fled to America. There he emained until he arrived in Paris 1 1798, and convinced the French at he was a man of influence hose mere arrival in Ireland ould raise a revolt; and he ecame the senior United Irish fficer in the French Army, though t odds with Tone, who regarded im as a drunken braggart. Never-heless, he was provided with a ship (*nacréon*), a small force of French roops and the munitions to equip a ebellion, arrived off Donegal at utland and landed on 16 eptember 1798. Finding that lumbert had surrendered and that here was no enthusiasm for a ising, the French realised the opelessness of the enterprise, 'andy was carried back to *nacréon* in a drunken stupor, and he expedition sailed away. He nded at Hamburg, was surren-lered to the British and sentenced o death, but he was allowed to eturn to France; pressure had een exerted by the French but probably the British realised that he to longer had influence, and was to danger. He was well-received in 'rance but died on 24 August 1803.

ARENTE (Tarentum), duc de, ee MACDONALD

AUENTZIEN (or Tauenzien), eneral Bolesas Friedrich manuel, Graf von Wittenberg 1760–1824)

n officer of the Prussian Army rom 1775, he served in the ampaign of 1793, attained the ank of general officer in 1801 and n 1806 commanded the left flank orps of Hohenlohe's army in the ena campaign; but is perhaps best emembered for his service in 813–14. He led IV Corps at Gross-Beeren and though practically

BOLESAS TAUENTZIEN VON WITTENBERG

defeated at Dennewitz, held on until assistance arrived. His best-known service concerned his besieging and capture of Torgau and Wittenberg in 1814, taking his title from the latter success. In 1815 he was given command of VI Corps but was not in time to participate in the Waterloo campaign.

TAYLOR, General Zachary (1784–1850)

Most distinguished as a general during the US–Mexican War, and twelfth President of the United States, he first came to prominence at the time of the War of 1812. Commissioned lieutenant in 1808, as a captain he gained considerable distinction in defending Fort Harrison against Indian attacks (4–5 September 1812), after which he was breveted major. He had less success in August–September 1814 when he led a small force up the Mississippi to attack the Indians in the Rock River region, but when they received British assistance Taylor prudently withdrew.

TCHITCHAGOV, see CHICHAGOV

TECUMSEH, Brigadier-General (*c*.1768–1813)

The great Shawnee chief Tecumseh, and his younger

brother Tenskwatawa (better known by his nickname 'the Prophet'), were leading personali-ties in attempts to resist the encroachment of settlers upon their traditional lands. His aim was to create a kind of democratic confederacy of Native American people in which old tribal conflicts would be negated, and from 1807 they were aided by the British from Canada. The plan was effectively destroyed by the defeat of the Prophet at Tippecanoe (17 November 1811), but upon the outbreak of the War of 1812 Tecumseh was appointed a brigadier-general in British service. His reputation as an orator, diplomat and warrior enabled him to exert considerable influence, and he behaved with great humanity, not common in frontier warfare. He aided Brock in the operations leading to Hull's surrender at Detroit, but relations with Proctor were less cordial, during that commander's retreat which led to defeat at the Battle of the Thames. In that action Tecumseh and his followers fought with great tenacity, but he was killed when the British line collapsed; it was said that he was shot by Colonel Richard M. Johnson, but the exact circum-stances of his death were in doubt. 'Had it been his fortune to have lived in a civilised country, and to have enjoyed the light of education, his memory would have been endowed with an immortality of honourable fame ... His character, full of strong savage talent and savage feeling, was free from coarseness in his manners or cruelty in his conduct.'[1] 'Tecumtha' was another spelling of the phonetic pronunciation of his name; 'the Prophet' (who died in 1834) may be found referred to as 'Elkswatana' or 'Pemsquatawah', the latter a version of 'Tensk-watawa', being a name he adopted, meaning 'the open door'.

1.*USJ*, 1839, vol. I, p. 489.

Drake, B. *The Life of Tecumseh and of his Brother the Prophet.* Cincinnati, 1841; Hook, J. *Tecumseh: Visionary Chief of the Shawnee.* Poole, 1989

TEIL, General Jean de Beaumont, Chevalier du (1733–1820)

Younger brother of Jean-Pierre du Teil, the Chevalier du Teil (as he is often styled) also served in the French artillery in the mid 18th century, and although rising to the rank of colonel in 1784, his principal fame arose from his publication *De l'Usage de l'Artillerie Nouvelle dans la Guerre de Campagne* (Paris, 1778), which was one of the works studied by Napoleon during his education under the elder du Teil at the artillery school at Auxonne. Unlike his brother, the Chevalier supported the Revolution, and having been retired in 1791 was appointed artillery commander of the Army of the Rhine, later serving in the Alps and Italy. In 1793 he became *général de division*, and despite age and ill-health was appointed to command the artillery at Toulon, where Napoleon was the leading figure, and in 1794 was again retired. In August 1799 he was recalled as inspector-general, and from 1800 until his final retirement in 1813 was commandant at Metz. His prime significance, however, was in the effect exerted by his military theories on the development of Napoleon's understanding of the art of war.

TEIL, General Jean-Pierre du, baron (1722–94)

Elder brother of the foregoing, he was an officer of the French artillery who had served with distinction in the Seven Years War, but his main significance in the context of the Napoleonic era arose from his appointment as commandant of the artillery school at Auxonne. His most celebrated pupil was Napoleon Bonaparte, who became something of his protégé, and benefited greatly from the encouragement and education he received from du Teil. Himself a disciple of Gribeauval, his ideas and those of the younger du Teil had a profound effect upon the formulation of Napoleon's military knowledge, as had his encouragement of the study of all aspects of the art of war. Ironically, du Teil was not in sympathy with the direction taken by the Revolution, and supported the opposition to it; he was captured and executed at Lyons in 1794.

THEROIGNE DE MERICOURT, Anne-Josèphe (1762–1817)

One of the more unusual characters of the Revolution, she was born in Marcourt in Luxembourg (from which place she took the name 'de Méricourt'). Well-educated and intelligent, she became a courtesan, but became famous for her support for the Revolution and her association with some of its leading figures. She maintained a political salon, and having been captured on a political mission to Liège, was taken to Vienna but released after an interview with Leopold II. She was thus even more celebrated (as '*la belle Liégoise*') on her return to Paris; she dressed in semi-military costume, equipped with pistol, sword and pike, and exerted considerable influence by her talent for oratory, being associated with the Girondins and the opponents of Robespierre, and led a corps of women. She was much involved in the riots of 10 August 1792, and was responsible on that day for the death at the hands of the mob of a political writer who had libelled her, one Suleau; but she was uninvolved in the September massacres, and in May 1793 was severely assaulted by a mob of Jacobin women. Shortly afterwards she lost her reason, an remained in that state until he death.

Reiset, Vicomte de. *La Vrai Théroigne de Méricourt.* Paris, 190

THIBAUDEAU, Antoine-Clair, comte (1765–1854)

The son of a Poitiers lawyer an member of the States-General, h too was a lawyer, and a supporte of the Revolution. Elected to th Convention, he voted for th death of the king, but declined t join the Jacobin Club and wa known for his firm principle rather than extremism, hence hi nickname 'iron bar'. In Octobe 1794 it was he who secured th recall of Paine to the Conventior and served on the Committee o Public Safety. In 1796 he wa appointed President of th Council of Five Hundred opposing Tallien, but retired t his legal career in 1798. Upon th establishment of the Consulate he became Prefect of the Girond and councillor of state, and wa subsequently Prefect at Mar seilles. Appointed a peer of France during the Hundred Days, he wa exiled as a regicide at the secone restoration, but returned t France after the 1830 revolution and became a senator during the Second Empire. While in exile he wrote his memoirs and a histor of the Consulate and Empire, o value in that he reported events o which he had personal knowl edge, being a close observer o Napoleon as well as a friend o Joséphine.

Thibaudeau, A. C. *Le Consula de l'Empire.* 1834; *Mémoires sur l Consulat.* Paris, 1827 (English edn titled *Bonaparte and the Consulate* trans. G. K. Fortescue. 1908) *Mémoires sur la Convention et l Directoire.* Paris, 1824

THIELMANN, General Johann Adolf, Freiherr von (1765–1824)

He was among those who had the

unusual distinction of fighting in two of the great battles of the age, within three years, on one occasion with Napoleon and on the other against him. Born at Dresden, he entered the Saxon Army in 1782 and served against the French in the Revolutionary Wars and in 1806; but after Saxony's alliance with Napoleon, he served with the French in 1807 (including Friedland) and 1809. In that year, as *Oberst*, he was extremely active and successful in defending Saxony against the Austrians, commanding a mobile force, even though he attracted something of a reputation for ambition and self-promotion; he became major-general, and lieutenant-general in 1810. In 1812 he gained great distinction at Borodino, when as commander of a brigade of Lorge's 7th Heavy Cavalry Division he led the charge which penetrated the Raevsky Redoubt; his troops included both Saxon heavy regiments (*Garde du Corps* and Zastrow Cuirassiers) and the 14th Polish Cuirassiers, and his conduct attracted Napoleon's attention and won the rank of *Freiherr* from the King of Saxony. In 1813 he was Governor of Torgau, and on the king's orders held it against both sides, but when Napoleon's threats brought the king back into line, Thielmann obeyed his orders to unite his command to the French, but himself went over to the Allies. Commanding a force chiefly of Cossacks, he defeated Lefebvre-Desnouëttes at Altenburg (28 September 1813) and, having been employed in re-organising the Saxon Army after Leipzig, commanded their troops in The Netherlands in 1814. Early in 1815 he became *Generalleutnant* in the Prussian Army, and in the Waterloo campaign commanded III Corps, covering the Prussian movement in support of Wellington after Ligny, by holding Grouchy at Wavre. Subsequently he served as commandant of Münster and Coblenz, and died at the latter place.

THOMIERES, General Jean-Guillaume-Barthelémy, baron (1771–1812)

Best known for his service in the Peninsular War, he had joined the army as a volunteer in 1793, was elected captain and served in the Pyrenees before transferring to the Army of Italy, with which he served in Napoleon's campaign of 1796, and in 1799–1801, including Marengo. In 1806–7 he served with Lannes, as ADC and from July 1807 as *général de brigade*. In Junot's army in Spain he led a brigade in Loison's 2nd Division and was wounded at Vimeiro; in Soult's army at Corunna he commanded a brigade of Merle's 1st Division. A baron from 1809, he led a brigade in Solignac's 2nd Division of Massena's Army of Portugal, and under Marmont succeeded to command of the 7th Division of the Army of Portugal at Salamanca. Disaster befell his command at that battle; despite being accompanied by Curto's light cavalry brigade, at the extreme left of the French position, no vedettes appear to have been posted so that he was completely surprised by the attacks from D'Urban and Pakenham which fell upon him. He was able to throw out his skirmishers and get his artillery into action, but a counter-attack in support of the skirmishers faltered, and the whole division was driven from the field in confusion, losing almost half its strength. Thomières was mortally wounded and died in the British lines.

THOUVENOT, General Pierre, baron (1757–1817)

He is best known as the instigator of virtually the last, and most pointless, action of the Peninsular War. Trained as an engineer, he was commissioned in the French colonial forces in 1780 and served in the West Indies until 1788. In the early Revolutionary Wars he was chief of staff to Dumouriez, who reported him as very expert in matters of reconnaissance, marching and camping, courageous and clear-headed in action, and a tireless worker, and similar opinions were held by Lafayette. He defected with Dumouriez and was in exile until permitted to return to France in 1800; he then served in San Domingo (becoming *général de brigade* in October 1802), and subsequently held a number of staff appointments. Wounded at Colberg, he then went to Spain, serving as Governor of Vittoria and later Bayonne. Here he came into the argument between Reille and Soult, the former objecting to Thouvenot (his junior) having command over some of Reille's troops by virtue of his Governorship. Thouvenot failed to mount an adequate resistance to the Allies' crossing of the Adour, and reacted passively to their operations against Bayonne until 14 April 1814, when he mounted a great sortie, almost the last action of the Peninsular War, and one entirely without purpose, for he surely knew that the war was by then over. The sortie, which cost the French 905 casualties and the Allies 838, was utterly pointless and was condemned by both sides as an inhuman waste of soldiers' lives; though Sir Charles Colville, who commanded after Hope was captured in the sortie, found him a gentlemanly, well-intentioned man and suggested that his action had been encouraged by his subordinates. It was surely, however, a pointless act of defiance, condemned by Wellington as the action of a blackguard, and Thouvenot confirmed his dissatisfaction at the outcome of events by refusing to surrender, in the face of all evidence, until he received incontrovertible proof of the armistice from his own side. He remained at Bayonne until his retirement in September 1815.

THUGUT, Johann Amadeus Francis de Paula, baron (1736–1818)

Born in Linz of humble origin, he made his career in the Austrian diplomatic service, notably in Constantinople, during which appointment he accepted a pension from France in the expectation that he might be able to render that country some service. On leave 1783–7 he resided in France, where he invested his fortune, then served as minister to Naples, and subsequently developed a hatred for the Revolution, partly upon ideological grounds and partly from the loss of his investments. Critical of the conduct of the early Revolutionary Wars, having been diplomatic agent with the Allied army, he was appointed Foreign Minister in March 1793, which aroused some opposition, from his non-aristocratic background as well as from his unsociable manner and an appearance once described as Mephistophelian. He pursued a policy of opposition to France and in the interests of Austrian territorial expansion, against Russia and Prussia, which diluted the military effort, his interference towards these ends causing some bitterness among his country's allies; though he retained British support, which may have had the effect of keeping him in office. He was blamed for the diplomatic breakdown between Austria and Russia over Suvarov's campaigns in Italy, though the view that left to himself Suvarov might have driven the French entirely from Italy perhaps over-estimates that general's resources. There was indignation over Thugut's acceptance of Campo Formio, and the defeats of 1800 made his position untenable; on New Year's Day 1801 the emperor wrote that as Thugut would always hold up the conclu-

sion of peace, being so disliked by France, he was to leave office, whereupon he retired from public life.

TOLL, Field Marshal Johan Kristoffer, Count (1743–1817)

The career of this notable Swedish statesman, who had begun his military service during the Seven Years War, was probably of most significance to the internal affairs of Sweden than in the wider context of the Napoleonic Wars. Having assisted in Gustavus III's *coup d'état* of 1772, he became a trusted adviser of that king and proved a most capable administrator, including in the position of commissary-general. Under Gustavus IV he was a skilled diplomat in the negotiations concerning Sweden's participation in the war against Napoleon; in 1807 he assisted at the defence of Stralsund, and after its surrender skilfully negotiated the withdrawal of the Swedish force, which would otherwise have been lost. A general officer under Gustavus III, for this exploit he was advanced to field marshal, and retained his position under Bernadotte, who made him a Count in 1814.

TONE, Theobald Wolfe (1763–98)

One of the most prominent of the United Irishmen, he was born in Dublin and became a lawyer, but politics became dominant in his life. In 1791 he was one of the founders of the Society of United Irishmen, the intention of which was to unite Roman Catholics and Protestants into a movement for parliamentary reform; but finding that prospect unlikely, the majority adopted the more extreme measures advocated by Tone from the beginning, being much influenced by the French Revolution. For a time the society was broken up after its contacts with the French government, and Tone's plan for revolution, be-

came known; but Tone, instead of being arrested like other leaders of the organisation, was permitted to emigrate to America (where he arrived in May 1795). In February 1796 he went to France to enlist help; he impressed Carnot and was given a French commission. He accompanied Hoche on the abortive expedition to Bantry Bay (December 1796), but the death of Hoche and the removal of Carnot was a severe loss of allies; Tone met Napoleon but did not receive much encouragement. He sailed for Ireland again aboard the 74-gunner *Hoche* as part of the French expedition; but she was intercepted by Sir John Borlase Warren and Tone was captured when *Hoche* was taken (12 October 1798). Tried by court martial, he made an impressive defence in his role as an officer of the French Army, and argued for the honour of being shot by firing squad; but he was sentenced to hang. On the day before the scheduled execution, he cut his throat (11 November 1798), from which injury he died on the 19th. Even in the country of his enemy sympathy was expressed: 'Every generous heart must feel for the mis-directed magnanimity of this Gentleman. His death is not to be ascribed to cowardice. He committed suicide in the fervour of a classical mind. Every scholar knows that it was the proud feeling of a hero to avoid public degradation.'[1] Tone's brother Matthew was captured before him, court-martialled and hanged; his son, William Theobald Wolfe Tone (1791–1828) served in the French Army and later emigrated to America, where he published a biography of his father, which completed an autobiographical study.

1. *Morning Chronicle*, 26 Nov 1798.

Elliott, M. *Wolfe Tone: Prophet of Irish Independence.* London, 1989; Tone, W. T. W. *Life of Theo-*

ald Wolfe Tone. Washington, 1826; *Autobiography of Theobald Wolfe Tone*, ed. R. B. O'Brien. London, 1893

TORRENS, Major-General Sir Henry (1779–1828)

Best known as military secretary to the CinC, to whom much correspondence regarding the Peninsular War was addressed, he was commissioned in 1793 and served widely, including the West Indies, North Holland 1799 (wounded) and the Peninsula (including Roleia and Vimeiro) before becoming the CinC's secretary in 1809. A lieutenant-colonel in the 3rd Foot Guards from June 1811, he became major-general in June 1814 and received the KCB in January 1815. He held the colonelcies of the 2nd West India Regiment 1818–22 and the 2nd Foot from 1822 until his death in August 1828; and was adjutant-general 1820-8. He should not be confused with the economist, Colonel Robert Torrens (1780–1864), who joined the Marines in 1797, was breveted major for Walcheren and commanded a Spanish unit in the Peninsula; he was an advocate of the repeal of the Corn Laws and presided over the colonial emigration commission.

TOUSSAINT L'OUVERTURE, General Pierre Dominique (1743 or 1746–1803)

'The Bonaparte of San Domingo' was born a slave, though of princely African descent, in the French colony of St. Domingue; but his family enjoyed some privileges which allowed him to acquire an education. He was originally named Toussaint à Breda (Breda being the estate on which he was born and to which he was tied); the name 'l'Ouverture' or 'Louverture' he adopted later for a reason which is uncertain. He came to prominence after the slave revolt of 1791, an orgy of massacre in which the rebels claimed to be supporting the French royal family against the revolutionary system in France, but in 1793 he changed allegiance to Spain (perhaps because that country still had a king), which controlled the other half of the island of Haiti. In 1794, however, he returned to the support of France because of their abolition of slavery, and in that year was appointed a French *général de brigade*, *de division* a year later. He opposed the British intervention in San Domingo, which was appallingly costly to them both by disease and from Toussaint's efforts; and then, seeing the opportunity for complete autonomy, sent away the French commissioners and subsequently, after another revolt involving virtual civil war, took over the Spanish portion of Haiti (1801). For a time the island enjoyed peace under his rule; he declared a constitutional government with himself Governor for life. Napoleon, however, determined to bring the colony to order (France having acquired title to the whole island by a treaty with Spain in 1795), and sent an expedition under his brother-in-law, Leclerc. The Haitians resisted; but Toussaint was seized treacherously at a meeting with the French, conveyed as a prisoner to France and died of neglect and despair on 7 April 1803. The French nevertheless failed to prosper; Leclerc died of fever and they quitted the island in November 1803, heralding a period of slaughter as various leaders fought for supremacy; which might have been avoided had not the career of the remarkable Toussaint not been so curtailed.

Alexis, J. S. *Black Liberator: the Life of Toussaint Louverture*. New York, 1949; Beard, J. R. *The Life of Toussaint Louverture*. London, 1853; Parkinson, W. *This Gilded African: Toussaint L'Ouverture*. London, 1980; Toussaint l'Ouverture, P. D. *Mémoires du Général Toussaint L'Ouverture*. Paris, 1850

TRANT, Major-General Sir Nicholas (1769–1839)

Although his British rank remained relatively lowly (brevet-colonel), he achieved considerable fame as a commander of Portuguese troops. Descended from an old Irish family, he served as a volunteer on the Duke of Brunswick's staff in 1792, and with the British Army in The Netherlands 1793–4, the Cape 1795, Portugal 1796, Minorca 1798 and in Egypt. As a captain in the Royal Staff Corps he was one of the first British officers sent to reorganise the Portuguese forces, served at Roleia and Vimeiro, and served in the Portuguese Army from April 1809 to 1813. Commanding a force of militia and volunteers, he harried Massena's artillery reserve at Vizeu (September 1810), though perhaps should have done more, and his troops let him down at Sardão later in the month,[1] but he captured Coimbra in October 1810. He defended that city in 1810–11, and during Massena's retreat, always daring, he engaged Claparède's division at Val de Mula (April 1811) and hastened their withdrawal. He covered Almeida in 1812 and conceived an audacious but impracticable scheme to surprise Marmont's headquarters with his militia division; Wellington issued severe criticism of Trant's expressed belief that 'the magnitude of the object would justify the attempt': 'nothing is so bad as failure and defeat. You could not have succeeded in that attempt; and you would have lost your division and that of General Wilson.'[2] As it was, Trant was himself surprised at Guarda but extricated his command. Having received a Portuguese knighthood by the bestowal of the Order of the Tower and Sword, after the war he went to France to recover his health, moving to Italy during the Hundred Days; and in 1819 declined command of a province of Brazil.

He died on 17 October 1839, 'a most gallant soldier and warm-hearted friend'.[3]

1. For his account of the event, in his whimsical style, see Oman, vol. III, pp. 399–400. 2. Wellington, 21 April 1812, vol. IX, p. 76. 3. *USJ*, 1840, vol. I, p. 100.

TREVISE, duc de, see MORTIER

TROUBRIDGE, Rear-Admiral Sir Thomas, Bt. (1758–1807)

SIR THOMAS TROUBRIDGE
(ENGRAVING BY HOLL AFTER BEECHEY)

From a relatively humble background (the son of a London baker), he joined the Royal Navy in 1773, and attracted some praise in the East Indies. Shortly before the Glorious First of June he was taken aboard Neilly's flagship *Sanspareil* after his own ship, HMS *Castor*, was captured, and was a prisoner aboard the French ship during the battle; when *Sanspareil* surrendered, he took command. He came to prominence in the Mediterranean, where Jervis reported that he was a most capable officer, the Bayard of the Royal Navy with honour and courage as bright as his sword. A close friend of Horatio Nelson from their days as midshipmen, he shared Nelson's passionate nature and hatred of the French;

though was to disapprove strongly of Nelson's affair with Emma Hamilton, which soured their previous close relationship. Commanding HMS *Culloden*, Troubridge led the line at St. Vincent, where his distinguished seamanship caused Jervis to exclaim that he manoeuvred as if the eyes of all England were upon him. He was less fortunate at Aboukir Bay, where *Culloden* ran aground and was unable to take any part in the victory. After further Mediterranean service (including the siege and capture of Fort St. Elmo at Naples, which Nelson said proved him to be a first-rate general), he received a baronetcy (30 November 1799). In 1800 he became ill and was posted home; he served as a Lord of the Admiralty 1801–4, was MP for Great Yarmouth 1802–6, and became rear-admiral. In 1805 he received a command in the East Indies, and was then appointed to the Cape; he sailed from Madras in the old and unseaworthy HMS *Blenheim*, which was lost in a cyclone off Madagascar. St. Vincent, like many others, deeply lamented his death. Troubridge's only son, Edward Thomas, who succeeded to the baronetcy, served as a midshipman in Nelson's ship at Copenhagen and himself rose to the rank of rear-admiral.

TURREAU DE GARAMBOU-VILLE, General Louis-Marie, baron de Linières (1756–1816)

Although he also had a diplomatic career, he is probably best remembered for his earlier military service. A captain in the Army of the Moselle in 1792, in June 1793 he was sent to the Vendée and in July became *général de brigade*. After some reverses at the hands of the Vendéen rebels – he was defeated and wounded at Coron, for example – he achieved some

success and was appointed to command the Army of the Eastern Pyrenees. From there he was recalled to the Vendée to succeed Rossignol as CinC, and organised the 'infernal columns' (*colonnes infernales*) which devastated the region in an attempt to annihilate opposition. In addition to harrying the rebel bands, Turreau burned villages and expelled the inhabitants to crush the rebellion, carrying out the orders of the Convention in its most extreme period. After the fall of Robespierre he was arrested and tried for the savagery of his conduct, but was acquitted; and while imprisoned wrote a valuable *Mémoires pour servir à l'Histoire de la Guerre de Vendée*. In 1799 he served in Switzerland, in 1800 with the Army of Reserve, and from 1803 to 1811 was French minister to the USA. Ennobled as baron de Linières, he held staff appointments 1813–14, latterly defending Würzburg, and retired in 1815. Despite his earlier hatred and persecution of the royalists, he accepted a decoration from the king upon the restoration of the Bourbons.

TWEEDDALE, Field Marshal George Hay, 8th Marquess of (1787–1876)

His parents both died in French captivity at Verdun: his mother, Hannah, in May 1804, his father, the 7th Marquess (1753–1804) on 9 August. He served in the Peninsular War; as a captain of the 1st Foot Guards he was wounded at Busaco while serving as deputy assistant QMG, and as a major in the 44th while serving as AQMG. He was wounded again in the War of 1812. In May 1875 he became field marshal. His younger brother, Lord James Hay (1788–1862), who as a captain in the 1st Foot Guards was ADC to Colville at Waterloo, and rose to the rank of lieutenant-general.

**XBRIDGE, Field Marshal
enry William Paget, 2nd Earl
, later Marquess of Anglesey
(768–1854)**

ne of the best British cavalry
ommanders of the period, he was
e eldest son of the 1st Earl of
Jxbridge, and until inheriting that
tle in 1812 he was known as Lord
aget. Beginning his military
areer as lieutenant-colonel in the
0th Foot which he raised from his
ather's estates, he served in The
Jetherlands in 1794 and 1799;
ntering the cavalry in 1795, he
ook command of the 7th Light
Jragoons and made it one of the
est regiments in the army. Major-
eneral from 1802 and lieutenanteneral in 1808, he commanded
Moore's cavalry in the Corunna
campaign, winning notable victories at Sahagun and Benevente;
but saw no further Peninsular
service by virtue of his having
eloped with the wife of
Wellington's brother, Henry
Wellesley, the cause of a quarrel
with the Duke's family (he married
the lady after divorcing his first
wife). Paget commanded a division
in the Walcheren expedition but
saw no further active service until
1815, spending the intervening
years in parliament (MP for
Milborne Port 1796–1810, and in
the House of Lords following his
father's death). With the animosity
evidently overcome (although he
had requested Cotton to
command his cavalry again),
Wellington accorded Uxbridge his
confidence and appointed him to
command the Allied cavalry and
horse artillery in the Waterloo
campaign, a task he accomplished
with distinction (if rather too eager
to become personally involved in
the fighting). Towards the end of
the battle Uxbridge lost his leg
when his knee was shattered by
grapeshot, giving rise to the
famous but perhaps apocryphal
exchange with Wellington, who
supported him in the saddle after
the injury; looking down,
Uxbridge supposedly remarked:
'By God, Sir, I've lost my leg!'; to
which Wellington replied, 'By God,
Sir, so you have!' Waterloo was
Uxbridge's last active service, for
which he was rewarded by the
title Marquess of Anglesey; but he
continued to serve in public office,
twice as Lord-Lieutenant of
Ireland (1828–33), difficult periods
in which he was criticised for
leniency towards Roman Catholics, and as Master-General of the
Ordnance (1846–52). He attained
the rank of field marshal in 1846.
His distinguished family included
his brothers Sir Arthur Paget
(1771–1840), the eminent diplomat; Sir Edward Paget (1775-
1849), one of Wellington's divisional commanders; and Vice-
Admiral Sir Charles Paget (1778–
1839). Anglesey's son Lord
Clarence Paget (1811–95) also
became an admiral, and another
son, General Lord George Paget
(1818–80) led the 4th Light
Dragoons at Balaclava and
commanded the Light Brigade
later in the Crimean War.

Anglesey, 7th Marquess of. *One-
Leg: the Life and Letters of Henry
William Paget*. London, 1961

ALMY, duc de, see **KELLER-MANN**

VANDAMME, General Dominique-Joseph-René, Comte (1770–1830)

DOMINIQUE VANDAMME
(PRINT AFTER J. S. ROUILLARD)

Renowned as a general for his courage, loyalty, frankness and plundering, he was born in Cassel, near Dunkirk, enrolled in the army in 1786 and served in Martinique before embracing the Revolution and forming a company of volunteer light infantry at his native town. His ability and extraordinary courage in the 1793 campaign led to his appointment as *général de brigade* in September of that year; after service in The Netherlands and Germany, and a suspension for looting (1795), he became *général de division* in 1799. Recalled from service again because of financial irregularities, he fell under Napoleon's spell and became a most loyal subordinate, his service in the Army of the Rhine, rather than under Napoleon in Italy, not counting against him. In 1805 he was greatly distinguished commanding the 2nd Division of IV Corps at Austerlitz; in 1806–7 he commanded Württemberg troops and was involved in the sieges of Glogau, Brieg and Schweidnitz.

Comte from 1808, in 1809 he again led his Württembergers, including at Abensberg and Eckmühl, and commanded at Vienna during the Wagram campaign. Notoriously ill-tempered and quarrelsome, when putting him under Davout's authority Napoleon warned the Marshal of his reputation, and for all his loyalty, Vandamme gave vent to his anger at not receiving the Marshal's baton which he thought he deserved. To Macdonald he raged at the appointment to the Marshalate of Oudinot and Marmont, and declared that Napoleon 'is a coward, a forger, a liar, and had it not been for me, Vandamme, he would still be keeping pigs in Corsica'.[1] Indeed, it was said that his rough and forthright manner was what blocked his promotion. In 1812 he served under Jérôme but returned home after quarrelling; and commanding I Corps in 1813, he was defeated and captured at Kulm. Although much admired for his bravery in this action, he had an awkward interview with the Tsar, after trading insults with the Grand Duke Constantine who, it was reported, snatched away Vandamme's sword. The Tsar accused him of plundering, whereupon Vandamme retorted that at least he hadn't murdered his father! (referring to the Tsar's supposed collusion in the assassination of Paul I). He was held in Russia until 1814, and exiled to Cassel by the Bourbons on his return to France, but rejoined Napoleon in 1815 and commanded III Corps in the Waterloo campaign. Again exiled at the second restoration, he was in America 1816–19 before being allowed to return to France; he died at Cassel in 1830, never having been re-employed. It was reported that Napoleon remarked that had there been two Vandammes, he would have had to make one hang the other; but for all his difficulties, Vandamme was one of Napoleon's most loyal and courageous subordinates.

1. Macdonald, vol. II, p. 6.
Du Casse, A. *Le Général Vandamme et sa Correspondance*. Paris, 1870

VANDELEUR, General Sir John Ormsby (1763–1849)
Son of Captain Richard Vandeleur of Rutland, Queen's County, he served in the British Army from 1781, including The Netherlands 1793–4, the Cape and under Lake in India, but is best remembered for his Peninsular and Waterloo service. He was appointed to command a brigade of the Light Division in September 1811, was slightly wounded at the storming of Ciudad Rodrigo, and was transferred to command of a cavalry brigade in July 1813, which he led to the end of the war. KCB from January 1815, in the Waterloo campaign he commanded the 4th British Cavalry Brigade; subsequently he rose to the rank of general. George Napier described him as 'a fine, honourable, kind-hearted, gallant soldier, and an excellent man. I never knew him say or do a harsh thing to any human being. No man can or ought to be more respected than he is.'[1]

1. Napier, G., p. 218.

VANSITTART, Nicholas, Baron Bexley (1766–1851)
A politician known for his financial expertise, he occupied a

number of posts in various British ministries, notably Secretary for Ireland under Pitt (1805), Secretary to the Treasury (1806–7) and, most importantly, Chancellor of the Exchequer under Liverpool (1812–22), during which time he was concerned with providing revenue for the pursuance of the war. He was ennobled as Baron Bexley in 1823 and left government in 1828.

VAN RENSSELAER, Major General Stephen (1764–1839)

Born in New York, he was a member of a most important and influential family, the fortunes of which had been laid by Killian Van Rensselaer in the second quarter of the 17th century. Stephen was an active and important politician, having been Lieutenant Governor of New York 1795–1801; his commission (by Governor Tompkins of New York) as major general of the state militia for the War of 1812 was overtly political: a prominent Federalist, it was hoped his appointment would gain support for the war from others of his party. Lacking military experience, it was agreed that he should be assisted by his kinsman, Solomon Van Rensselaer, a professional soldier who was expected to make the important decisions. As commander on the Niagara front, Stephen was defeated heavily at Queenston; he resigned his command and left the service shortly after, but resumed an active political career. He has been styled 'the last patroon', the original Killian being the first (a patroon being the recipient of a grant of land from the original Dutch government of New York and New Jersey). **Major General Solomon Van Rensselaer (1774–1852)** joined the US Army as a cornet at the age of 18, and became adjutant general of New York in 1801. He was in that office in 1812 when appointed to assist

Stephen, and the Queenston defeat effectively ended his military career, although subsequently he became a major general of militia.

VANSTABEL, Rear-Admiral Pierre-Jean (1744–97)

A native of Dunkirk, he served in the navy during the War of American Independence, and rose to the rank of rear admiral in 1793; but is probably best remembered for his command of the naval escort to the grain convoy which gave rise to the Battle of the Glorious First of June. With four ships-of-the-line he sailed to America in the winter of 1793–4, picked up the convoy and guided it successfully into Brest on 14 June 1794, a considerable triumph, having evaded the attempts by the Royal Navy to deny these vital supplies to France. He was appointed to command at Brest, and later in the year collaborated with Pichegru in securing Walcheren and thus the mouth of the Scheldt.

VAUBOIS, General Charles-Henri de Belgrand de, comte (1748–1839)

Although perhaps best known for his defence of Malta, he had a career considerably more extensive. Commissioned into the artillery in 1770, he advanced from lieutenant-colonel in 1791 to *général de division* in 1796. With the Army of Italy, he commanded the force which captured Livorno (Leghorn) (27 June 1796) just as the British residents were being evacuated in HMS *Inconstant*, which escaped unscathed despite being fired upon. He served at Roveredo and was pushed back after the two days' fight at Caliano; and made a fighting retreat at the same time as the Arcola operation, until supported. In 1798 he was one of the generals chosen to accompany Napoleon to Egypt,

but remained at Malta a Governor, where he stayed; when summoned to surrender by Saumarez, commanding an Anglo–Portuguese squadron in September 1798, he made a defiant reply, and they sailed away. After an insurrection by the inhabitants in that month, Vaubois was shut up in Valetta, and was blockaded by the British. He made a most gallant defence, continuing to issue defiant replies to calls to surrender (for example: 'I am too desirous to serve my country to listen to your propositions'). In February the British intercepted a relief-force and killed its commander, Perrée; so Vaubois tried to send a message to France by his ship-of-the-line *Guillaume Tell* that he could not hold out much longer, but she too was captured after a severe fight. In early September 1800 British reinforcements arrived and, with his supplies running out, Vaubois held a council of war which universally recommended surrender, and on 5 September he capitulated. He was retired upon his return to France, though in 1809 commanded a National Guard Division; he was made comte in 1808.

VEDEL, General Dominique-Honoré-Antoine-Marie, comte de (1771–1848)

Born in Monaco, the son of a French officer, the unfortunate Vedel is remembered for his association with Dupont's surrender. Enlisting in the army in 1784, he was commissioned in 1787 and served in the Revolutionary Wars (wounded at Rivoli). After Austerlitz he became *général de brigade*, commanded a brigade of Suchet's 1st Division of V Corps at Jena, served at Pultusk, Heilsberg and Friedland, and was promoted to *général de division* in November 1807. Sent to Spain with a division composed largely of recruits (six attalions of the *Légions de reserve* plus the 1/3rd Swiss Regiment) he was sent to reinforce Dupont (June 1808). On 17 July Dupont dispatched him, with his own division and four other battalions, to operate away from the main force, a fatal division of resources. This fault was Dupont's; but Vedel was responsible for unnecessary delays in marching to rejoin his chief when he heard the cannonade on 19 July. He finally got into action and was winning when Dupont sent a message that he desist, an armistice having been called. As negotiations proceeded, Dupont told Vedel to steal away and save his command, which he did; but when Dupont discovered that his negotiators had included Vedel's troops in their agreement for capitulation, and with the Spaniards threatening to destroy Dupont's force if the agreement were broken, he sent a message to Vedel to return. As Dupont was writing under duress, Vedel could have disobeyed orders and escaped; but he chose instead meekly to return to Bailen and lay down his arms, thus making Dupont's defeat even worse, and he even called in outlying detachments which were not officially included in the capitulation. When Vedel returned to France he was imprisoned and court-martialled; but was given further employment from late 1813 (serving in Italy and in 1814 at Lyons), and continued to serve under the Bourbons until his retirement in 1831.

VERGNIAUD, Pierre-Victurnien (1753–93)

One of the great orators of the Revolutionary period, he was born in Limoges and became a lawyer before his election to the Legislative Assembly, where his oratorical skills gained wide acclaim (though it was said that he was by nature indolent and would delay while others undermined him). The leader of the Girondins, he began as a supporter of constitutional monarchy but became critical of the king and a supporter of republicanism. His influence was used by those more extreme, whose actions were never part of his political philosophy; he denounced the September massacres, and spoke in favour of an appeal to the people in the matter of the trial of the king, though his own eloquence had helped create the anti-royal fervour which resulted. He voted for the death sentence, however (it was said that he spent the following night in tearful despair), and presiding over the Convention announced the result of the vote. (He later declared that he had voted for death, unjust though it might be, to avert civil war). He opposed the institution of a revolutionary tribunal, which aroused yet more hatred among those of more extreme views, who even plotted the death of Vergniaud's party; and though he at first defended himself with skill from the attacks of Robespierre, the fall of the Girondins was inevitable. In early July 1793 he was arrested, and together with his fellow Girondins was sent for trial, beginning on 27 October. Having been condemned to death on 30 October, the Girondins left the court singing *La Marseillaise*, and on the following day Vergniaud and the rest were guillotined. Napoleon remarked that in a sense they were the architects of their own downfall, for having gained great power in the Convention, the irresolution of their position concerning the fate of the king undermined their authority, so that, instead of them destroying 'the Mountain' (the extremists) and governing France, it was their faction which was overthrown.

Verdière, L. de. *Biographie de Vergniaud*. Paris, 1866

VERNET, Antoine-Charles-Horace (1758–1836), and Emile-Jean-Horace (1789–1863)

Antoine, known as Carle Vernet, was the son of Claude-Joseph Vernet (1714–89), a celebrated landscape and marine artist in the Claudian style. He became a distinguished historical painter and lithographer, perhaps best known as a painter of horses and as a caricaturist, but his military work was extensive, including battle-scenes (his painting of Austerlitz was rewarded by Napoleon with the *Légion d'honneur*). He also produced uniform-studies, such as the series of paintings illustrating the so-called 'Bardin' uniform-regulations of the French Army of 1812, and prints of troops involved in the occupation of France. His son, Emile-Jean-Horace, known as Horace Vernet, was also a most distinguished artist. Despite the guillotining of his aunt (Carle's sister), he became a fervent admirer of Napoleon, served in the National Guard and remained a Bonapartist even after the restoration. Like his father he was a battle-painter and also produced many uniform-studies; probably his best-known work was his *Barrière de Clichy*, which was refused by the Salon of 1822 for political reasons. Louis-Philippe commissioned his major work, the painting of many battle-scenes at Versailles. His sister married the renowned history-painter Paul Delaroche (1797–1856)

Dayot, E. *Les Vernets*. 1898

VIAL, General Honoré, baron (1766–1813)

After a short career at sea, he transferred to the army in 1792, serving in Corsica and in the Armies of the North and Alps before serving with distinction in the Army of Italy under Napoleon. *Général de brigade* from late 1796, he served at Arcola and Rivoli, and held the Governorship of Rome in 1798. In the expedition to Egypt he succeeded to the command of Menou's division after that general was wounded, and led it at the Battle of the Pyramids (the division was later commanded by Lannes). In 1802 he was sent as minister to Naples, became *général de division* in 1803, served as ambassador to Switzerland and in 1809 was appointed Governor of Venice; he became baron in 1808. Returning to active service, he commanded a division of Victor's corps in 1813, fought at Dresden and on 18 October was killed in the action near Probsthayda during the Battle of Leipzig. His younger brother, **General Jacques-Laurent Vial (1774–1855)**, earned considerable distinction as a cavalryman.

VICENZE, duc de, see **CAULAIN-COURT, General Armand**

VICTOR AMADEUS III, King of Sardinia (1726–96)

One of the least successful rulers of the house of Savoy, he succeeded his distinguished soldier father Charles Emmanuel III (ruled 1730–73), but could not emulate him; he was as extravagant and incapable as his ministers, and the state was not in fit condition to resist the armies of Revolutionary France, which Victor Amadeus opposed. (He was closely connected to the deposed French royal family, providing aid to *émigrés* and to his brothers-in-law, Artois and Provence (later Charles X and Louis XVIII of France) having married Marie Thérèse and Louise Marie Joséphine of Savoy respectively). Despite brave resistance by his Piedmontese troops, his forces suffered repeated defeats and by the armistice of Cherasco, and the Treaty of Paris (May 1796) which followed, he ceded Savoy and Nice

to France, and died shortly afterwards. He was succeeded by his three sons: Charles Emmanuel IV (ruled 1796–1802, and abdicated after losing the rest of Piedmont), Victor-Emmanuel I (1802–21, who remained in Sardinia until the Congress of Vienna restored his mainland possessions), and Charles-Félix (1821–31 who succeeded upon his brother's abdication).

VICTOR PERRIN, Marshal Claude, duc de Bellune (1764–1841)

Calling himself Victor, by which name he is generally known, he was born in La Marche (Vosges), of relatively humble parentage, and enlisted in the artillery in 1781. He left the army in 1791 and settled in Valence, but joined the local volunteers and advanced rapidly in rank; he became *général de brigade* and won recognition at Toulon, where he impressed Napoleon. After service with the Army of the Eastern Pyrenees and under Napoleon in Italy, he became *général de division* in March 1797. In 1800 he served again in Italy, notably as divisional commander holding the left of Napoleon's line at Marengo. In 1803 he commanded the Batavian Army, was plenipotentiary to Denmark 1805–6, in 1806 was Lannes' chief of staff and in January 1807 took command of X Corps. Taken prisoner and exchanged, he led I Corps at Friedland with such distinction that he was appointed Marshal (13 July 1807). After Tilsit he became Governor of Berlin, and in September 1808 was ennobled as Duke of Belluno; this title supposedly originated as a pun by Pauline Bonaparte. Victor was nicknamed '*le beau soleil*' because of his friendly nature (though Wellington thought it might originate from a round, red face), and hence the pun: from 'handsome sun' to

'beautiful moon' (*Bellune/belle lune*)! He was sent to Spain in command of I Corps, where his fortunes were mixed, though he enjoyed more success than some. In November 1808 he defeated Blake at Espinosa and in May 1809 Cuesta at Medellin, but was defeated at Talavera, and by Graham at Barrosa (where he was observed behaving with customary bravery, leading a column and waving his hat in encouragement). Withdrawn from Spain, Victor commanded IX Corps in the Russian campaign, initially operating in the rear of the *Grande Armée*, but playing a vital role in keeping open the escape-route for Napoleon's own force by sterling conduct at the Berezina. In 1813 he commanded II Corps, including Dresden and Leipzig, but was replaced in command in 1814 after being thought dilatory in his conduct before Montereau. Victor was appalled and refused to leave, declaring that he had not forgotten how to use a musket and would fight in the ranks if necessary; evidently affected by such a show of loyalty, Napoleon gave him a divisional command in the Imperial Guard instead, and in this position he was wounded at Craonne. He accepted the Bourbon restoration and accorded them the same loyalty he had shown to Napoleon; he accompanied the king to Ghent and on the second restoration became a peer of France. He even presided over a commission to investigate the conduct of officers during the Hundred Days, and voted for the capital sentence on Ney. Minister of War 1821–3, he was major-general of the Royal Guard, and despite being recalled from the Spanish expedition of 1823 he continued in favour until the 1830 revolution, when he retired into private life.

Arnold, J. R. 'Le Beau Soleil': Victor', in *Napoleon's Marshals*,

d. D. G. Chandler. London, 1989; ictor, Marshal. *Mémoires de Jaude-Victor Perrin*. Paris, 1847 covers only the early part of his service)

IGNY, Alfred de (1797–1863)
The son of a veteran of the Seven Years War, this poet and author was born in Loches (Touraine), and as a member of a noble family was a committed royalist. In 1814 he entered the reconstituted *Maison du Roi*, accompanied Louis XVIII on his flight to The Netherlands, and served in the Royal Guard until transferring to the 55th Line in 1823 in the hope of seeing active service in Spain, which was unfulfilled. He left the army in 1827. One of his most notable works, and that concerning contemporary military life, is *Servitudes et Grandeurs Militaires*, published in 1835. Sir Charles Napier edited a translation into English; a modern version is titled *The Military Condition*, trans. M. Barnett, intro. J. Cruikshank, Oxford 1964.

VILLARET DE JOYEUSE, Vice-Admiral Louis Thomas, comte (1748–1812)
Born in Auch of an aristocratic family, he was intended for the church, but preferred a military career. He entered the *Maison du Roi*, but after killing an opponent in a duel transferred to the Navy (1765). He was promoted after distinguished service at Pondicherry, and was favoured by Suffren, then commanding in the East Indies. Ordered to cruise in search of the British, he humorously requested letters of introduction to the British commander and Governor of Madras; and his joke was prophetic, for shortly after his frigate *Naïade* was captured by the British 64-gunner HMS *Sceptre* (June 1783). Villaret did not emigrate at the Revolution, and after commanding the 74-gunner *Trajan*, as rear-admiral flying his flag in *Le Montagne* led the fleet which was defeated at the Battle of the Glorious First of June. Despite his defeat – in which he had been burdened by the 'advice' of the commissioner Saint-André which can only have made his task more difficult – he insisted that it was worth the loss of a few ships to secure the safety of the vital grain convoy, and that he only determined to fight to distract the British from seizing it. Promoted to *vice-amiral* in the following September, in June 1795 he declined a full-scale action against Bridport's fleet, which outnumbered him, and lost three ships; and in 1796 turned to a political career in the Council of Five Hundred. In September 1797 he was sentenced to deportation as a royalist and took refuge in the island of Oléron, off the west coast of France. He was recalled, however, in 1801 commanded the fleet which took Leclerc to San Domingo, and in 1802 was appointed captain-general of Martinique; he became comte in 1808. He surrendered to the British in 1809 and upon his return from Martinique was unemployed under the shadow of this defeat, until Napoleon appointed him Governor of Venice in 1811; he died there in the following year. When conveyed home from Martinique aboard HMS *Belleisle*, her captain Edward Brenton reported him to be a polished gentleman of undoubted skill and bravery.

VILLELE, Jean-Baptiste-Guillaume-Marie-Anne-Séraphin, comte de (1773–1854)
This statesman, who came to prominence in the post-Napoleonic age, was born in Toulouse and served in the navy in the East and West Indies prior to the Revolution. He was arrested in the Ile de Bourbon during the Terror, but freed in 1794, acquired property and settled there, becoming involved in local politics, aiming to prevent malcontents from requesting British protection while resisting undue interference from France. He returned home and became involved in local politics, becoming mayor of Toulouse in 1814, when he declared for the royalists. He subsequently became one of the leading politicians in France, first in Richelieu's ministry, and from 1822 (ennobled as comte by Louis XVIII) as Prime Minister in the royalist interest, until he retired from public life in 1827 after defeat in a general election. Wellington, who knew him from his days at Toulouse, said that he was 'about the ablest man I saw amongst them'.[1]

1. Stanhope, p. 42.

Villèle, comte de. *Mémoires et Correspondance du Comte de Villèle*. Paris, 1887–90

VILLENEUVE, Vice-Admiral Pierre-Charles-Jean-Baptiste-Silvestre (1763–1806)

PIERRE-CHARLES VILLENEUVE

Known to history as the admiral defeated by Nelson at Trafalgar, he was a native of Provence who entered the Navy in 1778. After service in the West Indies, and despite aristocratic background, he sympathised with the Revolution and remained in the service. The shortage of experienced officers caused by emigration allowing rapid promotion for the capable, he was appointed captain in February 1793, survived suspension because of noble birth and became rear-admiral in 1796. He was appointed to a command in the abortive Bantry Bay expedition, but his squadron assembled too late to participate; but aboard his flagship *Guillaume Tell* did take part in the expedition to Egypt, and managed to escape from the destruction of the French fleet at Aboukir Bay (for which he received censure which was probably unfair). He reached Malta, where he was briefly taken prisoner when Vaubois' garrison surrendered to the British. Promoted to *vice-admiral* in May 1804, he took command at Toulon and was given the task of leading away the main British fleet before returning to assist in the French invasion of England. Much was against the plan, including his own belief in its success; but it might be argued that, having agreed to it, even while not approving, he should have carried it through, but he also considered the safety of his ships. Having returned to Europe (where he fought an indecisive action against Calder off Ferrol), despite orders to proceed, he took his fleet into Cadiz. After being informed that he was to be superseded in command, he left harbour and was defeated catastrophically at Trafalgar; Villeneuve himself was taken prisoner when his flagship *Bucentaure was* surrendered to Captain James Atcherley of the Royal Marines, representing Captain Israel Pellew of HMS *Conqueror*. He was taken to England but freed on parole; evidently overwhelmed by his defeat, shortly after returning to France he committed suicide by stabbing himself through the heart at an inn in Rennes on 22 April 1806. It was a sad end for a gallant officer who had been given a task which was probably quite impracticable.

VIVIAN, Lieutenant-General Sir Richard Hussey, Baron (1775–1842)

SIR RICHARD HUSSEY VIVIAN
(ENGRAVING PROBABLY AFTER E. M. WARD)

Descended from a very ancient Cornish family (his father was Warden of the Stannaries), he was intended for a legal career but preferred the army, purchasing his first commission in 1793. As a captain he served with the 28th Foot in The Netherlands in 1794, exchanging into the 7th Light Dragoons in 1798. He served with them in North Holland in 1799, and as lieutenant-colonel led them in the Corunna campaign, including Sahagun and Benevente; he was still commanding them when they returned to the Peninsula in 1813, until in that November he was placed in command of a cavalry brigade. Vivian was wounded severely in the arm in the action which secured the bridge of Croix d'Orade near Toulouse; and as major-general (June 1814) in the Waterloo campaign commanded the 6th British Cavalry Brigade. In January 1827 he was promoted t lieutenant-general, received baronetcy in January 1828 and i 1831 became CinC Ireland; he wa Master-General of the Ordnanc 1835–41 and MP for Trurc Windsor and East Cornwall fron 1820 until ennobled as Baron Vivian of Truro in 1841. He died c heart failure at Baden-Baden in August 1842, and was succeeded by Charles (1808–86), his eldest son by his first wife; his second son, John (1818–79), became Under-Secretary for War, and his natural son, Sir Robert John Hussey Vivian (1802–87), had a distinguished military career rising to the rank of general. As a brave leader of light cavalry, Sir Richard was much esteemed; his memorial at St. Mary's, Truro recorded that 'His nobleness of character, his charity, benevolence, and integrity endeared him to all who knew him. The widow and orphan never appealed in vain; and the deserving soldier always found in him a friend.' His reputation with his men can be gleaned from a remark made at Waterloo, when he asked the 18th Hussars if they would follow him: 'To hell, if you will lead us,' was the reply.[1]

1. Mackenzie, Col. R. H. 'Lieut General Richard Hussey, First Lord Vivian', in *Cavalry Journal*, 1920, vol. X, pp. 22, 25.

Vivian, C. H. *Richard Hussey Vivian, First Baron Vivian: A Memoir*. London, 1897

VORONTSOV, Field Marshal Mikhail Semenovich, Prince (1782–1856)

He was a member of a most distinguished and influential Russian family. His father was Semen Romanovich Vorontsov (1744–1832) who after service against the Turks became Russian Ambassador to London in 1785, where he spent the remainder of his life. Serving Catherine the Great, Paul I and Alexander I, he was an advocate of close Anglo–Russian relations and an opponent of France, and helped direct Russian policy in that direction; he fell from favour in 1800 but was reinstated by Alexander I, and remained ambassador until he resigned for reasons of health in 1806. His brother, Mikhail's uncle, was Alexander Romanovich Vorontsov (1741–1805), Imperial Chancellor 1802–4, like his brother a noted opponent of France, and an advocate of internal reform. Mikhail was educated in England, entered the Russian Army and served against the Turks, in the 1807 campaign (including Pultusk and Friedland), and in 1812 commanded the 7th Grenadier Division, being severely wounded at Borodino. In 1813 he commanded the small force which almost occupied Leipzig until stopped by the armistice, and served in the 1814 campaign, including Craonne. He led the Russian forces in the occupation of France (1815–18) and in 1823 was appointed Governor-General of New Russia (the southern provinces of the empire). He captured Varna in 1828, and as CinC and Governor of the Caucasus from 1844 his successes (including the capture of two-thirds of Daghestan) were rewarded by the title of Prince. He retired in 1853 and was advanced to the rank of field marshal shortly before his death. The family name may also be found with the spellings 'Woronzow', 'Voronzov' and 'Woronzoff'.

WAGRAM, prince de, see
BERTHIER

WAIRY, Louis-Constant, see
CONSTANT

WALEWSKA, Marie, Countess (1789–1817)

One of the most loyal of Napoleon's romantic conquests, she was the daughter of a Polish nobleman, who took her title from the husband she married in her youth, he being very much older. She met Napoleon in 1807, and although their liaison had been encouraged by those of her countrymen seeking to influence him towards the granting of Polish independence, it developed into a relationship of genuine affection. A child, Count Walewski, was born of the union in 1810, and Marie remained loyal to Napoleon, visiting him (with the child Alexandre) on Elba. After the death of her aged husband she married General (later Marshal) Philippe d'Ornano, but died at the very early age of 28.

Sutherland, C. *Marie Walewska: Napoleon's Great Love.* New York, 1979; Wilson, R. *Napoleon's Love Story.* 1935

WALEWSKI, Alexandre-Florian-Joseph-Colonna, Count (1810–68)

Napoleon's illegitimate child by Marie Walewska was recognised by her husband as his own offspring, and so inherited his name; even though the child accompanied his mother on her trip to Elba and had been acknowledged as Napoleon's son. With Philippe d'Ornano, Marie's second husband, as his stepfather, after Marie's death Alexandre was sent to Poland to be educated, but returned to France to escape service in the Russian army. In 1830 he was sent by Louis-Philippe on a mission to Poland; in 1831 while in England

he married Catherine, younger daughter of George, 6th Earl of Sandwich (and remarried after her death), and served in the French Army after taking French nationality. He resigned his commission in 1837, pursued a literary career, and under Louis Napoleon and the Second Empire was employed in diplomatic duties, including as envoy to London and as Foreign Minister (1855–60); he served as a senator 1855–65 and was President of the Chamber for two years. Some of his contemporaries were severely critical of his character and abilities.

Valynselle, O. *La Descendance Naturelle de Napoléon ler: le Comte Léon, le Comte Walewsky.* Paris, 1964

WALLACE, General Sir John Alexander, Bt. (*d.* 1857)

One of the best-known regimental officers of the British Army, he was commissioned in December 1787, served at Seringapatam, in Minorca (1798) and in Egypt, but is best known for his command of the 88th Foot in the Peninsula (lieutenant-colonel 6 February 1805). He was especially distinguished at Busaco, where he led most of his battalion and part of the 45th in a charge which repelled Merle's attack; Picton acknowledged that although he had led on the light companies of these two units, he claimed no credit, extolling Wallace as the victor. Wellington confirmed this by seizing his hand and exclaiming, 'Upon my honour, Wallace, I never witnessed a more gallant charge than that just now made by your battalion.'[1] He was also greatly distinguished at Fuentes de Oñoro. William Grattan (who believed Wallace to have been a descendant of the great Scottish hero Sir William Wallace (*d.* 1305)) described him as 'the very kind of man we wanted'

to lead a regiment like the 88th with its indomitable Irish composition; 'Although a Scotsman himself, he was intimately acquainted with the sort of men he had under him, and he dealt with them, and addressed their feelings, in a way that was peculiar to himself, and suited to them. In action he was the same as on parade, and in either case he was as he should be ... [he] was out of his place as a mere commander of a regiment; he was eminently calculated to head a division, because he not only possessed that intrepidity of mind which would brave any danger, but genius to discover the means of overcoming it.' An example of his homely oration to his men was on forming square in the face of enemy cavalry: 'Mind the square ... for by God, if you are once broken, you'll be running here and there like a parcel of frightened pullets!' He became major-general in August 1819, lieutenant-general in January 1837, and general in November 1851; awarded a baronetcy, he held the colonelcy of the 88th from October 1831 until his death.

1. This and subsequent quotations first pubd. in *USJ*, 1831, vol. II, p. 181.

WALTHER, General Frédéric-Henri, comte (1761–1813)

A well-known commander of Napoleon's Imperial Guard, he had enlisted in 1781; serving in the Berchény Hussars, he was commissioned in 1789, was wounded at Neerwinden, and became *général de brigade* in October 1793. After service in Italy and at Hohenlinden (wounded), he was promoted to *général de division* in August 1803. In 1805 he led the 2nd Dragoon Division at Austerlitz (wounded), and in the following year was appointed imperial chamberlain and given command of the *Grenadiers à Cheval* of the Imperial Guard. He commanded them (brigaded with the *Gendarmerie d'Elite*) at Jena, served in the 1807 campaign, and became comte in 1808. In the same year he commanded the Guard in Paris, led it into the Peninsula but returned to serve in the 1809 Danube campaign, commanding the Guard cavalry at Wagram. After serving throughout the 1812 campaign, he continued to command the *Grenadiers à Cheval* in 1813, though not having fully recovered from the exertions of the previous campaign. He led the 3rd Guard Cavalry Division at Leipzig, but after Hanau was en route to Metz to recover his health when he died suddenly at Kusel on 24 November 1813; Napoleon wrote to his wife, mourning the loss of one of his bravest and most trusted generals, testimony to his faithful service.

WARREN, Admiral Sir John Borlase, Bt. (1753–1822)

A member of an old Nottinghamshire family, he was educated at Cambridge University, went to sea in 1771, was MP for Marlow in 1774 and was created a baronet in 1775. In the early Revolutionary Wars he achieved much success as a frigate captain and commodore, taking a large number of French vessels, most notably the capture of the frigate *Pomone* (April 1794) and the destruction of the frigates *Andromaque* (August 1796) and *Calliope* (July 1797). His most important service, however, was surely that on 12 October 1798, when off the north coast of Ireland, in his flagship *Canada*, he intercepted the French squadron bringing reinforcements to the Irish rebellion, capturing the 74-gunner *Hoche* and the frigates *Embuscade*, *Coquille* and *Bellone*; among the prisoners was Wolfe Tone. In 1802 Warren went to Russia in a diplomatic capacity, but returned to sea, and as vice-admiral on 13 March 1806 his squadron captured the French 74-gunner *Marengo* and frigate *Belle Poule* off Brest. Admiral from 1810, he was CinC North American station 1813–14.

WATERS, Lieutenant-General Sir John (1774–1842)

One of the most remarkable intelligence officers of the period, he was a native of Margam, Glamorganshire, who during the Peninsular War (as an officer of the Portuguese Army and Wellington's QMG's Department) was a most valuable and practised spy, bringing intelligence to Wellington from behind enemy lines. Gronow stated that it was as if the war in Spain had been created for the express purpose of using his astonishing talents; not only a brilliant and perceptive observer, he had a chameleon-like quality which allowed him to impersonate a Spaniard of any class, any region, Asturian, Andalusian, Catalonian, and spoke French with such a perfect German accent that he was accepted unquestionably as an Alsacian when he mixed with their troops to gain information. Even when he was captured he not only made his escape but managed to secure the intelligence he had been seeking. He was wounded at Waterloo while lieutenant-colonel and assistant adjutant-general and became lieutenant-general in 1841.

WATHIER (or WATIER) DE SAINT-ALPHONSE, General Pierre, comte (1770–1846)

He was one of the second rank of Napoleon's cavalry commanders. A native of Laon, he was commissioned in 1792, his service including The Netherlands in 1799 and as commander of the 4th Dragoons was captured after Ulm and exchanged after Austerlitz. *Général de brigade* from December 1805, he led brigades in 1806–7, including Friedland, and in 1808 went to Spain as cavalry commander in III Corps; for his service there, notably as part of the covering force during the siege of Saragossa, in November 1809 he was rewarded with the title of comte de Saint-Alphonse. Arriving too late in the Danube theatre to command a brigade in the 1809 campaign, he returned to Spain in late 1810, and in July 1811 was promoted to *général de division* in command of the cavalry of the Army of the North. In Russia in 1812 he led the 2nd Heavy Cavalry Division of II Cavalry Corps, notably in the famous action around the Raevsky Redoubt at Borodino. In 1813 he joined Davout as cavalry commander and was besieged in Hamburg until 1814; unemployed upon the Bourbon restoration, he rejoined Napoleon in 1815 and in the Waterloo campaign led the 13th Cavalry Division of IV Cavalry Corps, composed of the cuirassiers with which arm he is most associated. From 1820 until his retirement in 1839 he occupied a number of administrative posts.

WEIMER, Marguerite-Joséphine (1787–1867)

An actress of striking appearance, who first trod the stage in Paris in 1802, Josephine Weimer, better-known by her stage-name 'Mademoiselle Georges', for a time became Napoleon's mistress; he devised an elastic garter for her which was easier to remove than the buckled variety. A decade after the end of their liaison, she made friends with Wellington during his time in Paris before the Hundred Days, and she claimed to have been his mistress as well. She was described as very large but an expressive actress who reminded Hobhouse of Mrs. Sarah Siddons.

Saunders, E. *Napoleon and Mlle. Georges.* London, 1958

WELLESLEY, Sir Arthur, see WELLINGTON

WELLESLEY, Sir Henry, Baron Cowley (1773–1847)

Wellington's youngest brother pursued a diplomatic career, serving in that capacity in Sweden in 1792. He was secretary to his brother Richard in India and Lieutenant-Governor of Oudh; First Secretary to the Treasury 1808–9, he was appointed British Ambassador to Spain, a position he held until 1822, where his influence was of assistance to Wellington's conduct of the Peninsular War. He was ambassador to Austria 1823–31 and subsequently to France; in January 1828 he was ennobled as Baron Cowley of Wellesley, Somerset. In September 1803 he married Charlotte (1781–1853), second daughter of Charles, 1st Earl Cadogan (her elder sister, Emily (1778–1839) having in 1802 married Henry Wellesley's brother, Revd. Gerald), but the marriage was not a success; Charlotte eloped with Henry William Paget, later Marquess of Anglesey, which was the cause of the family feud which prevented Anglesey from serving under Wellington in the Peninsula. Henry Wellesley obtained a divorce in 1810, and Charlotte married Anglesey; the child born to Charlotte in 1809, Gerald Valerian Wellesley (1809–82) was not acknowledged by Henry but was brought up by Wellington's

wife, and became Queen Victoria's much-esteemed Dean of Windsor. Henry had four other children (including a daughter by his second wife, Georgina, daughter of James, 1st Marquess of Salisbury), and he was succeeded by his eldest son Henry (1804–84), also a distinguished diplomat, who was created 1st Earl Cowley in April 1857.

Cowley, Lord. *The Diary and Correspondence of Henry Wellesley, 1st Lord Cowley, 1790–1816,* ed. Colonel F. A. Wellesley. London, 1930

WELLESLEY, Richard Colley, Marquess (1760–1842)

RICHARD, MARQUESS WELLESLEY
(ENGRAVING BY HUNT AFTER LAWRENCE)

Wellington's eldest brother was famous in his own right, not merely from his relationship with the Duke. Eldest son of the 1st Earl of Mornington, he succeeded to the title in 1781, and although involved in British politics as a supporter of Pitt (he was elected an MP in 1784, the peerage being Irish), it was in India that he made his name. In 1797 he was appointed Governor-General, and from his arrival in 1798 was involved in a very considerable extension of British power and influence, probably arising originally from the threat of French

intervention. Mysore was subdued by the capture of Seringapatam, but the Second Maratha War was still being fought when he was replaced as Governor-General by Cornwallis in 1805. Although the East India Company had been transformed from a trading concern into almost an independent power, Mornington's policies had brought him into conflict with the directors of the company, and his administration in India received much criticism. His rewards included an English peerage (Baron Wellesley of Wellesley, October 1797) and a marquisate, Marquess Wellesley in the Irish peerage (December 1799). Resolutions of censure over his tenure as Governor-General were defeated in both Houses of Parliament, and in 1809 he was appointed ambassador to Spain, where his brother was leading the British Army, but after a few months he became Foreign Secretary. He held this position until February 1812, when he resigned partly over a perceived lack of support for his brother in the Peninsula, and partly over his support for Catholic Emancipation. He returned to office as Lord-Lieutenant of Ireland 1821–8 and 1833–4. His first wife having died in 1816, in 1825 he married Marianne Paterson, the widow of the American merchant whose sister Elizabeth had married Jérôme Bonaparte. Wellington was upset by the marriage because he was believed to be fond of Marianne himself, and he disapproved of Richard's profligate habits; indeed, as early as 1810 he had remarked that he wished that Richard were castrated, to concentrate his mind upon matters of state! Having no legitimate successor, Richard's marquisate died with him, but the earldom of Mornington was inherited by his younger brother, William Wellesley-Pole (1763–

1845), who adopted the additional surname in 1778 and who became Baron Maryborough in his own right in 1821.

Butler, I. *The Oldest Brother: the Marquess Wellesley 1760–1842*. London, 1973; Hutton, W. H. *Lord Wellesley, Rulers of India* series 1893; Severn, J. K. *A Wellesley Affair: Richard, Marquess Wellesley and the Conduct of Anglo–Spanish Diplomacy 1809–1812*. Tallahassee, 1981; Torrens, W. M. *The Marquess Wellesley*. 1880; Wellesley, Marquess. *Despatches and Correspondence of the Marquess Wellesley KG during his Lordship's Mission to Spain ...*, ed. M. Martin. London, 1838; *Memoirs and Correspondence of the Most Noble Richard, Marquess Wellesley ...*, ed. R. R. Pearce. London, 1846

WELLINGTON, Field Marshal Arthur Wellesley, 1st Duke of (1769– 1852)

ARTHUR WELLESLEY,
1ST DUKE OF WELLINGTON

Arguably Britain's greatest soldier and one of the outstanding military commanders of his or any other age, he was the son of Garret Wesley, 1st Earl of Mornington (1735–81); the family name later reverted to its older form, 'Wellesley'. Arthur was born probably in Dublin (the exact location is uncertain), and educated at Eton and at a French military academy; but though the family had important connections there was little money, and as the least promising member of the Earl's sons he was consigned to a military career, the only thing for which he was thought fit. This was a mistaken perception, however; from the beginning he proved highly intelligent, with a penchant for hard work and no time for frivolity. Aided by the system of purchase of commissions he rose from ensign (7 March 1787) to lieutenant-colonel in command of the 33rd Foot (30 November 1793), led the regiment with distinction in The Netherlands (1794–5) where, he said, he learned 'how not to do it') and in 1797 went with it to India. This proved to be his real military education, and although his early appointments owed something to his elder brother Richard, who was Governor-General, the remainder of his military success was dictated by his own immense talents (indeed, as well as his family connections proving an advantage, he experienced some prejudice and hostility from opponents of his family). Service in India, where he first exercised independent command and learned every facet of military and diplomatic experience, established his reputation (though as a 'sepoy general' he had to some degree to re-establish it when he returned to Europe), and included some major triumphs, notably against the Marathas at Assaye (23 September 1803) and Argaum (29 November 1803). Returning to Britain in 1805, he resumed his political career (he had been an MP in Ireland as early as 1790 and served as Irish Secretary), until given a subordinate command under Cathcart for the Danish expedition. This confirmed his military talents, and he was appointed to lead the British forces in the Iberian Peninsula. He won the battles of Roliça and Vimeiro, but was superseded by both 'Betty' Burrard and 'Dowager' Dalrymple who prevented the exploitation of the latter victory, and (under protest from Wellesley) concluded the shameful Convention of Cintra. All three were recalled to face an enquiry, from which only Wellesley was vindicated; and after the death of Moore he was sent back to the Peninsula in April 1809 in supreme command.

From this time his fame increased with every success, but his task and responsibilities were immense. He commanded virtually the only army which Britain could deploy in Europe, yet had no 'unity of command', being dependent upon his own successes to retain the support of his political masters, and even as late as 1815 never had the freedom to appoint only those subordinates he wanted, but had to employ whomsoever was sent to him. That he was successful with these limitations, and with a staff so small that it might not have sufficed for a French *corps d'armée*, is testimony to his immense skill. These circumstances perhaps also explain his caution (he was compared with the Roman general Quintus Fabius Maximus, alias Cunctator, 'the delayer'), and why he tended to stifle burgeoning talent among his subordinates: with few officers completely trustworthy in independent command, Wellington insisted on overseeing everything himself. He was his own chief of staff and head of intelligence, acted as Britain's diplomatic representative in dealing with the allied governments, and superintended all details of operations. Astute, with a complete understanding of the military trade and a willing capacity for the hardest labour, his supervision of even the smallest concerns, together with the inherent qualities of the British Army and its Portuguese allies, produced what he described as 'the most complete machine for its numbers now existing in Europe'; but it was moulded by his actions and was very much his machine.

After Talavera, Wellesley was created a viscount (September 1809), his title 'Wellington' being taken from the old family estates in Somerset; his successive steps in the peerage were Earl (February 1812), Marquess (October 1812) and Duke (May 1814). His actions from 1809 to 1814 are virtually a history of the British involvement in the Peninsular War. His first priority was to establish a secure base in Portugal, French advances being frustrated by the Lines of Torres Vedras, the most effective fortification of the era, entirely his conception and to a considerable extent his design. In 1812 he assumed the offensive, winning a major victory at Salamanca but then being forced to retire after an injudicious attempt to take Burgos. The following year, however, there began the concerted driving of the French from Spain, Wellington crushing their main field army at Vittoria, penetrating the Pyrenees and invading southern France before the end of the war in 1814; on 21 June 1813 he was appointed Field Marshal of the British Army, accompanying his positions as Marshal-General of Portugal and Generalissimo of the Spanish armies. In 1815, acting in concert with Blücher's Prussian Army in The Netherlands, he blended successfully a heterogeneous army that included many inexperienced or perceived unreliable units into a force which defeated Napoleon at Waterloo, and this triumph established him as among the greatest of generals.

Wellington has been criticised for the defensive nature of his battles, and certainly his early Peninsula actions were not characterised by the spirit of offence which he had learned and employed in India (where he had advised a subordinate, 'The best thing you can do is ... dash at the first party that comes into your neighbourhood ... '[1] Some defensive tactics were largely forced upon him by circumstances, however, and within the overall concept of the 'defensive' battle his tactics could be quite aggressive; and the classic tactic of shielding his troops on a reverse slope not only concealed them from enemy reconnaissance and fire but proved an ideal counter to the French system of war. In the offensive sphere, he proved himself a master of opportunity (as at Salamanca) and manoeuvre (1813); he was truly a complete commander, rivalled only in his own time by Napoleon himself, yet was the opposite of Napoleon in virtually every way save personal courage, and was never defeated. His austere, aloof and even cold demeanour was partly an outward mask (he could be a most entertaining host despite the frugal nature of his dinners, and could be moved to tears by casualty-returns), but led to his being respected and trusted by his troops, but not revered in the way in which Napoleon and Marlborough were worshipped by their followers. Their trust in 'that long-nosed beggar that licks the French'[2] was total (in the words of two privates of the Light Division: Wellington's nose led to his nicknames of 'Hooky' or 'Beaky'). This trust was perhaps best articulated by John Kincaid, who paid tribute not only to Wellington's military skill but to his concern for the well-being of his men and their rations (the importance of logistics Wellington had learned in India):

'he was not only head of the army but obliged to descend to the responsibility of every department in it. In the different branches of their various duties, he received the officers in charge, as ignorant as schoolboys, and, by his energy and unwearied perseverance, he made them what they became – the most renowned army that Europe ever saw. Whenever he went at its head, glory followed its steps – wherever he was not – I will not say disgrace, but something akin to it ensued ... Lord Wellington appeared to us never to leave anything to chance. However desperate the undertaking ... we ever felt confident that a redeeming power was at hand, nor were we ever deceived. Those only, too, who have served under such a master-mind and one of inferior calibre can appreciate the difference in a physical as well as a moral point of view – for when in the presence of the enemy, under him, we were never deprived of our personal comforts until prudence rendered it necessary, and they were always restored to us at the earliest possible moment.' The entire army, in fact, would have agreed with Kincaid when he remarked that 'We would rather see his long nose in the fight than a reinforcement of ten thousand men any day.'[3]

After the end of his active military career, Wellington fulfilled every office of state from Prime Minister (1828–30) to CinC (1827–8, 1842–52) with the same uncompromising attitude as he had commanded in battle, sacrificing all for what he believed to be his duty and the public good, at one time even his personal popularity, when a mob broke the windows of his London home, leading to the erection of metal shutters which gave rise to the nickname 'the Iron Duke'. He became the mentor of the young Queen Victoria and transcended the ordinary status of public life to become a national symbol, and by popular acclaim the greatest Britisher of his age. When he died peacefully at Walmer Castle, his residence as Lord Warden of the Cinque Ports (14 September 1852), *The Times* described his career as 'one unclouded longest day'. A revealing remark was recorded by Lady Salisbury, who at Walmer in 1836 asked the Duke whether he realised that the victory of Waterloo 'had raised your name above every other'. Without a trace of false modesty, Wellington replied that he had never considered it, for 'That is a feeling of vanity; one's *first* thought is for the public service ... perhaps there is no man now existing who would like to meet me on a field of battle; in that line I am superior. But when the war is over and the troops disbanded, what is your great general more than anybody else? I am necessarily inferior to every man in his own line, though I may excel him in others. I cannot saw and plane like a carpenter, or make shoes like a shoemaker, or understand cultivation like a farmer. Each of these, on his own ground, meets me on terms of superiority. I feel I am but a man.'[4] A similar concern for the public weal over private success had characterised his conduct throughout life; when he was riding forward at the end of the battle of Waterloo, it was reported that an aide begged him not to risk himself. The battle was won, Wellington replied, so let them fire away – his life was no longer of consequence now that his job was done. As he was styled at the time, he was indeed the 'Great Duke'.

1.Wellington, vol. II, p. 210. 2. Tomkinson, p. 117. 3. Kincaid, pp. 36, 245–6. 4. Maxwell, vol. II, pp. 92–3.

Ellesmere, Earl of. *Personal Recollections of the Duke of Wellington*. London, 1904; Fraser, Sir William, Bt. *Words on Wellington*. London, 1889; Glover, M. *Wellington as Military Commander*. London, 1968; Griffith, P. (ed.). *Wellington Commander: the Iron Duke's Generalship*. Chichester, 1985; Hibbert, C. *Wellington: A Personal History*. London, 1997; James, L. *The Iron Duke: A Military Biography of Wellington*. London, 1992; Longford, Countess of. *Wellington: The Years of the Sword, Wellington: Pillar of State*. London, 1969, 1972 respectively; Maxwell, Sir Herbert. *Life of Wellington*. London, 1899; Stanhope, Earl. *Notes on Conversations with the Duke of Wellington*. London, 1888; Weller, J. *Wellington in India, Wellington in the Peninsula, Wellington at Waterloo*. London, 1972, 1962, 1967 respectively; Wellington, Duke of. *Dispatches of Field-Marshal the Duke of Wellington*, ed. J. Gurwood. London, 1834–8; Wellington, Duke of. *Supplementary Despatches and Memoranda of Field- Marshal the Duke of Wellington*, ed. 2nd Duke of Wellington. London 1858–72

WESTERMANN, General François-Joseph (*d.*1794)

This native of Alsace was an ardent supporter of the Revolution and a follower of Danton, and was conspicuous in the attack on the Tuileries. He served with Dumouriez, was arrested after the latter's defection, but having proved his innocence was appointed a general officer and sent to the war in the Vendée. His *Légion du Nord* became notorious for its excesses, and he himself had an equally bad reputation: contemporaries referred to him as a thief, devoid of military talents save acknowledged bravery, and as Robespierre described him, an untrustworthy, pretentious intriguer. Defeated at Châtillon, he was dismissed by the Convention (July 1793) but was reinstated upon appeal, and advocated a most savage and relentless form of war upon the inhabitants of the Vendée, involving massacres and widespread burnings. He and his troops performed their task with appalling efficiency, culminating with dreadful massacres at Le Mans and Savenay (December 1793), though it was claimed that they were unenthusiastic about engaging the enemy troops, preferring to slaughter the followers instead. Such appalling barbarity led to his becoming known as 'the butcher of the Vendée'. He was recalled to Paris, however, where he was proscribed with the Dantonists, and was executed on 5 April 1794.

WESTMORLAND, General John Fane, 11th Earl of (Lord Burghersh) (1784–1859)

Eldest son of John, 10th Earl of Westmorland (1759–1841), until he became 11th Earl upon his father's death, John Fane was known as Lord Burghersh. Commissioned in December 1803, his accelerated promotion to lieutenant-colonel by 1809 (against regulations and it was suggested because of his family connections) caused a minor furore in the House of Commons, and the promotion was revoked until he had completed the requisite period of service; not until December 1811 was his lieutenant-colonelcy approved. He served in staff capacities in the expeditions to Hanover 1805–6, Sicily 1806–7, with Duckworth's fleet at the Dardanelles, in Egypt and in the Peninsula, first as assistant adjutant-general and in 1809 as ADC to Wellington (including Rolica, Vimeiro and Talavera); and in 1810 with the 3rd Dragoon Guards, including Busaco. In 1813 he was appointed British commissioner to Schwarzenberg's army, and served from September 1813 and in the 1814 campaign in France, in many actions. As minister to the court of Tuscany he served with the Austrians in 1815, including Tolentino, and in conjunction with Bianchi signed the convention which restored Naples to the Bourbons. MP for Lyme Regis 1806–16, he became major-general in 1825, lieutenant-general in 1838 and general in 1854, and was ambassador to Berlin 1841–51 and to Vienna 1851–5. He was also a musician and composed several operas. In June 1811 he married Priscilla Anne (1793–1879), daughter of William Wellesley-Pole, 4th Earl of Mornington, who was thus Wellington's niece; she accompanied him to Germany in 1813. Burghersh wrote accounts of the Peninsular and 1813–14 campaigns. The third son who succeeded him as 12th Earl, Francis William Henry (1825–91), also had a military career, serving in India and as ADC to Raglan in the Crimea. The 11th Earl should not be confused with General Sir Henry Fane, who commanded a cavalry brigade under Wellington 1809–10 and 1813–14, was CinC India 1835–9, and held the colonelcy of the 1st Dragoon Guards from 1827 until his death in 1840.

Burghersh, Lord. *Memoir of the Early Campaigns of the Duke of Wellington in Portugal and Spain.* London, 1820; *Memoir of the Operations of the Allied Armies under Prince Schwarzenberg and Marshal Blücher, during the latter end of 1813 and the Year 1814.* London, 1822; *Correspondence of Lord Burghersh ... 1808–1840.* ed. Rachel Weigall (his granddaughter). London, 1912; Burghersh, Lady. *The Letters of Lady Burghersh (afterwards Countess of Westmorland) from Germany and France during the Campaign of 1813–14,* ed. Lady Rose Weigall. London, 1893

WHINYATES, General Sir Edward Charles (1782–1865)

He was the son of an army officer from Devon, and by his mother was related to Oliver Cromwell. Commissioned in the Royal Artillery in March 1798, he served in North Holland in 1799, in the Copenhagen expedition, and as a captain in the Royal Horse Artillery was distinguished in the Peninsula, including Busaco and Albuera. He is perhaps best known for commanding the Rocket Troop at Waterloo, where he was wounded severely. Knighted in 1823, he became a lieutenant-colonel in 1830 and rose to the rank of general in 1864.

WHITBREAD, Samuel (1758–1815)

One of the leading opposition politicians throughout the Napoleonic Wars, he owed his fortune to the family brewing business, and some of his political prominence to his marriage in 1789 to Elizabeth, eldest daughter of Sir Charles, later 1st Earl, Grey. In 1790 he was elected as Whig MP for Bedfordshire, and gained a reputation as a social and financial reformer, a critic of the government and a leader of the 'peace party' in British politics. An example of his rhetoric was a comment made in criticism of the government's policy for the suppression of the Luddite disturbances, describing measures to keep order as an attempt 'to stifle the cries of hunger by the point of the bayonet'.[1] Inveterate critic of the government though he was, Whitbread was not irrevocably opposed to all military matters: when in 1814 the government proposed to grant Wellington £300,000 and an annuity of £13,000 as a reward for his Peninsula victory, Whitbread objected on the grounds that the sum was insufficient; and he took seriously his own role as lieutenant-colonel of

the Bedford Volunteers, and from 1809 of the 1st Bedfordshire Local Militia. The esteem with which he was regarded in his own locality may be shown by an incident during the harsh weather of January 1814, when he was driving a horse-drawn sleigh. In Bedford High Street an 'honest labourer' ran out and seized the horse, stopping the sleigh, saying that he thought that 'his horse had run away, and kicked the wheels off, and hoped his honour was not much hurt'.[2] Whitbread thanked the man for risking his life and rewarded him with half a crown! Having opposed the renewal of the war in 1815, he lived to see its successful conclusion at Waterloo, but committed suicide on 6 July 1815.

1. *Gent's Mag.*, June 1812, p. 570. 2. *Edinburgh*, 31 Jan 1814.

Fulford, R. *Samuel Whitbread: A Study in Opposition.* London, 1967

WHITELOCKE, Lieutenant-General John (1757–1853)

JOHN WHITELOCKE AT HIS COURT-MARTIAL

An officer whose name was reviled throughout the British Army, he had been commissioned in 1778, served in the West Indies and held a number of staff appointments. He was colonel of the 6th West India Regiment 1795–1806, and of the 89th Foot thereafter; but despite active service in San Domingo, when as a lieutenant-general he was selected to command the South American expedition, he was wholly unfit for the task. He was described as arrogant, over-confident and rude, earning the contempt not only of his officers but also of the rank and file, with whom he attempted to ingratiate himself by the use of foul language; and worse, was militarily incompetent. His attempt to capture Buenos Aires ended in complete disaster and caused the abandonment of the whole sorry expedition; court-martialled, he was condemned as 'totally unfit and unworthy to serve His Majesty in any military capacity whatever', and was removed from command of the 89th, the 9th Earl of Lindsey being appointed in his stead (March 1808). So hateful was Whitelocke's reputation that a popular toast was 'Grey Hairs but no White Locks', and when the New Orleans expedition called to provision at São Miguel in the Azores in 1814, where it was rumoured he was living under an assumed name, a gang of soldiers and sailors chased an unfortunate inhabitant who happened to resemble him, who in fear of his life just managed to escape!

WILLIAM I, King of Prussia, Emperor of Germany (1797–1888)

One of the most significant of Prussia's monarchs, and the first German emperor, Wilhelm Friedrich Ludwig was the second son of King Frederick William III and Queen Louise. From an early age he demonstrated an interest in everything military, and despite his extreme youth received a commission in January 1807. A captain from October 1813, he accompanied the king in the campaign and was awarded the Iron Cross for bravery at Bar-sur-Aube; he became a major-general

WILLIAM I, EMPEROR OF GERMANY
(WILLIAM IV OF PRUSSIA)

WILLIAM I,
KING OF THE NETHERLANDS

at the age of 21. The remainder of his career is outside the scope of this work, but his experiences in the Napoleonic Wars must have exerted an influence on his subsequent life. He succeeded his brother Frederick William IV as king in January 1861, having risen to the rank of field marshal (1854) and having been acting as regent from October 1858; he was proclaimed German Emperor on 18 January 1871 at his headquarters at Versailles, having defeated France and with Bismarck established Germany as a great power.

WILLIAM I, King of The Netherlands; previously Prince William Frederick of Orange (1772–1844)

Son of William V, hereditary *Stadtholder* of the United Netherlands (who took refuge in Britain and died there in 1806), and Princess Sophia Wilhelmina of Prussia, he strengthened the ties between his family and that of Prussia by his marriage (1791) to Princess Frederica Wilhelmina, daughter of King Frederick II. He served in the early campaigns in The Netherlands during the Revolutionary Wars, and after his family was driven out settled in Berlin. He took part in the 1799 campaign in North Holland, and

after the Peace of Amiens came to an agreement with Napoleon, receiving some territory adjoining his family land of Nassau; but in 1806 took the part of his Prussian kinsfolk. He commanded a division at Auerstädt, after which he was deprived of his lands by Napoleon. In 1809 he joined Austria and was wounded at Wagram; and in November 1813 returned to The Netherlands, where he was proclaimed as sovereign prince in December, and subsequently (15 March 1815) was awarded the dignity of kingship of the united Holland and Belgium. The new King William I had the immediate problem of facing the Hundred Days campaign, and at first proved not especially co-operative with the Allied command in the area; only after an ultimatum from the Duke did he accede to Wellington's appointment as commander of his troops, with the rank of field marshal in Netherlands service. William was crowned in Brussels on 27 September 1815, and having surrendered his Nassau lands in exchange for Luxembourg, became Grand Duke of the latter state; but his reign was beset by conflict between his Dutch and Belgian subjects, culminating with the Belgian revolt of 1830. The two states became separate in 1831, but William invaded and only French intervention ensured Belgian independence. Faced with internal demands for liberalisation, William abdicated in favour of his son on 7 October 1840, retiring to his estates in Silesia.

WILLIAM II, King of The Netherlands, see ORANGE, William Prince of

WILLIAM IV, King of Great Britain, Duke of Clarence (1765–1837)

KING WILLIAM IV
(ENGRAVING BY AND AFTER W. SKELTON)

The third son of King George III, he pursued an active naval career from 1779, served at St. Vincent in 1780, and attained the rank of captain in 1786. On 20 May 1789 he became Duke of Clarence and St. Andrews and Earl of Münster. Although an ardent supporter of the war against France, and having attained flag rank, he was not permitted to play an active role in the war, so took the part of the Prince of Wales in his friction with the king. He became Admiral of the Fleet in 1811, but only in 1814 was he able to satisfy his enthusiasm for action, when he visited the British troops in The Netherlands. In the action at Merxem, near Antwerp, he flatly refused to go to the rear, and even helped the British skirmishers scramble through hedgerows and over fences; and but for a bayonet-charge which rescued him, led by Lieutenant Thomas Austin of the 35th Foot, would have been killed or captured by a French detachment. Throughout this terrifying affair he showed the greatest courage and composure. He succeeded his brother as king on 28 June 1830.

Ziegler, P. *King William IV*. London, 1971. An account of the affair at Merxem is in Austin, T. *Old Stick-Leg*, ed. Brigadier-General H. H. Austin. London, 1926, pp. 85–8.

WILKINSON, Major General James (1757–1825)

One of the worst generals – perhaps worst characters – of the period, he was born in Maryland and had a turbulent career as an officer of the US Army during the War of Independence. He became prominent in politics and commerce in Kentucky, and was a major figure in the 'Spanish Conspiracy' aimed at promoting the interests of that nation, probably intriguing both with and against them. His commercial ventures having failed, he secured a lieutenant-colonelcy in the US Army in 1791, intrigued against his superior Anthony Wayne and succeeded him as CinC in 1796. As Governor of Louisiana, he was involved in the Burr Conspiracy but evaded attempts to prove his implication and survived a court-martial in 1811. In March 1813 he was appointed major general and transferred from New Orleans to succeed Dearborn as commander on the northern frontier. His conduct of the campaign was highly criticised, and in March 1814 he was relieved of command for incompetence; but he was exonerated by a court of inquiry after he demonstrated the interference of his superiors and the failure of Hampton to support him at a critical period (the two were bitter enemies). In June 1815 he left the service, though without the censure which some might have considered his due. He published unreliable memoirs and subsequently went to Mexico in the hope of acquiring a land-grant, and it was suggested that his demise might have been hastened by the use of opium.

Shreve, R. O. *The Finished Scoundrel*. 1933

WILSON, General Sir Robert Thomas (1777–1849)

One of the most colourful characters of the age, and stated by Wellington to be 'a very slippery fellow [who] has not the talent of being able to speak the truth upon any subject',[1] he was the son of the artist Benjamin Wilson, through whom he gained his acquaintance with the King and friendship of the Duke of York. Commissioned in the 15th Light Dragoons in 1794, he fought at Villers-en-Cauchies, for which action he received the emperor's medal; he served in Ireland during the 1798 rebellion, in the expedition to North Holland, on a mission to Vienna in 1800, and in the Egyptian campaign, his published work on the latter beginning his career as a military author. He commanded the 20th Light Dragoons at the Cape in 1806, and in 1807 was sent as military commissioner to Berlin, serving with the Russians at Eylau and Friedland and writing an account of the campaign. In 1808–9 he formed and commanded the Loyal Lusitanian Legion, a Portuguese corps in British pay, but left the Peninsula in the latter year after some friction with Wellington and Beresford. Attempts by friends in parliament (notably members of the opposition) to magnify his achievements attracted some criticism; as William Warre (a Portuguese staff officer) commented: 'Nobody will deny him courage and talents as a Partizan, but to those who know the facts, the attempt at thanks in the House are more adapted to make him appear ridiculous, than to do him honour. He can never want a trumpeter while he lives, and no man better knows the *art de se faire valoir* ... He is a very good fellow as a companion, and a very able light troop Officer, and if he would not attempt to be more than he is, would be more respected.'[2] Sent on a diplomatic mission to Constantinople in 1812, he took the opportunity of joining the Russian Army in its fight against Napoleon, and as a liaison officer with the main army in the later stages of the campaign he exercised some influence upon the Tsar, and was critical of Kutuzov and others. He continued to serve with the Russians in 1813 (including Dresden and Leipzig), and was promoted to major-general on 4 June 1813; but, being somewhat mistrusted by Castlereagh, he was given the relatively unimportant post as liaison officer with the Austrians in Italy in 1814. Wilson's career after the war was equally colourful; he was sentenced to three months' imprisonment for assisting in the escape of Lavalette from his capital sentence in France, and in 1818 was elected MP for Southwark, only quitting parliament over his opposition to the Reform Bill. One of the queen's supporters at the time of her divorce from George IV, he further weakened his position when interfering in the attempted control of rioters at the queen's funeral, and as a result was dismissed from the service in September 1821. He returned to the Peninsula in 1823 (a tentative

suggestion that he might take command of the Portuguese Army came to naught), and was shot in the leg when the French besieged Corunna. His services to Canning in facilitating the formation of the 1827 ministry brought no immediate reward, but in 1830 he was promoted to lieutenant-general (back-dated to 1825), and in 1835 he received the colonelcy of the 15th Hussars. Having forsaken his Whig and Radical political affiliations – latterly he was more of a moderate Tory – for six years from 1842 he was Governor and CinC Gibraltar. He died in London in May 1849 and was buried in Westminster Abbey. If his principal military talent were bravery, and though he was vain and opinionated, his manner was such that even his opponents found him a charming companion.

1. Quoted in Glover, as below, p. 77. 2. Warre, p. 122.

Costigan, G. *Sir Robert Wilson: A Soldier of Fortune in the Napoleonic Wars*. Madison, Wis., 1932; Glover, M. *A Very Slippery Fellow: the Life of Sir Robert Wilson 1777–1849*. Oxford, 1978; Samuel, I. *An Astonishing Fellow: the Life of General Sir Robert Wilson*. London, 1985. Sir Robert Wilson's own writings include: *Brief Remarks on the Character and Composition of the Russian Army, and a sketch of the Campaigns in Poland in the Years 1806 and 1807*. London, 1810; *General Wilson's Journal*, ed. A. Brett-James. London, 1964; *History of the British Expedition to Egypt*. London, 1802; *Life of Sir Robert Wilson from Autobiographical Memoirs*, ed. Revd. H. Randolph. London, 1862; *Narrative of Events during the Invasion of Russia*, ed. Rev. H. Randolph. London, 1860; *Private Diary of the Travels, Personal Services and Public Events in the Campaigns of 1812, 1813, and 1814*, ed. Revd. H. Randolph. London, 1861

WIMPFFEN, General Georg Felix, baron (1744–1814)

The son of the King of Poland's chamberlain, he joined the French Army in 1757 and distinguished himself in the Seven Years War and subsequently. A general officer before the Revolution, he was Deputy for Caen in the States-General and served in the early campaigns of the Revolutionary Wars, notably at Thionville; but he is best remembered for his actions in June–July 1793. He accepted command of the troops collected by the insurgent Deputies who formed the 'Central Assembly of Resistance to Oppression', which intended to march on Paris; and when summoned there by the War Minister, Wimpffen threatened to arrive at the head of 60,000 Normans and Bretons. In the event the insurrectionist forces were scattered by troops loyal to the Convention (15 July 1793), and Wimpffen's advice to entrench at Caen and seek help, by implication from Great Britain even if that resulted in the restoration of the monarchy, was rejected. The insurrection having collapsed, Wimpffen was cashiered but evaded retribution under the Terror; he was granted retired status by Napoleon and subsequently held minor municipal office, receiving in 1810 an imperial barony to complement that which had been conferred by the *ancien régime*.

WINCHESTER, Brigadier General James (1752–1826)

A veteran of the War of American Independence, he was appointed brigadier general in the US Army in March 1812, but had spent the previous thirty years living in some comfort in Tennessee and was thus not an ideal candidate for an important field command, and was regarded as being too aristocratic by some of his troops. He agreed to serve under Harrison on the north-west front, but his command suffered from internal unrest and even mutiny, caused in part by conflict between regulars and volunteers. He was surprised at Raisin River (21 January 1813), captured when his right wing was overrun, and ordered those still fighting to surrender, apparently believing that this was necessary to prevent a massacre by the Indian allies of the British (some were murdered none the less). Winchester was taken to Quebec as a prisoner and exchanged in 1814; he left the service in the following year.

WINDER, Brigadier General William Henry (1775–1824)

A lawyer from Maryland:, he was commissioned lieutenant colonel in the US Army in March 1812, and brigadier general in March 1813. On the night of 5/6 June 1813, at Stony Creek, he wandered into the British lines and was taken prisoner, but was exchanged in early 1814, and in July was appointed to command the 10th Military District, responsible for the defence of Washington. He had not been Armstrong's choice, but he was overruled by the President; and perhaps it was an unfortunate appointment, for Winder was defeated at Bladensburg. He left the army in 1815, his health evidently undermined by his military service; he served as a state senator, but died at a relatively early age.

WINDHAM, William (1750–1810)

A member of an old Norfolk family resident at Felbrigg, he entered public life with a brief appointment as chief secretary to the Lord-Lieutenant of Ireland (1783) before being elected MP for Norwich in 1784. He generally supported the Whigs until after the outbreak of the Revolution,

WILLIAM WINDHAM
(ENGRAVING BY W. T. FRY AFTER REYNOLDS)

when he transferred his allegiance to Pitt, and was appointed Secretary at War (*not* the Secretary of State for War, or war minister) in July 1794, with a seat in the Cabinet, a distinction never previously attached to that office. He had some military experience himself, and was not devoid of personal courage: in 1773 he had embarked upon an exploration to the North Pole, but had to be landed in Norway after suffering unremitting sea-sickness; had taken a ride in Sadler's balloon in 1785; as a major in the Norfolk Militia he had helped quell a mutiny at Bury St. Edmunds in 1778, knocking down one of the miscreants and holding the rest at bay with his sword until rescued by his own company; and in 1793 had visited the siege at Valenciennes, touring the front within gun-shot of the enemy. In 1794 he visited the Austrian headquarters in The Netherlands, and, eager to help the French counter-revolutionaries, championed the disastrous expedition to Quiberon. In 1801 he left office with Pitt and opposed the peace with France, but declined to support Pitt in 1804; but upon the formation of Grenville's ministry became Secretary of State for War and the Colonies. He held this office as

long as the ministry lasted, notably introducing short-service enlistment; his impracticable plan for Robert Craufurd to occupy Chile fortunately was never put into practice. He raised objections to the volunteer system, though commanded the unit in his own locality, the Felbrigg Volunteers. He remained in parliament after relinquishing office; having lost his Norwich seat in 1802, he sat for St. Mawes, then New Romney (1806) and Higham Ferrers (from 1807). In July 1809 he sustained an injury to his hip while rescuing a friend's library from a fire; this, it was said, developed into a tumour and he died on 4 June 1810 following an operation to remove it. The king was said to have remarked, 'he was a genuine patriot, and a truly honest man'.[1] His father, Colonel William Windham (1717–61), had served as a volunteer with the Austrian Army, and as lieutenant-colonel of the Norfolk Militia had published the drill-book *A Plan of Discipline, composed for the use of the Militia of the County of Norfolk*, London, 1759, one of the most important publications of its type.

1. Obituary, *Gent's Mag.*, June 1810, p. 591.

Amyot, T. *Speeches in Parliament by the Rt. Hon. William Windham*. London, 1806 (ed. by his ministerial private secretary, and including a biography); Windham, W. *Diary of Rt.Hon. William Windham 1784–1810*, ed. Mrs. H. Baring. 1866; *The Windham Papers*, ed. Lord Rosebery. London, 1913

WINDISCHGRATZ, Field Marshal Alfred Candidus Ferdinand, Fürst zu (1787–1862)

He was one of those commanders of the later 19th century who gained his first military experience during the Napoleonic Wars. He entered the Austrian Army in 1804 and served with distinction in the wars of the period, notably at Leipzig and in 1814, but was most noted for his suppression of the 1848 insurrections in Prague and Vienna. Commanding against the Hungarian rebels, he successfully re-occupied Budapest in January 1849, but in April was relieved of command for his failure to defeat the Hungarian insurrectionists.

Müller, P. *Feldmarschall Fürst Windischgrätz*. Vienna, 1934

WINTZINGERODE (or WINZINGERODE), Field Marshal Ferdinand, baron (1770–1818)

FERDINAND WINTZINGERODE

Probably best known for his command in 1813–14, he was among those generals who combined military and diplomatic duties. After service in the Austrian Army in the earlier campaigns, he joined Russian service; as adjutant-general to the Tsar, he was sent to Vienna to help plan the 1805 campaign, and used his diplomatic skill to gain time by negotiating a provisional armistice with Murat, much to Napoleon's disgust. He fell from favour over his opposition to Tilsit but was restored in 1812 (when he was briefly captured), and in 1813 commanded a Russian corps in Bernadotte's army, including at

Leipzig. In 1814 he entered The Netherlands, and is perhaps most noted as being the Allied commander of the force that was defeated at St. Dizier on 26 March 1814, while probing south, unsupported, from Schwarzenberg's main position. His command was scattered in the action, which has the distinction of being the last of Napoleon's victories, albeit a minor success (if Ligny is excluded).

WITTGENSTEIN, Field Marshal Ludwig Adolf Peter, Prince of Sayn–Wittgenstein–Ludwigsberg (1769–1843)

A member of a family of Westphalian origin, his father had settled in Russia and served in the Russian Army. Wittgenstein himself followed suit, serving in Poland in 1794–5, in the Caucasus, and as major-general of cavalry had fought with Bagration's advance-guard at Austerlitz. Subsequently he served against the Turks and in Finland, but is best known for commanding I Corps of First West Army of the Russian forces in 1812, operating to the north of the main army to hold in check Napoleon's left. Upon the withdrawal of the *Grande Armée*, he pressured their left and attempted, with Chichagov, to cut the route of escape at the Berezina, which route was kept open only with the greatest difficulty. Upon Kutuzov's death in April 1813 Wittgenstein succeeded to command of the Russian and Prussian forces, but after Bautzen, and after much criticism from the Tsar, he relinquished command and led a corps instead, at Dresden and, commanding a large force, at Leipzig. He led VI Corps in 1814 until severely wounded at Barsur-Aube. In 1823 he was promoted to field marshal and in 1828 received command of the

Russian forces against Turkey, but resigned because of ill-health. In 1834 he was awarded the title of Prince by the King of Prussia.

WORDSWORTH, Captain John (1771–1805)

The great poet William Wordsworth (1770–1850) is not normally associated with the Napoleonic Wars, save for quotations such as, most famously, 'Bliss was it in that dawn to be alive/But to be young was very heaven!' (on the French Revolution, from *The Prelude*, IX), and for his condemnation of the Convention of Cintra; but as an example of how the wars affected much of society, it is worth noting the career of his younger brother. John Wordsworth entered the maritime service of the East India Company, and as captain of the ship *Earl of Abergavenny* was one of few EIC officers to be awarded a sword by the Patriotic Fund at Lloyd's, for service in an action against a French squadron in the China Seas in February 1804. In February 1805 he was lost when his ship sank in Weymouth Bay.

Wordsworth, W. *Tract on the Convention of Cintra, published 1809*, intro. A. V. Dicey. London. 1915

WORONZOW, Prince Mikhail *et al.*, see VORONTSOV

WRANGEL, Field Marshal Friedrich Heinrich Ernst, Graf von (1784–1877)

This distinguished Prussian commander was another of those leading soldiers of the later 19th century whose early experience was in the Napoleonic Wars. He entered the Prussian cavalry in 1797, as a subaltern was awarded the *Pour le Mérite* after distinguished service at Heilsberg, and the Iron Cross for service at Wachau (Leipzig), and attained field rank during the 'War of Liberation'. He is best known for his command of II Corps of the German federal troops in the Schleswig–Holstein campaign of 1848, the suppression of disturbances in Berlin in the same year, and, as field marshal from 1856, for commanding (despite his age) the Prusso–Austrian Army in the Danish war of 1864, for which he was ennobled as Count. On the seventieth anniversary of the beginning of his military career, his regiment (3rd East Prussian Cuirassiers) was awarded the title of 'Graf Wrangel'.

WREDE, Field Marshal Karl Philipp, Prince (1767–1838)

The outstanding Bavarian soldier of his time, he was born in Heidelberg and was intended for a career in civil administration, but in 1799 raised a volunteer corps and was appointed its colonel. At Hohenlinden he commanded a Palatinate brigade with distinction, and after the Peace of Lunéville was appointed lieutenant-general in the Bavarian Army. He served alongside the French from 1805, with distinction at Pultusk, but the attitude of the French towards the Bavarians turned him against the French alliance, although the king's tact prevented an open split. In 1809 he commanded in the bitter Tyrol campaign, and was wounded at Wagram when a ball grazed his side. Slightly dizzy after his fall, he declared to Macdonald, 'Tell the emperor that I die for him; I recommend to him my wife and children'; on realising the nature of the injury, Macdonald replied with a laugh that his wife would continue to be able to have his children![1] In that year Napoleon made him a count of the empire (but was said to have remarked that although he could make him a count, he couldn't make him a general), but Wrede's sympathies

lay instead with the anti-French faction. He commanded the 20th Division of the *Grande Armée* with distinction in the 1812 campaign, at one point marching on foot when suffering so badly from diarrhoea that he was unable to ride, but survived. After re-organising the Bavarian forces in 1813, he took the field against his erstwhile allies after his country's change of allegiance (which he approved), was severely defeated at Hanau, but led the Bavarians in 1814, including at La Rothière, Bar-sur-Aube and Arcis-sur-Aube. Created a Prince in 1814, he represented Bavaria at the Congress of Vienna and became a leading figure in Bavarian politics as an opponent of Montgelas, whom he succeeded in 1817, and as CinC and head of the council of regency during the king's absence in 1835 remained a figure of considerable influence.

1. Macdonald, vol. I, p. 343.

Heilmann, J. *Feldmarschall Fürst Wrede*. Liepzig, 1881

WURMSER, Field Marshal Dagobert Sigismund, Graf von (1724–97)

A member of an old noble family from Alsace, he served originally in the French Army, but transferred to Austrian service after his father left Alsace. During the Seven Years War he was distinguished as an expert 'outpost' commander and leader of hussars, and attained the rank of general officer. He was further distinguished in the War of the Bavarian Succession, in 1793 drove the French forces from Alsace, and participated in the siege of Mainz, winning an action at Weissenberg (13 October). Following a period at Vienna, in August 1795 he was given command of the Army of the Rhine, recovered Mannheim and, promoted to field marshal, was sent to command in Italy. Despite

his great experience, at his considerable age he was unable to match the skill of the young Napoleon; attempts to relieve Mantua led to defeats, notably at Castiglione and Bassano, and he was himself besieged in Mantua with the remains of his army. Forced to capitulate in February 1797, he was sent home by Napoleon (who was impressed by Wurmser's resolution), and even though he had been defeated he was not retired but given command in Hungary; but his health collapsed and he died at Vienna in the summer of that year. His earlier distinction was not entirely obscured by his later failure, at an age when he willingly risked losing his reputation in the cause of the service.

WURTTEMBERG, Frederick II and I of, see FREDERICK I

WURTTEMBERG, Eugene (Eugen) Frederick Charles Paul Louis, Herzog von (1788–1857)

Eugen of Württemberg, who may be found referred to as either Duke (*Herzog*) or Prince, was a brave and competent field commander despite his youth. Son of a general in Prussian service (also named Eugen of Württemberg), he accompanied his father in the 1806 campaign and then entered Russian service. Promoted to general officer, he commanded the 4th Division of Baggovut's I Corps at Borodino where he had three horses shot from under him in immediate succession. A dauntless individual, he displayed great personal bravery here and in succeeding actions; he was present at Lützen and Bautzen, commanding the rearguard after the latter; took command after Ostermann-Tolstoy was wounded at Kulm and was distinguished at Leipzig, notably in leading the attack on

Wachau (16 October 1813) which he had predicted would run into more opposition than was anticipated. Here, Eugen provided inspirational leadership under the greatest trial; he also served in the 1814 campaign, notably at Arcis-sur-Aube, thereafter retiring to his Silesian estates, later writing important memoirs.

Württemberg, Prince Eugen. *Erinnerungen aus dem Feldzuge des Jahres 1812 in Russland von dem Herzog Eugen von Württemberg*. Breslau, 1846

YORCK, Field Marshal Hans David Ludwig, Graf von Wartenburg (1759–1830)

HANS DAVID LUDWIG YORCK VON WARTENBURG (PRINT AFTER VON GEBAUER)

A Prussian commander of the greatest distinction, Yorck (whose name is often rendered as 'York') is perhaps best known for an action which proved a watershed in the history of his country. The son of a Prussian officer, he entered the Prussian Army in 1772 but was cashiered for complaining about the plundering of a fellow-officer. Instead he entered Dutch service, campaigned in the East Indies and returned to Europe in 1785, being reinstated in the Prussian Army after the death of Frederick the Great (who had personally sanctioned his earlier dismissal). In 1794 he served in Poland and gained a reputation as a commander of light infantry, and in 1806 was distinguished as a rearguard commander, until wounded and captured at Lübeck. He played a leading role in the re-organisation of the Prussian Army, becoming inspector-general of light infantry, and succeeded the pro-French Grawert in command of the Prussian corps which participated in Napoleon's invasion of Russia in 1812, operating on the extreme left of the *Grande Armée*. As a devoted

patriot, this duty was objectionable to him, but he fulfilled his task with skill until the opportunity arose for a decisive move. By the Treaty of Tauroggen, which he negotiated, the Prussian corps became neutral; it was received with acclaim by the anti-French party, and although at first denounced by the king and government, precipitated the Prussian change of allegiance which had so vital a bearing upon the subsequent campaigns. Yorck declared Prussia's hostility to Napoleon before the king did, and led his men with considerable effect in the 'War of Liberation', notably in the withdrawal after Bautzen, at the Katzbach and in the Leipzig campaign; his title (awarded 1814) was from his victory at Wartenburg on 4 October 1813. He was also much involved in the 1814 campaign, notably at Montmirail and Laon. He appears not to have been an easy companion (he especially disliked Schwarzenberg), and Clausewitz described his nature. He noted his bravery and talent, and that his colonial experience had 'enlarged the sphere of his intellectual observation. A fiery and passionate will, concealed beneath apparent coldness; a powerful ambition, suppressed by constant resignation; and strength and boldness of character distinguished him. He was honest; but gloomy, choleric, and reserved, and a bad subordinate. Personal attachment was not congenial to him. The stimulus of his actions was fame, and the means were supplied by strong natural abilities. His worst feature was, that under the appearance of being downright and straightforward he was, in fact, close and reserved. He talked loud when his hopes were lowest, and assumed despondency when he entertained no apprehension.'[1] At times, however, he displayed good

humour, and was dauntless in action; his troops nicknamed him *der alte Isegrim*, the fairy-tale equivalent of 'the big bad wolf'. Despite his abilities, he was not employed in the 1815 campaign (so as not to supplant Gneisenau, who was junior to him), and being given command of reserve formations in Prussia, decided to retire from active duty. He was advanced to the rank of field marshal in 1821.

1. Clausewitz, p. 225.

Droysen, J. G. *Leben des G.F.M.* [Generalfeldmarschall] *Grafen Yorck von Wartenburg*. Berlin, 1851; Paret, P. *Yorck and the Era of Prussian Reform 1807–1815*. Princeton, 1966

YORK, Field Marshal Frederick Augustus, Duke of (1763–1827)

The second son of King George III was elected to the bishopric of Osnabrück at the age of six months (which he retained until 1803), but thereafter his career was largely military in character. Gaining considerable experience by attending the Prussian and Austrian manoeuvres, he became a major-general in the British Army and colonel of the Coldstream Guards in 1784 (transferring to the 1st Foot Guards in 1805, which colonelcy he held until his death), and was appointed Duke of York and Albany in the same year. Having spent some years in Germany, he returned to Britain in 1787, took some part in public affairs in the House of Lords,

FREDERICK, DUKE OF YORK (ENGRAVING BY
SKELTON AFTER SIR WILLIAM BEECHEY)

fought a duel with Lennox (later Duke of Richmond) and in 1791 married the Princess Royal of Prussia, Frederica Charlotte Ulrica Catherine (1767–1820), daughter of Frederick William II. He commanded in the field in two campaigns, both in The Netherlands (1793–5 and in the expedition to North Holland 1799), in neither case with distinction; but his real value was in military administration, and his tenure as CinC witnessed many important reforms (though not all were at his instigation). On his return from his first Netherlands campaign he was appointed field marshal (February 1795) and served as CinC until 1809, when he had to resign over the scandal involving his mistress, Mary Ann Clarke, who had been using her connection to promise military and other preferments. Although it was proven that the duke had no knowledge of this, much less that he had actually connived at the attempt to extort money in return, he was censured and displaced as CinC by Sir David Dundas, until in 1811 he was restored to the office, which he held until his death. He was popular with the ordinary soldiers and known as 'the soldier's friend'; indeed, even James Hadfield, the insane ex-soldier who took a shot at the king at Drury Lane Theatre in 1800, when escorted under arrest into the duke's presence, exclaimed 'God bless him! he is the soldier's friend, and I love him!' His marriage was unhappy and there was a separation (the duchess retired to live in Weybridge), and the duke had no legitimate children; but it was believed that Lieutenant Joseph Stilwell, alias 'Scamp', of the 95th killed at Waterloo, was a natural son, and that Charles Hesse of the 18th Hussars, also a lieutenant at Waterloo, was another. If so, it was a remarkable coincidence that Hesse, who would thus have been a grandson of the British king, was killed by Napoleon's illegitimate son, Léon Denuelle, in a duel.

1. *Gent's Mag.*, July, 1800, p. 687.

Burne, A. H. *The Noble Duke of York: the Military Life of Frederick, Duke of York*. London, 1949; Watkins, J. *A Biographical Memoir of His Late Royal Highness Frederick, Duke of York and Albany*. London, 1827

ZARAGOZA, Agostina (1788–1857)

AGOSTINA ZARAGOSA
(MEZZOTINT BY H. MEYER)

Heralded as representing the incarnation of Spanish resistance to French invasion, 'the Maid of Saragossa' was celebrated in prose, in verse by Byron and was portrayed by Goya in his print *Que Valor!* Agostina was a young woman who came to prominence, it was said, by manning a cannon at the siege of Saragossa, after her lover or fiancé had been killed in its defence. Her name, 'Zaragoza', which is usually that given, is representative of the spirit of the city; Belmas calls her 'Augustina d'Aragon' and other versions include 'Maria Agostina' and 'Augustina Sarzella'. Palafox claimed to have witnessed her bravery, commissioned her as a sub-lieutenant of artillery and gave her a pension for life; she continued to serve in the artillery, escaped the French capture of the city and appeared at Cadiz, in uniform, where she acted as a patriotic symbol. Certainly her appearance suited the purpose of presenting her as an example for emulation; young and attractive, if not quite as ravishing as Byron suggested ('her long looks that foil the painter's power/Her fairy form, with more than female grace'), Sir John Carr described her face as 'remarkable for its sweetness'. Admiration was not entirely universal; William Napier inclined to doubt all the stories of a number of heroines at Saragossa, though admitted that 'when suddenly environed with horrors, the delicate sensitiveness of women, driving them to a kind of phrenzy, might produce actions above the heroism of men',[1] and Carr reported that at Cadiz some thought that Agostina should have left war to men. He added, surely with some truth, that 'happy would it have been for your country, if many of your soldiers, and most of your chiefs, had acted

with the undaunted intrepidity of this young female!'[2]

1. Napier, W., vol. I, p. 70. 2. *Gent's Mag.*, Dec, 1811, p. 549.

ZIETHEN, Field Marshal Hans Ernst Karl, Graf von (1770–1848)

Possessing one of the most famous names in the history of the Prussian Army, his chief fame rests with his actions in the 1815 campaign. Although he held a brigade command in 1813, including Leipzig, it was as *Generalleutnant* in command of I Corps in 1815 that he was most prominent, both at Ligny and in the march to Mont St-Jean, supporting Wellington's left flank late in the day. He later commanded the Prussian forces during the occupation of France, and attained the rank of field marshal in 1835.

HALFTITLE ILLUSTRATIONS

Page 1: 'They grumbled but
they kept on following him', after Raffet.
Page 13: Italy 1796, after Raffet.
Page 21: Arcola, after Vernet.
Page 55: Bonaparte in Egypt, after Suchodolski.
Page 89: 18 Brumaire, by Bouchot.
Page 109: Napoleon at Eylau, after Gros.
Page 115: 23rd Dragoons parade at Tilsit.
Page 127: Somosierra, after Kossaka.
Page 145: Somosierra, by Motte after Grenier.
Page 161: Vimeiro, after L'Evéque.
Page 163: Raszyn, after Suchodolski.
Page 169: Raszyn, after Kossaka.
Page 177: Wagram, after Kossaka.
Page 199: Wagram, after Vernet.
Page 231: Prisoners of war at Wagram, after Rosen.
Page 243: The Review (Place du Carousel), after Vernet.
Page 249: Uhlans of the Légion de la Vistule c.1811–14,
after Gembarzewski.
Page 271: Napoleon at Moshaisk, after Wereschtschaguine.
Page 289: The Report, after Rosen.
Page 317: Napoleon's escort, after Cherminski.
Page 325: The Retreat, after Wereschtchaguine.
Page 327: Episode at Reims, after Rosen.
Page 335: Two Grenadiers, after Rosen.
Page 349: The Return from Elba, after Steuben.
Page 351: Retreat of the Bataillon Sacré at Waterloo,
after Raffet.